INDIA'S URBAN FUTURE

INDIA'S URBAN FUTURE

Edited by Roy Turner

SELECTED STUDIES FROM AN
INTERNATIONAL CONFERENCE SPONSORED BY
KINGSLEY DAVIS, RICHARD L. PARK,
CATHERINE BAUER WURSTER

1962

BERKELEY AND LOS ANGELES
UNIVERSITY OF CALIFORNIA PRESS

University of California Press
Berkeley and Los Angeles, California

Cambridge University Press
London, England
© *1961 by The Regents of the University of California*
Library of Congress Catalog Card Number: 62–9459
Printed in the United States of America

PREFACE

The present book, like most collective enterprises, is partly the out-growth of particular circumstances. In 1959 the three undersigned, although representing different academic fields, found ourselves at the same university (California, Berkeley campus) and interested in the same subject, urbanization. We also found ourselves inter-ested in the same country, India. What could be more natural, then, than our decision to join together in a study of urbanization in India?

Behind our interest lay some developments in the world which gave significance to, and thus explained, our joint concern with this specific topic. For one thing, the process of urbanization is now more rapid and massive and affects a greater part of the world than ever before, mainly because it is now rampant in the less developed countries, which still embrace some three fourths of the world's people. The migration of hundreds of millions of rural folk to cities in these still chiefly agrarian countries is revolution-izing the life of humanity just as surely as are the other major aspects of economic and social modernization, and the unprece-dented rates of over-all population growth are helping, along with the rural-urban migration, to swell the populations of individual cities to figures hardly known anywhere a half century ago. Neces-sarily, social, economic, and political problems of major significance are being created by the huge rural-urban migration and the rapid rise of giant cities in countries whose main orientation has until recently been agricultural.

Seeing that the major trends and problems of urbanization occur now in the less industrial countries, we thought that India should make a good case for analysis, not only because of the size and obvious importance of this country, but also because it is located in the world's largest and most populous continent, possesses a considerable body of information on economic and demographic subjects, and enjoys a group of leaders who take a responsible and intelligent interest in the country's destiny. To make a study of Indian urbanization on our own, however, would have involved more time and more talents than the three of us could supply; besides, it would probably not have made much impression on those in India who are called upon to act in the nation's behalf. Accordingly, we came to the conclusion that the best plan would be a week-long seminar in which experts and officials concerned with Indian urbanization, drawn from India as well as from the West, and from several academic disciplines as well as from government, would discuss the problems on the basis of papers prepared in advance by most of the participants.

The Ford Foundation was kind enough to give us support for this project, which was organized with the invaluable assistance of Edward G. Echeverria, Albert Mayer, Asoka Mehta, P. R. Nayak, and Tarlok Singh. The seminar was held from June 26 to July 2, 1960, in Berkeley, California, with thirty-three participants. (A list of the participants will be found elsewhere in this volume.) We were extremely pleased with the frank but cordial character of the discussion, and with the remarkable absence of disciplinary or regional parochialism. The Indian participants showed a gratifying tolerance to having their urban problems discussed by Americans; more than this, it seemed that the participants really forgot they were from different countries in their absorption with Indian urbanization from the standpoint of India.

After the conference, Roy Turner fortunately accepted our request to edit a volume of the proceedings. A planning specialist from the University of Chicago and currently on the staff of International Population and Urban Research, he was eminently qualified for this task. The job has been arduous and long, not only because the papers were not all in final shape but also because correspondence spanned great distances and the exigencies of publication limited our space far below the amount required to accommodate all the papers. Mr. Turner has performed his editorial duties with skill, patience, and tact. He profoundly regrets, as we do, that some papers had to be shortened and others omitted altogether because of the costs of publication.

The detailed work of the conference itself fell heavily upon the staff for the Center for South Asia Studies, particularly upon Mrs. Akiko Owen, who deserves our sincerest thanks. In addition, we received important administrative aid from the Extension Division and from the central office of the Institute of International Studies of the University of California. The manuscript was typed with unusual efficiency and good nature by Mrs. Anne Cohen of the IPUR staff, with assistance from the Institute.

Above all, we wish to thank our Indian friends who did so much to make the seminar a success. Not only did many of them come all the way from India for the seminar, but they brought along a willingness to discuss their country's problems and complexities in the combined spirit of scientific inquiry and responsible concern for the future. They taught the other members of the seminar a great deal, and we hope that they will feel this volume to be a fitting tribute to the effort they made.

Finally, to the American as well as the Indian contributors of papers, we wish to acknowledge unusual tolerance and coöperativeness with respect to editorial changes. If the present book stimulates further interest and research into the problems of urbanization in the world's newly developing countries, if it serves as a point of departure, as a demonstration of the close interweaving of practical and scientific questions, it will greatly please us.

KINGSLEY DAVIS
International Population and Urban Research
University of California

RICHARD L. PARK
Department of Political Science
University of Michigan

CATHERINE BAUER WURSTER
Department of City and Regional Planning
University of California

SEMINAR PARTICIPANTS

The following persons attended the Seminar on Urbanization in India at the Claremont Hotel, Berkeley, California, from June 26 to July 2, 1960. Those marked with * contributed papers.

Bapat, S. B., Director, Public Administration Division, United Nations Technical Assistance Administration.

Breese, Gerald, Bureau of Urban Research, Princeton University, and Consultant, Delhi Regional Plan.

*Brush, John E., Department of Geography, Rutgers University.

*Chatterjee, B., Director of Urban Community Development, Delhi Municipal Corporation.

*Chaudhuri, Sachin, Editor, *Economic Weekly*.

*Clinard, Marshall B., Department of Sociology, University of Wisconsin, and Consultant, Urban Community Development, Delhi.

*Davis, Kingsley, International Population and Urban Research, University of California, Berkeley. *Sponsoring Committee*.

*Echeverria, Edward G., City Planner, and Consultant, Delhi Regional Plan.

Echeverria, Paula, Economist.

*Ellefsen, Richard A., International Population and Urban Research, University of California, Berkeley; now of Department of Economics and Geography, San José State College.

*Harris, Britton, Institute for Urban Studies, University of Pennsylvania, and Consultant, Delhi Regional Plan.

*Hoselitz, Bert F., Research Center in Economic Development and Cultural Change, University of Chicago, and Consultant, Delhi Regional Plan.

Karve, Irawati, Department of Anthropology, Deccan College, Poona, and University of California, Berkeley.

*Lambert, Richard D., South Asia Regional Studies, University of Pennsylvania.

Loshbough, Bernard E., ACTION-Housing, Inc., Pittsburgh, Pennsylvania.

Mandelbaum, David G., Department of Anthropology, University of California, Berkeley.

*Manickam, T. J., Director, School of Town and Country Planning, New Delhi.

*Mayer, Albert, Architect and Planner, New York City, and Chief Consultant, Delhi Regional Plan.

*Mehta, Asoka, Member of Parliament, Government of India.

*Meier, Richard L., Mental Health Research Institute, University of Michigan.

*Misra, K. N., Town and Village Planner to Government of U. P., Lucknow.

Mitra, Ashok, Economist, International Bank for Reconstruction and Development.

*Nayak, P. R., Commissioner, Managing Director, Indian Refineries Limited, and member, Oil and Natural Gas Commission.

*Pant, Pitambar, Head of Perspective Planning Division, Planning Commission, Government of India.

*Park, Richard L. Park, Department of Political Science, University of Michigan. *Sponsoring Committee.*

Sethi, Prakaschand, Mayor of Ujjain, and member, All-Indian Congress Committee.

*Singh, Tarlok, Joint Secretary, Planning Commission, Government of India.

*Sovani, N. V., Gokhale Institute of Politics and Economics, Poona.

Spate, O. H. K., Department of Geography, Australian National University.

Staley, Eugene, International Industrial Development Center, Stanford Research Institute.

*Tangri, Shanti, Lecturer in Economics and Social Science, University of California, Berkeley.

Turner, Roy, International Population and Urban Research, University of California, Berkeley.

*Wurster, Catherine B., Department of City and Regional Planning, University of California, Berkeley. *Sponsoring Committee.*

The following persons contributed papers but did not attend the Seminar:

Barve, S. G., Irrigation and Power Department, Government of Maharashtra.

Bogue, Donald J., and Zachariah, K. C. (joint paper), Department of Sociology, University of Chicago, and Department of Sociology, University of Pennsylvania, respectively.

Bose, Ashish, Demographic Research Centre, Institute of Economic Growth, University of Delhi.

Bredo, William, Stanford Research Institute.

Nath, V., Collector, Sawai Madhopur, India.

Rao, V. L. S. Prakasa, and Learmonth, A. T. A. (joint paper), Indian Statistical Institute, Calcutta, and Department of Geography, University of Liverpool, respectively.

CONTENTS

1. CHANGES IN THE URBAN POPULATION

   I. Urbanization in India: Past and Future   3
      Kingsley Davis
  II. Urbanization and Migration in India   27
      Donald J. Bogue and K. C. Zachariah

2. URBAN STRUCTURE AND URBAN SOCIETY

  III. The Morphology of Indian Cities   57
      John E. Brush
  IV. Urban Community Development in India: The
      Delhi Pilot Project   71
      Marshall B. Clinard and B. Chatterjee
   V. City-Hinterland Relationships in India   94
      Richard A. Ellefsen
  VI. The Impact of Urban Society upon Village Life   117
      Richard D. Lambert
 VII. The Village and the Community   141
      V. Nath

3. URBANIZATION AND ECONOMIC DEVELOPMENT

 VIII. The Role of Urbanization in Economic Development: Some International Comparisons   157
      Bert F. Hoselitz

IX. Urbanization and the Long-Range Strategy of Economic Development 182
Pitambar Pant

X. Urbanization, Political Stability, and Economic Growth 192
Shanti Tangri

XI. Centralization and the Alternate Forms of Decentralization: A Key Issue 213
Sachin Chaudhuri

XII. Industrial Decentralization in India 240
William Bredo

XIII. Urban Centralization and Planned Development 261
Britton Harris

XIV. Urban Living Conditions, Overhead Costs, and the Development Pattern 277
Catherine Bauer Wurster

Appendix: Data from the Delhi Studies 296

XV. Relations of Technology to the Design of Very Large Cities 299
Richard L. Meier

4. GOVERNMENT AND PLANNING

XVI. Problems of Integrating Rural, Industrial, and Urban Development 327
Tarlok Singh

XVII. National Implications of Urban-Regional Planning 335
Albert Mayer

XVIII. Urbanization in Maharashtra State: Problems and a Plan of Action 347
S. G. Barve

XIX. The Challenge of Urban Growth to Indian Local Government 361
P. R. Nayak

XX. The Urban Challenge to Local and State Government: West Bengal, with Special Attention to Calcutta 382
Richard L. Park

XXI. Some Operational Problems in Urban and Regional Planning and Development 397
Albert Mayer

XXII. The Future of Indian Cities: National Issues
and Goals 413
Asoka Mehta

5. CONCLUSION

XXIII. A Survey of the Literature on Urbanization in
India 425
Bert F. Hoselitz

EDITOR'S POSTSCRIPT 444

INDEX 457

Part 1

CHANGES IN THE URBAN POPULATION

URBANIZATION IN INDIA: PAST AND FUTURE

Kingsley Davis*

Looking at urbanization from a demographic point of view—that is, as the proportion of the population living in towns and cities—we know that India is in the midst of a gigantic urban increase. Her situation in this respect resembles, at least in a general way, the stage that other countries either are in now or have passed through at an earlier time. We know this because an increase in urbanization is closely linked with industrialization, or over-all economic development. The process of urbanization exhibits a pattern in which the rate of change is slow at first, then rises steeply as the early stages of industrialization are reached, and tapers off gradually when the proportion urban begins to reach a saturation point. In other words, as the lines in Figures 1 and 2 show, the process describes an attenuated "S," or logistic, type of curve during the progress of industrialization. Eventually the urbanization curve approaches a plateau, because the trend, coming to include most of the population, can go no further. At this point urbanization fails to keep pace with economic development, which can proceed after a country has become virtually completely urbanized.

In the United States, for example, the fastest rate of urbanization occurred during the years from 1820 to 1870, when the average gain in the proportion urban was 29.3 per cent per decade, in contrast to 4.9 per cent per decade between 1920 and 1950. A similar pattern, as the figures and Table 1 show, was characteris-

* Richard B. Gamble and O. Andrew Collver, both on the staff of International Population and Urban Research, gave invaluable assistance in the computations on which this paper is based.

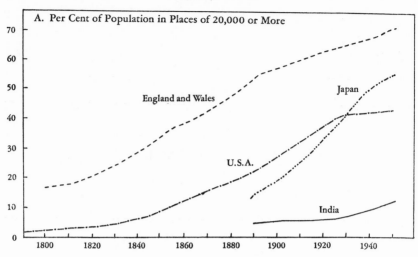

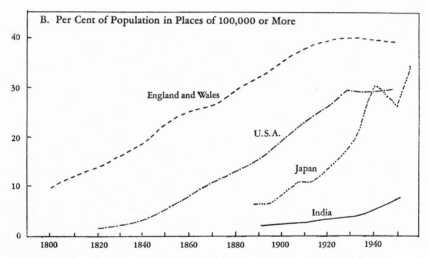

Figure 1. The Rate of Urbanization in India Compared to That of
Certain Other Countries.

tic of England and Wales, and of Japan. This pattern manifests
itself regardless of which index is taken to measure urbanization—
the proportion in places over 2,500, over 20,000, or over 100,000.

Of course, the eventual tapering off of the rate of urbanization
with advanced economic development does not mean that the urban
picture undergoes no further change. On the contrary, just about
the time that the rate of over-all urbanization begins to decline
another change begins—namely, the deconcentration of city popu-

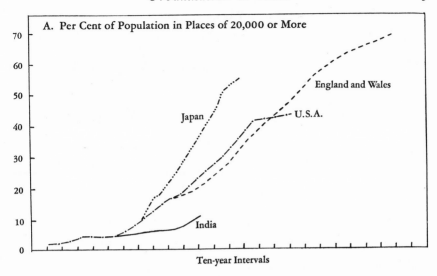

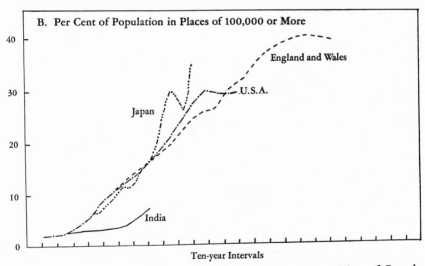

Figure 2. The Rate of Urbanization in India Compared to That of Certain Other Countries. Each Starting Point Placed on the U.S.A. Line.

lations. This deconcentration, which starts at the center of the city, gradually spreads outward from the center until it eventually causes the periphery to move out much faster than would be expected from the rate of population growth itself.

Normally, the great rise in the *proportion* of the population in towns and cities can take place only by rural-urban migration. An

TABLE 1

MAJOR PERIODS OF FAST AND SLOW URBANIZATION, VARIOUS COUNTRIES

Country	Period	Average per cent gain per decade in proportion		
		In urban places	In places of 20,000 or more	In places of 100,000 or more
India..................	1881–1931	3.7[a]	4.2[b]	7.3[b]
	1931–1951	19.7[a]	19.7	49.4
U.S.A.................	1790–1820	12.6[d]	16.3	...[c]
	1820–1870	29.3	35.9	54.9
	1870–1930	14.0	17.3	18.5
	1930–1950	2.4	2.3	6.1[e]
England and Wales.....	1811–1891	...	14.4	14.3
	1891–1951	...	4.8	3.9
Japan.................	1888–1930	33.3[f]	...	37.3
	1930–1955	16.5[g]	...	22.7

[a] For the period 1881–1901, the data relate to prepartition India (without Burma), and are taken from Kingsley Davis, *Population of India and Pakistan* (Princeton, N. J., Princeton University Press, 1951), p. 127. For the period 1901 to 1951, the data are from Ashish Bose, "The Process of Urbanization in India: 1901–1951" (Doctoral dissertation, University of Delhi, 1959), p. 46. The definition of "urban" includes places of 5,000 or larger, but makes numerous exceptions. See Appendix H of Davis, *op. cit.*

[b] The data are for 1891 to 1931 and for 1891–1901; they relate to prepartition India (without Burma). Later periods from Bose, *op. cit.*, p. 50.

[c] No cities in this class prior to 1820.

[d] Incorporated places of 2,500 or over.

[e] Standard Metropolitan Areas of 100,000 or more.

[f] Places of 10,000 and over.

[g] 1930–1950 only.

exception would exist if the surplus of births over deaths were far greater in the towns and cities than in the rural areas, but this is never the case. In virtually all countries the most rapid phase of urbanization occurs at a time when the differential in natural increase between country and city is at, or is approaching, its maximum. The cities during this period are deadlier than the countryside and yet also have fewer births, with the consequence that, from natural increase alone, the trend would be *deurbanization*.[1] In con-

---

[1] We realize that this is a broad generalization about urban-rural vital rates, and one difficult to substantiate. It may have been truer for countries that industrialized earlier than for those now undergoing the process of industrialization. It can hardly be denied that the cities of 1820 to 1870 in the United States were more unhealthy than the countryside, or that their birth rates dropped more rapidly after that than did rural birth rates. But a case can be made for saying that in some underdeveloped countries today the cities are healthier than the countryside, and that this partly compensates for the lower birth rate there. The result is that the difference in natural increase between city and country may be less extreme than at a comparable stage of development in the Western nations.

sequence, the rapidly urbanizing nation is involved in a huge and troublesome geographical shift of its population. To put it succinctly, about 60 per cent of its population must move from the countryside to the cities. This is a problem so formidable that few governments seem willing to face it realistically; yet, if *rapid* economic development is to be achieved, the territorial shift must also take place *rapidly*. The problem may be complicated by additional factors. For instance, in many less-developed countries today it is complicated by an already heavy rural population density and by an extremely fast rate of over-all population growth.

WHY HAS INDIAN URBANIZATION BEEN SO SLOW?

With this typical general pattern in mind, let us now take a brief look at the past trend of Indian urbanization. Such a glance shows at once that the process in India has been relatively slow. This is brought out in Figure 2, where the same data as in Figure 1 are plotted, but this time the starting point for each country is placed on the United States line, in order to compare its subsequent path with that of the United States after the latter had reached that level. It can be seen, for example, that Japan's urbanization moved faster than that of the United States, whereas British and Indian urbanization moved more slowly.[2] To find a level of urbanization corresponding to that in India in 1901, one must go back in the United States to about 1839. During the next fifty years after that level was reached in the United States, the proportion in cities of 100,000 or more rose more than five times, whereas in India it rose less than three times. Much the same lag is shown by the proportion in places of 20,000 or more.[3] In other words, India was farther behind the United States in urbanization in 1951 than she was in 1901. Since Japan's urbanization was faster than that of the United States, its case highlights the slowness of Indian urbanization.[4] Figure 2 brings out the relative speeds, as does Table 2.

As a general rule, it is true that the more recently in history the process of industrialization has occurred, the faster is the rate,

---

[2] The dates of the lines are contained in Fig. 1.

[3] See both panels of Figs. 1 and 2. We do not propose to deal here with the relative merits of different indices for measuring urbanization. This question is discussed in the references cited below in note 5. It is also dealt with in a paper by Jack P. Gibbs and the present writer, "Conventional versus Metropolitan Data in the International Study of Urbanization," *American Sociological Review,* XXIII (October, 1958), 504–514.

[4] In the case of Japan, however, we do not have satisfactory data going back to a period when the country was as little urbanized as India was prior to 1951. Comparison when both countries were at the same level is therefore ruled out.

Kingsley Davis

TABLE 2

COMPARATIVE SPEED OF URBANIZATION IN INDIA, JAPAN, AND U.S.A.

Country	Places of 20,000-plus			Places of 100,000-plus		
	Starting date	Per cent of popu-lation	Years for pro-portion to rise 112 per cent	Starting date	Per cent of popu-lation	Years for pro-portion to rise 179 per cent
India............	1901	5.6	50	1901	2.8	50
U.S.A............	1838	5.6	21	1839	2.8	19
Japan...........	...	...	...	1893	6.0	35
U.S.A............	...	...	...	1853	6.0	41
England and Wales	1801	16.9	53	1901	9.7	73
U.S.A............	1875	16.9	43	1865	9.7	48

including the rate of urbanization.[5] If this rule holds in a majority of cases, then India's slowness is more clearly exceptional, because her development is still today in a comparatively early stage.

Accordingly, an important question is this: why has India's urbanization been so slow? The answer, I suggest, is the relative slowness of economic development in India. Although nobody knows the past Indian rate of economic development, the evidence seems to indicate that it is not likely to have been rapid, compared to that of most other countries at roughly similar stages:

Presumably, if India's per-capita income had fallen 50 per cent, or had doubled or trebled over the years from the 1870's to the 1940's, then such a change would have been reflected in the national-income estimates, no matter how crude, unreliable, or noncomparable they may be. As a matter of fact, the basic data on India's production . . . indicate that no change of such magnitude has occurred. Whatever *real* change there has been has taken place within much smaller limits. It is the cardinal weakness of the existing national-income estimates that they are hopelessly inadequate to indicate these less drastic changes. We simply cannot tell from them whether total national income has increased proportionately with the rate of population growth, has slightly exceeded it, or has lagged somewhat behind.[6]

[5] For fuller discussions of this point, together with the reasons therefore, see other papers by the writer: "Urbanization and the Development of Pre-Industrial Areas," (with Hilda Hertz Golden), *Economic Development and Cultural Change*, III (October, 1954), 6–26; "Population and the Further Spread of Industrial Society," *Proceedings* of the American Philosophical Society, XCV (February, 1951), 8–19; "The Origin and Growth of Urbanization in the World," *American Journal of Sociology*, LX (March, 1955), 429–437.

[6] Daniel Thorner, "Long-Term Trends in Output in India," in Simon Kuznets *et al.* (eds.), *Economic Growth: Brazil, India, Japan* (Durham, N.C.: Duke University Press, 1955), p. 119.

Basing his view on research done under his supervision, Daniel Thorner comes to the conclusion that per capita output in India over the long run may have declined.[7]

Turning from the long-run to the short-run trend, we are particularly interested in the last two or three decades. Unfortunately, our latest census data end in 1951, so that we are unable to gauge the effect of the apparently enhanced rate of economic growth under the two Five Year Plans. It is significant that the rate of change in urbanization from 1941 to 1951 in the Indian Union was faster than that experienced by Japan and about two thirds as fast as that in the United States at roughly the same level:

PER CENT IN 100,000-PLUS CITIES

Country	Decade	Start	End	Per cent increase
India.................	1941–1951	5.4[a]	7.8[a]	44
U.S.A................	1850–1860	5.0	8.4	68
Japan...............	1888–1898	6.0	7.7	28
	1898–1908	7.7	10.7	39

[a] The census data are for metropolitan areas as delimited by International Population and Urban Research. If IPUR delimitations of metropolitan areas are not used, the percentage increase in proportion urban is the same, but the percentages in cities for the two dates are 5.0 and 7.2. In the long-run comparison of Tables 1 and 2, the MA delimitations for 1941 and 1951 have been used, because the "cities" of 1901 were comparable (as an index of urbanization) to the MA's of 1951.

It may be, then, that the 1961 data will show India to be urbanizing now, in contrast to earlier periods, at a rate more comparable to that of other countries at a similar level. If this proves to be the case, it will be a sign, though not an absolute proof, that economic growth has accelerated. It will also be a sign that India is in for a greatly increased rate of internal migration, an intensification of urban problems, and perhaps a rise in political unrest.

Some preliminary results from the 1961 census show, however, that urbanization has not moved rapidly since 1951. Unfortunately, the information is not sufficiently detailed for us to use metropolitan areas, as we have done for 1951. However, by using metropolitan figures given us or estimated for Calcutta, Bangalore, Bombay, and Delhi, we can arrive at some modification in the direction of including large urban aggregates. On this basis we calculate that in 1961 at least 8.9 per cent of India's population was living in places of 100,000 or more, and 13.3 per cent in places of 20,000 or more. The two figures for 1951 were 7.8 and 11.9 respectively.

[7] *Ibid.,* pp. 120–128.

It seems, then, pending further information, that the rise in urbanization during 1951–1961 was not so rapid as we anticipated. The gain in the proportion in places of 100,000 or more was only 14 per cent, in contrast to the 44 per cent rise from 1941 to 1951. However, when fuller information is available, it may turn out that the gain was greater than that shown by preliminary figures which prevent our dealing with metropolitan areas except in a few instances. In this regard it is noteworthy that the combined population of five big metropolitan areas, made as comparable as possible with available data from the 1951 census reports and the 1961 preliminary report, increased by 33 per cent from 1951 to 1961 as against 52 per cent from 1941 to 1951. The figures (in 000's) are as follows:

| | | | | Per Cent Increase | |
	1941	1951	1961	1941–51	1951–61
Greater Calcutta.....	3,534	4,578	5,550	30	21
Greater Bombay.....	1,695	2,839	4,146	68	46
Hyderabad..........	739	1,086	1,252	47	15
Delhi..............	696	1,437	2,344	107	63
Bangalore..........	496	939	1,208	90	29
Total..........	7,160	10,880	14,501	52	33

FUTURE URBANIZATION IN INDIA

Projecting the future urbanization of India can be done by assuming that the proportion living in towns and cities will describe the same sort of curve—an "S," or logistic, curve—in India that it has described in the past in more advanced countries. This assumption can be applied in at least two ways: either by fitting a logistic curve to the six points available in India from 1901 to 1951 and extrapolating to the year 2000, or by taking some fully industrialized country as a model and assuming that India, from 1951 on, will urbanize at the same rate. The results will vary according to how each technique is applied. They will vary somewhat, for example, according to the assumption made concerning the asymptotes in the logistic fit; and they will vary according to which industrial country is chosen as the model in the "follow-the-leader" technique. In the present research, we have tried both methods to project India's future urbanization.

PROJECTION OF URBAN PROPORTION BASED ON UNITED STATES HISTORY

Since the United States has had a slower rate of urbanization than Japan, and yet a faster one than Britain or France, it seemingly represents a middle-of-the-road basis for estimating India's future urbanization. The United States reached India's 1951 percentage in cities 20,000-plus and its percentage in cities 100,000-plus in 1858–59. Following the United States curves from that date, we get the following estimates for India:

	Percentage in Places	
Year	20,000-plus	100,000-plus
1975...................	19.3	13.1
2000...................	30.8	21.2

What this would mean in terms of people depends, of course, upon the future of India's total population. If we take the United Nations estimates, we obtain the results shown in Table 3. It will be noticed that, if the projections hold true, the population in urban

TABLE 3

ESTIMATED PROPORTION OF INDIAN POPULATION IN CITIES AND METROPOLITAN AREAS IN 1975 AND 2000, BASED ON UNITED STATES MODEL

Year	Total population (thousands)	In places 20,000-plus		In MA's of 100,000-plus	
		Per cent	Number (thousands)	Per cent	Number (thousands)
1951...........	356,879	11.9	42,448	7.8	27,927[a]
1975...........	563,000[c]	19.6	110,000	13.9[b]	78,257
2000					
Low.........	745,000[d]	...	229,000	...	158,000
Medium.....	1,000,000	30.8	308,000	21.2[b]	212,000
High........	1,000,000	...	339,000	...	233,000

[a] Includes metropolitan areas for the larger places delimited by International Population and Urban Research. The figure for cities proper in this size class comes to 25,829 thousand, or 7.2 per cent.

[b] Obtained by "grafting" the 1951 Indian percentage onto the United States curve. Method explained in text.

[c] United Nations, *The Future Growth of World Population* (New York: United Nations, 1958), p. 74. The UN, in a later publication, *The Population of Asia and the Far East* (New York, 1959), pp. 100–102, adopted the projections which Ansley Coale and Edgar M. Hoover published in their book *Population Growth and Economic Development in Low Income Countries.* (Princeton, N. J.: Princeton University Press, 1958). According to these, the 1975 figure would be 587 million on the high-fertility assumption, 560 million on the medium-fertility assumption, and 524 on the low-fertility assumption. The later UN publication gives no estimates beyond 1981.

[d] *Ibid.*, p. 71. Strictly speaking, this source does not give estimates by single countries for the year 2000. It does, however, give estimates for broad regions. If we assume that India will have in the year 2000 the same proportion of Central and South Asia that it had in 1975 (namely, 76.4 per cent for the medium estimate), then we get the estimates given here.

aggregates of 100,000 or more inhabitants will be about triple in 1975 what it was in 1951, and in the year 2000 it will be two to four times the 1975 figure. As far as places 20,000 and over are concerned, the population living in such places by the end of the century may almost equal India's total 1951 population.

PROJECTION OF URBAN PROPORTION
BY LOGISTIC EXTRAPOLATION

As a basis of predicting India's future, the United States pattern, if not conservative, is at least middle-of-the-road, because America's development preceded India's by three-quarters of a century and, therefore, represents the older rather than the newer pace of industrialization. Evidence that the United States model is conservative is found when we fit a logistic curve to the data on the urban proportion in India from 1901 to 1951. As Figure 1 illustrates, the rise in the proportion in towns and cities was actually so steep from 1931 to 1951 that, when used to work out the logistic equation, it causes the extrapolated line to ascend rapidly.[8] As a consequence, we get the following projected proportions:

	Percentage in Places	
Year	20,000-plus	100,000-plus
1975...................	26	24
2000...................	52	50

These proportions are more than double those found by taking the United States pattern as a future model. Using the same population estimates as before, we find, accordingly, that the absolute population in places of 100,000 or over would be more than double the number estimated before. In the year 2000, for example, there might be half a billion people in India living in such cities.

THE FUTURE VOLUME OF
NET RURAL-URBAN MIGRATION

The nature of our estimates is such that they all assume the UN projections of *total* population growth in India. In addition, they all assume that the *urban* population will grow faster than the rural. This faster urban growth will hardly be due to superior natural increase on the part of the urban people. On the contrary,

---

[8] The line for cities and metropolitan areas over 100,000 was fitted by assuming an upper limit of 65 per cent, a lower limit of 2.6 per cent. By changing the assumptions, one can get a different line. If an upper asymptote of 75 per cent and a lower one of 2.7 per cent are assumed, the proportion in 1975 turns out to be 34 per cent, and in the year 2000 it is 66.

the towns and cities will almost certainly exhibit a *lower* natural increase than the rest of India. This means that the volume of rural-urban migration will have to be great enough (assuming the accuracy of our estimates of urbanization) not only to compensate for the urban deficiency in natural increase, but also to supply the urban advantage in growth.

The estimated volume of future rural-urban migration, therefore, depends on three factors: first, the UN estimates of total population growth; second, our estimates of the rising proportion of the population in towns and cities; and, third, our assumptions as to how much the city natural increase will fall below the non-city rate. The first factor is constant up to 1975 in all the estimates, and then breaks into three possibilities (high, medium, and low) from 1975 to 2000. The second factor divides into two possibilities according to whether or not the logistic pattern or the United States pattern is assumed. The third also divides into two basic alternatives, the one assuming *no* difference in natural increase as between city and non-city and the other assuming that the cities' natural increase is substantially lower. Throughout our estimates, we utilize two conceptions of the city population: those in towns and cities of 20,000 and over, and those in cities (or metropolitan areas) of 100,000 or more. In each case, the non-city category refers to the rest of the population.

The crisscrossing of the numerous alternative possibilities gives a variety of future estimates. We shall start with the most conservative assumptions with respect to the second and third factors —that is, we shall assume that urbanization rises in the future in India as it did in the United States and that there is no difference in natural increase as between the city and non-city populations.

MINIMUM ESTIMATE OF NET RURAL-URBAN MIGRATION

Assuming: (1) UN estimates of total population growth
(2) U.S. rate of urbanization
(3) No rural-urban difference in natural increase

By ignoring any differential in natural increase, the estimated migration is basically obtained by subtracting from the projected population in towns and cities (as obtained above) the population they would have had if their inhabitants had increased in number at exactly the same rate as the total estimated population of India. For the sake of accuracy, however, this basic computation must be modified for two reasons. In the first place, some of the apparent movement into cities is not really such, but is simply a function of the rise of certain places into the status of cities. In other words, some non-city people will become city inhabitants simply by staying at home. In the second place, another part of the apparent movement into cities will be due to the fact that, during any specifiable period, the migrants who move to cities prior to the end of the period will have a natural increase of their own *in the cities,* which it would be a mistake to count as migration.

To facilitate correction for these two sources of error, we have made our computations in terms of ten-year intervals. With respect to the first source of error (due to reclassification of cities), our problem was to find the population at the beginning of the decade living in places which, by the end of the decade, became cities. To do this we took the estimated population in cities at the beginning and end of each decade, and from this obtained the *number* of cities at each date by assuming that the rank-size rule applied.[9] The difference in number between the start and the close of each

---

[9] The rank-size rule is the generalization that, in any country or region, the size of a particular city is equal to its rank divided into the population of the chief city. In other words,

$$R_i S_i = M \tag{1}$$

where R is the rank and S the size of the ith city and M is a constant. The rank of the chief city being 1, its size is equal to M. Although the formula never holds perfectly, it fits the actual distribution of cities in large countries well enough to serve our purpose.

Since the lower class-boundary of the places considered in our calculations is arbitrarily set at either 20,000 or 100,000, the size of the smallest city S_n, is known. Using the case of the 20,000-plus class as an illustration, we have:

$$S_n R_n = M$$

$$20,000 R_n = M$$

$$R_n = \frac{M}{20,000} \tag{2}$$

Now, since R_n is the rank of the smallest city, it is also the same as the number of cities in the distribution. Furthermore, in view of the fact that we know the total population in cities (ΣS), we can find R_n, as follows:

From (1) above,

$$S_i = \frac{M}{R_i}$$

$$\Sigma S = \Sigma \frac{M}{R}$$

$$M = \frac{\Sigma S}{\Sigma \frac{1}{R}} \tag{3}$$

Given (2) above, we can substitute for M and have:

$$R_n = \frac{\dfrac{\Sigma S}{\Sigma \dfrac{1}{R}}}{20,000}$$

decade was taken to be the number of places that grew into the city class during the period. Their population at the start of the decade was computed from the rank-size formula,[10] and by adding this to the "city" population at that time, we eliminated it from the estimated migrants.

With regard to the second source of error (the natural increase of migrants themselves), we took the estimate of migrants left by correction of the first source and assumed that their natural increase was equal to that of the nation as a whole and that half of it occurred *before* they migrated to the cities. Subtracting this from the corrected estimate of migrants, we reached our final (doubly corrected) estimate for the decade.

By repeating this procedure for each decade, we came out with a set of estimates that could be summarized for any particular period between 1950 and 2000. The results—it should be remembered we are now assuming the U.S. rate of urbanization and no rural-urban difference in natural increase—are shown in Table 4. It can be seen that, by the lowest possible estimate that our assumptions allow, there will be during the last half of the present century more than 55 million migrants into cities of 100,000 or more, and more than 85 million into cities of 20,000 or more. In the twenty-five years from 1975 to 2000 there will be over 37 million and 57 million into the two classes of places, respectively. Even the highest figures in this table are conservative, because they are based on the assumption of no rural-urban differential in natural increase and a rate of urbanization that is less than that shown by Japan or by a logistic extrapolation.

When the absolute figures in Table 4 are related to the populations involved, we have a set of projected migration *rates*. These

$$R_n = \frac{\Sigma S}{20,000 \, \Sigma \frac{1}{R}} \tag{4}$$

In this equation, the R on one side is the same as the R on the other. Therefore when, as in our case, ΣS is known there is only one value of R which will make the two sides identical. With a table of reciprocals we can find the number of reciprocals which, when summed, will yield the identity.

[10] Since, from the previous footnote, $\Sigma S = \Sigma \frac{1}{R} \cdot M$, we can get the population in the cities in any segment of the distribution by summing the reciprocals of the ranks in those cities and multiplying by M (the population of the chief city in the distribution). In other words, for the segment:

$$\sum_{h}^{b} S = \sum_{h}^{b} \frac{1}{R} \cdot M$$

where h stands for the highest and b for the lowest rank of the cities in the segment.

TABLE 4

Four Estimates of Net Migration into Cities and Towns

Period and population estimate	Net migration from outside (in millions)							
	Minimum estimate[a]		First medium estimate[b]		Second medium estimate[c]		Maximum estimate[d]	
	Into places 20,000+	Into cities 100,000+	Into places 20,000+	Into cities 100,000+	Into places 20,000+	Into cities 100,000+	Into places 20,000+	Into cities 100,000+
Decades:								
1950–1960......	11.2	7.9	12.4	9.3	14.5	13.7	15.7	15.0
1960–1970......	7.9	5.4	10.2	8.0	25.0	27.7	30.4	30.7
1970–1980								
High.........	19.1	10.0	22.8	14.6	42.4	48.6	46.8	55.5
Medium......	19.2	10.0	22.7	14.6	42.2	48.7	46.6	55.4
Low.........	19.4	8.6	21.0	12.8	41.2	47.4	43.4	50.7
1980–1990								
High.........	22.2	17.0	28.5	24.8	63.2	66.4	71.1	79.9
Medium......	22.4	16.8	27.8	23.4	62.0	66.0	68.8	77.6
Low.........	20.6	15.4	23.7	19.4	54.6	58.2	58.6	64.9
1990–2000								
High.........	32.2	20.8	42.4	34.0	80.8	69.8	93.8	92.8
Medium......	31.2	20.7	39.0	30.8	77.3	67.6	87.4	85.1
Low.........	26.6	17.6	30.4	22.2	63.5	56.0	67.2	64.2
25-year periods:								
1950–1975......	28.7	18.3	34.0	24.6	60.6	65.7	69.4	73.4
1975–2000								
High.........	64.0	50.0	82.3	66.1	165.2	160.5	188.3	200.5
Medium......	63.2	38.0	78.2	61.5	160.4	157.9	179.5	190.4
Low.........	56.9	37.3	64.6	48.0	138.7	137.9	147.5	154.5
50-year period:								
1950–2000								
High.........	92.7	68.3	116.3	90.7	225.8	226.2	257.7	273.9
Medium......	91.9	56.3	112.2	86.1	221.0	223.6	248.9	263.8
Low.........	85.6	55.6	98.6	72.6	199.3	203.6	216.9	227.9

[a] Assuming U.S. rate of urbanization and no rural-urban difference in natural increase.

[b] Assuming U.S. rate of urbanization and natural increase of 20,000+ places to be 80 per cent and of 100,000+ places 67 per cent of that outside such places.

[c] Assuming logistic rate of urbanization and no rural-urban difference in natural increase.

[d] Assuming logistic rate of urbanization and natural increase of 20,000+ places to be 80 per cent and of 100,000+ places 67 per cent of that outside such places.

are shown in Table 5. Again, it must be stressed that these are our most conservative estimates; yet they lead to the result that in each decade between 100 and 230 migrants will enter the cities and towns per 1,000 average population in those places. Since the population outside the towns and cities is greater, the migrants will be fewer in proportion to it. The "rural" rates, however, tend to rise during each decade. Thus Table 5 illustrates the fact that, in the early stages of a country's urbanization, the net rural-urban migration rate is much greater when measured in terms of the urban population than when measured in terms of the rural. Ulti-

TABLE 5

Four Estimates of Rates of Net Migration into Cities and Towns from Outside

Period and population estimate	Minimum estimate[a]				First medium estimate[b]				Second medium estimate[c]				Maximum estimate[d]			
	Into places 20,000+		Into places 100,000+		Into places 20,000+		Into places 100,000+		Into places 20,000+		Into places 100,000+		Into places 20,000+		Into places 100,000+	
	Per 1,000 pop. outside	Per 1,000 pop. inside	Per 1,000 pop. outside	Per 1,000 pop. inside	Per 1,000 pop. outside	Per 1,000 pop. inside	Per 1,000 pop. outside	Per 1,000 pop. inside	Per 1,000 pop. outside	Per 1,000 pop. inside	Per 1,000 pop. outside	Per 1,000 pop. inside	Per 1,000 pop. outside	Per 1,000 pop. inside	Per 1,000 pop. outside	Per 1,000 pop. inside
1950–1960	33	215	22	228	37	238	26	269	43	275	39	376	47	297	43	412
1960–1970	21	104	13	105	27	135	20	155	67	282	71	391	82	343	79	434
1970–1980																
High	42	168	20	131	50	201	30	191	102	274	113	348	113	302	129	397
Medium	42	169	20	131	50	200	30	191	102	273	114	349	113	301	129	397
Low	45	184	19	121	49	199	28	180	106	287	117	367	111	302	126	392
1980–1990																
High	40	125	28	141	52	161	31	206	138	233	141	255	155	262	170	307
Medium	41	130	28	143	51	161	39	216	138	234	144	260	153	260	169	306
Low	45	140	30	155	51	161	38	195	142	244	148	271	153	261	165	302
1990–2000																
High	47	116	27	109	62	153	44	179	161	175	135	156	187	203	180	208
Medium	49	121	29	117	61	151	43	174	165	180	140	163	187	204	176	205
Low	53	133	31	128	61	152	40	162	173	191	148	174	183	202	170	200

[a] Assuming U.S. rate of urbanization and no rural-urban difference in natural increase.

[b] Assuming U.S. rate of urbanization and natural increase of 20,000+ places to be 80 per cent and of 100,000+ places 67 per cent of that outside such places.

[c] Assuming logistic rate of urbanization and no rural-urban difference in natural increase.

[d] Assuming logistic rate of urbanization and natural increase of 20,000+ places to be 80 per cent and of 100,000+ places 67 per cent of that outside such places.

mately, the relationship is reversed as the rural population becomes smaller than the urban.[11]

FIRST MEDIUM ESTIMATE OF NET RURAL-URBAN MIGRATION

Assuming: (1) UN estimates of total population growth
 (2) U.S. rate of urbanization
 (3) Natural increase in 20,000-plus places four fifths, and in 100,000-plus places two thirds, of that outside such places

A low-medium estimate of the future net flow of non-city to city migration can be obtained by keeping the assumption that future urbanization will follow the past United States path, but allowing urban natural increase to be lower than the rural. There is no good basis for predicting how much difference in natural increase there will be between village and city, but if we assume that the population in places of 20,000 and over will have an excess of births over deaths that is 80 per cent of that of the population outside of such places, we shall perhaps not be far wrong. More drastic is the assumption that the natural increase in cities of 100,000 or more will be only two thirds of that outside these cities,[12] but the decline in fertility usually starts in the cities.

The results of calculations based on these assumptions are given in Table 4. The allowance for a differential in natural increase causes the estimates of net migration to be from around 20 to 50 per cent higher than those in the minimum estimate. The net migration rates (as shown in Table 5), computed by dividing the estimated migrants by the same mid-populations in urban places and nonurban places, are larger in much the same ratio as the absolute numbers. On the basis of the first medium assumptions, then, the prospective net rural-urban migration in India rises from about

---

[11] See Kingsley Davis, "Internal Migration and Urbanization in Relation to Economic Development," in United Nations, *World Population Conference, 1954* (New York, 1955), II, 783–801.

[12] Research by Richard B. Gamble, on the staff of International Population and Urban Research, shows that in 1951, according to data for 53 metropolitan areas in India with more than 100,000 inhabitants, the age-standardized child-woman ratios in cities were practically as high as the rural ratios. The average child-woman ratio for the 53 MA's is 534, and that for the rural population is 538. The under-reporting of children may be greater, however, in rural areas. If the death rate of children is lower in cities, this argues against our assumption concerning natural increase. Our knowledge of mortality differences, however, is even less than our knowledge of fertility differences between country and city. The main argument for our assumption of a future rural-urban differential in natural increase rests, then, on the general rule that the decline of fertility with the demographic transition starts in cities, and that mortality, if not worse in cities, is usually no better than in the country.

30 per 1,000 of the nonurban population in the 1950's and 1960's to about 60 in the 1990's. The rate per 1,000 persons already in places of 20,000+ decreases somewhat.

SECOND MEDIUM ESTIMATE OF NET RURAL-URBAN MIGRATION

Assuming: (1) UN estimates of total population growth
(2) Logistic rate of urbanization
(3) No difference between city and non-city in natural increase

A logistic curve fitted to the previous urban history of India yields an extrapolated trend of future urbanization so steep that the estimated migration becomes very high. Indeed, even when no rural-urban difference in natural increase is assumed, the logistic yields higher estimates than does the U.S. model with an assumed difference in natural increase. This can be seen by examining Table 4. The table shows the number of migrants, using the second medium estimate assumptions, as being more than 200 million between 1950 and 2000. The rates, as exhibited in Table 5, are correspondingly higher. Due to the rapid urbanization assumed, the number of migrants in relation to the city population begins at a high point (nearly 400 per 1,000 per decade between 1950 and 1970) and diminishes rapidly, especially after 1980. For the same reason, the number in relation to the non-city population rises rapidly, reaching 135 to 175 per 1,000 in the decade from 1990 to 2000.

MAXIMUM ESTIMATE OF NET RURAL-URBAN MIGRATION

Assuming: (1) UN estimates of total population growth
(2) Logistic rate of urbanization
(3) Difference in rate of natural increase of city and non-city populations in first medium estimate

Although the assumptions underlying our logistic extrapolation of India's future urbanization are not extreme (with an upper asymptote of 65 per cent in places 100,000 or over and of 80 per cent in places of 20,000 or more), the rate is nevertheless so fast that, if rural-urban differences in natural increase are also assumed, the resulting estimated net migration is extremely large. For instance, as Table 4 shows, there would be around 70 million net migrants during the first twenty-five-year period, and around 150 to 200 million during the second. Similarly, the rates (Table 5) climb to the point where, in the 1960–1970 decade, the migrants will equal 34 to 44 per cent of those already in cities and towns, and, in the 1990–2000 decade, they will equal 17 to 19 per cent of those outside cities and towns.

The estimates arising from our varied assumptions necessarily cover a considerable range. As could be expected, the range tends to widen as the period in question becomes more remote; but it widens much more in absolute difference than in proportional difference.

Despite the width of the range in each period, the projections all indicate that India is likely to have a tremendous shift in the location of its people. Even the lowest estimate calls for a net shift in residence of 85.6 million people during the 1950–2000 period. This is more than a fifth of India's entire estimated population gain during that period (according to the low population projection, which should be assumed if we accept the low estimate of rural-urban migration). The highest estimate, 258 million, is equal to 35 per cent of India's population increase (according to the high population projection). By the lowest estimates, we find that there will be periods when 5 per cent of the non-city population will be shifting residence each decade, and by the highest estimates it will be 19 per cent. In cities of 100,000 or more, the low estimate finds decades when the stream of newcomers contributes more than 20 per cent of the population already there; and possibly this may be, by the highest estimate, over 40 per cent in some decades.

The fact should be emphasized that we are *not* estimating the total movement back and forth between city and country. We have talked throughout about *net* migration only. The actual movement will be far greater than the net figures, because many people will move back and forth several times. Furthermore, we have not precisely estimated the rural-urban net movement. Our figures concern only the movement into cities of 20,000-plus or 100,000-plus from outside those cities. Necessarily, the outside population contains some urban people in the first case and many urban people in the latter case. The actual net rural-urban movement will be greater than the non-city to city movement.

In view of these considerations, we feel that our migration estimates point to a substantial movement in India. The higher figures doubtless seem fantastic, because, in sheer absolute numbers of human beings on the move, they have no equal in human history. The volume of new housing, water supply, transportation, and urban employment that will be required to accommodate this mass movement of 86 to 258 million people into cities is staggering.

When we realize that this will be only part of the growth of cities, that the cities will also be growing rapidly from natural increase, we see that the work of accommodation in Indian cities almost defies imagination.

HOW PROBABLE ARE THE ESTIMATES
OF CITYWARD MIGRATION?

Naturally, the question arises as to the probability of the estimates. Which figures are likely to be the actual ones?

Unfortunately, there is no way of answering this question. The actual course of cityward migration in India may fall outside our range, because of catastrophic events not included in the assumptions. It may be objected that we have overestimated the rate of urbanization in India and consequently the volume of rural-urban migration. This view could rest on the argument that, for such developments as we picture to occur, a fairly rapid rate of economic development must characterize India during the rest of this century. Our answer is that by contemporary standards the rate of economic growth achieved in the United States during the period 1858 to 1908 (which is the period that furnished us with one of our models for urbanization) is slow, not rapid. To put it another way, if India is to have the population growth projected for her by the United Nations or by Coale and Hoover (see Table 3), she cannot have a slow economic development. If she is to solve her present economic problems in the face of population growth, she must move, if not at a revolutionary speed, at least at a speed equal to that achieved by Japan.

It may again be argued that our estimates are too high on exactly the opposite ground—namely, that we assume urbanization will necessarily be tied to economic development. India may, according to this view, have a moderate or an extremely rapid rate of economic growth without a corresponding rate of urban expansion. If this is possible, the present writer has yet to find any evidence of it. There is no nation in history which has made the economic transformation which has not also experienced the urban change. Developments thus far in India give no indication whatever that India will be an exception to the rule. Until some hard evidence to the contrary is produced, the writer believes that in this regard neither India nor any other country can have its cake and eat it too.

Such considerations lead us to the view that, barring catastrophic developments, the more probable estimates of migration into cities are the medium ones we have set forth. If we take the mean of these two as being the single most probable, we have the following:

Net Migrants (millions)

Years	Into places 20,000-plus	Into places 100,000-plus
1950–1960.............	13.4	11.5
1960–1970.............	17.6	17.8
1970–1980.............	32.4	31.6
1980–1990.............	44.9	44.7
1990–2000.............	58.2	49.2
1950–1975.............	47.3	45.2
1975–2000.............	119.3	109.7
1950–2000.............	166.6	154.9

It should be noted that if any of our projections prove true, the big period of internal migration in India is yet to come. The quarter century between 1975 and 2000 will see two to three times the amount of such movement in 1950–1975.

THE FUTURE POPULATION OF INDIAN CITIES

As yet we have said nothing about particular cities in India. It is time now that we turn to the question of their future populations, and some of what has been said will, I think, help us in this difficult task. Other things being equal, the smaller the areal unit under consideration, the more difficult it is to estimate the future population. The reasons for this are as follows:

1) The size of the geographical unit tends to be inversely related to the proportional role of migration. A small country like Israel may double its population in a few years by immigration, but this is most improbable for a country the size of Brazil or the United States.

2) Among the components of population change, migration is the most difficult to predict, evidently because it is the least constrained by biological factors. Whereas the lower limit of the death rate and the upper limit of the birth rate are biologically conditioned, there is little of such conditioning in either the upper or the lower limits of the migration rate. In other words, migration is more purely socially determined, therefore affected by a greater variety of factors, and consequently more unpredictable.

If this line of reasoning is accepted, we can understand why there is less confidence in future population estimates for cities than for countries. Indeed, the growth of cities in modern times has depended greatly on precisely the most unpredictable of the demographic components—migration. Although the total volume of future rural-urban migration within an entire country may be estimated with some confidence, the flow into a particular city may not be.[13] The more rapid the rate of urbanization being experienced by a country, the greater is the role of rural-urban migration in the growth of its cities. Accordingly, it is in this kind of country that estimation of the future growth of individual metropolises is especially difficult. The future populations of British metropolitan areas, for example, can be estimated with more confidence than the future populations of Indian metropolitan areas. Yet it is in the underdeveloped, rapidly urbanizing country that there is most need for planning and hence most need for population forecasts. The difficulties and pitfalls cannot be allowed to dissuade us from trying such individual city forecasts.

The best method of making city population forecasts depends upon the length of the period involved and the purpose in view, as well as the kind of data available. If the chief purpose is to forecast the population only for the next few years, the recent growth rate of the city itself will be a good basis of prediction.[14] This will be true regardless of the technique used in extrapolating past total population growth. We may call this kind of projection the "autonomous" type, because it uses solely material having to do with the particular city or metropolis under consideration. The trouble with it is that any particular city is an integral part of a larger system. Therefore, especially for long-run projections, it does not pay to ignore the total system. To take an extreme case, if one knew in advance that the seat of the Indian government were going to be moved within two years from Delhi to Nagpur, one would not wish to predict the population of Delhi ten years from now solely on the basis of the past growth of this city.

Recognition that any given city is part of a larger system, and that its growth depends on what happens to that system, is the logical basis for estimating future populations by the so-called "ratio" type of projection. Like the "autonomous" type, there are various specific techniques for "ratio" projections. They all depend on hav-

---

[13] Sometimes an attempt is made to predict the future population of a city or metropolitan area on the basis of the number of the jobs estimated to exist in the future. This was done, for example, with respect to the metropolitan area of Washington, D.C. See *Mass Transportation Survey,* a report made by the National Capital Planning Commission and National Capital Regional Planning Council (1959). But the trouble is that the number of future jobs in an urban area is as unpredictable as population itself, if not more so. See, for example, the criticism of the Washington population estimates made on this basis in *Hearings* of the Joint Committee on Washington Metropolitan Problems, Congress of the United States, November 9–14, 1959, pp. 31–57.

[14] Bogue found, for example, that the best predictor of decade growth in standard metropolitan areas of the United States was the growth of the area during the previous ten years. See Donald J. Bogue and Dorothy L. Harris, *Comparative Population and Urban Research* (Oxford, Ohio: Scripps Foundation for Population Research, 1954), p. 24.

ing a population projection for a larger area than the city under
study, but the character of the larger area and the manner in
which the ratio is treated may differ from one case to another.[15]
In what follows we shall use a novel method for making long-run
population estimates for Indian cities. This is essentially a "ratio"
method, but it makes use of "autonomous" data as well. The logic
of the method is this: the future population of any particular city
depends not only upon the prospective population growth of the
country as a whole, but also upon the changing degree of urbanization in that country. To project the population of particular Indian
cities we shall, therefore, make use of our projections of India's
future urbanization.

It will be recalled that, having the United Nations population
projections for India and our own estimates of the degree of
urbanization, we are able to compute the projected population in
cities at various dates. Our present problem, then, is somehow to
estimate the *number* and the *sizes* of the cities that compose this
population. To do this we have once more to call upon the rank-
size rule. In fact, for the purpose of estimating rural-urban migration, we have already had to compute the number of cities at each
date.[16] Also, the size of the chief city has been computed, and from
this it is easy to get the sizes of the next ranking cities. We thus
come out with an estimate of the sizes of the major cities in India
at various dates in the future.

This method, however, does not tell us the *identity* of the cities.
It merely says that, say, the first ten cities, whatever and wherever
they are in India, will have approximately certain sizes. What is
required in addition is some procedure for determining which
Indian cities will have the ranks in question. To accomplish this,
we have made two assumptions: first, that the major cities at future
dates will be cities which already exist in India; second, that the
relative growth of these cities over the last fifty years, when extrapolated over the next fifty years, will give the *ranking* of these
cities in the future. Note that we do not use the past growth of the
particular city to say what its future population will be. We merely
use its past growth, relative to that of other cities in India, to say
what its *rank* will be among them. When one is given this rank for

---

[15] An elementary discussion of various techniques of projections for cities is contained in United Nations, "Estimates and Projections of the Population of Large
Cities and Their Use in Urban Development Planning," UN Seminar on Evaluation
and Utilization of Population Census Data in Latin America, Santiago, Chile,
November 30–December 18, 1959 (unpublished; limited distribution). This document
also contains an extensive bibliography. In the United States a recent application of
the ratio method to metropolitan areas is Jerome P. Pickard, *Metropolitanization of
the United States* (Washington, D.C.: Urban Land Use Institute, 1959).

[16] See note 9.

some future date—say, 1975—one can then assign it the population that goes with this rank, according to our estimates of the urban population.

The procedure just described yields the results set forth in Table 6. The largest metropolis, which will perhaps be Calcutta, will have

TABLE 6

ESTIMATED SIZE OF THE TEN MAJOR CITIES IN INDIA IN 1970 AND 2000
(In millions of inhabitants)

Metropolis[a]	Type of estimate of proportion in cities[b]			
	Low		High	
	1970	2000	1970	2000
Calcutta..............	12.0	35.6	16.0	66.0
Delhi................	6.0	17.8	8.0	33.0
Bombay..............	4.0	11.9	5.3	22.0
Madras...............	3.0	8.9	4.0	16.5
Bangalore............	2.4	7.1	3.2	13.2
Ahmedabad...........	2.0	5.9	2.7	11.0
Hyderabad...........	1.7	5.1	2.3	9.4
Kanpur..............	1.5	4.5	2.0	8.3
Poona...............	1.3	4.0	1.8	7.3
Nagpur..............	1.2	3.6	1.6	6.6

[a] Ranked according to their relative position in the year 2000. (See text.)

[b] Each type of estimate yields two series of figures for the specific cities, according to whether the 20,000+ or the 100,000+ class is utilized. On the whole, however, the differences are not great; we have accordingly taken the mean of the two. Furthermore, for the year 2000, we have three additional bases for different estimates, according to whether the high, low, or medium population projection is used. In all cases, for purposes of the present table, we have used the *medium* population projection.

according to the calculations between 12 and 16 million inhabitants in 1970 and between 36 and 66 million in the year 2000. The next city, probably Delhi, will have between 18 and 33 million at the latter date. If these figures seem high, it has to be remembered that no country the size of India and with its projected population growth has ever undergone the urban transition. If India has the development that the population projections imply and that the economic plans envisage, it will doubtless have cities of a size never equaled up to now. The largest city in the world today is New York, with approximately 15 million people. The projected population of India's largest city, even on our "high" assumption, is not out of line with India's scale at that time. With an estimated population of one billion in the year 2000, the country's principal city, with 66 million, would constitute only 6.6 per cent of the total population. This is a modest percentage for the chief city. The main city in the United States constitutes about 8.4 per cent of the population, and the chief city in the United Kingdom constitutes about 20.5 per cent of the total. Whether human beings will want to live in such huge urban agglomerations is another question. The answer depends in part on the structure which these agglomerations have. The metropolitan deconcentration found late in the process of urbanization is in part a response to the inhuman impact of high urban densities in large aggregates. A high density over a little space can be tolerated, because escape seems easy. But a high density over a great amount of space seems oppressive. For this and other reasons, as urban agglomerations become larger—reaching sizes of two or more millions—we may expect the center to remain static or lose population, while the periphery expands rapidly outward at a lower average density. This process has the effect of lowering the density and, therefore, making urban life somewhat more tolerable, but it also has the effect of introducing another depressing feature, the difficulty of escaping from the city. A metropolitan aggregate of 66 million might well cover an area that would take four hours to drive across. Our projections do not say that such cities *will* exist, but merely that if other things occur which people foresee as probable, then these too will occur.

URBANIZATION
AND
MIGRATION IN INDIA

Donald J. Bogue and K. C. Zachariah

A discussion of urbanization in India (and, in fact, almost every-where in the world) fundamentally is a discussion of net rural-to-urban migration, and an analysis of the forces that underlie ur-banization is also an analysis of the migration-stimulating effects of various demographic, economic, and social forces which are at work. The demonstration of this contention is neither difficult to give nor to understand. Urbanization usually is said to be taking place when the proportion of total population that is residing in places defined as urban is rising, or when urban population is grow-ing at a faster rate than the average rate of growth for the nation. All population growth is composed of two components: (*a*) "re-productive change" (also called "natural increase"), which is the excess of births over deaths, and (*b*) net migration. If one assumes a situation wherein there is no net international migration, then the migration component for each community within that nation must be due entirely to net internal migration.

THE MIGRATION-URBANIZATION RELATIONSHIP

In India today, as in most nations of Asia, the rate of reproductive change is not very different in rural and urban areas. In the cities death rates may tend to be somewhat lower than in rural areas, but birth rates also tend to be somewhat lower, so that the rate of growth from reproductive change is roughly the same. Hence, very little urbanization can take place as a result of vital processes alone. In fact, in many epochs of history, and probably in many Asian cities, there would be a net decline in urbanization if vital processes alone were at work. (For example, in Calcutta city, the registered number of deaths was always greater than the registered number of births up to 1951.)

The reclassification of places as urban or rural may not be negligible, and it may, therefore, be a factor in the growth of urban population. In India during the period 1941–1951 the number of towns increased from 2,390 to 3,018. The increase of 628 towns in 1951 was a result of the exclusion of 122 towns of 1941 and the inclusion of 750 new towns. However, for any country where this factor is neglible, or is considered to be unimportant for a particular type of analysis, the rate of urbanization is equal to the rate of net in-migration to towns. In most instances, the total urban population gained from redefinition will be a comparatively small fraction of the total gain to the urban population. We may make the assertion, therefore: *Rural-to-urban migration is by far the major component of urbanization and is the chief mechanism by which all of the world's great urbanization trends have been accomplished.* This being the case, there is great potential profit in focusing on rural-to-urban migration as a way of deepening one's understanding of the urbanization process.

Until very recently, almost no data for attempting such an analysis were available, and the opinion was rather widely held that valid migration estimates could not be prepared from the rather deficient statistics available for most nations of Asia. Experimental work performed by one of the authors has led to modified and improved methods which appear to overcome most of the difficulties, and which yield estimates that appear to be reasonably precise and highly useful.[1] Further exploratory work by the authors jointly, and its use by students at the Demographic Centre, have yielded estimates of net migration for almost every major city of southeastern Asia, and rural-urban migration estimates for the states and regions of several nations, in which India was the prototype for later work. The present paper summarizes briefly the content of these calculations, and tries to interpret them and from them build a somewhat more sophisticated view of urbanization in nations that are simultaneously undergoing economic development and rapid population growth.

[1] K. C. Zachariah, *Internal Migration in India, 1941–51* (Bombay: Demographic Training and Research Centre, 1960).

POPULAR MISCONCEPTIONS CONCERNING THE IMMOBILITY
OF TRADITIONAL AGRARIAN SOCIETIES

Many works written from an anthropological point of view emphasize the strong hold which the Indian village has over the hearts and minds of the population. It has been widely accepted that the rural population of India is comparatively non-migratory, because it is too strongly tied to its village origins by bonds of kinship, marriage customs, language, and centuries of in-group living to be easily diverted to the comparative insecurity and strangeness of the city. Similar views have been expressed about the agrarian societies of other Asian nations. In India, so widely has this viewpoint been accepted that urbanization has almost come to be regarded as being inconsistent with the Indian way of life, with the corollary that the urban form of social organization ought to be kept suppressed and minimized to the greatest extent possible while trying to raise standards of living. This has been expressed in proposals to "bring jobs to the people" in the individual villages in the form of cottage and other handicraft industries—an alternative to erecting establishments at those points and on a scale that would assure low unit costs and high worker productivity, as has been the spatial pattern of economic development in Europe and America. "Factories without cities" seems to be a slogan that represents much of the current attitude toward urban migration in India.

Statistical evidence in support of the view of population immobility has been cited from the data for state of birth, which show that in all of India, in 1951, only 3.1 per cent of the total population was living outside the state of birth. This very low percentage has also been found to hold at earlier censuses.

PER CENT OF POPULATION LIVING OUTSIDE
STATE OF BIRTH, 1901–1951

1951	3.1
1931	3.6
1921	3.7
1911	3.6
1901	3.3

These data[2] seem to indicate that the great mass of India's population is born, lives, and dies in or very near its birthplace; that this situation has persisted throughout the span for which

---

[2] The percentage for 1951 is computed from Table D-IV, *Census of India, 1951,* I, Part II-A; for other years the percentages are taken from Kingsley Davis, *Population of India and Pakistan* (Princeton, N.J.: Princeton University Press, 1951), and refer to unpartitioned India.

statistics are available; and that the 1951 census gave no indication of any change in this pattern. The regional barriers of differences in language, marriage customs, food habits, social status, and
reliance upon one's relatives for mutual assistance have been said
to explain these statistics. Only such dramatic events as great
famines, floods, or political upheavals (such as the partition with
Pakistan) have been thought capable of driving the Indian peasant
from his village to seek his fortune in strange environs, and the
place-of-birth statistics seem to prove it.

Without trying to assess whether this situation ever actually
existed in India in the past (at least in the extreme form described),
we suggest that there is much evidence that it did not exist in the
decade 1941–1951, and that there is a very rapidly rising tempo
of rural-to-urban migration under way throughout India. Experimental work has shown that state-of-birth statistics have a built-in
bias toward understating the volume of movement that has taken
place, especially in recent years.[3] Moreover, India's history has
certainly been one of great invasions and migrations, with much
circulation of population, so that it is doubtful whether the conditions of near-perfect immobility ever really existed. Indian peasants
have anxiously rushed into new plantations as they were opened
up (for example, in Assam), and into foreign lands wherever they
would be admitted (Burma, Ceylon, Malaya, Africa). It is quite
possible that the great dominance of the village over the residential
desires of the average Indian citizen (especially those feeling the
pinch of population pressure the most) has been greatly exaggerated, and that deficient statistics have perpetuated this bit of
misinformation. Certainly it would be a serious error of fact to
attribute immobility to the rural population of India in the current
and prospective future situation, as the data of the next section will
show.[4]

GROWTH OF URBAN POPULATION IN INDIA, 1941–1951

In 1951 there were 3,018 towns[5] with a combined population of
about 61.9 million persons. During the intercensal period 1941–

---

[3] Donald J. Bogue, "The Use of Place-of-Birth Statistics and Duration-of-Residence
Data for Measuring Internal Migration," in *Seminar on Evaluation and Utilization
of Census Data* (Bombay: Demographic Training and Research Centre, 1960).

[4] Zachariah, *op. cit.*

[5] According to the definition followed in the 1951 census, "A Town is normally
an inhabited locality with a total population of not less than 5,000 persons, but, places
with a somewhat larger population which do not possess a *definite* urban character
may not be treated as towns. At the same time, places with a smaller population with
definite urban character (including generally all municipalities and cantonments and
other places having a local administration of their own) may be treated as separate
towns." *Census of India, 1951,* I, Part II-A.

1951, the urban population increased by 18 million persons, or by 41 per cent. Simultaneously, the proportion of urban population in the country increased from 13.9 per cent in 1941 to 17.3 per cent in 1951. This increase is made up of (1) the natural increase in the 3,018 towns, plus (2) net migration during the decade, plus (3) the population in 1941 of 750 areas which were towns only in 1951, minus the population in 1941 of the 122 areas which were towns only in 1941.

The second component gives the total net rural-to-urban migration plus the balance of international migration in the urban areas. Certain limitations of the data make the estimation of migration to some of these towns difficult. The population in 1941 of 321 of these towns is not given in the census reports; this makes it impossible to estimate the migration to these towns.

TOTAL RURAL-URBAN MIGRATION IN INDIA, 1941–1951

The 2,697 towns (urban places) for which the relevant data are available had a total population of 60 million persons in 1951, or about 96.9 per cent of the total urban population of the country. An estimate of net migration among persons ten years of age and above in these towns is 7.1 million (3.7 million males and 3.4 million females). A rough estimate of net migration among persons under ten years is 1.1 million persons. The total population in 1951 in the 321 towns for which the relevant data for 1941 are not available is about 1.9 million. In some of the bigger towns among these (such as Faridabad or Ulhasnagar) the entire population may be migrants, and in some of the smaller ones only a very small fraction may be migrants. Taking into consideration the contribution of this group of towns also, *the rural-to-urban migration in India (including balance of international migration in the urban area) during the period 1941–1951 may be estimated to be a little under 9 million persons.* This is a rate of net in-migration to cities equivalent to 20 per cent of the 1941 urban population. It is a rate of net out-migration from rural areas equivalent to 3 per cent of their 1941 rural populations.

URBANWARD MIGRATION IN INDIA BY STATES, 1941–1951

The breakdown of the total net rural-urban migration by states is given in Table 1. This table gives the migration only of persons ten years of age and above to the 2,697 towns for which relevant data are available.

During the decade under consideration, the largest migration has been to Madras—about 1.7 million persons. Bombay comes

TABLE 1

URBANWARD MIGRATION BY DISTRICTS

Name of district and state	Urbanward migration, 1941–51			
	Volume		Rate (per 100, 1941 population)	
	Male	Female	Male	Female
UTTAR PRADESH.............	+253,851	+212,514	+6.57	+6.84
1. Dehra Dun............	+24,772	+21,351	+40.52	+70.59
2. Saharanpur...........	+4,635	+16,053	+2.94	+14.31
3. Muzaffarnagar........	+4,301	+2,640	+4.39	+3.41
4. Meerut..............	+49,484	+32,178	+25.02	+21.16
5. Bulandshahr..........	−5,265	−4,173	−4.62	−4.33
6. Aligarh..............	+2,180	+3,433	+1.61	+3.14
7. Mathura.............	+2,879	+2,123	+3.35	+3.03
8. Agra................	+26,698	+14,893	+13.00	+8.72
9. Manipuri............	+1,656	+1,090	+4.76	+3.77
10. Etach...............	−1,491	−1,217	−2.27	−2.18
11. Bareilly.............	−4,442	−3,756	−3.13	−3.21
12. Bijnor..............	−3,988	−3,961	−3.73	−4.10
13. Budaun.............	−4,392	−5,050	−5.89	−7.67
14. Moradabad...........	−220	−4,598	−0.12	−2.80
15. Shahjahanpur........	−10,672	−5,695	−12.76	−5.96
16. Pilibhit.............	−2,524	−2,388	−6.49	−7.20
17. Rampur.............	+12,083	+13,874	+18.78	+24.57
18. Farrukhabad.........	−2,335	+1,978	−3.33	+3.57
19. Etawah.............	+1,600	+792	+3.35	+1.99
20. Kanpur.............	+74,204	+49,056	+24.57	+25.09
21. Fatehpur...........	−2,674	−2,705	−11.50	−11.63
22. Allahabad...........	+14,409	+13,950	+8.78	+11.02
23. Jhansi.............	+3,333	+3,753	+3.86	+4.85
24. Jalaun.............	+133	+225	+0.41	+0.78
25. Hamirpur...........	−2,006	−1,356	−5.98	−4.22
26. Banda..............	+269	−3,369	+1.00	−1.53
27. Banaras............	+33,029	+44,145	+20.07	+34.02
28. Mirzapur...........	+1,245	+89	+2.42	+0.19
29. Jaunpur............	−1,138	−569	−2.87	−1.63
30. Ghazipur...........	−4,305	−1,746	−7.83	−3.37
31. Ballia..............	−482	+1,685	−1.01	+3.83
32. Gorakhpur..........	+11,009	+3,473	+16.40	+5.93
33. Deoria.............	+626	+1,101	+1.87	+3.81
34. Basti..............	+3,478	+2,208	+18.05	+14.13
35. Azamgarh..........	−2,864	+94	−5.41	+0.21
36. Naini Tal..........	+1,259	−1,663	+1.82	−6.04
37. Almora............	+2,896	+715	+26.77	+10.85
38. Garhwal	−307	+472	−3.85	+15.84
39. Lucknow...........	+24,599	+22,629	+10.33	+12.75
40. Unnao.............	−649	−761	−2.30	−3.13

TABLE 1 (Continued)

| Name of district and state | Urbanward migration, 1941–51 | | | |
| | Volume | | Rate (per 100, 1941 population) | |
	Male	Female	Male	Female
41. Rae Bareli	+511	−611	+2.12	−2.84
42. Sitapur	+1,656	−233	+3.46	−0.60
43. Hardoi	−2,994	−3,257	−4.72	−6.07
44. Kheri	+56	+5	+0.18	+0.02
45. Faizabad	+9,077	+10,936	+15.79	+25.41
46. Gonda	−5,080	−4,432	−9.69	−9.85
47. Bahraich	+1,148	−2,107	+3.57	−7.40
48. Sultanpur	+1,553	+626	+20.69	+11.14
49. Pratapgarh	−127	−499	−0.98	−4.42
50. Bara Banki	−1,695	−1,907	−4.05	−5.31
BIHAR	+111,618	+76,183	+10.40	+8.57
51. Saran	−3,120	−1,015	−6.97	−2.58
52. Champaran	−3,545	−810	−11.82	−3.17
53. Muzaffarpur	+3,012	+3,677	+5.55	+8.40
54. Darbhanga	−2,602	+7,471	−3.91	+13.43
55. Monghyr	+7,992	−5,994	+7.39	−6.05
56. Purnea	+10,665	−785	+27.27	−3.08
57. Patna	+29,648	+22,033	+15.41	+13.92
58. Gaya	+6,103	+6,169	+6.85	+8.10
59. Shahabad	+8,175	+4,513	+10.73	+6.51
60. Bhagalpur	+4,287	+828	+7.71	+1.87
61. Santal Parganas	+7,857	+7,951	+21.35	+25.83
62. Hazaribagh	+5,988	+6,806	+13.34	+17.77
63. Ranchi	+15,954	+10,241	+39.02	+28.40
64. Purulia	+152	+5,129	+0.46	+18.24
65. Dhanbad	+4,012	−1,390	+16.95	−8.80
66. Palamau	−400	+843	−3.40	+7.74
67. Singhbhum	+17,233	+10,516	+13.72	+11.33
ORISSA	+36,238	+15,395	+14.81	+6.86
68. Cuttack	+15,508	+9,184	+26.56	+18.82
69. Balasore	+243	−617	+1.19	−3.33
70. Puri	+8,011	+7,306	+27.06	+29.51
71. Sambalpur	+4,438	+2,733	+21.85	+13.96
72. Ganjam	−1,055	−9,135	−2.34	−20.27
73. Koraput	+8,998	+4,823	+55.98	+30.13
74. Dhenkanal	+1,204	+1,160	+10.78	+11.07
75. Keonjhar	−1,140	+428	−23.89	+10.12
76. Phulbani	−400	−383	−14.14	−13.15
77. Bolangir	+566	+334	+3.12	+1.86
78. Sundargarh	−443	−457	−5.70	−6.44
79. Kalahandi	−15	−251	−0.28	−4.56
80. Mayurbhanj	+296	+270	+6.18	+7.73

TABLE 1 (Continued)

| Name of district and state | Urbanward migration, 1941–51 | | | |
| | Volume | | Rate (per 100, 1941 population) | |
	Male	Female	Male	Female
BENGAL AND CHANDERNAGORE	+415,482	+389,629	+13.94	+23.54
81. Burdwan	−2,822	+18,639	−2.12	+20.68
82. Birbhum	+804	+2,077	+2.48	+7.45
83. Bankura	−652	−2,251	−1.35	−5.15
84. Midnapur	+7,985	+20,020	+7.63	+23.99
85. Hooghly	+20,124	+13,674	+13.37	+14.41
86. Howrah	+19,596	+21,115	+6.97	+14.22
87. 24 Parganas	+164,595	+124,621	+29.87	+38.82
88. Calcutta	+137,539	+143,805	+9.47	+21.90
89. Nadia	+28,206	+23,269	+47.87	+40.57
90. Murshidabad	+3,452	+2,312	+5.78	+4.22
91. Malda	+1,625	+1,466	+10.92	+11.92
92. West Dinajpur	+2	+344	+0.05	+13.45
93. Jalpaiguri	+4,480	+3,164	+25.72	+30.58
94. Darjeeling	+15,508	+8,608	+46.30	+34.90
95. Cooch Behar	+10,213	+6,751	+61.21	+66.60
96. Chandernagore	+3,945	+2,015	+18.53	+11.86
ASSAM	+56,401	+32,459	+36.52	+34.05
97. Cachar	+12,255	+8,426	+70.56	+83.18
98. Goalpara	+5,410	+3,011	+34.51	+28.41
99. Kamrup	+5,862	+2,104	+17.40	+9.72
100. Darrang	+3,138	+1,647	+33.43	+35.93
101. Nowgang	+10,438	+6,838	+98.73	+109.16
102. Sibsagar	+3,610	+980	+21.06	+8.92
103. Lakhimpur	+7,695	+3,177	+32.63	+24.59
104. United K. & J. Hills	+6,474	+5,566	+28.52	+35.92
105. Naga Hills	−39	−80	−1.83	−5.81
106. United Mikir–North Cachar Hills	+208	+210	−22.32	+39.03
107. Mishmi Hills	+1,333	+580	+105.04	+73.65
108. TRIPURA	+8,580	+7,104	+85.08	+93.34
MADRAS AND COORG	+854,844	883,039	+20.76	+21.56
109. Srikakulam	−3,737	−3,674	−4.34	−3.89
110. Visakhapatnam	+18,144	+24,627	+16.14	+21.79
111. East Godavari	+29,459	+34,207	+17.20	+19.86
112. West Godavari	+13,970	+15,285	+10.48	+11.12
113. Krishna	+36,941	+37,600	+29.14	+30.90
114. Guntur	+38,513	+38,401	+20.46	+20.41
115. Nellore	+12,373	+11,616	+15.22	+14.43
116. Cuddaph	+5,965	+6,510	+11.07	+12.53
117. Kurnool	+13,269	+9,738	+16.92	+12.57
118. Bellary	+16,544	+14,886	+15.53	+14.62

TABLE 1 (Continued)

| Name of district and state | Urbanward migration, 1941–51 | | | |
| | Volume | | Rate (per 100, 1941 population) | |
	Male	Female	Male	Female
119. Anantapur	+16,224	+13,370	+19.81	+17.23
120. Madras	+248,377	+242,080	+60.95	+65.43
121. Chingleput	+20,995	+22,326	+17.05	+18.68
122. Chittoor	+8,240	+9,270	+12.25	+13.91
123. North Arcot	+24,167	+32,105	+11.71	+15.53
124. Salem	+42,637	+46,100	+25.79	+28.67
125. Coimbatore	+64,597	+54,939	+28.72	+25.18
126. South Arcot	+12,566	+12,739	+9.32	+9.42
127. Tanjore	+37,728	+42,349	+17.18	+18.71
128. Tiruchirapalli	+26,917	+26,764	+11.87	+11.82
129. Madurai	+55,732	+53,710	+18.73	+17.96
130. Ramanathapuram	+19,151	+24,279	+8.70	+10.34
131. Tirunelveli	+35,154	+41,055	+11.82	+13.13
132. The Nilgiris	+4,327	+4,443	+11.91	+14.11
133. Malabar	+32,695	+39,727	+17.53	+21.10
134. South Kanara	+23,557	+27,374	+30.22	+34.88
135. Coorg	+2,045	+1,213	+32.30	+24.83
MYSORE	+262,710	+232,545	+37.00	+35.81
136. Bangalore Corp	+139,019	+118,545	+64.90	+61.57
137. Bangalore	+11,475	+10,788	+24.58	+24.22
138. Kolar Gold Field City	−1,702	+5,958	−2.42	+9.40
139. Kolar	+7,888	+7,259	+17.64	+16.90
140. Tumkur	+12,708	+4,764	+36.99	+15.21
141. Mysore City	+30,642	+32,184	+38.80	+44.97
142. Mysore	+8,325	+7,840	+18.79	+18.27
143. Mandya	+7,153	+6,618	+25.94	+26.00
144. Chitaldurg	+15,640	+11,458	+33.97	+27.18
145. Hassan	+9,194	+7,774	+30.78	+27.86
146. Chikmagalur	+5,570	+3,835	+22.24	+16.97
147. Shimoga	+17,400	+15,522	+36.37	+37.07
TRAVANCORE-COCHIN	+59,659	+76,253	+12.86	+16.91
148. Trivandrum	+22,252	+25,047	+14.78	+16.75
149. Quilon	+22,305	+27,317	+17.49	+22.32
150. Kottayam	+3,322	+6,062	+6.16	+12.00
151. Trichur	+11,690	+17,827	+8.85	+13.87
BOMBAY	+978,805	+615,062	+22.43	+17.03
152. Greater Bombay	+571,689	+240,280	+53.93	+37.84
153. Banaskantha	+2,115	+1,958	+9.67	+9.64
154. Sabarkantha	+599	+1,608	+2.78	+8.42
155. Mehsana	−2,792	+6,153	−1.89	+4.39
156. Ahmedabad	+67,743	+56,715	+16.21	+18.16
157. Kaira	+9,049	+12,093	+4.54	+6.73

TABLE 1 (Continued)

| Name of district and state | Urbanward migration, 1941–51 | | | |
| | Volume | | Rate (per 100, 1941 population) | |
	Male	Female	Male	Female
158. Panch Mahals.........	+5,142	+2,591	+9.28	+4.92
159. Baroda...............	+13,352	+15,400	+10.74	+14.85
160. Broach...............	−2,494	−440	−4.04	−0.79
161. Surat................	+8,542	+11,468	+5.11	+7.45
162. Amreli...............	−2,344	+305	−5.82	+0.80
163. West Khandesh........	+10,144	+8,070	+13.34	+11.09
164. East Khandesh........	+7,389	+8,795	+3.69	+4.68
165. Nasik................	+30,416	+23,513	+23.06	+19.75
166. Ahmednagar...........	+16,207	+12,376	+20.21	+16.43
167. Poona................	+89,318	+69,339	+30.87	+27.77
168. Satara North.........	−549	+867	−0.79	+1.30
169. Satara South.........	+4,758	+7,353	+3.95	+6.42
170. Kolhapur.............	+14,240	+13,654	+13.22	+13.90
171. Sholapur.............	+16,924	+12,607	+8.91	+7.14
172. Belgaum..............	+11,198	+13,434	+6.53	+8.42
173. Bijapur..............	+11,022	+14,070	+8.44	+11.21
174. Dharwar..............	+16,227	+16,607	+8.10	+8.75
175. Thana................	+86,387	+57,493	+72.94	+56.93
176. Kolaba...............	+2,662	+2,756	+6.57	+7.18
177. Ratnagiri............	−1,223	+4,606	−1.84	+6.63
178. Kanara...............	−1,250	+1,391	−2.34	+2.52
SAURASHTRA................	+27,636	+48,977	+5.19	+9.41
179. Halar................	+7,832	+8,305	+12.06	+12.73
180. Madhya Saurashtra....	+13,502	+20,894	+9.30	+14.61
181. Zalawad..............	+2,704	+5,117	+4.96	+9.53
182. Gohilwad.............	+9,283	+12,390	+7.65	+10.82
183. Sorath...............	−5,621	+2,271	−3.83	+1.57
184. KUTCH................	−782	+1,131	−1.80	+2.38
MADHYA PRADESH............	+128,309	+140,414	+11.00	+13.18
185. Sagar................	+9,062	+9,604	+13.49	+15.29
186. Jabalpur.............	+13,847	+20,373	+11.63	+22.42
187. Hoshargabad.........	+4,677	+5,051	+8.38	+10.11
188. Nimar................	+6,381	+6,594	+13.15	+15.00
189. Mandla...............	−114	+85	−1.82	+1.43
190. Betul................	+3,821	+2,560	+33.52	+23.23
191. Chhindwara...........	+1,314	+458	+4.16	+1.51
192. Raipur...............	+9,358	+9,541	+19.63	+20.50
193. Bilaspur.............	−193	−780	−0.65	−2.70
194. Durg.................	+981	+3,560	+3.18	+11.46
195. Bastar...............	+152	−158	+1.86	−1.91
196. Raigarh..............	+2,268	+3,180	+10.59	+15.22
197. Surguja..............	+559	−32	+5.69	−0.37

TABLE 1 (Continued)

Name of district and state	Urbanward migration, 1941-51			
	Volume		Rate (per 100, 1941 population)	
	Male	Female	Male	Female
198. Chanda...............	+269	+1,552	+0.66	+3.99
199. Bhandara.............	+5,993	+5,326	+17.41	+16.36
200. Balaghat..............	+2,086	+2,325	+15.62	+18.07
201. Wardha...............	+3,960	+6,916	+7.62	+14.29
202. Nagpur...............	+39,058	+43,999	+17.84	+22.08
203. Amravati.............	+8,827	+7,952	+7.28	+7.15
204. Akola.................	+6,793	+5,418	+7.54	+6.62
205. Buldana..............	+4,097	+4,182	+6.68	+7.31
206. Yeotmal..............	+5,503	+2,708	+11.58	+6.17
MADHYA BHARAT AND BHOPAL	+87,468	+94,904	+13.83	+17.44
207. Bhind................	+636	+458	+5.83	+5.05
208. Gird..................	+13,122	+16,376	+12.99	+19.46
209. Morena...............	+1,365	+955	+8.21	+6.82
210. Shivpuri..............	+1,562	+1,280	+19.13	+17.47
211. Goona................	+2,937	+2,263	+13.01	+10.85
212. Bhilsa................	+1,209	+993	+10.65	+9.95
213. Rajgarh..............	-2,120	-845	-10.19	-4.48
214. Shajapur.............	+671	+1,325	+4.81	+10.07
215. Ujjain................	+16,763	+15,376	+26.49	+28.18
216. Indore...............	+30,451	+32,618	+22.18	+30.82
217. Dewas................	+548	+1,493	+3.67	+11.38
218. Mandsaur.............	+4,790	+6,080	+9.82	+13.32
219. Ratlam...............	+6,620	+7,332	+14.80	+17.86
220. Dhar.................	-1,288	-655	-6.14	-3.36
221. Jhabua...............	+367	+535	+11.47	+18.34
222. Nimar................	+2,281	+2,828	+5.79	+7.68
223. Sehore...............	+7,070	+6,030	+13.47	+13.34
224. Raisen...............	+568	+462	+25.54	+21.39
HYDERABAD.................	+237,912	+258,644	+18.81	+21.74
225. Aurangabad...........	+8,081	+7,077	+12.13	+11.60
226. Parbhani.............	+6,378	+8,085	+10.40	+14.14
227. Nanded...............	+9,749	+10,673	+17.18	+19.79
228. Bidar................	+3,778	+5,933	+6.01	+9.75
229. Bhir.................	+1,988	+1,817	+5.32	+5.29
230. Osmanabad...........	+341	-198	+0.65	-0.41
231. Hyderabad...........	+103,646	+122,832	+26.27	+33.75
232. Mahbubnagar.........	+5,619	+4,513	+12.41	+10.27
233. Raichur..............	+16,686	+13,803	+21.07	+18.15
234. Gulbarga.............	+15,413	+17,519	+16.72	+19.69
235. Adilabad.............	+12,354	+12,234	+34.70	+36.31
236. Nizamabad...........	+9,553	+10,418	+19.61	+22.83
237. Medak...............	+3,082	+3,732	+9.02	+11.23

TABLE 1 (Continued)

Name of district and state	Urbanward migration, 1941–51			
	Volume		Rate (per 100, 1941 population)	
	Male	Female	Male	Female
238. Karimnagar............	−990	+559	−1.66	+0.94
239. Warangal.............	+32,757	+31,024	+34.58	+35.53
240. Nalgonda.............	+9,712	+8,623	+22.27	+20.93
VINDHYA PRADESH...........	+3,870	+604	+2.78	+0.46
241. Datu.................	+334	+788	+2.01	+5.14
242. Tikamgarh............	−1,464	−1,047	−12.77	−9.29
243. Chhatarpur...........	+394	−704	+1.72	−3.02
244. Patna................	−1,666	−2,145	−13.66	−17.18
245. Satna................	+3,873	−2,709	+15.80	+11.41
246. Rewa.................	−38	−203	−0.13	−0.73
247. Shahdot..............	+2,407	−1,206	+10.67	+5.50
RAJASTAN..................	+79,883	+110,881	+8.02	+12.33
248. Jaipur...............	+55,378	+55,897	+37.20	+40.46
249. Tonk.................	+1,114	+1,340	+3.51	+4.53
250. Sawaimadhopur........	+1,418	+3,789	+3.99	+11.87
251. Bharatpur............	−7,457	−7,580	−11.12	−13.19
252. Alwar................	−4,490	−4,952	−9.98	−12.21
253. Jhunjhunu............	−5,604	−106	−11.68	−0.23
254. Sikar................	−2,881	+844	−5.33	+1.56
255. Bhilwara.............	+5,398	+4,654	+26.34	+24.09
256. Bikaner..............	−13,677	−6,673	−18.28	−10.77
257. Churu................	+9,431	+12,125	+11.76	+16.37
258. Gangangar............	+5,232	+6,509	+19.28	+31.03
259. Jodhpur..............	+10,263	+14,345	+11.19	+17.73
260. Barmer...............	+3,337	+3,132	+29.15	+29.70
261. Jalore...............	+200	+352	+2.47	+4.78
262. Pali.................	+3,756	+5,039	+13.38	+18.74
263. Nagaur...............	+5,960	+4,478	+14.48	+11.60
264. Jaisalmer............	−411	−427	−10.56	−12.37
265. Udaipur..............	+9,364	+10,139	+19.71	+24.31
266. Dungapur.............	−944	−429	−9.72	−4.56
267. Banswara.............	+308	+450	+3.73	+5.60
268. Sirohi...............	+1,026	+1,408	+14.48	+21.39
269. Chittorgarh..........	+594	+1,484	+2.20	+5.84
270. Kotah................	+4,697	+5,436	+9.57	+12.50
271. Bundi................	−1,032	−276	−5.72	−1.62
272. Jhalawar.............	−817	−97	−6.98	−0.89
273. AJMER................	+14,851	+15,425	+12.80	+15.73
PUNJAB H.P., BILASPUR, AND PEPSU.....................	−84,650	−18,242	−6.12	−1.74
274. Simla................	+10,153	+5,153	+62.23	+73.56
275. Kangra...............	−1,183	+382	−17.39	+13.41

TABLE 1 (Continued)

| Name of district and state | Urbanward migration, 1941–51 | | | |
| | Volume | | Rate (per 100, 1941 population) | |
	Male	Female	Male	Female
276. Hissar.................	−3,023	−2,220	−4.07	−3.63
277. Rohtak...............	+309	+3,809	+0.50	+7.09
278. Gurgaon..............	−4,309	−3,239	−8.01	−6.83
279. Karnal................	+304	+4,533	+0.43	+8.08
280. Ambala...............	+4,034	+5,659	+3.94	+7.91
281. Hoshiarpur...........	−6,566	−5,331	−14.57	−14.42
282. Jullundur.............	−5,600	+7,368	+4.80	+8.50
283. Ludhiana.............	−2,157	+4,521	−2.36	+6.58
284. Ferozepur.............	−18,745	−3,807	−14.96	−4.47
285. Amritsar..............	−64,693	−40,619	−23.99	−20.61
286. Gurdaspur...........	−3,505	−2,733	−6.67	−6.44
287. Patiala...............	+8,071	+7,203	+11.74	+13.91
288. Barnala...............	+1,033	+2,116	+2.32	+5.86
289. Bhatinda.............	−4,549	−2,364	−9.15	−6.02
290. Kapurthala...........	+863	+3,451	+2.95	+14.91
291. Feteh Garh Sahib......	−2,313	−1,866	−15.49	−15.31
292. Sangrur...............	−1,036	+4,099	−2.68	+14.03
293. Mohinder Garh........	−4,712	−5,378	−21.98	+26.74
294. Kohistan..............	−568	−1,086	−6.08	−17.87
295. Mahasu...............	+1,004	+565	+38.09	+43.68
296. Mandi................	+280	+1,208	+3.58	+21.25
297. Chamba..............	−292	−96	−7.61	−3.47
298. Sirmoor..............	+1,250	+85	+31.41	+2.69
299. Bilaspur..............	+27	+345	+1.52	+31.56
300. Delhi.................	+196,277	+168,735	+47.32	+60.08

Source: K. C. Zachariah, *Internal Migration in India*, 1941–51 (Bombay: Demographic Training and Research Centre, 1960).

next, with 1.6 million. Urban areas in West Bengal also received a fairly large number of migrants. Punjab is the only state having a net outward movement.

In terms of the rate of urbanward migration, there is a good deal of variation between the states. The highest rate is for Tripura, where from the migration of persons above ten years (in 1951) the population increased by as much as 85 per cent among males and 93 per cent among females. Delhi comes next, with 47 per cent and 60 per cent for males and females, respectively. Among the major states, Mysore has the highest rate—37 per cent for males and 36 per cent for females. In Assam too, the urban-ward migration has been large in terms of the urban population in 1941./The rates are very near those of Mysore. The states whose rates are below the all-India average are the Punjab, Pepsu, Himachal Pradesh, Bhilaspur, Ajmer, Rajasthan, Vindhya Pradesh, Madhya Bharat, Bhopal, Madhya Pradesh, Saurashtra, Kutch, Travancore-Cochin, Orissa, Bihar, and Uttar Pradesh.

The breakdown of urbanward migration by sex is also given in Table 1. Net in-migration among men outnumbers that among women in ten states. On the whole more males moved into urban areas than females, the difference being about 0.3 million. In terms of the 1941 population of these areas, however, the rate of migration is more among females—16.3 per cent for females and 15.2 per cent for males.

Zonal differences are also noticed in the sex differences among rural-urban migrants. Urban areas of the north and east zones have attracted more males than females. In other zones, on the whole, the females outnumber males. Industrialized areas, like Bombay and Mysore, are exceptions. In Delhi also the male migrants outnumber the female migrants.

When we consider the rate of migration, the predominance of female migration becomes more conspicuous. In Uttar Pradesh, West Bengal, Tripura, and Delhi, where the volume of migration is greater for males, the rate of migration is greater for females. The largest difference is observed in West Bengal, where the rate for females is higher than the corresponding male rate by as much as 10 per cent. The evidence available suggests that the first phase of rapid rural-to-urban migration in India was predominantly masculine in composition, but now that channels and connections have been established it is coming to have a more balanced sex composition.

URBANWARD MIGRATION IN INDIA
BY DISTRICTS, 1941–1951

The diversity shown by the various states from the point of view of urbanward migration conceals to some extent the greater diversity in the rate of urbanward migration in the various districts. The range of variation of district rates is much greater than that of the states. The volume and rate of urbanward migration by districts are also given in Table 1. Some of the highest rates of urbanward migration for districts are noticed in Assam. For example, the Mishmi Hills experienced an in-migration rate of 105 per cent; the net migration among males aged ten years and above in the urban areas of this district is higher than the total urban population in 1941. Similarly, in Nargong district the urbanward male migration is more or less equal to its male population in 1941. Tripura State had a male migration rate of 85 per cent, and Goalpara District in Assam had a rate of 71 per cent.

Though the rates of migration have been high in these districts, the volumes are small. For example, the in-migration to the Mishmi Hills, cited above, consists of only 1,330 males and 580 females. There are, however, a number of other urban centers attracting quite a large number of migrants during the decade. Migration among persons aged ten years and above exceeded 100,000 in the urban areas of each of the districts given below:

Name of district	Volume of migration among persons ten years and above (in thousands)
Greater Bombay	812
Madras	490
Delhi	365
24 Parganas	289
Calcutta	281
Bangalore Corporation	258
Hyderabad	227
Poona	158
Thana	143
Ahmedabad	125
Coimbatore	120
Madurai	119
Jaipur	110

Among the urban areas which lost population by migration during the decade, Amritsar in the Punjab comes first from the point of view of both volume and rate of migration. The urban areas in this district lost about 65,000 males and 41,000 females. Ferozepur, Bikaner, and Shahjahanpur are a few other districts in which the urban areas experienced a fairly large volume (more than 10,000 males in each of these districts) of out-migration. Most of the urban centers which lost population by migration are in Northwest, North, and East India. In Madras, for instance, only Srikakulam District had an outward movement. Similarly, in Mysore, only Kolar Gold Field City experienced out-migration. None of the Travancore-Cochin districts come under this category. In Bombay, out of 27 districts, six showed out-migration for males and only one for females. Even from these areas, however, the volume and rate of out-migration are small.

MIGRATION TO METROPOLITAN CITIES IN INDIA, 1941–1951

The volume and age-sex distributions of the net migrants to the four metropolitan cities of India derived by the census survival ratio method are given in Table 2. In terms of the total volume of migration, Bombay leads the other three cities. In comparison to the number of persons enumerated in 1941, however, the migration has been greatest in Madras City, where the net migration was more than two thirds of the population, at the beginning of the decade. Though the population of Calcutta in 1941 was greater than that of any other city, the volume and rate of migration there has been small during the decade. The situation in Calcutta can be

TABLE 2

NET MIGRATION TO METROPOLITAN CITIES

Age as on Census day 1951	Volume of migration (in thousands)							
	Bombay		Madras		Delhi		Calcutta	
	Male	Female	Male	Female	Male	Female	Male	Female
10–14........	+66.3	+41.0	+38.6	+36.6	+34.2	+24.8	+45.4	+39.7
15–19........	+116.1	+52.9	+44.5	+33.9	+39.1	+30.7	+89.9	+39.7
20–24........	+165.8	+61.7	+39.4	+23.3	+34.7	+24.1	+96.2	+26.1
25–29........	+152.8	+49.6	+34.4	+20.5	+21.3	+17.1	+55.7	+14.7
30–34........	+81.6	+20.6	+23.9	+19.0	+8.2	+13.0	−7.4	+7.8
35–39........	+28.1	+6.2	+15.5	+17.8	+6.4	+9.6	−32.2	+5.9
40–44........	+5.5	+4.6	+12.8	+17.0	+10.2	+8.2	−25.4	+3.6
45–49........	−3.0	+5.5	+10.4	+15.0	+10.3	+8.7	−19.3	+1.9
50–54........	−0.7	+6.3	+8.7	+13.6	+6.8	+7.4	−13.2	+2.8
55–59........	+1.0	+5.1	+7.5	+12.4	+5.4	+4.9	−7.6	+3.0
60+........	−5.6	+5.0	+16.2	+25.7	+2.9	+1.3	−13.5	−1.3
Total 10+...	+607.9	+258.7	+251.8	+234.9	+179.7	+150.1	+168.6	+143.8

0–9.........	Volume of migration under 10 years (in thousands)							
	+87.1		+53.2		+75.8		+38.6	

	Rate of migration (per 100 average population)							
10–14........	+59.32	+46.69	+60.84	+60.97	+57.65	+52.10	+36.36	+44.43
15–19........	+83.85	+60.41	+72.16	+59.92	+66.41	+67.91	+55.08	+46.11
20–24........	+91.97	+63.67	+66.78	+44.71	+58.92	+58.56	+48.60	+31.96
25–29........	+79.22	+53.38	+60.73	+42.25	+39.76	+47.97	+27.34	+19.95
30–34........	+48.78	+27.85	+47.93	+44.95	+18.51	+44.49	−4.14	+12.34
35–39........	+21.31	+11.25	+37.61	+50.30	+17.75	+42.67	−22.63	+11.36
40–44........	+5.62	+11.24	+37.63	+57.27	+33.48	+46.53	−23.64	+8.70
45–49........	−4.40	+17.64	+37.95	+61.05	+42.17	+58.80	−24.85	+6.01
50–54........	−1.55	+26.49	+41.48	+68.29	+38.51	+64.88	−25.04	+10.80
55–59........	+3.35	+29.47	+48.87	+79.17	+43.78	+62.81	−22.54	+5.30
60+........	−16.36	+18.28	+62.93	+90.50	+19.08	+15.77	−30.05	−3.80

explained in terms of the pattern of movement of displaced persons, and that in Madras, to some extent, in terms of the return migration of persons of Madras origin from Burma, Malaya, and other countries in southeastern Asia (and even from areas within the country).

The main features of the age-sex distribution of the net migrants to these cities are evident from Graph 1. The maximum numbers of net migrants are in the age-group 15–19 years or 20–24 years (age as of 1951), usually the latter. The rate of migration also reaches the maximum at about the same age. The similarity between the curves for Calcutta and Bombay is noteworthy. The pattern of movement to Madras or Delhi is different from that to Bombay or Calcutta.

SOCIOECONOMIC CORRELATES OF URBANWARD MIGRATION

The urbanward migration rates given for the 300 districts of India vary from as high as +109 per cent to as low as −27 per cent. It is therefore natural to inquire how much of this variation can be explained in terms of the socioeconomic characteristics of the urban and rural areas of the districts. Such an inquiry can lead to a better understanding of the factors affecting rural-to-urban migration. The scope of the analysis is very much limited, as the data on socioeconomic variables available by district for the period under study are few in number. In the following analysis the migration rates used are those of male population.

The partition of the Indian subcontinent into India and Pakistan has been one of the important stimuli for the movement of population in India since 1947. Between 1946 and 1951 about 6.2 million Muslims left India for Pakistan, and 7 million Hindus came to India from across the border. Thus, refugee movement resulted in considerable change in the population structure of certain towns, districts, and states. The high rates of urbanward migration observed in certain districts, and the low rates observed in some other districts in North India (and especially in the Punjab), can both be traced to the movement of displaced persons. Some of the other factors with which migration rates were found to be associated are (1) size of the biggest towns in the district, (2) unemployment rate, and (3) proportion of population in nonagricultural occupations.

The correlation coefficients between migration rate and the size of the largest town in a district were fairly high and consistent in the various states. Statistically, only those of Madras and Bombay were significant. For other states, where the correlations were not

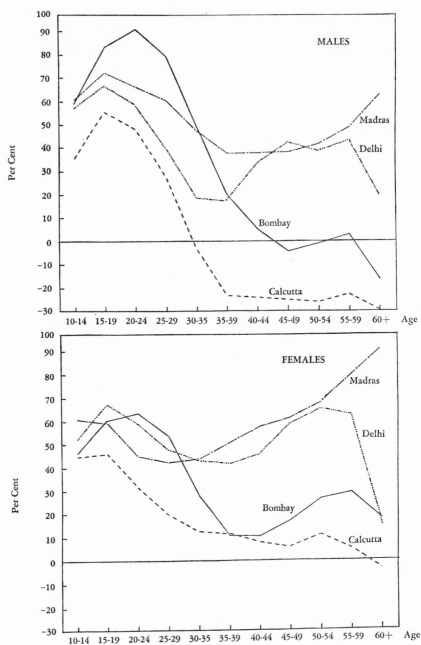

Graph 1. Male and Female Migration Rates, by Age, Metropolitan Cities.

statistically significant, the low value was due to the disturbing effect of one district in each state. If these districts are omitted, the correlations become significant. On the whole it can be concluded that, apart from the disturbing effect of the partition movement and the extreme values observed in some of the minor urban areas, the rate of migration to the urban area of a district is associated with the size of the biggest town in that district.

Unemployment rates were obtained by district for only three states in the 1951 census. The correlation coefficient between migration rate and unemployment rate in all three states was positive and statistically significant. The most probable interpretation of the positive correlation is that people migrate because of the distress in the rural areas and contribute to the problem of unemployment in the urban areas.

The correlation between migration rate and proportion in non-agricultural occupation is positive and statistically significant in most states in the south and west zones.

The migration estimates which have been summarized above support the following conclusions:

a) Rural-to-urban migration in India is not negligible, but is a very widespread phenomenon.

b) Streams of migration are flowing not only toward the very largest cities, but also to hundreds of medium-size and smaller cities in all regions, except those adversely affected by partition.

c) Although originally this migration may have some of the aspects of a "pioneering" movement, comprised predominantly of males, the 1941–1951 decade witnessed the removal to the cities of almost as many women as men.

d) There is little evidence of reluctance on the part of the villagers to seek their fortunes in the city. In fact, the unemployment data suggest that they crowd into the cities seeking work. Very possibly, unemployment in the cities, rather than the restrictive effect of cultural tradition in the villages, is the major brake upon rural-to-urban migration at the present time.

e) This upswing in urbanward migration probably is a fairly recent phenomenon which began in the late 1930's. It has now progressed to a point where the residents of almost every village have relatives or fellow villagers living in at least one (and possibly several) of the major cities. Family and village ties are sufficiently strong to create an obligation upon the successful migrant to help sponsor new entrants to the city. With villagers becoming progressively more oriented toward the new urbanized economy, and with migration channels firmly established, the nation seems to be all set to enter a phase of unprecedented urbanization, assisted by the prevailing family system and culture rather than hindered by it.

Livelihood and Educational Characteristics
of Internal Migrants in India

When Indian people leave their villages and move to another region, what kinds of jobs do they get? Are the persons who move the better educated villagers or the poorest, most desperate, and least educated villagers? Unfortunately, important as these questions are, there are only sparse data with which to attempt to answer them.

LIVELIHOOD CHARACTERISTICS OF THE MIGRANTS

At the time of the 1951 census a special tabulation was made of the "livelihood class" of self-supporting persons, by state of birth. These statistics make it possible to compare the livelihood class of migrants (persons living in a different state from that in which they were born) with that of the general population of the state to which they moved. Table 3 summarizes this information. It was prepared as follows:

a) A percentage distribution by livelihood class was prepared for all migrants to each state for which data were available.

b) A percentage distribution by livelihood class was prepared for the general, self-supporting population of these same states, most of whom were born in the state.

c) The percentage distribution for the general population was subtracted from the percentage distribution for migrants, and the differences were recorded in Table 3.

The results of this calculation are a set of percentage point differences that show the extent to which migrants differ from the general population. A summary, over-all measure of the extent of this difference is the "coefficient of dissimilarity," which is simply the sum of differences of either sign for each set of data. On the basis of this evidence, it is permissible to draw the following inferences:

a) In every state for which there is information, the in-migrants are found preponderantly in *nonagricultural* industries. There is a substantial excess of migrants in livelihood classes V, VI, VII, and VIII—with a compensating deficit in the agricultural classes I through IV. Even in states that are quite rural, the residents who were born out of state tended to be overwhelmingly in nonagricultural occupations. This demonstrates, in yet another way, that internal migration in India is urban oriented, and that movement from one state to another is intimately related to movement from rural to urban areas.

b) Although migrants tend to enter all four of the nonagricultural classes, *manufacturing* (nonagricultural production) and *services* (which comprise most of class VIII) are the two major migrant-employing branches

TABLE 3

LIVELIHOOD CLASSIFICATION OF TOTAL SELF-SUPPORTING MALE POPULATION COMPARED WITH THAT OF THOSE BORN OUTSIDE THE STATE OF THEIR RESIDENCE, 1951 (PERCENTAGE POINT DIFFERENCES, SELECTED STATES)

State	Coefficient of dissimilarity	I Cultivation of owned land	II Cultivation of rented land	III Cultivating laborers	IV Non-cultivating owners and rent receivers	V Production, non-agricultural	VI Commerce	VII Transport	VIII Professions, services, and miscellaneous
Uttar Pradesh	51	−47	−2	−2	0	11	8	6	26
Bihar	51	−32	−3	−16	0	26	6	6	13
Orissa	33	−23	−2	−8	0	7	7	4	15
West Bengal	46	−27	−9	−9	−1	20	9	9	8
Assam	57	−47	−8	−1	−1	41	4	3	9
Tripura	41	−33	−4	−3	−1	6	13	1	21
Madras	29	−21	+1	−8	0	4	4	4	16
Mysore	52	−49	−2	+3	−1	19	5	2	23
Travancore-Cochin	37	−23	−4	−10	0	30	1	0	6
Coorg	35	−27	−5	−1	−2	24	2	0	7
Bombay	53	−37	−8	−6	−2	19	13	4	17
Saurashtra	31	−24	−5	−2	1	3	3	6	18
Madhya Pradesh	48	−35	−2	−11	1	10	11	7	19
Hyderabad	37	−24	−5	−8	0	4	9	3	21
Vindhya Pradesh	53	−46	0	−7	4	11	8	7	23
Average difference		−33	−4	−6	−0.2	16	7	5	16
Average percentage of composition in state of residence		46	8	12	1	13	6	2	12
Ratio of average difference to average composition		−72	−50	−50	−20	123	117	250	133

of livelihood. Manufacturing and services are, however, also the two largest branches of all urban employment.

c) If one adjusts the differences of Table 3 to make allowance for the comparative size of the various livelihood classes (last line of the table), it is discovered that migrants are disproportionately concentrated in *transport* industries. Migrants to the city appear to meet the greatest resistance in entering commerce. All but a few types of commerce, such as street vending, seem to be relatively closed to them.

Additional information about the kind of employment which migrants get may be derived from a special tabulation of a sample of the working population in the Greater Calcutta Industrial Region, according to birthplace and type of industry.[6] It was found that 30 per cent of all workers were born in the Calcutta Industrial Region, 7 per cent in other regions of West Bengal, and 63 per cent in other states of India. The following industries, however, had more than 75 per cent migrants, and hence might be defined as "migrant-hiring" industries:[7]

Processing and manufacture

    Canning and preservation of fruits and vegetables
    Other processers of grain and pulses
    Makers of butter, cheese, ghee, and other dairy products
    Brewers and distillers
    Toddy drawers
    Cotton ginning, cleaning, and pressing
    Cotton spinning, sizing, and weaving
    Jute pressing, baling, spinning, and weaving
    Tanners and all other workers in leather
    Cobblers and all other makers and repairers of boots, shoes, sandals, and
        clogs
    Manufacture of paints, varnishes, and lacquers
    Manufacture of bricks, tiles, and other clay products
    Sawyers
    Stone cutters and dressers
    Gas supply
    Works and services—domestic and industrial water supply
    Sanitary works and services, including scavengers

Commerce

    Hawkers and street vendors, otherwise unclassified
    Vendors of wine, liquors, aerated waters, and ice in shops
    Hawkers and street vendors of drink and foodstuffs

---

[6] *Census of India, Paper No. 6* (1955), "Working Population in Calcutta Industrial Region—Distribution by Industry, Place of Birth, and Educational Attainment—1951 Census."

[7] *Ibid.,* Appendix A.

Transport, storage, and communications

Transport by road
Transport by water
Railway porters
Storage and warehousing

Health, education and public administration

Police (other than village watchmen)
Village officers and servants including village watchmen

Services not elsewhere specified

Cooks
Gardeners

Contrast with the preceding this list of industries where more than 50 per cent of the workers were born in West Bengal:

Processing and manufacture

Canning and preservation of fish
Other food industries
Millers of cereals and pulses
Fur dressers and dyers
Tentmakers
Makers of other made-up textile goods, including umbrellas
Woollen spinning and weaving
Hemp and flax spinning and weaving
Manufacture of rope, twine, and string
Workers in copper, brass, and bell metal
Workers in other metals
Cutlers and makers of surgical and veterinary instruments
Nonferrous metals
Manufacture, assembly, and repair of railway equipment, motor vehicles, and bicycles
Manufacture of all other transport equipment
Manufacture of electric fans and other accessories
Mechanics (unspecified)
Engineering workshops engaged in producing machine and equipment parts
Manufacture of professional, scientific, and controlling instruments
Photographic and optical goods
Repair and manufacture of watches and clocks
Workers in precious stones and precious metals, and makers of jewelry and ornaments
Manufacture of musical instruments and appliances
Stationery articles other than paper and paper products
Toy makers
Coke ovens
Carpenters, turners, and joiners
Veneer and plywood makers

Basketmakers
Furniture and fixtures
Other industries of woody materials
Printers, lithographers, and engravers
Masons and bricklayers
Painters and decorators of houses
Construction of buildings
Construction and maintenance—telegraph and telephone lines

Commerce

Dealers in drugs and other chemical stores
Publishers, booksellers, and stationers
Wholesale trade in commodities other than foodstuffs
Real estate—house and estate agents, and rent collectors

Transport, storage, and communications

Postal services
Telegraph services
Telephone services
Wireless services

Health, education and public administration

Registered medical practitioners
Vaids, hakims, etc.
Midwives
Vaccinators
Nurses
Assistant veterinary surgeons
Professors, lecturers, teachers, and research workers

Services not elsewhere specified

Production and distribution of motion pictures; other recreation services
Lawyers of all kinds
Clerks of lawyers
Architects, surveyors, and engineers
Public scribes, stenographers, and accountants
Artists, sculptors, and image makers
Photographers
Servants in religious edifices and burial and burning grounds; pilgrim conductors; circumcisers, etc.

A careful comparison of the types of items included in each list leads to the conclusion that in the Calcutta Industrial Region a disproportionately large share of migrants are working at low-status, lower paying, unskilled-laborers' jobs and in places where large quantities of labor are used on a mass scale. Industries where skill, high status, higher incomes, and artisanship are involved tend to be reserved for Bengalis. It is impossible to determine whether this is due to lower educational and other qualifications of migrants, to the operation of the status system, or to both. In any event, it is clear that the migrants have poorer work status and less income, on an average, than the nonmigrants. In the absence of data for any other place, it is impossible to test whether this finding for Calcutta is representative of the situation in other urban places of India. General observation and a knowledge of the prevailing status system would suggest that it is an example of a general process that is at work in most, if not all, cities; but this is only speculative at the present time. *It is quite possible, however, that the rural migrant to the large cities of India is forced to bear hardships and undergo suffering to a much greater extent than is generally appreciated. As population pressure mounts, it may be neither the villagers nor the city dwellers who bear the major burden of the misery, but the displaced rural population that can neither be accommodated on the land nor find an economic connection in the city.*

EDUCATIONAL CHARACTERISTICS OF MIGRANTS

In India, data with which to evaluate the educational level of migrants are available only for one area, the Calcutta Industrial Region, derived from the report cited above. Though we do not know how representative it is with respect to India as a whole, the following principle summarizes the major finding for the Calcutta region: migrants to the large metropolis possess a considerably *higher* average level of educational attainment than the general population of the states from which they are drawn, but they tend to have a *lower* average level of educational attainment than the population of the place to which they migrate.

The following tabulation of the educational attainments of the working population in the Calcutta Industrial Region according to place of birth supports the contention that the in-migrants are less well educated than the native-born population.

Place of Birth	Total	Educational attainment			
		Illiterate	Below matriculation	Below degree	Above degree
Total working population.....	100.0	45.2	43.8	8.0	3.0
Calcutta Industrial Region.	100.0	27.6	54.9	13.2	4.3
Rest of West Bengal.......	100.0	35.7	47.1	11.9	5.3
Other East India..........	100.0	63.4	35.1	1.1	0.4
South India..............	100.0	51.2	34.6	10.0	4.2

Source: *Census of India, Paper No. 6* (1955), "Working Population in Calcutta Industrial Region—Distribution by Industry, Place of Birth and Educational Attainment—1951 Census," Table II-A, p. ii.

The proportion of illiterate workers among in-migrant groups is clearly higher than among workers born in West Bengal. The migrants differ widely in this characteristic; the proportion of illiterates is much higher among those coming from near-by states in East India outside Bengal than among those coming from South India. The migrants from South India, in contrast, had almost as high a percentage of workers above matriculation as the native-born Bengalis. (There was an insufficient number of migrants from North and West India to make a separate analysis for these regions.) The above finding was tested for each specific industry by comparing the per cent of illiteracy among Bengalis and among migrants. In all but a small fraction of the several hundred industry groups, the native-born workers in a given category had less illiteracy than the in-migrants. Table 4 summarizes this relationship. If one studies this table by columns he will discover that, in general, within each of the four nonagricultural livelihood classes the proportion of illiteracy is smaller among workers born in the

TABLE 4

PER CENT OF ILLITERACY AMONG SELF-SUPPORTING MALES IN THE
CALCUTTA INDUSTRIAL REGION, ACCORDING TO PLACE OF BIRTH
AND LIVELIHOOD CLASS

| Place of Birth | Per cent of illiteracy among general population, aged 15–64 | Per cent of illiteracy among male workers in Calcutta Industrial Region by livelihood class | | | | |
		Total, all industries	Livelihood class V	Livelihood class VI	Livelihood class VII	Livelihood class VIII
Calcutta Industrial Region.	62.5	27.6	34.8	17.4	28.5	28.3
Rest of West Bengal	. . .	35.7	31.8	44.0	15.1	34.4
Bihar	77.2	67.0	67.2	52.2	81.8	65.2
Orissa	76.3	50.1	54.7	40.2	56.3	46.4
South India	59.7	51.2	66.0	18.8	54.1	38.7
West India	57.5	13.6	24.2	7.6	25.9	31.0
Central India	77.4	67.6	81.6	41.4	68.7	53.4
Northwest India	80.1	21.8	29.4	14.6	27.3	29.0
East Pakistan	. . .	20.8	24.5	12.3	27.8	20.6
East India (total)	71.5	46.2	50.4	31.7	62.0	44.5
North India	78.2	63.6	71.1	43.2	71.5	55.6
Total	. . .	45.2	52.3	29.2	58.5	42.0

Source: *Census of India, Paper No. 6* (1955), "Working Population in Calcutta Industrial Region—Distribution by Industry, Place of Birth and Educational Attainment—1951 Census," pages 2–223.

Calcutta Industrial Region than among workers from other states.

Table 4 is equally important when studied by rows, for it validates the other part of the conclusion stated above. The first item in each row specifies the per cent of illiteracy in 1951 among the population residing in each of the several regions. The succeeding items in each row report the extent of illiteracy among the persons who had migrated out of that place into the Calcutta Industrial Region. For each row, it is readily apparent that illiteracy is less among the out-migrants than among the populations of the states in which the migrants were born. Certain additional findings emerge from an analysis of this table by rows:

a) Illiteracy is not a strict bar to migration, for if a state has a high rate of illiteracy, there tends also to be a high rate of illiteracy among its out-migrants. For example, Bihar and Orissa both have illiteracy rates in excess of 75 per cent, and in all livelihood classes the workers in Calcutta who came from these states were more poorly educated than were the workers from other states. Had illiteracy been a bar to movement, the illiteracy rate within each livelihood class would have been approximately the same, irrespective of the state of origin.

b) The greater the distance which a migrant must move to reach a metropolitan center like Calcutta, the less illiteracy there is among migrants. Conversely, the shorter the distance to be covered, the higher the rate of illiteracy is in comparison with the place of origin. For example, in Northwest India, North India, and West India illiteracy is very much higher than among the migrants who left these places and traveled to Calcutta. The major variable involved here seems to be one of distance. In other nations it has also been found that people with more education tend to travel greater distances to seek work, while those with little education are inclined to travel shorter distances.

In summary, from the one instance for which evidence is now available, it appears that in India the propensity to migrate to urban areas is much higher among literate and educated people than among the illiterate, and that as the level of education rises the tendency to travel greater distances to seek employment increases. If this is true as a general pattern throughout the country, it may be expected that as school attendance in the villages increases, there will be an increased flow into the cities of literate rural youths seeking their fortunes. Many people fear that as a result of economic development Indian cities will soon be flooded with illiterate, unskilled, and inexperienced agriculturalists who will only burden the labor market with large quantities of manpower that cannot be absorbed. This may not be a correct picture. Instead, during the coming decades, rural-to-urban migration in

India may deliver large numbers of young men and women who have no prospect of a decent livelihood in the village because of population pressure on the land, but who have received a minimum education in the expanding educational system and are ready to be absorbed in the expanding economy.

Part 2

URBAN
STRUCTURE
AND
URBAN
SOCIETY

THE MORPHOLOGY OF INDIAN CITIES

John E. Brush

Interpretation of the morphology of Indian cities begins with mapping the existing layout of streets, the arrangement and characteristics of buildings, and the associated patterns of land use. It necessitates study of their relationships to site and situation, and ultimately investigation of the historical circumstances influencing their origins and evolution. The inertia of the site and build of an Indian city is undoubtedly greater than the persistence of the functional aspects of its economy. India has a long tradition of urbanization, and an understanding of present-day cities must be based upon historical geography.

In this paper I have attempted to draw conclusions from the body of urban studies written by geographers, social ecologists, and city planners. More than 80 cities and towns have been analyzed during the past thirty to thirty-five years, and it seems appropriate to compare the results and to deduce generalizations, if possible. I am not placing primary emphasis on a few large cities, because it is apparent that the greater the geographic distribution and range of population represented, the more valid the conclusions. Perhaps in this way the merits of further urban studies in India can be enhanced and the value of existing work can be made known to agencies now undertaking to modify the traditions of urban dwellers and to increase their welfare.

City Landscape and Functional Areas

Indian cities have been well characterized by Deshpande as lacking in basic unity of layout and function. About twenty years ago he wrote:

A dilapidated fort, an old but partly revived "Peth"-market—, a prominent but partly neglected temple, the vestiges of past prosperity, and administrative offices, such as the Collector's or Mamlatdar's Katcheri, schools and shops, the marks of modern time, characterize almost every town of [Bombay] Province.[1]

Prabhu describes the geographic pattern of Dharwar as loosely woven and adds that, "Like most other Indian towns, it is a collection of 'period' pieces." [2]

Every city or town with pre-British origins which has grown at all during the last century shows a striking contrast between the indigenous part and the Anglicized part. The great port cities of Calcutta, Bombay, and Madras, which developed exclusively under British rule, exhibit a remarkable blending of Indian and European urban traditions, producing a modified kind of European townscape in which Indo-British culture evolved and still continues to flourish. It is also true that some inland cities, such as industrial Jamshedpur and governmental Chandigarh, have almost purely European antecedents. But the typical Indian urban center contains a congested old section, adjacent to which may be found *carefully planned* and

---

[1] C. D. Deshpande, "Cities and Towns of Bombay Province: Aspects of Urban Geography," *Indian Geographical Journal*, XVI, No. 3 (1941), 284.

For the basis of the following description I am indebted to Howard F. Hirt, Noel P. Gist, Pradyumna Prasad Karan, R. V. Joshi, V. R. Prabhu, and R. L. Singh, particularly in the works cited below.

Hirt: "A Study of the Urban Geography of Aligarh," *The Geographer*, V, No. 2 (1952), 24–27; "Aligarh, Uttar Pradesh: A Geography of Urban Growth" (Doctoral dissertation, Syracuse University, 1955), *Dissertation Abstracts*, XVI, No. 5, 942; "Spatial Aspects of the Housing Problem in Aligarh, U.P., India," *Population Review*, II, No. 1 (1958), 37–45.

Gist: "The Ecological Structure of an Asian City (Bangalore): An East-West Comparison," *Population Review*, II, No. 1 (1958), 17–25.

Karan: "Patna and Jamshedpur," *Geographical Review of India*, XIV, No. 2 (1952), 25–32; "The Pattern of Indian Towns: A Study in Urban Morphology," *Journal of the American Institute of Planners*, XXIII, No. 2 (1957), 70–75.

Joshi: "Urban Structure in Western India: Poona, A Sample Study," *Geographical Review of India*, XIV, No. 1 (1952), 6–19.

Prabhu: "Dharwar: A Study in Indian Urban Landscapes," *Bombay Geographical Magazine*, I, No. 1 (1953), 56–63.

Singh: "Evolution of Settlements in the Middle Ganga Valley," *National Geographical Journal of India*, I, Part II (1955), 69–114; "Gorakhpur: A Study in Urban Morphology," *ibid.*, I, Part I (1955), 1–10; *Banaras: A Study in Urban Geography* (Banaras: Nand Kishore & Bros., 1955); "Mirzapur: A Study in Urban Geography," *Geographical Outlook*, I, No. 1 (1956), 16027; "Ballia: A Study in Urban Settlement," *National Geographical Journal of India*, II, Part I (1956), 1–6; "The Trend of Urbanization in the Umland of Banaras," *ibid.*, II, Part II (1956), 75–83; "Two Small Towns of Eastern U.P.: Sultanpur and Chunar," *ibid.*, III, Part I (1957), 1–10; "Faizabad-*cum*-Ayodhaya," *ibid.*, IV, Part I (1958), 1–6; with Mrs. B. Mukherjee, "Functional Zones of Ranchi," *ibid.*, III, Parts III–IV (1957), 117–124; with K. N. Singh, "Development of Twin-Township of Dehri-Dalmianagar," *ibid.*, II, Part III (1956), 121–127.

[2] "Dhawar . . . ," p. 63.

often spacious sections dating from the British period. The urban morphology of India thus shows either conflict or blending of indigenous features and the hybridized European features.

INDIGENOUS PATTERN

The old cities of distinctively Indian character in the northern plains and desert borders or in the Deccan region usually exhibit a number of common features, some of which derive in part from southwestern Asia through Muslim influence. The streets are irregular in pattern, narrow, and crooked. The main vehicular thoroughfares are rarely more than thirty or forty feet in width, often without sidewalks, and encroached upon by booths and the projecting open fronts of the shops which line them. The side streets and alleys are usually much narrower and so crooked as to be almost impassable for wheeled vehicles. The ground is completely covered by structures, except for the streets, the interior courts of some dwellings, and the occasional market areas and open spaces around public buildings. One- or two-story construction is predominant, although "lofty" buildings of three, four, or even six stories may exist along the main streets. The common types of masonry construction, known as "pucka," are brick or stone laid with mortar and often covered with plaster and roofed with semicylindrical tiles. But *"kutcha"* construction of mud walls with thatch roofs is found in the peripheries. Historic palaces of Hindu or Muslim rulers often rise on a near-by hill or stand by the river. Sometimes the battlements and moats of the pre-British walled city survive. The domes and minarets of mosques and the pinnacles of temples are prominent features.

There is usually some evidence of British influence in the form of the town hall, the municipal office, an enclosed and roofed central market, and the clock tower. Bicycles and automobiles push aside pedestrians and bullock carts. There may be ferroconcrete structures belonging to the prosperous merchants and modern flats for the wealthy residents standing side-by-side with traditional structures. But one passes abruptly into dim by-lanes and secluded courtyards which appear not to have been reached by modern influences.

The main bazaar, called "chowk" or "chauk" in northern India, is not quite equivalent to the central business district of an American city. It is crowded with numberless small retail shops which deal in foods or cloth, hardware, jewelry, and other consumers' goods. Groups of competing merchants tend to occupy a particular section. Thus, there is a bazaar for grain merchants and perhaps another for greengrocers. There is a street where brassware is sold and another for pottery. Another street is inhabited by goldsmiths, or silversmiths, and so forth. Native bankers and moneylenders, health practitioners, oculists, dentists, and public letter-writers congregate in the vicinity of the central bazaar, sometimes occupying second-story rooms above shops. But generally the upper and rear rooms are used as dwelling places by the merchants. The wholesale grain and other bulk-commodity markets are usually to be found near by. Retail business establishments may extend a mile or two along the main arteries of traffic, and subsidiary bazaars are usually developed, especially in the cities and large towns.

Surrounding and adjacent to the commercial streets are the primarily residential neighborhoods. There is a high degree of community consciousness and personal identification of the inhabitants with these neighborhoods. Brahmins and other high castes are usually in the best-built residential areas in or near the center of the old cities. Muslims are clearly separate from Hindus and are themselves subdivided into quasi castes and economic classes. The laboring castes and menial outcastes of lowest socioeconomic status occupy the poorest houses and tend to be located in the outskirts rather than the center. Gist, however, thinks this kind of segregation in Bangalore is less sharp than the segregation of Negroes in American cities.[3]

Wards, or larger and more inclusive sections of a city called "mohallas," are recognized. They usually take their names from the predominant caste or occupational group, from the founder's name or that of the original rural village on the site, or from a market, a public building, or an old city gate. The population of a mohalla may be several thousands or tens of thousands.

While segregation by commodity in business areas and by socio-economic or religious group in residential areas is a well-developed state of affairs in Indian cities, there is not the clear-cut separation of residential land use from business or industry which is normal in the cities of Europe and America. Merchants live in the bazaars and small shops; service industries and manufacturing of all kinds are located in predominantly residential areas. In some areas, manufacturing and retail or wholesale trade are carried on in the same establishments.

EUROPEAN PATTERNS

In contrast to the patterns of the indigenous urban settlements, the former British military contonments, civil stations, railway colonies, and company towns were laid out often on preconceived plans with definite functional areas. The tree-shaded streets are

---

[3] "The Ecological Structure of an Asian City . . ."

broad, metaled or paved, and the buildings are set well back. Structures are almost exclusively pucka, and many of them stand in the midst of large fenced compounds with much space devoted to trees and grass or landscaped in formal gardens. The typical British-built residence, called a bungalow (from Bengali *bānglā*), is a large rambling house with thick walls and high ceilings, large windows, and a wide veranda (from Hindi *barandā*) with pillars running all around, and is either flat cement-roofed or sloping tile-roofed. There are, of course, the modest row-house quarters for servants, mercenary troops, and other employees.

The inhabitants of these urban areas originally were the British soldiers, officers, civil administrators, businessmen, and missionaries. Some few of the foreigners were of non-British origin. There was probably always a preponderance in numbers of native population, including Christian converts and Eurasians (Anglo-Indians), who naturally tended to congregate in such areas and still do so. Today the Indian population is strongly dominant, although made up more largely of the governmental and professional intelligentsia and less markedly segregated by caste or religion than is true in the old cities.

The military cantonments are characterized by a fairly regular alignment of streets and comprise barrack blocks with rows of living quarters for the soldiers and their families, separate bungalows for the officers, hospitals, churches, and officers' clubs, together with drill grounds and rifle ranges, ammunition depots, and military supply warehouses. Sometimes there would be manufactories for armaments and other equipment and executive offices of regional military headquarters. Cantonments were built chiefly during the 19th century and had permanent garrisons in the beginning. Most of them have long since been abandoned for military purposes.

The civil stations, with which the cantonments now tend to become functionally merged, originally contained the offices and residences of nonmilitary branches of government at the district or province (now state) level. These areas still serve the same functions for which they were established in the late 19th and early 20th centuries, although Indian officials have entirely replaced the British. Public offices, often housed in strictly European-style structures little adapted to India, usually include the administrative (district magistrate's) headquarters, the tax collector's office and court, the law court, and the police barracks and jail. Sometimes there are other public institutions, such as the government printing presses, public libraries, and mental hospitals. Post and telegraph offices, foreign banks, insurance offices, hotels, cinemas, colleges and secondary schools following English curricula, and stores carrying goods of European types and fashions, all of which originally served the needs of the British governing class, now cater to the Anglicized native population.

The older cantonments and civil stations dating from the days of the East India Company present a good deal of irregularity in plan, and there is less predilection for straight or grid-pattern streets. The most irregular are the hill stations, situated in the mountains or uplands for climatic reasons to serve as health sanatoria and summer resorts and, because of the rough terrain of the sites, characterized by winding roads and widely dispersed stone and wooden houses. It was in the hill stations that a type of cultural landscape most resembling that of the British Isles was created. But every civil and military station, on the plains or in the hills, has its bazaar section which shows virtually all the features of indigenous urban settlement, although restricted in area and relatively small in population.

The railway colonies and other company towns probably show the greatest regularity of plan and the highest degree of separation between functional areas and economic classes. In most instances these urban settlements originated after 1870. The land was owned by the companies or held on long-term lease. The streets, dwellings, and all other structures were fully and exclusively controlled by the management. The rail depot and yards, the company offices, the extensive plants for the manufacture or maintenance of rolling stock, are common features set apart in such a settlement, e.g., Kharagpur, built after 1900 by the Bengal Nagpur Railway about seventy miles west of Calcutta.[4]

But the most distinctive features of the railway towns are the perfectly uniform grid of streets and the monotonous rows of brick dwellings, graded and rented strictly according to the wage scale and occupational status of the employees. For the lowest-paid semi-skilled workers, who were from the start invariably Indians, a single room with attached kitchen and enclosed courtyard was considered sufficient. These dwelling units are built in contiguous rows of ten and twelve, or multiples thereof, allowing little or no open space between street and entrance. The quarters designed for the intermediate grades of personnel, often including Eurasians as well as Indians, have more rooms, some in a second story, and are set back farther from the street. The two-story bungalows built

---

[4] The following description of a railway town is based on the author's experience in Kharagpur, West Bengal, in the period before World War II. It would be instructive to observe changes subsequent to nationalization of the railway and political independence from Great Britain.

for the employees with the highest technical skills or managerial capacity and receiving the highest salaries, who at first were mainly British, stand amid spacious landscaped grounds with small row houses for the servants in the rear.

Each grade and wage level was assigned to a specific section of town, creating an economic and, originally, a racial or national hierarchy of status differing from the traditional caste and socioeconomic segregation of the indigenous cities. The system was unlike Indian tradition, especially at the intermediate and low grades, in that families of different religions, castes, and mother tongues found themselves living side-by-side. A Punjabi Sikh would be assigned quarters beside a Telegu Christian or a Maratha Hindu. The Muslims were mixed with Hindus. The system also differed from tradition in that the highest ranks would be found farthest out from the center of town, usually on the opposite side of the railway tracks from the lowest ranks and the native bazaar. The commercial and industrial areas would be much less congested in a railway-owned settlement than in a typical Indian city. Broad streets were laid out, planted with trees alongside, and, if not paved with macadam, probably metaled with gravel and clay rolled hard.

Some company towns, e.g., Jamshedpur, resemble Kharagpur in grid pattern and segregation of employees according to wages and skills. This city has been created since 1907 on an undulating site formerly occupied by rural villages, and has grown to nearly 250,-000 in population under the benevolent capitalism of the Tata Iron and Steel Company. It covers about twenty-five square miles and achieves homogeneity without monotony and rapid growth without crowding. In the words of Karan,

. . . . Jamshedpur is distinct from other urban centers in Bihar in respect to modern layout, a marked segregation of functions and consequent absence of congestion. The factories are so widely spaced that it is not the chimneys but gardens which dominate the landscape.[5]

Extreme congestion and haphazard urban development in India are not confined to the old cities. One has only to visit the big manufacturing centers of Sholapur, Ahmedabad, Kanpur, or the Hooghly industrial towns to see irregular, narrow streets and closely built structures of indigenous types spreading rapidly in modern times. The twin township of Dehri-Dalmianagar, a commercial and manufacturing center of some 25,000 in southern Bihar which has multiplied in population eightfold since the 1920's, is an example described by K. N. Singh:

---

[5] "Patna and Jamshedpur," p. 32.

There is a promiscuous panorama of chance-directed and chance-erected . . . houses of different character[istics,] aspect and layout; some are brick-built [and] tiled, some mud-walled and tiled, while on the outermost fringe of this zone come the thatched brick-built or mud-walled cottages and also some first-class modern buildings of well-to-do people. . . . On the inner side are to be found some slum residences with all their abominable characteristics and it is here that the urban proletariat lives.[6]

Such is the landscape of the inner commercial zone of Dehri. Yet, only a mile distant is Dalmianagar, developed under the direct control of the Dalmia congeries of industrial firms, in which there is

Segregation of factories and offices from the residential colony on the one hand, and [grading] of residences on the basis of economy and status from one-room twelfth-class labor quarters to first-class large bungalows of the management.[7]

POPULATION DISTRIBUTION

Two facts about urban population distribution stand out clearly from the data obtained in recent censuses.

First, extremely high densities occur in both the indigenous inland centers and the Indo-British seaports. The maximum residential concentrations were reported to be 400,000 to 454,000 persons per square mile in some wards of Calcutta during 1941 and Old Delhi during 1951. Thus, there are at least 650 to 700 people living in the area of an acre in these two large cities, which ranked first and fourth, respectively, in terms of their total metropolitan population in 1951. On Bombay Island, as a whole, the mean population density must have approached 100,000 per square mile in 1951, but Greater Bombay averaged only one fourth as much. The maximum density reported in Bombay during 1941 was 256,000 persons per square mile (400 per acre), and in 1951 it may have exceeded 300,000. The comparatively low maximum of 112,000 persons per square mile (175 per acre) recorded for Madras in 1931 must have been at least doubled by 1951 in proportion to the growth of the population in the city as a whole. It is not only in these four largest cities of the country that high densities occur. One observes that the number of persons per square mile in Poona went as high as 160,000 and in smaller cities such as Banaras and Aligarh it exceeded 90,000.

The second notable fact about population distribution is the

---

[6]K. N. Singh, "Morphology of the Twin Township of Dehri-Dalmianagar," *National Geographical Journal of India*, III, Parts II–IV (1957), 176.

[7]*Ibid.*, p. 178.

sharp density difference between wards in the central or old urban areas and the peripheries, particularly where there are suburbs, as in the case of Calcutta, or cantonments and civil stations, New Delhi being an obvious example. The ratio of maximum to minimum densities may be as high as 300:1 (Banaras) or 100:1 (Calcutta). In general it appears that only in Bombay and Calcutta are the central business districts less densely populated than the surrounding residential areas, as is almost always true in American cities. In the commercial center of Bombay the large business blocks of the "Fort" and the open spaces of the adjacent Esplanade bring down the density of this inmost zone of the city to 19,200 persons per square mile (30 per acre). A similar lessening of density occurs in downtown Calcutta around Dalhousie Square below Howrah Bridge and north of Fort William and the park area of the Maidan. Population data by wards do not exhibit the true details of distribution. Information regarding the actual areas of habitation would permit mapping of the real geographic patterns.

The original causes of such extreme concentration and abrupt gradients of population density can be summed up in three words: protection, prestige, and proximity. In medieval and early British times the imperial cities were wholly or partly enclosed by walls or ditches for defense. Many local rulers also fortified their chief towns. Soldiers and retainers, merchants and craftsmen crowded inside the walls for military protection and safety from robber bands. The palace, being the seat of power and wealth, became a focal point around which the people of highest status gathered for royal patronage as well as proximity to trade with all who came into and went out of the city. The levels of prestige and wealth became progressively higher along the thoroughfares going toward the city center, and the least privileged and poorest people were relegated to the back lanes and marginal areas, which sometimes were outside the city walls.

This pattern of urbanism was a pronounced feature of the pre-British period in northern India and the Deccan when Muslims and Hindus of official rank or merchant castes lived inside the walls. Despite the vicissitudes of Poona under the Hindu Marathas in the 18th and 19th centuries and the disappearance of the old walls, the most congested central ward—where a fort had been built and occupied by Muslims in 1631—still goes under the name of Kasbe-Pune ("Walled Poona").[8] In Aligarh the ancient Koil mound, which was fortified during the period of Muslim rule, is the nucleus

---

[8] Joshi, "Urban Structure in Western India . . . ," pp. 7–9.

of the city today. It is the site of the chief mosque and the seat of municipal government and is solidly covered with buildings and streets, although the walls are gone and urban development has spread far out on the plain below.[9] Old Delhi, built under the Mogul Emperor Shah Jahan's rule in the 17th century, is a prime example of survival of the pattern more or less intact.

' From the 16th through the 18th centuries small forts and trading "factories" established by several European nations on the coast of India served similarly as points of attraction. Native Indian employees and entrepreneurs concentrated especially in Madras, Bombay, and Calcutta as British influence grew at the expense of the Portuguese, Dutch, Danes, and French. In the case of Madras, the concentration was in George Town (formerly Black Town), north of Fort St. George on a narrow peninsula of land acquired in 1639 and protected by swamps and the little River Cooum. On Bombay Island, ceded by the Portuguese to the British in 1661 and occupied in 1665, the earliest concentration was in the Fort. This nucleus was actually enclosed by a wall from about 1720 to 1862. Urban development had, however, spread outside the Fort even before it was completed, and further concentration was encouraged by the natural isolation of Bombay from the Maratha-held mainland. In Calcutta, which was permanently occupied by the British in 1690 and protected by two successive Fort Williams, the water barrier of the Hooghly River on the west was reinforced by a ditch enclosing an area two or three miles in width and nearly five miles in length. Within this area the commercial core of the city and some elite residential sections are still found.

During the 19th century, as the power of native rulers declined in India and the need for such military defenses was outmoded, proximity remained the chief advantage for city dwellers—proximity not simply to the retail trade of the central bazaar or trading "factories" on the water front, but also to the amenities of European life at first available only in the cities.

In 20th-century India, poverty must be added as the fourth and main cause of urban congestion. The unsanitary and degraded living quarters in the Bombay chawls and the Calcutta bustees must be seen to be believed. Yet, the lowest-paid factory laborers and service workers crowd into a few square feet of space, glad for mere shelter. Housing conditions are equally appalling in certain jute-mill towns along the Hooghly near Calcutta, and perhaps in the places of temporary refugee concentration in the Punjab and Delhi.[10]

---

[9] Hirt, "Spatial Aspects . . . ," pp. 38–39.
[10] For a description of Indian slum life, see chap. iv—*Ed.*

DECENTRALIZATION AND URBAN FRINGES

The lack of centralization in urban functions and the comparatively slight development of fringe areas are two features which appear contrary to what could be expected in India in the light of the sharp density gradients and residential crowding.

The strongly dominant central business districts so long familiar in Europe and America, in which large retail and wholesale trading establishments are located along with banking, insurance, hotel, entertainment, and communications industries, can scarcely be said to exist, except in the Indo-British seaports. In part the lack of central services can be accounted for by the tastes and traditions of the people, whose requirements are met in the small bazaar shops of the conservative inland cities. It is also to be explained by the low income of a vast majority of the inhabitants and by the development of separate business areas in the British-built cantonments and civil stations, where wealth became concentrated.

In reality, many cities functioned as dual entities during the British period and still do so. India Chauk (formerly Connaught Circus) in New Delhi and Chandni Chauk in Old Delhi are examples of a binuclear commercial pattern. Polynuclear patterns are described in Bangalore by Gist[11] and in Poona by Joshi.[12]

Such geographic patterns of double or multiple business districts are unlike the new American pattern of outlying shopping centers which compete with the central business districts in retail trade and some personal services, but remain largely subsidiary in relation to financial and professional services and communications industries. The central bazaars in the large cities of India are supplemented by neighborhood bazaars. But the Anglicized business areas—with their fashionable stores dealing in European types of goods, their banks, cinemas, hotels, and various public agencies—complement rather than compete with the indigenous bazaars. Their outlying and sometimes scattered locations seem incongruous and even inefficient as a way to provide for the needs of urban dwellers today. Centralization of all modern goods and services, however, could only intensify bazaar congestion.

It remains to be seen what patterns of business location will develop as the demand for goods and services increases in the India of the future. Two tendencies are already evident. First, there is the unrestricted accretion of small shops along the main roads and particularly along the arteries of traffic leading from the old bazaars and residential areas to the railway stations or new factories. Second, there is the haphazard filling-in of the open spaces

[11] "The Ecological Structure of an Asian City . . ."
[12] "Urban Structure in Western India . . ."

of the cantonments and civil stations. Bungalows are adapted or enlarged for offices and stores. The spacious grounds are built upon without consideration for aesthetic values or sanitary conditions. Prabhu[13] expresses concern for the future welfare of the citizens of Dharwar, a small Mysore city, where the average density is already twice as great as in many cities of comparable population and where incessant change is obliterating the basic contrast between the indigenous part and the Anglicized part, much to the detriment of the latter.

Another distinct pattern less frequently met with is that of self-contained cells. This is found in some of the new settlements which have developed under the aegis of private industry or the control of government. Modinagar, U.P., a small town twenty-eight miles northeast of Delhi, which is economically supported by the Modi family mills, is described by A. B. Mukherji as a linear grid-pattern settlement, paralleling the rail line, "with the residential units on one side and the factories on the other side of the trunk road that runs as the base line of the town." [14] The business core, near the railway station, "consists of long lines of box-type shops situated on two sides of the trunk road." [15] But there are several secondary nuclei—more or less self-contained, with stores and residential units—near the various factories. In Jamshedpur, while there is a modern business district serving the whole city, a series of industrial suburbs, with factories and adjoining workers' settlements separated from one another by open spaces and parks, is developed on a large scale.[16] At Chandigarh[17] the fifteen-square-mile site is divided into sectors by a grid of straight roads. Each sector is a self-contained residential area, with commercial and recreational services. One sector is the city center, with the complete range of specialized services. The buildings to house the functions of the Punjab state government are grouped separately.

The fringes around all but the largest urban agglomerations as yet show remarkably little alteration of the traditional forms of rural settlement. In 1951 many small towns of 50,000 or less had as much as 12 or 15 per cent of their population engaged in or supported by agriculture. Farm villages and cultivated fields are observed within the municipal limits of cities of 200,000 or 300,000

---

[13] "Dharwar . . ."

[14] A. B. Mukherji, "Modinagar: A Study in Urban Geography," *Geographical Review of India,* XV, No. 4 (1953), 11.

[15] *Ibid.,* p. 13.

[16] Karan, "Patna and Jamshedpur," pp. 31–32.

[17] R. M. Panjabi, "Chandigarh: India's Newest City," *The Geographical Magazine,* XXXI, No. 8 (1958), 401–414.

population. The rural look of the urban fringes may be more apparent than real, because some of the inhabitants of villages close to a city or town may have taken up urban employment—as, for example, in Modinagar[18] and Allahabad.[19] There is also intensification of farming, of course, in response to the heavy demand of city dwellers for fresh vegetables, fruit, and milk. Any American observer of India's urban fringes, however, cannot fail to be impressed by the absence of the urban sprawl so prevalent around the cities of the United States. This feature of urban morphology at first seems inexplicable in view of the persistent urban congestion of old cities and the intensified overcrowding in rapidly growing centers.

Centrifugal forces are relatively weak in India for the simple reason that most urban dwellers must walk to work. Although mass transportation by train or trolley and bus is cheap and rapid in the large cities, there are many small cities where modern means of local transportation are inadequate or almost nonexistent. Furthermore, the low wages received by the workers do not permit the expenditure of even a few *paise* for fare. They must live within a mile or two of their places of employment. Hence, most city dwellers cannot afford to escape to the less densely occupied fringes.

Contiguous urban extensions and separate suburbs have appeared around some of the most prosperous centers of commerce and trade or governmental activity. Persons of middle income, the white-collar workers, lesser civil servants, and skilled factory workers can afford public transportation or use bicycles for daily travel. It is they who are populating the modest ferroconcrete bungalows built on lots of a quarter acre or more described by Joshi[20] on the margins and in outlying sections of Poona. Rarely do persons of upper economic classes have private automobiles for daily travel; if they do, the street congestion inside the old cities makes the vehicles impractical to use. In Calcutta, Bombay, Madras, and New Delhi automobile commuting has begun, but remains relatively unimportant. Most of the automotive vehicles seen on the streets of Indian cities are public conveyances for people or goods, and they are far less numerous than bicycles and animal-drawn vehicles. The low density of extra-urban automotive traffic is indicated by the fact that only 20 to 30 buses a day travel the main roads of the 3,500-

---

[18] Mukherji, *op. cit.*

[19] Ujagir Singh, "Banaras—A Note on Its Urban Geography," *Indian Geographical Journal,* II, Part I (1956), 36–47.

[20] C. B. Joshi, "The Historical Geography of the Islands of Bombay," *Bombay Geographical Magazine,* IV, No. 1 (1956), 5–13.

square-mile service area around Agra.[21] H. H. Singh[22] thinks that one automobile is to be expected to pass every ten minutes on the heavily traveled streets of Jaunpur, U.P.

Local railway service is rapid and frequent to and from Calcutta, Bombay, and Madras. The growth of true residential suburbs outside these cities has been stimulated during the past three or four decades. As many as 200,000 passengers are carried daily by rail into Bombay, and suburban development is occurring as far as ten to fifteen miles from Bombay Island along the two railways crossing Salsette Island. There is a suburban belt outside Madras stretching fifteen miles or so southwest along the railway to St. Thomas Mount and Guindy and served by 70 trains a day in each direction.[23] Dormitory suburbs are flourishing on the basis of trolley or bus services north, east, and south of Calcutta as far as five or six miles from the central business district.[24, 25] The rail lines paralleling the Hooghly River for thirty miles or more northward from Howrah and Sealday have long been used by white-collar workers traveling into Calcutta. But the three-dozen urban municipalities, extending fifteen miles downriver as well as thirty miles upriver from the City, and together with it comprising a conurbation of 4.6 million inhabitants in 1951, are industrial satellites rather than residential suburbs. The Hooghlyside conurbation has an industrial base, primarily jute textiles, dependent upon the advantages of the river and parallel railways for raw material assembly and access to seagoing vessels. Most of the 1.8 million urban people living outside Calcutta are dependent directly or indirectly upon employment in the local mills and do not commute to the City.

[21] Lal Singh, "The Umland of Agra," *National Geographical Journal of India*, II, Part III (1956), 149–152.

[22] Hari Har Singh, "Evolution of the Townscape of Jaunpur City," *ibid.*, IV, Part I (1958), 35–46.

[23] N. Subrahamanyam, "Some Aspects of the Growth of Greater Madras: A Study in Suburban Geography," *Journal, Madras Geographical Association*, XIII, No. 1 (1938), 22–31.

[24] Meera Guha, "The Morphology of Calcutta," *Geographical Review of India*, XV, No. 3 (1953), 20–28.

[25] *Idem*, "Transport in and Around Calcutta: An Analysis of Traffic Conditions," *ibid.*, XVII, No. 2 (1955), 1–9.

URBAN COMMUNITY DEVELOPMENT
IN INDIA:
THE DELHI PILOT PROJECT

Marshall B. Clinard and B. Chatterjee

On the basis of previous census reports and what other limited data are available, it is estimated that the slum population constitutes from 10 per cent to as high as 60 per cent of the total population in the large Indian cities. Were these slums to be judged by Western standards the percentage would undoubtedly be greater. A conservative estimate would place urban slum dwellings which are totally unfit for human occupation at about 1.15 million.[1] In the sample survey carried out by the State Statistical Bureau of the government of West Bengal in 1956, it was estimated that nearly 600,000 people lived in slums in the city of Calcutta alone.[2]

Urban slum dwellers reside in *katras,* lanes, chawls, bustees, *ahatas,* and *cheris. Katras* are small, single-room tenements, normally constructed in rows, within a courtyard or enclosure and with a single entrance. Lanes are narrow, winding, and often damp, with densely populated houses on either side. Multistoried buildings, called chawls in cities like Bombay, house numerous families, with many persons (often more than one family) normally residing in one room. Latrines and water taps are common. Bustees are located in quite open areas of the city, or outwards from the center, usually on unauthorized sites. They are generally thick clusters of

[1] "Report of the Advisory Committee on Slum Clearance" (New Delhi: Government of India, July 18, 1958), p. 5.
[2] *Ibid.*

small, dilapidated mud huts, often with roofs or sides made of scraps of wood, gunny sacks, metal, or other waste materials. In some cities, such as Kanpur, bustees are built within a compound or enclosed walls and are called *ahatas*. In the southern cities of India slums usually consist of rather neat mud or thatched huts similar to village huts. In Madras they are called *cheris*.

Typically in slum areas the streets, lanes (gullies), and drains —which are open—are filthy, and people sleep as many as six to twelve in a room, hovel, or shack. The Indian slums, however, are more than the aggregate of the physical surroundings: they are also a way of life. Disease rates, poor health, and infant mortality are high, and there is little adequate knowledge of health and sanitation, nutrition, or child care. Illiteracy is exceedingly high, cultural and recreational activities are usually lacking, except as provided by such commercial enterprises as the cinema, or gambling, and most slum dwellers feel apathetic or even antagonistic to local authorities, whom they often blame for their plight. Seldom do slum dwellers coöperate with civic authorities to improve either the local area or the city as a whole, and they generally lack community consciousness.

Apart from the various physical and social conditions which are characteristic of the urban slums, the bazaars which are located in or near all residential areas pose their own particular problems. They seem to have an ageless past and an aimless future. These colorful places, through which countless people pass and repass many times each day, are sources of much chaos and confusion as well as dirt and disease in the locality. Bazaars are congested, their drains are often choked with garbage and filth, and dirty water flows in all directions. A broken water tap may continue to spread and waste water for days without anyone's doing anything to correct it, and in some bazaars children and some adults urinate and defecate near drains adjacent to the shops. In general appearance bazaars in urban areas are unattractive and need much improvement. Articles and food are dumped indiscriminately, food handlers display an amazing disregard for sanitary and hygienic principles, and signboards are haphazardly and insecurely erected. Extensive and unauthorized encroachments on the pavement are chronic features of any bazaar and are a source of great inconvience.

A common feature in many bazaars, as well as in the central shopping areas, temples, and railway stations, is the inevitable beggar who makes his rounds in all Indian cities. Mendicancy has become institutionalized due to chronic unemployment and the lack of organized charity or public relief. One survey reported that in the city of Bombay alone there are about 10,000 beggars,[3] some 47 per cent of whom are able-bodied. Of the remainder 18 per cent are aged and infirm, 12 per cent are lepers, and 10 per cent blind and crippled. The total beggar population of Delhi has been estimated at about 3,000, of whom 44.5 per cent are able-bodied.[4] Many beggars earn a rupee or more a day, which is almost equal to, or in excess of, the daily wage of some workers. It has been estimated that Bombay citizens spend some 3,500,000 rupees annually on indiscriminate charity to beggars, and Delhi citizens 918,000 rupees. If such sums were to flow through welfare channels, adequate care and rehabilitation services might be provided not only for all beggars, but for many others also. While many cities have various types of legislation against begging, institutional facilities are not adequate to cope with all beggars even if they are arrested.

Despite the deplorable physical conditions, the Indian urban dwellers do little themselves to correct the situation. Either they are apathetic or they feel that the solution is entirely a responsibility of government and welfare institutions. In fact, the people have little faith in their own capacities to do anything. Although they feel dependent upon local authorities, they are antagonistic toward the local government because situations are seldom improved, and they do little to coöperate with the municipal authorities. Water taps, dustbins, electric bulbs in public places, and manhole covers are stolen, and streets and public places are dirtied in numerous ways.

In part, these situations are due to a general lack of unity among city dwellers, and several factors have contributed to this lack of cohesiveness in the social relationships in Indian cities. In pre-British India the city population was largely distributed geographically by religion, caste, and subcaste, and by occupational and regional groups forming social islands.[5] These social characteristics had real meaning and developed such extensive exclusiveness that the groups often constituted cities within cities. These cities appear to have had a fairly stable population, giving residents greater opportunity to know one another intimately. All this has vastly changed with rapid industrialization and the migration to the cities of village people or refugees of partition. Increasingly, people living in local areas of the city are mixed by caste, or by regional grouping and occupation. Although groups of persons may

---

[3] M. V. Moorthy, ed., *Begger Problem in Greater Bombay* (*A Research Study*) (Bombay: Indian Conference of Social Work, 1959), p. 14.

[4] *The Beggar Problem in Metropolitan Delhi* (Delhi: Delhi School of Social Work, 1959).

[5] A. K. Nazmul Karim, *Changing Society in India and Pakistan* (Oxford, 1956).

live in close proximity, or a larger area may be even predominantly of a certain group, housing pressures have made it increasingly impossible for large numbers of persons with similar social characteristics to form exclusive groups in any one area. Thus caste groups, regional groups, or occupational groups may well be scattered all over the city.

While caste is still important in the villages of India, it appears to be declining in the cities today.[6] Such changes vary according to the particular caste and social stratum of society.[7] Urban living conditions are rapidly modifying strict adherence to caste regulations. In cities, for example, it is often impossible for each caste to follow its traditional occupation, and there are no caste procedures for certain new occupations in an industrial urban society. In place of caste, the city is becoming differentiated more and more by a class system.

THE COMMUNITY DEVELOPMENT APPROACH TO URBAN PROBLEMS

A realistic approach to the enormous problems of Indian cities will attempt changes in the lives of the people within the present framework and with the resources now available. It will lead to limited physical improvements—better drains, water facilities, and latrines, etc.—as well as changes in the way of life, and will aim chiefly at using the human resources of the community. Such is the urban community development approach, which attempts to develop community feeling and shared objectives among city people. Self-help and citizen participation are to be fostered. Such a program is not offered as a substitute for government action on a large scale in improving housing and increasing economic opportunity; it is limited to those areas and those problems where there is a possibility of self-help.

There are important differences between urban community development and rural community development. The primary goal of the latter is economic improvement, particularly in agricultural production, whereas in the former it is the amelioration of living conditions and community life that predominates. New social patterns must be found to replace the relatively well-organized village social structure. In the villages, organizations must be revitalized and change be brought about within a traditional frame-

---

[6] See, for example, P. N. Prabhu, "A Study on the Social Effects of Urbanization," in UNESCO Research Centre on the Social Implications of Industrialization in Southern Asia, *The Social Implications of Industrialization and Urbanization: Five Studies in Asia* (Calcutta, 1956), pp. 90–94.

[7] K. M. Kapakia, *Marriage and Family in India* (Bombay: Oxford University Press, 1959), pp. 119–120.

work; in the city, on the other hand, adaptations need to be made to new conditions, and urban people must be helped to regain intimacy in their impersonal surroundings.

PILOT PROJECT IN URBAN COMMUNITY DEVELOPMENT

In view of the magnitude of the task, any large-scale slum clearance or improvement of the slums is clearly beyond the financial capacity of the government at this time. It has been felt, however, that something could and must be done to improve the situation. The present pilot project in urban community development was designed to stimulate citizen participation and self-help activities to cope with slum conditions and prevent further deterioration in the areas, as well as to develop a feeling of civic consciousness. Delhi was chosen as the site of the pilot project for several reasons. First of all, as the nation's capital, its conditions are of particular concern to the national government. Secondly, the problems of Delhi are comparable to most Indian cities', with perhaps those of Calcutta being greater and those of Bombay and Madras less. Thus, any procedures found to be suitable to the capital city might be transferred to other Indian cities.

The project instituted in Delhi was made possible by a grant from the Ford Foundation to the Delhi Municipal Corporation, through the Health Ministry, and work was initially started in September, 1958, with the appointment of a director and consultant. The original grant was for $25,000, with a subsequent grant of $155,539 for the continuation of the experiment until March, 1962. Over the three-and-a-half years the Delhi Municipal Corporation contributes an increasing share of the cost annually.

GOALS AND OBJECTIVES

The goal of the Delhi Pilot Project has been to promote the growth of healthy, harmonious, and satisfying community life, and to encourage the development of citizens' participation in programs of civic improvement.[8] The objectives are:

---

[8] The first national Seminar on Urban Community Development, held in Hyderabad December 24–30, 1959, has stated the objectives of this type of work as "(*a*) to create community consciousness and to encourage the people to participate actively in efforts to improve their level of living with as much reliance as possible on their own initiative and by the provision of technical and other services in ways which encourage self-help and mutual-help in order to make efforts more effective [and] (*b*) process of developing community consciousness: (i) utilization of existing common institutions and the creation of new ones to meet the growing needs of the community, (ii) utilization of existing services or the creation of new ones for the community, (iii) creation of common facilities, (iv) recognition of the changing needs of the community and common efforts to meet them."

1. The social integration of the communities on a local neighborhood basis through participation in *self-help* and mutual aid programs
2. Development of a sense of *civic pride* by stimulating local interest in civic betterment campaigns
3. Preparation of the ground for *democratic decentralization* of municipal services through the organization of Vikas Mandals (people's development councils) fostering local leadership
4. Creation of the necessary climate for undertaking programs of *economic betterment,* based on maximum use of community resources and local initiative

GENERAL PLAN

The Delhi Pilot Project involves seven types of improvements: (1) the creation of a Department of Urban Community Development as part of the Delhi Municipal Corporation; (2) the organization of the first six citizens' development councils or Vikas Mandals; (3) the establishment of neighborhood councils involving the organization of 32 Vikas Mandals into three large neighborhoods; (4) improvement of the typically poor sanitary conditions and general disorder in the local bazaars, through community organization; (5) an attempt to improve the work of the local voluntary groups, called mohalla committees; (6) the development of a health and welfare council and community chest to coördinate the welfare services in Delhi and integrate them with the citizen development councils;[9] and (7) various civic campaigns to improve the physical appearance and conditions of the city.

Planning began in October, 1958, and actual field work began in February, 1959, on the organization of the first Vikas Mandals, or citizens' development councils.[10] The councils consist of elected representatives of small groups ranging from 250 to 400 families. These development councils then discuss the problems of the local area and formulate self-help action programs. In the third phase of the plan, the six original pilot projects have been increased to three neighborhoods involving altogether about 50,000 persons. This will furnish experience in coördinating citizen participation

---

[9] There is no community chest in any Indian city. The only health and welfare council in the country is located in Poona.

[10] The plans were developed in a detailed "Manual for Urban Community Organizers." This manual, which explains the philosophy and procedures of the work, has been a useful tool in orienting and training new staff members. It has been issued in mimeographed form by the Delhi Municipal Corporation and is now being revised by the authors for publication.

and self-help among a larger group of people. The plan might be divided into four phases:

Phase I.   (September, 1958–March, 1959.) Planning Phase.
Phase II.   (April, 1959–March, 1960.) Action Phase— Six Vikas Mandal Pilot Projects.
Phase III.   (April, 1960–March, 1961.) Neighborhood Extension Phase, Bazaar Project, Mohalla Committees, Health and Welfare Council, and Community Chest.
Phase IV.   (April, 1961–March, 1962.) Consolidation and Evaluation Phase.

VIKAS MANDALS

The six pilot project areas were selected, according to typological representativeness, out of thirty possible areas that were studied. The working unit has been set up as 250 families, about 1,250 persons, although in actual practice it has sometimes gone as high as 400 families, or 2,000 persons. It was felt that a larger unit would be ineffective for the development of meaningful relations among people. Although each area is a geographic whole, it is artificial in the sense that, with one exception, there was not initially even a partial semblance of organization of the residents or consciousness of being a community. The one area with some identity among its members had, however, no recognized community organization in the accepted sense.

Each project area has a distinctive population composition and physical condition, with local factors which might help or hinder community organization; and each project varies in caste, religion, occupation, and length of residence. On the whole, the projects were designed to recognize the social differentiation and the complexity of life which generally exist in most large urban areas in India. The six areas are as follows:

1. *A colony built for rehabilitation of squatters from shack bustees.*—This project consists of families who formerly lived for years in the worst shack bustees in different parts of Delhi and who have recently been relocated in a completely new area with relatively good physical planning in terms of drains, water, and latrines.[11] The colony was built on a self-help basis, each squatter being given a small piece of land, building material worth 200 rupees on loan, and a standard design for a one-room hut. The project area covers 429 families and the average number of persons

[11] A real "shack" bustee was not taken for a project because most of them are unauthorized occupants on government land. It would be almost impossible for the municipal government to encourage self-help improvements in the area and then later force the residents to move.

in a family is 3.9. The total population is 1,629 persons and the social composition of the group is complicated and heterogeneous. The people come primarily from Rajasthan and Uttar Pradesh, and some are Sansis (ex-criminal tribe) and Marathas. The men and women who work are mostly building workers and unskilled laborers who have a high (93) per cent) illiteracy rate. Although this area is hardly a slum physically, the slum mentality brought from the bustees pervades the people's lives. Fights are common, and there is much social tension. The Corporation's position as the landlord has created some difficulties in urban community development work in the area.

2. *Slum area in a highly congested, low-income part of the city with relative unity in occupation and religious background (Muslim).*—This old Muslim locality adjoins a mosque in the western extension of the old walled city. Although the houses are situated in a planned way in a fairly compact block, they are in a dilapidated condition. The single-story hutlike structures line both sides of narrow lanes. The property now is under the Custodian of Evacuee Property. This project consists of 303 families with a population of 1,890 persons, 75 per cent of the adults being illiterate. The area is much neglected and the main occupation is trunk making, many of the houses being used as workshops. Lack of basic amenities and feelings of uncertainty in the area have been crucial factors in its neglect, and unsanitary conditions fostered a severe cholera epidemic two years ago.

3. *Slum area in a highly congested part of the city in a lower-income bracket, with relative unity in occupational and religious background (Hindu).*—The project area consists of two major *katras* and one *ahata,* housing 273 families with a total population of 1,014 people. The people belong to the scheduled castes with very low incomes, and their plight becomes still worse in the slack season during the monsoons. Over four fifths of the people are illiterate, and the level of education of literates is low. They work mainly as potters or construction workers. Their apathy was due to a number of factors.

4. *An area of predominantly industrial workers.*—The area covers about 238 families, or 1,200 people, who live mainly in *katra*-type housing. Industrial workers employed in two large textile mills form 60 per cent of the population. There are a large number of immigrants from West Pakistan who mainly occupy one part of the project area. Literacy is rather high (42 per cent), about one in eight being matriculates or above. The average monthly earnings of a family is about Rs. 100. Their preoccupation with union activities, the tiresome nature of the occupation, and

their regional affinities combined to make them originally somewhat indifferent to organized community activities.

5. *Slum area in a highly congested, low-income part of the city with considerable diversity in occupation, caste, and religion.*— This area consists of two sides of a long and fairly wide lane with three smaller lanes branching off. The lane was once connected to the rampart wall of the old city. The population of the lane is heterogeneous both as to caste and class. Those of the upper castes tend to live at one end of the lane farther from the city wall, as was the custom long ago, with the Harijans (Untouchables) and lower castes at the other end nearer the city wall. Included in this project are 265 families, the majority of whom (73 per cent) are illiterate. This figure rises to as high as 90 per cent illiterate among the Harijans. The caste and class heterogeneity (Brahmans, Khatiks (butchers) and Harijans) is an important factor in social relations; their integration is the chief problem. The lower groups (Khatiks) have tended to follow their traditional and customary leaders, who in many ways do not work well with people of the higher social and economic groups.

6. *Housing colony for displaced persons with chiefly cultural and recreational problems.*—The houses in this area, about ten miles from the center of the city, were built by the displaced persons themselves with financial help from the government. Some 275 families (1,360 persons) live in the compact area which was chosen for the project. The colony has good housing, an adequate water supply, electric lights, and many facilities, such as a school. The men are largely engaged in occupations outside the area. The problems of the area are a lack of cultural and recreational activities, a lack of unity among the people, and a feeling that they are not really a part of the city after all the years since partition.

ORGANIZATIONAL PROCEDURES

After the areas were selected, a male and a female community organizer were assigned to each project. These organizers are carefully selected on the basis of personality, motivation, and education. About half have an M.A. in social work and the rest are from a variety of fields. All are given an in-service training course of about six weeks in urban sociology and the philosophy and procedures of urban community development. These organizers interviewed the heads of the families individually and attempted to stimulate the people's interest in solving some of their local problems. After the initial interview the organizers called zone meetings of approximately 15 to 25 families living in a lane, *katra,* or other small area, to discuss problems at this level and to elect a council representative. This council, when constituted for the 250 families, numbers 10 to 15 people who, in turn, nominate office-bearers—president, vice-president, secretary, and treasurer. A meeting is next called of all the adults in the area, who formally elect the officers and adopt a simple constitution. (A somewhat similar and parallel organization is also established for women.) The council then sets out on various self-help activities. Almost the entire responsibility, and all the credit for the work, is given to the Vikas Mandal, the organizers simply serving as stimulators and counselors. After a Vikas Mandal has been established the organizers move on to another area, keeping close contacts with the first Vikas Mandal. This process continues until eventually each organizer's responsibility is four projects with about 1,000 families.

Each organizer follows certain specific procedures in organizing an area:

1) A preliminary study is made of the area. Information is secured about physical features, such as lanes, schools, temples, playgrounds, and community centers; the types of dwellings, the physical amenities, and the cleanliness of the area; population composition according to caste, religion, region, and occupation; organized groups; common activities or celebrations and the nature of social relations in the area. A detailed survey is not possible because of time, and also is not advisable because it might unduly arouse among the residents suspicions which could interfere with later organizational work.

2) Following this general survey the organizers call on all residents, door to door, to discover what they think of the area and its problems and whether they would like to do something about them. In addition to securing some factual data, six questions are asked on the initial interview. The questions are phrased to stimulate the people to think about self-help in relation to local problems, and to discover natural leaders in the local area. The questions are:

   a) What are some problems in the local area which you think the people here might be able to do something about?

   b) How long have the problems existed?

   c) Would you like to do something about the problems of the area?

   d) Have you had any experience in mutual aid, coöperative welfare, or voluntary organization?

   e) To whom do you turn in the area in times of crisis?

f) Would you be interested in attending a group meeting of persons in the area to discuss neighborhood problems?

3) Natural leaders of the area, through whom the organizers can work, are identified. These are persons who want to see improvement and changes made in the local community, are resourceful and articulate, tolerant of others' opinions, and whose judgment is highly regarded.

4) Regular meetings of the council are held, committees ap-appointed, and citizen discussion-groups organized—particularly at the zone level.

5) Finally, there is the development and implementation of specific action programs devised by the local community and carried out by them.

STIMULATING SELF-HELP

In nearly all projects the initial contacts were met with suspicion, hostility, and apathy. The people of the slums have been so exploited by political parties and welfare organizations and have become so dependent upon government that, in the beginning, they did not believe in the workers or visualize the possibilities of self-help. This situation improved after about three weeks of daily visits to the local areas. The workers found that some small incidents often stimulated the people. In the following field report, an urban community organizer early in the work used the problem of unhinged latrine doors to "sell" the possibilities of self-help to a group of local people:

On the worker's inquiry about the latrines, one of the persons of the last lane led the community organizer to the main *katra.* In there are twelve dry latrines, six for males and six for females. The doors of the male latrines were all unhinged from the wooden brackets. The chairman of the mohalla committee, who was along with the community organizer, started again his harangue against the landlord and the Municipal Corporation. The worker patiently heard him and when he finished, she asked the person who had led them to the latrines, "For how long has the condition in the latrines been like this?" The reply was "Since the last two or three months." The worker said, "To repair these doors I think we need only a few nails." "Yes, you are right," came the immediate reply. "What do you think we have to spend on the nails sufficient to repair the door?" again inquired the worker. "Only three or four annas (five cents)," replied everyone crowding around.

"Let us make the expense one rupee—how many families use the latrines?"

"About a hundred or more."

"Don't you think this much money can be contributed by the *katra* people to get the doors repaired, or should we wait for the landlord or the Corporation to come and repair it?"

The chairman of the mohalla committee was hearing everything. He at once was enraged, and pushed his hands in his pockets and said, "I will pay three annas, four annas, or any amount from my pocket, but, sister, do you think we should start fixing the latrine doors? We would be working in filth and dirt." The worker then politely said that she was just asking about the possibilities because it is inconvenient to the residents and not to the landlord and also the cost involved was meager. If they could get a person who was professionally a blacksmith or like that, he could help them fix the door. Anyway, it was just an idea and they could drop it.

But the others in the group were already thinking and were quiet. At least, the emphasis was laid on the over-all responsibility and not on the Municipal Corporation.

DEVELOPING COMMUNITY FEELING

In the areas selected for the pilot self-help projects a crucial task has been the stimulation and development of a "community feeling" among the people who merely live in an area without feeling any ties or pride in their surroundings. The development of such a feeling of pride and civic sense has required much ingenious planning. The very fact that the council members meet together to deliberate on their common problems gives them a sense of importance and local pride. Such a feeling is further enhanced through such devices as giving each council representative a zone name-plate to have in front of him at the council meeetings; printing letterheads with the names of the office-bearers, receipt books for payment of annual membership fees of one rupee per individual member, and milk distribution cards; and the use of zone numbers demarcating the project area. All project areas have a small Vikas Mandal office with the name of the organization above the door.

As early as possible in each project, in order that the residents can see tangible results of their combined efforts in improving their areas, such self-help projects are undertaken as applying whitewash, placing dustbins with the name of the project area painted on them, installing bulletin boards, repairing water taps and lanes, and putting up such signs as "Keep This Place Clean." As the areas begin to feel some cohesiveness, such projects as sewing and literacy classes are begun, and recreational projects are instituted, through the help of other personnel such as the public health nurse and the recreational and handicraft field-program organizers attached to the Department.

The identification of the local residents with the community organizers and the other personnel further supports a feeling of unity. This common identity is even greater when most of the city is not as yet involved in urban community development projects.

Visits between Vikas Mandal representatives have also been arranged by the Department, and this has tended to foster a sense of healthy competition, pride, and loyalty in one's own area. Such inter-project contact has proved to be an effective technique which has often led to the exchanging of gifts between people from one area and representatives of other areas. Athletic contests, such as volley ball, have been held between teams representing various project areas. Other Vikas Mandal projects, such as common picnics or sight-seeing programs, have strengthened friendly ties on a locality basis. Finally, meetings have been arranged at which the office-bearers of all the projects report in the City Council Chamber to the chairman of the Standing Committee and the city commissioner on what the people of the projects have been doing, giving them a feeling of importance in their joint efforts.

SELF-HELP ACTIVITIES

Up to March 1, 1960, the first six Vikas Mandals launched about 200 self-help activities, covering a wide range of community needs.[12] They have encompassed such varied projects as improvements in the sanitation of the area; beautification of the area; institution of health, nutrition, and first-aid classes; and recreational activities for children and adults. In addition, singing groups, women's clubs, literacy groups, and women's handicrafts have been initiated, and group celebration of national days and festivals has been promoted. In all projects the emphasis is on the group and not upon the individual. There is no set pattern to the activities, the self-help projects being developed purely on the basis of the needs felt by the community.

Many diverse activities have been undertaken in this manner. Dustbins have been provided and drains built and cleared; broken water taps have been replaced and hand pumps repaired; lanes have been leveled, and courtyards have been paved with brick; houses have been repaired. In the way of beautification, houses have been whitewashed and there has been some attention to gardening. There have been sanitary improvements (e.g., construction of latrines and prevention of children from defecating in drains), and such activities to improve health as pre- and post-natal classes, instruction in personal hygiene for children, and mass vaccination campaigns. Recreation and handicrafts have been stimulated by self-help means. Volley ball, singing, sewing, weaving, and soapmaking are but a few examples. It is impossible here to give any comprehensive idea of all the activities that have

---

[12] In addition to urban community organizers there is a small staff of field program organizers in public health, recreation, and handicrafts. These technically trained persons assist the Vikas Mandals when requested to do so. All field program organizers are given an orientation in terms of a citizen self-help program.

blossomed through self-help, but final mention must be made of educational and welfare improvements, including the education of preschool children, literacy classes, reading rooms, and the formation of a women's volunteer corps, among whose activities are the preparation and distribution of free dried milk.

NEIGHBORHOOD COUNCILS

Each of the six pilot project areas has from 250 to 400 families. The realistic problem of integrating these small communities into a larger human organization must be faced. The second step, therefore, was to set up an organization on a scale corresponding to a neighborhood. Three pilot Vikas Mandals have been extended into neighborhood areas. In one case the extension has been delimited by four main roads passing on the four sides of the project area. In the other, there has been a smaller but more established geographical entity with a fair degree of exclusion from other areas. The coördination of the Vikas Mandal is in the charge of two neighborhood organizers who in turn are responsible to one of the chief community organizers.

The functions and organization of the neighborhood councils.— Just as attempts have been made to build a strong Vikas Mandal after integrating smaller zones by informally bringing their representatives into a council, efforts have been made to create a neighborhood council in the same fashion. Each neighborhood council consists of representatives of approximately ten to fifteen Vikas Mandals. The area of each Vikas Mandal is drawn according to physical boundaries, and the composition of the population is kept as homogeneous as possible. Later adjustments in the boundaries are made, if needed. In the development stage this neighborhood council is expected to be a loose confederation and may be given a name like "Kshetra Panchayat" (Area Council). Also included on the council are representatives of established mohalla committees and welfare organizations and institutions functioning in the area. Municipal government employees such as schoolteachers, sanitary inspectors, and health officers can serve as ex-officio (nonvoting) members on the council to develop a spirit of coöperation between the authorities and the people in improving local services.

One objective of these neighborhood councils is the decentralization of municipal services, so that they can become more effective at the more intimate and personal level of 250 to 400 families, which is the primary unit of organization. The larger organization can make this decentralization of municipal services meaningful and effective. Matters such as the handling of private sweepers, common usage of limited open spaces in the neighborhoods, or the establishment of institutions, such as a library, can be made only by a larger group of people at the neighborhood level. Likewise, in overcrowded parts of any city a number of problems—such as the presence of unauthorized manufacturing units, small trades and commercial establishments, dairies and cattle nuisance, besides antisocial activities like illicit drinking, prostitution, juvenile delinquency, etc.—can yield only to the organized forces of the larger neighborhood. The three neighborhoods in the Delhi projects are:

NEIGHBORHOOD I. This area, located in an old part of the city with many winding lanes and houses of various types, consists of 37 acres. Although there are electricity, drainage, and water connections, these are not adequate. Drains are open, there is generally poor sanitation in the area, and there are very few open places. In the monsoons certain places are waterlogged for long periods because of choked drains. About 4,000 families, or about 20,000 persons, live in this area. About 20 per cent are Muslims; of the Hindu population about 5 per cent are displaced persons, some 5 per cent belong to higher caste and economic levels, and the remainder belong to a lower economic group having three different subcastes; Chamar, Nais, and Julahan. They are engaged in weaving and *thela*-pulling (hand carts), and belong to such occupations as hawkers, unskilled laborers, porters, and factory laborers.

NEIGHBORHOOD II. This locality is situated on private land, which was developed only about twenty-five years ago and consists mainly of *katras* located along lanes. The area has a good shopping center and a fair degree of such amenities as water, light, and latrines. Although the local civic amenities and facilities are fair, the sanitary conditions and community life need great improvement. About 2,500 families or 7,500 persons live there, and about 60 per cent of the population are displaced families. Industrial workers, such as weavers, spinners, and dyers, and nonindustrial workers, such as washermen, small-factory workers, shopkeepers, and hawkers, make up about 25 per cent of the total work force in the area.

NEIGHBORHOOD III. The third neighborhood, consisting of about 12,500 persons, is also situated on private land. The total area is about twenty-three acres and has a very zigzag layout of houses, with narrow and blind alleys. The area has a mixed type of structure—single- as well as double-storyed houses, big *katras,* dilapidated houses as well as good and new houses. The area is heterogeneous in caste and class, and people have more or less settled affiliations to a certain political group. The existing local associations are restricted in their scope and need reactivating. A part of this neighborhood developed only about thirty years ago; two other parts developed earlier. The newer area, representing roughly 25 per cent of the population, consists primarily of people in the lower economic group, mainly occupied in construction work. It lacks adequate provision of the basic amenities, water and light, and the sanitation is poor. One of the older areas, comprising about 50 per cent of the total, is a fairly good locality in terms of basic amenities and general sanitation. The people belong to middle and upper middle groups and are in business, government, and service. The third part is mainly occupied by displaced persons. These people are petty shopkeepers, hawkers, shop assistants, and government servants.

Educational aids.—In order to stimulate coöperative efforts in local areas and to demonstrate what can be accomplished through pooling modest resources, financial grants have been made in the form of educational aids for some projects. Although in many projects no subsidy at all has been given, grants generally have ranged from a 10 to a 50 per cent subsidy. These subsidies have also made it possible for citizens to undertake more and larger projects than would otherwise have been possible. In the case of sewing machines, for example, if fifteen women in an area wish to buy a sewing machine they are given some assistance providing each agrees to teach at least one other person in the area. They each pay one rupee a month for six months and contribute up to 100 rupees toward the total cost of 180 rupees. The machine then belongs to the Vikas Mandal and can be rented out again to other women. Since the machines are owned by the group, they are well cared for. Subsequently machines may be purchased by other groups coöperatively on an installment basis.

Originally it was felt that it might be difficult for people to contribute any money, since most individuals earn only two to five rupees a day. Despite this, they have been able to undertake many shared projects where individuals' contributions are small. Given a good project which they want badly enough, and which is not too expensive, they are somehow able to find the necessary funds.

BAZAAR PROJECT

Since bazaars are integral parts of neighborhoods it would be unfortunate to deal with neighborhood conditions while neglecting the unsightly and unsanitary state of most of the bazaars. Bazaar conditions arise from such factors as overcrowding and extensive encroachments, but most of the chaos is due to a lack of organization. If the shopkeepers and the public coöperated, even to a limited extent, many bazaars could be transformed into better shopping centers. Whereas the initial appeal is expected to be largely in economic terms, namely that profits could be increased, it is hoped that improvements will foster a feeling of local pride and a realization of the necessity for better sanitation measures.

A typical bazaar with some 300 shops has been selected as a pilot project, and two organizers were assigned in February, 1960, to the task of developing a local organization which through self-help, rather than governmental or police action, could make local improvements. A project contact card was prepared, asking such questions as "Would you like your bazaar to be more beautiful and attractive?" "What are the problems of the bazaar?" "Would you help to do something about the problems?" and "Would you attend a meeting called for this purpose?" It is hoped that this approach will win the confidence of the bazaar shopkeepers and overcome many suspicions.

So far the project is too new for more to be said than that the response has been encouraging—particularly in the attitude of the shopkeepers toward mutual coöperation, and their own recognition that a bazaar often represents a situation of "antagonistic symbiosis." Shop owners have shown an interest in improving the sanitation and general cleanliness by providing dustbins. Some also recognize the need for removing encroachments and providing water taps, urinals, and cycle stands, as well as keeping animals away by some means. Already they pay their electric and water bills in a coöperative manner to save time, and it is possible that they might employ a common person to tackle their many legal problems, at a cheaper cost. The advantages of group advertising might also be demonstrated. Although some of these goals may be accomplished before too long, it may require a longer time to encourage eating houses and dealers in sweets to cover their food and to use soap and hot water for washing dishes.

Mohalla committees.—Mohallas are Indian equivalents of neighborhoods. Residents of these areas in the past have come together in times of crisis or need to form mohalla committees (residents' associations) or mohalla sudhar committees (residents' welfare committees). In some cities there was from Mogul times a system of "mir mohalla" (chief of the locality), wherein the help of heads of families in a neighborhood was enlisted by authorities for law and order.

Today mohalla committees vary considerably in size, coverage, and membership, some having as many as 25,000 families and others less than 100. Some of them are quite effective; others exist in name only. Many mohalla committees encounter difficulties, including a lack of trained workers and effective continuity in leadership. At a recent meeting of the representatives of the mohalla committees, called to discuss matters of common interest, some 21 representatives of 11 mohalla committees (representing about 600,000 people) attended. It was suggested that joint meetings be conducted to stimulate and learn from each other and that a newsletter be issued.

Accordingly, the Department has started training programs for mohalla committee men and women workers who will act as auxiliary community organizers on a voluntary basis. A periodic newsletter for mohalla committees is issued from time to time, and inter-mohalla committee meetings are held periodically. Workers from the Department are deputed to the executive committee meetings of these mohalla committees on request, so as to offer them consultation and guidance. Thus, existing institutions can be used for urban community development.

CIVIC CAMPAIGNS

Since it is felt that civic campaigns can be effectively used in working toward the goals of the pilot projects, various civic campaigns have been worked out. These civic contests and "Keep Delhi Clean" campaigns help to create an awareness of the civic problems and to stimulate an emotional attachment to the city, its history and beauty. If this use of mass-media communications can help to stimulate civic pride there will be a better climate for the work in the local community.

The first project of this type was carried out in connection with World Health Week. Donations amounting to Rs. 7,500 were secured from various companies and a series of advertisements was placed in the newspapers, carrying their names and that of the Department of Urban Community Development. The advertisements dealt with such topics as making Delhi a cleaner and neater place, the need for prevention of diseases, and the necessity for public coöperation in improving the city.

CITY WELFARE COUNCIL AND FUND

It has also been proposed that a city welfare council be promoted to coördinate health and welfare services in the city and to make it possible for citizen self-help projects to secure encouragement from other agencies.

One of the most important functions of this council will be the pooling of all community resources to meet the financial needs of voluntary agencies and services in the city. Although community chests are well known all over the world, India has never experimented with such a program.[13] City dwellers at present are pestered with scores of "appeals" from many agencies throughout the year. Some people are approached often in a year, whereas hundreds of thousands of citizens, whose small individual contributions would total a large sum, are hardly ever tapped. Unauthorized collections by exploiters are common, causing leakage and wastage of community resources. Thus the city welfare council and fund is envisaged as an integral part of the urban community development program. Such a council will consist of representatives of all social service agencies in the city, both public and private, working under its own constitution.

ADVISORY COUNCIL

An Advisory Council on Urban Community Development, appointed by the mayor, consists of representatives of the municipal government and a number of social agencies in the city. As soon as neighborhood councils have been formed, their representatives will also be included in this council. The Advisory Council is an *ad hoc* body which advises the Department and is preparing the ground for a full-fledged health and welfare council and community chest. This type of coördination would enable a number of important welfare agencies in the city to render better service.

SOME TENTATIVE CONCLUSIONS

Although the period of experimentation has been short, the results have been encouraging. People have responded readily to self-help. Although slum people are largely illiterate, they possess common sense, shrewdness, and ability. With encouragement and stimulation, they show interest in their own betterment. Though poor, they are not happy to live in filthy surroundings or remain illiterate, and they are aware of the contrasts between their own lives and those of many others they have seen in the city. Much knowledge has been gained about the nature of slum life and the difficulties of developing an organization for self-help. The generalizations outlined below will require further testing by the evaluation and research unit.

Initial suspicion.—In the beginning it was found hard to establish relationships with the people in the local communities. This was thought to be due to the fact that in the past many a political candidate has talked glibly about their betterment as a vote-catching

---

[13] Recently the papers reported that 600,000 members of a tribal group in Orissa had contributed a rupee each systematically to collect 600,000 rupees for their welfare. This should be possible of achievement in cities as well, through the organization of community chests.

device without any follow-up. In addition, many social welfare agencies and governmental groups have made promises which have never been fulfilled. The people's feelings toward the municipal authorities and their inability to meet the problems faced by the community have created a general atmosphere of lack of faith. This initial suspicion was usually overcome after two or three weeks' organizing work.

The poverty of the Indian slums is not as great as it first appeared.—Our original idea was that there would be relatively little in the way of surplus funds available to the population for self-help. This has not been the case. Most slum dwellers seem to have money available for the purpose, providing their contribution individually is small, e.g., one rupee per month available for literacy, or a few annas to construct a water tap, and so forth. The explanation lies partly in the fact that the average monthly rent is only a few rupees in the cities, representing a much smaller proportion (less than 10 per cent) of total income than in the West. Many people spend money on gambling, alcohol, and the cinema. Also, as several of the members of the family are working, the *total* income is sometimes greater than one would expect. This statement does not imply that there is that much money available for self-help, but rather that a small contribution from each person would make it possible for a Vikas Mandal to have available a substantial sum of money.

Political feelings are skin deep.—The political feelings of the Indian people of the slums appear to be skin deep. Moreover, affinity with political parties does not appear to be primarily on ideological grounds, but rather for the purpose of exploiting the political party for whatever benefit can be gained. Political considerations seem to be unimportant for achieving improvement in the local community. So far, politics do not appear to have played any important role in either facilitating or hindering the organization of a Vikas Mandal.

Improvements in caste and regional relationships must be primarily on a geographical basis.—The Vikas Mandal seems to furnish a means by which different groups, whether on the basis of caste or region, can be brought together on a geographical basis within a city. Suggestions that there should be changes in caste relationships are largely ineffective unless different castes are brought together on a local basis. Community activities appear to be the primary way to deal with caste difficulties.

Closer Muslim-Hindu relationships can be promoted through Vikas Mandals.—Many Muslim communities in Indian cities tend to be isolated from the larger Hindu community. Association of Muslims with the activities of Hindu Vikas Mandals has helped to remove the barrier of isolation and made the Muslims feel that they are an integral and contributing part of the total community.

Limited mobility of people in Indian cities is favorable for the formation of organized activities on a local basis.—A large proportion of the people of Indian cities, and in particular the women, live and often work in a relatively limited area, and one can say that the world of an Indian is a relatively small area within the city. This is largely due to the fact that Indians do not have good transportation. We have found in some cases that women rarely leave a *katra* even to go to the *katra* adjoining. This is quite different from much of the Western world. It seems that perhaps we can expect more success in organizing Vikas Mandals because of this limited mobility.

Women are more highly motivated for self-improvement than men.—Men are so much away from home and their relationship to their family is such that the women must take greater responsibility for the sanitary conditions of the area, for the health of the children, and even for much of the cultural, educational, and recreational activities of their families. Whether or not change will be produced in Indian cities in the long run will depend primarily upon the women, not upon the men, at least as regards the type of change envisaged in this project.

The women of the slums are much more highly motivated for self-improvement than we had originally expected. At first we rather opposed the idea of women organizing themselves into groups of their own, because we thought that perhaps the men would oppose such an organization. In many cases, particularly in the case of the younger women, they have responded more actively than have the men. The situation indicates that Indian women of the lower class are not satisfied with either the conditions under which they live or their subordination to men. Several effective women's groups have been formed. In a Muslim area, where the women live in purdah, a women's group which meets weekly has been formed and three women have been accepted by the men as associate members of the council. There is no question that women in India carry the brunt of social change.

Organizing the Vikas Mandal on the basis of zones rather than on the total group of people.—One of the major changes in the original plan has been the organization and structuring of a Vikas Mandal on the basis of zones of 15 to 25 families rather than on a total group of 250 as originally planned. A council is now developed from representatives elected by lanes, *katras,* or other groupings. This organization has developed for two reasons. In the first place, it became clear that even the small size of the

Vikas Mandal is larger than the typical Indian's "world," at least in terms of the problems they would like to solve. Indians of the cities think primarily in terms of the lanes, *katras,* and chawls where they live. The second reason for this type of organization is that one can get council members elected quite easily if it is done in terms of 15 to 25 families. If the elections are carried out with a group of 250 families, one is likely to get political considerations and encounter difficulty in electing a council. A special procedure was devised for getting unanimous elections at the zone level.

Should economic improvement be the major objective of the Vikas Mandal?—Many persons have felt that economic improvement should be the major objective of a Vikas Mandal. So far, this appears to be quite difficult to achieve. The great diversity of occupations in an area and the fact that the economic problems of India primarily arise from larger considerations make it difficult to work for economic improvements at the local level. Something can be done, of course, to improve the economic and earning possibilities of women through certain types of work, but it is difficult to do much for the men. Economic improvement can also be achieved indirectly through coöperative purchasing of food, wise planning of nutritious meals, more effective expenditure, and coöperative credit unions. The project will continue to try to find ways of improving economic conditions in the Vikas Mandal, and perhaps more can be done after a Vikas Mandal has been organized effectively for some time.

FUTURE CONSIDERATIONS

It seems likely that the general pattern outlined here, since it has been developed in areas of different types, should provide a framework for other Indian cities, with modifications to suit local variations.[14] The project goals and objectives, for example, have generally been supported by the National Seminar on Urban Community Development.[15] It was concluded that in order to secure more effective and lasting benefits, the people should be encouraged to participate actively to improve their level of living, as much reliance as possible being put on their initiative, with the technical and other services being used only to encourage self-help and mutual aid. The process of discovering and training local leaders was also stressed.

[14] A second pilot project in urban community development has been started in Ahmedabad with a grant of $170,000, in August, 1960, from the Ford Foundation. The plan calls for a large-scale series of projects involving 200,000 persons in a major industrial city of a million population.

[15] See note 8.

It has been suggested that voluntary welfare agencies should be entrusted with this work. In view of the many local problems involved in a task which traditionally concerns local administration, however, the best agency appears to be the municipal corporation or municipality in any city. This view has been strongly supported by the Seminar on Urban Community Development, which has categorically stated that the municipal corporation or municipality should be in over-all charge of this work, setting up a department of urban community development with an advisory council of ward councilors, representatives of Vikas Mandals, and voluntary agencies.

The problems of urban areas are so appalling that they need guidance and direction from the national level, in addition to attention at the local level. For this purpose some machinery should be established at the center to effect over-all direction and coördination between cities operating such programs. Its structure and location, however, present some difficulties. National government interests in municipalities—such as town planning, housing, public health, education, and social welfare—are divided among several ministries. If a program of urban community development is to succeed, it should have the unstinted support of all the ministries concerned. Perhaps the establishment of a separate autonomous body would solve the problem more effectively than charging any existing central ministry with this work. In any event, one or two research and training institutes for urban community development workers need to be established, preferably on a regional basis.

V

CITY-HINTERLAND RELATIONSHIPS
IN INDIA

WITH SPECIAL REFERENCE TO THE HINTERLANDS
OF BOMBAY, DELHI, MADRAS, HYDERABAD, AND BARODA

Richard A. Ellefsen

Indian cities today are experiencing rapid change. They are growing in area and population, and at the same time they are acquiring a new character as their peoples perform new tasks in a physical environment that increasingly reflects the use of Western technology. The economic activity of Indian cities is increasing in response to the over-all influences of independence, overseas trade, and a planned development program. These influences are manifested in individual cities by the construction of factories and increased commercial activity, by the expansion of governmental functions in the national and the state capitals, by the construction of new housing at the city's edge, by the growth of distribution centers, and by the rapid expansion of motorbus service into the surrounding countryside. It seems reasonable to suppose that a larger urban periphery implies a larger hinterland and that the city's increased activity is effecting a regional transformation.

Any attempt to predict or, through policy, to influence the course of future urbanization surely requires some knowledge of city hinterlands. In particular, an understanding of their extent and their functional relationships with their nuclear cities is called for, together with an analysis of the complex of human activities in the hinterland. This paper presents the results of a preliminary investigation of some fundamental relations of Indian cities with their hinterlands, and also develops a methodology for hinterland studies in underdeveloped countries.

The fact that little importance has been attached to the hinterland is apparent from the few attempts in India at planning a whole city region. A major exception was the Town Planning Organization, founded in 1956 to prepare a master plan for Delhi[1] and its region. The direction of study taken by the T.P.O. indicates their awareness that knowledge of the hinterland, the nodal city region, is requisite to comprehensive planning. It is necessary to know such things as the area of greatest city influence, the economic activities of hinterland residents, the pattern and use of transportation systems, the agricultural pattern, and the market potential of the region.

In addition to the T.P.O.'s work, a few individual papers have discussed the hinterland. Of these, only R. L. Singh's study on the "Umland" (hinterland) of Banaras[2] fulfills the objective of first delimiting the area and then analyzing its relationships with the city. Singh's studies, however, and those of other North Indian cities by his students, deal with each city as a unique entity, making comparability on a nationwide basis most difficult. Moreover, dependence on personal observation and survey for each specific case has not resulted in the development of a widely applicable method.

Singh attempted to use Western techniques by measuring bus service and newspaper circulation in addition to the areas supplying milk, vegetables, and grain to the city. The limited value of borrowed methods is evidenced by Singh's use of the area in which Banaras Hindi newspapers were circulated to determine the outer boundary of the hinterland, even though this circulation area was at least five times larger than that covered by the other criteria of delimitation. In the absence of circulation figures, the circulation area was determined by mapping what the newspapers considered as their "main reading areas." The value of newspaper circulation as a regional index is further reduced by a general low level of literacy.

Studies of hinterlands in Western countries have had the advantage of using data covering many characteristics of the population, both demographic and economic. The more comprehensive and complete data available in the West for hinterland study include such items as the volume of retail and wholesale trade, receipts from services, value added by manufacture, rental values,

---

[1] *Master Plan for Delhi*, published in 1960 by the Ministry of Health, Government of India. See appendix to chap. xiv.

[2] *Banaras—A Study in Urban Geography* (Banaras: Nand Kishore & Bros., 1955).

number of professional workers, newspaper circulation, locations of specialized services, radio and television audiences, and telephone networks.

Unfortunately, since economic data for hinterland places in India are not universally available, it is necessary to use, first, basic demographic materials and, second, locally available data on land use, food supply, and transportation networks. The hinterland, as thus delineated, continues outward until the point is reached where the factors measuring the degree of urbanization equal the average for the rural areas of adjacent districts, or district subdivisions.

As a result of heavy reliance on demographic data, the measurement is more one of the reaction to urban influence than it is of economic interdependence (as in Western studies). Therefore, the measurement of Indian city hinterlands and their relationships with the city in this study employs a somewhat different technique from that used elsewhere. The developed state of the rural economy in Western countries has meant that specialized goods and services available to city dwellers are also available to people in the outlying areas. The problem of delimitation then becomes one of determining from where, and to what degree, the people of the hinterland derive urban-produced goods and services. The assumption is made that all rural areas are under the influence of some city, whether directly or indirectly through a satellite center.

But in India, with a large rural population dependent mostly on primary activities, and where rural-urban differences are sharp, the hinterland may best be studied at this early stage of its development by regarding it as that area adjacent to the contiguously built-up area which exhibits physical, economic, and demographic characteristics resembling the city more than the isolated rural areas. Much of the area fairly close to the city, even for the large cities in this study, which would be an active hinterland for a comparable Western city, remains as isolated and tied to agriculture and a barter-type economy as many points lying at great distances from any major city.

The relative smallness of the surrounding area manifesting urban influence, and therefore the steepness of gradients in our five cases, requires a detailed examination of the smallest possible units, namely the revenue, or areal, villages. From these villages, as units of observation, sectors have been constructed. This affords the possibility of measuring the slight but critical differences in the values of the indices of urbanization.

Use of the next-largest census unit, the district subdivision (such as tahsil, taluk, taluka) would conceal the significant differences. A

contrast of the city population with the rural population of surrounding districts would surely be striking, but would only measure
basic rural-urban differences. A fine shading of the grays, ranging
from black to white, is required, and this can only be done by using
the hinterland village as the unit of observation. Since the entire
rural area of India is composed of over half a million villages,
treated as minor civil divisions, it is possible, by using village data,
to discern extremely fine-grained patterns. Researchers dealing with
the United States usually have access to data only for whole coun-
ties and for urban places. Bogue,[3] for instance, was compelled to
use county units in sectors and zones, and Kish[4] encountered difficulty in not having enough urban places in some zones to permit
comparability. Thus, for India, the disadvantage of working with
fewer reported items in the census is partly offset by their availability for each and every village as well as the towns and cities.

The small areal extent of Indian city hinterlands is probably
attributable to the stage of development of the country. The regional city of the West is, after all, relatively new and almost
wholly a product of a high level of living and modern means of
transport. This difference in stage of development means that concepts used in the United States by researchers such as Bogue, who
"assumes that the entire area of the United States is blanketed with
metropolitan dominance," [5] are not applicable to India. The hinterland of an Indian city need not, however, be thought of as including only that immediately adjacent area where interdependence is
the keynote, as it is in this study. Indian cities, like Western cities,
also exercise a certain degree of influence over broad regions and
occasionally even nationally. This loosely united hinterland is composed of many single-factor regions. Food, for example, comes into
the city from both near and far. Bombay receives about a third of
its milk supply from Anand, over 250 miles away, while the balance
is produced within the limits of Greater Bombay itself. Although
most of the fresh vegetables for the Delhi market come from local
sources, large supplies of fresh fruit come from as far away as
Kashmir, Madras, and Bombay. But these are secondary spheres of
influence, and to measure them would require the type of demographic and economic data used in the West for similar purposes.

The presence or absence of physical amenities is frequently used
as an indicator of the sharp differences between urban and rural
India. Only to a very limited extent do electric-power lines, tele-

---

[3] D. J. Bogue, *The Structure of the Metropolitan Community: A Study of Dominance and Sub-Dominance* (Ann Arbor, Mich., 1949).

[4] L. Kish, "Differentiation in Metropolitan Areas," *American Sociological Review,* XIX, No. 4 (August, 1954), 288–298.

[5] *Op. cit.,* p. 17.

phones, city bus service, and water and sewage lines extend into the hinterland. The absence of amenities in villages contiguous to the urbanized area has prompted observers to say that modernism stops at the edge of the city. A survey the present writer made of the physical amenities available in 16 villages in the Delhi area, all of which are located within two miles of the city limits, revealed that a definite lag exists between the demographic characteristics of an outlying, practically "surburban" village and its physical appearance. Although the 16 villages as a whole had 75 per cent of their population dependent on nonagricultural occupations as reported in 1951,[6] this survey in 1959 showed that only 6 were even partially electrified; 12 had the minimum in hard-surfaced streets, while the balance had only dirt lanes; and only 10 had even the most primitive of sanitation systems. The impetus of increased economic activity in the area, and more traffic on the roads passing by, had prompted 8 villages to build roadside shops, forming in miniature the sort of development along highways seen in the United States. Most of the agricultural land formerly worked by the villagers had been converted to urban use. The contrast between modern and ancient was completed by the presence of imposing new housing projects standing beside the crumbling walls of a centuries-old village.

Likewise it is misleading to assume that a village does not possess specialized goods and services simply because there is neither a commercial core nor any institutionalized place of business. The villagers' needs are served by traditional forms of medicine, law, finance, religion, personal services, education, and trading, the availability of which not only reduces dependence on the city but acts as a deterrent to the spread of Western forms of products and services.

Delimitation of Hinterlands for Five Cities

Based upon the village data available in the 1951 census,[7] factors were sought which would best reveal the changing degree of urbanization from city to rural areas, and from which city influence could

---

[6] *District Census Handbook, Delhi State, Census of India 1951* (Delhi State Government, 1953).

[7] Available in the Primary Census Abstracts of the *District Census Handbooks*, published for the first time in 1951 for most of the districts of India, are: village area, number of males and females, number of houses and households, number of literates, and number of males and females in each of eight livelihood classes. The Livelihood Classes are divided into two groups. The first includes four divisions of the agricultural classes; the second breaks into the four nonagricultural classes: production other than agriculture, commerce, transport, and other services and miscellaneous sources. Each of the Livelihood Classes includes both the active workers and their dependents.

be inferred. It was decided that the following demographic factors were the best available indicators of city influence: (1) density of population, (2) the sex ratio stated as a percentage of males in the population, (3) the proportion of literates in the population, (4) the proportion of persons dependent on nonagricultural occupations for their livelihood, and (5) the proportion of persons dependent on commerce stated both as a percentage of the total population and as a percentage of the nonagricultural population.

As a first step in studying the degree of urbanization—and hence city influence—in the hinterland, raw demographic data were converted to proportions, ranked and grouped in quintiles. A map was then prepared of the administrative units[8] surrounding each city, placing a value for each village in its exact location. An overlay of transportation arterials placed on the completed maps revealed a striking visual correlation between high values of the indices of urbanization and roads and railways entering the city. There was also a prominent zone of high values immediately adjacent to the city. Intermediate values could be discerned for villages located along minor roads. Map study also revealed that many areas of the lowest values were associated with places where access was most difficult.

The map study strongly suggests that not only is accessibility a key factor in spreading the effects of urbanization in the hinterland, but that there exists a grading of the degree of urbanization with accessibility. Furthermore, there is a suggestion that accessibility naturally falls into grades based on location relative to the city and the roads, the types of which are known from field study and map reading. The area immediately adjacent to the city is ideally the most accessible, followed by the major highways and railways, the secondary roads, and finally the isolated villages. The areas of the hinterlands in this study only extend to an average distance of eleven miles outward from the city edge. Within these limits there is no clear pattern of regression with absolute distance.

This use of sectors shows an advantage over the conventional method of computing indices of urbanization for circles drawn concentrically from the center of the city. Zonation yields what appears to be a sharp drop with distance. However, examination of

---

[8] Administrative units chosen were generally district subdivisions for which both data and map coverage were available, and were as follows: Madras—all of Saidapet Taluk, with the addition of a "panhandle" section of Sripurumbudur Taluk; Delhi—the entire area of Delhi State; Hyderabad—all of the 3 talukas of Hyderabad West, Hyderabad East, and Medchal; Bombay—villages of Greater Bombay District beyond the outermost ward, Borivali Taluka, Thana Taluka, and Bassein Taluka; Baroda—parts of Baroda, Padra, and Waghodia talukas.

the areas included in each of the zones reveals that, since lines of communication and transport converge upon a city in a spokelike fashion, the first zone is not only closest to the city in absolute distance—it is also so highly penetrated by railways and highways that nearly all of its minor civil divisions are within easy reach of the city. Proceeding outward, the zones increase in total area and toward the rim of the wheel the spokes become farther apart. Since this means that the ratio of villages in contact with roads to those that are isolated ranges from very high in the innermost zone to very low in the outermost, the question is whether the ranging of values should be attributed to increasing distance or decreasing accessibility. The answer given by the sector analysis is that accessibility is the correlative factor.

A description of each of the sectors follows and they are schematically illustrated in Figure 1. The sectors are (1) the City— (*a*) Inner Wards and (*b*) Suburban Wards, (2) Belt, (3) Ribbon, (4) Secondary Roads, and (5) Interstitial Villages.

DIVISIONS OF THE CITY

All of the cities in this study, except Baroda, are large in area, ranging from forty-nine square miles for Madras to sixty square miles for Hyderabad. Wide variations in demographic characteristics exist between the small, crowded electoral wards of the old parts of the cities and the frequently more dispersed wards at the edge of the cities, where recent expansion has taken place. This difference is taken into account by dividing the city into Inner Wards and Suburban Wards. Since it has been Indian city administrative practice to annex territory surrounding the more established parts of the city as it grows and becomes developed, these outermost sections of the city contain an interesting mixture of old village centers (which often persist in their rural form even though surrounded by new city development), government and private housing projects, scattered private housing, improvised village-type housing of refugees and in-migrants, scattered industrial and commercial developments (including, perhaps, government-founded industrial estates), and patches of agricultural land, usually referred to as "undeveloped land."

The fact that the Suburban Wards are only about a third as densely populated as the Inner Wards is largely a result of legislative annexation practice. In order to maintain ward populations at about the same size, the legislators included about three times as much area when forming the less built-up sections at the edge of the city into wards.

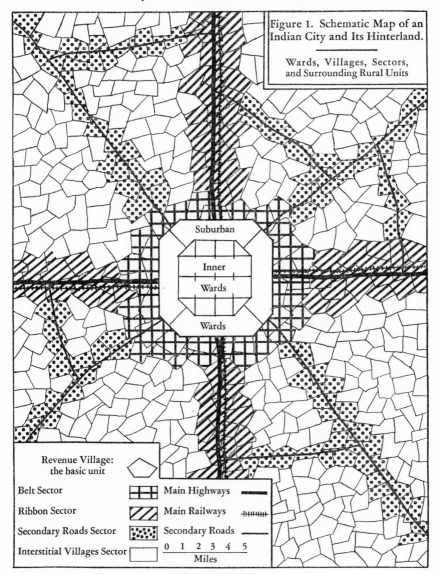

Figure 1. Schematic Map of an Indian City and Its Hinterland.

Wards, Villages, Sectors, and Surrounding Rural Units

Suburban

Inner

Wards

Wards

Revenue Village: the basic unit

Belt Sector

Ribbon Sector

Secondary Roads Sector

Interstitial Villages Sector

Main Highways

Main Railways

Secondary Roads

0 1 2 3 4 5
Miles

THE BELT

The outer boundary for the Belt was drawn at a point just two miles from the outer limits of each city as of 1951. For the inland cities of Baroda, Delhi, and Hyderabad, the Belt extends around the city in all directions. For Madras, facing the Bay of Bengal on an even coast line, all sectors, including the Belt, extend in only three directions. Bombay, lying as it does on the southern tip of a

peninsula (actually an island) has almost a one-directional hinterland. The area across the bay to the east and south of the city is
quite isolated because of the physical barrier.

THE RIBBON

Next in importance in degree of urbanization is the sector extending outward from the edge of the Belt and including an area a
mile wide on each side of the major routes of transportation—the
Ribbon. Within this distance villagers are in a position to be influenced by any ribbon development outward from the city. Indigenous forms of transportation are more efficient, encouraging
travel to and from the city. Villages were only considered to fall
within the Ribbon if they were either within one mile of the main
highway or within a mile of a rail station. Obviously, many villages,
although lying on the rail line, remain quite isolated if there is not
ready access to a station.

SECONDARY ROADS

The emphasis on accessibility is continued in the grouping into a
sector of all villages touching on secondary roads. It is of prime
importance that these roads are metaled and capable of all-season
use. Most agricultural rural areas in India are crisscrossed with a
network of dirt roads and trails, quite suitable for carts and cycles
during the dry season, but almost impassable during the rains. The
presence of the hard-surfaced road, even if only one motor-vehicle
lane wide, is an undeniable isolation breaker. With increased accessibility, the village way of life will change as it becomes possible
to set up regular bus service to the city; an outlet is furnished for
village products; the village in turn becomes a more accessible
market for the city; and the way is open for possible daily commuting to city jobs. Perhaps the most significant meaning of the
construction of secondary roads is that not only do the larger
villages, which the road was designed to connect, come into closer
contact with the city, but all the villages along the road have new
vistas opened to them. The secondary roads may be either feeder
lines connecting with the main highways and railroad stations, or
roads leading directly in and out of the City or the Belt.

INTERSTITIAL VILLAGES

Falling last in terms of potential contact with the city is the
sector listed as Interstitial Villages. Villages making up the sector,
whether near or far from the city in air miles, all have isolation as
a common factor. For the resident of such villages a trip either to
the city itself, to a satellite center in the Secondary Roads sector,

or to the Ribbon means going by foot, cycle, or cart over a distance of one to ten miles of unmaintained dirt track.

To determine if values for the factors of urbanization have reached their minimum point at the Interstitial Villages, surrounding rural units have been examined for comparison. For this purpose, values were averaged for the rural population of all district subdivisions contiguous to the administrative units used in this study.

URBAN CHARACTERISTICS
OF HINTERLAND POPULATIONS

The demographic characteristics employed each measure a different aspect of urbanization. Some are more reliable than others as indicators of the degree of urban influence in the hinterland. The proportion not in agriculture, at one extreme, is a bold indicator, with a wide and constant variation; sex ratio, at the other, varies radically among the hinterlands and records only subtle differences from sector to sector. Application through all the sectors for all the hinterlands in the following section affords an opportunity to test the indices and to make an appraisal of their suitability for the case studies. It also suggests the possibility of broader application in other underdeveloped countries.

DENSITY

The construction of density patterns on a minor civil division basis is much more meaningful in India than it would be in most of the United States, where the county, as the smallest rural areal unit, is many times the size of an Indian village. Indian rural densities are, of course, quite high in the heavily cultivated areas, often approaching a thousand persons per square mile. Above this general plane of high density stand peaks of intense crowding in the cities. Although these peaks have rather steep sides, the grades do extend a short distance into the hinterlands of at least the large cities.

All five cities exhibit a very rapid drop in density from the Inner Wards through the Suburban Wards to the Belt, where the first villages are encountered. The sharp difference between the densely built-up city and the agricultural countryside is quite apparent on the landscape. The long ribbons of housing, shopping areas, and industries that extend outward from the American city are not present in India to warn the traveler that he is approaching a major city, perhaps one with a population of a million and more people. Only in Bombay is a Western-type ribbon approximated. Otherwise, only minor ribbon development is discernible to mark the city's edge. The low silhouette of the Indian city does not even project a sky line as a guide to the city's center.

Relatively high Belt densities (Figure 2) reflect the recent growth of the urban fringe. Old village centers have become more densely populated, and pockets of agricultural land are the sites of new building. Both of these methods of "densification" are noticed particularly in the case of Delhi, where densities drop from the Belt to nearly the rural low in the Ribbon.

Since the mean area for all 896 villages in the study is 1.7 square

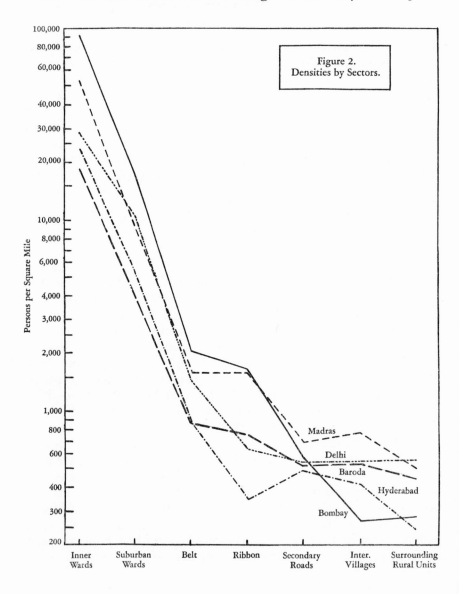

Figure 2.
Densities by Sectors.

miles, and with little variation between sectors, a regression of density from the Belt to the Interstitial villages is almost entirely a function of population size. This results in nearly identical regression patterns for densities and population sizes. Mean deviations of village areas for each city hinterland are further reflection of areal uniformity, as Table 1 shows.

TABLE 1

MEAN DEVIATIONS IN VILLAGE AREAS

Hinterland	Mean village area (in square miles)	Mean deviation (in square miles)
Delhi	1.5	0.2
Madras	1.4	0.2
Hyderabad	1.8	0.2
Bombay	2.2	0.4
Baroda	2.6	0.4

Beyond the Secondary Roads sector, densities are controlled largely by the type of agriculture practiced. Farming areas around Delhi, Madras, and Baroda, quite homogeneous in degree of cultivation, are capable of supporting high agricultural densities, while lower rural densities are found in the less uniformly cultivated hinterlands of Bombay and Hyderabad.

As villages of the hinterland come increasingly under the influence of the city, this contact should be reflected by absolute village populations that are higher than more distant and isolated villages. The population growth of the hinterland villages is probably due to forces operating from both the city and the rural areas. On the one hand, some overflow city population takes up residence in accessible hinterland villages, while, on the other, people from the most isolated rural villages move closer to the city, where they can benefit from city contacts but are not forced to surrender all of their traditional forms of living.

NONAGRICULTURAL LIVELIHOOD

Traditionally, the shift of an economy from emphasis on primary industries to nonagricultural activities has been considered as a sensitive indicator of progress in underdeveloped countries. It seems safe to infer that areas adjacent to cities, where the proportion of the nonagricultural population grades off to the rural average, must reflect a continuum of urbanlike activity.

Nonagricultural livelihood in the hinterland population includes the activity not only of those living in outlying villages and towns who commute to the city, but also of those engaged in producing or marketing items for direct consumption in the city, such as building materials, fresh foods, and milk.[9] Certain industries are finding it profitable to move from the crowded bazaars to railside and roadside locations out of the city. Workers living either in near-by villages, or in factory housing, boost the census totals for the total nonagricultural population. Besides the workers who are lured out of the city, part of the local surplus agricultural labor force is tapped for factory work. Family dependents also take advantage of the new urban contacts by producing handicraft products for the city market. Unfortunately, this latter type of activity, recorded under the census heading of "earning dependents," is not published for the primary census units used in this paper.

Figure 3 shows the distribution of nonagricultural livelihood in

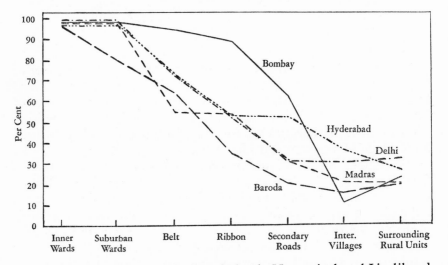

Figure 3. Per Cent of the Population in Nonagricultural Livelihood Classes by Sectors.

the five hinterlands. The steep drop in the curve from Suburban Wards to the Belt indicates the lack of a fringe area occupied by a rural non-farm population so characteristic of the regional city of the West. The only exception is Bombay, with its more highly developed immediate hinterland, and this is due largely to the city's position at the end of a peninsula, where suburban development is concentrated into a narrow finger of land. The concentration of Bombay's nonagricultural activity is further accented by the ex-

[9] Many occupations in the rural area, such as those including persons solely engaged in keeping milk cattle and persons who act as agents for fresh foods, fall into the nonagricultural livelihood category of the Indian census.

treme rurality of its Interstitial Villages, where 89 per cent of the population is dependent on agriculture—a figure higher than for any of the other four hinterlands.

In a nation where great rural-urban differences occur, one expects people in the city to be much more literate than those in the country. Higher literacy is obviously associated with cities because of the wider availability of education and the need for education to handle complex urban functions. A degree of literacy in the hinterland intermediate between that of city and remote rural areas shows up in Figure 4. There are several possible reasons for this,

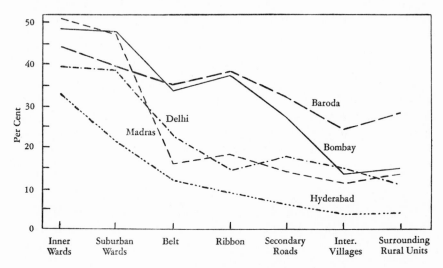

Figure 4. Per Cent Literate by Sectors.

all of which seem to validate the use of literacy as a measurement of urban influence. Literates are likely to be prominent among rural in-migrants to the city and its environs; commuters will take part in occupations requiring literacy; educational facilities are perhaps more numerous close to the city. Aspirations towards literacy, in general, are probably encouraged by the proximity of urban facilities.

There is, however, no evidence from the case studies that there is an even gradient in moving from sector to sector. In fact, in three of the cases (Delhi, Madras, and Hyderabad) literacy drops off very steeply from City to Belt, causing the cities to stand out in sharp contrast to their surroundings, while the curves for Bombay and Baroda drop sharply only beyond the Ribbon, suggesting either that the influence of these cities is stronger or that the level of literacy in the rural areas of their regions is high. It appears that both factors are in operation. In the case of Bombay, a high level of literacy through the Ribbon is caused by the presence of extensive middle-class suburbs on Salsette Island. (Much of the suburban area has been made a part of the city by annexation since 1951, the year for which our data are taken). The low point for literacy in the Interstitial Villages of Baroda, at least ten percentage points above the same sector for the other hinterlands in the study, is a reflection of the rural mean for Gujerat, higher itself than all other sections of India with the exception of Kerala, when only the rural population is considered. This is a good example of the sizable regional differences in demographic characteristics in India which necessarily affect the comparative assessment of city influence.

SEX RATIO

Indian cities, and particularly those of over 100,000 population, have a much larger proportion of males than the rural average (53.3 per cent as against 50.9). There are conflicting expectations concerning the sex ratio of the hinterland. One view is that the hinterland is supplying males to the city, leaving male-deficit areas. Others see the hinterland, like the city, as a reception area for male in-migrants. Moreover, the effect of city overflow has been mentioned as a modifying factor.

According to the findings, the hinterlands do generally possess male dominance, although to a lesser degree than in the city, and they exhibit a clear gradient from sector to sector in most cases. The sex ratios for Delhi and Bombay, which fall from an abnormally high proportion of males (up to 63 per cent) in the city to about 52 per cent in the rural areas, reveal a sharp regression. Since the population of the two southern cities, Hyderabad and Madras, has about as many females as males, only an abnormal deficit of males in the countryside would permit a steep grade of the curves. Therefore, the use of sex ratio as an indicator of city influence is the most revealing for cities which are highly masculine, although slight differences between city and hinterland, as in the case of Madras, might prove significant upon examination of more cases.

COMMERCE

The proportion of the population receiving their livelihood from commerce was selected as an index of urbanization because of its potential value as a measurement of the settlement as a trade center. Many villages, especially those most accessible to the city, are taking on certain urban ways, manifested by a larger proportion in commerce than is found in the more isolated villages. As the influence of the city reaches out into the hinterland, there is a growing market for goods and food produced by the villagers. The money that comes back to the village in turn forms a local market for items previously considered luxuries. This approaches the situation in the advanced country with a generally high economic level in both large and small places, where one might expect the proportion of those engaged in commerce in the small trading centers to be about the same as in the city, simply to carry on the ubiquitous trade function.

In the more isolated villages, however, the small proportion of persons in commerce (even if taken as a percentage of the non-agricultural population) implies that the buying power of the villager is so low that few people can be supported by this activity. Also, with greater dependence on subsistence agriculture, there is less need for trading. The proportion in commerce varies from a high of about 25 per cent in the City down to about 12 per cent in the Interstitial Villages, with a gradation through the intervening sectors.

The Regression of Demographic Characteristics

Average values for all of the factors measured decrease outward from the city as places become less accessible, varying from the highest values for the inner wards of the city to the lowest for the interstitial, isolated villages of the hinterlands. The rate of decline is approximately constant for the four factors of sex ratio, non-agricultural livelihood, literacy, and dependence on commerce. Simultaneously, density and absolute population are declining at a decreasing rate, dropping steeply to the Belt and then falling gradually to the rural low. From this pattern, the inference may be made that the sectors of the hinterland with greatest access to the city—the Belt, the Ribbon, and Secondary Roads—possess values of the indices of urbanization that are relatively higher than might be expected from their densities and populations. This implies that these sectors are interdependent with the city, even though their populations and densities more closely resemble the rural level. Although 98 per cent of the change of density and population occurs between the Suburban Wards and the Belt, only from 33 to 65 per cent of the total change has been reached by the other four factors.

For most factors there is first a relatively slight drop from the Inner Wards of the city to the Suburban Wards (Figure 5). The rapid drop of density, the notable exception, is due entirely to the

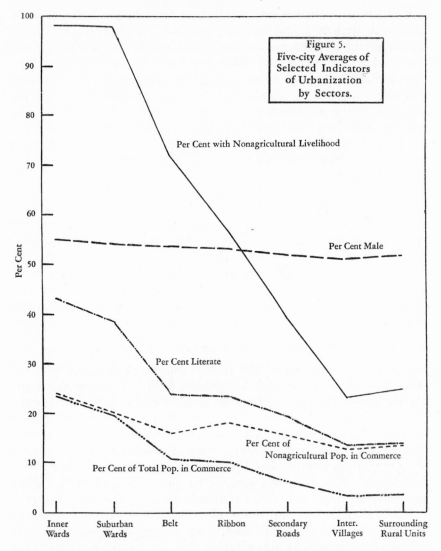

Figure 5.
Five-city Averages of
Selected Indicators
of Urbanization
by Sectors.

previously mentioned outsize area of the suburban wards. A relatively larger drop in values is anticipated in moving from the Suburban Wards to the two-mile belt around the city. This is realized in literacy, per cent in commerce, and per cent dependent on a nonagricultural livelihood; 35 to 49 per cent of their total drop falls between these two points. It is this rather steep falling-off of characteristics associated with an urban way of life that leads to the often-made statement that urbanism stops at the city's edge. Indeed, literacy does drop from 38 to 24 per cent of the total population, the dependence on commerce is cut nearly in half, and agriculture claims 25 per cent of the population compared to the 2 per cent in Suburban Wards. Still, the values of these characteristics remain considerably higher than in the more remote areas.

A plateau of values is encountered in going from the Belt to the mile-wide ribbon of villages along each side of the major routes of transportation. Only the percentage of persons dependent on the nonagricultural occupations continues its steady drop. In the Ribbon, the advantages of possible contact along railroads and hard-surfaced highways equalizes the absolute proximity to the city enjoyed by the Belt. The Belt, of course, includes all villages that fall within the demarcated areas, some of which are located on main roads while many are quite isolated.

The importance of the all-weather road is illustrated by the drop to the next unit, Secondary Roads. Though values are lower than those in the Ribbon, these villages are still in a more advantageous position than the rural isolated villages for establishing and maintaining contact with the city. As these lesser roads do not always go directly into the city, but are frequently feeders into the main roads, or to railway stations, the Secondary Road sector represents the smaller branches of the tree that is tapping the countryside. Values of urbanization falling about midway between the Ribbon and the Interstitial Villages reflect this function. (Local governments, recognizing the need for providing access to the rural areas, have entered programs of surfacing existing dirt roads.)

The only factor to reach its maximum drop between the Ribbon and the Secondary Roads is the sex ratio, with the per cent male falling from 53.4 to 51.8. This probably means that the non-agricultural economic activity in Secondary Roads and Interstitial Villages is only capable of supporting local surplus agricultural labor and that male in-migrants from all areas are required to bypass the Secondary Roads sector and go on to City, Belt, or Ribbon to find nonagricultural employment. The proportion of males in Secondary Roads is about the same as in the Interstitial Villages and the surrounding rural units.

Finally, all factors, with the exception of village size and density, fall to their lowest values in the Interstitial Villages. The regression from Secondary Roads is strikingly uniform, ranging from between 15 per cent and 21 per cent of the entire decline. It appears almost as if all the factors of urbanization, after having reacted differently in different sectors in their losing battle to stave off India's all-powerful rural dominance, finally meet at the Secondary Roads sector and sink together to their rural low, where all attempts to put up an urban "front" are abandoned.

A look at the values for the Interstitial Villages sector helps one to realize its isolation and backwardness, relative to the rest of the hinterland. On the average for all five hinterlands, 51 per cent of its population are male, 14 per cent are literate, and only 3 per cent are dependent on commerce. Density is a relatively low 491 persons per square mile, and 77 per cent of the people are dependent on agriculture.

How does this complex of factors compare with the national average for rural areas? The Interstitial Villages sector for the five hinterlands studied emerges slightly higher than the national rural mean for all factors considered, suggesting that the sector is still feeling a slight amount of urban impact. The relatively high value for the nonagricultural population is probably the best indicator that the sector falls under a degree of city influence.

The relative low position of the Interstitial Village sector is emphasized by the slight upturn in values for the rural parts of surrounding district subdivisions. These values should be somewhat higher, since all villages are included in the surrounding rural units without any knowledge of whether or not they lie on transportation routes. If the same delimitation method could be continued to these units, values for the most isolated villages would probably be below the national rural average.

Variations Among the Hinterlands

The variables studied do not all exhibit the same reaction to declining accessibility in all hinterlands. Still, there is enough consistency to make a few generalizations. The indices of urbanization experience a fairly sharp drop between the outer edge of the city and the belt surrounding it, they then continue at a reduced level, although varying locally, and finally show a lesser but relatively important drop in going from Secondary Roads to the most isolated sector, Interstitial Villages. All of the hinterlands, with the notable exception of peninsular Bombay, experience the largest drop in the indices of urbanization between suburban Wards and the Belt. Delhi, in particular, has its greatest decline for all four factors occurring between these two sectors. Moreover, for all hinterlands combined, literacy, nonagricultural livelihood, and commerce all experience their greatest percentage variation of decline between the Suburban Wards and the Belt. Only sex ratio has its largest drop occurring between the Ribbon and Secondary Roads.

Among the five hinterlands, two distinct patterns of fluctuations of values and variable village size emerge. In the first, Bombay, Madras, and Baroda all show a leveling of values between the Belt and the Ribbon. This stems from the maintenance—or even moderate increase—of average village population size in moving from Belt to Ribbon, as Table 2 indicates.

TABLE 2

AVERAGE VILLAGE POPULATIONS IN THE
BELT AND RIBBON OF THE HINTERLANDS

City	Average village population	
	Belt	Ribbon
Bombay...............	2,069	2,326
Madras...............	1,938	1,970
Baroda...............	1,752	1,903
Delhi................	1,752	1,024
Hyderabad...........	1,263	674

The presence of larger villages in the Ribbon is a further indication of the importance of transportation arteries, whose influence in the above three cases outweighs that of proximity, the chief advantage of the Belt.

The leveling for Delhi and Hyderabad, on the other hand, occurs between the Ribbon and the Secondary Roads and for much the same reason. Average village size shows relatively little decline for Delhi, and registers an actual increase for Hyderabad, as indicated in Table 3. Delhi's behavior is probably due to the

TABLE 3

AVERAGE VILLAGE POPULATIONS IN THE RIBBON
AND SECONDARY ROADS OF THE HINTERLANDS

City	Average village population	
	Ribbon	Secondary Roads
Delhi................	1,024	980
Hyderabad...........	674	871
Bombay...............	2,326	1,432
Madras...............	1,970	1,144
Baroda...............	1,903	1,619

fairly good secondary-road system of Delhi State, responsible for tying some large villages to the main transportation routes and providing others with an impetus for growth. This suggests that large villages have a more urban character than small villages. It may be argued that any settlement of several thousand people is urban, even if not so delineated by an arbitrary census definition.

CONCLUSIONS

The apparent differences between Western and Indian hinterlands resolve, upon examination, into a difference of the rate at which city influence declines outward from the city. The regional city in the United States falls into fairly distinctive sections starting from the city and moving outward through the urban fringe, the rural-urban fringe, and the immediate and remote hinterlands. Conversely, the whole area around an Indian city where urban influence is strongly felt is so small that such a classification is impractical, except in a condensed way for the largest cities. The urban fringe of these cities is usually restricted to small and sporadic residential and commercial developments at the city's edge, ruling out the possibility of a rural-urban fringe. The immediate hinterland is proportionately smaller in area than its Western counterpart, and might prove to be not much larger in area than the urban fringe and rural-urban fringe of an American city of about the same population. The outer hinterland, with its nebulous connections with the city, remains the most difficult to delimit and analyze.

Published economic data for hinterland measurement do not exist for India as they do in the West, and in the absence of extensive field work the elementary demographic data must be employed. Findings in this paper indicate that the area under city influence can be inferred from the reaction of population characteristics to the dual forces of declining accessibility and increasing distance from the city.

It is believed that the methods employed in this paper could be extended and used to measure hinterlands of other Indian cities. Greater availability of maps, indispensable for this type of study, together with the acquisition and field checking of more extensive economic data, would add considerable scope and reliability to similar studies within India. Such measures as sample traffic counts, locations of milksheds, volume of bus and train passenger-travel, and both highway and rail freight-movement statistics would add quantitative substantiation. The work would be facilitated by the publication of more data on a village basis in the *District Census Handbooks*. For instance, the reporting of at least the Divisional units of the Industrial and Service classification by small areal units would yield useful information on the way of life in the hinterlands. Comparative analysis could then attempt to discover patterns of human activity peculiar to all Indian hinterlands.

Additional testing and refinement of this research method could produce a system for comparative measure of urban hinterlands in other underdeveloped countries. Such a system would be designed for and restricted to countries with highly differentiated rural and urban economies. (A measure such as literacy would be unusable in a country with a nationally uniform education level, for example.)

The conventional use of zones appears to be an entirely inadequate method of measuring accessibility. In countries such as India it is necessary to use the smallest minor civil divisions for which demographic data are available to establish sectors graded as to their potential accessibility to the city. The use of sector analysis appears quite satisfactory in the limited areas involved here and would probably be workable in other underdeveloped countries.

The sector analysis of hinterlands allows us to take account of the physical site and location of the individual city and to give due importance to the location of lines of transport and physical barriers in the interpretation of the patterns resulting from the mapping of demographic phenomena. Moreover, if the differences in demographic characteristics between the city and the most agricultural part of the hinterland are to be understood, it is necessary to know the character of the particular rural area as well as that of the city and its functions.

Finally, a working knowledge of the functions of the hinterland and of its interaction with the city is going to become increasingly important in the planning of the future course to be taken by urbanization in India. If the city of the future in India is going to resemble the regional city of the Western type, understanding of the hinterland at this time will permit the establishment of policies that will insure its efficient and profitable regional development.

Richard A. Ellefsen

APPENDIX TABLE

INDICES OF URBANIZATION BY WARDS, AND HINTERLAND SECTORS

City	Inner Wards	Suburban Wards	Belt	Ribbon	Secondary Roads	Inter-stitial Villages	Sur-rounding Rural Units
Density (Persons Per Square Mile)							
Delhi	28,834	10,402	1,421	628	523	538	527
Madras	53,003	9,445	1,547	1,595	676	756	484
Bombay	92,056	17,638	2,062	1,661	580	262	270
Hyderabad	23,248	5,506	812	318	467	395	249
Baroda	19,395	....	885	737	510	505	440
Sex-Ratio (Per Cent Male)							
Delhi	56.7	58.1	55.9	55.6	53.4	52.1	53.3
Madras	52.2	51.5	51.0	51.1	51.2	50.4	50.8
Bombay	63.5	59.1	57.2	56.5	54.2	51.2	50.3
Hyderabad	50.6	48.5	49.7	51.7	49.2	50.1	50.8
Baroda	53.7	....	55.8	52.2	51.1	51.7	52.2
Literacy (Per Cent Literate)							
Delhi	39.4	38.2	22.4	14.6	17.2	14.9	9.6
Madras	50.9	46.9	16.3	18.4	14.3	11.5	13.5
Bombay	48.3	47.1	34.0	37.5	27.4	13.6	14.9
Hyderabad	33.2	21.4	12.0	8.9	5.3	4.1	4.7
Baroda	44.3	....	34.9	38.3	31.8	24.2	28.2
Non-Agricultural Livelihood (Per Cent of Total Population)							
Delhi	99.6	98.9	72.6	52.2	31.2	30.5	32.8
Madras	98.5	96.4	54.4	54.4	30.4	20.4	20.4
Bombay	98.4	99.2	94.6	88.9	62.2	11.0	22.8
Hyderabad	98.3	97.1	73.4	52.7	51.6	35.9	26.8
Baroda	97.0	....	63.9	35.1	19.4	16.0	19.0
Per Cent of Total Population Deriving Livelihood From Commerce							
Delhi	27.2	20.0	9.4	5.2	4.3	2.9	4.7
Madras	23.8	13.9	9.1	9.9	4.7	3.3	2.8
Bombay	24.9	22.7	18.5	18.6	8.3	.5	2.5
Hyderabad	20.8	21.4	11.1	7.2	9.4	5.4	3.5
Baroda	21.5	....	7.8	9.0	3.1	2.5	3.4
Per Cent of Non-Agricultural Population Deriving Livelihood From Commerce							
Delhi	27.3	20.2	13.0	10.0	13.8	9.6	14.3
Madras	24.2	14.4	16.8	18.2	15.5	16.3	13.9
Bombay	25.2	22.9	19.6	20.9	13.3	4.4	10.8
Hyderabad	21.2	22.0	15.1	13.8	18.1	15.1	12.9
Baroda	22.1	....	12.2	25.8	15.8	15.7	17.7

VI

THE IMPACT OF URBAN SOCIETY
UPON VILLAGE LIFE

Richard D. Lambert

Implicit in the concept of social change in India is the notion that the urban areas will change more rapidly than the villages and that the cities will act as catalysts introducing changes in rural areas, perhaps more slowly, but nonetheless inevitably. It is the thesis of this paper that while the first part of this notion may be true, and changes are more rapid in the urban areas, there is considerable slippage between urban-based changes and the more stable rural areas. In part, this is a simple function of numbers. The forces of change which may be potent when viewed from the city quickly lose their impact when spread over the vast number of villages that have to be affected. But, more than this, there are buffers which attenuate and divert this impact as it moves against the grain of traditional urban-rural relationships.

The urban-rural dichotomy is as untidy a sociological concept in India as it is elsewhere in the world. The census cutoff point in size is at 5,000 population; but there appears in each census a long list of settlements which, although they have more than 5,000 inhabitants, in the eyes of the local authorities are still sufficiently agricultural in their pattern of livelihood and habitation to be called villages. In other cases, communities of less than 5,000 which are said to possess "urban" characteristics are classed as towns. This blurring of the line of demarcation occurs not only in demographic, but in geographic delimitation of cities as well. Many villages at the fringes of the great metropolises are rural or urban only in the fact that the most recent legal demarcation of the municipal limits does or does not happen to include them. Such accidents may have important consequences, as any bullock-cart driver paying octroi duty can testify, but it is not very helpful to the serviceability of the urban area as a descriptive category. The fluidity of the boundary between urban and rural aggregates is a familiar problem to demographers, but in most countries it affects only the twilight zone where one or another aggregate could reasonably be put on either side of the line.

In India, however, the web of society is cut by so many other cleavages and composed of so many distinctive strands that the separate grouping of urban centers as contrasted with rural areas is considerably less efficient for the purposes of social analysis than many other ways of partitioning the society. This becomes apparent the moment we begin to deal with variables such as occupations or industries. Of eighty-eight subdivisions of the Indian census economic classifications,[1] only thirteen have less than 25 per cent of their work force in the rural areas, and none of the thirteen employs a total work force as high as 500,000 workers. Even those economic activities which are normally considered to be urban activities—textile manufacture, metal work, construction, the manufacture of chemicals and fertilizer, electric machinery and supplies, cement, wholesale and retail trade, wearing apparel and food processing—have large segments of their labor force in rural areas.

If heavily urban economic activities were further restricted to those in which the ratio of employees to independents was high, the limited scope of what might be called fully urbanized occupations would be even clearer. Nor are activities normally classified as rural absent from even the largest cities. Even a metropolis such as Madras had 32 persons per thousand engaged in primary industries (cultivation and livestock tending) in 1951, and the many smaller cities had even more. Allahabad, with a population of 332,295 in 1951, had 71 per thousand of the working population engaged in primary industries; Moradabad with 161,854 had 146 per thousand; and Rampur with 134,277 had 174 per thousand.

The proportion of the work force in primary industries has fluctuated wildly in some cities, rising to 30.3 per cent in Allahabad in 1931. Even allowing for the notorious inconsistencies of Indian occupational statistics, it is surprising to note that in six of the thirteen largest cities in Uttar Pradesh the proportion of the work force engaged in primary industries has substantially increased rather than decreased since 1911.

Sociological variables such as the prevalence of joint families have in some cities showed little differentiation from the sup-

---

[1] *Summary of Demographic and Economic Data, Census of India, 1951* (Paper No. 3, 1953). Calculations limited to males.

posedly rural tradition, and then in the unanticipated direction of greater prevalence in the cities.[2] Moreover, detailed studies of neighborhoods in Indian cities have found much in common with rural social patterns.[3] Gertrude Woodruff in her study of a Pariah slum in Bangalore[4] found that this enclave, while not duplicating the complete social structure of the few villages from which it drew its inhabitants, retained enough of the rural base to serve as a "resting stage" in the process of adjustment to city life.

On the other hand, in the entire area around the Asansol industrial complex, villages as well as towns might well be considered one unified urban area as rapid industrialization turns the hinterland of each large factory into dormitory settlements for its workers.[5]

While it is true that the overlap of rural and urban areas is greater in India than in the West, for purposes of analysis it may still be useful to treat them as if they were mutually exclusive. This is, in fact, what the vast majority of village and city surveys have done. In reading among the village studies it often appears that the author has drawn an imaginary line around the village and that he is interested only in intravillage affairs, even when villages are very close to cities. There are, of course, persuasive reasons for this, among them the limitations of the resources of a lone investigator. But this limitation of perspective occurs even when teams of investigators are employed. Aside from considerations of manpower, however, the general theoretical orientation of the village studies which are mostly, in Redfield's[6] terms, synchronistic and holistic, treats extra-village influences as either irrelevant or disturbing factors in a stable, structurally equilibrated microcosm. The urban surveys, for entirely different reasons, tend to stop at the municipal limits.[7] Here the main limitation is in the definition

---

[2] Cf. K. M. Kapadia, "Rural Family Patterns," *Sociological Bulletin* (Bombay), V (September, 1956), 111–126.

[3] Cf. A. Bopegamage, "Neighbourhood Relations in Indian Cities—Delhi," *Sociological Bulletin* (Bombay), VI, No. 1 (March, 1957), 34–42.

[4] Gertrude Marvin Woodruff, "An Adidravida Settlement in Bangalore, India" (Doctoral dissertation, Radcliffe College, 1959).

[5] Vithal Babu, *Report on a Preliminary Inquiry on the Growth of Steel Towns in India* (Calcutta: UNESCO Research Centre, 1959).

[6] Robert Redfield, *The Little Community* (Chicago: University of Chicago Press, 1955). The argument for the unity of the village is made explicit in Rudra Dutt Singh, "The Unity of an Indian Village," *Journal of Asian Studies*, XVI (November, 1956), 10–19. It is implicit in the debate over the "great" and "little" tradition in McKim Marriott (ed.), *Village India* (Chicago: University of Chicago Press, 1955).

[7] Exceptions to this are found in R. L. Singh, *Banaras—A Study in Urban Geography* (Banaras: Nand Kishore & Bros., 1955), chap. viii, where the hinterland (Umland) is considered an extension of the city, and in B. R. Misra, *Report on Socio-Economic Survey of Jamshedpur City* (Patna: Patna University Press, 1959), where Misra compares the city and rural residents of families that fall in his sample.

of the sampling universe for the questionnaire surveys so characteristic of urban studies in India. Between the two streams of research, urban and rural, lies a doab relatively unwatered by the rising flood of social research in India. In at least one village study it is argued that the urban-rural gap is not just an oversight arising out of research strategies, but is a reflection of a real barrier between town and village. D. N. Majumdar[8] writes as follows:

> An Indian village is not merely a way of life, it is also a concept—it is a constellation of values and so long as our value system does not change, or changes slowly and not abruptly, the village will retain its identity, and so it has done till today. The continuity that one finds in other parts between rural and urban living—a "continuum," as a noted anthropologist has described it —does not necessarily exist between villages and towns in India. There are two distinct constellations of values and there are sharp dividing lines between the two levels of living and experience. Even villages situated on the outskirts of towns have maintained the value system, and thus our villages do not become townships. Even villages of 5,000 inhabitants or more, which the Indian Census defines as "urban," retain the rural value system and differ from cities and towns, a fact which even casual observers will not fail to notice. We see in Mohana people who have an adequate knowledge of, and contacts with towns; they are the know-alls in the village, and in many matters they have special prestige status in the village. People listen to them, admire them for their experience, receive assistance and advice when they need the same, but they regard the village as distinct and socially distant from the town.

This ideological barrier, then, is supposed to operate to inhibit the permeation of urban influence in the villages.

In a slightly different vein, Opler,[9] starting from the vantage point of a single village, discusses a number of "extensions" of the village which link it with the outside world. In brief catalogue, his extensions include: common origin and descent shared with a cluster of surrounding villages; village exogamy creating kinship ties with other villages; caste assemblies cutting across village lines; customary work obligations of practical and ritual services in another rural community; participation in national religious movements such as the Arya Samaj or political movements such as the nationalist drive; pilgrimages to distant shrines and religious centers, and the visits of itinerant shrine priests; connections with the market towns and with the courts, land records office, officials, and government seed and agricultural-implement stores; and temporary out-migration for education.

---

[8] *Caste and Communication in an Indian Village* (Bombay: Asia Publishing House, 1958), p. 329.

[9] Morris Opler, "The Extensions of an Indian Village," *Journal of Asian Studies*, XVI (November, 1956), 5–10.

Three things should be noted about this list. First, the center of gravity is clearly in a single village; conceptually, Opler envisages a village and its hinterland. Second, many of these extensions connect with other rural areas. Urban contacts are only one special kind of relationship in the external affairs of a village. And, third, most of the extensions follow very old patterns. As Opler himself comments:

> Another point that seems worth noting is that the basic articulation of Senapur and Senapur people with other communities and far-flung places which we have noted is not a recent development or a consequence of modern systems of communication and transportation. They rest on ancient practices and patterns.[10]

The same general picture, however without the single-village-centered outlook, emerges in an article by Cohn and Marriott in which they speak of supralocal rural networks of social relationships. They list "networks of trade, networks of marriage, political networks, and networks of contacts formed by many kinds of religious travellers." Like Opler, they comment that these networks are not new.

> But trading networks beyond the village have been well-developed in India at least since Muslim times. Cash was in use for taxation and transactions in agricultural produce. Trade routes were extensive and protected over large areas. Itinerant traders and in some areas itinerant markets still do a large share of all business. Networks of marriage ties are extensive, especially in northern India, where as many as 100,000 persons spread over hundreds of square miles are often linked directly or indirectly. Political networks consist primarily of ties of clan and kinship among rulers and dominant landlord groups of the countryside.[11]

The specifics of external relations are rarely documented in the many village studies which are at hand. When "foreign affairs" are mentioned it is usually the intrarural networks that are most likely to be emphasized. The most detailed catalogue of specifically urban contacts may be found in D. N. Majumdar's study[12] of a village, Mohana, situated only eight miles from Lucknow. He reports that one of the most important continuing contacts with the city is in the marketing of village surpluses—fruits, milk, grain, animal products. For this purpose each individual may own or hire his own bullock cart, or he may deal with one or more of the middlemen who gather the material in the village and sell it in the

---

[10] *Ibid.,* p. 8.
[11] Bernard Cohn and McKim Marriott, "Networks and Centers in the Integration of Indian Civilization," *Journal of Social Research* (Ranchi, Bihar), I, No. 1 (August, 1958).
[12] *Caste and Communication in an Indian Village.*

city. Surrounding the village is a set of market villages, some of them specializing in particular products and meeting only one or two days per week. These markets serve the function of redistributing products throughout the rural areas and act as gathering places for job lots to be taken into the city. Majumdar reports that villagers like to sell their product in markets nearest the city or proceed into the city itself because of the higher prices there. As an aside it might be noted that this rapid price gradient as one moves away from the city was noted in some of the early District Gazetteers, where it is also pointed out that the initial effect of the extension of transporation into the rural areas was to permit urbanites to set up rural markets rather than to encourage the villagers to come into the cities.

Continuing with Majumdar's account of urban contacts, marriage fields vary by caste, but all of them encompass urban areas. Many rites of passage and religious ceremonials take place at major shrines in large cities. Cremation near the Ganges requires a trip to Kanpur in a hearse car, or, if the *Gomti* will suffice, to Lucknow City. The god Hanuman has many worshipers in Majumdar's village, but to worship him villagers must go to Alliganj in Lucknow. Other special pujas can only be performed at urban shrines. On festive occasions such as Holi, Shiv Ratri, or Jagan Nath ki Puja, ritual supplies are bought in the city and on the festival day processions of bullock carts make a long day's outing into the city. Among the villagers a few go to the city regularly—for instance, those who are employed there and others who vend the surplus milk. Village dhobis have some clients in the city, and shopkeepers do their purchasing there. A number of students attend the higher secondary school at tahsil headquarters. Villagers also travel into the city to visit well-known Ayur-Vedic physicians in lieu of or in addition to a trip to the allopathic physician in a village about a mile and a half away.

All of these instances could well be fitted into Opler's or Cohn and Marriott's general formulations with little difficulty. Majumdar summarizes the extent of the urban contact as follows:

> It is not an absolutely communicating village, it is not urbanized, as could be expected, but it lies on the periphery of an urban area—it communicates through the many individuals who have contacts with the town, and who go out and return to the village regularly and occasionally.[13]

Corroborating the traditional, stable nature of the urban-rural relationships, Cohn and Marriott look at the pattern from the urban end of the networks. They make the point that urban areas

---

[13] *Ibid.*, p. 327.

(or "centers" as they call them) have different hinterlands for each of their functions, and that towns differ among themselves as to which function or functions predominate.

Centers perform specialized functions and are typically the abodes of specialists. Following a marriage network, for example, one finds in the town center the marriage broker, the most learned astrologer who can determine the suitability and time of marriage, sometimes the genealogist, and certain higher types of sacramental priests, musicians, and entertainers for the wedding. Commercial networks have their nexes in markets and fairs and in the shops of wholesale traders and bankers. Centers in the network of pilgrimages naturally display many orders of shrine priests, teachers and other religious experts of all sorts.[14]

In spite of these differences in emphasis, when the society as a whole is viewed in cross section each urban area performs a hinge-like function. Its greater heterogeneity connects the less urbanized areas below it with the larger center above it in "multilevel hierarchies" of specialists. The specialties which they describe as urbanized are administrative and political, commercial, religious and educational. In other data there is some evidence that many artisans and small manufacturers, formerly distributed among the villages, are becoming urbanized, so that villagers must either go into the towns to get carpentry done, for instance, or must hire an urban dweller to come to the village temporarily.

So far, I have indicated that the evidence from the village studies argues both for the integrity of the village and for a series of traditional links of this separate whole, the village, with alien territory, including the city. What are the consequences of this portrayal for predicting the effects of urban impact on the rural areas of India? To the extent that these traditional connections with the town predominate, we are likely to have less urban-induced change in the villages than their proximity to the city and the comparative ease of transport would indicate. The village is held to have not only an internal structure and a value system resisting urban intrusion, but also a set of middlemen who mediate between it and the city. Traditional routes of contact outside of the village are mostly with other villages, and travel is in the time-honored pathways or "networks" which lessen the impact. So far, then, urban impact for village change seems very little.

Evidence for this stability does, in fact, appear in the few longitudinal comparisons of the same village at an earlier and a later point of time. One of the fullest of such studies is the survey of Bhadkad,[15] a village of 1,516 population in Kaira District in the

---

[14] *Op. cit.,* p. 5.
[15] *Bhadkad* (Bombay: Indian Society of Agricultural Economics, 1957).

center of Gujarat. The village is only two miles from the railway station of Deva, on the Bhadrad-Nadiad line which connects with the main railway routes to Bombay, and it is also within easy reach of four other railway stations. Bhadkad was surveyed in 1913 and again in 1955, and the remarkable feature of this inquiry is the small amount of change which had taken place. In forty years the village has increased by some 300 persons, but the number of families has remained almost constant in spite of the fact that some 31 families have migrated, mostly for other places in Gujarat, but also to distant places within as well as outside of India. The pattern of caste composition has not changed significantly, nor have the customs and traditions regulating marriage. Village artisans still get a share of the produce if they are following the traditional occupations. Some changes have occurred, particularly in consumption goods. Changes in food habits include: greater consumption of rice, dal, wheat, vegetables, milk, sugar and condiments, and tea. In dress the turban has disappeared to be replaced by caps, particularly Gandhi caps; the long coat is rarely seen; small girls now wear frocks instead of *gagharis* and *kabjas,* and the use of fine cloth is increasing. Windows are appearing in village houses; decorations have decreased; separate kitchens and bathrooms are increasingly common, although no latrines have appeared; cement or tile floors have replaced the cow-dung-plastered mud floors; kerosene lanterns have replaced castor oil lights; and some chairs and tables have begun to appear. More fundamental changes include the displacement of some of the poorer nonagricultural pursuits—hand-loom weaving, smith work, ornament making, shoemaking, and dyeing. Debt has increased, but credit sources have become more local. Health has gone from bad to worse. Institutions which were traditionally designed for coöperative work have become defunct, and the new *gram panchayat* is an uneasy graft.

In spite of these changes, many of them superficial, the overwhelming impression is one of stability. The authors comment: "The facts, on a comparative review of the socio-economic position of the village in the first survey period and the second survey period, show the stark reality that the progress in development either in the economic sphere or in social change has been very slow." [16] Those changes which have occurred seem not to be linked to the urban centers, but to reflect broad changes in the whole society. Examination of the retrospective accounts of change found in other village studies emphasizes the broad features of social change. Bailey, in his account of an Orissa village, emphasizes change brought about by the arrival of political administra-

---

[16] *Ibid.,* p. 66.

tion, the development of a commercial economy, and the breakdown of the joint family system. He writes:

> The arrival of the Administration has brought the village into the larger economy of India and from this time a new process of change began. The method by which the village as a whole exploited the material world was altered. The traditional economy rested on agriculture. Wealth still is largely derived from the land, but this is no longer the only source. There are also the profits of trading and the work on behalf of the Administration. The economy no longer is exclusively agricultural. It now also is mercantile.

> In the new economy wealth can be got by other means than owning land. This led to the breakdown of joint-families. Estates were reduced in size by constant partitioning until some of them became uneconomic and land was sold. The land was bought by those who had profited in the new economy.

> Individuals both among the newcomers and among the old residents have profited in this way. But there has been a tendency for the WARRIOR caste-group, who formerly monopolized the land to lose property in favour of the other castes, particularly the two groups of DISTILLERS and more recently the Board OUTCASTES.

> This change in the distribution of wealth has brought about an adjustment, which still is taking place, in the traditional political structure of the village.[17]

One of the most extensive discussions of village change is M. S. A. Rao's *Social Change in Malabar*.[18] Like Bailey, Rao takes as his central focus the decline of the traditional economy, especially the displacement of the older arts and crafts, and the increasing importance of traders and middlemen. Kathleen Gough[19] reports that Kumbapettai, a village some miles north of Tanjore City, "has moved about halfway in the transition from this relatively stationary feudal subsistence economy to a much wider-scale, expanding capitalist economy and a great increase in economic transactions with the outside world." As a consequence, the power of the Brahmans has been decreased, the lower caste groups have emerged in "economic rivalry rather than cooperation," and social relations have extended in increasingly wider circles beyond the village. This picture of the decline of the monopoly of economic power of the landed aristocracy, the growth of a cash economy, and the enmeshing of village affairs in a broader regional and national context is mentioned in almost all of the village studies in one way or another. In most, it is taken to be the prime mover, the major structural shift from which other changes flow. One might suspect that the temptation to follow a highly idealized Western model of social

---

[17] F. G. Bailey, *Caste and the Economic Frontier* (Manchester: The University Press, 1957), pp. 42–43.

[18] (Bombay: Popular Book Depot, 1957.)

[19] "The Social Structure of a Tanjore Village," in Marriott (ed.), *Village India*, pp. 36–52.

change had made this paradigm a little exaggerated. Market networks and the predominance of cash transactions are of long standing in many sections of India, and the earlier isolation of the village was surely not so complete as these retrospective accounts would have us believe. Nevertheless, even if we interpret these statements to refer to matters of degree, the fundamental shifts discussed reflect changes in the entire society. While groups outside a particular village are having an increasing voice in internal affairs, only some of these groups are urban, and their urbanness is an incidental rather than a prime factor. For instance, the spread of the Marwari moneylenders through rural Maharashtra before the Deccan Riots of the 1870's was not urban-based, and was urban-induced only in the sense that the British contract law which supported it had its seat in the towns and cities. Moreover, villages usually conduct their external economic affairs through specialized middlemen, part of whose talents is their knowledge of other, particularly urban, markets. Frequently these intermediaries were ethnically separate, specializing, religion-based groups ("communities" in Indian usage), and their style of life was not likely to be copied by their fellow villagers.

My comment, above, that these broad changes in the over-all structure of the society are not functions of urbanization needs some refinement. One increasingly popular area of research is the fringe village, so called because it is on the edge of a town. The city is seen as the locale par excellence of the newer society, with its influence radiating into the surrounding villages. General social change is seen as a consequence of proximity to the city, and the farther from the city the village is, the less its degree of change is presumed to be. In its simplified form, one has the image of a stone dropped in a pool, with ripples traveling in concentric circles and disturbing the calm surface with gradually decreasing effect. I emphasize that the fringe-village approach is a point of view and not a descriptive reality because, as pointed out above, many of the villages whose unity and isolation have been emphasized lie very close to towns and cities. It will be recalled, for instance, that Majumdar's village, discussed earlier, is only a few miles from Lucknow.

Nonetheless, this approach has produced some concrete evidence of change in villages near cities and towns. In the main its proponents have concentrated on broad structural changes in these villages, in particular the form of the family and the effect of an extra-village focus of economic activities. One of the clearest of the studies under the former category is K. M. Kapadia's article[20]

---

[20] "Rural Family Patterns," *Sociological Bulletin*, V (September, 1956), 111–126.

comparing family patterns in the town of Navsari (pop. 44,663 in 1951) in Gujarat, five "impact" villages within three miles of the town, and ten "rural" villages outside of this ring but still in the same taluka. In general, Kapadia finds that the joint family is more common in the urban area as compared with the rural area, and that even the average size of family is greater in the former. The five impact villages lie in between. Town families have an average size of 7 persons, impact villages of 6.2 persons, and rural areas of 6 persons. It must be said that there is some doubt as to the meaningfulness of this trend in view of the difficulties in precise definition of the joint family[21] and the likelihood of sampling errors' erasing the differences, and the picture might well be different if a large metropolitan center were studied instead of a small traditional town; but at least these data do not support the general thesis of urban erosion of traditional rural social structure.

M. S. A. Rao comes to a different conclusion in his study[22] of a village seven miles to the northwest of Delhi. He finds in his fringe village that "there is a greater number of nuclear families, but they do not approximate to those in the urban areas. The brothers get separated more for the sake of convenience, to avoid conflicts between their wives. The joint family system is still respected and its advantages are praised. The family organisation shows a level of adjustment which is not found either in the urban or in the rural society." [23] William A. Morrison[24] tries to test further the impact of the "urban-industrial individualizing values and attitudes" on a village near the town of Kalyam, itself a way station on the main railway route out of Bombay. He finds that the joint and quasi-joint family patterns are normally restricted to the traditional village middle class. The nontraditional middle and upper status caste-groupings, touched most by the "urban-industrial" values and most exposed to education, have nuclear families. So also do the lower socioeconomic levels of the village, but in this group the predominance of nuclear families reflects their "poverty-stricken way of life."

In summary, then, we can conclude that it is not clear in which way the urban–fringe–rural continuum runs on family types and size, but that in any event urban impact is selective within fringe villages and among them.

---

[21] See I. P. Desai, "The Joint Family in India—An Analysis," *ibid.*, V (September, 1956), 144–156; also M. F. Nimroff, "Some Problems Concerning Research on the Changing Family in India," *ibid.*, VIII (September, 1959), 32–38.

[22] "Fringe Society and the Folk-Urban Continuum," *ibid.*, pp. 13–18.

[23] *Ibid.*, p. 17.

[24] "Family Types in Badlapur: An Analysis of a Changing Institution in a Maharashtrian Village," *ibid.*, 45–67.

There is more general agreement on the effects of the urban market-oriented economy on village life. Mrs. Hemalata Acharya[25] writes of the "metropolitan aura" of the city of Nasik, which extends for only six miles: "This limit has been fixed because I have found that the expansion of the city has not gone beyond this, and though the transport facilities have provided means for visiting Nasik often, these facilities have not been availed of by many." The four villages she studied lie on two major arteries leading into the city. On each road, the nearer village is almost totally absorbed into the urban economy, while the more distant one, at the most three or four miles farther out, is relatively untouched. About Anandavali, three miles from Nasik, she says that "Anandavali does not seem to be either a traditional village or a changing village. It is a parasitic village and its people have lost interest in the village itself. They look to Nasik for their daily sustenance. There are no occasions on which people come together; the community life among them has disappeared. And yet the dress of the people, food and houses have changed but little." Gangapur, three miles farther down the same road, falls within the Nasik economic area in that its production is geared to the Nasik market, but it deals with the city through truckers who serve as middlemen:

The village on the whole has changed but little in spite of its being very near the city. The cash-nexus is coming into prominence and the villagers are getting interested in Bombay market, because it brings more rewards. This in itself is sufficient to bring about changes in the life of the villagers. But these are today imperceptible. Of course, there are changes due to the beginning and the end of the daily cycles, life cycles and seasonal cycles. Farmers have taken to improved seeds, have introduced pumping machines on their farms. The social distance between the Mahars and other castes is not conspicuously observed, although it persists. Outsiders influence their daily activities and the villagers do accept advice though not without doubts.

The same general contrasts hold true for the two villages separated by three miles on the other road. Generalizing about all four villages, Mrs. Acharya says:

In all these four villages one notices the continuous flow away from them of money, in the form of taxes, rent, prices and revenues. The predominance of one occupation in the villages and the lack of other sources of livelihood bring down the standard of living of the villagers. The introduction of money economy and the production for the market have brought in their train the middlemen and moneylenders. The terms of trade weigh against the rural areas. The four villages studied show their tendency and it is clear that they are being engulfed by the city. It is to the city that they look for employment,

[25] "Urbanizing Role of a One-Lakh City," *ibid.*, V (September, 1956), 89–101.

for market, for money and therefore, the villages remain merely food production centres.

An interesting example of villages, even more distant than those in Mrs. Acharya's study, entering into the urban market economy is given in Y. B. Damle's forthcoming study entitled "Impact of Industrialization on Rural Society," [26] which concerns the effects of the establishment of a nonprofit milk-collection center which daily sends milk to the Poona market, some twenty-two miles away. Farmers from 21 villages lying within a radius of five to six miles bring their milk into the center, where it is tested for quality and transferred to special trucks for transport to the city. One of the important consequences of the establishment of the center was the formalizing of the economic relationships between the rural hinterland and the city. At the same time it insulated the villagers from many of the less desirable side-effects of urban contact. In listing the benefits of the scheme, Damle mentions:

> The producer of milk, especially within the vicinity of 20 to 30 miles, used to go to the city for selling his milk and thus was wasting his whole day. Villagers in going to cities used to spend a considerable amount of money on transport and other incidental though largely non-essential expenses such as those on hotels [restaurants], cinemas, etc. This expenditure is now altogether saved. In visiting the cities daily, the producers used to sell milk either in the open market on cash or supply the same to customers on credit basis. In the former cases, there was the temptation of utilising the sale proceeds for purchases of luxuries, while in the latter case, the producers were in constant threat of not receiving their dues at the end of the month.

The social by-products of this scheme are the usual consequences we found in the increasing predominance of a cash economy in the rural area. The impact of the urban area on village change is at least one step removed in the Damle study, lending further support to the thesis that major rural changes are occurring not so much because of urbanization per se, but because of general changes in the society, some of which reach their most extreme form in the urban areas. Mrs. T. S. Trent's[27] study of the impact on the village of Manhalli in Mysore of the extension of canal irrigation and the change to sugar-cane cultivation under the aegis of a sugar factory is a clear illustration of the occurrence of the changes we have been discussing without the presence of large aggregates of population in the immediate vicinity.

The change producers, then, are not the city or town per se, but the newer forms of economic organization as well as a modernized,

---

[26] Paper, to be published by UNESCO, now in typescript.

[27] Described in M. N. Srinivas, "Industrialization and Urbanization of Rural Areas," *Sociological Bulletin*, V (September, 1956), 79–88.

more cosmopolitan set of values characteristic of some sections of the urban population. Morrison, in the article discussed earlier, implies this when he speaks of the "urban-industrial individualizing values and attitudes," and when he shows that changes in family styles are directly correlated with the educational level of the villager. The diffusion of modernism and cosmopolitan values into the rural areas is studied directly by Damle.[28] Selecting seven villages arranged in a rough ranking of distance from Poona, from one to eighty miles away, he inquired in each of the villages about the diffusion of information concerning: the national political scene, national policies, world political structure, international policies and events, and modern ideas on social organization and recreation. Although Damle tempers his comments with what he calls a "structure-functional" analysis to explain the difference in absorption of new ideas, the rankings of information flow reflect the distance from the city. In addition to the support for the urban radiation theory of the spread of modernization, the surprising thing about this study is how quickly one encounters ignorance of even such major national events as the Five Year Plan, or in the most distant village (some seventy-two miles northwest of Poona City) of the existence of Jawaharlal Nehru. D. N. Majumdar gives the following account of the resistance in the village to the acquisition of "useless" information:

Newspapers are not popular among the villagers, and even if they were supplied to them free of cost, they would not benefit them. One reason for this unpopularity of newspapers is the illiteracy of the villagers. If one reads out the news to them they listen, but that only for a short while. There is so much work to be done that they cannot afford to waste their precious time in such "trash" (so it appears to them). One of the investigators of the Department of Anthropology used to read out the papers to them sometimes. The first day, there were many people sitting around him, then as days passed by their interest ebbed, and the investigator had to give up reading the papers to them.[29]

One more type of concern with the radiation of influence from urban centers might be mentioned. A few of the city surveys, following the pattern of Western urban geography, have tried to define the area which is connected with the city by various kinds of linkages. R. L. Singh, a student of Dudley Stamp, tries to define the "Umland" of Banaras.[30] In attempting to delimit this hinterland, Singh considers the various regions which supply vegetables,

---

[28] Y. B. Damle, *Communication of Modern Ideas and Knowledge in Indian Villages* (Cambridge, Mass.: Massachusetts Institute of Technology, 1955).

[29] *Op. cit.,* p. 296.

[30] *Op. cit.,* chap. viii.

milk, grains, and other agricultural products, and the areas reached by bus service and newspapers. The vegetable zone which supplies fresh produce for urban consumption extends about twelve miles along its longest axis and about six miles on the shorter one, and includes about 72 square miles. The milk-supply zone extends farther, including some 180 square miles; the grain and other agricultural products zone includes some 4,000 square miles, and the bus zone extends about the same distance. The largest of the zones, defining the limits of the Umland for Singh, is the newspaper circulation zone, which "exhibits the cultural integration of the Umland" and includes more than 20,000 square miles, or almost ten times the territory included in the district. He adds the interesting comment that "the religious sphere of influence of Banaras is so wide and so extensive that it has penetrated into almost all parts of India. So it is of little use in defining the Umland of the city." [31] It might be added that it is a good example of the limitations of the Umland approach for a study of impact. Another attempt to determine the domain of a city is Bopegamage's[32] mapping of the traffic and transport nexus of Delhi, which, when the airways are added, embraces the world.

It is a little doubtful what these areas, even if they could be defined precisely, would represent. Certainly, in view of Mrs. Acharya's comments about the effective impact zone of Nasik extending no more than six miles from the city limits, it is a little difficult to consider these as "impact zones" except in the most attenuated form. It is also clear that within each of these extended areas are a sizable number of other urban clusters. Perhaps it is useful to consider them as the complement to Opler's "extensions" of the village, where the surrounding world was seen as a field of operation for a single village. Singh and Bopegamage have substituted a city for Opler's village-centered universe.

We come closer to what most people seem to think of when urban impact is discussed when we consider, not the radiation of influence from cities into rural areas, but rather the presumed radical change in life style which confronts the villager when either he moves to the city or the city reaches out to encompass his village. Our concern, however, is with the way in which the urban flow may make itself felt on the villagers who are left behind. What little evidence there is indicates that this effect is not very substantial. In the first place, out-migration may have a stabilizing effect, permitting the village to cast off members whose presence would other-

---

[31] *Ibid.,* p. 118.
[32] A. Bopegamage, *Delhi: A Study in Urban Sociology* (Bombay: University of Bombay Press, 1957). (See also Richard Ellefsen's study, chap. v.—*Ed.*)

wise be disturbing to the stability of the structure—behavioral deviates, those whose aspirations are too high to be comfortably satisfied in the village, and also economic supernumeraries. In the second place, although most residents in any particular village have been born there, many villages have long-standing pathways of out-migration, sometimes to very distant places, and village life closes quickly behind the departees. Migration to Ceylon or Malaya is a tradition in many a South Indian village, and the stream from western India into Africa and the Arabian Sea area is well known. Some districts consistently send out their residents to other areas for work. For instance, Ratnagiri District in Maharashtra has sent out a major portion of its adult male population to Bombay for at least several decades. Gertrude Woodruff [33] reports that for the Pariahs in South India:

/ Going to the city is not so much a move of desperation as it is an alternative way of life. There is no stigma attached to migration, and it is by no means the unsuccessful family only that makes the move. In Pariah conversation, the phrase "to see the world" is a common one. This is considered the natural prerogative of every man, and to a lesser extent of women. Bangalore, and indeed Penang, are not remote strange places. Bangalore, particularly, is constantly discussed and knowledge of it is fairly detailed—the gardens and parks and bright night-lights have a romantic tinge, but reality corrects romance. One young man, back from a visit, said to his sister, "I have seen your Bangalore—it is nothing but a river of sewage."

There is hardly a boy in the cheri who does not know the bus and train timetables, expenses, and the address and place of work of several relatives. Intervisiting and postcards are frequent. Some villagers regularly go to Bangalore during the hot season to enjoy the city's superior climate.

The same pattern of alternation between village and town life is emerging in a study of blacksmiths in Howrah being conducted by the UNESCO Centre in Calcutta. For several generations, blacksmith families have rotated various family members between work in a family unit in the city and employment on the family land in Bihar villages. Many of the migration streams have not been urban-bound, but intrarural. In the early decades of this century, for instance, the cities of the Punjab remained almost constant in size, while the great migration streams moved toward the new canal colonies. In short, for many villages out-migration is not a new phenomenon, and the flexible pluralistic structure readily closes behind the departees. Perhaps the deepest effect of migration might be expected to occur when villages fall within the commuting orbit of a major metropolis and sizable segments of their population work in the city and use the village only as a

[33] *Op. cit.,* p. 78,

dormitory or for weekend residence. I recently visited several villages near the East Pakistan border, some twenty-five miles east of Calcutta, where about half the adult males work in the city. It would be interesting to determine what the effects of this were on village structure. I can only report that the visible impact upon at least the externals of village life seemed to be very little indeed.

If we may conclude that the general effect of out-migration, even in substantial numbers, is at least an open question, it is possible that the selectivity of the loss disturbs the balance of the village. The most common generalizations concerning the segment of the rural population which does leave are expressed in terms of such "push" factors as man-land ratio, suggesting that it is those displaced economically who are forced out of the villages. A classic statement of this point of view is found in Prabhu's report:

> Poverty and pestilence in rural areas have been the major causes of the cityward movement of villagers. Small landholders and labouring classes had been the worst sufferers in the time of famines and bad seasons in Deccan and Konkan . . . In the famine of 1876–77, large numbers of lower caste people from Satara, Ratnagiri and Kolaba came to Bombay in search of work.[34]

Morris, in his trenchant critique[35] of this study, points out that while economic reasons may be those most often given by respondents in explaining their move, the "push" factors operated across the board and the willingness of people to leave the rustic idyl for the urban "Inferno" only under severe economic distress is, at least in part, mythology. An argument similar to Prabhu's is given by Srinivas for the nonagriculturalists. He remarks that, "When there are too many persons in a non-agricultural caste group, the excess may migrate to a nearby town." [36]

The first look at data, however, begins to qualify these general statements. The most frequent instance of selectivity is the high proportion of males among the migrants. The effect on the rural area is to produce an imbalance in the sex ratio. In fact, the forthcoming Bombay survey conducted by the University of Bombay uses sex ratio disparities among the different districts in Bombay

---

[34] Pandhari Nath Prabhu, "Bombay: A Study on the Social Effects of Urbanization on Industrial Workers Migrating from Rural Areas to the City of Bombay," in *The Social Implications of Industrialization and Urbanization: Five Studies in Asia* (Calcutta: UNESCO Centre on the Social Implications of Industrialization in Southern Asia, 1956), p. 53.

[35] Morris David Morris, "The Myth of 'Paradise Lost,'" *The Economic Weekly*, July 6, 1957, pp. 857–862. For Prabhu's rejoinder see his "UNESCO Study of Bombay Labour: A Rejoinder," *ibid.*, September 7, 1957, pp. 1157–1158.

[36] M. N. Srinivas, "The Social System of a Mysore Village," in Marriott (ed.), *Village India*, p. 16.

State to estimate the extent of urban migration from each district. This would seem too uniform a criterion, in that some districts—for instance, Ratnagiri—have mostly lone male migration, while the Ghat districts are more prone to family migration. Nonetheless, the depletion of young male adults in the village is one of the most important of the by-products of selective migration. Mrs. Dandekar[37] investigated the demographic effects of the long-standing out-migration of husbands upon the village of Mithbaon in Ratnagiri District. While the age of marriage had been appreciably raised, the surprising finding was that the fertility of the 388 women in Mithbaon whose husbands were away in Bombay was in no way less than that of the rest of the village wives. I am not sure what to make of her finding that the female insanity rate in this village was higher than the combined rate in five other villages in different districts of Maharashtra. She explains this on the basis of the out-migration of males.

Edwin Eames,[38] in a study of urban-bound migrants from a single village in Uttar Pradesh, belies the general picture of the economically distressed sections of the populace moving. He notes that the different castes not only differ in their propensity to mobility, but in the level of occupation they find in the city. Not only do the upper caste men migrate more often, but they prosper more than others. This would suggest that the "pull" takes precedence over the "push" factor.

Eames's inquiry was specifically concerned with the effects of out-migration on the traditional jajmani system. He finds "all of those leaving the village are either jajmans (employers) or purjans (employees), but the general feeling is that there has been little effect upon the system in general." Other studies support the thesis that migration from the village does not destroy the joint family system, but rather that a new type of joint family emerges whose seat is still in the ancestral village and whose urban wing is an integral part of both the ceremonial and economic unit. In time, the largest proportion of this kinship unit may be in the city, but the extended kin ties persist and the system in the village remains intact. An older statement of this pattern is found in the Baroda census of 1911.[39]

The ordinary course of permanent migration is as follows:—A family finds its ancestral land or business insufficient for its increasing numbers or is unable

---

[37] Kumudini Dandekar, *Demographic Survey of Six Rural Communities* (Poona: Gokhale Institute of Politics and Economics, 1959).

[38] "Some Aspects of Urban Migration from a Village in North Central India, *Eastern Anthropologist*, VIII (September–November, 1954), 13–26.

[39] Report volume, p. 43.

to obtain local employment for all its members and a son accompanied perhaps by a cousin or two goes off in search of land or work to places where he knows he can find them. He starts as a tenant or a clerk and after a time, becomes an owner, and sends for his wife to join him in his new home. Her brothers and cousins follow her on the same errand which brought her husband to the place, knowing that they will find friends. His sons look for wives and his daughters for husbands in the neighbourhood of the old home, and so a small colony is formed which serves as a nucleus for further migration. As time goes on, the colony expands, its numbers increase, migration ceases or assumes the reciprocal form, until at length, the ties connecting the colony with the people of the neighbourhood grow stronger and those with its original home relax and wives are no longer sought for at a distance.

This quotation points up the associational nature of migration— few travel into a strange environment without welcoming kin or caste groups to ease the way. Gertrude Woodruff reports that out of 793 people living in the Pariah *jopadi* in Bangalore, 467 had migrated from rural areas, mostly from only three villages: "38 percent of jopadi migrants came to Bangalore as children under 15 with one or more parents, another 38 percent came as married couples and 11 percent were brought to the city as wives." [40] A study by B. R. Misra,[41] in which he compares the members of Jamshedpur families resident in the city with those left behind, gives further support for this family-centered associational migration.

The major point of the above paragraphs is that the migrational flow, for a variety of reasons, has had less impact on the villages than might appear likely if viewed from the receiving urban end of the process. Villages show the same resiliency in the face of what might be called "urban feedback"—that is, the continuing village contacts of out-migrants and the intrusion of urban ways brought by those who return. Most home visits are for brief periods and frequently occur under circumstances when the returnee is least likely to affect village ways. Festival, marriage, and funeral visits are so encrusted with ceremonials that the role of each person is clearly defined along traditional village patterns. In cases of sickness, when return to the village is likely, the convalescent returnee is not in a position to dominate his rural environment. The occasional triumphal return of the ex-villager who has succeeded in the city is so brief in duration and so indicative of the separateness of the urban world that its impact in the village is limited to a temporary flow of urban gadgets and consumption goods.

Permanent returnees are rarer. The educated tend to remain in

[40] *Op. cit.*, pp. 21–22.

[41] *Report on Socio-Economic Survey of Jamshedpur City.* (Patna: Patna University Press, 1959), pp. 10–26.

the cities. The dream of retiring to the village is not often realized, except in cases of ill health or in refuge from urban unemployment. Woodruff notes,[42] "There is considerable evidence that the flow of wives to the city is essentially a one-way process. Certainly, women who have been in Bangalore since early childhood do not adjust easily to rural life where there is a very different set of expectations for them—particularly as regards skills."

Perhaps the most potent agents of change among the urban returnees are those returning to the village on small pensions, such as retired clerks, petty officials, or ex-servicemen, who bring to the village not just an urbanized but a partially Westernized life style. Their return to the village, sometimes with cash to buy land, lends them prestige in village circles and their leverage for change is considerable, although all too often their life style is considered suitable for them, but not one to be copied by their less cosmopolitan neighbors.

The example of the pensioners leads us back to one of the basic points that has been made throughout the paper. The traditional urban-rural relations tend to minimize the potential forces for rural change which might have flowed from the cities. In some things, particularly in religious practices, the prestigeful cities did serve as models for village patterns, but their influence was brought to the village by mediating middlemen and was tempered to fit with little dislocation into established patterns. This is not to argue for a lack of change in the village, but only that such changes were usually changes in the broad structure of society, a good portion of which was rural both in its origin and impact.

On the other hand, as cities have taken on new functions, especially those resulting from contact with the West, it is the diffusion of the effect of these new functions which has constituted the most severe of the rural dislocations. High on the list of these new functions is the growth of industrialization and the organization of a monetized, rationalized economic structure. Studies looking at the village from the viewpoint of the city have tended to concentrate upon these functions and consequently to exaggerate the extent of rural change. We would anticipate, therefore, that the greatest dislocation of rural patterns by a town would follow when the town has grown suddenly and almost exclusively around one of the newer economic functions for which there is no provision in the traditional networks of relationships. Even here, the word "suddenly" needs emphasis, for long-settled administrative centers which add a few industrial units are not nearly so disturb-

---

[42] *Op. cit.,* p. 75.

ing.[43] The combination of new industrialization and urbanization, if we may step a little across the border, is examined in a lengthy study by A. F. A. Husain entitled *Human and Social Impact of Technological Change in Pakistan*.[44] Husain collected some 75 widely scattered cases to measure the effects of the newly developing jute-processing industry and industrial base in East Pakistan. In general he found a favorable, if discriminating set of attitudes among the villagers toward the towns and factories. If one has land, he will prefer to stay in the village. If not, a steadily paying job in the city is considered superior to agricultural labor. Urban jobs employing the ability to read and even peon jobs are considered superior, and those holding them are respected. Factory employment, if the job is permanent, is considered slightly lower in rank, and coolies, rickshaw drivers, and domestic servants are not thought well of. Husain reports that such people frequently pretend to be peons when they return to their villages. The so-called moral and religious dangers of urban life are not taken seriously. In any case, they are identified with English education. In fact, Husain reports, religious observances have, if anything, increased in the factories as worship becomes institutionalized as part of the factory routine.

This generally favorable orientation toward the towns is turned to hostility only in those areas immediately contiguous to new factories and urban sites. A few selected passages from Husain will indicate the general nature of such observations.

Mosquitoes have greatly increased in the locality; the case cannot sleep at night due to their biting. On account of the construction of ditches necessitated by the building of the factory which have not been filled and the presence of insanitary latrines in the factory, mosquitoes breed easily. Cholera is also prevalent in the factory quarters but not in the villages. (II, 77.)

Many factory people (particularly Noakhali people) are ruffians, they precipitate trouble. Recently at the time of the elections, the factory people did violence in a meeting organised in his village. (II, 77.)

The factory has taken land and has not paid compensation adequately or promptly. It has meant higher prices for food and necessaries. But the villagers have not benefitted from the food prices; due to smoke from the factory chimney yield of crops, vegetables have been impaired. The health of the locality has been adversely affected, mosquitoes have increased and one gets bad smell due to insanitary and congested living conditions in the factory. Few people from the villages have got jobs in the factory as people from India and the outlying districts of East Bengal have been employed mostly. (II, 89–90.)

[43] Cf. Richard D. Lambert, "Factory Workers and the Non-Factory Population in Poona," *Journal of Asian Studies*, XVIII (November, 1958), 24–42.

[44] (Two vols.; Dacca: Oxford University Press, 1956.)

In sum, the objections seem to be: a decline in sanitation, loss of ethnic homogeneity in the area, and disruption of the local economic balance. It might be added that the effect of smoke on the crops was probably imaginary, but it was a viewpoint widely held. Villages in the immediate vicinity of the town claimed that the benefits of higher prices for agricultural products went to distant villages and that many of the local people had been forced to become nonproducing consumers at the inflated prices.

In addition to these highly personal inconveniences, the rural social structure is most sensitive to changes in the relationships between people and land. Therefore, it is not surprising that the bitterest sentiments against the intrusion of towns and industries arose over the extent and manner of the acquisition of village land by these new factories and towns. Several hundred acres may be required for an extensive factory, and the displacement of large numbers of families from their land is almost inevitable. Not infrequently, the government forces the sale of land to the factory through a Land Acquisition Department. In such a case, compensation is always less than villagers expect and compensation is very slow in coming.

Conceivably, those displaced might be absorbed by the new economic opportunities in the factories. Husain reports that

few people from the villages in the neighbourhood of the mills had, in fact, been employed in the mills although extravagant promises had been made by government spokesmen at the time of the acquisition of the land that the mills would mean a new era of prosperity for the locality. The villagers alleged that the mills had employed mainly people from the distant districts of the province as well as people from outside the province. (I, 263.)

In short, then, we find that the impact of sudden industrialization and urbanization is not to draw the villagers into the new economic pursuits so much as to displace them from their old occupations without absorbing many of them into the new ones. This is not surprising in view of our discussion up to this point. Only a minority of the people ever left the village to be absorbed into urban pursuits. Had a whole village migrated en masse to the city, selective absorption would have taken place and severe dislocations in the social relations would have resulted among the people. The setting-up of a new factory or town on village lands has the same effect. Moreover, the high degree of ethnic and regional specialization of skills and the castelike structure of occupational classifications within factories (or, for that matter, in the construction of dams, the building of railroads, or the tilling of plantations) inhibits the absorption of local workers who, when it is a fresh area of penetration, are not likely to have the requisite skills. The village economic dislocation occurs at the same time that the traditional devices for keeping the city or the factory at a safe social distance no longer avail.

A spectacular example of displacement without absorption occurred at Rourkela and Durgapur with the construction of the new government-sponsored steel plants. Vithal Babu[45] reports that in the four years prior to October, 1958, land acquisition took in 20,488 acres, affecting 32 villages, of which 16 were fully evacuated. The government of Orissa was given the responsibility of resettling the 12,878 people displaced. Babu reports:

> Out of the 2,400 displaced families, nearly 800 families have been re-settled in the Jalda colony and about 400 in the Jhirpani colony. The rest of the 1,200 families are still in the villages which were partially evacuated till November 1958, while a few families have gone to the twelve reclamation colonies in the interior forests. We found that only old people are going to the reclamation areas to carry on agriculture, while the able-bodied men and women are either in urban resettlement colonies or in the surrounding areas in search of job opportunities. (P. 229.)
>
> [But,] out of 5,973 able-bodied men and women, the project authorities recruited 161 for regular employment, 223 as the work charged [315] and 630 as the muster roll. The rest of the people in these colonies, it can be assumed, have been idle and unemployed, living from day to day on the money paid by way of compensation by the Steel Project Authorities . . . It was reported that skilled, semi-skilled and even unskilled workers were brought by the contractors and sub-contractors from different parts of the country, mainly from outside the province. (P. 237.)

Displacement in Durgapur has had disorganizing effects similar to those it had in Rourkela:

> Agriculture is no longer the principal source of income for the displaced people . . . The displaced people do not seem to have taken advantage of the avenues of employment as 54 percent of them are reported to be unemployed . . . The middle classes, who previously constituted the largest majority in the traditional system of economy with 5 to 20 bighas of land have, in general, developed a tendency for avoiding manual labor as something appropriate only for lower caste people . . . Side by side, it is noticed that the commercial opportunities expanding in the context of the growing town, have been neglected by the displaced persons, while outsiders have captured the market. (P. 323.)

On the other hand, Bhilai, where a similar problem of settling 2,000 displaced families was met and where the surplus cultivable land is considerably less than in Orissa, seems not to have shared

---

[45] *Report on a Preliminary Inquiry on the Growth of Steel Towns in India* (Calcutta: UNESCO Research Centre, 1959).

the problem. By some process which Babu calls a "mystery," the displaced villagers seem to have scattered without the aid of the government into other agricultural areas; almost none of them showed up in the contractors' labor force.

In summary, then, the impact of urban areas per se on villages seems from the available literature to be less than might be expected. Such changes are maximal (1) in areas where displacement is sudden and substantial, and (2) where the independent variable is not just urbanization, but the introduction of large-scale industrialization as well. The consequences of these impressions for Indian policy are, I think, clear and already expressed to some extent in government programs. Each village must be reached separately and on its own terms; the diffusion from urban areas of changes is too slow a process. On the other hand, many of the difficulties currently experienced in such undertakings as the Community Development Program (or such social legislation as the Hindu Code Bill or land-reform legislation) attest to the remaining difficulties facing urbanized elites, even when they deliberately attempt to induce change in the countryside.

VII

THE VILLAGE AND
THE COMMUNITY

V. Nath

The concept of the community is of fundamental importance for the Community Development Program. This program is based on the belief that economic and social advance in rural India can best be secured through rural people working coöperatively as members of communities; and that, for this purpose, it is necessary to strengthen and revitalize the existing communities and to foster the community spirit to the extent that it is deficient. Also, in much of the thinking on community development it is implicit that the "village" is a "community." Concepts like people's participation, or the collective endeavor of a village in undertaking programs of common benefit, and the development of the three basic institutions—the panchayat, the coöperative society, and the school—are concepts basic to the Community Development Program and they all assume that the "village" is the "community."

In view of this assumption, it is worth while asking: to what extent is the Indian village a community today? This will involve an examination of the nature of the village and of the rural community as well as an analysis of the factors on which the village's role as a unit of community life rested in the past. We shall also discuss how these factors have been affected as a result of the social and economic changes of the last 100 years or more, and whether new units of community life are emerging in rural India.

THE VILLAGE AS THE UNIT OF SETTLEMENT

For a definition of the term "village" we must go to the Indian census, which says: "It should be borne in mind that the concept of a village is not demographic, but administrative. As a general rule, it represents a parcel of land, the boundaries of which are defined and settled by a Revenue Survey or by a Cadestral Survey. It may be, but need not always necessarily be a single house cluster with a local name, marking its distinctiveness as a residential locality." [1]

It will be clear from the above definition that the term "village," strictly speaking, does not stand for a social or a settlement unit. It is a term used to express what is primarily a revenue-administrative unit. It is true that in most parts of India this is also a unit of settlement or habitation. The village in these parts conforms to the popular picture of a cluster of houses (or more than one cluster of houses, adjoining) situated amid its cultivated fields which define its boundaries, separate it from other similar units, and give it a distinct identity. It is necessary, however, to emphasize that this picture does not obtain in all parts of the country: that there are important variations from it in several areas, and that in some parts of the country the village as a settlement unit does not exist at all.

The identity between the revenue village and the unit of settlement is closest in northwestern India and in the "dry" areas of the country generally, e.g., Punjab, Rajasthan, Western U.P., Bombay, Mysore, and parts of Madhya Pradesh. In these areas, the village is a tightly nucleated unit of settlement, distinctly marked out from other similar units. The main variation from this pattern is that frequently the Harijan Basti is not contiguous with the main village and is located at a small distance from it. But, as we move away from these areas, there is a trend towards a more dispersed settlement pattern, with the village being composed of a "main village," which is usually inhabited by the landholding castes, and one, two, or more "hamlets." In the Gangetic plain, this pattern is already well established in Central U.P. and becomes more marked as we move farther east. Thus, over large parts of eastern India (Bihar, Orissa, and West Bengal) the revenue village consists of the main village and a number of small clusters of households (*thollas*), each situated within its own grove of trees, having its own source of water supply, and separated from the others by some distance. Village boundaries are not clearly discernible in these areas, because the clusters which form part of one village are hardly distinguishable from those forming part of the next. A somewhat different situation is found in Madras and parts of Andhra Pradesh. Here the pattern of settlement is generally similar to what would be called the tightly nucleated village type,

---

[1] *Census of India, 1951* Part II-A, Demographic Tables, p. 2.

i.e., a distinct cluster of houses surrounded by cultivated fields. But these "clusters" are not called villages, but "hamlets." The revenue village in these areas consists of a number of such hamlets and generally has a large population, up to 10,000 or 15,000.

The extreme departures from the pattern of the tightly nucleated village are found at the two extremities of the country, Kerala and Himachal Pradesh. In Kerala the unit of settlement is the individual homestead situated within its own compound and agricultural lands. These homesteads extend in almost unbroken lines along the roads and in other areas suitable for settlement. The "village" here is a purely artificial unit created by the revenue administration and has no existence on the ground. Generally, a large population of 5,000 to 15,000 is included in it. In the other parts of the west coast, between Kerala and Bombay City, the settlement pattern can be considered to be intermediate between the homestead type found in Kerala and the "village" type. Villages here are often no more than somewhat more concentrated clusters of homesteads. At the other end of the country, in Himachal Pradesh, where the population is very sparse, the typical unit of settlement is the "hamlet," consisting of a very few houses, sometimes not more than two or three. Himachal Pradesh represents the extreme in this respect, but in hilly and mountainous areas all over the country the "hamlet" type of settlement exists, especially where the population is sparse, and true "villages" begin to appear only in valleys and other areas of more concentrated population.

These examples have been given *not* to prove that the village is not the unit of settlement over most parts of the country. There is no question about this. They have been given merely to show that this is not universally true and that there are important differences from this pattern in some parts of the country. An adequate appreciation of these differences is of great importance for all policy makers and workers in community development and other rural development programs, because almost every physical task of development—ranging from agricultural improvement measures, such as irrigation, to location of community facilities, such as schools and *panchayat ghars*—is vitally affected by them. The planning of rural development programs has obviously to be very different in Kerala, where each household lives in its own compound, from that in Punjab with its tightly nucleated villages. Certain programs, like the pavement of village streets and drains, so important in Punjab, are scarcely necessary in Kerala. On the other hand, the cost of such a program as rural electrification is much higher in Kerala, because of the necessity of taking electric lines to every individual homestead. The efficiency of *gram sevaks* and other development workers is also influenced by the settlement pattern. In Punjab, the task of the gram sevak is relatively easy, because he has all the families living in a village potentially within his reach every time he visits the village. In Kerala, on the other hand, his work is much more difficult, because for propagation of any program he has to visit individual homesteads.

The rest of this discussion relates only to areas where the "village" is the unit of settlement, including those areas where the "village" consists of a central unit and one or more hamlets. The feeling of community centering on the village is strongest in these areas, and we feel that by concentrating attention on them we shall be able to see more clearly the factors on which this feeling is based, and also understand its limitations. Areas like Kerala and Himachal Pradesh in which the settlement pattern is very different have been excluded, because the feeling of community centering on the village is very weak or virtually absent in them.

THE VILLAGE AS A SOCIAL UNIT

The assumption that the "village" is the "community" has a strong basis in historical and even present fact. The people living in a village did not (and do not) have the comparatively superficial or transitory ties which bind the residents of a neighborhood or a residential suburb in a modern Western city. They had (and still have) intimate economic and social relationships which were (and are) regulated by traditions and institutions which have evolved over centuries. The main bases on which these economic and social relationships (and the feeling of community focusing on the village) have rested are three: isolation of the village, the jajmani system, and caste and kinship.

The isolation of the village severely limited the contacts of the villagers with the outside world and made it necessary for them to confine their economic and social relationships within the village or within a group of neighboring villages. Caste and the jajmani system provided the social and economic bases on which these relationships rested. The two institutions were intimately related and mutually supporting. Caste defined the occupation and the social status of the different individuals and groups living in the village. The jajmani system defined their economic relationships and bound the cultivators, on the one hand, and the artisans and other non-agriculturists, on the other, in a system of economic interdependence. The system was organized with the village as the basic unit. Most of the artisans and others who supplied goods and rendered services to the cultivators were resident within the village. Moreover, the practice of fixed payments in kind at the time of harvest, which constituted the core of the jajmani system, represented in fact a sharing of crops by those who rendered services to cultivators. As a result, all the residents of the village, both cultivators and noncultivators, acquired a feeling of direct dependence on the lands of the village, a strong sense of belonging to the village and of sharing in its destiny.

This does not mean, of course, that every village was self-sufficient in every respect or was completely isolated from the outside world. Contacts between neighboring villages must have been of considerable importance in most areas. Cases of artisans of one village, especially a large village, serving a few neighboring villages must have been frequent. Marital and other social relationships extended over a number of neighboring villages, the number of villages and the distances involved being much larger among those groups (e.g., Jats in northern India) where there are restrictions on marriage within the village. Social scientists who have made village studies in recent years have analyzed the patterns of such intervillage relationships and have also referred to organizations of a specified number of villages (four, twenty) which had judicial and administrative functions and which must have been well developed in the past.[2]

The administrative, economic, and social changes of the last hundred years or so have profoundly affected these three bases on which community feeling centering on the village rested. The isolation of the villages has been broken and they have now important administrative, economic, social, and political contacts with the outside world. The jajmani system has been greatly weakened. In some parts of the country where it existed before, it has practically disappeared. In most others it exists in an attenuated form, with jajmani relationships preserved best in the cases of those artisans whose services are most necessary for cultivation (e.g., carpenters) or those whose wares have not been completely replaced by factory-made goods (e.g., potters). Caste has also undergone important changes. Further, the processes which have brought about these changes are operating with ever increasing vigor. This is very clear from the experience of the post-independence years. In this period, as a result of the operation of community development and other development programs, communications in rural areas have been greatly improved, with the result that the range and magnitude of the villagers' contacts with the outside world have greatly increased. Also, systematic efforts are being made to

---

[2] Oscar Lewis, *Village Life in Northern India* (Urbana, Ill.: University of Illinois Press, 1958), pp. 29–30. This is a study of a Jat village in Delhi State.

break the mental isolation of villagers and to help them acquire a modern and progressive outlook in the interest of greater production, higher income, and higher levels of living. This is the sole aim of the extension part of the Community Development Program. Thus, the isolation of the village, both physical and mental, has been effectively broken. The process of substitution of cash transactions for those in kind, which implies breakdown of the jajmani system, is being completed at a rapid rate as the villagers are more effectively brought within the orbit of the national market economy. Accordingly, to the extent that the feeling of community centering on the village rested on these two factors—isolation and the jajmani system—it is being further weakened at a rapid rate.

The case of caste is different and more complex. The changes of the last hundred years or so have undoubtedly weakened the outward manifestations of caste. Thus, they have greatly reduced the rigors of caste taboos and regulations, and weakened organizations, such as the caste panchayats, which were responsible for enforcing them. Identity between particular castes and occupations has also been affected by the decline of certain occupations (most village crafts), growth of opportunity in others (e.g., trade, and certain service occupations like tailoring), and consequent occupational mobility. Hence the role of caste as a socioeconomic-political institution imposing a certain way of life, rules of behavior, and code of conduct on its members has suffered a decline. But the position of caste as the basic unit of social organization in rural India has not been affected. On the contrary, it is maintained by some sociologists that caste has been strengthened in some ways and is playing entirely new roles which are required and have been made possible by the changed conditions of modern times.[3]

The role of caste in contributing to community feeling centering on the village is rather complicated. The social and economic stability which caste provided was an essential prerequisite of the jajmani system: it is doubtful whether the system could have existed in the absence of caste. Therefore, through its support to the jajmani system, caste may be seen as an important factor contributing to the feeling of community centering on the village. On the other hand, caste itself provides a primary focus for community feeling which is a rival to loyalty to the village. In this connection, the discussion in a recent publication, *Village India*,[4]

---

[3] The role of caste in influencing elections and political alignments is most frequently noted.

[4] McKim Marriott (ed.), *Village India* (Chicago: University of Chicago Press, 1955); articles by M. N. Srinivas, pp. 32–34, and Marriott, pp. 174–181.

is interesting. Srinivas, discussing the social system of a Mysore village, refers to the vertical unity of the village as against the horizontal unity of the caste and says that the village may be described as "a vertical entity made up of several horizontal layers each of which is a caste." Marriott, describing a village in Western U.P., analyzes in considerable detail the nature, extent, and limitations of the feeling of community centering on the village and the extent to which the village is a unit. It is interesting to note that both these views, which bring out the limitations of community feeling centering on the village, are based on field work in parts of the country where the village is a distinct unit of settlement and this feeling is the strongest. In areas where the settlement pattern is dispersed and the village consists of a number of hamlets, each composed either exclusively or predominantly of members of a single caste, the feeling of community in the sense of belonging to the village is considerably weaker.

THE PRIMARY COMMUNITY

This brings me to the question of the primary community in rural India. After a study of observations made in several village studies which have been published in recent years, and an analysis of experiences with development programs which required collective effort and contributions from the whole community, I have come to the conclusion that the primary community in rural India is today constituted not by the "village," but by the members of a single caste living within a village. In areas of dispersed settlement where the village consists of several settlement units (*thollas*), the existence of this primary community is very clear, because these *thollas* are organized primarily on the basis of caste. But even in areas where the tightly nucleated village is the settlement unit it is often found that houses of members of different castes concentrate in different sections of the village, the concentration of Harijan households in a wing of the village being most marked. In my view, the multicaste village—most villages in India are multicaste—should more appropriately be called a "secondary community" because the feeling of belonging to it represents the first extension of the primary loyalty to the smaller unit mentioned above. There is considerable support for this view in recent experiences with the Community Development Program. For example, in many villages participation in such programs as the pavement of streets and the construction of school buildings or drinking-water wells has been organized primarily on the basis of *thollas*, mohallas, or caste groups. This is particularly true where the participation has meant a spontaneous mobilization of local resources of labor, materials, or cash. The whole village might have come together to take a decision for participation in the activity; but the execution of the decision and the actual mobilization of resources has been generally on the basis of the smaller unit. This leads me further to think that one reason why development programs based on the assumption that the village itself is the community meet with considerable difficulties in the field is that, as soon as any such program is presented to the village, the different primary communities within it begin to think not only of the interest of the village as a whole, but of their own interests, which are often in conflict with the former. Institutions such as panchayats, based on the village as the unit, meet with difficulties for the same reason. The fact has to be faced that the village is a plural society consisting of a number of primary communities, each of which thinks of its own interest at the same time as—or even before—it thinks of that of the village.

CONFLICT BETWEEN HIERARCHICAL AND EGALITARIAN CONCEPTS

Not only is the village not the primary community, but its traditional hierarchical organization, in which the status, rights, and obligations of individuals and groups differ, is in fundamental conflict with the egalitarian principles on which India seeks to build new institutions and the new "community." It is necessary to grasp the existence of this conflict and to realize that Indian rural society will have to resolve it and rebuild itself along egalitarian principles. This is no small task, and the difficulties which confront the panchayats, coöperatives, and other institutions requiring coöperative endeavor, can be more readily understood if this fundamental conflict is kept in view. Take the case of the statutory panchayats. Their constitution is based on the two principles that (*a*) each adult resident in the village has a vote and through it an equal share in the governance of the village, and (*b*) the entire population of the village shall be governed by the same laws and rules.

Neither of these principles has held for the traditional organization of the village, in which certain groups have had far higher status and far more rights than others, and in which different standards of behavior and codes of conduct have applied to different groups. The point is so obvious that it is not necessary to elaborate it any further. Therefore, if the village people, the greater part of whose life continues to be governed by the traditional hierarchical organization, have difficulty in grasping the egalitarian principles underlying the statutory panchayats and in working through these institutions, this is not surprising. Similarly, the unsuccessful working of many coöperatives will be found to originate in this conflict between the egalitarian principles which underlie the institution and the hierarchical concepts which govern the rest of village life. In this case, however, the difficulties of bringing the different social and economic groups composing the village into one coöperative society are better appreciated, and it is recognized that separate coöperatives, each catering to the interest of different economic or occupational groups (cultivators, weavers, tanners, carpenters, etc.), are more satisfactory. It is also recognized that it is more feasible to combine the same class of artisans living in adjoining villages in a coöperative society than to combine cultivators and noncultivators living in the same village. In other words, the bonds of economic life (occupation) with which those of social life (caste) are inextricably mixed are stronger than the community feeling centering on the village.

The hierarchical character of rural life, and the economic and social distances between different sections of the village, are likely to constitute an even greater difficulty in developing organizations of young people and women. Unlike the panchayat, which is a statutory organization, these organizations are voluntary in nature. Moreover, their functions, being mainly cultural and recreational, affect those aspects of social life in which deep-seated traditions, emotions, and prejudices play a dominant part. Of the two, the women's organization will encounter greater difficulties, because the outlook of women is more tradition-oriented than that of the young people. But there is no doubt also that the successful working of these organizations would itself prove a powerful factor in social change and in reorienting the pattern of rural social life from the hierarchical to the egalitarian principle.

It is necessary, therefore, to understand clearly the real nature of the task involved in organizing these institutions successfully. The task is not merely one of getting rural people to come together to perform certain civic and developmental functions (through panchayats) or economic functions (in coöperatives), or of getting rural women and young people to come together for recreational or cultural programs. It is really the task of making a fundamental change in the existing basis of social organization of the villages.

SOME FUTURE TRENDS

This analysis of the village as a community and the changes to which its social organization has been subjected brings us to the question: what changes in the structure of the village can be anticipated in the near future, and what kind of a community is likely to emerge in rural India? This is a large question, an adequate discussion of which is not possible within the scope of this paper. The following observations may, therefore, be taken as no more than a projection of a few trends which are already observable.

CHANGES IN PHYSICAL STRUCTURE: EXPLOSION OF VILLAGES

The village will undoubtedly remain the unit of settlement in most parts of the country, but there will be important changes in its physical structure and socioeconomic composition. The physical changes will be especially marked in areas where the tightly nucleated village is the unit of settlement (i.e., the northwest and "dry" areas generally). In most villages in these areas there is acute congestion and shortage of housing, with the result that the villages are under pressure to expand. This pressure is increasing rapidly, because with population growth the demands for housing are increasing and with a rise in living levels people wish to have better, more spacious, and more comfortable houses. The pressure will mount steadily, and there might well be an explosion of villages similar to that which we are seeing today in the case of metropolitan areas like Delhi. This explosion would create a serious land-use situation in many areas. Expansion of villages in most cases can take place only at the expense of cultivated lands. And, since in most fertile areas there is already intense pressure of population upon cultivated lands, any large-scale diversion of these for house-building purposes will aggravate the population pressure still further. Careful land-use planning will, therefore, be necessary.

The expansion of villages will normally mean bringing contiguous areas just outside the village boundaries under habitation. At times this is bound to present serious difficulties, because lands just outside the village may be especially prized for agriculture and, therefore, difficult to obtain; or there may be physical or topographical factors which make such expansion difficult. Consequently, new villages situated at some distance from existing ones will arise. Also there will be a tendency for cultivators to live, homestead fashion, on their fields. This tendency should be particularly marked in areas of well irrigation in which intensive cultivation can be practiced. The factors favoring this tendency are (a) the disappearance or reduced importance of factors such as water supply and need for defense, which favored nucleated villages in the past, and (b) an appreciation of the advantages, both economic and hygienic, of living on the fields (e.g., more efficient use of farmyard manure; ease of intensive cultivation and production of high-value crops—vegetables and fruit; no need for such facilities as pavement of streets or drains).

The pattern of settlement in these areas is therefore likely to become more open and dispersed, with large numbers of new villages and homestead settlements developing side-by-side with the older, tightly nucleated villages, which would themselves be expanding.

CHANGES IN SOCIOECONOMIC COMPOSITION: RISE OF THE SERVICE CENTER

The socioeconomic composition of the villages is also likely to undergo important changes. It is most probable that, as the breakdown of the jajmani system becomes complete, more and more artisans and others rendering nonagricultural services will concentrate in the larger villages or small towns. This will have two results:

1) Progressive *agriculturation* of the small and medium villages. With the artisans and other nonagriculturists concentrating in the larger villages or small towns, the small and medium villages will become more purely agricultural and thus more nearly homogeneous in both occupational and caste composition.
2) Growth of the larger villages and small towns into units, which for want of a better name we may call "service centers."

A concentration of artisans in these service centers is essential for technological advance in the crafts and for improvement in the economic and social conditions of the artisans. All the measures needed to achieve these objectives—industrial extension and training of artisans in improved techniques, the provision of common service facilities (e.g., dyeing in fast colors, in the case of hand-loom weavers), supply of electric power, bulk purchase of good-quality raw materials, provision of credit, standardization of product, and efficient marketing—can be provided economically only if the artisans are concentrated in a limited number of service centers instead of being dispersed in every village. Further, innovation, which is necessary for continued technological advance in any industry, can flourish only when artisans are freed from the stagnation imposed by the jajmani system, and this can be achieved effectively only when they move from their present locations.

Apart from concentrating the existing artisans, the service centers will supply the large and increasing range of *new* goods to meet the demands of modern agriculture and rising levels of living. Examples of goods which will be needed in increasing quantities as agriculture is modernized are: improved seed, fertilizers, pesticides and other plant-protection aids, improved implements (including tractors and pumping sets), and such materials as steel, cement, and diesel oil. The supply of these items and the servicing and repair of modern equipment can be arranged efficiently only at service centers. The larger villages and small towns are already centers for the marketing of agricultural produce and the distribution of consumers' goods. Both these roles will assume greater importance as agricultural production, rural incomes, and standards of living rise. Many of the centers will also attract processing industries based upon the agricultural production of the surrounding villages. Some, which have a locational advantage for a particular industry (e.g., availability of raw material or skill in craft), or are caught in the general process of decentralization of industries from the cities, will also develop small- or medium-scale industries having a wider market. Facilities for agricultural credit —especially medium-term, long-term, and specialized credit needed for making investments in land or improving agricultural techniques—will also tend to be concentrated at such centers. Further, as coöperative societies for marketing, distribution, and processing grow in importance, these societies will also be located in them.

Social and administrative services already concentrate in the larger villages and small towns. This concentration will continue, and these will be the centers from which all the more advanced services and facilities will be provided to the rural people. While such elementary services as primary education and first-aid medical care can be provided in every village, the more advanced facilities of secondary schools, dispensaries, and hospitals can, obviously, not be thus duplicated. Administrative, recreational, and cultural functions will also follow the concentration of economic and social-service functions in service centers.

The above is not a hypothetical picture; it only represents a projection to the near future of the trends which are already visible. Artisans and others providing goods and services to the cultivators already concentrate in larger villages or small towns. Expansion of welfare services is rapidly proceeding to a stage where "service centers" catering to the needs of a number of villages are emerging. The beginnings of these can be seen in many Community Development blocks where a number of facilities are being concentrated in a few large villages which are the natural trade and communication centers for the surrounding villages.

It is difficult to generalize about the size of these centers or about the number of villages or the population that a center will serve. There will undoubtedly be much variation in these respects in different parts of the country, because of differences in density of population and stage of economic development. In most parts of the country, however, the service centers will have a population ranging between 2,500 and 10,000 (with most falling between

4,000 and 7,500), and will serve a population of 5,000 to 10,000 in their constituent villages. Thus, we visualize that a population of 10,000 to 20,000 (including the population of the service center itself) will be served by a center. A normal Community Development block with a population of about 70,000 will therefore have three to six such centers, with the block headquarters itself being a bigger center.

With this development of the service centers, rural society will have two major constituents: (*a*) a large number of villages, or such smaller units as hamlets or homesteads, and (*b*) a much smaller number of service centers. The population of the former will be predominantly agricultural, because the artisans and other nonagriculturists will tend to concentrate in the service centers. It will also be more homogeneous socially, because, as explained above, caste and occupation are still closely related in rural India. *The villages will therefore be predominantly agricultural, with fewer castes and much less social distance between the castes than is the case with villages today.* The population of the service centers, on the other hand, will be mixed; besides the artisans and others engaged in service occupations, many cultivators will be living in them. Many of the original cultivator residents of these centers whose lands are close by will continue to live there. In addition, many prosperous cultivators who can afford two establishments will keep their families there (e.g., for the sake of the children's education), while they themselves live on their lands.

THE SERVICE CENTER: FOCAL POINT OF THE NEW COMMUNITY

The service center with its constituent group of villages will constitute a real community. The basis of this community will be functional: the feeling of belonging to it will rest on the wide range of services—economic, social, administrative, cultural, and recreational—which the center performs for the entire community and on the relationships of mutual dependence (even though based on cash transactions) which will have been established between the artisans and other nonagriculturists on the one hand and the agriculturists on the other. It must not be assumed, however, that such a community will be completely or even largely self-sufficient, as the village was of old. For higher social and administrative services, as well as for all economic transactions, the center will be connected with larger centers—the block headquarters, *mandi* towns,[5] and distribution centers—and through them with the wider national life and economy. It will, however, for the reasons ex-

---

[5] Markets for agricultural produce.

plained above, be a very real community, the recognition of which will be of immense assistance for planning all rural development programs.

Such transformations of the structure of the rural society into predominantly agricultural villages on the one hand and service centers on the other, and the emergence of the latter as focal points of the new communities, are essential for an efficient organization of economic functions and for the creation of modern social and administrative purposes. They will also assist in making an effective change from the present hierarchical to the new egalitarian social structure which is the aim of the Community Development Program. So long as the present economically heterogeneous multicaste village persists as a basic unit in rural India, the establishment of efficient economic organization and an egalitarian sociopolitical system will be faced with difficulties. But, with the differentiation of the type described above, the change will be easier of achievement. The socioeconomic composition of the villages being more homogeneous, social equality will be easier to establish, and, since the relations between agriculturists in the villages and nonagriculturists in the service centers will be primarily cash-based, considerations of caste and social status will be much less important than they are today.

Part 3

URBANIZATION AND ECONOMIC DEVELOPMENT

VIII

THE ROLE OF URBANIZATION
IN ECONOMIC DEVELOPMENT:
SOME INTERNATIONAL COMPARISONS

Bert F. Hoselitz

Rapid urban growth is a relatively new phenomenon in India. Up to the end of the First World War some urban growth took place, but neither the proportion of the total population in urban places nor the rate of increase of the urban population itself was startling. With the decade 1921 to 1931, urbanization became a noticeable phenomenon in India, and the rate of urban growth has accelerated with each decade since then. Moreover, the cities and larger towns (i.e., urban places with more than 20,000 inhabitants) have grown more rapidly than those with only quasi-urban features. These trends of urban growth in India during the last few decades are presented in Table 1.

Two facts, above all, should be noted: (1) The percentage variation of the total population living in urban places has been increasing each decade since 1901, and (2) the rate of increase during the five decades 1901 to 1951 in towns with 20,000 or more inhabitants has been almost twice as fast as the rate of growth of all urban places together (i.e., 112 per cent as against 59 per cent). These data apparently understate the rate of urban growth somewhat, since the Indian census, on which these data are based, does not list population of metropolitan areas, but only of towns and town groups, and we may assume that data for metropolitan areas would show a more rapid rate of growth, especially of the larger cities and towns.

A datum which is often selected from these figures is the fact that

TABLE 1

URBAN GROWTH IN INDIA SINCE 1881

Year	British India	India (boundaries of 1948)			
		Percentage of urban population	Per cent variation per decade	Percentage of urban population in towns 20,000+	Percentage variation per decade in towns 20,000+
	(1)	(2)	(3)	(4)	(5)
1881........	9.3	...	...	...	...
1891........	9.4	...	...	...	...
1901........	10.0	10.91	...	5.61	...
1911........	9.4	10.57	−3.12	5.48	−2.32
1921........	10.2	11.38	7.66	6.08	10.95
1931........	11.1	12.13	6.59	6.97	14.64
1941........	12.8	13.91	14.67	8.88	27.40
1951........	...	17.34	24.66	11.89	33.90
1901–51.....	...	...	58.94	...	111.94

Sources: Column 1, Kingsley Davis, *The Population of India and Pakistan* (Princeton, N. J., 1951), p. 127; columns 2–5, Ashish Bose, "The Process of Urbanization in India" (Doctoral dissertation, University of Delhi, 1959), p. 167.

in 1901 (or 1891) the proportion of the urban population of India was around 10 per cent, and that this proportion was roughly similar to the share of the urban population in the United States in 1840. But, whereas in the five decades between 1840 and 1890 the share of the urban population in the United States rose from 10.8 per cent to 35.1 per cent, in India it rose only from 10.9 per cent in 1901 to 17.3 per cent in 1951. Hence the rate of urbanization in India was much slower than in the United States, though the parallel is somewhat vitiated by the fact that in India the rate of urbanization accelerated from 1901 onwards, whereas in the United States from 1840 to 1890 it tended to slow down gradually.[1]

The purpose of these comparisons is either to determine the comparative speed of urban growth in India, as against the United States, or to extrapolate from American past experience the future trends of Indian urban growth. But there are a number of reasons why comparisons between the United States and India have serious

[1] See Ashish Bose, "The Process of Urbanization in India" (Doctoral dissertation, University of Delhi, 1959), pp. 168–169. A similar comparison between Indian and United States urban growth, although not with the period 1840–1890, but an earlier period (1790 to 1850), is made by Kingsley Davis, *The Population of India and Pakistan* (Princeton, N.J., 1951), pp. 127–128.

shortcomings. Culturally the United States and India are very different, and it would be difficult to select two countries more different in social structure. The growth of the United States falls entirely in the period of modern capitalism; there are no survivals in American culture of previous feudal or tribal systems of social organization; moreover, though an overwhelming proportion of the American population did live in rural areas in the 18th and early 19th centuries, rural America was at that time culturally an outlying province of Britain and Europe. Even in the early stages of American history, the urban centers played an overwhelming role culturally, and, as Lampard has pointed out, from the very early times the United States had an essentially urban civilization.[2] Finally, and most importantly, the growth of American society in the 19th century took place through the settlement of new land. Urban growth was not merely a process of already existing urban centers growing larger; new cities were founded, and this was possible and necessary because of the spatial expansion of the population over previously uninhabited country. The experience of urban growth in countries like the United States, Canada, or Australia is relevant if comparisons are made with Siberia or Brazil, or perhaps even the western portions of China, but not if our concern is with India, a country which in its main outlines has maintained a fairly stable settlement pattern for hundreds and even thousands of years. Moreover, unlike American society, which fundamentally is a modern society, Indian society has roots which go back deep into its past. Though Harappa and Mohenjo Daro are irrevocably gone, we should not forget that Banaras was a principal urban center in the time of the Buddha; that Patna, a state capital in modern India, is located on the site of Pataliputra, the capital of the Magadha empire; and that Delhi, the national capital of India, was once Indraprastha, one of the legendary capitals of the Mahabharata.

Comparisons between India and the United States, whether they deal with historical or contemporary trends, must, therefore, be highly imperfect, because of the profound differences in culture and traditions of the two societies. Similar though somewhat less profound differences exist if India is contrasted with Europe. Europe had a feudal social structure not so long ago, and its society was organized along tribal lines at a time when India had seen the rise and fall of empires which embraced a large portion of the subcontinent. Moreover, in many European countries we will en-

---

[2] Eric Lampard, "Urban-Rural Conflict in the United States, 1870–1920: An Ecological Perspective on Industrialization," a paper read at the University of Michigan, May, 1959. [Mimeographed.]

counter manifold traditions which date back to a time in which most of the population lived in more or less self-contained village communities and in which the few scattered urban centers, rather than specializing in the production of finished goods and exchange with the countryside, performed mainly administrative functions for surrounding territories. As we shall see later, a wide distance separates the European and the Indian city culturally and administratively. But, in terms of social structure and even in terms of demographic developments, the countries of Europe in the 19th century are less distant from 20th-century India, and hence patterns of urbanization in 19th-century Europe are more appropriate as a yardstick of developments in modern India than corresponding data from the United States.

In Tables 2 and 3 are presented some data on the rate of urban growth in various countries during the 19th and 20th centuries. In Table 2 urban places with more than 20,000 inhabitants are

TABLE 2

POPULATION IN CITIES WITH OVER 20,000 INHABITANTS IN SELECTED COUNTRIES
(in per cent of total population)

Country	c. 1800	c. 1850	c. 1890	c. 1920	c. 1950
England and Wales.............	16.9	34.9	53.7	. . .	. . .
Scotland.....................	13.9	27.7	42.4	. . .	. . .
Ireland......................	5.9	8.7	15.3	. . .	. . .
France.......................	6.8	10.7	21.1	. . .	. . .
Belgium......................	8.7	16.6	26.0	. . .	. . .
Netherlands..................	24.5	21.6	29.4	. . .	. . .
Germany.....................	4.6	13.0	21.9	. . .	. . .
Prussia....................	6.0	7.8	23.0	. . .	. . .
Bavaria....................	3.7	6.1	15.8	. . .	. . .
Switzerland..................	1.5	5.4	13.2	. . .	. . .
Sweden......................	3.0	3.4	10.8	. . .	. . .
Denmark.....................	10.9	9.6	20.2	. . .	. . .
Norway......................	0.0	4.2	13.8	. . .	. . .
Scandinavia...............	4.1	4.9	13.8	. . .	. . .
Spain........................	9.8	9.6	18.0	. . .	. . .
Portugal.....................	10.4	10.6	8.0	. . .	. . .
Iberian peninsula............	9.9	9.8	15.5	. . .	. . .
Austria......................	4.4	4.2	12.0	. . .	. . .
Hungary.....................	2.3	4.6	10.6	. . .	. . .
Austro-Hungarian Empire.....	3.5	4.4	11.5	. . .	. . .
Russia.......................	2.4	3.6	7.2	. . .	. . .
United States.................	3.8	9.8	23.8	. . .	. . .
India........................	. . .	. . .	4.8	6.1	11.9

Sources: For countries other than India, Adna F. Weber, *The Growth of Cities in the Nineteenth Century* (New York, 1899), *passim*; for India, Bose, *op. cit.*, p. 170.

TABLE 3

INCREASE OF POPULATION IN CITIES WITH MORE THAN 100,000 INHABITANTS
(selected countries, selected periods)

Country	Factor by which population multiplied in cities of 100,000 in 1925			Factor by which city population is multiplied in period cited	
	c. 1815 (1)	c. 1870 (2)	c. 1925 (3)	Period (4)	Multiplicand (5)
England and Wales........	1.0	5.4	12.5	1800–1850	5.3
Scotland.................	1.0	3.7	6.7	. . .	. . .
Ireland..................	1.0	1.8	3.0	. . .	. . .
France...................	1.0	2.3	4.2	1850–1890	2.8
Belgium.................	1.0	2.9	7.4	1850–1890	2.3
Netherlands..............	1.0	1.7	4.8	1850–1890	3.4
Germany (frontiers of 1914)	1.0	3.0	11.8	1850–1890	6.0
Prussia.................	. . .	. . .	. . .	1850–1890	8.6
Bavaria.................	. . .	. . .	. . .	1850–1890	4.5
Switzerland..............	1.0	3.3	10.6	. . .	. . .
Scandinavia..............	1.0	2.3	8.4	. . .	. . .
Austria (frontiers of 1914)..	1.0	2.7	8.1	1850–1890	3.4
Hungary (frontiers of 1914)	1.0	1.6	4.3	1850–1890	3.2
Russia...................	. . .	. . .	. . .	1850–1890	3.2
Poland..................	1.0	2.7	14.1	. . .	. . .
United States.	. . .	. . .	. . .	1850–1890	7.0
		1901	1951		
British India.............	. . .	. . .	. . .	1890–1955	6.1
India...................	. . .	1.0	2.84	1901–1951	4.9

Sources: Columns 1–3 (for all countries except India), Helmut Haufe, *Die Bevölkerung Europas* (Berlin, 1936), pp. 225–226; columns 4–5 (for all countries except India), Weber, *op. cit., passim;* columns 1–5 (for India), *Census of India, 1951,* I, Part II-A, and International Urban Research, *The World's Metropolitan Areas* (Berkeley and Los Angeles: University of California Press, 1959), pp. 47–49, 52.

considered, since smaller towns frequently do not exhibit genuine urban characteristics in terms of social structure or even economic specialization. Though in many countries the census authorities have designated much smaller central places as "urban," it was decided to confine our comparisons to places with 20,000 inhabitants or more, in order to avoid differences arising from different definitions of "urban" and "rural," and in order to enhance the probability that only places with genuine urban features would be included.

Table 2 shows that the share of population in these effectively urban places increased in India during the sixty-year period 1891 to 1951 from 4.8 per cent to 11.9 per cent, or in round figures from almost 5 per cent to almost 12 per cent. In most European countries the rate of growth was somewhat faster. If we omit from consideration those countries which already had more than 10 per cent of their population in urban places of more than 20,000 inhabitants at the beginning of the 19th century, we find that in Germany the rate of population increase in these effectively urban centers during the fifty years from 1800 to 1850 was faster than in India, and that in Austria-Hungary the rate of population growth was about the same as in India, but took only forty years, from 1850 to 1890. Proportions of the effective urban population similar to those in India in 1890 were found in Scandinavia in 1850, and in Switzerland in 1850. In both regions the rate of urban growth was faster than in India during the last sixty years, since in Scandinavia the effectively urbanized share of the population grew to 13.8 per cent in forty years, and in Switzerland to 13.2 per cent in the same forty years. On the other hand, the rate of urban growth in Russia was approximately equal to that of India.

Considering the entire experience of European urban growth during the nineteenth century we may conclude, however, that with the exception of a few cases (e.g., Britain, Germany, Belgium and the Netherlands, and, to a lesser extent, France) India's rate of effective urbanization during the last fifty to sixty years follows, on the whole, the same pattern as that established in Europe during the period of incipient industrialization in each country. Thus, although India's urban population in the first half of this century grew at a somewhat slower rate than the urban population of Europe during most of the 19th century, the rate of urbanization in India is not abnormally slow, and is commensurate in general magnitude with European growth rates. Moreover, the speed of urban growth in India (as can be seen from column 5 of Table 1) has increased considerably in successive decades, and this pattern again repeats the experience of most European countries. Hence from the purely demographic standpoint India's progress of effective urbanization shows approximately the same characteristics as the corresponding trends in the various European countries.

In Table 3 are presented some data on urbanization in still larger urban centers, i.e., in places with populations of more than 100,000 inhabitants, which in conformance with Indian practice we will designate as "cities." Table 3 is composed of two parts; the first three columns show the rate of multiplication of population which at the end point was residing in cities of more than 100,000 inhabitants, and the last two columns show the multiplication of population resident in urban centers with more than 100,000 population at the starting and the final points of the period indicated. In other words, in the first three columns are described the growth rates of cities which ended up with populations of more than 100,000, though at earlier dates some might not have contained 100,000 inhabitants. In the last column we take the population resident at the beginning of the period in all places with more than 100,000 inhabitants and compare it with the population resident at the end of the period in all places having more than 100,000 inhabitants. (The beginning and end dates of the period are given in column 4.) On the whole, the two parts of Table 3 show a fairly high concordance; the periods selected for the last two columns of Table 3 are those which showed in each country the fastest rate of city growth as compared with other periods.

Table 3, like Table 2, shows that the demographic trend in India's large cities in the last half-century resembles rather closely that of the large cities in European countries. In the first fifty years of this century the population living in Indian cities which now have more than one lakh population almost tripled. This record compares roughly with that of Belgium, Austria, and Germany in the first half of the 19th century, and exceeds the rate of growth of population of large cities in Hungary, Ireland, and Scandinavia in the same period.

Similarly, the rate of growth of the city population in India during the 20th century does not fall behind comparable growth rates in European countries during the period of their most rapid urbanization. From the sociological standpoint this section of Table 3 is more significant than the first three columns. It shows by what factor the population resident in large cities was multiplied over a period of forty to fifty years. In other words, it shows that in the first fifty years of this century the population of India in cities of one lakh or more population increased almost fivefold, and that in the sixty-five years from 1890 to 1955 this population in the territory of the former British India increased more than sixfold. Not many European countries show such high rates of growth, though in the United States the population in cities of more than 100,000 inhabitants increased sevenfold in the forty years from 1850 to 1890 and in Prussia the rate of increase in the same period was even more than eight-and-a-half-fold.

These rates of growth are of great significance. Students of urbanization are agreed that, to the extent to which the process of modernization is mediated through urban centers, the larger cities play a more crucial role, and that, in general, the larger a city, the more important is its general mediating function in the process of social change and acculturation. To some extent, therefore, the rapidity with which a country modernizes, or at least with which psychological attitudes favorable to modernization are created, is dependent upon the growth of its cities and especially the large cities. And here the performance of India in the most recent past does not seem to lag behind analogous periods in many European countries; if we add to this, moreover, that urbanization has been increasingly rapid in the last two or three decades (a fact which emerges from Table 1) and may be expected to continue at even higher speed than in the recent past, the gradual development of a large urban sector in Indian society will constitute one of the important "environmental" preconditions for rapid modernization.

II

We may conclude that on the strictly demographic level the over-all trends of Indian urbanization in the first half of the 20th century show substantial similarities with analogous periods in the urbanization process in Europe. We now shall turn to the consideration of whether the social and economic conditions of the process of urbanization also show analogies, and what similarities and differences in the two processes may appear.

An important difference between European countries in earlier phases of economic development and India at the present is revealed by Table 4. There the approximate distribution of the labor force in eight European countries is presented at a time when the proportion of their population in urban centers with more than 20,000 inhabitants was roughly the same as that of India in 1951. Some of these countries were substantially industrialized, but other countries were chiefly producers and exporters of primary products, as shown in Table 4.

What is important to note is that at a time when the degree of urbanization was roughly the same in these countries as in India now, the share of the labor force in manufacturing was substantially larger than in India in 1951 and the share of the labor force in agriculture was substantially smaller. In more explicit terms, whereas at a roughly equivalent degree of urbanization in the European countries only a little more than half of the population derived its livelihood from agriculture, more than two thirds of the population derived their livelihood from agriculture in India in 1951; and whereas more than a quarter of the European population derived its livelihood from manufacturing, only a tenth of India's population depended upon manufacturing for its livelihood.

It is, of course, true that precise comparisons of this kind are

TABLE 4

DISTRIBUTION OF LABOR FORCE AND SHARE OF URBANIZATION
(selected countries)

Country	Year	Percentage of working force			Per cent of population in towns with over 20,000 inhabitants
		Agri-culture	Manufac-turing	Services	
Austria.............	1890	43	30	27	12.0
Ireland.............	1851	47	34	19	8.7
France..............	1856	53	29	19	c. 10.7
Norway.............	1890	55	22	23	13.8
Sweden.............	1890	62	22	16	10.8
Switzerland.........	1888	33	45	22	13.2
Portugal............	1890	65	19	16	8.0
Hungary............	1900	59	17	24	c. 10.6
Average (unweighted)....		52.1	27.3	20.6	11.0
India..............	1951	70.6	10.7	18.7	11.9

Source: Columns 1–3, Simon Kuznets, "Quantitative Aspects of the Economic Growth of Nations, II: Industrial Distribution of National Product and Labor Force," *Economic Development and Cultural Change*, V, No. 4 (July, 1957), Supplement, pp. 77, 82–90; column 4, Table 2 of this paper.

imperfect, that the classification of the labor force is somewhat arbitrary, and that the differences may be somewhat smaller than shown in the table. But the difference in the relative weight of industry and agriculture is so striking between late-19th-century Europe and mid-20th-century India that even the correction of inaccuracies in classification would not lead to a very substantial change in the picture.

Given the degree of urbanization, the countries of Europe were more industrialized than India is now. The lag in industrial development, as compared with late-19th-century Europe, is not only exhibited by the lesser degree of industrialization in India's countryside, but also in her cities. A rough composition of the urban occupational structure can be gained from the distribution of livelihood classes among which the urban population is distributed. The Indian census presents eight livelihood classes, the first four of which are designated as "agricultural classes" and include farmers, tenants, agricultural laborers, and landowners. The fifth class is composed of persons depending upon manufacturing, the sixth on commerce, the seventh on transport, and the eighth on miscellaneous services. Only 40 per cent of India's total population in livelihood

class V resides in cities, and the corresponding figures for livelihood classes VI, VII, and VIII are 60.2 per cent, 66.3 per cent,
and 50.2 per cent, respectively. In other words, the majority of
persons depending upon manufacturing live in rural areas, as do one
half of those depending upon services, two fifths of those depending upon commerce, and one third of those depending upon transport.

If we look at these data from a different standpoint, i.e., from
that of the occupational composition of the urban population, we
find that 25 per cent of this population depends upon manufacturing, 20 per cent upon commerce, 6 per cent upon transport, 35
per cent upon miscellaneous services, and the remaining 14 per cent
upon agriculture and landownership. To be sure, the proportion of
population dependent upon manufacturing increases as the size of
the city increases, but even in cities of the largest size (i.e., cities
with more than 100,000 inhabitants) only 29 per cent of the
population derives its livelihood from manufacturing, and the proportion of this class declines to 24.9 per cent in towns with population of 50,000 to 100,000 inhabitants and to 22.9 per cent in towns
with 20,000 to 50,000 inhabitants. Similar decreases of a few percentage points with declining city size can be noted in other typically
urban occupational groups, i.e., transport, commerce, and other
services. In towns with populations below 10,000 inhabitants less
than one fifth of the population depends upon manufacturing for a
livelihood and more than one third on various forms of agricultural
occupations.[3]

In contrast to this, the proportion of persons deriving their livelihood from manufacturing and mining in Germany in 1882 showed
the following numerical characteristics: in cities of more than 100,-
000 inhabitants 47.3 per cent derived its livelihood from what the
Indian census would call class V livelihood (manufacturing and
mining), in towns between 20,000 and 100,000 inhabitants this
proportion was 52.8 per cent, and in towns between 5,000 and
20,000 inhabitants it was 53.6 per cent. In other words, roughly
half the urban populations (rather than a quarter as in India)
depended upon manufacturing and mining.[4]

In brief, one of the characteristics of India's economy, as compared to that of late-19th-century Europe is its lower level of industrialization, not only in the rural areas, but also in the cities.
This means that urban growth has proceeded with a smaller relative accumulation of industrial capital in urban centers, and this in

---

[3] All data in this and the preceding paragraph are from Bose, *op. cit.*, pp. 217–218.
[4] See A. F. Weber, *The Growth of Cities in the Nineteenth Century* (New York, 1899), *passim.*

turn has the consequence that relatively fewer employment opportunities in manufacturing and related occupations become
available in urban areas for immigrants to the cities. To this should
be added that the external aspects of manufacturing in India and
in late-19th-century Europe are also different. We have no comprehensive data on the distribution of persons occupied in manufacturing in India as between plants of different size. But it is well known
that a large portion of the Indian labor force in manufacturing is
employed in the so-called "unorganized" sector, i.e., in small cottage
or handicraft-type shops, employing usually few, if any, employees
who are not members of the owner's family. Though this is true of
almost all enterprises located in rural areas and small towns, it is
also true of a large proportion of enterprises engaged in manufacturing in cities and large towns. Important reasons for the preponderance of so many small-scale enterprises are the very inefficient capital market, the absence or malfunctioning of effective
institutions for combining many small capitals into one of larger
size, and the over-all low level of saving in the community. These
factors tend, moreover, to inhibit the development of many external
economies in urban areas which are generally acknowledged to have
been important factors in the economic development of Western
countries. Moreover, the small size of many industrial firms also
prevents the exploitation of internal economies, i.e., economies of
scale of production. Thus, the comparatively low level of urban
industrialization, combined with the preponderance of many small
enterprises in industry, places impediments in the path of economic
development in India which were either absent or much less significant in comparable periods in the Western more highly developed countries.

The scarcity of capital and the small size of many industrial
enterprises is the result of yet another difference between India
and the countries of Europe during their early phase of industrialization. Both in 19th-century Europe and in present-day India a
sizable portion of the urban population is composed of migrants.
We have noted earlier the very rapid rates of growth of large
towns and cities, and it is quite clear that a multiplication of the
urban population by several times in a few decades can take place
only because constant sizable migration to the cities occurs. In
Europe, capital formation in urban areas occurred with sufficient
rapidity so that the new arrivals sooner or later could find employment in industry or associated occupations. To be sure, there were
often violent fluctuations in industrial employment due to the business cycle, and, quite apart from this, there was never a smooth
correlation between additions to the urban labor force and additions

to the urban capital stock providing employment for the new-comers. This means that during the 19th century, when European cities grew so rapidly, there were sometimes prolonged periods of excess labor supply in urban areas; but in the long run the period of European industrialization and urbanization must be regarded as one characterized by a shortage of labor—especially if it is compared with present-day India. In other words, in spite of temporary hardships and misery which new arrivals to the urban labor force may have encountered in 19th-century Europe, in the long run profitable employment opportunities opened up for them.

This, in turn, had the result of creating an open and well-functioning labor market in European cities, and also made possible a substantial degree of upward social mobility through economic achievement. In present-day India these conditions are absent in most cities, or at best present only to a very limited degree in a few. The simultaneous presence of small, cottage-type enterprises and large factories producing similar or identical commodities, but with a much lower net productivity of labor in the former, leads to great variations in earnings between the large, modern plants and the small, more primitive ones. This disrupts the labor market, and strong tendencies favoring the development of noncompeting groups make themselves felt. This development, in turn, impedes social mobility and at the same time tends to contribute to mis-allocation of resources and, often, to prolonged unemployment. A fractionalized, internally disrupted labor market exists in many Indian cities not only for unskilled or semiskilled labor, but even for more highly skilled (especially white-collar) occupations; and a portion (though by no means all) of the so-called "educated unemployment" of Indian cities is attributable to the imperfections in the mechanism of allocating human resources.

Compared with European cities during a corresponding period of economic development, the cities of India, therefore, show the following economic features: urban industry is less developed and is characterized by a larger number of small-scale and cottage-type enterprises; the urban labor force, therefore, is made up of a smaller portion of industrial workers and a larger portion of persons in miscellaneous, usually menial, unskilled services; the urban labor market is fractionalized and composed of mutually non-competing groups, thus impeding optimum allocation of resources and preventing upward social mobility and relief in the amount of unemployment. All these features make economic development more difficult in India today than was the case in Europe in the 19th century. They also are a cause for the lower level of earnings and productivity in Indian urban occupations.

Why, in view of these relative disadvantages, do urban centers, and especially the larger urban centers, grow at approximately the same pace as did the cities of Europe in the 19th century? Though part of the growth is due to the natural increase of population, we have seen that sizable migration to the cities does take place. Moreover, the bulk of cityward migrants are young males in the early ages of their active working life.[5] There is considerable discussion of whether "push" factors or "pull" factors prevail in inducing persons to move to the cities of India, and this discussion is somewhat repetitive of arguments raised in Europe in the 19th century. I believe that in both cases the proponents of the preponderance of push factors are more accurate, but the actual conditions and developments in rural areas, which tended to push the population out, are different.

The main reason for Indians leaving the villages is the high population density in agricultural regions and the smallness of the amount of land available to cultivators—in brief, the sheer excess of human resources on the land. In Europe there also developed an imbalance between human and nonhuman resources in agriculture, not because of excessive agricultural population density, but because of the rationalization of agriculture and the creation of larger-sized farms. By the end of the third quarter of the 19th century, 74 per cent of all farmland in England and Wales was in farms of 100 acres and more. At around 1890, 44.9 per cent of all agricultural land of France was in farms of that size, and in eastern Germany between 55 and 60 per cent of all agricultural land was in farms of more than 100 hectares (about 250 acres).[6] In other words, in Europe large-scale agriculture was on the rise. The small- and middle-sized grain farmers became increasingly squeezed and turned to the production of specialized crops (wine, vegetables, or fruits) or high-grade foods (meat, dairy products, eggs). This had the result of improving greatly the efficiency of agriculture, and, though the total income of small farmers and agricultural laborers did not catch up with that of urban workers and employees, the rural population did, on the whole, participate in the rising living standards resulting from economic growth. The rationalization of agriculture also caused them to participate in technical progress and the associated rise in the productivity of

---

[5] Estimates of recent migration to the large cities of India have been published in S. N. Agarwala, "A Method for Estimating Decade Internal Migration in Cities from Indian Census Data," *Indian Economic Review*, IV, No. 1 (February, 1958), 59–76; a comprehensive study of rural-urban migrations in later-19th-century Europe is found in P. Meuriot, *Les agglomérations urbaines dans l'Europe contemporaine* (Paris, 1897), pp. 309–332.

[6] See Meuriot, *op. cit.*, pp. 285–287.

labor. Thus, the agricultural sector participated fully in the fruits of the industrial revolution, although in many parts of Europe there appeared various lags and leakages in relative farm incomes. Protection was resorted to in order to overcome, at least partially, these frictions. The important point, however, is that not only was more capital applied to agriculture as economic growth progressed, but education spread to the countryside rapidly, communications were swiftly improved, the rural population became increasingly familiar with machines and their operation, and the cultural gap which divided city and country became narrowed.

In India the pressures which are operative on the cityward migrants are of a very different kind from those predominant in 19th-century Europe. Here it is not the modernization of agriculture which leads to a geographical and functional redistribution of the labor force of the country, but the sheer pressure of population—the low (and declining) man-land ratio.[7] Some idea of the contrasting pressure of human resources on land, as between European countries in the 19th century and present-day India is presented in a paper which appeared elsewhere and which shows that the countries of northern and western Europe had available roughly from 3 to 5 times as much cultivable land per farm household in the mid-19th century as is available today for each Indian farm household.[8] This means not only that the short-run effects of population growth exerted less pressure on existing agricultural resources in Europe than in India, but also that it was easier to produce and mobilize a food surplus on European farms which could be made available for the urban population. This, in turn, meant that the entire outlook of the European farmer, from the outset of rapid industrialization, could be more directly oriented toward marketing all or part of his crop, rather than producing primarily for his subsistence. Here, again, the most important aspect is not the purely economic one, but the sociocultural one. The greater degree of commercialization of agriculture produced attitudes among the farm population which made them more responsive to fluctuations in relative prices and more receptive to innovations in techniques of agricultural production. Hence European agriculture showed a much greater degree of flexibility in its re-

---

[7] The increasing population pressure on agricultural resources in India is the main theme of the Report of Shri R. A. Gopalaswami, I.C.A., the census commissioner of the last census; see *Census of India, 1951*, I, Part I-A, 138–150, and Part I-B, Appendixes I and V. For a more recent analysis see *Report on India's Food Crisis and Steps to Meet It* (Delhi, 1959), pp. 9–20, by the Agricultural Production Team of the Ford Foundation.

[8] See Bert F. Hoselitz, "Population Pressure, Industrialization and Social Mobility," *Population Studies*, XI, No. 2 (November, 1957), 126. This paper is also reprinted in Bert F. Hoselitz, *Sociological Aspects of Economic Growth* (Glencoe, Ill., 1960).

source-allocation patterns, and could therefore take part more effectively in the all-pervasive process of economic growth than can Indian agriculture, which today is so largely oriented toward subsistence production.

These conditions determine differences in the reasons for rural-urban migration in Europe and India, as well as differences in the quality of migrants. Though some European writers in the 19th century made much of the socio-cultural rural-urban differences which were presumed to prevail then, these were different from those prevailing in India today, since in over-all attitudes and values the newcomers to European cities and towns were little different from those of the urban population. In India, on the other hand, the cultural impact exerted by the city on the countryside is small, and the attitudes of a large part of Indian urbanites towards educational standards, innovation, capital formation, and entrepreneurship are little different from those of the rural population. In brief, in Europe urban cultural values tended to overwhelm and gradually eliminate those of the countryside. In India we find a small, highly urban sector with very new and modern values, and close beside it a mass of urbanites whose distance from rural culture and social structure is almost nil. It is often said that India lives in her villages. This is true not only of her rural population, but also of a large sector of her urban people.

III

These observations bring us to the third aspect of the role of the cities, their cultural and social impact. It has been shown in the preceding sections of this paper that, although the demographic patterns of urban growth in 20th-century India and in 19th-century Europe were rather similar, the underlying economic conditions accompanying this process of urbanization differed considerably. Social and cultural conditions are associated more closely with economic than with demographic changes, and for this reason it would not be surprising to find that differences between European and Indian urbanization in the sociocultural sphere also are greater than in the demographic field. One of the factors which contributes to this difference is that many of the largest and most important cities of India were foreign creations, imposed upon Indian society from the outside, rather than natural growths within the native social structure. This is not to say that Bombay, Madras, and Calcutta—and other large cities of India—are not thoroughly Indian today. But the outlook of the urban elite in these and other large centers differs from that of the rural elite and the elite in small towns. And in a country like India, where educated persons are still in a minority, the attitudes and opinions of the elite play a very important role in setting the general cultural framework for a society. The urban elite in the large centers is Westernized, has a European or at least European-style education, often uses English as a language of communication, and is far removed in attitudes and style of life from the peasants and the mass of poorer urban workers. The elite in the rural areas and in smaller towns is less removed from the common people, it speaks one of the vernacular languages, and in its religious practices, its social views, and even its ordinary daily behavior patterns is closer to the masses. To be sure, there are differences in wealth and power between the elite and the common people even in the countryside or the small towns, but the cultural and behavioral gap is narrower and in many instances completely absent. This means that the distance between the dominant ideology in Indian cities and the Indian countryside is great, and that the overcoming of this gap for the newly arrived migrants is difficult, often requiring more than a generation to be accomplished.

This has the consequence that the urban population in India is made up of several layers of differentially "urbanized" persons. In particular, there exist within the confines of large cities considerable sectors of persons who culturally—i.e., in attitudes, values, and behavior—are villagers. Some of them have come recently from a village, others may have resided in a city for some time, and still others may have been born there. Since these persons have still a village outlook, they often have not severed their ties with the village. Many of them return more or less regularly to their villages. Even though they were born in the city, some keep alive their interest in property in the village their parents came from and maintain close ties with the extended family, parts of which continue to live in the ancestral home. These groups also have not overcome the general economic outlook of villagers. They are employed as unskilled workers, and they form usually the most poorly paid sector of the population. They have unsteady and irregular employment, a large proportion of them is illiterate, and, in spite of the impact of the demonstration effect upon them, they have patterns of consumption which are little removed from those of villagers.

In Indian cities there are several intermediate groups between these completely village-like "urbanites" and the sophisticated, Westernized members of the metropolitan elites who resemble in many aspects persons in similar social positions in the great cities of the West. These intermediate groups tend to narrow the gap somewhat between the extremes. Moreover, there existed a cultural gap even in the cities of 19th-century Europe. But it was never so wide and so persistent as in India.

Next in importance to the wide gap between urban elite and rural culture in India is the great variety of particularistic groups. Indian society is notably dissected into groups whose behavior patterns, customs, occupations, and even food practices vary. Some of the lines separating these groups are the result of linguistic and tribal differences, but within the linguistic or tribal grouping there are sharp differences of caste, or jati. It is irrelevant for our purposes how this variety of small caste groups, each with its own rules and norms, has originated—i.e., whether it is the result of fission and segmentation of earlier larger groups or, as Iravati Karve argues, is the result of a process of constant addition and agglomeration of new groups. It is equally irrelevant whether this great variety of small subgroups is the result of some religious or ritual theory or is the outcome of the political heterogeneity and absence of effective political control over large areas in India's history. It is a fact that caste is important in many parts of India, especially in the rural parts; that caste is hierarchically organized; that it tends to establish barriers to free movement and free interaction; and that—in spite of official condemnation of "communalism"—caste still manifests its strength in many fields of social action.

In urban centers, largely through the impact of Western values, but partly also under the influence of economic necessity, the divisive features of caste have become greatly mitigated in many public contacts, but have been largely maintained in private, more intimate relations. Persons of different castes will work together and visit the cinema or theater together, but they will not (or only rarely and in unusual circumstances) visit each other's homes, intermarry, or form close friendships. The migrants who come to the city, and who usually leave behind a strongly caste-ridden society, come into a situation in which their caste relations are ambiguous. They soon learn, however, that in private relationships the ordinary divisions set up by caste are, on the whole, valid also in the city. In more concrete terms, neighbors, friends among whom one may visit, and persons from whom one can receive aid or counsel in adversity or difficulty are normally only persons belonging to the same caste or, at most, a related caste. Hence arrangements for living are made in which the rural settlement patterns are, in part, transferred to the city. In Europe, in contrast, caste never existed. Discrimination in the choice of living space took place there also, but a person could and did move out of certain neighborhoods if and when his economic and social position permitted. Though there is a tendency for this to happen also in India, it is usually possible only for persons in the highest social positions or with relatively great wealth, and many Indian cities, especially many of the smaller cities and medium-sized towns, are spatially comparable to agglomerations of larger and smaller villages rather than to organically interrelated population centers.

There is yet a third sociocultural difference between Europe and India, relating primarily to the cultural tradition of towns and cities. In Europe, at least in western and central Europe, towns very early became independent political bodies. In territories where the central power was weak, e.g., Italy and Germany, the degree of political autonomy of urban centers was high, but it was also in evidence in the more highly centralized monarchies of England and France. The city-state is a European invention, and the city-state was never formally stronger than in medieval Europe. Moreover, the medieval city-state, unlike the ancient city-state, did not arise out of a combination of tribes, but through contract. One of the points forcefully stressed by Max Weber, in describing the uniqueness of the European medieval city, is the fact that its origin is an usurpation of rights by burghers who formed a sworn fraternity, thus exempting themselves from the effective overlordship of some territorial ruler. To be sure, city charters often appeared as grants of a lord, who in this way saved face, but, as Weber points out, the effective instrument in the formation of the Occidental city was the *conjuratio,* the sworn contract by the citizens for purposes of joint protection and defense, even—in extreme cases—against the lord.[9] This resulted in the establishment of an independent government of the urban community which could own property and tax the citizens. It meant that some representative body of the citizens was charged with taking measures for the common defense, that this body could impose laws and ordinances, that it provided for special economic privileges of the citizens, and that it was responsible for the construction of walls and moats and streets and squares—in brief, for public works for and on behalf of the citizens.

Thus, in Europe, urban institutions developed which made for the unified rational administration of the city; city governments developed which had as their function the regulation of relations among citizens and between citizens and strangers; and authorities were constituted which were responsible for the provision of structures and other public works in the common interest of all citizens. Though this cannot be called planning in the modern sense, it was

---

[9] See Max Weber, *The City,* trans. and ed. Don Martindale and Gertrude Neuwirth (Glencoe, Ill., 1958), chap. ii.

the forerunner of modern city planning. One needs only to look at maps showing the successive extensions of city walls in medieval cities to see that these new walls were planned with the ecological pattern of the entire city in mind; that not only the economic and civic-political needs of the community, but also its recreational and aesthetic needs, were considered.[10]

India never had a tradition of urban self-government of this kind. The Indian cities always were appendages to a court or other administrative center, to a temple or other place of worship or pilgrimage, or to a colony of merchants. To be sure, many of the functions which were performed by European cities were also performed by Indian cities. Just as the preindustrial cities of Europe, so the cities of India had principally governmental or religious, educational or cultural functions, but at the same time were economic centers, i.e., nuclei of trade. Especially the cities newly founded by Europeans were markets, and the victory of the British over the Dutch and French in Bengal ultimately decided the rise of Calcutta. But, although Indian cities functionally performed a role similar to that of the preindustrial cities of Europe, they never had the political and administrative autonomy of European cities, never developed governments of their own, and never created institutions representing exclusively the civic interests of their inhabitants. Even where we have instances of city planning in India —as, for example, in Jaipur or Lucknow—the plan embraces not the city as a whole, but merely a small area around the court or a central area in which the royal palace and the main cult buildings had their site. Ecological planning of the city as a whole is a concept which first was introduced into India with the foundation of New Delhi in 1911.

Let me summarize. When we turn to the sociopolitical sphere and contrast the process of urbanization in India with that of 19th-century Europe, again we find several crucial differences. First, the cultural gap between the dominant city elite and the rural masses is even greater in India than was the case in Europe in its early stages of industrialization. This makes the adjustment problems for cityward migrants in India more difficult, but it also produces in the urban population an intermediate sector of very imperfectly committed urbanites. Secondly, Indian society is much more broken up into mutually exclusive groups than was European society. Class barriers in 19th-century Europe were high and often difficult to surmount, but caste barriers are even more nearly impervious.

---

[10] For a publication which graphically represents some planned urban growth in medieval cities see F. L. Ganshof, *Étude sur le développement des villes entre Loire et Rhin au moyen âge* (Brussels, 1943), especially the Appendix (maps).

Though in certain urban roles caste tends to lose its vigor, it maintains itself in others and hence continues to play a divisive role, fractionalizing the urban population—especially in housing and community-living aspects.[11] Thirdly, India has no tradition of urban autonomy and urban independence in administration. Such concepts as zoning or the provision of parks, open spaces, and other public amenities for community use have been absent from Indian thinking and are only now being introduced. Urban finances have, in the past, been deplorable, and urban tax receipts continue to be insufficient even for the installation and maintenance of vital services. Major public works in urban areas, to the extent to which they were undertaken at all, were the result of action not by the citizens or their representatives, but by some ruler or other powerful person who had his residence in a city or town. Indian cities, even in the very recent past, thus have not grown in any orderly fashion, but—like Indian society as depicted by Iravati Karve—by addition and agglomeration.

The result is that Indian cities—even some of the largest ones—show sizable quarters which have preserved their rural character and in which life is carried on under general conditions only little different from those of the village. This in turn is reflected in the style of life and attitudes of that part of the urban population which has not broken its ties with village life and is only partially and incompletely "urbanized." Hence the cultural impact of the "city" in the modernization process in India is exerted upon a population which is culturally and psychologically farther removed from accepting change than was the European population in the 19th century and hence under much less favorable environmental conditions than was the case in Europe. Moreover, whereas the cultural elements produced in the European city were elaborations of already indigenous culture complexes, in India many of the new cultural elements come from a foreign culture. These cultural impediments are added to other obstacles in the path to rapid economic growth in India.

IV

In the preceding sections we have attempted a comparison between urbanization in India today and the process of urban growth in the early stages of European industrialization, and have found that these two episodes show significant differences in the economic and social spheres, though the demographic picture is very similar. In

---

[11] For some examples of this see the sections on "Neighborhood Relations," and "An Indian 'Ghetto,' " in A. Bopegamage, *Delhi: A Study in Urban Sociology* (Bombay, 1957), pp. 93–109.

order to round out our analysis of Indian urbanization in a world setting it is incumbent upon us now to examine the similarities and differences that exist between Indian urbanization and this process in other developing countries. Unfortunately, a comparison between India and other developing countries must remain brief and perhaps somewhat superficial. In part this is due to limitations of the available data; even demographic data are scarce and of doubtful validity, and economic and sociocultural data are in even more imperfect state. But in part it is also due to the limitations of this writer, who must rely for comparative material primarily on second-hand and third-hand sources.

The demographic picture, as one might expect, does not differ very much in other developing countries from that of India. The African experience is still very recent; though urbanization has been rapid there, it is mostly a postwar phenomenon. In fact, some African cities have grown in the recent past at a more rapid rate than has been recorded almost anywhere else. It seems that a number of factors are responsible, chief among them the growth of political self-determination and the economic development of the region. Whether and to what extent African patterns of urban growth will ultimately resemble those of other countries, it is as yet premature to say, though some field studies have been made which seem to indicate that in the sociocultural sphere many phenomena familiar from the urbanization process of India and other Asian countries also tend to occur in Africa.[12]

In Latin America, also, the demographic trends of urban growth have been similar to those of India. In fact, cities and towns there have grown even more rapidly. In Venezuela, for example, the proportion of the population in places with more than 20,000 inhabitants was 5.3 of the country's total in 1891. By 1951 this proportion had risen to 31.3 per cent. Similar trends were observable in Mexico, Chile, Puerto Rico, and Panama.[13] In Latin America it is also the large cities which have grown most rapidly. For example, whereas in 1940 there were four metropolitan areas with more than a million inhabitants in all Latin America, and another five with 500,000 to one million inhabitants, in 1955 there were eight metropolitan areas with more than a million and another ten with 500,000 to one million inhabitants. Moreover, in 1940 there were altogether twenty cities with more than 200,000 inhabitants

[12] See the reports in International African Institute, *Social Implications of Industrialization and Urbanization in Africa South of the Sahara* (Paris, 1956).

[13] See Kingsley Davis and Ana Casis, "Urbanization in Latin America," *Milbank Memorial Fund Quarterly*, XXIV (April, 1946), 197–198. For Venezuelan data see Ministerio de Fomento, Oficina Central del Censo Nacional, *Octavo Censo de Población* (Caracas, 1954), *passim*.

in all of Latin America, whereas in 1955 this number had increased to forty-six. Their population rose from 13,423,000, or 10.8 per cent of the total population, in 1940 to 36,895,000 or 19.2 per cent of the total population, in 1955.[14] This is a very rapid increase, no matter with what other region or period we compare it.

All these data show that during World War II and the postwar period urban growth has proceeded rapidly in Latin America, and that, above all, the additions to the larger urban centers have been even greater than in India. It is interesting to consider whether in the socioeconomic field the Latin-American pattern resembles more that of 19th-century Europe or that of present-day India. In many ways the countries of Latin America are intermediate between those of Europe and those of South and East Asia. Capital is relatively scarce, but not as scarce as in Asia. Average incomes in most countries are several times above those of the countries of Asia, but (with the rather spurious exception of Venezuela) well below those of Europe. The elites of Latin-American countries are Westernized, deriving their culture from that of the Iberian peninsula. The masses in many Latin-American countries are Negroes, Indians or mestizos, many of whom are culturally far apart from the urban upper-class elites. In fact, though caste does not exist in Latin America, the cultural differences between urban elites and rural masses are as wide as those in India and the gap, though primarily one of economic and social class, is as difficult to surmount as that in the poorer countries of Asia and Africa. Some upward social mobility does exist, especially in countries like Mexico or Brazil which have shown rapid economic growth in the last few decades, but, on the whole, the cleavages in Latin-American society have remained as severe as they were upon the attainment of independence.

Evidence on the socioeconomic impact of urban places in Latin America is scanty. Some of the most perceptive work on sociocultural change in Latin-American cities has been done by Oscar Lewis, who has found, on the whole, a remarkable persistence of rural behavior patterns and attitudes among recently urbanized populations.[15] Lewis's studies have been made mostly among the lower-class urban dwellers of Mexico City. He found, among other

---

[14] Based on data presented in Davis and Casis, *op. cit.*, pp. 192–194, and International Population and Urban Research, *The World's Metropolitan Areas* (Berkeley and Los Angeles: University of California Press, 1959), pp. 43–45.

[15] See his "Urbanization without Breakdown: A Case Study," *Scientific Monthly*, LXXV, No. 1 (July, 1952), 31–41; and "The Culture of the Vecindad in Mexico City: Two Case Studies," *Actas del III Congreso Internacional de Americanistas* (San José, Costa Rica, 1959), I, 387–402.

things, that peasants who had recently arrived in Mexico City maintained and, if anything, strengthened the extended family ties they had before; religious life became more disciplinary and all pervasive, and their religious outlook, contrary to the preconceived ideas of some urban sociologists, did not become more secular; the use of village remedies and beliefs persisted, and the system of *compadrazgo* remained strong; above all, these recent migrants tended to settle in so-called *vecindades* which tended to become small, socially more or less self-contained communities within the city, enhancing cohesive and personalized ties among their members. Lifetime friendships were established within the *vecindad*, and the daily face-to-face relationships resembled those of a village situation. Most marriages occurred within a *colonia* (a group of neighboring and related *vecindades*), and most members of *vecindad* were related by either kinship or *compadrazgo* ties.

This picture, which has been underlined by Joseph A. Kahl (who also found similar sociocultural relations among recent immigrants and, indeed, large portions of the poorer inhabitants of African cities), seems to indicate that culturally the cities of Latin America have close resemblances with those of India, and that Lewis may not be far wrong when he speaks of a "culture of poverty," i.e., a generalized pattern of sociocultural relations typical of peasants and poor urbanites in the developing countries of Asia, Africa, and Latin America.[16]

Finally, we may ask whether the urbanization process in Latin America (and other developing countries) is associated with economic features similar to those of India. We have seen earlier that the main economic problems arising in Indian urbanization are partly a result of the low degree of industrialization in both urban and rural areas, combined with a dense agricultural population and with a scarcity of capital, which moreover becomes available often only in small, fractionalized amounts. The economic environment in which urbanization in Latin America has proceeded has in part been different. Indigenous capital also is not abundant and, as in India, investment in agricultural land or urban real estate or even in commerce is preferred, as compared with investment in industry. But population pressure on agricultural resources is less severe than in India, and relatively larger amounts of private foreign capital —mostly in the extractive industries, but during the last few years increasingly in manufacturing—have become available. Much of

---

[16] See J. A. Kahl, "Some Social Concomitants of Industrialization and Urbanization: A Research Review," *Human Organisation*, XVIII, No. 2 (Summer, 1959), 53–74; also the works by Oscar Lewis cited in note 15.

this capital has come from the United States.[17] Thus, the scale of operations of modernized industry is relatively larger in Latin-American cities than in India. Though many handicrafts and small industries continue to exist, their output frequently is not competitive with that of the modern, more highly mechanized factories; even though small and large plants may be found in the same industry, the output of each tends to find a market among different social or local groups. To be sure, we witness also serious imperfections in the labor markets of Latin-American cities; we find many aspects of labor-management relations there which are also encountered in India—e.g., a sharp division between blue-collar and white-collar occupations, or a high degree of paternalism on the part of the employers; and we find relatively labor-intensive methods of industrial production.[18] But, whereas the relative backwardness of urban industry in Latin America is the result of the imperfect and partial adoption of a modern technology imposed upon a population which still lacks many of the skills and educational endowments required for its efficient operation, the relative backwardness of urban industry in India is primarily an outflow of the general conditions under which Indian industry functions. Some of the causes for the industrial backwardness of India are the same as those in Latin America, but in addition the very different resource endowment and the structure of capital and industrial investment resulting from it are superimposed in India (and also other countries of South Asia) to compound the impediments in the path of rapid economic development.

Summarizing this very sketchy overview of the comparative role of the urban impact in various developing regions of the world, we may conclude that developments in sub-Saharan Africa are as yet unclear and difficult to predict, but are likely to show—in the realm of social adjustments—some of the features now encountered in India. Latin America appears to be in an intermediate position between India (and other South Asian countries) on the one hand and the advanced European countries on the other. Demographic patterns of urbanization showing an early rapid growth which gradually slows down appear to parallel one another in all regions, with the European and other advanced countries being in a decidedly later phase of the urban growth process than Latin

[17] See Research Center in Economic Development and Cultural Change, *United States Business and Labor in Latin America* (a study prepared at the request of the Committee on Foreign Relations, U.S. Senate, 86th Congress, 2nd Session [Washington, 1960]), pp. 9–35, especially pp. 28–33.
[18] See, for example, United Nations, Department of Economic Affairs, *Labour Productivity of the Cotton Textile Industry in Five Latin-American Countries* (New York, 1951), *passim,* but especially pp. 6–10, 13–16.

America, Africa, or Asia. In social relations the differences between the advanced countries and the underdeveloped countries appear greatest, perhaps because the cultural complex of industrialism is indigenous with western and central Europe and is a foreign importation into the underdeveloped countries. The economic function and impact of cities in various parts of the world appears to be greatly modified by the general resource endowment of the various nations. In densely populated Asia, where demographic pressures are higher than elsewhere in the world, the relatively low ratio between nonhuman and human resources creates conditions of poverty which prevent the full impact of urban centers from exerting itself sharply. In Latin America, where the ratio between resources and population is more favorable, urban centers provide more of the amenities and external economies for a well-functioning industry, although the level of skill and education of the human resources in these countries is yet inadequate to make full use of the opportunities created by the urban environment. It appears, therefore, that the model to be followed by urban developments in India is not the pattern established by the United States, Europe, or Latin America. Rather, India must work out her own solutions in the framework of her own sociocultural and economic conditions. Perhaps the history of urban growth in China and Japan may provide some more useful guidelines for India than the experience of Western countries. But it would go far beyond the limitations of this paper and the knowledge of this writer to attempt to substantiate this suggestion in greater detail.

URBANIZATION AND
THE LONG-RANGE STRATEGY
OF ECONOMIC DEVELOPMENT

Pitambar Pant

Urbanization is an important aspect of the process of economic and social change in India, and its future role can be studied best with reference to the long-range strategy of development. The long-range strategy has the objective of securing a progressive rise in the level of consumption per capita by methods which will make possible an indefinite continuance of the process, and which will also satisfy certain political and social ends, such as liberty and reduced inequality. Increased capital formation, industrialization, and urbanization are the means and necessary conditions of achieving the desired objective.

This rise in consumption can of course be secured only by a large and continuous rise in production. For an underdeveloped country with widespread underemployment, low productivity, and a rapidly growing population the obvious requirement for securing a large rise in output is more capital. So that the average worker may have more and better equipment with which to work, better sources of power and energy and better facilities of transport are required for larger outputs (and larger consumption later on). There is scope for raising output by introducing better methods (for example, in agriculture) and by more intensive use of existing capital (for example, in certain manufacturing industries), but, essentially, progress will depend on the willingness of the community to divert an adequate part of each year's flow of income from immediate consumption to capital formation.

Obviously, there are difficulties in stepping up the rate of investment when incomes are as low in relation to subsistence requirements as they are for the vast masses of people in India. A balance has to be struck between the contending consideration of larger current consumption and still larger consumption in the future. Further, the rate of investment has to be built up progressively to a permanently high level which will be considered satisfactory for the optimum growth of the economy. There has been progress in this regard during the last ten years of planning in India: net investment has been raised from about 5 per cent of national income in 1950 to about 11 per cent in 1960, with 8 per cent financed out of domestic savings. The Third Plan envisages this rate to be stepped up to above 14 per cent by 1965, with more than 11 per cent domestically financed, and to about 16 to 17 per cent by 1970, almost wholly financed out of domestic savings. With this level of domestic savings, a steady increase of national income of the order of 5 to 6 per cent per year may be realizable.

A sustained increase of income of at least 5 per cent a year together with a much higher level of investment will imply a very large increase in the use of machinery, steel and cement, fertilizers and chemicals, power and fuel, transport, etc. Owing to the small size of the domestic capital-goods and intermediate-goods industry, this implies either a very large expansion in exports or a large increase of import substitution, or both. A close study of the export prospects highlights the difficulty of expanding exports, in spite of the best efforts, to anything like the level of increased imports in the absence of timely measures to replace imports by domestic production. In the initial period, however, when the foundation is being laid for a strong capital-goods and intermediate-goods industry in India, the country has inevitably to face a serious balance-of-payments problem, and progress is dependent on the availability of sufficient foreign loans to meet the gap.

The program for agricultural production is of overwhelming importance in the present phase of Indian economic development. It has to meet the requirements of food and fibre, which account for nearly two thirds of the total consumer expenditure, for a growing population having increasing income—apart from contributing to a modest increase in exports. Deficiency in output in this sector cannot be made good by increased output of manufacture, either by way of diverting demand or through increased exports. The rate of rise of food production, in effect, determines the maximum rate of rise of national income which is compatible with a satisfactory balance of payments, within the framework of a policy which seeks to prevent inflationary increases in prices of food grains and to avoid rationing or imposing additional taxes on low incomes.

From the maximum rate of increase of per capita income derived in relation to the maximum rate of growth of agricultural production considered technically and organizationally feasible, it is possible to project the demand for final goods and services by consumers at the end of a given period. To this have to be added the output for exports, and the goods and services for use by government and for investment. The estimates of demand of final products thus obtained provide the basis for working out the demand for intermediate goods, and the raw materials which are required in the process, by making use of appropriate economic-technical coefficients supplied by studies of interindustry relations. Some of these items, which could not be domestically supplied in view of domestic cost and resource availability, would have to be imported. Finally, the computed total output for separate industries and sectors of development are checked against the amounts of related investments and the figures of employment. The process has to be repeated several times to get a consistent and reasonably balanced picture. There has to be balance "within the productive system" between the supplies of various materials, intermediate products, essential services (for example, power and transport), and trained personnel and the requirements of using industries and sectors; between supplies of different goods and services and the demand for them at higher levels of income; between savings of the community and investment in the economy. From a very rough sketch to begin with, the exercise can be improved and elaborated at successive stages by bringing in more careful analysis, better information, and the more intimate association of a large number of experts.

We may now present very briefly the results of some speculative thinking about the course of economic development in India during the next twenty years. The purpose is to put together some crucial magnitudes in order to evaluate in quantitative terms some problems the growing economy may have to face which have special reference to urbanization.

The population of India is estimated at 430 million in 1961 and about 620 million in 1981, the annual increase being at the rate of 2.1 per cent at the beginning of the period and 1.4 per cent by the end.[1] For simplification, a constant growth rate of 1.8 per cent has been assumed for the entire period. On a realistic appraisal of

---

[1] On assumption of fertility declining linearly by 50 per cent, 1966–81, A. J. Coale and E. M. Hoover, *Population Growth and Economic Development in Low Income Countries* (Princeton, N.J.: Princeton University Press, 1958), Appendix A, Table A 9.

possibilities, it seems likely that agricultural production may be increased over the twenty-year period at a rate of 4 per cent a year, the rate being somewhat faster at the beginning and slower toward the end. The index of net output of agriculture will be 220 and of food grains 200 in 1981, as compared to 100 in 1961. Corresponding to this rate of growth of food grains production, the balanced rate of growth of national income per capita may be calculated as 3.5 per cent, assuming an average income elasticity of demand for food grains as 0.5 over the period.[2] These results are summarized in Table 1.

TABLE 1

SELECTED INDICES OF A GROWTH MODEL, INDIA, 1961–1981

Indices	1961	1981	Average annual increase, 1961–1981
Population in millions....................	430	620	1.8
Index of net output of agriculture...........	100	220	4.0
National income at 1960 prices (Rs., billions)..	140	392	5.3
Per capita income at 1960 prices (Rs.).......	326	630	3.5
Index of nonagricultural output.............	100	335	6.3

The rate of growth of national income is 5.3 per cent per year, and the estimated growth of income and of investment over the twenty years, 1961–1981, are given in Table 2.

Starting from the figure of a national income of Rs. 140 billion in 1961, the income has been estimated after intervals of five years on the assumption of 5.3 per cent rise per year. Net investment as

TABLE 2

GROWTH OF NATIONAL INCOME AND NET INVESTMENT, 1961–1981
(At 1960 prices)

Indices	1961	1966	1971	1976	1981
National income (Rs., billions)...............	140	180	235	304	392
Net investment as per cent of national income..	11	14	16	17	18
Net investment (Rs., billions)...............	15	25	39	52	70
Net investment during each Five-Year Plan period....................................	100	160	230	310	...

[2] This assumes that the natural demand for food grains will not be restrained by physical controls, or by increase of relative prices of food grains or increased taxation of the poor.

per cent of national income is the same as assumed in the Third Plan for 1961 and 1966. For subsequent years the rates correspond to projections given in the Second Plan. The over-all net investment for the twenty years may be put roundly at Rs. 800 billion.

The allocation of this investment for 1961–1981 may follow the following pattern (in billions of rupees, 1961 prices) :

	Rs., billions
Mining and manufacturing		320
Mining, including oil exploration and production	35	
Electric power	65	
Metallurgy	65	
Production and transport equipment . . .	60	
Chemical fertilizers	12	
Cement	5	
Sugar	8	
All others	70	
including small-scale production . . .	25	
Transport and communications		130
Agriculture and rural development		110
Irrigation and land improvement	65	
Other agriculture, forestry, fishing, animal husbandry and dairying, and ancillary industries	25	
Rural housing, water supply and civic amenities (monetized)	20	
Urban housing and municipal services		150
Education, health, culture, and recreation		50
Others—services, trade, etc.		40
Total		800

Table 3 gives an idea of the volume of production in 1961 and 1966 (as outlined in the Third Plan) and in 1981 corresponding to the preceding scheme of investment.

Progress in agriculture will call for a large expansion in area under irrigation (from 70 million acres in 1961 to 200 million acres in 1981), extensive use of chemical fertilizers (production of 5 million tons of N in 1981 is designed to meet the requirements of all areas and crops), land improvement and addition to net sown area, better implements and machinery and better techniques and organization. All of these are taken into account in the scheme of investment. With these facilities production may increase as envisaged, but the migration to urban areas will not be checked.

TABLE 3

TARGET OF PRODUCTION OF KEY INDUSTRIES, 1961, 1966, AND 1981

Industry	Unit	1960–61 anticipated	1966 planned	1981
Electricity.............	billion K.W.H.	21.0	42.0	200
Crude-oil refining.......	million tons	4.6	9.0	40
Coal.................	million tons	53.0	97.0	320
Steel ingots...........	million tons	3.5	10.0	42
Aluminum.............	thousand tons	17.0	75.0	320
Cement..............	million tons	8.8	13.0	40
Fertilizers (in terms of nitrogen, N).........	thousand tons	210.0	1,000.0	5,000
Production and transport equipment...........	Rs., billions	3.0	7.5	35
Cotton textiles (incl. hand loom)..........	billion meters	6.6	8.5	20
Sugar (refined)........	million tons	2.3	3.5	10

From the point of view of labor required for agriculture, the somewhat larger area brought under cultivation, the wider practice of double cropping, and the more intensive operations should give fuller employment to cultivators and agricultural laborers—and may even absorb some increase in their number. Because of the widespread underemployment among the agricultural laborers, who are also the poorest, there is little scope for addition to their existing number, and the bulk of the natural increase in this class may be expected to move into non-farm occupations in rural areas or migrate to urban areas. A similar tendency, but less pronounced, may be observed among the cultivator class. The non-farm rural population may be expected to grow because of the large expansion in rural activity—in transport, construction, crafts, and services. Urban population has been estimated to have been increasing at about 4 per cent per year for some years past, the transfer from rural areas accounting for half of this increase. This trend is likely to continue. Table 4 gives a rough idea of the distribution of population underlying the assumptions of the present model.

The average income in the agricultural sector is about half of that in the rest of the economy. Increase in productivity per person in agriculture should be not less than in nonagricultural occupations if this ratio is not to become even more unfavorable to the agriculturists. The nonagricultural population (urban and non-farm) is shown in Table 4 to increase from 155 million to 295 million in twenty years, which is an annual increase of 3.3 per cent. Non-

TABLE 4

DISTRIBUTION OF ESTIMATED POPULATION, RURAL AND URBAN, 1961 AND 1981

Distribution	Estimated percentage distribution*		Estimated population, 1961 (millions)	Average annual rate of increase	Estimated population in 1981 (millions)	Increase in 20 years, 1961–81 (millions)
	1951	1961				
Rural						
Non-farm.....	16	15	65	2.0	95	30
Cultivators ...	44	42	180	1.0	220	40
Laborers......	23	22	95	0.5	105	10
	83	79	340	1.1	420	80
Urban..........	17	21	90	4.0	200	110
Total........	100	100	430	1.8	620	190

* Percentage for 1951 from Coale and Hoover, *op. cit.*, Table 21.

agricultural income has been estimated to rise by 6.3 per cent per year (Table 1), which gives a per capita rise of 3.0 per cent. For the same order of productivity rise in agriculture, the cultivator population should not increase by more than 1 per cent. As a result, there may be an increase in the population of urban centers (of population 5,000 and more) by 110 million and of rural areas by 80 million. Even this large increase in urban population will change the proportion of urban population only from about 21 per cent in 1961 to slightly over 32 per cent in 1981.

It is estimated that at least 38 million new jobs will be required to absorb this increased population in urban areas. The investment scheme is designed to create job opportunities as shown in Table 5.

TABLE 5

DISTRIBUTION OF INCREASE IN URBAN WORKING POPULATION, 1961–1981

Expected addition to working population in:	Millions of persons	Per cent of increase
Mining and manufacture.............	13	34
including small scale industries......	5	16
Construction......................	4	10
Transport and communication........	3	8
Trade and commerce................	7	18
Services..........................	11	30
Total........................	38	100

It has been estimated that the cost of housing per person in urban areas, not counting the cost of land,[3] is about Rs. 1,600. The different elements of cost are divided broadly as follows: site development, 16 per cent; community facilities (including educational, health, and cultural facilities), 9 per cent; cost of dwelling unit, 75 per cent. The area of dwelling unit has been worked on the basis of one hundred square feet of floor space per person, and the average size of an urban household is assumed as 4.6 persons. The cost of construction is taken as Rs. 12 per square foot, two thirds of which is building cost, with the rest including the cost of water supply and electricity installation, external services, etc.[4] Assuming that about one half of the total provision of Rs. 90 billion in the investment allocation under the items "Education, health, culture, and recreation" and "Others" is available for expanding community facilities in the urban areas, the total amount available for urban housing and community facilities will be Rs. 195 billion,[5] which should meet the housing requirements of the additional population of 110 millions and leave about Rs. 10 billion to alleviate overcrowding and to bring about some measure of improvement in urban facilities. As for improvement in rural housing and water supply, sanitation, drainage, and civic amenities, the provision of Rs. 20 billion (under "agriculture and rural development") will go toward meeting the cost of construction materials and hired labor and is exclusive of the contribution of the village communities by way of self-labor. It is estimated that this amount should be adequate to meet the requirements of modest housing arising out of the increase of 80 million in the rural population. It may also be noted that a part of the increase in urban population is due simply to a change of classification when the population of a rural center rises above 5,000. To this extent the provision of "urban" housing serves the purpose of bringing about a steady improvement in housing condition of erstwhile villages.

In view of the low standard of housing in general and the severe overcrowding in urban areas, even a larger program of housing could be justified. Resources for it, however, must be mobilized in a manner which will not divert unduly the amount of resources needed to maintain continuing growth in other sectors of the economy and for providing fuller and better employment to the

---

[3] The average cost of land per person housed in urban areas is about Rs. 350. For the economy as a whole, the cost of land is not included in net investment shown in Table 3.

[4] Cost figures are drawn from a paper on "Housing and Urban Services: Status, Standards, Costs" contributed by Edward G. Echeverria to the Seminar on Urbanization in India [not included in this volume—Ed.].

[5] See investment allocation, p. 186.

growing population. A stepping-up in the rate of investment may be considered, but there are serious limits on grounds of both political and physical feasibility. Utmost importance, therefore, attaches to devising methods of low-cost urbanization. The task has to be approached from several directions. There is urgent need for evolving a positive urban land policy which will provide for the control of land value and use and for the speedy acquisition of land at low prices. Specifications and standards should be critically reviewed and new ones formulated which will be more economical and more in consonance with the requirements of the situation. Every encouragement should be given to the use of local building materials and the manufacture of new materials which will reduce the cost of construction. Scientific research should be directed to finding new materials, new designs, and new ways of construction, and there must be adequate arrangements to bridge the gap between the results of laboratory research and their application in the field. Ways and means will also have to be found to direct investment in housing and urban development in such a way as to serve the real need of the community, so that, when the priority is for the construction of houses for the masses, the limited investment does not find undue outlet in luxury construction and expensive overheads.

The long-run strategy of planned economic development should not be limited to a phasing of investment and production over time, but should also take into account the locational aspects of development. A positive approach is necessary to foster agriculture and industry, power and transport, and distribution and density of urban centres in a spatial pattern so as to achieve the optimum results in relation to the social and economic goals of the society. By way of illustration, Table 3 gives an indication of the order of magnitude of production in selected key industries during the next two decades. Further studies can provide clues as to the likely size of the plants and their location for a much larger number of industries. This tentative exercise would suggest new considerations and reveal new relationships, each successive round bringing fresh insight into the problem. Thus will be brought together the multifarious aspects of development in a balanced temporal and spatial pattern. As new facts are disclosed, new methods are developed and new resources are discovered; as horizons expand, the design of development will also undergo a change.

The over-all strategy of economic development has to draw support and sustenance from regional studies of resources and possibilities; it must in turn give direction and balance to regional planning and reveal the impact of one development on many related aspects. In the absence of such studies covering the entire field, it would not be possible to guide development rationally, avoid costly mistakes, and anticipate future contingencies wisely and constructively. Problems of this type require close and concrete consideration and need continuous attention.

X

URBANIZATION, POLITICAL STABILITY, AND ECONOMIC GROWTH

Shanti Tangri

Sociologists and economists have in general tended to agree about the mutually beneficent influence of urbanization and economic development. The argument runs in terms of economies of population aggregation and value transformations conducive to economizing, enterprising, and innovative behavior. Generalizations in this field are based largely on the historical experience of Western developed economies.[1]

I have argued elsewhere that urbanization is neither a necessary nor a sufficient condition for economic growth.[2] Under certain conditions, however, and up to a point, it can be a desirable condition for growth, while under other conditions, or beyond a certain point, it can be a factor in slowing down growth. In contemporary India the process of urbanization, in both magnitude and nature, seems to be a factor retarding rather than accelerating growth.

Here I do not propose to review the highly important but well-

---

[1] For a brief (and unsympathetic) review of non-Weberian theories of the city see Don Martindale and Gertrude Neuwirth's Prefatory Remarks (pp. 9–62) in their translation of *The City*, by Max Weber (Glencoe, Ill.: Free Press, 1958). For a more limited and relevant discussion see William L. Kolb, "The Social Structure and Functions of Cities," *Economic Development and Cultural Change*, III, No. 1 (October, 1954), 30–46.

[2] "Patterns of Investment and Rates of Growth, with Special Reference to India" (Doctoral dissertation, University of California, Berkeley, 1960). For a historical criticism of the "industrialization through urbanization" thesis see Carl Bridenbaugh, *Cities in the Wilderness* (New York: Ronald Press, 1938), and *Cities in Revolt* (New York: Knopf, 1955).

discussed issues of social overhead capital, economies of scale for industrial plants and cities as a whole, external economies, consumer densities, pools of labor, skills and knowledge, centers of communication and innovation, etc.[3] My contention is rather that we cannot determine the role of urbanization without estimating the economic costs or benefits of such urban phenomena as *anomie,* political and ideological ferment, and transformation of cultural and social values. For drawing policy conclusions we need also to know comparable costs and benefits associated with social change among rural populations. I have been unable to find comparative studies of this nature. Reviewing the literature on social and economic change leads me to believe, however, that the socio-economic costs of tradition-oriented rural attitudes, though never measured, are usually assumed to be prohibitive enough to make growth extremely slow, if not impossible, while similar costs of urbanization are seldom considered to be high enough to prevent or retard change. Indeed, this is what the historical experience of Western societies seems to indicate.[4] That perhaps is not and will not be the case in India and some other underdeveloped countries. As the benefits of urbanization have been discussed extensively in the literature, I will discuss primarily the other side of the case. In this context a few words about the relative rural-urban potential for economic development are in order.

THE RURAL-URBAN POTENTIAL FOR ASSET FORMATION

In the cities, the savings of entrepreneurial and managerial classes tend to be high, and those of middle and lower classes to be low or negative, because of low incomes and/or higher consumption standards and lower earner-dependent ratios in families. Thus, while the proportion invested out of industrial incomes tends to be relatively high, compared to investments out of agricultural income,[5] it is not clear how the total urban savings-income ratio compares on a per capita basis with the rural savings-income ratio.

[3] See, for example, Eric Lampard, "The History of Cities in Economically Advanced Areas," *Economic Development and Cultural Change,* III, No. 1 (October, 1954), 81–136.

[4] *Ibid.,* p. 132.

[5] P. N. Rosenstein-Rodan thinks the former ratio is often as high as 35 per cent and the latter between 10 and 15 per cent. (This and other references to him are based on personal conversations and a seminar he gave at the Massachusetts Institute of Technology in the spring of 1959.) Wilfred Malenbaum derives the figure 10 per cent for the latter ratio from sample data on India; cf. *The Non-Monetized Sector of Rural India* (Cambridge, Mass.: Center for International Studies, M.I.T., 1956), p. 11. He thinks the figure may be a slight overestimate. Some economists think the figure is much lower. For an argument that most estimates of rural capital formation are downward biased see Basil S. Yamey, and Peter T. Bauer, *Economics of Underdeveloped Countries* (Chicago: University of Chicago Press, 1957), pp. 16–31.

Lack of empirical information precludes judgment on the relative rural-urban potential for asset formation out of internal savings.

However, the possibilities of asset creation without prior or concomitant savings are quite extensive and impressive in rural areas[6] and insignificant in urban areas. In the villages people often cooperate to help each other in building houses or fences, or in other acts requiring group effort; not so in the cities, where exchange of labor is monetized and thus involves problems of financing. Again, in the villages there are unused resources—such as common village lands, forests, tanks, wells, ponds, labor, and skills which can be used for asset creation given an appropriate program of mobilization. A villager repairs his own home more readily than a city dweller. Also there is a lesser expectation, on the part of an idle villager, as compared to an urbanite, of finding alternative sources of income, whether the relative expectations of the urbanite and villager are justified or not by the realities of job markets.[7] Thus, lower opportunity costs of the villager make it easier for him to donate his labor to his neighbor or to his community. Finally, many materials and assets which the villager has use for are not desired by the urbanite. The villager can dig up clay and lime and bring palm leaves from the outskirts of the village and husks from his fields, to thatch his roof or plaster his walls or add a room to his house. The urbanite will live in a crowded brick hovel rather than in a thatched mud house. He may not be able to afford a new brick house, but a mud house is not an asset in his eyes—and if it were, the municipal authorities would probably not tolerate, much less encourage, its construction.

The deepening, cleaning, and lining of village tanks and wells as sources of water supply for humans and animals and for irrigation and the construction of warehouses for storing agricultural produce—a vital step for stabilizing agricultural prices and increasing output, for preventing significant losses in food supplies, and for freeing the cultivator from the usurious controls of money-

---

[6] Yamey and Bauer, *op. cit.* A detailed analysis of the rural-urban potential for capital formation in the underdeveloped countries is given in my "Patterns of Investment and Rates of Growth . . ."

[7] Whether people are pushed or pulled to towns, one can argue that economic opportunities in towns must be better than in villages, that potential migrants must believe them to be so, and that in the long run their perception must be validated by experience, otherwise the flow of population would cease or reverse itself. If this reasoning is correct, differentials in reality and perceptions of reality by villagers about relative opportunities become irrelevant for long-run population flows. This reasoning assumes that migration can be based on "irrational" considerations only in the short run. In fact, only a small minority of the migrants need realize their expectations in order for the myth to survive that opportunities in the city are greater than in the country—in other words, people's irrational behavior in regard to spatial mobility can persist even in the long run.

lenders—involve the use of local labor, materials, skills, and organization. Constructing schools, clinics, and community centers, digging ditches and canals and building roads, terracing, bunding, and hedging fields, planting suitable trees on fallow land, controling soil and wind erosion, and developing village ponds as sources of fish supplies: these also are dependent on similar uses of labor and skills.

In addition, the potentialities of increased agricultural output resulting from better practices and marketing, and the consolidation of holdings, net of expenses of innovation, seem impressive.[8] Addition of new facilities, such as brickkilns, multiplies this potential several times, brickmaking being one of the simplest and least expensive operations, ideally suited for local production, distribution, and use in most communities.[9]

In ten years of planned development India has not come anywhere near to exploiting this potential fully, and this in spite of the demonstration by Communist China of its powerful role in the initial phases of development.[10]

THE COST OF THEOLOGIES AND IDEOLOGIES

Around the theory of indivisibilities, ably propounded by Professors Rosenstein-Rodan, Nurkse, and others, has grown an almost mystical complex of belief with many variations.[11] Crudely put, it amounts to this: in underdeveloped countries you have got to have a "big push" if you want to generate self-sustaining growth (enough to outstrip population growth). The big push is then related to big projects and the most up-to-date technology.

All of these ideas have some validity. But political beliefs and historical associations have taken this discussion partly from the realm of theory and reality into that of dogma. Many Marxists are for this way of thinking because it fits the Russian model. Some ardent nationalists are for it because other theories seem to stress rural and agricultural development, a thing which the British rulers used to stress.

---

[8] See, for example, Albert Mayer, McKim Marriott, and Richard L. Park, *Pilot Project, India: The Story of Rural Development at Etawah, Uttar Pradesh* (Berkeley and Los Angeles: University of California Press, 1958), pp. 233–287.

[9] *Kurukshretra: A Symposium on Community Development in India, 1952–1955* (New Delhi: Community Projects Administration, 1955), pp. 298–308. The facts reported here are also cited in Mayer *et al., Pilot Project, India*, pp. 272–278.

[10] Wilfred Malenbaum, "India and China: Contrasts in Development Performance," *American Economic Review*, XLXI, No. 3 (June, 1959), esp. pp. 305–307. See also Durdin Tillman, "Red China Plans Vast Irrigation," New York *Times*, November 3, 1958, and other similar reports in the *Times*.

[11] For a brief review of these theories see Benjamin H. Higgins, *Economic Development, Principles, Problems and Policies* (New York: Norton, 1959), pp. 384–408.

Rightly or wrongly, to many this British attitude was an indication of Britain's desire to keep India a nonindustrial, raw-material-supplying colony. To some, like Pandit Nehru, the big dams are "temples of a new faith" in India.[12] To others, steel mills are the crux of economic development. To yet others, steel mills and shipyards are the symbols of national power and autonomy. Psychological symbols and national power may legitimately compete with economic goals. Steel mills, unlike shipyards, are perhaps economically justified in India. The point, however, is this: if economic criteria indicate that a network of rural feeder roads is more productive for the economy than an airline, or fertilizer factories are more remunerative than steel mills, it needs to be explicitly stated that the choosing of steel mills and airlines involves the adoption of other criteria. Indeed, the commitment of the bulk of the nation's resources to construction of dams and irrigation systems with long gestation periods is not easy to justify on economic grounds, when the urgent problems of food, shelter, and clothing can be solved much more quickly with simple technologies, less capital, and more labor.[13]

The example of big dams illustrates that gigantomania is not always biased toward urbanization. However, due to the correlations between economic development, industrialization, and urbanization which most people carry in their minds, it tends to favor urbanization and industrialization, particularly capital-using industrialization at the cost of labor-using, agricultural, and industrial development. It results in inefficient use of resources for the "short run" (which may extend to fifteen or twenty or more years) in exchange for added but more uncertainly anticipated benefits in the "long run." In an economy like that of India, when high interest rates of 40 or 50 per cent per annum,[14] reflecting the scarcity of

---

[12] Takashi Oka, "Dam in India Looms as 'Temple of Faith,'" *Christian Science Monitor*, January 28, 1958.

[13] If it is assumed that both the production of more consumers' goods and the labor-intensive mode of production for consumers' as well as capital goods will only stimulate population expansion and not raise per capita incomes, and that population growth cannot be checked otherwise, then a "capital-intensive" investment program may be the only economically feasible program for development. Cf. Walter Galenson and Harvey Liebenstein, "Investment Criteria, Productivity and Economic Development," *Quarterly Journal of Economics*, LXIX, No. 3 (August, 1955), 343–370. As I have argued elsewhere (see note 2), such a program is not politically feasible in a democracy. It amounts to controlling population growth by starving a section of the people (the unemployed) or spreading consumption goods more thinly over an expanding population, thus keeping general mortality rates high. Even in Communist Poland such a program was overthrown by the people, and only terror and purges enabled Stalin to carry it through in the Soviet Union.

[14] Rates of interest as high as 5 or 6 per cent per month have been reported to the author by several people in villages and traditional sections of old cities.

capital (and not the artificially controlled low rates of interest, such as 3 or 4 per cent in the imperfect capital market), are used to discount the flow of future outputs, it is not at all clear that such long-run investments are always more productive, even in the long run, than a series of short-run, quick-maturing, and quickly depreciating investments.

I am not aware of any published information which attempts to justify long-run projects in India on such economic grounds. When people are so wedded to their theories that they apply them without even trying to test them, wasteful allocation of resources is likely to occur—and the theories take on the character of theologies. Thus, very often the zeal for setting up the most modern factories and transportation systems increases the real costs of industrialization and urbanization.

Another important reason for the increased expensiveness of urbanization in India is the modern and egalitarian ideology of public welfare. England in the 18th and 19th centuries could ignore the social costs of slums, unsanitary conditions, and fire hazards to a greater extent than can India in the 20th century.

Because of bad sanitation, Josiah Strong believed, there were 156,600 "unnecessary" deaths in U.S. cities in 1890.[15] Today, public health measures are introduced first in the cities. The resulting population growth, with overcrowding of housing, schools, hospitals, and transport systems, and shortages of food and other necessities, is a well-known story. Thus are being built the pressures, the strains, and the tensions which may lead to political turmoil or to an authoritarian regime. And hence, as Rostow has stated, the responsibility of the "non-Communist literate elites in . . . transitional societies [to] ensure that the humane decision to save lives does not lead to an inhumane society." [16]

This welfare philosophy is affecting villages also. Describing wastages of cement and steel in one Indian village, René Dumont wrote, "Even European villages do not yet possess all these amenities. India has tried to become a welfare state before creating the basic economy required to sustain it. Comfort has been given priority over production."[17] But this priority of comfort over production becomes operative first in the cities and then radiates out.

Most experts expect housing conditions to get worse in the urban

---

[15] *The Twentieth Century City* (New York: Baker and Taylor, 1898), p. 58.

[16] W. W. Rostow, *The Stages of Economic Growth: A Non-Communist Manifesto* (Cambridge: Cambridge University Press, 1960), p. 144.

[17] "Agricultural Defeat in India," *New Statesman and Nation*, LVIII, No. 1501 (December 19, 1959), 871.

areas of the underdeveloped areas in the coming decade or two.[18] This certainly appears to be the prospect in India.[19] As congestion and slums grow, the need to spend more on urban areas to provide for public health services and social amenities will also increase. The amenities are more expensive because of higher standards expected by urbanites. And if, in addition, a city has already exceeded the population mark of 400,000–500,000, which Rosenstein-Rodan considers optimal from the point of view of social overhead capital, per unit costs of social services may rise rapidly. The number of cities in excess of this size is likely to increase very rapidly in the coming decades in India, thus making urbanization an increasingly expensive process.

If many of the economic, social, and political troubles of the developed economies flow from the fact that ideology lags behind technology, the troubles of the underdeveloped areas become more acute because ideology outruns technology.

ECONOMIC FRUSTRATIONS: UNEMPLOYMENT, UNDEREMPLOYMENT, AND MISEMPLOYMENT

In spite of all the deficiencies in the available employment statistics,[20] it is evident that the trend of growing unemployment in India is not likely to reverse itself in the near future. Urban unemployment accounts for perhaps half of the total. In the larger cities, Malenbaum points out, of all the employed 51.8 per cent were literate and only 3 per cent had any college education, while of the unemployed 78.4 per cent were literate and 5.1 per cent had college education. Some 46 per cent of all the educated unemployed are concentrated in the four major cities of India.[21]

The interval between completion of education and first employment is often quite long. "Thus, while some 50 per cent of the illiterate unemployed have been out of work for at least a year, 75 per cent of the matriculates and intermediates are in this category." [22] Majumdar's study of a large sample of alumni of Lucknow University holding Master's degrees indicates that the more highly educated are unemployed longer. Of the unemployed

---

[18] See, for example, Burnham Kelley (ed.), *Housing and Economic Development* (Cambridge, Mass.: Massachusetts Institute of Technology, 1955).

[19] Pitambar Pant's confident optimism about the housing situation is based on minimal average-cost estimates for the Third and Fourth Plans, far below those actually achieved in the first two Plans.

[20] For a review of these see K. N. Raj, "Employment and Unemployment in the Indian Economy: Problems of Classification, Measurement and Policy," *Economic Development and Cultural Change*, VII, No. 3, Part I (April, 1959), 258–278.

[21] Wilfred Malenbaum, "Urban Unemployment in India," *Pacific Affairs*, XXX, No. 2 (June, 1957), 138–150.

[22] *Ibid.*, p. 146.

in this sample, 44 per cent had been unemployed for over two years, 18 per cent for a year and a half, and 27 per cent for a year. A somewhat similar pattern emerges from a sample survey conducted by the Delhi Employment Exchange.[23]

Corresponding to underemployment and seasonal or disguised unemployment in the villages, there is considerable disguised unemployment and/or misemployment in the cities, as reflected in the rapid growth of the low-productivity service sector in which unskilled, uneducated workers, and especially the transients, seek means to subsist. Among the educated in the Majumdar sample, "about three-quarters of those who sought service in a firm and a substantial majority of those who sought service in government or sought a profession of their own failed to achieve it." Economic frustration can only be high in such situations. None of the 237 who answered Majumdar's question as to the factors responsible for difficulty in getting a job blamed it on their own shortcomings. While only about 12 per cent blamed it on bad luck, the rest blamed society in one way or another, to wit: "government," 48 per cent; "society," 13 per cent; "lack of proper and systematic training," 26 per cent—which usually meant lack of opportunities for these.

If the educated unemployed provide leadership, these transients, whom Hoselitz calls the *lumpen proletariat,* provide the raw material for mobs. Political parties, trade unions, business and religious groups, displaced landlords, and princes willing to provide ideological, financial, and organizational resources for making effective use of these two groups are not scarce in the cities.

Rapidly increasing enrollments in colleges and schools, and demographic and economic trends, are likely to swell the ranks of both of these groups in the coming decade. This *lumpen intelligentsia,* as Lewis Feuer calls it, with little skill, opportunity, or capital for entrepreneurship in economic activity, turns to political entrepreneurship where, with less capital, training, and skills, a man can manage to exist, if not get ahead. Moreover, opportunity costs in economic enterprise are higher than in political enterprise. Social values, historical associations, and ideological fashions make economic enterprise a less and political a more desired activity as a means to status and power.

Physical densities, communication, and other facilities make political organization relatively easier in cities. Groups with re-

[23] For the Lucknow sample see D. N. Majumdar, *Unemployment Among the University Educated: A Pilot Inquiry in India* (Cambridge, Mass.: Center for International Studies, Massachusetts Institute of Technology, 1957). For the Delhi survey see Motilal Gupta, "Problems of Unemployment in India" (Doctoral dissertation, Netherlands School of Economics, Rotterdam, privately published, 1955), p. 43.

sources and tightly knit organizations, like the Communists or the Rashtriya Swayam-Sewak Sangh (R.S.S.) are at a relative advantage in such situations. Part of the success of Communists in Kerala and Bengal, two of the most densely populated areas in India, may be due to this reason.[24] The R.S.S. similarly is, by and large, an urban lower-middle-class movement. Psychological densities—intense interchange of ideas, rumors, and stimulations in crowded situations—are conducive to demagoguery and crowd formations. Speakers and audiences tend to stimulate each other into states of irresponsibility and frenzy in situations of crowding and anonymity which are more easily obtained in cities than in villages. Extremist groups with less scruples and more resources stand to gain from situations in which crowds can be turned into mobs.

NONECONOMIC FRUSTRATIONS: SEX, SPORTS, RECREATION, AND THE ARTS

Education, urban environment, increasing interregional and international contacts, and foreign and native motion-pictures are either widening the gap between the old and new generations, or promoting a double standard of morality among many. Students and some illiterates watch Hollywood movies—the former partly and the latter mainly—for their sex appeal. And these very people often turn around to criticize American society, as depicted in these movies, as lewd, materialistic, and corrupt, while describing their frustrating cultural framework as spiritualistic and pure. There is less segregation of the sexes in big cities, particularly among students. But economic insecurity and intellectual fashion, by preventing early marriages, are choking off the traditionally accepted avenues for sex gratification, while extramarital sex gratification is severely limited because of strong social mores, joint family living, overcrowded housing and the consequent lack of privacy, and relative immobility of most people (due to the lack of money, motorcars, "metros," and motels). Strong cultural sanctions also operate against prostitution among the educated middle classes. Sexual frustration in this group is, thus, quite high. In addition, there are neither sufficient opportunities to participate in sports nor to attend sports spectacles where, on weekends, like their American counterparts, they may work off their steam by yelling some team to victory. There are few opportunities for youth to develop and display its talents in the theater, literature, or other forms of creative life—the market for art being limited. Rowdy politics be-

---

[24] Benjamin Higgins explains the success of the Communist party in the crowded sections of Indonesia partly on the same grounds.

comes a channel for youth's repressed exuberance. For many it is an inexpensive substitute activity, and for some an attractive avenue to social climbing and psychic satisfaction. The dictatorships of Russia, Nazi Germany and Latin America have well demonstrated their understanding of the role of sports and stadia in politics. Even in an affluent democracy like America, one wonders to what extent the political apathy of college students may be attributable to the existence of vast opportunities for economic, artistic, romantic, and extracurricular satisfactions. In the contemporary Indian urban context, political apathy is conducive and activism is detrimental to political stability. Unless there is a change in the nature of this activism, or in economic trends, the politics of irresponsibility are likely to increase in the cities.

Sources and Patterns of Extremism

Cities either give birth to political and other leaders or draw them there. A major consequence of Western education has been the growth of nationalist and culturally revivalist, as well as socialist and Communist, ideologies.[25] A conservative-liberal coalition is in power in India, but liberalism has as yet not taken deep roots there. It is from the villages that the ruling Congress party derives its support. In the cities it has been losing steadily. Calcutta, though not quite typical of other cities, may yet turn out to be the model of political sickness likely to spread in other cities.

Revolutions, Brinton has remarked, leave behind both a uniting tradition and a memory of successful revolt.[26] The process of winning independence developed self-confidence in the common man and it trained cadres of politically active workers. Students participated more heavily than perhaps any other group in the revolutionary struggles. Theirs were the highest aspirations—theirs also the deepest disappointments—and theirs the strongest and most emotive reactions. Education, youth, and unemployment produce explosive mixtures.

A political party in India, Weiner has pointed out, is often an alternative social structure vis-à-vis the traditional family.[27] Some bolt from the discipline, frustration, and pettiness of the joint family wedded to the past to take sanctuary in the discipline, dedi-

---

[25] For the Indian case see Bruce T. McCully, *English Education and the Origins of Indian Nationalism* (New York: Columbia University Press, 1940).

[26] Crane Brinton, *The Anatomy of Revolution* (New York: Vintage Books, 1957), pp. 262–264.

[27] Myron Weiner, *Party Politics in India: The Development of a Multi-Party System* (Princeton, N.J.: Princeton University Press, 1957), p. 8. He treats this theme at length in "Politics of Westernization in India," (Institute of East Asiatic Studies, University of California, Berkeley, April, 1957). [Mimeographed.]

cation, and intrigues of the political party devoted to the future. Purposelessness of life is transformed into a cause and an overriding loyalty that makes many young persons sacrifice health, money, and other careers. The more demanding the discipline of a party, the greater the dedication of its members. Again, in India, dedication and self-sacrifice, per se, as Singer has noted, are time-honored traditions.[28] Thus, the same person will often respect and admire a liberal humanist like Nehru, a conservative reformer like Gandhi, a fascist like Subhash Bose, and a rightist revolutionist like Savarkar. This ethos of dedication, though quite useful for maintaining political unity around charismatic symbols like Nehru and Gandhi, is dangerous for democracy. Fanaticism can grow more easily and nondemocratic charismatic symbols can replace the present ones, in this psychological climate. The tradition has not lost ground in the cities. If anything, it has been intensified by two puritanic movements—Gandhism and Marxism. The saving grace of the villager is his belief in many gods—often warring gods. Through the centuries he has learned to pray to them and yet live without them. Divergences of professed and practiced faith do not generate serious anxieties. But the urbanite is a monotheist, and a true believer. His rationalism leads him to a passion for consistency, and in the context of limited knowledge, poor education, poverty and insecurity, and an atmosphere of superstition, this often leads to intolerance. Educated, urban middle classes provide most of the political leadership, including that of the Communist party.[29] The strongholds of Muslim fanaticism before the creation of Pakistan were in educational centers like Aligarh, Dacca, Lahore, Calcutta, Karachi, Peshawar, and Rawalpindi. Hindu conservatives and reactionaries have derived large numbers of their leaders and workers from Delhi, Nagpur, Poona, Lahore, and Benares. The chances are that in India, if dictatorship comes, it will be of the Left. Left radicalism appeals more to the science-worshiping mind of youth. It also offers a more complete and intellectually satisfying credo. It has international support as well as internationalist ideology. The first yields tremendous organizational advantages, while the second appeals to urban cosmopolitanism.

The ruling party has a reservoir of material resources in its business supporters, but it lacks youthful manpower. The socialists have manpower, but lack material resources. The rightists get their financial backing from feudal social classes which are on the way

---

[28] Milton, Singer, "Cultural Values in India's Economic Development," *The Annals of the American Academy of Political and Social Science*, CCCV (May, 1956), 81–91.

[29] Gene D. Overstreet, and Marshall Windmiller, *Communism in India* (Berkeley and Los Angeles: University of California Press, 1959), pp. 357–364.

out. Only the Communists have access to both youthful manpower and finances in ample and increasing quantities. The budget of the Communist party in one state alone is reported to be larger than that of the Praja Socialist party for the entire country. Moreover, the Communist credo has "worked" elsewhere. Communist countries are developing rapidly. To the man in a hurry to change the world, communism seems the wave to ride.

Few young men seek political activity in the ranks of the party in power. To defend the *status quo* is not heroic, especially when there are unemployment, poverty, crime, waste, inequalities, and corruption all around. Besides, the party in power has a fairly well-established hierarchy with large numbers of older people, wherein social climbing is more difficult, while opposition groups have use for any man—trained or untrained. There is more room for expansion of the party machinery—hence more opportunities for status or power within the party structure, and, if one has faith enough in the rightness of one's cause, in society at a later date. Communists, in general, are in a better position to absorb newcomers. Well integrated, well financed, with a ready-made ideology tailored to all levels of comprehension, they have a well-designed program for action, so that each new entrant finds plenty to be busy with. The newcomers work like missionaries for a cause and a judgment day. Their internal and external supporters give finances in a big and religious way. Living in a democracy, they are free to organize and operate. When their irresponsible actions are repressed, they acquire a halo of martyrdom. This adds another dimension of romance and adventure to oppositional politics, which thrives in an atmosphere where jailgoing has acquired social prestige.

Whether urban educated youth goes Right or Left,[30] it is not likely to be the standard-bearer of liberal democracy if social and economic conditions continue to worsen. It is perhaps the lower middle class in the cities, unskilled and semieducated, culturally conservative or confused, and politically adrift, whose politics are the most volatile. This floating population in the political arena makes it easier for opportunistic (as well as idealistic) politicians to resign from and reënter political parties, and to reshuffle political alliances with a staggering and confusing frequency. A kind of unrestrained laissez-faire politics prevails. Individuals as well as parties seek to maximize their political gain with little regard to rules and

[30] For the view that the collapse of democracy would lead, initially, to the emergence of a Rightist or military rather than a Communist dictatorship in India see M. F. Millikan and W. W. Rostow, "Foreign Aid: Next Phase," *Foreign Affairs*, April, 1958, pp. 418–436. For the opposite view see Taya Zinkin, "India and Military Dictatorship," *Pacific Affairs*, XXX, No. 1 (March, 1959), 89–91.

principles essential for the maintenance and growth of a responsible representative political system.[31]

Cities also reveal patterns of mutative extremism. After the death of S. P. Mukerji, the leader of the rightist Jana Sangha, his parliamentary seat was captured by a Communist. Aligarh University, which was a hotbed of rightist Muslim politics, became a center of Communist activity after the creation of Pakistan.[32] Egalitarian, populist, and welfare-state ideas are shared by most, it not all, political parties. Emotive issues, like language or corruption, unite radicals of the Right and the Left against all moderates. All kinds of opportunistic alliances between all kinds of political groups take place all the time, but the spiritual and psychological affinity of what Hoffer calls the "True Believers"[33]—the fanatics of all faiths, political and otherwise—makes the actual or potential union of Right and Left radicals more dangerous. As the power of the ruling party declines and as youth becomes increasingly disillusioned with the *status quo,* the liberals and moderates are likely to lose. It may be that the old administrative, religious, and cultural cities like Delhi, Banaras, and Ajmer will move to the Right and industrial-commercial cities like Calcutta, Madras, and Bombay to the Left. Where responsible and strong trade-unions take root, as in Bombay, socialists rather than Communists may gain by this shift. But if unemployment and living conditions continue to worsen, the greatest gains will ultimately be for the extremists.

In such conditions even the villages are likely to go over to extremist politics—but perhaps with a time lag. The swastika may appeal to the peasant and the hammer and sickle to the intellectual,

---

[31] For a description of such politics see S. L. Polai (ed.), *National Politics and 1957 Elections in India* (New Delhi: Metropolitan Book Company, 1957), esp. pp. 12–15; also, Margaret W. Fisher and Joan V. Bondurant, *The Indian Experience with Democratic Elections* (Indian Press Digest, No. 3 [Berkeley: University of California, December, 1956]), pp. 69 ff. For Pakistan see K. S. Newman, "Pakistan's Preventive Autocracy and Its Causes," *Pacific Affairs,* XXXII, No. 1 (March, 1959), 18–33.

[32] For the Calcutta by-election see Polai (ed.), *op. cit.,* p. 157. The social, historical, and political causes for this political mutation of Leftist into Rightist extremism, and vice versa, differ from situation to situation. For the Italian case see, for example, "Party-Ocracy versus Democracy: An Exchange Between Ignazio Silone and J. K. Galbraith," *Radical Humanist,* XXII, No. 45 (November 9, 1958), 527–528 and 531.

The psychological factors that make this mutation possible are, however, fairly constant. See Eric Hoffer, *The True Believer: Thoughts on the Nature of Mass Movements* (New York: Harper, 1951) and *The Passionate State of Mind* (New York: Harper, 1955), and Brinton, *op. cit.;* also, T. W. Adorno *et al., The Authoritarian Personality* (New York: Harper, 1950), and A. H. Maslow, "The Authoritarian Character Structure," *Journal of Social Psychology,* XVIII, 2nd half (November, 1943), 401–411.

[33] In his book of that title, previously cited.

but their transmutation or alliance is not inconceivable—and if it comes it will, like plague and cholera, come from the cities.

INTELLECTUALS AND SLUMS

Growing slums, worsening sanitary conditions, lowering living standards, and unemployment concentrate misery visibly, not in inaccessible villages, but in areas which are the habitat of writers, social reformers, artists, poets, teachers, religious preachers, humane societies, dreamers, city planners, sociologists, journalists, and economists. They arouse the concern and the ire of these and other socially sensitive and articulate individuals and groups. Some of their protest—especially when it comes from professional groups— helps rectify some evils, such as graft, inefficiency, and waste. But, by and large, it merely adds to feelings of dissatisfaction with the *status quo.* Believing that they are bystanders, not participants, in processes of social change, many intellectuals become angry men— young and old. Their anger, in turn, leads only to callousness on the part of authorities, who dismiss their criticism as "destructive." A vicious circle of irresponsible and angry criticisms on both sides is thus initiated.

A society in a perpetual state of anger is not a stable society.

TRANSIENTS AND *Anomie*

Because of housing shortages, low incomes, transportation costs, and other factors, immigrants from rural areas are primarily males. In the four biggest cities, 60 per cent of the population is male as compared to 51.4 per cent for India as a whole.[34]

This ratio is even higher among working classes and migrants. Gambling, racing, dope peddling, prostitution, and cult religiosity tend to spread in rapidly growing cities. The result is a demoralized, unhealthy, pitiful mass which, unlike an industrial reserve army, Hoselitz asserts, is not easy to convert into a disciplined factory work-force.[35] It is true, as Knowles points out, that these people can be converted into an effective labor force if fed and trained properly.[36] But it is easier to turn them into a riotous mob; it needs less training and discipline, and the demand for this alternative is fairly high and frequent in the cities.

---

[34] Malenbaum, "Urban Unemployment in India." The number of women per thousand men is as follows: Calcutta, 602; Bombay, 569; Ahmedabad, 764; Kanpur, 699. See also Bert F. Hoselitz, "The City, the Factory, and Economic Growth," *American Economic Review*, XLV, No. 2 (May, 1955), 178–179.

[35] *Ibid.*

[36] William H. Knowles, "Discussion on 'Urbanization and Industrialization of the Labor Force in a Developing Economy,'" *American Economic Review*, XLV, No. 2 (May, 1955), 188–190.

Opportunity costs of political rioting are very low for these marginal people. Crowded housing or, more commonly, lack of any housing whatsoever (one quarter of Bombay's population sleeps on the streets) makes physical access to them very easy. They are eager to talk about their troubles. Political workers find the uprooted urban "rice-roots" receptive to their ideas and leadership. The Communists often have the most convincing explanations for all the troubles of these unfortunates, even though at times, as among the refugees from Pakistan, the rightists manage to get a foothold.

There are no estimates of the total economic costs of social disorganization that arise in such contexts. Juvenile delinquency, drunkenness, murder, theft, and robbery involve increased costs, including those for police and justice administrations and for institutions for the detention, reform, and rehabilitation of convicts. Some sketchy information available for three rural-urban districts in Bombay State indicates that over-all crime rates and their economic costs are much higher in the cities.[37]

Besides, political demonstrations and rioting dislocate traffic, trade, and production and result in loss of property and sometimes even of life. No cost estimates for these are available. The greater frequency and magnitude of these in the cities suggests that these costs are higher there.

WORKERS AND ENTREPRENEURS

Per capita output and income are generally higher in cities than in villages. This is, however, largely a result of the higher per capita investment and the associated modern technology in cities. Effects of urban environment, per se, as distinct from those of more investment or superior technology, on labor morale, productivity per man-hour, hours of work, quality of work, and mobility of the labor force need to be ascertained. It is not inconceivable that the proportion of time lost due to strikes (many for noneconomic reasons) increases while the pace of work slows down—at least in the very big cities where relatively more workers are unionized. Unions in India, being largely controlled by political workers from outside their ranks, can and often do use labor for organizing

[37] See, for example, *Annual Police Administration Report of the State of Bombay, Including Railways for the Year 1957* (Bombay: Government of Bombay, Police Department, 1959), pp. 96–101, 160–171.

Several limitations of the data, as published, do not permit a more definite conclusion, or an exact statement of comparative costs. Available data for 1925 indicate that drunkenness is increasing and social maladjustment is more rife in industrial cities. See B. S. Haikerwal, *Economic and Social Aspects of Crime in India* (London: Allen & Unwin, 1934), p. 46. Haikerwal, however, is inconsistent about his feelings regarding the relative incidence of crime in cities and villages; see, e.g., pp. 12, 48.

strikes, protest marches, and demonstrations for furthering their political ends. Language riots in Bombay are a case in point.[38] Husain's study of industrial location in East Pakistan indicates that social disorganization is minimal and workers' morale is maximal where workers are not torn away from their rural habitat.[39] In this respect trade unions can play an important role in reducing rather than aggravating costs of urbanization. By providing a new sense of community and a web of social relationships and activities, they can integrate immigrants into new meaningful and satisfying life-patterns and help build their morale. The responsibility of the unions is high, because in Indian cities there are few secondary social organizations or religious institutions which can create a sense of belongingness corresponding to that provided by the growth of sects like Methodism and Presbyterianism during the Industrial Revolution in England.[40] There are no such significant movements for creating a new social milieu for immigrants in place of the one they left behind. The operation of caste panchayats in cities to some extent prevents the alienation of the worker from his traditional society. In the years to come, however, the strength of this institution is likely to diminish.[41] And to the extent it does not diminish, city society will merely duplicate village society on a large scale. Cities then become collections of villages. The argument for urbanization as a vehicle for value transformations conducive to industrialization then disappears.

Cities, by concentrating the labor force in relatively small areas, and by making possible the organization of labor, are creating conditions in which the clash of labor and entrepreneurial interests becomes more well-defined. Unions are already exercising an influence on governmental policies much greater than is warranted by the size of their membership.

The consequent upward pressure on wages and consumption may

---

[38] For the crucial role of unions in precipitating such disturbances in the autumn of 1956 see Marshall Windmiller, "The Politics of States Reorganization in India: The Case of Bombay," *Far Eastern Survey*, XXV, No. 9 (September, 1956), 129–144.

[39] A. F. A. Husain, *Human and Social Impact of Technological Change in Pakistan* (Dacca: Oxford University Press, 1956). This study contradicts the contrary view expressed by Hoselitz, *op. cit.*, pp. 181–184.

[40] On the role of religion in both resisting and aiding social change, and that of Protestant sects in reintegrating communities disrupted by rapid industrialization and urbanization see W. Arthur Lewis, *The Theory of Economic Growth* (Homewood, Ill.; Richard D. Irwin, Inc., 1955), pp. 101–107.

[41] The role of caste in economic development is the subject matter of much writing which is excellently reviewed by Morris Davis Morris in "Caste and the Evolution of the Industrial Workforce in India," *Proceedings of the American Philosophical Society*, CIV, No. 2 (April, 1960), 124–133; also, see his "The Recruitment of an Industrial Labor Force in India, with British and American Comparisons," *Comparative Studies in Society and History*, II, No. 3 (April, 1960), 305–328.

not be a bar to increased investment, if such wage increases result in equal or larger productivity increases. The relation of wages to productivity in India, however, has not been empirically explored. Again, if entrepreneurial consumption can be kept in check, it will be somewhat easier to restrain workers' consumption. In practice, it has not been easy to restrain the consumption of either group.

Successful measures to keep both wages and profits—or, strictly, the share of wages and profits that goes into consumption—from rising would necessitate greater regulation of both groups by government, entailing more political, economic, and social controls, more administrative personnel, and increased costs. It would also necessitate a greater capacity for public agencies to fulfill roles of entrepreneurship if private enterprise should become discouraged as a result of such measures. How far the new educated groups, pouring out of colleges and universities with largely a nontechnical and half-baked education and with a tradition of averseness to economic enterprise and initiative, will make better managers, directors, and planners of enterprises under public rather than private control is yet an open question.

EXPOSURE EFFECTS: SOCIOLOGICAL, ECONOMIC, AND POLITICAL

Cities are being integrated into a growing network in and outside the country more rapidly than villages. With rapidly increasing contacts between different groups, tensions are mounting. Patterns of in-migration tend to heighten the tensions associated with regionalism in India.

Increased intergroup contacts are raising the levels of aspiration, without increasing levels of achievement. Consequently, the sense of *absolute deprivation* is increasing among urbanites. Closer contact with upper classes and their modes of living increases the sense of *relative deprivation*. At the same time, urban political and social ideologies are sensitizing the norms whereby people evaluate "social injustice," thus increasing the intensity of resentment and hostility. English commoners may derive satisfactions from the luxuries that their Queen enjoys—as Samuelson suggests[42]—but commoners in India are becoming averse to such "vicarious consumption" in proportion to the degree of their urbanization. Indian motion-pictures and literature, platforms of political parties and political speeches, and the sermons of preachers and social reformers often reflect as well as stimulate this emergent social ethos. The

---

[42] Paul A. Samuelson, "The Dilemmas of Housing," in Kelley (ed.), *Housing and Economic Development*, p. 35.

darshana-seeking villager loses his sense of awe and respect for political and other heroes and elites as he observes them from closer quarters and imbibes urban egalitarian ideas. As the erstwhile demigods look more human to him, their actions appear more inhuman. Both the numbers of malcontents and the intensity of discontent increase.

Patterns and levels of consumption also change as a result of exposure or demonstration effects. Lower expenditures on food within some income groups, and a substitution of refined-processed foods and sugar for more nutritious foods, have implications for the health and productivity of urbanites. But the changed pattern, particularly among middle- and upper-income groups, also involves more use of luxuries and foreign goods. Thus, there is the flow of scarce resources away from socially useful expenditure into the manufacturing of luxuries, and also a drain on foreign exchange. Levels of consumption also tend to rise, affecting the volume of internal savings available for capital formation.

Successful revolts in some countries raise the morale of revolutionists in others. The revolution of communications transmits knowledge as well as social unrest across oceans.

SLOWING DOWN THE DYNAMO

W. Arthur Lewis has said,

Towns tend to be prominent in organizing most political movements, whether their aim is greater freedom or less, if only because government is usually done from cities to which the politically ambitious are attracted. . . . Town is the home of the mob, and mobs are as prone to sweep tyrants into power, who reduce the opportunities for economic freedom, as they are to take part in liberating movements. The town is also the home of monopolists—the traders' associations, the guilds, the workers' combinations—whose aim is to restrict opportunities and to keep out new men. The town takes the lead in movements for reducing the amount of work done, and for working sullenly or resentfully. . . . If therefore a case can be made for saying that towns lead out of stagnation into growth, as good a case can be made for saying they lead out of growth into stagnation.[43]

In India, towns are not likely to lead into stagnation, but they can lead into slower economic growth and political instability, because of the diversion of resources from more to less productive investments. Urban populations have more access to, and influence on, political processes. As conditions worsen, towns are likely to demand and get progressively larger proportions of the national pie at the cost of the countryside.

---

[43] *Op. cit.,* pp. 150–151.

As the international economy developed, disparities of income grew between the rich and the poor nations, in the past century or so. Now, as the Indian economy develops, disparities are likely to grow between the village and the city. But what worked politically in the 19th-century world of colonial powers is hardly likely to work in the egalitarian 20th century. This trend can be reversed by appropriate allocations and actions for development of the countryside. There is little reason to believe that the rural exodus would continue if economic and social opportunities for advancement were expanding rapidly enough in the villages. In the Majumdar study, out of 327 respondents, 35 per cent were rural in origin. Of these, 35 per cent were willing to return to their villages after the completion of their studies. The other 65 per cent, who were unwilling to do so, were largely motivated by economic considerations. When the entire group of former students from rural areas was asked whether they were willing to return to villages if given a job similar to the one they held, 61 per cent said yes. Of the rest, 63 per cent again gave an economic reason for their answer—they expected chances for their economic advancement to be better in the cities.[44] If a majority of these highly educated (they all had Master's degrees), "westernized," urbanized Indians of rural origin were willing to return to the villages, given proper opportunities there, it is not unreasonable to assume that unskilled and tradition-oriented migrants can be persuaded to return with as much, if not greater, ease under similar conditions. And it should certainly be easier for those who are still in the villages to keep on living there.

Economic measures for correcting the pace and nature of urbanization can be supplemented by an ideological campaign, especially, because the village still has a romantic, emotional, political, or philosophical attraction for many, even among the intelligentsia and other groups of urban origins. There is no reason to believe that many idealistic and educated men will not choose to work in villages if they are assured that it is not the end of the road for their careers.

CONCLUSION

There are more opportunities for making a person a participant in economic planning and development in rural than in urban areas. This, by itself, reduces political disaffection. Also, in villages there is a greater level of tolerance for the old and familiar problems of unemployment and poverty. By exporting these problems to cities, political instability is increased. There are many avenues for sig-

---

[44] Majumdar, *op. cit.,* pp. 33–34.

nificant increases in agricultural and rural industrial output. There are greater opportunities for capital formation with the use of idle labor and other resources in villages. The levels and patterns of consumption unfavorable to economic growth can be prevented from emerging with less difficulty in rural than in urban areas.

Higher direct and indirect costs of social disorganization, welfare ideologies, and overhead capital in cities are reducing the flow of output obtainable from investment of available resources—some of which, like labor, are going to waste partly because of a pattern of development which is urban-oriented. If these trends continue, political discontent will grow in the cities, and if public discontent fails to change governmental policies peacefully, streets may become the arbiters of political destiny. But the problem cannot be solved by expanding employment only or largely in urban areas. The employment elasticity of urbanization may be greater than one—every new job in the city is likely to attract more than one person from the country, thus worsening the problems and tensions in cities.

Increased sports, circuses, sex, spectacles, festivals, cultural shows, and demonstrations of military prowess can provide some substitute satisfactions and distractions to discontented youth. But the real effective solvent of tensions is rapidly expanding social and economic opportunity for advancement through orderly processes, in rural as well as in urban areas. The former have progressively lost their human and material capital to the latter. This flow can and needs to be reversed for the benefit of both. Communist China is doing it by coercive measures.[45] India has to do it by economic inducement and persuasion.

Meanwhile the great march of men from the backwoods to the metropolises continues at an ever accelerating pace. The new frontier—albeit a dangerous one—is not the wilderness with its promise of freedom, gold, or virgin lands, but the skyscraper with its promise of food and shelter.

Unlike the promise of the wilderness, the promise of this frontier may turn out to be an illusion. Like the countless who fell by the wayside or collapsed after reaching the streets of Calcutta in the Bengal famine of 1942, many more are likely to discover that escaping from the stagnation of the village does not necessarily mean salvation in the city slum.

Development patterns which cannot slow down this explosive and skewed growth of cities (big ones growing faster than the

---

[45] Gordon Walker, "Old Chinese Socialism Tested," *Christian Science Monitor*, February 8, 1958.

others) will involve a great wastage of human resources. "A social order is stable," Hoffer has said, "so long as it can give scope to talent and youth. Youth itself is a talent—a perishable talent." [46] This is one resource which if not utilized for development is likely to become political lava in a country where the social fabric of democracy is still very inflammable.

[46] *The Passionate State of Mind*, p. 20.

XI

CENTRALIZATION AND THE ALTERNATE FORMS OF DECENTRALIZATION: A KEY ISSUE

Sachin Chaudhuri

History seems to have assigned to the Indian people the unique task of translating a fundamental unity which is cultural and spiritual into a workable proposition of government and administration. This is not a problem that could be solved once and for all by drawing up a constitution or a national economic program. The integration of India neither begins nor ends with the framing of the constitution; the attempt has to be renewed every day as various interests clash and collide. It has been asked and it is likely to be asked more insistently in the next few years: will India hold together? Some have read in the political scene signs that India is falling apart. Why India? Everyone is falling apart —some effort has continuously to be made to hold oneself together. In this process of integration the issue of centralization versus decentralization crops up again and again—in matters of administration, economic planning, education, and so on, as also in day-to-day politics.

The conflict between centralization and alternative forms of decentralization is at the moment a very real issue in India. It appears at different levels of government and in widely separated spheres—the amount of autonomy to be allowed to the management of industrial enterprises in the public sector; the degree of freedom which the state governments should have in planning development in their own states, and how to reconcile state projects with the priorities of an all-India plan; the extent to which rural development programs should be handled by villagers themselves. The issue of decentralization of political power inherent in these conflicts merges with the basic economic issue of removing regional disparities. One aspect of this is the posing of the problem as a choice between two different patterns of economic development, one village-based and the other urban-centered. Presented thus, it is neither a key issue nor a real one. It is only to the extent that there is scope for choice that one must ask if such choices are key issues. The nostalgic, sylvan, village-based-culture arguments for decentralization do not stand up to either Indian history or modern development. The balance between industrial growth and urban development, the postulates of equality between rural and urban standards of living, and the costs and benefits of regional dispersal of industries—these are the elements that make decentralization a real but still undecided issue.

There is a great deal of ambivalence in the Indian attitude to urbanization which is derived from Indian experience of the British days. It is not true that Indian civilization was primarily rural. The cities of old performed their "orthogenetic function" of converting folk culture into its civilized dimension. If we leave out the very early period, the relics of which have disappeared, and come to the times of the Buddha, we read about many cities which are already the meeting place of various cultures and influences and also centers for the transmission of such influences. In the most flourishing periods, we find that city life was well developed; and university towns had acquired such world-wide reputation as to attract scholars and monks from distant China and South Asia.

Among close students of the Upanishads, there are some who believe that philosophical speculation of such a high order would be possible only in an urban setting, where material progress had already attained a high standard. The interaction of minds which releases thought from its fixed molds was a constant and recurring reality. True enough, then as now, the bulk of the people lived in villages; some of the villages developed into centers of learning, others acquired fame for their various crafts. But the transmittal points of culture, political authority, and economic influences, through which passed traders, pilgrims, and scholars wandering in search of knowledge, must have been urban centers of the size and pattern set by the material advancement of those times, by the means of transport, by the progress of construction, sewerage, and city planning. Such were the factors that went into the building of Banaras, a pilgrim center and center of crafts, the history of which goes far back into the past, and Delhi, Agra, and Dacca in later times—all seats of government as well as centers of trade and crafts. Side-by-side with trade, pilgrimages progressed, as in Tanjore or Madura. These cities would not compare unfavorably with the medieval cities or towns of Europe of these times.

The break comes with the advent of colonialism. The older urban centers fell into decay instead of benefiting from the opening-up of the new type of trade. The colonial cities developed where the East India Company had obtained concessions and set up trading and military establishments which were combined and later became the seats of government—Calcutta, Madras, Bombay, all belong to this category. While these cities grew and the new type of trade flourished—a new type, because it was trade in products other than those on which medieval cities had grown— the old economy collapsed, the socioeconomic structure was destroyed. Colonial rule was exploitive, not because trade developed on new lines and old crafts decayed, but because the effect of industrialization in the West which it transmitted was not moderated or softened by appropriate social policies and governmental action; in any event, the impact was not such that the oncoming changes could initiate development. As a result, India, known for her manufactures the world over, was reduced to a predominantly agricultural country; pressure on land increased, and profits of agriculture were not plowed back into the land; no attempt was made to rehabilitate the old industries, or to adapt them to the needs of the changed times and revitalize them by grafting modern technology on them.

There was another aspect to colonial urbanization. The culture of the new city was an imported culture; for a long time it failed to take root. But the reason was again the same: such cities were foreign "enclaves," not the product of internal development—economic, social, and cultural. This was the basic reason for the isolation of Calcutta from the social life of Bengal in the early British days. The preindustrial cities of Europe were cultural centers and so much more advanced than the surrounding countryside that "urban" and "rustic" implied wide cultural difference and the undisputed superiority of the one over the other. Not so with the parvenu culture of Calcutta, as compared with the village life of the time. Rural society was highly developed, it had carried status differentiation to the utmost degree, and it did not easily acknowledge its inferiority. In fact, it had no need to, until, through the inevitable process of intersection of minds and such opportunities as the colonial power gave to the development of Western education, urbanization gradually made Calcutta the city of new learning. It was only then that Calcutta gained the position of leadership in the social and political life of Bengal. Calcutta did not, however, come to be any less exploitive, and its leadership lacked a firm economic base. The emerging middle class was numerically small and consisted largely of professional people who derived their income directly or indirectly from land, and not from trade or industry.

Calcutta's position in the life of Bengal is unique. Today the city and its environs contain nearly a third of the population of West Bengal, but even before Partition it had the same position. In fact, to quote Sudhin Datta, "during the last two hundred years the capital has so dominated the province as to become one with it; and this is untrue of another city in the country." [1]

While the cultural transformation, coupled with progress in transport and communications, broke down some of the barriers between the urban and rural societies, it was only one of the contributing factors. New forces on the political and economic fronts led to a widening of the gulf between urban and rural standards of living, drawing people away from the villages. In the process, the character of the problem changed—from that of a conflict of interest between "foreign" cities and "Indian" villages to a conflict between the rates of urban and rural development. The self-conscious turning-away from the cities, which was so characteristic of the early days of national awakening, derived as much from their being administrative capitals of foreign rulers as from their exploitive nature. This distrust of exploitive urban life was a major strand in Gandhian thought. City dwellers were the agents of exploitation of the people of India—every pice that went into their pockets was tainted money. The "back-to-village" slogan raised at the time of the first Swadeshi movement remained a popular slogan throughout the period of the national struggle. The form it takes in the present debate is that of centralization versus decentralization—spatial dispersal of industries, balanced regional growth, equitable distribution of economic power.

For a discussion of these issues from the standpoint of Indian goals, it would be helpful to start with a sweeping view of the recent past, from which to focus on the future. An outstanding landmark was the Congress session of 1934, at which Gandhi moved his famous resolution for organizing the All-India Village Industries Association for "resuscitating the dead and dying village industries." A delegate, who happened to be an economist, moved an amendment which for "the dead and dying . . ." would substitute "such village industries as have an economic future." Gandhi would not accept the amendment; he laughed it out. Speaking in Hindi, he said that he wanted to go to the villages to help the

---

[1] "The World's Cities: Calcutta," *Encounter*, VIII, No. 6 (June, 1957), 45.

villager by fixing a nail to the wheel of his creaking cart, by design-
ing for him a clay lamp which would burn vegetable oil instead of
kerosene and yet give a flame without too much soot, improve the
village *ghani* (the oil crusher operated by bullocks), and so on.
What need did he have of great economists or big financiers? That
resolution initiated the program of village industries to build up the
self-sufficient village economy of his conception, based on self-help,
dignity of labor, and limitation of wants through voluntary restraint. In the Third Plan, these village industries figure as a part
of the Decentralized Sector, with dwindling importance.

Then there was Rabindranath Tagore. In his reminiscences, re-
calling the happy days he had spent in his childhood in a garden
house on the banks of the Ganga (known to others as the Hooghly)
some miles from Calcutta, he writes with deep feeling of the river
defiled by the jute mills emitting their effluence into it, dirtying its
water, and of its banks desecrated by ugly chimneys and factories.
But Tagore's denunciation of the ugliness and squalor which modern industry inflicts on cities did not stop with aesthetic revulsion.
He had grown up in one of the most crowded, most completely
unplanned, and most over-built parts of Calcutta, Chitpur, within
a stone's throw of Burra Bazaar, where the concentration of trading was at its highest. He chose a rural retreat at Santiniketan,
where he spent his life to develop it into an international university.
But, along with Santiniketan, he also worked unceasingly building
up Sriniketan, another village only two miles away, into a center for
agriculture and handicrafts. This was to be a model, village-based,
for the socioeconomic regeneration of India. The lamp he had lit at
Sriniketan, he hoped, would someday light other lamps. Tagore's
desire for reviving the village can be partly traced back to his love
of the Upanishadic ideal; it was in forest retreats that India's
highest thoughts had been conceived and given immortal expression.
But Tagore never shunned or drew away from science or modern
industry. Santiniketan generated its own electricity; it was not far
from a railway station; it was not cut off from the world.

Let us pass then to Pandit Jawaharlal Nehru. The sight of the
slums in which most industrial workers live in so many of the
Indian towns and cities always makes him fly into a passion, and
his denunciation of this indignity to human beings has gone on
ringing: "I believe in no argument, economic or other, which is
based on the creation of slums . . ." [2] Not that slum-clearance
programs have progressed much in consequence; but that is quite
another story. It is not merely the slums, however, which worry
Nehru; he is as deeply perturbed by the difference between the

[2] Statement at Bangalore, October 6, 1956.

city and the village. This was "one of the most terrible things in India," he has often said, and "there could be no balanced economy in the country from any point of view, more especially psychological point of view, if this vast difference remained." "When bright people migrated from villages to city," he adds, "they did no good to the city but they did a lot of bad to the village by coming away from it. It must be stopped." [3] But how?

URBANIZATION IN INDIA

Can the rural-urban differences be removed or even significantly reduced without migration on a much greater scale than now? Can planned effort made in advance hope to cope with it and regulate its pace?

The process of economic development and the social change which accompanies it leads to a shift of population from rural to urban areas. As was observed earlier, in the period immediately preceding the advent of modern industry the impetus for urbanization came from (1) centralization and modernization of administration, and (2) opening-up of foreign trade. The resulting pattern of urbanization was different from that of the preindustrial society. Old cities decayed and new ones came up—often cheek by jowl, as in Delhi—and the character of urbanization changed between the beginning and the end of the 19th century, though at the end of the century, because of the decay of old cities, the percentage of the urban to the total population had probably not changed at all. The port towns became administrative capital cities, the growth of a middle class gave rise to residential towns; railway townships came in the wake of the development of railways; trading towns arose for the assembly of raw materials for export and for the distribution of imported manufactured goods.

The rate of urbanization is generally slow in the early phase of development; it then becomes faster, until a point is reached after which it slackens to a steady pace. India is passing through this intermediate stage of fast growth. Population pressure and stagnation of the rural economy have made rapid urbanization precede, rather than follow, industrialization. It is likely that the rate of migration will increase, and that urbanization will be even faster until it levels off after about, say, 40 per cent of the total population becomes urban, as against 17 per cent at the 1951 census. By that time the Indian economy, on present showing, is expected to reach the stage of self-sustained growth; the national income will be sufficiently high to ensure large-enough savings to

---

[3] AIMO (All India Manufacturer's Organization) Annual Meeting, April 3, 1960.

meet the cost of urban development of this order, on the one hand, and that of the dispersal of economic overheads, on the other, without impairing thereby the further growth of the economy through the maintenance of an adequate rate of investment.

In the present phase of transition, however, urbanization has gone ahead of economic development, leaving a wide "development gap." It appears in two different forms: in the form of "overurbanization," i.e., urbanization exceeding the range of economic development, and in that of a marked deficiency of urban facilities and services, akin to the scarcity of consumption goods in an economy in the initial stage of planned development. Urban development and the provision of urban services fail to keep pace with the growth of urban population; and the competing demand on available resources raises the problem of choice between provision of urban amenities to ensure tolerable living conditions for the mass of urban population, on the one hand, and a faster rate of growth of the economy, on the other, by channeling as large a part of the resources as possible to productive investment and creation of capital assets. It has been contended that the supposed conflict between urban development and economic growth is misconceived; that urban development is itself a capital asset with high production potential; that urban centers are nurseries for the growth of entrepreneurship and points of transmission for the diffusion of improved techniques of production, etc. And in so far as urbanization plays this role, of course, it should be given a high priority in an economy which aims at industrializing and modernizing itself rapidly.

But how high should this priority be? It is by no means a simple question to answer. Though urbanization is related to economic development, there is no unique relationship between the two, and varying degrees of the one can be in association with the other. The optimal degree of urbanization and its character will depend, therefore, on the extent to which concentration of population can be expected to bring about the changes which urban sociologists associate with it, viz., rational utilization of labor, uninhibited by noneconomic factors, the development of a committed labor force, and so on. The basis for the sociological argument in favor of urbanization is pretty weak in India. Urbanization promotes economic development, not primarily through the social transformation of labor and the changes in attitudes it brings about, but by providing the economic overheads, the infrastructure of development, and external economies, creating thereby the conditions favorable for industry. It is industry-based urban development that exhibits these features, not urbanization of whatever sort. Where urban growth is a direct adjunct of industrial development, as in the case of new steel towns, the question of choice does not arise. In other cases, it does.

The desirable degree of urbanization has to be determined by a balance of factors: costs of overheads (capital costs of urban amenities, housing, etc.), as also social costs in terms of social dislocation and adjustment, on the one hand, and resulting advantages —economic (improvements in productivity, creation of surplus, nurturing of entrepreneurship) and cultural (diffusion of new values and changes in attitudes)—on the other. Again, given the degree of urbanization, the same criteria may be applied to the choice of the most desirable pattern of distribution of the urban population among (*a*) towns and cities of different size groups and (*b*) industrial, trading, and commercial towns, administrative centers, residential and university towns, and small towns as servicing centers for rural areas.

Forecasts of the situation that is likely to develop over the next few years or decades are reasonably certain. Those based on the projection of the rate of increase of urban population experienced in recent years are fully confirmed by others made on a different basis, namely that of the degree of urbanization which other countries went through when they were at a stage of development comparable to that of India today. The assumption in the latter case is that India will also attain the same high rate of development achieved by those countries.

As industrialization is being speeded up, a certain pattern of urban development is emerging. Efforts toward and investment for developing industries tend to be concentrated on urban centers which have already attained some development. This is because the cost of infrastructure is high and external economies are difficult to reproduce; industries in the private sector are more likely to succeed if they are located where these facilities already exist, and where a market has already developed. The dispersal of industries that is being thought of, and that may be feasible, will also favor concentration rather than bring industries to the villages. Planned development of industry, however, may avoid the much greater concentration in a few places which would be inevitable in the absence of this limited but deliberate program of dispersal. It should be noted that dispersal in this context means a more desirable pattern of growth, not the reversal of the trend toward concentration; decentralization, in this sense, does not attempt to reverse or slacken the pace of migration. To the extent that villages develop into townships, urbanization will not involve internal migration. Making due allowance for such natural growth of villages into towns, statistical estimates suggest, nevertheless, that the movement of population into the larger cities in the next few decades is going to be staggering. Demographers threaten that, in sheer numbers, it will have no parallel in human history. All this time, cities will also be growing rapidly from the natural increase of their own population.

Countries which have launched upon development later than others have generally completed the transformation of their respective economies in progressively shorter time. With the experience of other countries before her and the advanced techniques of production available to her, it is not unreasonable to expect that India, as one of the last to enter the field, will be able to complete the transformation of her economy in a shorter period than, say, Japan. In fact, having decided upon planned development, the period of transformation should be much shorter and comparable to that of the countries in the Communist world. India has the further advantage of keeping out of the "cold war" bloc; and, if this advantage continues, she should be free from the kind of strain which distorted the planning effort of Soviet Russia, forcing her to divert to the building-up of her war potential resources which could have been utilized for speeding up economic development under more favorable auspices.

Japan's example is particularly worth noting, and it will be found to be disconcerting. Many in this country look upon Japan as the model for development of small-scale industries and, therefore, of a decentralized economy. The point to emphasize here is that decentralization—whether the place of small industries in Japan's economy entitled her to this distinction or not—has not slackened or held up urbanization in the least. As a matter of fact, Japan is more highly urbanized than the United States. The degree of urbanization does not, of course, depend on that of economic development alone; it has also to do with geography and the distribution of natural resources. It is possible that planning may enable India to attain a high rate of development without as high a rate of urbanization as, say, that of Japan. But there is nothing in the geographical features of the country and the distribution of the natural resources to suggest that India's urbanization could be less than, say, that of the United States. On the contrary, the density of population, the high concentration of coal and iron, for example, and the inadequacy of capital which militates against wider dispersal of economic overheads—all these go to suggest a higher rather than a lower rate of urbanization than that attained by the United States in a comparable period of its growth.

The Quest for Balance

Political thinking in the country overwhelmingly favors the view that though India may not be able to do altogether without big industry and towns and cities, the Indian economy, like Indian culture, should remain predominantly village-based; and that once the rural economy is rehabilitated, and nonagricultural employment found for the people not needed in agriculture, the rural-urban balance, which was destroyed by the British Raj, will be restored. There are differences about the means to be adopted for achieving this end, and there is controversy enough about the right method of raising agricultural productivity: whether peasant farming is to be encouraged or replaced gradually by coöperative farming; whether village industries, which are to provide nonagricultural employment, should be mechanized and, if so, to what extent; whether greater employment or higher productivity should have the prior claim; and so on. But all are agreed that the rural-urban balance can be restored and the wide differences now prevailing between urban and rural standards removed, without much further migration. If rural-urban differentials in productivity and living conditions are removed, and there is neither push from one end nor pull from the other, it may be legitimate to conclude that there will be no movement. A misconception persists, however, about the distribution of rural and urban population at the end point, and the path to it has not been critically examined.

When the economic development that we are aiming at has been substantially achieved, per capita real income raised sufficiently to ensure a fairly high and rising standard of living, and the economy set firmly on the path of self-sustained growth, how will our villages, towns, and cities look? Villages are certain to be much better places to live in, and quite prosperous. But perhaps there would be fewer of them—bigger, compact, and better laid out, with an adequate network of common amenities and services. The pressure on land and the density of population in the rural areas may conceivably be reduced to a substantial extent. The grass would be greener, eroded hillsides covered with forest, rivers better cared for; and though the entire countryside may not be laid out like a landscape garden, improved patterns of land use and conservation of water resources would significantly alter the appearance of the land. The land would certainly support those who work on it much better. But it may not need so many people as it does now to till it and to take care of it, even after due allowance is made for diverting the labors of those who are now underemployed to land development and construction of rural capital assets such as drainage, contour bunding, minor irrigation, afforestation, etc. The villages would doubtless have their complement of light industries and productive services, too.

But if the villages are to have a better life, more and more goods and services for them will have to come from the towns and cities. In short, the present rural-urban distribution of population will have to change drastically and that, too, within the next few decades. As economic development gathers momentum, the rate of urbanization will progressively rise, whatever the pattern of development that is aimed at. While setting the goal of a higher standard of living and rising per capita income for the Indian people, policy makers have not thought out fully its implications. There is a great deal of hangover from the past in beliefs and values which are held today. Why so many people should hold on to a system of ideas which is manifestly impossible to square with reality, why what they *think* they are doing is patently different from what they are actually doing, can perhaps be explained as a projection from the past; but it does not mitigate in the least the conflict that is arising today and which is bound to deepen as the years roll on.

A Problem of Resources?

Broadly, it is reasonable to assume that the resources necessary for urban development would be created in the process of economic development. This would, however, be true only in the long run, at the end of the time span which planned development has in view. The creation of resources for urban development does not synchronize with the requirements at every point of time. There is inevitably a development gap in this as in other aspects of planning. This gap can be measured in financial terms also, but it appears much more tangibly in the deficiency of the physical resources for town planning and urban development. The situation can be illustrated from the provisions made in the Draft Outline of the Third Plan for urban development.

In the five years ending in 1966, the growth of urban population is estimated at 18 million. Taking the cost of urban housing at Rs. 1,600 per head suggested by one of the members of the Delhi City Planning Team (which is much lower than the standard cost incurred by government departments), the cost of housing these 18 millions alone works out at Rs. 2,880 crores. This is exclusive of the cost of land, which is ignored as being not a social cost at all. If the cost of land is included, Rs. 3,500 crores will be required for urban development on this basis, against which the provision under the Third Plan[4] amounts to only Rs. 1,000 crores.

[4] *The Third Five Year Plan: A Draft Outline* (New Delhi: Planning Commission, Government of India, June, 1960), p. 26.

This figure of Rs. 1,000 crores is estimated on the assumption that half the Public Sector outlay under social services would be for urban housing and development, and that about Rs. 675 crores would be private investment in housing during the Third Plan.

If the picture is dismal in financial terms, it is even more so in terms of all-round shortages of steel, cement, and other construction materials. Recently a high-powered committee was set up by the prime minister to speed up slum clearance. The committee was hard put to find finances for even short-term ameliorative measures. It worked out a modest scheme for the provision of minimum amenities, such as water supply and sewage disposal, leaving to the future the larger tasks of remodeling and new construction. Even for this minimum program, however, materials such as steel, corrugated iron sheets, and cast-iron and galvanized-iron pipes would be necessary—and all these were scarce. The alternatives were to import or to wait till domestic production caught up.

Another form in which "development gap" appears is "overurbanization"—the growth of urban population in excess of what is required for economic development and what could be supported by the rate of growth of national income. The overurbanization thesis does not rest merely on the particular distribution of the labor force of the country between agricultural and nonagricultural occupations. Though that evidence is bad enough, the thesis is supported even more strongly by the character of urban employment in India today. Employment in secondary and tertiary sectors seems to be disproportionately high, judged by the experience of other developing countries and that of advanced countries at a stage of their development comparable to India's today. The extent of urban unemployment and unduly high employment in unproductive service industries, which merely masks unemployment, is today as distressing a feature of the economic scene as rural stagnation. True, much greater industrialization is necessary for absorbing the urban unemployed and the underemployed, e.g., those engaged in spurious service industries, as also for raising agricultural productivity. The case for diversion of resources for the creation of social overheads in urban areas will not be apparent, however, as long as there are no corresponding returns from them in terms of economic value.

On the other hand, however undesirable the occupational structure of urban labor might be, the average income of such labor is, nevertheless, higher than that of rural labor. If only for this reason, it may not be desirable to put obstacles in the path of migration. This is further supported by the consideration that the social cost involved, or rather the social overheads for providing urban amenities, are much lower in India than elsewhere; instead of thinking of trying to bring down the costs from the impossibly high Western standards which dominate the thinking of Indian town planners and engineers ("Cutting down the Western standard of cost to the size of the Indian pocketbook"),[5] much better results could be obtained by evolving indigenous solutions to these problems, by systematic utilization of local materials and labor. It will further aggravate rural unemployment and underemployment, which is already very high, if any attempt is made to interfere with or restrain migration. The character of urban employment and the existence of floating populations, moving from town to town and back and forth between towns and villages, urgently calls for a deliberate social policy for the rehabilitation of both urban and rural labor. It is futile to assume that industrial development has only to be speeded up and there will be an automatic solution to both these problems. Returns on investment on the rehabilitation of urban population which is surplus—in the sense of being in excess of the requirements of economic development—have to be weighed against returns from investments in other areas of the economy, including those on rural development.

In this assessment of the desirability of urbanization on the basis of social costs and economic returns, the rural bias observable in Indian political attitudes to such questions does not come into play. Indian opinion is neither impressed by the high potentiality for economic development claimed for urbanization, on the grounds that it creates what the sociologists call a "universalist-achievement-oriented value system," nor too depressed by the findings of the social anthropologists that urbanization in India does not produce the social changes necessary for economic development. It is true that if sheer density and heterogeneity of population were the criteria of urbanism, Indian villages have known both—to a greater extent perhaps than in the city of Calcutta—and absorbed both without turning a hair.[6] Neither density nor heterogeneity of the Indian villages has brought about the cultural transformation that is associated with urbanization. Perhaps the controversy is somewhat pointless, since the desired change here is obviously modernization and a change in the traditional attitudes which inhibit development. The merits claimed for urbanization from the standpoint of economic development, such as increase in labor efficiency through the development of a committed

---

[5] The remark of Catherine Bauer Wurster.

[6] McKim Marriott, "Some Comments on William L. Kolb's 'The Structure and Functions of Cities' in the Light of India's Urbanization," *Economic Development and Cultural Change*, III, No. 1 (October, 1954), 50–52.

labor force, cultivation of habits of disciplined work, etc.—an urban environment is not needed in India to develop these attitudes. It is not the development of certain attitudes which makes the urban environment necessary, but the combination of economic overheads, markets, complementary skills and services, credit institutions and transport, which cannot be brought together except in urban centers. Provision of training facilities rather than the creation of an urban environment is what Indian labor needs to develop efficiency. Indian labor does not have to learn the habits of application, discipline, and capacity for sustained work in factories. It is not entrepreneurship, either, which India is lacking today conspicuously. It is the inadequacy or nonavailability of economic overheads which retards development, and, since external economies can be created only in areas of concentration, economic development in India cannot be primarily rural-based. But urban development must meet the test of costs and returns.

Aspects of a Dilemma

It is as much the demand which urban development makes on the country's resources—and the poor returns it has given in terms of production and productive employment—as it is rural stagnation that compels attention to the devising of means to moderate or slow down the pace of migration at the rural end. The factors behind the exodus are mainly economic: excessive pressure on land, stagnation of village industries, lack of nonagricultural occupations and job opportunities. There are some noneconomic factors also— attraction of city life, lack of medical and educational facilities in villages, the social disabilities of some sections which they can get rid of by moving to towns. The impact of these factors on the rural elite is particularly important. When those who are best able to take the initiative in improving conditions of village life and provide the intellectual stimulus for change tend to leave the villages, the effect on the volume of migration is much more than in proportion to their number. Migration statistics show that most of those who get some kind of schooling leave the village.

Urban-rural wage differentials and relative earning opportunities are the crux of the problem. Agricultural development is, of course, a prime concern. Taking a long view, however, increase in agricultural productivity cannot be a factor making for any substantial increase in rural employment. On the contrary, economic development necessarily means that smaller and smaller numbers would be engaged in food production, so that labor is released to produce other things, to support and sustain the growth of the economy. Mass underemployment in agriculture being our most acute problem, some alleviation can be expected for a time from developments in agriculture—but only up to a point, and only until development has really caught on. If two crops are grown where only one was grown before, more labor will be needed in processing and transporting the crop, and for ancillary services. To the extent that underemployment is reduced and the income of the agriculturist is raised, there will also be demand for products and services, some of which the labor released from fields can profitably supply, provided it involves no significant capital investment.

But even if there should be appreciable progress in agriculture, the scope for employment and earning opportunities created thereby would soon be exhausted. The Draft Outline of the First Plan had looked upon development of industry and trade as the key to agricultural development: by absorbing the surplus from agriculture, industrial development would accelerate the development of agriculture. The main reliance, therefore, will have to be on non-agricultural occupations and rural industries, if the exodus is to be arrested or slowed down. Which industries can be taken to the village and to what extent? A reorientation of the pattern of industrial location has been suggested as technically feasible. There is an economic case for choice of techniques in the direction of labor-intensive and small-scale industrial processes, and much of recent thinking has been concentrated on these possibilities. Lower social overheads and the substantial scope for economizing on such overheads is a major argument in favor of this pattern of location. If villagers could work not far from their homes, investment in housing could be saved, that on transport considerably reduced, and the social problems faced by uprooted migrants crowding into urban areas altogether eliminated. The sentimental appeal of this solution is not difficult to imagine, but its economics faces serious hurdles.

There are not many noncapital-using rural industries which can be developed in addition to those already existing. The latter are overcrowded, and labor productivity in them is low. As a welfare measure, subsidization of these rural industries could be a substitute for the social insurance which India is unable to provide. When underutilization is ended and idle capacity is fully utilized, new techniques can be introduced gradually to transform the "household and hand industries" of Professor Mahalanobis's Draft-Plan-Frame for the Second Plan. The Second Plan, however, went much further. One of its cardinal principles was that, during the Plan period, the bulk of the increased supplies of consumers' goods should be reserved for village and small-scale industries so that employment in these industries should progressively increase:

The basis of the above decision is not a general opposition to technical improvement such as is implied in the view, *if held anywhere,* that a less advanced technology is in itself the more desirable. Its main purpose is to rehabilitate, in their own occupations, persons possessing traditional productive equipment and skills; to protect those who are at present employed and to offer to the unemployed and the underemployed, additional or fuller employment in their traditional occupations though their productive effort here will be so meagre that it will have to be supported by direct and indirect subsidies to yield to them a minimum level of subsistence income. An advantage in providing such part relief employment within traditional occupations is that by its means existing capital equipment and trained personnel can be put to some use, howsoever uneconomic, and be made to produce the needed supply of consumer goods.[7]

One has to enter a caveat: there *are* people who oppose technological improvement because of the social changes associated with it. Subject to this, the above is a perfectly justified rationalization of village and small-scale industries in the initial stage of development. But it does not answer the question whether industrial development can be village-based when resources become available at a later stage to carry out technological changes.

The impact of agricultural development on rural employment in nonagricultural occupations needs exploration. Village studies show that diversification of employment does not by itself indicate that type of development which can be expected to hold back rural exodus. It is only in those villages which are exposed to semi-urban influences that nonagricultural employment may indicate the development of some industry that is really remunerative. In a village where there is a mixture of occupations, one cannot say that this is an indicator of progressive economic change and a symptom of development gaining momentum as well as direction—when agriculture is poor, there is pressure in so many villages to engage in nonremunerative service industries.[8] If, however, agricultural conditions are favorable for improved farming, better land utilization calls for the performance of many kinds of services connected with agriculture, and the increase in prosperity encourages the development of a service sector in the village scheme. In villages where a significant proportion of the households are engaged in "arts and crafts," the wider employment opportunities which this signifies are

---

[7] V. M. Dandekar, "Rationale of the Ambar Charkha," *Economic Weekly,* July 6, 1957, 863–867. Italics supplied.

[8] B. N. Ganguli, "Rural Economic Development," *Economic Weekly,* Annual Number, 1960, pp. 193–198.

explained by the presence of prosperous villages in the neighbor-hood.[9] The emergence of demand from agricultural developments or better agricultural prices is not in question. What scope is there for meeting such demand through rural industries or location of industry in predominantly rural areas?

Whatever the professions about decentralization and the faith in it as the ultimate ideal, it will be fatal to turn our face against reality and disregard what is happening today and what is bound to happen tomorrow and the day after. Dispersal of industries be-ing limited by the shortage of capital and the inevitable channeling of such capital into the most productive uses in the short period, we have to be prepared for massive urban growth in the coming decades. While every effort should be made to control this flood, by the known methods of flood control and river training—to press the imagery further—action at the highest level is urgently needed to cope with migration by the advance planning of urban develop-ment. There is an apparent paradox in this: that while migration cannot be effectively checked and economic activities cannot be ade-quately dispersed in the last analysis because of inadequacy of capi-tal, urban development should be allowed to make heavy demands on the limited resources for social overheads. In fact, to the extent the latter demand is met, less resources will be available for pro-ductive investment, defining the latter in the narrow terms dictated by the present state of underdevelopment and crushing poverty.

The location of industries, agglomeration, and urban concentra-tion tend to follow the same set pattern everywhere. However un-desirable on social or even economic grounds—the latter from the standpoint of long-term growth potential—the tendency powerfully resists all but massive ameliorative measures. It cannot be wished away. It is tempting for a country on the threshold of industrializa-tion to look back at the mess in which others landed themselves in the past, to want to profit from their mistakes, and to resolve to keep to the straight and narrow path. But maximization of returns has still to remain the sheet anchor of policy, and that inhibits too wide a dispersal of the economic overheads basic to industrial de-velopment. A greater dispersal may be possible at a later stage, when more resources have been created; but by then enough harm may already have been done in a mixed economy with an enormous private sector. For, the creation of economic overheads alone does not foster industry; a combination of several other factors is neces-sary—markets, complementary skills, services. The environment in which newly sprung industry can gain nourishment and grow is found, if at all, in that very combination usually despised as an

---

[9] *Ibid.*

agglomeration. Slums and city blight may not be an essential ingredient of economic growth. They have unfortunately been its natural concomitant, if not its sponsors.

It is not true that economic development, once initiated, automatically spreads in ever widening circles, or that by appropriate social policies industries can be easily dispersed. A wide dispersal of industries is prevented in the beginning by scarcity of resources. After development has been initiated, there may be greater scope for choice. But, over large areas of the economic field, decisions are individual and are taken with a horizon too narrowly circumscribed by short-term economic considerations. Even small industries tend to be started where the environment is favorable and congenial to their growth. Attempt at wider dispersal, or even deliberate sponsorship of multicentered development, encounters serious obstacles from the forces which are already developed and which are so difficult to counter:

Within India, under the Second Plan, the trend in practice has perhaps been for the developed areas to become more developed and for the backward areas to fall behind, at least in relative terms. (This trend would probably have been similar or even stronger under a free-enterprise economy.) This is not an unnatural concomitant of the emphasis placed on physical planning in the sense of giving priority to basic industries from which other industries will be born or benefited in the next phase of development.[10]

Regional development embraces such things as improvement in land uses, development of agriculture, and fuller utilization of the natural resources. It is not possible, therefore, to find a ready measure on which can be based a comparison of the relative position of the different regions at the beginning and the end of a Plan period. The development of industries, however, lends itself more easily to statistical computation, and figures have been cited from time to time, e.g., of the regional issue of industrial licenses, to point to the direction of change. A cursory glance at these figures shows that the tendency toward concentration in areas where industries are already developed has not been checked, and it suggests the helplessness of the licensing authority to counter this tendency effectively. To the extent that licenses are issued for substantial extension of established industries, there is little scope for choice. Even the licensing of new industries does not show any significant departure from the established pattern of localization.

The reasons are obvious. There would be few wanting to set up industries in a location which does not have the necessary infra-

---

[10] A. T. A. Learmonth, "Regional Planning in India," *Economic Weekly*, Annual Number, 1960, pp. 241–244.

structure. Industry in the private sector cannot disregard private costs, however high may be the social cost of their decisions. In the circumstances, there is hardly any initiative on the part of the government to interfere with the choice of location, except perhaps where political pressures from the states become difficult to resist. When the location is fixed with an eye to wider considerations, even a confirmed socialist like Professor Balogh comes down on it:

> Policy aimed at a greater equality of income is often conducted through restrictions which interfere with efficient production in the private sector, e.g., through regional dispersal of industries in unsuitable units, pressure to establish factories in unsuitable areas.[11]

Enterprises in the public sector are less heavily fettered in their choice, but when limitations of transport, availability of power, and some other factors are considered, and due allowance is made for the normal human weakness for choosing a place of work which should also be congenial and convenient to live in, it will be seen that freedom in this case is also severely restricted. Major shifts in location are retarded by cost considerations even when an element of subsidy would be fully justified in locating a plant where external economies are yet to develop, with the deliberate intention of creating such economies and inducing further development centered on this point. Here, as elsewhere, conflict arises between short-term and long-term returns, and there is also the all-too-human desire not to risk the criticism of setting up one more unremunerative unit in the public sector. That spread effects are ignored where they could be easily provided for, with a more forward-looking planning of the new steel towns, however, does not appear to be a valid criticism, since the main purpose of decentralization is to discourage concentration and encourage light industries to move to where the markets are and where labor is. In fact, if there were a conscious and deliberate decision to plan the steel towns in such a manner as to prevent steel-using industries from clustering around the steel plants, that would be an example of foregoing quick returns in the interest of more balanced growth!

Primarily, the case for decentralization arises from a desire to make economic development as broad-based as possible. Decentralization is also a deliberate policy for preventing disparities between regions or different social groups from becoming wider with the progress of economic development. The desire for moderating the flow of migration does not spring from value-loaded judgments based on nostalgic longings for a dead past. It is not

---

[11] Thomas Balogh, "Economic Strategy for Third Plan," *Economic Weekly*, Annual Number, 1961, pp. 241–249.

deliberately turning one's face against reality, but a deeper understanding of that reality, which leads to the quest for appropriate economic policies based upon such an understanding. Decentralization, however, is used in so many different senses in India that, even at the risk of being obvious, it would be useful at this stage to digress on these.

The Content of "Decentralization"

There is, to begin with, the concept of devolution of decision making which is sought to be realized in the scheme of democratic decentralization or establishment of the Panchayat system. There is decentralization of economic power implicit in the aim of establishing a socialistic pattern of society which is India's professed goal. Again, there is decentralization in the sense of location of industries away from points of concentration. As a spatial concept, decentralization in the Indian context undergoes a very big transformation when the idea of dispersal of industries is carried to the extreme form of making the village the base of economic development. There are various shades of meaning in between, and centralization sometimes appears as its inseparable associate, as in the idea of decentralized production which can be made effective and workable only by centralized marketing and financing.

It is easy to see why these different aspects of decentralization get mixed up in the process of planning. Any plan worth the name would seek to provide employment for as many people, and in as wide a region, as possible. This, obviously, means that the creation of employment opportunities should be widely spread, so that lack of mobility of labor would not result in the existence of pockets of unemployment and labor shortage side-by-side. Decentralization is, in this sense, a spatial concept amounting more or less to prevention of geographic unevenness in the development of the labor market. In the particular Indian context, it would mean taking industries to the rural areas. Related to this is the view that concentration is undesirable on social grounds and that excessive concentration creates problems which can well be avoided without any social costs. Among the reasons advocated for the dispersal of economic activity is that drawing large masses of people into a few urban centers widens the gulf between urban and rural society, which is undesirable as much from the angle of living space and provision of urban services as from that of prevention of concentration of economic power and, therefore, ought to be a matter of concern to any government or people aiming at a socialistic pattern of society.

Stemming from these reasons, decentralization of economic

activity becomes a policy of locating industries in a proper manner. The program has necessarily to be centered on those activities in which there is a real choice. There is, for instance, no question but that mines have to be where the minerals are found, or, in the case of heavy industries such as steel, that the location is more or less determined by the occurrence of raw materials and that economy of operations requires the unit to be large. But, with efficient transport and adequate power facilities, there is room for influencing the other industries to spread out. Decentralization thus becomes in effect a program for ordered location of light and consumers'-goods industries.

There is, however, more to it. Precisely because a choice in regard to dispersal of consumers' goods exists, other questions arise in respect to these industries. While decentralization in the spatial sense is conceivable, its practicability depends on its leaving the economy no worse than it would be under conditions of agglomeration of units of production. That is to say, in terms of quantity and quality of output, and in terms of costs, the decentralized industries should do at least as well. Where dispersal of units does not imply a change in methods of production in a significant manner, this merely amounts to saying that facilities such as transport, power, and finance are available in an adequate measure in rural areas. Alternately, even if some additional expenses are to be incurred in respect to these, they ought to be more than compensated by lower labor costs.

It is essential to note that decentralization in the above sense is not directly linked with any modification in methods of production. The average unit of production may be no smaller, or use no less advanced techniques of production, than its counterpart in an industrial concentrate. All that has happened in this scheme is that instead of asking labor to come to it, the industry has gone where labor is available. One could, of course, go farther in this direction, adjusting the type of industry to the sort of labor available in different localities. But this is an adjustment which often means more than what it seems prima facie.

This is so because at this stage decentralization takes on a second meaning, in the sense of combining changes in methods of production with changes in location. The industry should be such that it can bring into effective use hitherto untapped labor resources through a variation in the organization of the production process. In other words, the unit, whatever its size in terms of financial investment or final output, would differ significantly in status and in the plan of operations from units elsewhere. And, if it is to succeed and flourish, these adjustments should make it equally competitive. We have, therefore, two reasons for decentralization and two interpretations of the term. While the two reasons, namely provision of work over a wide area and avoidance of colossal concentrations of people, can be treated as aspects of a bid to prevent unnecessary movements of labor, it is not always helpful to fail to distinguish between the two interpretations of the term, viz., dispersal in space and decentralization of productive operations. The former is quite consistent with uniformities in size and techniques between different units; the latter, however, may often not be. The likelihood of such confusion being widely prevalent is illustrated by the debate in India regarding the program for cotton textiles. Decentralization is for all practical purposes identified with encouragement of the hand loom and hand spinning. Apart from the other reasons that may justify such a move, the point to note is that such "decentralization" involves a choice in regard to the process of production and not merely in regard to location. Indeed, there can be, and are, concentrations of hand looms themselves in particular areas, so that any effort to develop them may not fully meet the criteria of spatial dispersal of the demand for labor. But it does mean a change in production techniques.

Because of this, discussion regarding decentralization becomes involved with questions of efficiency and productivity of labor and other resources. There is no necessary reason for a decentralized industry in either of the two senses discussed above to be less efficient than centralized industry. But that would imply an adaptation of the processes of production in such a way that a multiplicity of workshops should not impair the quality or quantity of output. Technically, the saving in terms of overheads arising from the spreading-out of work should not be counterweighed by an increase in prime costs per unit of the same product. How this is to be assured is a major problem, both of organization and of technique. The problem is yet to be solved. There has been a considerable effort of late to develop small-scale industries, but they, too, have tended to cluster—largely for reducing overhead costs. On the other hand, the mere dispersal of units may not mean a dispersal of economic power. Large corporations in the American economy have many productive units under their control, and these units are not all located in any one place. The power, therefore, lies not in the factory, but in the firm. It is, in other words, control in the sense of finance and decision making that matters. Even more pertinent to the question is the fact that spatial and process decentralization does not lead to decentralization of power, as is evidenced in Japan by the famous zaibatsus. In the hand-loom and power-loom sector of the textile industry in India, a comparable type of control has already appeared in the form of contracting merchants or financiers farming out power looms, thus taking advantage of the subsidy given to small units and shifting some of the risks in the process. As long as a process of industrial growth implies the creation of large markets and a high degree of monetization of the economy, economic power goes along lines of financial and organizational control. Therefore, it follows that, to be effective, decentralization of power should extend to these fields also. And this has to be achieved without impeding the widening of markets, increased specialization, and all other concomitants of industrial progress.

Comprehensive decentralization, therefore, means redistributing power without affecting adversely the operations necessary for supplying an ever widening market. The relocation of industrial units and the adoption of suitable techniques of production have of necessity to be accompanied by rationalization of certain other processes, viz., financial and marketing organizations. Hence the usual association of decentralized production with coöperative or state organization of marketing and credit supply. The alternative to this is acceptance of a change in the nature of the market in the direction of small entities supplied by groups of small producers, in which case decentralization reaches its logical conclusion—at the cost of technical and industrial progress. Those who favor decentralization have, therefore, to accept either (*a*) concentration of great power in the hands of the state as regards finance, trade, large-sized industrial operations, etc., or (*b*) breaking up the market into local units, with an inevitable trend toward sluggishness. To deny this choice amounts in effect to a denial of the main purpose of decentralization, which is the avoidance of an unequal distribution of economic power between individuals and groups in society.

When decentralization is associated with changes in production methods and, consequently, differences in capital-labor ratio, etc., considerations of employment potential may convert the conflict into one of greater efficiency versus greater employment. The latter links up logically with the objective of avoidance of concentration of economic power in the hands of individuals or sections of the community. Those who have this pattern of development in mind are prepared to concede that a minimum of large-scale industries would be necessary, but not too many: a few selected ones suitably dispersed and preferably under public ownership would be enough to supply the key materials which could not be produced on a small scale. This conception of economic development aims at much more than "spatial dispersal"; it aims at the same time at a more even and equitable distribution of wealth and at prevention of concentration of economic power. Broadly, this may be described as the Gandhian viewpoint, though Gandhiji himself, with his habitual penchant for emphasizing a point sharply, put it as the ideal of self-sufficient village economy. This he did in order to turn the direction of economic development from the city to the village.

The Gandhian view apart, what emerges from this digression is this: the several distinct elements which are gathered together under the common rubric of "decentralization" all find expression, in varying degrees of vagueness, in the objectives as well as the instrument of planning in recent years.

CONCLUSION

The "Directive Principles of State Policy" laid down in the Constitution of India, according to which the Planning Commission is to act, are (*a*) that the citizens, men and women equally, have the right to an adequate means of livelihood; (*b*) that the ownership and control of the material resources of the community are so distributed as best to subserve the common good; and (*c*) that the operation of the economic system does not result in the concentration of wealth and means of production to the common detriment.

To what extent is the aim of achieving a decentralized economy incorporated in the above directives? This is a matter of interpretation. In the Draft Outline of the First Five Year Plan, for example, the chapter on small-scale industries had this paragraph:

The importance of small scale production in the predominantly agricultural economy of this country need hardly be stressed. Reference has already been made to the Directive Principle of State Policy in the Constitution of India, laying down that the operation of the economic system should not result in the concentration of wealth and means of production to the common detriment. What is essential for economic development on democratic lines is a diffusion of sources of power and instruments of production, which would release new springs of energy among the people and make them participate actively, in however small a sphere, in the functioning of a planning economy. It is now widely recognized that local autonomy and devolution of economic power are imperative in order to offset overcentralization which saps initiative and enterprise.[12]

But the case for small-scale industries was not supported exclusively or primarily on ideological grounds, as the reference to the

---

[12] Government of India, Planning Commission, *The First Five Year Plan—A Draft Outline, July 1951* (New Delhi, 1952), p. 162.

Directive Principles might suggest. A number of factors were mentioned in their support, such as, that they constituted an important source of employment to the middle class, that shortage of capital and a plentiful supply of labor favored them, that setting up small but efficient units of production at suitable locations would reduce cost of transport, that they would use local resources, etc. But in the final report of the First Plan, the reference to Constitutional Directives was deleted and the subject was broken up into two separate chapters—one on village industries, and another on small industries and handicrafts. The village-industries chapter outlined state policy in regard to such industries in terms of a common production program for regulating the relation between large-scale and small-scale industries by (1) reservation of spheres of production, (2) nonexpansion of the capacity of large-scale industry, and (3) imposition of cess on the latter, etc.

The approach, therefore, in short, may be called pragmatic rather than ideological. The Second Plan, which was oriented to heavy industry, retained the common production program and provided for expansion of capacity of consumers' goods, subject to the requirements of this program and the production targets for the decentralized sector. But, as the attainment of a socialist pattern of society had been adopted as one of the basic objectives before the Second Plan was drawn up, the Constitutional Directive has naturally to be interpreted in the light of this change.

In the ten years of planning, what direction development has taken is not, however, a question of interpretation, but of facts. If this experience is analyzed, we clearly get a pattern of development which is difficult to square with that suggested by the "Directive Principles of State Policy." These directives may not be specific enough to be regarded as policies that are capable of being applied to practice. They are, rather, to be regarded as goals. And goals are not always where we arrive eventually, though they might be held up all the time as the destination. Human evolution is not teleological, but emergent. Neither decentralized development nor reduction of regional disparities has been achieved to any significant extent. True, the decentralized sector forms an important part of the Plan; but the development of large-scale industries has progressed far enough in these ten years to reduce the decentralized sector into a progressively contracting sector of the economy. There has been no absolute reduction, nor is the investment proposed for this sector smaller, but its share of the total has been going down. This is hardly to be regretted, for low productivity or economic inefficiency, which marks the decentralized sector, is not a value in itself. The experience of the last decade, however, certainly brings out the patterns of development aimed at and achieved in sharp contrast.

By and large, economic development in India has proceeded more or less on the lines of other countries in the early stages of their industrialization; and urbanization has come in as its counterpart, though it may not, especially its rapid rate of growth, be accepted as desirable or welcome. The crippling inadequacy of urban services, the heavy and fast-growing backlog of housing, the increasing attention that slums and overcrowding have been drawing from the government, as also the mounting burden on municipal budgets which municipalities cannot bear—all these highlight the seriousness of the problem. The projections of our urban growth in the coming decades raise it to a scare.

A country yet in the early stages of development has certain advantages. Since it launches upon planned development, it must have a social philosophy. To the extent that a social philosophy informs its economic policy, the instruments of control that planning provides can be used for making urban development conform to the desired pattern. These instruments are power-production programs, transport—especially road-transport—policies, and the creation of other overheads. It is easier to influence the location of new industries than to remove or disperse old established industries. By and large, in the planning of urban development, the necessity of rebuilding would be comparatively small, though it would not be negligible by any means.

Some of the political factors should help. A federal government itself implies a certain measure of dispersal. Despite the natural desire of the central government to go strictly by economic and technical considerations in the location of power projects or industrial plants in the public sector, as also in the planning of transport, pressures from the states have effected some degree of decentralization. This involves perhaps the sacrifice of short-term gains, but it does help to build up a higher growth potential in the long run and a more desirable pattern of distribution of economic activities and, therefore, of urbanization. Not that regional disparities have been narrowed as a result, but they are perhaps less wide than they would be without such pressures from the states, however undesirable the latter might be in other respects.

Also, dismal forebodings of demographers notwithstanding, India may yet have a bit of respite before migration assumes vastly greater proportions, and there is no reason why she should not take advantage of it. It is possible that the programs of rural development, which are being pursued with increasing determination and vigor, may bring in a period—stretching over some years,

ot a decade or two—during which the absorptive capacity of
rural economy will significantly increase, and this in its turn
help to moderate the rate of migration and soften somewhat
difficulties of adjustment which too rapid urbanization im-
es. To try to resist or reverse the long-term trend of migration
urbanization, banking on the hope of building up a viable
1omy which is primarily village-based, would be worse than
le; it would mean inviting disaster. But that does not mean that
flood cannot be held for some time. The experience of other
1tries goes to show that the rate of urbanization accelerates
after agricultural productivity begins to rise.
'his will leave the country quite unprepared to cope with the
flood when it breaks, i.e., when agricultural productivity—not
unit of land but per unit of labor—begins to rise. When this
pens, it will add a new dimension to the rate of migration,
ely determined hitherto by the growth rate of population
e. There may be time till then for planning urban develop-
t in advance and in an orderly manner. The sheer magnitude
he problem, and the grave social consequence of neglecting it,
e it imperative that, instead of being treated as isolated items
ocial expenditure under the heads of "slum clearance," "public
th," and "industrial housing," urban development should be
grated into the Plan.

XII

INDUSTRIAL DECENTRALIZATION
IN INDIA

William Bredo

The Government of India has recognized the problem of excessive urbanization and concentration of industry, and has taken a number of measures aimed at promoting rural industrialization. The policy pronouncements seem to have had definite social motivations, but it is not clear to what extent the government has taken economic considerations into account. It is quite apparent that the social goals associated with preferring to have the people live in villages, towns, and small cities may be in conflict with the economic objectives of obtaining the maximum impact for a minimum expenditure on the industrialization of the country. Quite conceivably, industry might be promoted too far into the rural areas, with the result that few new enterprises would be generated and too large a proportion might fail, with considerable wastage of economic resources. If the process of decentralizing industry were better understood, presumably effective methods could be devised for working out an industrialization program which could achieve a good compromise between social goals and the goal of conserving economic resources and achieving a high-level impact from industrialization.

The Karve Committee, reporting in 1955, made a strong plea for the decentralization of industry.[1] It visualized the following kind of decentralized industrial pattern:

[1] Government of India, Planning Commission, *Report of Village and Small Scale Industry Committee* (New Delhi: October, 1955).

The pattern of industrial activity that should gradually emerge is that of a group of villages having its natural industrial and urban center. These small urban centers will be similarly related to bigger ones. Thus a pyramid of industry, broad based on a progressive rural economy will be built up. In such an organization small centers can experience a cooperative interest in the bigger ones and these latter would develop a genuinely supporting instead of an exploitational relationship towards the smaller towns and the countryside.[2]

This report helped pave the way for the Indian small-scale industry development program. It had a great deal to do with the philosophy that has since guided the execution of this program.

A number of clearly experimental types of programs have been undertaken with the special aim of obtaining rural industrialization.

During the past four years, 25 industrial projects have been undertaken by the Ministry of Community Development in areas covering one to three Development Blocks.[3] Three examples of good results are reported by a recent study team. At Kakinada, Andhra Pradesh, with intensive promotion of the Ambar Charka and improvement in other industries in 40 nonelectrified villages, employment was created for 3,000 people at an average wage of close to one rupee daily. In the electrified area of Neyyattinkara, near Kerala, progress was achieved entirely through small-scale industry. The investment was four times that of the Kakinada Block, but twice as many people were employed at daily earnings of about Rs. 2 in manufacturing pump parts and in assembling pumps and making coconut sprays and bicycles. In the Sharif Block in Bihar, progress in both village and small-scale industries was achieved. Besides problems in the organization of production, major problems were encountered in marketing and in reducing production costs.

It may be concluded that the experience so far gained in developing industry through the Community Development Program from the village level up has not been a general success. The appropriateness of extending industry to such small and predominantly rural areas may be questioned on both social and economic grounds. From an economic point of view, the probability of achieving successful industrial promotion is comparatively low. The cost of the promotional effort is relatively high and there is great danger of wasting economic resources in such efforts. The Delhi Seminar on Rural Industrialization agreed that the relevant question in this context was "What size of plant and production

---

[2] *Ibid.*, p. 22.
[3] Seminar on Rural Industrialization and Economic Development, held in New Delhi, March 14–15, 1960. Summary prepared by Richard Morse, p. 2.

technique is required for economic manufacture of a given prod
and which centers serve large enough markets to absorb the ou
of such a plant." [4]

The Small Scale Industries Organization has been condu
intensive campaigns recently with the aim of using the distric
an operational area for developing rural industry. The appr
is to make an area-development survey of industrial opportun
in the district. Publicity is then given concerning the findings
the kinds of assistance that the government is prepared to prov
Prospective entrepreneurs are sought out by technical persor
Then assistance is offered in the procurement of raw materials
in providing credit, marketing, and production guidance.

In the Warangal District of Andhra Pradesh, industrial grd
was stimulated over a period of several months at both the dis
headquarters and in several villages, with the aim of achie
interdependent growth. Village artisans were introduced into m
anized work, and factories were modernized in the small t
where agricultural and forest products were processed. Carper
trained in the near-by Rural Arts and Crafts Training Centr
Mulug placed orders for woodworking machinery through t
Coöperative Society. At the district headquarters of Warang
city of well over 100,000 people, 15 to 20 new small factories
being established on an industrial estate. These units will n
bicycle parts, builders' hardware, rice-mill and oil-engine s
parts, agricultural implements, bolts and nuts, and similar arti
The growth of industry at Warangal is expected to increase
demand for the products of village artisans. Warangal is vi
ized as an intermediary link between markets and raw mater
since it is a transport junction. A place such as Warangal prom
more opportunities of economic linkage than villages and s
towns, and for that reason offers greater chances of success th
smaller or more remote center.[5]

INDUSTRIAL ESTATES

The Indian industrial-estates program may be considered a
significant feature of the program for the planned decentra
tion of industry. The device of industrial estates is used as a m
anism for fostering small industry on a dispersed basis. The in
trial-estates program was actually initiated in 1955. Early in 1
96 estates had been sanctioned, of which 32 had been comple
another 28 should have been finished by the end of the year. W
completed, these estates would cost about Rs. 110 million

---

[4] *Ibid.,* p. 3.
[5] *Ibid.,* pp. 3–4.

ld establish 3,600 factories employing about 50,000 people.
present program calls for the development of 110 industrial
tes, widely distributed over the nation. Only small-scale enter-
es—defined as plants having a capital investment of no more
 Rs. 500,000—are permitted to settle on these government-
sored industrial estates.

he estates projects usually provide for factories of several
s, which may be obtained on rental, rental purchase, or direct
hase basis. The land is leveled, streets and access roads are
tructed, and public utilities, including water, sewage disposal,
electricity, are provided. In addition, special assistance is given
e industrialists who receive permission to settle on the estates,
ding the long-term rental of factories, high priorities for the
hase of equipment and machinery, hire-purchase loans for the
isition of machinery, and technical assistance from the Small
stries Service Institutes and Extension Centres. Frequently
kshops, demonstration centers, common facilities centers, and
r services are furnished on the estates with the aim of raising
luctivity and encouraging growth.[6]

uring 1959, the Central Committee on Employment of the
an Ministry of Labor recommended "the creation of employ-
t opportunities in rural areas by the establishment of rural
strial estates . . . and that development of small-scale cot-
 industries as a source of employment should be planned on a
onal basis as 'feeders to large-scale industries' on a pilot
s."[7] It is not known the extent to which the Indian govern-
t has embarked upon this program, but it indicates the inten-
 to push industry in the direction of the regional underdevel-
d areas and the rural communities.

lso during 1959, the National Planning Commission circu-
d a document prepared by Dr. Malhotra proposing a program
 "town-centered" small-industry development, with the aim
) to avoid further strain on the basic facilities where large
ustry is already concentrated, and (2) to bring employment as
 as possible to the doors of the unemployed."[8] The aim of this
posal is to seek industrialization of towns with a population
ging between 20,000 and 50,000, since by the end of the Second
e Year Plan most of these towns will be electrified. Surveys
ld be conducted to determine which of these towns would con-

William Bredo, *Industrial Estates—Tool for Industrialization*, a study made for
International Industrial Development Center, Stanford Research Institute, Menlo
k, California (Glencoe, Ill.: Free Press, 1960), pp. 28–29.
ndian Economic Newsletter, I, No. 12 (June, 1959), issued by the Embassy of
a, Washington, D.C.
eminar on Rural Industrialization, Summary, p. 5.

stitute natural economic foci of the surrounding rural areas. An Integrated Assistance Centre would be established to provide the various kinds of help needed to promote industrial growth in the towns selected. Industrial estates might be established. Village-centered industry would be supported—e.g., through the establishment of common facility centers. A variation of the proposal suggests that the grain market towns (*mandis*) are logical centers where growth might be stimulated, in view of the function of these market towns to assemble farm produce and serve as distribution points for village products. These *mandis* are normally linked by transportation to the villages and to the outside. It is expected that entrepreneurship and capital would be available from the established traders.[9]

One would tend to agree with the seminar group (the Seminar on Rural Industrialization and Economic Development, held in New Delhi in 1960) that cities of 20,000 to 50,000 population are probably too small to use as economic nuclei, unless there is evidence that industrial activity is developing. It does not seem feasible to consider every district town or city as a potential focal point for industrial development. As was pointed out in the seminar, an economic survey should study an area of perhaps five or six districts, so as to observe all of the economic interrelationships within a larger area before selecting a community to be promoted industrially.[10]

This brief introductory summary suggests that the approaches taken by the Indian government in looking for successful means of decentralizing industry have been rather diverse, experimental, and only partially successful. There is, however, strong indication that the industrial-estates program is going to be very successful, and this looks like a hopeful approach to the problem. In addition, a great deal is being learned from the various types of approaches, so that a successful program eventually may be put together.

The Basic Approach to Decentralization

Instead of letting the location of industry happen in a "natural" way, without any attempt at direction, it is considered possible and desirable to use various means of stimulating or guiding industry to communities where it is believed to be in the interest of a region or the nation. Effective methods can be developed for affecting industrialization in accordance with policy. In the past, policies have been indirect in their application within the framework of laissez faire. An industrial laissez-faire policy has operated in such

[9] *Ibid.*
[10] *Ibid.*, p. 6.

a way that it was in the interest of an enterprise to move toward the existing large economic agglomerations. The large cities developed the necessary infrastructure, and provided the external economies and the incentives of large markets to attract industry, all working together to encourage the clustering attribute of economic activity. There were the attractions of finance, of highly skilled management and technical personnel, of a trained pool of labor, and of highly developed transportation facilities. In the course of time, there developed also slums, traffic congestion, social problems, and political discontent, not to mention the high cost of social overhead facilities. These costs have never been reckoned in evaluating the role of laissez-faire policies in the process of economic development.

It must not be forgotten that in the process of city growth, public investments have always been large in the infrastructural facilities and in the social services, such as education and health. It is, therefore, important in looking at the components of the process of growth to evaluate especially the public investments which could be made as well in one community as in another. Moreover, there should be an evaluation of these costs in the large cities, compared with communities of smaller size, especially in the construction of housing and the provision of public utilities of water, sewage disposal, and electricity. But a complete evaluation should consider the total economic effects, including the induced agglomeration of industry in cities of different sizes. Nor can social and political costs and benefits be neglected.

Since public investments would have to be incurred, anyway, to provide the facilities and services for the population migrating to the cities and for the industrial enterprises stimulated there, the aim should be to establish the necessary infrastructure and the external economies needed to enable industry to survive. Industrial estates, improved financing, research, and industrial extension services are some of the devices necessary for attracting industry and for fostering industrial growth. Besides these, there may be the need to offer special inducements for attracting industry to underdeveloped areas, such as ready-built factories on industrial estates, favorable financing of equipment, tax concessions, possibly partial payment for the costs of shipping equipment, help in training staff, and so on. Such special assistance may be justified on the grounds that the comparatively high economic and social investments of the cities would not be required in the villages and small towns of the countryside.

It has been found through experience that investments in social overhead facilities and a favorable attitude on the part of govern-

ment do not in themselves induce industrial investment. Var
incentives and measures of assistance are needed to make inv
ments sufficiently attractive. It has been suggested that busi
might be required to pay a special assessment for the additi
costs of social overhead investments to accommodate the pop
tion of large metropolitan centers, compared to the cost of acc
modating the same populations in smaller urban or rural comm
ties. The levying of such direct tax assessments, however, in a
tion to the normal taxation of large cities, could be discoura
to investment. Besides, the approach is essentially negative,
rather than encouraging investment in dispersed locations it m
constitute a general hindrance to investment. Consequently
would seem much preferable for government to provide a w
gamut of incentives to induce industry to establish itself away f
the big cities.

In encouraging industry to settle in smaller urban centers,
ceivably additional investments could be justified, and certain t
of industry-assisting institutions should be established to put
potential industrial locations on a comparably attractive basi
industrialists.

REDUCING REGIONAL DISPARITIES IN ECONOMIC CONDITION

In India, as in most of the newly developing countries, there
wide regional disparities in per capita income and living lev
Speaking generally, such great regional differences within count
tend to create strains of substantial political dimensions, so tha
some instances the very existence of the nation is threatened
other cases, sizable segments of the population are still living ur
tribal conditions, and the government may be interested in draw
them into the main stream of national development to increase t
social contribution and to reduce social tensions in the future.
decentralization, industrial centers may be established to cr
nuclei of economic activity in underdeveloped regions. The imp
of industrialization on the less developed regions can be maximi
and the advantages of spreading out and dispersing the popula
will be gained.

Furthermore, to reduce the attraction of the large cities, i
essential to make village life more attractive. It may be true i
the attraction of the cities has been less of a factor in dome
migration than the lack of opportunities in the villages. By bring
industry closer to the villages, industrial jobs are going to be av
able near at hand. In many cases, rural workers may be able to c
mute to industrial jobs by bicycle from their villages. Industria
comes higher than other rural incomes, coupled with more

lier employment, should substantially affect rural living con-
ns. Moreover, the increase in the goods available from expand-
industrial centers should also improve the life in the homes.

conomical transportation systems and facilities are essential for
ling industry to penetrate into the less developed interior re-
s of the country, and to link them to the metropolitan com-
ties. Communication systems need to be provided for the ex-
ge of essential information by developing adequate mail serv-
elegraph, and telephone systems. In some regions there may be
eed for extending an electrification grid systm, in order to make
r accessible, although in the very early stages of development
onary power units may be adequate. In some areas, water sup-
and disposal of effluent may be essential for industrial purposes
will have to be developed on an adequate scale. The cost of
iding all these essential facilities needs to be taken into account
eighing the advisability of encouraging industrialists to pene-
into less populous communities.

establishing industry in less developed regions, the kind of
prise should be weighed perhaps even more carefully than
l in evaluating its possible impact on the chances for success.
rever possible, industry should develop local resources to re-
transportation costs, as well as to use resources that would
rwise be unutilized or would have to be imported. Further-
, wherever possible, the kinds of industry selected should be
as would produce for local consumption or assist in local
uction, so as to provide consumers' goods for improving the
uctivity of the household and the content of living, and pro-
rs' goods for increasing the productivity of agriculture and
industry, or to increase the demand for local products. Of
se, there will be many cases where the products of a regional
rce will be unique and plentiful, and will be able to supply
ational or even international market, such as certain mineral
rces, forestry and paper products, and fisheries. Such in-
ies should provide an opportunity for spearheading industry
derdeveloped areas.

basic consideration in establishing a regional industry is the
ion of size of the enterprise to the size of the market. Since
regional market is usually limited, it is of more than normal
rtance to evaluate the size of the market. Too frequently in
lishing industry, enterprises have been handicapped by the
lness of the market or by the fact that the size of the market
unknown. Ignorance of the market is probably one of the
test deterrents to industrialization, since prospective en-
eneurs are faced with the high risk of establishing an enter-

prise in a situation where a large degree of uncertainty exists and the testing of the market may involve economic hazards.

INTERDEPENDENCE OF THE
RURAL AND URBAN ECONOMIES

It would be fair to say that the Community Development Program, so far, has failed to come up to expectations with respect to progress in promoting agricultural production and in developing rural industry. Considerable progress has been made in improving the sanitary conditions of the villages, in improving the roads to connect the villages with the larger economy, and, perhaps most important, in promoting the spirit of village self-help. On the other hand, progress in agriculture has been indifferent. The failure of the agricultural sector significantly to increase the food supply, to reduce food imports, to increase agricultural exports, or to provide increased revenues for development has had sharp repercussions on the execution of the Second Five Year Plan.

In the view of the writer, the role of industrialization in bringing about change in agriculture, especially in an underdeveloped economy, has been generally misunderstood. Outside of biological improvements in crop and livestock production, reflection will suggest that improvements in agricultural productivity are dependent upon the farm machinery and the inputs of fertilizer and pesticides produced by industry. The application of most improved cultural practices in farming is dependent upon equipment manufactured by industry. The improved technology derived from industry is the source of the dynamic elements responsible for transformation of agriculture and of major aspects of village life. This factor has been missing in the Community Development Program. In the provision of agricultural implements, there are still vast gaps and many technological steps to be traversed in India. In the operations of harvesting and threshing, for example, it is unfortunately impossible to record any progress over the ancient methods.

Similarly, improved equipment is essential for raising the productivity of the village artisan. Better methods of using traditional tools and equipment will have only negligible effects on improving productivity and income.

If this kind of analysis is accepted, the role of industry in the process of economic development is placed in a new light. Industry provides the dynamic characteristic of the economy which is responsible for improvements in the productivity of the human person and of agricultural land.

If satisfactory measures can be developed, it will be possible to bring the rural areas into the main stream of technological development. The rural areas will be brought into the monetary market economy, and improved transportation will bring about closer and more competitive price relationships between regions. The traditional separation of the two segments of the economy will be ended. In a variety of ways, economic linkage between the urban and rural economies needs to be developed for the purpose of increasing the impact of industrial development on agriculture and the rural people.

In one direction linkage should be obtained by providing the producers' goods—the implements, equipment, and tools—required by farmers and village artisans for increasing their productivity and improving rural living. This will be the mechanism for increasing incomes and enlarging rural expenditures on industrial goods.

The linkage of agriculture to industry, on the other hand, is developed by encouraging the establishment of firms processing farm products and by improving marketing services. These are essential for increasing the demand for farm products and increasing the diversification of agriculture. Agricultural processing (including the processing of agricultural wastes into feeds and food products) is also the basis for improving the utilization of many farm products. In addition, farm products should become the base for many industrial commodities.

A further linkage with the industrial economy is obtained by strengthening the producers'-goods industries which manufacture the equipment required for processing and handling farm produce. In addition, machine and repair shops need to be provided close to the agricultural areas to service farm and processing equipment.

Another linkage between industry and agriculture is in the employment opportunities created for rural labor. This will have two aspects: first, the provision of equipment to permit more effective use of labor in agriculture and cottage industry, and, secondly, the provision of agricultural employment. The latter point raises the important question as to how far industry should move to the villages to tap the supply of rural underemployed labor.

Such a program of economic linkage will have the effect of establishing that upward spiral in the circularity of production and marketing which is essential in order to bring the rural economy to new levels of output.[11]

By approaching rural development in these terms, the question of industrial location is introduced into the problem of economic development strategy. This brings a new dimension into the

---

[11] Ragnar Nurkse, *Problems of Capital Formation in Underdeveloped Countries* (New York: Oxford University Press, 1953).

philosophy of economic development. It means that in econo
planning it is necessary to think in terms not only of what kin
industry is to be developed, but of where industry is to be loca
Thus, appropriate principles and policies need to be devised
locating industry geographically with the purpose of ensuring
full impact upon less developed regions and the country
whole.

THE PROCESS OF ECONOMIC GROWTH
AND INDUSTRIAL LOCATION

The process of urban growth appears to be self-stimulating.
large cities seem to provide the conditions essential for the r
accumulation of capital, the stimulation of industrial entrepren
ship, and the creation of the institutions that foster indus
growth. Apparently, certain external economies support and st
late the growth of industry, and once this process is under w
tends to stimulate itself. Attention has been drawn by student
the fact that this process has operated not only within nations,
also, with significant consequences, in international trade.

Both in interregional and international trade the process
tended to work so that, in effect, industrialization is transmi
only slowly to underdeveloped areas.

There is an extremely heavy concentration of industry in
bay and Calcutta, where close to half of the larger Indian m
facturing plants are located. Both of these cities were develope
a result of trade with the West. At first only trading centers,
grew in the course of time into populous cities with heavy
dustrial concentrations which have encouraged further growth
a sense, they have a closer relation to overseas economies tha
the rest of India. The limited analysis presented in the Appe
to this paper supports this hypothesis, as reflected in the fact
no major shift has occurred in the dispersion of industry from
high concentration in these two large industrial complexes. It
supports the thesis that the economic process seems to work in
direction of further bolstering the growth of centers where t
is already a clustering of industry or commercial activity.

Once this process is understood it raises the possibility of ta
a creative approach to economic growth by fostering industry
different spatial pattern and perhaps at a more rapid pace
would take place in the absence of such deliberate action. I
effective approach of this kind can be developed, it may be pos
to achieve a better compromise between desirable social and
nomic goals without the serious problems that have histori
arisen when the location of industry was controlled.

here has been some tendency in professional and scientific circles
ccept prevailing patterns of population distribution in urban
ers, on the basis that the existing pattern is the result of the
of natural forces, and that therefore it is inevitable, if not
rable. A rule has been formulated to rationalize this tendency
populations so to arrange themselves as to result in a certain
ing of population centers by size.[12]

oresters, biologists, and agronomists are realizing that an exist-
distribution of population of plant life may not necessarily be
, and that there may be more than one optimum distribution
population. We may note that Pareto's Law of Income Dis-
ution has a great measure of validity, as far as we know, in its
lication to comparatively advanced societies. Yet we know also
there are considerable deviations from this norm and that the
uency distribution changes considerably even within the same
try with changing business conditions. Pareto's rule was formu-
d before the income tax was in vogue, which has important
lifying effects on the size structure of income. Thus there are,
easingly, grounds for believing that, up to certain points, im-
tant economic aims may be achieved by egalitarian measures
as income taxation and from greater access of the people to
cation and economic opportunity.

y analogy, perhaps the same arguments may be applied to the
distribution of cities. This is not to say that an equal size
ribution of cities is necessarily desirable, but that some sig-
ant deviations from the distribution implicit in the rank-size
m may be in the interest of countries from economic, political,
social points of view. It is conceivable that by a policy of de-
tralization economic growth may be stimulated in many places,
hat the over-all gain may be greater than would have been the
if the process of industrialization had been allowed to con-
e under conditions of laissez faire.

This paper proceeds from the hypothesis that it is feasible to
uence the course of urbanization during the process of in-
trialization of a country, and that this can be done without using
sures that are unduly restrictive or costly. It also proceeds from
value judgment that it may well be desirable to change the
sent pattern of urbanization of the population toward one that
ld improve the social and economic welfare of the nation.

CONSIDERATIONS IN ESTABLISHING INDUSTRIAL NUCLEI

One of the most important issues is where to locate the industrial
lei spearheading industrial decentralization in certain areas. It

See chap. i, note 9, for an explanation of the rank-size rule.

is not to be assumed that industry should be established from "scratch." A very large private or public corporation may be able to withstand losses for as long as four or five years, while the market is being developed and production is pushed to capacity; but for most types of industry that would be promoted in a decentralization program, especially industry developed by private enterprise, it would be necessary to establish the operation on a viable economic footing right from the beginning. Viability is, therefore, an important determining factor, dictating where industry should be located.

While experience has been comparatively limited concerning the possibility of developing industry in the villages, there is enough to support a relatively firm hypothesis that such attempts are going to be faced with considerable handicaps. Village industry could be costly to establish from the standpoint of finding the entrepreneurs, putting them into business, and then having a high proportion of failures. The chances of commercial success probably are against the village entrepreneur unless there is uniqueness in the resources locally available, the market, the source of financing, or the entrepreneur's own qualifications. On the other hand, where the village entrepreneur has shown initiative and good judgment, and appears to have prospects, he should be assisted to grow and become a success.

The basic problem in establishing industry is that of finding a market large enough to permit the operation of an enterprise upon an economical scale. The usual bottleneck encountered in initiating village-based industry is that of too small a market for the operation of an enterprise using comparatively modern technology. For this reason some would argue that the prospects of establishing strong industrial nuclei are definitely enhanced if the program is based on cities with a population in the neighborhood of 100,000 or larger.

Clearly, there can be no simple prescription for selecting nucleus communities where industrial enterprise may be promoted with a high chance of success. Good entrepreneurs have grown up in much smaller cities, though this achievement is generally difficult under Asian conditions, where the infrastructure and the external economies are not usually sufficiently developed. Therefore, the communities selected should preferably contain some enterprises already operating successfully. The presence of successful enterprises indicates that the market has been tested, that the management has ingredients of success, and that the community provides conditions essential for the growth and survival of industry. The community should have a progressive tone, as reflected in the attitudes of its businessmen and leaders. There should be a buoyant outlook toward the future, resulting from recent growth and good future prospects.

There should, also, be indications that entrepreneurship can be found in the area. While there will be possibilities for interesting entrepreneurs from outside the area, especially for the establishing of branch plants, the main reliance will probably need to be placed on obtaining local entrepreneurship. Wherever possible, there should be several local resources or a number of market opportunities which could be feasibly developed.

The presence of local educational institutions, such as universities, schools of technology, vocational institutions, Community Development training schools or academies, and industrial research and extension facilities, will be a material supporting condition. These institutions will be a means for training potential managers, supervisors, and skilled workers, and may even be a training ground for the development of entrepreneurs.

The potential industrial nucleus should be well located on good transportation facilities and services. Good road connections are essential, but rail service is not vital unless bulky or heavy minerals or other industrial raw materials or finished products require to be transported.

Finally, it is well to have rather well-developed banking and credit facilities, not only to mobilize local capital, but to assist in bringing the advantages of a modern credit system into less developed areas.

Wherever possible, large firms should be encouraged to establish smaller branch plants in dispersed locations, provided this can be done on an economic basis, instead of enlarging an existing plant. This is an excellent method of spearheading decentralization, since it permits an extension of existing entrepreneurship, management, and finance—all scarce resources. Such encouragement of large industry is more likely to be successful if it is planned as part of an industrial-estates program. Furthermore, an industrial estate comprised principally of small-scale and medium industry has better chances of developing and becoming successful if one or more larger enterprises are also situated there.

Larger firms should also be encouraged to procure repair parts and semifabricated materials by subcontracting. In the underdeveloped countries, particularly, firms frequently desire to place as little dependence on outside suppliers as possible, and may aim to become self-sufficient in view of the uncertainty of obtaining parts or materials when needed and of the kind and quality required. The small supplying firm is frequently dependent upon uncertain

raw-material supplies. It is also beset by many other problems
conditions over which it has no control. On the other hand,
contracting is of supreme importance to the economy, and is, th
fore, a method of doing business that should be encouraged.
government could take the lead in its own procurement prog
by providing some concessions or preferences to firms that do
contracting.

Subcontracting provides a number of advantages. In many c
a domestic source is created in place of a foreign supplier. F
competition is increased as more firms are put into the same l
of business. In addition, atomization of production may be gener
desirable, as it reduces the need for regulation. The know-how
production is transmitted to other industrial units. The opport
ties for extending entrepreneurship are expanded to a ma
which would otherwise be retained within a large firm. The
curing firm may also provide financial assistance to the new f
It is conceivable, too, that economies in production may be achie
through specialization.

It should be clear that the major bottleneck in achieving a
cessful program of industrial decentralization comes from
absence or inadequate development of the local infrastructure
the external economies considered essential by industrialists. I
difficult at this stage to identify the particular features of a com
group of external economies. This is a matter that needs to
studied in existing industrial concentrations and perhaps exp
mentally by building certain external economies into new indus
nuclei. The problem of identification should not be insurmounta
Nor should the cost of providing the minimum external econo
be financially excessive. Quite conceivably, there are economie
scale, based on the size of the industrial complex.

It is believed that the industrial-estate concept provides the
to the solution of this problem. It is the means by which a la
cluster of enterprises can be brought together to benefit from
common pool of managers, supervisors, and skilled workers,
from the exchange of goods. Economies of scale are possibl
the construction of the estate and in providing the public util
more cheaply than these could be provided by industrialists. '
industrial estate provides a complex sufficiently large to mak
economical to provide good transportation and communica
services. For the same reason, it becomes economically feasibl
provide a whole variety of contributing services, to small
dustrialists especially, such as research, industrial extension, tr
ing, and credit facilities. Where the industrial complex or
community is large enough, it may even be feasible to provide t

nological institutes, vocational training schools, and possibly institutions of higher learning from which many of the future managers and entrepreneurs may be expected to come. The industrial estate, therefore, may well be the means whereby the local infrastructure and the external economies demanded by entrepreneurs as a precondition for industrial clustering can be deliberately created and used for executing an industrial dispersal program.

THE POSSIBILITY OF A PHASED
DECENTRALIZATION PROGRAM

A developing country, even a comparatively advanced country, will be handicapped in executing a program of industrial decentralization, due to the inadequate development of the infrastructure in dispersed and outlying communities. To penetrate into the less developed areas it is necessary to construct or improve transportation facilities, especially roads; to extend the electric power grid; and to provide a water supply, telephone communication, and other facilities. Since these investments are costly, comparative economic studies must be made to determine whether to develop dispersed industrial outposts to accommodate new industry, or whether to add on to the public utilities and roads of existing industrial centers.

While industrial decentralization undoubtedly can be justified, the real question may be the pace at which it can be economically and effectively promoted in areas away from established centers of economic activity. This question is also related to another issue— whether it may be better economic strategy to plan on a phased penetration of less developed areas. Such an approach may be more economical and more feasible from a financial standpoint. It may also permit a more certain impact by developing urban centers close to existing industrial centers where growth is already well started. Then, as investment resources permit, the infrastructure would be extended and the necessary external economies would be built in, so that successful industrial nuclei could be established in places where the industrial spark is beginning to flicker. Implicit in such an approach is the possibility of extending the coverage of industrial urbanization into underdeveloped areas where there are opportunities for developing important natural resources, such as minerals, or to develop ports, railway junctions, or other significant infrastructural features. These investments should have important multiplier effects on the regional economies in themselves and, in addition, should serve to encourage the clustering of industrial and commercial activity, once the basic investments have been made. Such developmental and infrastructural investment should present opportunities for pushing the creation of industrial nuclei into the interior or to distant points, from which further industrialization may radiate. In this way investments in the development of resources and important infrastructural features can be used effectively and in an integrated way with the industrialization program, so that a phased development of the interior may be achieved in an economic and effective manner.

APPENDIX: A NOTE ON INDUSTRIAL-LOCATION TRENDS IN INDIA*

Since the future pattern of urbanization will be shaped largely by industrial development, it is of basic importance to understand present trends in the location of industry, including the forces and criteria that determine these decisions. Although such studies have probably been made in connection with the formulation of the Third Plan, no factual analysis seemed to be available at the time of writing. A list of licensed industries had been issued by the Indian government,[1] however, and some tabulations were made from this raw material.

The government's list gives the names and addresses of plants licensed to produce various types of manufactured products scheduled under the 1951 Act. Several qualifications should be noted. (1) Plants must have more than 50 employees (100 if no power is used), and an investment of over Rs. 500,000, but no size indication beyond these minima is given. (2) Listing is under 36 different product classifications, and a plant may appear under more than one heading if its products are varied.[2] (3) The different types of license are not fully explained, but they all seem to signify either new, enlarged, or revived production; or a change in plant locale, and hence expanded manufacture of a particular type in the listed location. The data, therefore, appear to indicate places where certain kinds of production, in plants of substantial size, have increased between 1951 and 1957. If these judgments are correct, our rough tabulations should serve to suggest recent location trends for growing industries of various types.

The distribution of licenses for selected industries by city size is shown in Table 1. The total number of licenses issued under the Industry (Development and Regulation) Act of 1951, was 1,882.

---

* This Appendix is based on material prepared by William Bredo and Richard Ellefsen.—*Ed.*

[1] Government of India, Ministry of Commerce and Industry, *List of Industrial Undertakings Licensed by the Central Government under the Industries (Development and Regulation) Act, 1951 (65 of 1951), as on 31st December, 1957* (Delhi: Government of India Press, 1959).

[2] For an interesting critique of this method of classification, see "Industrial Censuses," *Economic Weekly,* November 28, 1959, pp. 1608–1610.

TABLE 1

DISTRIBUTION OF URBAN POPULATION AND MANUFACTURING-ENTERPRISE LICENSES (TOTAL FOR SELECTED SCHEDULED INDUSTRIES AND BY-PRODUCT GROUPS) BY SIZE CLASS OF CITY, INDIA, 1951–1957

Size class of city	Per cent of urban population, 1951[a]	Licenses issued to selected scheduled industries		Per cent distribution of licenses among product groups								
		Number	Per cent	Metallurgical industry	Bicycles	Electric lamps and fans	Chemicals, pharmaceuticals, and drugs	Glass, ceramics, cement, and gypsum	Agricultural products processing			
									Total[b]	Veg. oils	Sugar	Cotton textiles
Class I (100,000 and over)	41.8	680	47.6	45.6	51.0	70.2	72.8	43.0	41.2	46.9	4.6	50.8
Cities over 1,000,000:												
Calcutta and Bombay	12.0	328	23.0	30.8	16.3	48.9	47.2	22.6	13.9	19.0	1.3	15.8
Madras, Delhi, and Hyderabad	6.3	42	2.9	1.6	8.2	...	5.6	3.2	5.5	...	0.7	3.4
Cities 100,000–1,000,000	23.5	310	21.7	13.2	26.5	21.3	20.6	17.2	21.8	27.9	2.6	31.6
Class II (50,000–100,000)	10.1	103	7.2	9.9	...	...	1.5	4.3	9.7	10.1	6.6	10.8
Class III (20,000–50,000)	16.7	173	12.1	15.9	18.4	10.6	6.2	11.3	12.6	10.1	14.5	15.7
Classes IV, V and VI (less than 20,000)	31.4	471	33.1	28.6	30.6	19.2	19.5	41.4	36.5	32.9	74.3	22.7
Total	100.0	...	100.0	100.0	100.0	100.0	100.0	100.0	100.0	100.0	100.0	100.0
Total number of licenses issued for each product group	...	1,427	...	182	49	47	195	186	768	79	152	406

NOTE: Licensed establishments are those employing 50 workers and using power, or employing 100 workers if no power is used; the figures include licenses granted and subsequently revoked. The "selected scheduled" industries are those reported in the Census of Indian Manufactures of 1951; they include metallurgical industries; bicycles; electric lamps and fans; chemicals, drugs, and pharmaceuticals; glass, gypsum, cement, and ceramics; and selected agricultural-products processing industries, including jute, woolen, and cotton textiles, vegetable oils, sugar, timber, leather goods, soaps, food processing, and paper.

[a] Based on the 1951 census.

[b] Includes jute, woolen, and cotton textiles; vegetable oils; sugar; timber; leather goods; soaps; food processing; and paper.

The table is based on the classification of 1,427 licenses arranged according to the 29 selected industries included in the 1951 Census of Indian Manufactures.

Turning to the four broad city size-groups, it is interesting to note that the percentage of licenses in each group was rather similar to the proportion of the total urban population in each category, although somewhat higher in cities over 100,000 (almost double in Bombay and Calcutta), and somewhat lower in cities of 20,000 to 50,000. In different industrial categories, the variation was, of course, high.

From this, it would appear that the general distribution of growing industries among different city size-classes was fairly even. This, however, raises an important question. How much of the growth in small communities was within the metropolitan orbit of the major industrial centers? Further tabulations are shown in Table 2. These are not strictly comparable with Table 1, since this table includes additional industrial categories and hence more licenses. By determining the location of licensed firms within metropolitan Calcutta and Bombay,[3] it was found that 35 per cent of the total was in these two centers, which comprised 14 per cent of the urban population in 1951. Since these metropolitan plants may also be larger, on the average, than those in smaller cities, it would appear that there is still a very strong trend toward industrial expansion in or near the old major centers, despite the efforts toward wider dispersal. If some of the inherently localized processing industries such as sugar and cement are excluded, the share of industry in these two metropolitan areas is even greater.

The uneven distribution of growing industry by states is indicated in Table 3, which compares the geographical distribution of industry derived from the Census of Indian Manufactures of 1951 with the licenses issued to "scheduled" industries over the period 1951–57. The 1951 census shows 6,978 factories in existence which "employed 20 or more workers on any day and used power in the manufacturing process." [4] As referred to earlier, the scheduled industries licensed under the Industries (Development and Regulation) Act of 1951 include plants having more than 50 employees (or 100 if no power is used), and an investment of over Rs. 500,000. A total of 1,882 licenses was issued for this industrial group (second column), and a total of 1,427 licenses was issued to

---

[3] Metropolitan areas as delimited and listed in International Urban Research, *The World's Metropolitan Areas* (Berkeley and Los Angeles: University of California Press, 1959).

[4] Government of India, Ministry of Commerce and Industry, Department of Commercial Intelligence and Statistics, "Summary of Census of Indian Manufactures 1950–54," special supplement to *Indian Trade Journal*, August 24, 1957, p. 2.

TABLE 2

LOCATION OF INDUSTRIAL-PRODUCT GROUPS IN THE BOMBAY AND CALCUTTA METROPOLITAN AREAS

Code number	Industrial-product group	Total number of licenses (all India)	Per cent of all-India licenses in:	
			Bombay MA	Calcutta MA
1	Metallurgical industries.........	231	20	26
2	Fuels........................	9	22	...
4	Prime movers (nonelectric)......	14	29	...
5	Electrical equipment...........	164	26	26
6	Telecommunications...........	29	24	17
7	Transportation................	127	17	18
8	Industrial machinery...........	82	19	18
9	Machine tools.................	13	23	23
10	Agricultural machinery.........	21	29	10
12	Miscellaneous mechanical and engineering.................	30	30	40
19	Chemicals (excluding fertilizers)..	113	21	12
21	Dyestuffs.....................	17	82	...
22	Drugs and pharmaceuticals......	102	52	14
23	Textiles......................	569	20	9
24	Paper and pulp (including paper products)...................	45	7	13
25	Sugar........................	154	...	...
26	Fermentation industries.........	25	...	...
28	Vegetable oils and *vanaspati*.....	92	18	4
29	Soaps, cosmetics, etc...........	15	33	27
30	Rubber goods..................	36	22	69
31	Leather goods.................	10	...	...
33	Glass........................	53	42	15
34	Ceramics.....................	79	3	32
35	Cement and gypsum products....	73	...	...
36	Timber products...............	16	...	19
	Total Establishments.........	2,119	...	...
	Without sugar and cement.......	1,892	...	...

the group of "selected scheduled" industries (first column). The data reflect a very close correspondence in the patterns of distribution of industry among the various states between the census and the licensing statistics. Some higher concentrations of the scheduled industries are shown for the states of West Bengal, Madras, Punjab, Mysore, and Madhaya Pradesh. But it is obviously not clear whether these are attributable to shifts of industry over the 1951–57 period or due to differences in the industrial classification.

This is a field where systematic research is badly needed, not

TABLE 3

PER CENT DISTRIBUTION BY STATE OF CERTAIN LARGE INDUSTRIES
AND OF LICENSES IN SELECTED SCHEDULED INDUSTRIES
AND IN ALL SCHEDULED INDUSTRIES

State	Licenses, 1951–1957		Industry (factories) in 1951
	Selected scheduled industries[a]	All scheduled industries[b]	
Andhra	. . .[c]	. . .[c]	. .[d]
Assam	1.4	1.0	1.1
Bihar	4.6	4.4	5.6
Bombay	23.8	28.3	29.4
Kerala	3.1	2.4	3.3
Madhaya Pradesh	5.0	4.9	0.6
Madras	20.2	17.5	15.9
Mysore	1.8	3.9	. . .
Orissa	5.7	1.9	3.3
Punjab	5.2	6.8	4.8
Rajasthan	1.7	1.3	2.4
Uttar Pradesh	10.1	8.7	11.6
West Bengal	14.6	17.9	14.6
Delhi	2.2	2.6	2.0
Other	0.6	0.1	1.1
Total	100.0	100.0	100.0

NOTE: The large industries are those reported in the Census of Indian Manufactures of 1951.

[a] Licenses issued under the Industries (Development and Regulation) Act of 1951 for the 29 industries included in the Census of Indian Manufactures of 1951.

[b] Licenses issued under the Industries (Development and Regulation) Act of 1951.

[c] Included in Madras are 4.5 per cent for "selected scheduled industries" and 3.8 per cent for all scheduled industries.

[d] Included in Madras.

only in terms of industrial location data per se, but also on the public and private bases for decision making that determine economic geography.

XIII

URBAN CENTRALIZATION
AND PLANNED DEVELOPMENT

Britton Harris

It is impossible to consider the importance of urban and metropolitan development in relation to industrialization and economic
development as a whole without some reference to the more general
problems of the goals which Indian society is setting for itself, and
to their possibilities of achievement. In briefly discussing these
goals, it is not my intention to trespass on the capacity and responsibility of our Indian colleagues to consider and evaluate
them. I propose to speak only as a reporter in presenting impres-
sionistically a few of the major goals which appear to have been
adopted or considered for adoption in India, and to speak, in my
capacity as an economist-planner, as to their relations with urban
patterns. Since I agree that centralization versus decentralization *is*
a key issue facing government at the highest level within India, the
determination of an appropriate policy in relation to this issue
necessarily involves the highest goals of, and the most important
measures of developmental control available to, India as a whole.
Any failure to state my impression of the structure of goals and
my opinion as to their implications would leave open the possibility
that I might inject my own values in a manner not readily identifi-
able.

THE GOALS OF INDIAN DEVELOPMENT

It is hardly necessary to say that the over-all goal of Indian society
and the Indian nation is human welfare, welfare being considered
in the broadest sense to include not only material goods, but also

human dignity and cultural values. To make this statement does not substantially advance the analysis except to make it clear that no one could impute to India any goal of national aggrandizement or power aside from the moral power which would inhere in attaining this primary goal.

Obviously, the attainment of human welfare requires implementation through the establishment of major subsidiary goals. I take it that the paramount such goal in India is, for the present, material progress, subject to certain restraints or bounds to be mentioned. To a certain extent, the achievement of cultural and spiritual welfare is recognized to be dependent on a minimal level of physical welfare which, in turn, depends upon productive capacity. It appears to be implicit in Indian planning that social and cultural goals cannot adequately be achieved without a necessary physical base in the production of food, housing, clothing, and cultural materials. Although the levels to which these things may need to be supplied in India could be substantially below levels sought by the advanced Western countries, they are substantially above levels now prevailing in India. From this it follows that India faces a long period of substantial effort to effect the necessary economic transformation.

In the realm of political and cultural values, India is committed to a fundamentally democratic, and to some extent socialist, pattern of society. At the very least, the term "socialist" is to be taken to imply that vested property interests shall not be permitted to impede the satisfaction of human needs. At the most, it apparently should be taken to mean that government shall own and develop transportation, communications, irrigation, and all or part of critical manufacturing industries. It would appear that most commerce and finance and a very large proportion of manufacturing industry, as well as all agricultural production, are to be privately owned and managed, though regulated.

The democratic commitment of Indian policy, in the exigencies of daily political life, demands that not all increments of production be devoted to development, but that some of the benefits be provided in the form of rising consumption standards. Such improvement in the level of living is in itself a necessary prerequisite to economic development, since education, nutrition, health, and shelter are needed for improved productivity.

Any consideration of these broadest goals indicates immediately certain sources of conflict in hammering out current policy. There is no automatic balance between investment and consumption. Likewise, the growth of private-interest groups through economic development in the private sector leads to potential conflicts in the determination of policy. What may be democratic development for one group may appear undemocratic to another. Such conflicts are unavoidable with the differentiation of economic function, ownership, and interest accompanying economic growth.

The desire to preserve certain existing Indian cultural patterns and values presents a special problem worthy of more extended consideration than is possible here. Such respect for existing patterns of culture is implicit in the general view of the leaders of India. It is, however, apparent that since preëxisting cultural values have not resulted in sufficient economic progress, some new values and cultural patterns must be adopted and adapted in India. The extent and pace of this adaptation are serious policy problems.

Judgment on most of the foregoing issues has to be based on the question of urgency in economic development, and it would appear that most conflicts over policy can ultimately be traced back to deep differences in the evaluation of this urgency. In my own estimation, the choices which face India are extraordinarily difficult, because at present levels of population and resources, including existing capital resources, the chances for the success of an economic development effort are dangerously low. Failure of the present effort could lead to political, social, and economic chaos. These would induce widespread suffering of the bitterest kind; and at a later date the further increase of population and attenuation of resources would increase the conflict between measures to achieve desired development and the democratic presuppositions currently in force in India. Thus, in my view, those policies which in so far as possible postpone present consumption and push speedy development at the cost of some present cultural values are fundamentally justified. They would, in the long run, provide a better chance for higher levels of living and a coherent, self-directed national cultural development.

URBANISM AND ECONOMIC GROWTH

In this general picture of Indian development problems, urban development occupies a special place. Urbanism and industrial development are, in my opinion, closely linked but not wholly interdependent phenomena. For reasons which will be developed below, cities provide certain outstanding advantages for the development of industry. At the same time, the capital needs of urban development and the expanded and revalued consumption patterns of the urban population are in part satisfied by industrially produced commodities. The reduction of rural population pressure through rural-to-urban migration facilitates the adoption of improved agricultural methods which require manufactured fertilizers, tools, and capital goods. Higher levels of income in rural areas may

create a demand for manufactured articles of consumption. Together with taxation, the increased rural demand for manufactured
goods is an essential prerequisite for the exchange needed in the
provisioning of cities.

It is thus apparent that urbanization and industrialization are
concomitant parts of a much larger process which vitally involves
the rural areas. In this process, we wish particularly to focus upon
the developmental role of cities and metropolitan areas, first as they
constitute growing points in the economy which are particularly
well suited to industrial development, and, second, as they place
heavy demands upon the developmental resources of the nation as
a whole. These demands already are so great, and give evidence of
increasing so rapidly, that their importance cannot be overlooked.
In the context of the earlier remarks as to the urgent nature of development, urbanism would not merit the detailed attention given
here, were it not a problem of such magnitude as could gravely en-
danger the successes of developmental planning.

In order to review these problems in better perspective, some
estimation of the major magnitudes involved is needed.

Urban areas are growing at approximately 4 per cent per year,
or over 40 per cent per decade. It is thus predictable that if the
1961 census reveals a total population of over 435 million, it will
likewise reveal an urban population of approximately 90 million.
Over the three decades from 1951 to 1981, in which the population of India will increase to 600 million, urban population will
probably increase to at least 180 million.

The economic attraction of urban areas may not yet have exhibited its full potency. The Third and Fourth Five Year Plans
now in prospect will represent a critical period for industrial development. With the increased availability of basic metals and with
more locally produced machine tools, a rapid spurt of development
is hoped for and is entirely possible. This spurt may be accentuated
if vigorous foreign-exchange restrictions accelerate local production of desired commodities. Such a rapid multiplication of new
industry may greatly enhance the attraction of urban areas and, in
fact, touch off during the next ten years a much more rapid movement of the potentially available rural migrants.

In the face of the implication that 35 to 40 million persons might
migrate into urban areas in the coming decade, many people in-
stinctively infer that such migration must be directly or indirectly
controlled. Some consideration is given to possible indirect control
in the later discussion. Direct controls, however, are explicitly
rejected as undemocratic and unworkable. Even in more highly
controlled societies where residence permits have been issued and

direct controls attempted, the results have been unsatisfactory. In India, such an expansion of governmental controls is contrary to established policy. In the rural areas, it would especially have the undesirable effect of restricting personal mobility and subjecting the underprivileged more than ever to the control of petty local tyranny.

The predictable wave of urban growth has inescapable conclusions for investment policy, public and private. A total increase of at least 40 million persons in urban areas in the coming decade means approximately 8 million new households and 13 million new jobs or, per quinquennium, 4,000,000 and 6,500,000, respectively. The cost of providing one new dwelling-unit is estimated in the Second Five Year Plan at Rs. 5,000, but this estimate does not apply to the unorganized and unaided "self-help" housing which represents little social investment. The average cost might better be placed at Rs. 2,000 per house. The provision of employment opportunities requires the provision of working space and equipment; the latter will be largely disregarded as being provided for elsewhere in the Plan. Space requirements, however, will amount to between 100 and 200 square feet per employee, excluding hawkers, vendors, transportation employees, public-administration employees, public-school teachers, hospital employees, and others who either work in the open or whose space is otherwise provided. The incremental growth of urban population under favorable circumstances will be more heavily weighted with manufacturing employees and organized commercial employees whose space requirements meet the foregoing standards and are not otherwise provided for in the Plans. A rough workable assumption would be that 40 per cent of all employees added in urban areas will require 100 square feet of work space each, at a cost of Rs. 20 per square foot. The extension of urban services, mainly roads, utilities, and the improvement of existing facilities required by the added volume of use, as associated with both residential and employment activities, may very conservatively be estimated at a cost of Rs. 1,000 per family. Thus, a rough global estimate of the five-year urban investment consequent on the addition of twenty million population in five years is:

Housing . . . . 4.0 million at Rs. 2,000 = Rs. 8.0 billion
Workplaces . . . . 2.6 million at Rs. 2,000 = Rs. 5.2 billion
Urban improvements . . . . . . 4.0 million at Rs. 1,000 = Rs. 4.0 billion

The approximate total of two thousand crores of rupees required for investment not otherwise provided for in the Plan may, on the whole, be regarded as a relatively conservative estimate, implying as it does a large proportion of low-standard housing and restricted workplaces for industrial and commercial employees. Such an investment would have represented one third of the total public and private investment in the Second Five Year Plan; it would, of course, be a substantially lower proportion of the resources of the Third Plan, but it would still remain a major item and a severe competitor with more directly productive investments.

INDUSTRIAL GROWTH AND DECENTRALIZATION

As distinct from the investment costs of urban areas, there are direct and partially measurable benefits. We may take our departure from the fact that urban incomes in India range from two to three times the level of rural incomes, even including the unemployed and underemployed urban population, whose existence is sometimes pointed to as evidence that the cities do not provide real economic opportunity. This superior level of income must be attributed in the main to the different mix of activities in urban places. The high proportion of jobs in government, railways, and organized commerce and industry is not, and probably can never be, duplicated in the rural areas. To a very considerable extent, the price which must be paid for urban development is a price paid for conducting these activities at all in the Indian economy.

It might be argued that, if possible, these activities should be dispersed into rural areas, in the extreme case to avoid the problem of urbanism altogether, and in the "impure" case to channel the bulk of urban development into smaller centers and drastically to revise the size distribution of Indian cities. The question of principle at the root of these two arguments is essentially the same, and deserves further elaboration.

First, however, we may also mention the peripheral argument that a great proportion of the activities undertaken in cities are "parasitic" in character, that these parasitic activities should be dispensed with, and that an effective approach is to deal with them by dealing with urban gigantism. The conjectured parasitism of large Oriental cities combines more than one concept. In some measure we have already demonstrated that a sound and greatly expanded industrial and commercial community, most probably concentrated in cities, will be a necessary and desirable concomitant of Indian economic growth. In so far as some of this activity, as viewed in the West from India, is wasteful, competitive, and unhealthy, it may be controlled by other measures, and the productive resources thus released might be devoted to other purposes more in accord with Indian desires.

The parasitism is sometimes imputed to ideological and cultural activities whose purposes are desirable, but whose content partakes to an objectionable degree of nonindigenous elements. The desirability and necessity of such cross-cultural influences and the form of their organization is a major policy problem. In any organized society with a national government and national purposes, the formation of leading cultural centers cannot, however, be avoided, and I suspect that this observation applies the more, the more consumption might be directed away from material objects.

Finally, after dealing with these somewhat dubious characterizations of parasitism, I am forced back to the conclusion that the main source of urban gigantism and parasitism susceptible to direct treatment is the overwhelming inefficiency of petty trade, petty services, and petty manufacturing in their urban manifestation, and the tremendous following population which this inefficiency implies for any vital and central activity in the urban scene. This symptom can only be treated through the rationalizing effects of development and its consequent redistribution of employment.

We can now return to the question of completely or partially decentralizing urban activities with a view substantially to reducing the implied costs of urban development in the process of economic development. During my months in India, I was fortunate in being able to visit many industrial and nonindustrial cities throughout the country, to inspect manufacturing conditions under a wide variety of circumstances, to assess very roughly the levels of commercial services and utilities in communities of different sizes, and to talk with a fair variety of industrial entrepreneurs and managers. I have had some considerable experience with industrial conditions and industrial location in the United States and Puerto Rico, and my contact with Indian conditions was rendered more susceptible to analysis and comparison with these more advanced countries through the friendly assistance of the Indian government technicians with whom I worked.

Industrial conditions in India are varied and multiform. At one end of the scale, handicraft industries are surviving in localities of all types, frequently with government assistance. Such industry provides a meager livelihood, and conditions range from poor to execrable. Further, such industry does not appear readily to survive transplantation into rapidly growing centers from other localities. At the other end of the scale, large self-contained industrial plants have been established and successfully operated in conditions up to the point of virtual isolation from the urban environment. Such isolation is not, however, the general rule. Once established, such industry tends to create an umbrella of operating utilities, power supply, regular transportation outside the area, and an industrially disciplined labor force, which attracts the location and growth of other industries. In Jamshedpur (Tatanagar), and apparently in the new government steel towns, land ownership and local controls can make this umbrella ineffective. But in localities like Bangalore the attraction established by the pioneering activity of the Government of Mysore and the Indian government's defense manufacturing activities has a snowball effect in the absence of other controls. The climate so created influences not only private industry, but also additional governmental locational decisions.

As between urban areas, and within the larger of these, conditions similarly vary over a wide range. The reliability of power and communication services, the accessibility of cultural and educational facilities, the resourcefulness of local service technicians, the passability of the roads, and the work outlook of the labor force tend to fall off with movement down the scale of size and outward from the metropolitan center. As between independent cities of different sizes, those under a present population of 200,000 tend to be unable to supply so many of the desirable features of an environment which stimulates manufacturing growth that they cannot at present be seriously considered as potential growth centers. Where cities are satellite to and partially dependent upon a larger metropolitan center, this lack of facilities may be partially overcome from that center, and an industrial-growth environment may be established in centers of 50,000 people or less or in relatively new townships, such as Modinagar. The viability of industrial growth is, thus, directly correlated with the size of the city or with the size of an adjacent metropolitan center, inversely correlated with the distance from a large center, and positively correlated with the size and self-contained character of the industrial establishment.

We may take note of the fact that if one or two large plants can become established in an already existing and predominantly nonindustrial town without restrictions on other industrial growth or on the establishment of a normal Indian commercial and service economy, then 10,000 industrial employees implies a population of close to a quarter of a million people, approaching, therefore, the size necessary for an independently viable industrial environment. This conclusion may be reached as follows. One third of the total population will be employed. About one third of the employed population can be in manufacturing, still preserving the "balanced" character of urban activities. Of this manufacturing employment, about one third will be in normal, necessary, and traditional lines. The other two thirds would be divided between the "umbrella" industries and the new growth attracted by their success and their stabilization of the environment. The population multiplier of the *initial* new employment is therefore about 25 to 1!

None of the foregoing observations would apply where the substantial industries being examined are old and traditional industries with limited growth potential and restricted effects on the environment, as in Kanpur, Allahabad, and Ahmedabad. The industrial mix of such towns is not necessarily favorable to further growth. In the contrary case, the above line of reasoning cannot be applied to new towns, because these are not ordinarily permitted to expand in the expected pattern. In both of these cases, but for different reasons, industrial employment will form a higher percentage of the total and the growth leverage of industrial growth will not be so great. For cities like Madras, Bangalore, and Coimbatore, recent development patterns would seem to confirm in rough terms this ratio between viable total population and new manufacturing employment in large plants.

So far, we have not specifically discussed the problems of industry of intermediate size in modern lines of production, such as may be expected to grow up in some larger metropolitan areas or in cities larger than one quarter million population under the umbrella of the successful establishment of one or more modern plants. Such establishments represent a hitherto not fully appreciated reservoir of very great growth—a component heavily dependent upon the environment for meeting its needs and therefore sensitive to its proximity to urban centers. The Third and Fourth Five Year Plans, if successful, will receive a heavy contribution from the growth of such establishments. At the same time, cities in metropolitan and middle growth ranges can receive a similar impetus. Since, by virtue of their size, these establishments draw more heavily upon entrepreneurial skills and the hothouse development of these skills in centers of rapid cultural and technological change, their relocation and wide distribution throughout the economy of India is but little susceptible to policy determination.

On the basis of the foregoing insights, it would appear that the benefits of higher income due to improved employment-mix which can now be observed in Indian urban areas, by comparison with rural areas, cannot be diffused throughout the economy directly by the stimulation of industry in a rural setting, nor can we take an optimistic view of the possibility of decentralizing to a limited degree, below a city size of one quarter million persons.

INDIRECT COSTS AND BENEFITS

Aside from the direct and partially measurable economic costs and benefits of urbanism in India, there is a whole series of related indirect costs and benefits, some of which deserve further comment.

Conditions of city living throughout India are very bad, especially on the basis of an unfair comparison with Western cities. It is frequently assumed that on a purely physical basis such conditions are worse than rural conditions and, hence, imply very large social costs for further urban growth. Owing to the great differences between the environments, such differences are very difficult to measure, and undoubtedly some of the statements regarding them represent value judgments rather than evaluations. If Indian experience parallels the American, there may be a romantic tendency to misjudge actual rural physical conditions. The actual extent of these physical differences is an appropriate subject of research, and should be measured not only in terms of the conditions themselves, but also in terms of their effects on health and mortality. Beyond physical conditions themselves, however, there is an area where personal and social effects are not so readily measured. This is sometimes generally characterized in terms of "social disorganization," and many value-laden judgments are passed upon its prevalence, its importance, and its correlation with the size and type of urban community. In so far as this social disorganization can be related to specific indices, such as the sex ratio in the working-age groups, its importance can be weighed and measures may be recommended to change conditions. In so far as this social disorganization is associated with the process of reorienting the population in part to an urban industrial society, it should be viewed in the larger context of development goals and methods. From this point of view, the educational environment of the city operates in conditions such that increased social mobility provides opportunity, increased aspirations provide motivation, and the existing productive institutions and labor force are the campus and faculty. It is very doubtful whether these educational conditions could be reproduced so as to have the same effect at reasonable cost in the environment of the smaller cities and the rural areas. While it might be desirable to revise this process and to mitigate or remove its undesired effects, it is certainly not desirable to throw the baby out with the bath water.

THE DEVELOPMENT OF POLICY
IN RELATION TO GOALS

We have now established a general framework within which the Government of India and of the Indian states could attempt further research and experimentation with policy designed to fit urbanism and urban growth into national development policies at various levels and in ways appropriate to maximizing the attainment of goals, or to reducing the costs and increasing the benefits to be derived in the process of urbanization.

I have attempted to establish the following salient points:

1) The Government of India is developing policy in a framework of values which leads to immediate emphasis on rapid economic development so conducted as not to do violence to the long-term goals of a materially and culturally improved democratic way of life.

2) Industrialization plays a key role in this development.

3) Rural-to-urban migration is the main cause for the rapid emergence of the urban problem; this migration cannot substantially be controlled by democratic means and may accelerate with agricultural development.

4) Urban costs in the upsurge of urban growth must be a major element of planned investment.

5) Urban growth cannot be fully decentralized to reduce these development costs, since such decentralization would excessively undermine the prerequisites of sound industrial development.

These considerations are the most fundamental factors constraining the further development of policy with respect to urbanism.

Indian urban growth is largely without precedent from the pure planning point of view, because cities of this size have not existed in India prior to very recent times, and because cities with India's problems have not existed at any time in the West. Given a sufficient program of research and activity in urban planning, related on the one hand to the continuing function of local government and on the other hand to the fact gathering and general planning of the Indian government, India should rapidly be able to accumulate the needed information for informed policy formation. At the same time, regardless of other aspects of policy, intelligent city planning should be able to economize substantially on the costs of urban development at fixed levels of amenity, health, and the provision of physical facilities. These fixed levels, consonant with available development resources, will not only be lower than presently acceptable minimum standards in western Europe, but will also fall below standards now being employed in experimental programs for government housing, workers' housing, and low-income housing on a limited basis by the Union Government, the states, and a few urban governments.

More intimate contact with the actual problems of urban and

metropolitan development will provide more satisfactory answers to the differences in costs and productivity which are argued in this paper for centers of different size in India. My own conclusion, generalized from the preceding section, would be that there is probably a saving to be realized by stimulating economic growth in cities presently less than one million but more than 250,000 in size. Such stimulation will increase the populations of these cities, and within twenty-five years will move most of them into the class of over one million in size. This does not imply that the growth of cities now over one million should be actively discouraged, but only that they should not continue to enjoy so strong a relative monopoly on the conditions favoring growth and expansion. For all cities in which growth may be anticipated, and especially for those now over one million in population, tremendous savings of developmental expenditure are to be anticipated through more careful and orderly organization of growth. Such organization will include an active development of satellite centers surrounding the main metropolitan center and partially depending upon it for the establishment of adequate environmental conditions for urban growth.

It is quite apparent that one of the main instrumentalities in achieving this type of objective will be the control of industrial location. As the "growing tip" of the Indian economy, industrial location is more easily "bent" in the desired directions, and, to a substantial extent, the location of tomorrow's development will reflect the new directions to which impetus is given today. This capability of industrial location in influencing growth is already recognized in part in the execution of policies designed to equalize economic opportunity as between broad regions of India. To a limited extent, it can be used during the establishment of "umbrella" industries to influence the relative speed of development of urban centers in the size ranges appropriate to development.

Increasingly, however, it is to be expected that larger industrial establishments, instead of being subject to arbitrary locational decisions, will grow out of smaller establishments in suitable industrial environments. As this happens, the relocation of industry will take place largely within, rather than between, urban centers. In this context, industry becomes the most flexible locational element in the metropolitan complex, and the natural process of growth, expansion, and relocation can be used to structure the expansion of the metropolitan area itself.

Studies of Delhi and other Indian cities have elucidated somewhat the rationale of the rather obvious intense concentration of population and activity in the central portions of these cities. This intense concentration is a straightforward consequence of poverty, resulting both from the low expenditure on housing (which promotes the formation of high-density slums), and from the low expenditure on transportation (which reinforces the advantage of a dwelling place near work opportunities). Poor communications and competitive market conditions tend to keep business enterprises drawn close together. None can afford the costs of moving outward and stabilizing their own necessary environment. The industries serving residential sections tend in this situation to amalgamate with the centrally located "downtown" industries; even in the larger cities, the downtown shopping center pulls trade from the entire metropolis.

The development of lower-density housing and the interjection of public open spaces has been tried as a solution to this problem, first with British planning and the development of civil lines and cantonments, and later with government housing and other subsidized housing under the Indian Union. These efforts have not been entirely successful, because directly and indirectly they throw a transportation burden upon the Indian worker, whose close tie with his work is disrupted either when he remains within the new community or is forced to move beyond it. The only reasonably mobile and rapidly changing element in this picture is private manufacturing industry at the medium scale, which may, within limits, be forced to relocate and draw its labor force with it. In so far as new industrial communities so created are too far removed or too cut off from the metropolitan environment, however, this approach will likewise fail. Large-scale internal decentralization, especially through satellite towns, can succeed only if special efforts are made to strengthen the nonindustrial portion of the local employment, if the employer has ready access to the larger market for labor, inputs, and production, and if the secondary workers in households can be occupationally mobile by commuting to the city center and other subcenters.

As locally generated industrial growth becomes more prevalent, redistribution as between metropolitan areas will come to depend less on the establishment of umbrella industries in specific localities and more upon the improvement of the environment for economic growth. When efforts are made to analyze and implement this opportunity it will, I believe, become ever more apparent that such efforts must be focused in a few centers of intermediate size, rather than distributed widely over the full spectrum of urban places in India.

Since at present migration to urban places is far in excess of the rate of growth of industrial production proper in India, it would appear that a major element of policy should be the maximizing of the capacity of industrially growing areas to absorb in-migrant populations. This means that, in so far as is possible, opportunities should exist for the expansion of employment opportunities according to patterns now normal in most Indian urban areas, even though these patterns reflect the poverty and inefficiency of the economy as a whole. In both types of location or relocation discussed in the preceding paragraphs, neglect of this principle is a serious danger. For a variety of reasons, there appears to be a tendency to attempt complete isolation of industrial development, both in establishing new industrial communities and in planning for satellite development. Under alternative conditions, the very large industrial undertakings of the Union Government and the construction of new industrial townships for the production of steel and other basic industrial goods would provide an excellent umbrella for the further expansion of related industries, the training of an industrial labor force, and the growth of associated services and residential-service activities. Through wholly inappropriate planning, in my view, these new towns have essentially been zoned against further spontaneous industrial development and against an adequate spectrum of nonindustrial employment—for which neither adequate housing nor adequate business accommodations are ordinarily provided. In effect, this planning throws an additional burden of expansion upon other preëxisting cities. Similar errors appear inherent in the planning of satellite industrial communities when they are designed mainly to siphon off industrial employment and to remove it out of the sight and smell of the more squeamish sectors of the economy. Inadequate attention to the desirability of expanding the employment in satellites beyond pure industrial activities leads to placing them too far from the metropolitan center and constricting too severely their access to goods, services, and personnel in the center. To the extent that this happens, even the primary, as well as the secondary, purpose of the establishment of satellite towns may be defeated.

Because of their obvious application, two major types of planning activities have been considered briefly in relation to the execution of policy with respect to urban growth: urban planning itself, and the planning of industrial location and relocation. These activities, however, should be only a small part of the instruments available to the Union and state governments of India in pursuing any goals which may be established in this area of action. In fact, it is perhaps useful to point out that the definition of goals implied above —for example, the goals of more rational internal organization of cities and of a somewhat wider distribution of industrial growth—

is not synonymous with an articulation of policy. How often we hear it said that the Government of India "already has" a policy of industrial decentralization, when a study of the facts reveals that it has a *goal* of decentralization which is but imperfectly implemented in policy and is, sometimes, negated by other policies.

Viewed in this light, the goals here being discussed must constantly be reëvaluated in terms of their feasibility, and in terms of the effects of policy sets, each designed to serve a particular goal, upon the whole structure of goals.

Many conclusions can be drawn from this formulation. Throughout this discussion there has been the implication that the realistic setting of goals is constrained not only by the conditions of the problem itself as they have been enumerated here, but also by the existence of many other interrelated problems in social and economic development in India. In this realm, I have not been able to devote space to the problems implicit in a statement such as "Our goal [policy?] is to provide adequate housing for all classes in India." Current housing policy has derived its definition of adequacy from experience alien both to India's culture and to India's level of living. As a result, the experience gained has been of limited applicability in any larger context, and the problem has been growing more rapidly than the government has been able to move toward a solution. At the same time, the execution of these same housing policies has created conditions running counter to other values—for example, by creating one-class communities. This illustration must suffice to indicate that major problems of harmonizing goals exist in the operation of many specific programs which impinge on urban development. And all of these programs must be harmonized in a larger framework with the resources available and the various values which realistically can be satisfied.

At the same time, when we explore the reconciliation of goals and policies, we obtain a clue to another valuable line of approach. Policies aimed at achieving the goals which we may tentatively set up can be executed through many different instrumentalities and powers of the Government of India and its component parts. These include not only the powers of capital expenditure which are inherent in large-scale government planning, but also many powers of taxation, landownership, land control, allocation of materials, allocation of transportation facilities, and the like. Unfortunately, the powers and programs which are influential in urban development are widely diffused through the Union and state governments, and their appropriate coördination for policy purposes is very difficult. Even more unfortunate, however, is the fact that urban problems have not been viewed as a whole, and the force and ap-

propriateness of different measures in influencing urban development have never been fully evaluated. Thus, in Delhi at the moment
when the Ford Foundation team was concluding that real estate
taxes could play an important role in controlling development, the
Delhi Corporation was preparing without further consideration to
abandon the house tax as a source of revenue. Since it is now evident
that the problems discussed in this paper will not yield to expediency
or opportunistic solutions, it is quite evident that problems of urban
development and policy development associated therewith require
the elevation of urban planning to a level of major consideration
within the total planning effort. In this context, I believe that a
suitable set of policies harmonized with the development needs of
India will be developed, and I believe that in outline it will follow
some of the conclusions of this analysis.

XIV

URBAN LIVING CONDITIONS,
OVERHEAD COSTS, AND
THE DEVELOPMENT PATTERN

Catherine Bauer Wurster

Rapid urban growth is inevitable in India, and essential for progress, but it is also very costly. This was the consensus of the seminar,[1] and much of the discussion centered around the three-horned dilemma which must somehow be resolved: (1) city living conditions are increasingly intolerable and must be improved, (2) the urban population will double, at the very least, in the next twenty years, and (3) urban social-overhead expenditures must be kept as low as possible during this critical period if productivity is to be adequately increased. As Pitambar Pant summed it up: "The utmost importance attaches to devising methods of low-cost urbanization."

The demographic, economic, social, and political factors which pose this issue so sharply in India are analyzed elsewhere in this book, and need not be discussed here. Moreover, Mr. Pant's paper[2] courageously fits the problem into the framework of national economic trends and requirements, suggesting the scale of expenditure on future urban improvements that might be feasible. The estimate is modest, but by no means hopeless: about ten billion rupees a year for the next twenty years, on the average, which comes to a thousand rupees per capita of the urban population in 1981

---

[1] Meetings held June 26–July 2, 1960. Mrs. Wurster's paper was written after the seminar.—*Ed.*

[2] Chap. ix.—*Ed.*

(assumed to be 200 million), or about Rs. 1,800 per person added to the urban population between 1961 and 1981.

The need for economy accounts for some further assumptions made by many of the seminar participants, which are the particular concern of this paper: that large, congested metropolitan centers are a relatively expensive method of urban expansion, and that some form of urban-industrial decentralization should be encouraged. This view was highlighted by Professor Davis's projections, which suggested that Calcutta might conceivably reach a population of 12 to 16 millions by 1970, and over 50 million by the year 2000. (It has probably also been reinforced by the rising Calcutta emergencies which have attracted international attention since the seminar.) There were some participants, however, who believe that continued metropolitan concentration is either essential to maximum productivity, or impossible to prevent in a free society such as India's.

But "decentralization" is a very vague term which can mean a great many different things: spreading suburbs, satellite communities, new independent towns of varied size and purpose, the expansion of existing small towns, village industry, the strengthening of local government in general, or entirely new forms and methods of development which have not yet been tried or even thought up. And if the physical pattern of urban and economic development really does have a significant effect on living conditions, improvement costs, and productive efficiency, then it is necessary to know what kind of pattern has what specific effects under a given set of conditions, and why.

Decentralization has been a major issue in many parts of the world for half a century or more, and one might expect that some systematic knowledge had been gained from the varied trends, policies, and experiments which have promoted it in one form or another. The fact is, however, that very little is known about the comparative costs and benefits of different development patterns. In any event, the conditions and purposes have usually been quite different from the situation in India today. The dispersion of homes and industry in American suburbs was made possible by the automobile, while the British New Towns were carefully planned to accommodate a relatively small "overspill" from old congested districts, not a vast flood of rural in-migrants. In both cases the results appear to be quite expensive, but there was no compulsion to minimize overhead costs if other values seemed to be worth the price.

This is, therefore, a pioneering realm for research and policy in India. But if those who try to guide India's future urban growth confront some special and difficult problems, they also have special opportunities which many of their Western confrères might envy. For one thing, most of India's urban expansion and economic development is still to come, which means that the pattern is not yet set and many alternatives are potentially open. Given adequate agreement upon and understanding of desirable goals and suitable criteria, it should be relatively cheaper and easier to achieve these goals in new development than in the redevelopment and reorganization of obsolete cities, which is the frustrating problem that confronts most Western planners.

Also, powerful tools are available to Indian planners, which hardly existed in the 19th century, when the rate of Western urbanization was at its peak, and are somewhat weaker even today in many Western countries. Economic planning is fully accepted and well developed. Comprehensive physical planning is less advanced, but the basic decisions and expenditures that actually shape the urban-industrial pattern, whether consciously or unconsciously, are largely public: resource-development projects, transportation and utility lines, housing and other urban improvements, as well as numerous public measures to develop, encourage, or control industry. Moreover, these programs are largely administered by state governments, which would facilitate physical planning on a regional basis.

Before this can be done very effectively, however, there needs to be better understanding of cause and effect, the comparative costs and benefits of alternative patterns for civic welfare and productive efficiency, and how best to balance these factors under a given set of local conditions.

This paper merely suggests an approach. In the section on the Urban Pattern an effort is made to isolate the more obvious variables in the pattern, with examples of how they seem to affect the cost of certain elements, such as housing and transportation. The result is some rough hypotheses, in the section on Comparative Cost, which will have fulfilled their purpose if they stimulate controversy and real research. First, however, it may be worth while to look at the present situation in Indian cities in relation to their size.

URBAN CONDITIONS: SOME EVIDENCE BY CITY SIZE GROUPS

If certain aspects of Indian cities are roughly compared, it appears that the biggest centers do seem to present the most difficult problems, whatever may be the cause, despite their continued attractiveness to rural in-migrants and economic enterprise.

OVERCROWDING AND SANITATION

The correlation between size and crowded living conditions is evident from some national survey figures:[3]

Families living in one room or less:

Rural...................... 34%
Urban..................... 44%
Four biggest cities.......... 67%
Calcutta................. 79%

Households with per capita floor area of less than 50 square feet:

Rural...................... 14%
Urban..................... 21%
Four biggest cities.......... 33%
Calcutta................. 70%

Private *outdoor* space, an important factor in living conditions in warm climates, would, of course, decrease even more rapidly with city size.

Size, however, is not necessarily the cause of these conditions. The fact that the biggest cities have also been growing fastest certainly contributes to overcrowding. But it is likewise evident that the opportunity for rural in-migrants to provide themselves with simple shelter by cheap traditional methods tends to decline as cities grow larger, for a number of reasons.

The proportion of the population residing in pucka structures, with access to a clean water supply and water-borne sewerage systems, tends to increase with city size. But these benefits are none too prevalent even in the metropolitan centers, and as far as health is concerned they merely help to offset some of the evils and dangers that are caused by congestion. Despite better sanitation systems, medical care, education, and incomes, the crude death rate was higher in urban than in rural areas, as of 1954, although the differential was decreasing.[4] The cholera situation in Calcutta, considered an international menace by the World Health Organization, is dramatic evidence on this point:

Significantly, cholera incidence in rural areas of West Bengal is now greatly diminished by virtue of a highly successful environmental sanitation programme for providing safe water over the past few years. Endemicity, how-

---

[3] National Sample Survey, 7th Round, 1953–1954, quoted in National Buildings Organization, *Monograph on the Housing Situation in India* (1959).
[4] *Statistical Abstract, Government of India, 1957*, p. 61.

ever, continues unabated in the Greater Calcutta area, which still forms the nucleus of the disease spread in other parts of West Bengal State.[5]

URBAN PUBLIC EXPENDITURES

It would be interesting to know the trends in total public outlay in cities, by comparison with national and rural expenditures, and by city size groups. Data are available on municipal budgets, but these include only part of the cost, since many urban expenditures (particularly for education and public housing) are made directly by the state and national governments, whose published budgets do not indicate where the money is spent.

But there are many indications that per capita costs have gone up, and that they are higher in big cities—despite the evidence that living conditions are relatively worse. Judging from surveys by the Federal Reserve Bank,[6] disbursements by local authorities serving cities with over 100,000 population as of 1951 probably doubled between 1952 and 1959. Expenditures in 1958–59 by fifty-six large municipalities came to Rs. 940 millions. In terms of their 1951 population of around 22 millions, per capita expenditure therefore averaged about Rs. 43, although it would have been considerably lower in actual fact due to population growth in the meantime. In the same rough terms, however, the per capita figure for the thirteen big City Corporations was Rs. 57, while it was less than half, or Rs. 25, for the forty-three smaller cities. Moreover, the large expenditures by Improvement Trusts, Port Trusts, and other independent authorities are not included, though they would greatly increase the gross figure for the big cities. As for the cities under 100,000, comparable data are not readily available, but it can be assumed that their per capita outlays were much lower than Rs. 25.

The major items of municipal expenditure are for sanitation, health, and public works, including roads, and local resources are supplemented by outside aid for various purposes. Under the Second Five Year Plan, Rs. 630 millions of national and state funds were allocated for urban water supply and sewerage systems.[7]

Public expenditures on urban housing, for the most part constructed by state and national agencies, have been quite high. The National Buildings Organization estimates that the dwellings facilitated (or at least planned for) by public authorities under the First and Second Plans were as follows:[8]

[5] World Health Organization, *Assignment Report on Water Supply and Sewage Disposal, Greater Calcutta,* January, 1960, p. 1.

[6] *Reserve Bank of India Bulletin,* February, 1959, and April, 1958.

[7] India Planning Commission, *Development Volume on Health Programmes in India* (c. 1959), chap. xi, sec. 19.

[8] National Buildings Organization, *Monograph on the Housing Situation in India* (1959).

	Number of Dwellings
Purposes	
National programs for industrial workers, slum clearance rehousing, and low- and middle-income groups........	431,000
National program for refugees........................	323,000
Primarily by various ministries for their employees, but also miscellaneous state and local programs...........	1,053,000
Total..	1,807,000

The allocations for the first group were Rs. 1,465 millions, or Rs. 3,400 per unit. It may be assumed that the cost of the other programs averaged at least Rs. 4,000 per unit, which would come to around Rs. 6,500 millions. Total expenditures would, therefore, be roughly Rs. 8 billions, averaging Rs. 800 million per year for the decade. (All unit costs would be much higher now, it should be noted.)

Although no figures are available as to the distribution, it may be assumed that most of this housing expenditure was in the larger cities, for various reasons: their social needs are the most urgent, refugees and government employees are concentrated there, and unit costs are relatively high.

ECONOMIC CONDITIONS: EMPLOYMENT AND INCOMES

Comparative analysis of economic trends, limitations, and opportunities in different sizes and types of cities would illuminate many aspects of the urban picture. The 1961 census will show the occupational structure, and there is a mine of potentially useful information on industrial location in the licensing records which could lead to more intensive studies of locational criteria.

Dr. Bredo includes some rough tabulations from the licensing directory in the Appendix to his seminar paper.[9] Of the licenses granted for new and expanded production in major industrial categories in recent years, 23 per cent were apparently for plants located within the corporate limits of Bombay and Calcutta, about 35 per cent within their metropolitan areas, and almost 50 per cent in Bombay State and West Bengal. These figures suggest that the two biggest centers still exercise powerful attractions, but that there is also strong evidence of industrial growth in their fringe areas and in the larger regions around them.

Industrial development brings other types of enterprise, and the big metropolitan communities are also major centers of business, cultural, and government employment. They include, therefore, a

---

[9] Chap. xii.—*Ed.*

large portion of the profitable new undertakings and the people with high or rising incomes. Then why, it might be asked, is it so difficult for them to pay for the necessary improvements in their physical environment, even if the price tags are relatively high?

Part of the answer lies in the fact that these very qualities tend to attract hopeful or desperate in-migrants at a much more rapid rate than the new jobs to support them are provided. In 1956 the percentage of unemployment in the four largest cities was double the rate among the rest of the urban population.[10] There is also a great deal of marginal employment in ill-paid and uncertain "service trades." The big centers are, therefore, almost as poor as they are rich, and the median income is not much higher than in towns with little modern development. Some comparisons of consumer expenditures are available from a sample survey conducted in 1953 by the Taxation Enquiry Commission:[11]

Size of community	Average per capita monthly expenditure (in rupees)
15,000–50,000	28.2
50,000–1 million	30.4
Over 1 million	39.6

The unemployed or underemployed in-migrants tend to make living conditions worse and overhead requirements more costly per capita, although they can contribute little toward increased productivity. It is this picture, with the threat of worse to come, that leads to the push for some form of "decentralization." But exactly what kind of development pattern might be better than the present trend toward metropolitan centralization? Or are the problems and conflicts inevitable at this stage of India's development, only to be solved by gradual economic progress and not subject to any important degree of alleviation by physical planning? These questions can only be answered effectively by a systematic analysis of various factors in the development pattern, in terms of their social and economic implications. The following section merely suggests the type of approach required.

How the Urban Pattern Affects Conditions and Costs: Some Variables

City size, in population terms, is only one of the significant factors. Density and area are just as important, and also functional struc-

---

[10] Wilfred Malenbaum, "Urban Unemployment in India," *Pacific Affairs*, XXX, No. 2 (June, 1957), 138–150.

[11] Government of India, *Report of the Taxation Enquiry Commission*, 1953–54, I, 67.

ture, particularly the relation between homes and workplaces. If the comparative costs and benefits of different patterns are to be weighed, the effect of these variables on specific elements in the urban environment must be considered.[12]

The following material is necessarily rather generalized. In the Appendix to this paper, however, there are some concrete cost estimates for housing and utilities in the Delhi area (from an analysis of Delhi Plan studies by Edward Echeverria), which provide pertinent examples).

HOUSING: THE EFFECT OF DENSITY

City size per se has little direct influence on housing costs. But the high land-prices and related accessibility problems which are often prevalent in large cities both tend to increase the required density of residential development. Density is a critical factor in the cost of housing construction.

Even in countries with the most advanced technology, elevator apartments are much more expensive per unit of floor area than low structures. But in India the differences in housing cost due primarily to density and dwelling type seem to be much wider. In recent years, under the Works Ministry's standard regulations for a minimal one-room unit with sanitary facilities and balcony or veranda, the price range for typical examples would be about as follows:[13]

> In a four-story tenement on an expensive site at maximum density (primarily in Bombay and Calcutta)............................... Rs. 6,000 to 7,500
>
> In a two- or three-story structure on moderate-priced land............................... Rs. 4,000 to 5,000
>
> In a one-story structure on cheap land, in smaller towns or in the outlying fringe of larger cities.. Rs. 2,500 to 3,500

These costs are for ordinary contract construction. Under the Slum Clearance Program, however, local authorities have been encouraged to provide plots with pucka sanitary facilities and a supply of kutcha building materials, for more or less self-help construction. With space standards often above the minimum, these units cost only Rs. 900 to Rs. 1,500, even in Madras and Bangalore. Of course, they are only feasible where very cheap land acces-

---

[12] The basic influence of geographic factors, in terms of resource availability, topography, climate, etc., is not considered here. Their fundamental importance to urban planning has long been recognized, and their effects are much better understood than the spatial aspects of the development pattern.

[13] From materials provided the author by the Ministry of Works, Housing and Supply, 1959.

sible to employment is still available—a rare and diminishing resource in all large cities.

The range is, therefore, tremendous. High-density tenements cost two to three times as much as ordinary one-story homes, and five to six times as much as self-help units with more space and equal sanitary facilities. The local variations in official building-cost indices of the National Buildings Organization are rather small and do not account for these differences. Land cost has a direct influence in some cases, but density appears to be the most significant factor—probably because, in general, higher densities mean dwelling types which require increasing dependence on modern materials and technology, and skilled labor and supervision, which are all relatively expensive in India, sometimes imported, and often in short supply.

On the other hand, low-density housing can utilize various noncompetitive and nonmonetary resources: the homeownership incentive to invest labor and savings otherwise unproductive; kutcha materials (which a minimum of technological ingenuity might improve); unskilled in-migrant labor with knowledge of traditional building methods; and the Indian climate, which makes private outdoor space useful for many family activities and makes traditional methods of construction and design more suitable in many cases than imported Western practices.

Housing is by far the biggest factor in urban overhead costs, and community facilities such as schools, hospitals, parks, and playgrounds are affected by the same influences. If tolerable urban living conditions are to be achieved at Mr. Pant's price, it seems likely that planning for low-density development will be an important prerequisite, besides a substantial program of public land acquisition or other controls to prevent speculative price rises.

SANITARY FACILITIES: THE EFFECTS
OF SIZE AND DENSITY

The two major elements, water supply and excreta disposal, must be considered separately although they are interrelated. An adequate supply of clean piped water is a basic essential for community welfare, and here local geography plays a particularly important role in costs, which may rise steeply if readily accessible resources no longer meet the need. Indeed, Richard Meier suggests that in India the cost of water may often be *the* determinant in the future urban pattern. Apart from geographic variables, however, increased city size and density probably tend to make for economy in a water distribution system, up to a point.

To some extent this would also be true for a piped water-borne sewerage system, although a large, expanding urban area is likely to meet with increasingly serious and costly problems of disposal. For any alternative method—septic tanks, "aqua privies," pits, composting, night-soil collection—relatively low density is usually an essential factor in its feasibility for decent and healthy urban living. Under suitable conditions such methods may be economical, particularly in their demands on skilled labor and high-quality industrial products, and as a means of conserving water. The fact that science can improve the simpler systems without losing their economical advantages is evident from the Japanese experience.

Size and density can, therefore, work both ways to some degree. Although housing is a much larger item in urban overhead expenditures and consumer costs than sanitary facilities, the latter are a major factor in municipal budgets. The Planning Commission estimated a few years ago that it would cost Rs. 3.3 billion to provide modern water and sewerage systems for the urban population *as of 1951,* with no allowance for growth.[14]

TRANSPORTATION: THE EFFECTS OF SIZE, DENSITY, AND FUNCTIONAL STRUCTURE

Getting from home to work, particularly, is an important element in both family and public budgets, and in productive efficiency. The journey to work is greatly affected by the urban pattern in several different but interrelated ways. In so far as more population means going a greater distance to work, city size makes for a rapid increase in costs, both to the worker and to government. More mileage means a shift from walking (free, except in time and energy cost), to bicycle (a considerable investment for many low-income Indians), to bus (fares, plus subsidy, plus better roads), and finally to expensive rail lines in many cases. Commuting by private automobile is still infrequent in India, but it is already producing new traffic problems and rising highway expenditures. The transportation item is usually the biggest single factor in the high per capita budgets of big cities. In the Delhi area, requirements for the next five years are estimated at Rs. 120 millions.[15]

The effect of size on transportation costs is qualified, however, by two other factors. One is density, which in this case makes for economy until traffic jams begin to counterbalance geographic proximity. The other is city structure, particularly in terms of the relationship between homes and work opportunities. If most people live fairly close to an adequate job market, whether in the main

---

[14] India Planning Commission, *op. cit.,* chap. xi, sec. 13.
[15] Estimate from Delhi Town Planning Organization.

center or elsewhere, commuting costs will not be high even if the city is enormous. But where employment in a large city is either highly centralized or so dispersed that job markets tend to be spread over a wide area, or are otherwise unrelated to places of residence, transportation problems and costs are likely to be maximized.

The urban pattern affects transportation needs, but it is equally true that transportation systems have a direct effect on the whole development pattern, and on land costs and density in particular. Roads and transit lines open up new areas for development, and thereby reduce the pressure on sites in older districts. In most developing countries, including India, land prices tend to be much higher in relation to other economic indices than they are in the United States. This difference is due to our high degree of mobility, which continually expands the area of potential development and thus helps to curb monopolistic price tendencies in land.

In the cases where a large and highly integrated metropolitan community is inevitable or essential in a country like India, a big investment in transportation might conceivably lower land and housing costs to such a degree that it would be an economy rather than an extravagance.

THE TIMING OF URBAN OVERHEAD REQUIREMENTS:
LOCATIONAL FACTORS

The number of people dependent on industrial or other urban types of employment will inevitably double within the visible future. Where they live, and where the new jobs are located, however, will affect not only the scale of urban overhead expenditures, but also the *time* when they must be made. In some patterns, the immediate requirements for public and private investment are maximized, while in others some of these costs may be postponed.

In an entirely new town built by government or industry, all the housing and essential community facilities must be provided at the start. To accommodate an equal volume of growth in an existing city, the same number of additional dwellings may be required immediately if there is a severe shortage, but community facilities of some kind are already there and can be supplemented gradually. Of course, cheap land in the new town may outweigh this advantage in many cases, but it should nevertheless be taken into account in balancing costs and benefits for different locations and patterns.

There is also a third type of situation, where people work in cities or outlying industry while remaining in their villages. Sooner or later, such communities are likely to become "urbanized," with attendant overhead costs, but this will happen gradually, with modest improvements along the way and with a minimum of capital expenditure required at the outset.

PRODUCTIVITY, EMPLOYMENT AND THE DEVELOPMENT PATTERN: THE NEED FOR KNOWLEDGE

Little enough is known about the social and civic aspects of the urban environment. With respect to the other side of the picture—the effect of the development pattern on economic enterprise, productive efficiency, and employment—there is even less understanding and far greater confusion. This was recognized at many points during the seminar discussions, and there was a general consensus that more research on industrial location experience and criteria, in particular, is a prime necessity for effective planning.

The fundamental importance of such knowledge can hardly be overemphasized. The pattern of urbanization is ultimately determined by the location of economic development and employment opportunity, and it would be useless to reduce overhead costs at the price of economic efficiency. The most sophisticated knowledge and policy with respect to housing and civic problems will be ineffective unless they are closely integrated with sound planning for industrial location and the pattern of economic development.

The Indian problem is in many ways a new one. Western knowledge and experience have little to contribute, and are often positively misleading. In any case, the present author has no qualifications for expert judgment in the field, but it is possible to identify some of the confusions and controversies.

In the continuing debates over basic economic policy, it has often been assumed by both Indian and foreign theorists that emphasis on the stimulation and gradual modernization of small industry would tend to favor decentralization, with lower overhead costs. The obverse assumption has also been made: that all-out industrialization, with big modern plants, would go hand in hand with great metropolitan concentrations. There is mounting evidence, however, to support diametrically opposite deductions. It is the small semimodern industry that may often require the nursery of the crowded big-city bazaar area, or the nearest equivalent that can be provided in an industrial estate. On the other hand, large-scale heavy industries are inherently more self-sufficient. They can often be established successfully in rural isolation, as has frequently happened in India.

Modern industry, however, seldom provides much employment for unskilled villagers. But this raises another question. Many economists now argue that part of the function of large-scale modern factories should be to stimulate smaller transitional enterprises in their environs by a kind of "umbrella" influence. If this is true, then the one-industry, single-purpose enclave needs to be reconsidered. In that case, "it will be worth while to consider ways and means for the integration of different kinds of industry on a regional basis and then to provide a township to cater to their combined requirements, instead of establishing an *ad hoc* township for every industry." [16]

There is another potential fallacy in the fatalistic attitude toward private enterprise location. It is often assumed, implicitly or explicitly, that the trend toward industrial and population concentration in a few major areas cannot be diverted, whatever the resulting social costs, because any different pattern would require such arbitrary controls that enterprise would be dampened and productivity reduced. This view tends to ignore the effect of public decisions on locational attractions. Industry and business require many services and facilities—from utilities to good schools —which are largely provided by government. If these expenditures are mainly concentrated in a few big cities—as they probably are today—then increasing economic concentration is a likely corollary. If the magnets are located elsewhere, with due respect for other business requirements, another kind of pattern can be shaped.

Finally, there is the fact, increasingly recognized, that urban overhead costs are a critical element in economic progress, particularly in the present stage of Indian development. The resources required for minimal urban improvements will mount very rapidly, in any case. Any substantial economies that might be feasible would mean a significant increase in the resources available for more immediately productive investment in industry and agriculture.

THE COMPARATIVE COST OF DIFFERENT PATTERNS: SOME SPECULATIONS

The variables in the devolment pattern seem to have a substantial effect on urban costs and resource-saving potentialities, and the key factors are probably housing and transportation. The range of minimal investment per additional household dependent on urban employment may run from close to zero where no new housing or transport facilities are required, to well over Rs. 10,000 where the cost of both is necessarily high. In many cases, however, they are in obverse relationship, and the optimum balance between housing and transportation costs will often be the key consideration.

---

[16] N. K. Gandhi, "New Towns Construction in India," *Quarterly Journal of the Local Self Government Institute*, October, 1957, p. 438.

The discussion of the variables and their effects on certain elements can be applied to various types of urban-industrial patterns. No effort is made in the following to weigh the potential merits of different patterns for economic enterprise, but it is evident that most patterns offer economic opportunities under certain circumstances, and concrete examples are noted from the variegated Indian experience, with some of their implications.

VILLAGES WITH INDUSTRIAL EMPLOYMENT

This is obviously the cheapest pattern, from the viewpoint of overhead costs. An ultrasimple example would be the villages in the Etawah Pilot Project, whose small brickkiln provides local employment, enhances local income, and supplies material for village improvement.

Coimbatore District, on the other hand, exemplifies advanced industrial development in the country, with its expanding modern mills up to ten or more miles outside the city, most of whose employees walk or bicycle from neighboring villages, while the managers may either live on their cotton farms or commute from town.

In both cases, however, villagers have acquired new employment without leaving their old homes and without adding to urban overcrowding or overhead costs. Later on, the whole area around Coimbatore will probably be urbanized, but the present pattern postpones these costs, and it may also lead to a relatively economical, "subcentered" type of metropolitan community.

In both areas, the villages show many signs of gradual physical improvement, paid for out of increased local income with little if any outside assistance. To whatever extent this pattern is feasible for industry, or satisfactory to potential industrial workers, it is certainly economical.

INDEPENDENT NEW TOWNS

The opposite form of decentralization, from the viewpoint of initial costs, is the entirely new and modern community, built as a unit by government or a big corporation. There are many different types in India, and they all offer certain advantages: cheap land, with maximum freedom to plan its future use, and little or no transportation problem within the community. Living conditions are often excellent in these towns.

All the essential facilities, however, must be provided at the start, generally from the top down, and their cost is frequently quite high, too high to be feasible for the vast majority of future urbanites. This is undoubtedly true of Chandigarh, and also of most model industrial communities. A good example is Mohone, the community built by the National Rayon Corporation about twenty miles north of Bombay, where the total (nonindustrial) investment per household was well over Rs. 10,000, although most of the dwellings cost only Rs. 4,000.[17]

An entirely different type of new Indian town is the refugee community, of which Faridabad is probably the best example. This has none of the social and civic weaknesses inherent in a company town, but until recently it also lacked the basic advantage of local employment for the residents. Here the potential economies of cheap land and low density were fully utilized. Housing and community facilities are quite as good as in any model industrial community, but the cost was greatly reduced by the use of refugee labor, with self-help ownership incentives, on a well-organized basis. Economically, Faridabad seems to be over the hump, and it may become one of the major outlying subcenters in the Delhi region. Kalyani, north of Calcutta, was not so fortunate. The major problem for new independent towns is the fact that all the elements—employment, housing, utilities, schools, etc.—have to be ready at approximately the same time if a frustrating period is to be avoided.

THE EXPANDING METROPOLITAN COMMUNITY

Here is where housing and transportation costs need to be balanced, and the balancing will be greatly affected by metropolitan structure—particularly the employment pattern, the residential pattern, and the relationship between them.

Three general types of employment pattern may usefully be distinguished—centralized, dispersed, and subcentered—in terms of their probable effects on housing and transportation requirements. If a great deal of additional employment is provided in an existing downtown center such as Bombay City or Old Delhi, housing costs are likely to be maximized for those who live near by and transportation costs for those who choose cheap outlying land, while both costs may be relatively high for those who live in intermediate locations. If employment is widely dispersed throughout the metropolitan area, as it seems to be in Calcutta, some people may be able to minimize both housing and transportation costs, but in general the scattering of the job market is likely to increase transportation problems. And, if people must have ready access to

---

[17] From J. J. Mehta, National Rayon Corporation, Ltd.

work opportunities in widely dispersed locations, they may have to live in the central area and, thus, add to its costly congestion.

Probably the most economical pattern for metropolitan expansion is a network of more or less self-sufficient subcenters, their size varying with their functions, but each offering a fairly wide range of employment opportunities and related housing accommodation. Such a pattern would also permit a great many more villagers to commute from their present homes to urban types of employment than is possible in a highly centralized type of large metropolitan community, as Albert Mayer has argued.[18]

If Bangalore can find the water, it might readily develop such a pattern in its future growth. Richard Meier's theoretical model, suggested in his seminar paper,[19] reflects the same general concept, with many ingenious additions. As he also suggests, transportation systems are likely to play a key role in shaping such a pattern. The rail transit line in Madras provides a good example. It made possible the Guindy industrial estate, which could form the nucleus of a balanced satellite community. It also permitted the rehousing of central slum dwellers in self-built, minimum-cost homes on cheap land. The fact that this land was in public ownership points up another issue. In big metropolitan areas, particularly, speculative land prices are likely to frustrate rational plans and economical development patterns unless they are drastically curbed. The public acquisition of land needed for future development, well in advance, would be a fundamental economy measure.

THE EXPANDING CITY OF MODERATE SIZE

Aside from strictly rural industry, the most economical alternative for future development (if the least dramatic and the most frequently forgotten) is probably an existing city whose population is, let us say, between 50,000 and 500,000. There were around 160 cities in this category in 1951; doubtless there are many more by now. Land would still be fairly cheap, densities relatively low, resource-saving experiments feasible, and transportation problems minimal (at least for another decade or two). At the same time, such cities are big enough in most cases to support and administer adequate services, and to provide leadership, enterprise, and a fairly wide range of economic opportunities, particularly with positive encouragement from the state and national Governments.

In his seminar paper[20] Britton Harris suggests 200,000 as the

---

[18] Chap. xxi.—*Ed.*
[19] Chap. xv.—*Ed.*
[20] Chap. xiii.—*Ed.*

breaking point, but Hoselitz has elsewhere proposed that even towns of 20,000 can offer an effective base for a well-organized industrial complex.[21]

At present these moderate-sized cities and towns are often very weak in the economic services and cultural facilities required to attract new enterprise, since most expenditures for these tend to be made in the major centers (and, in turn, largely account for their more rapid industrial development and growth). Despite these drawbacks, many moderate-sized cities *are* attracting and stimulating new productive enterprise, perhaps particularly in the East Punjab and in Bombay State. One example is Rajkot, in Saurashtra, with a 1951 population of 132,000, whose metalworking tradition can be followed through all the technological stages from the old central bazaar area to the new and mechanized industrial estate on the outskirts. Another is Baroda, a university community whose development has been stimulated by the restrictions on industrial expansion in Bombay City.

In 1951–1952, municipal expenditures were around Rs. 10 per capita in Rajkot, Rs. 15 in Baroda, and Rs. 40 in Bombay (excluding the independent public corporations).[22] If the critical civic needs of all three communities were met, the differential would probably be greater. Similar evidence is available on the cost of typical one-room public housing units, built to national standards by Bombay State in the three communities a few years ago: Rs. 2,800 in both Rajkot and Baroda, and Rs. 4,500 to 7,500 in Bombay, depending on density and land cost.[23] According to their respective *Socio-Economic Surveys,* incomes were somewhat higher in Bombay than Baroda, but housing congestion was far worse.

CONCLUSIONS AND IMPLICATIONS

Although these rough bits of evidence and broad hypotheses do not lead to conclusive answers, and there never will be any one ideal or optimum pattern to fit all conditions, there is enough evidence to indicate that "decentralization" is a real issue. Certain variables in the development pattern—including city size, density, and structure, and whether industry is stimulated in new towns, expanded towns, satellites, old centers, or rural areas—apparently have a substantial effect on living conditions and urban overhead costs, as well as on productive efficiency for different kinds of enterprise.

[21] Bert F. Hoselitz, "Economic Growth and Rural Industrialization," *Economic Weekly,* February 22, 1958, pp. 291–301.

[22] *Statistical Abstract, Government of India, 1957,* Table 97.

[23] From materials provided the author by the Ministry of Works, Housing and Supply, 1959.

If this is true, how can the future pattern of urban-industrial development be guided so that limited overhead expenditures will produce maximum social and economic benefits? The problem here lies not so much in any inherent difficulty as in the fact that there are few precedents for the kinds of planning and research that are probably required. Innovations will be necessary.

BROAD AREA PLANNING BY THE STATES?

What seems to be needed is a broad kind of physical planning concerned with the pattern of economic development, the pattern of urban growth, and, above all, the interrelationships between the two. None of the established types of planning quite fills this bill. National and state economic planning, exceptionally well developed in India, are primarily concerned with over-all economic policy in budgetary terms, not with locational patterns or interrelationships. (Mr. Pant's estimates are probably a pioneering attempt to consider even the over-all costs of future urbanization.) Public-works planning is focused on resource development, utility and transportation systems, and other overhead facilities, often in regional terms, but unrelated to future patterns of activity or population distribution in any concrete sense. The Damodar Valley scheme includes no plan for future urbanization in West Bengal or Bihar, any more than its prototype did for the Tennessee Valley. Rural planning for village development has tended to be equally specialized, although rural industrialization means urbanization sooner or later. (In his paper on rural development,[24] however, V. Nath suggests that village planning should be related to the service center, since it is the focal point for a developing rural area.) Finally, urban planning is either solely concerned with the area within present municipal limits or, as in the Delhi Plan, with a metropolitan region for which there are no unified public controls to assure effectuation of the plan. Indeed, all regional planning, everywhere in the world, suffers from the fact that a "region," almost by definition, is usually an area for which there is no effective governmental structure.

But there is an obvious and relatively simple answer, particularly in India, where state governments are strong and well developed. The states are already active partners with the Center in economic planning, each with its own Five Year budget. They also make most of the major decisions and expenditures with respect to resource development and public works, industrial location and industrial estates, village development, urban housing, and city planning. All that would seem to be needed is to coördinate these

---

[24] Chap. vii.—*Ed.*

programs in terms of a general area-development plan for the state, or for subregions which require particular concern, such as the Calcutta area or the major section of the Damodar Valley which lies within West Bengal. A start was made in this direction by the Mysore Survey, prepared by Prakasa Rao and A. T. A. Learmonth for the Indian Statistical Institute and the National Planning Commission. If the states were merely to *map* their Third Plan budgets, this could be a highly significant step toward the integration of rural, industrial, and urban development which has been so eloquently promoted by Tarlok Singh in his seminar paper[25] and elsewhere. There are a few good precedents for this kind of planning, in Israel and Holland particularly, although the scale of these nations is smaller than that of most Indian states.

NEW KINDS OF RESEARCH-CUM-ACTION?
THE DYNAMIC INDIAN LABORATORY

At present, it must be admitted, much of the basic knowledge required for planning is not available in readily usable form. Here also there is all too little to be learned from the West, even in terms of research method.

It would not, however, be difficult to gain some systematic working knowledge of comparative overhead costs and potential economies for tolerable living conditions in different types of urban patterns. Nor would it be difficult to develop usable criteria for the effective location of different kinds of economic enterprises. India has excellent statistics, and a great deal of basic data is potentially available in the public records, sample survey cards, etc. There is also a tremendous range of experience to be analyzed, not only in India itself, but in other countries with comparable climate, resources, and economic conditions. And there are numerous plausible hypotheses to be tested, some of which are suggested in this book.

In the main, however, the needed research job will not be of an academic kind, to be carried out in libraries, offices, and laboratories. Additional scientific analysis and surveys will be needed, but real knowledge will largely come from *systematic experiments and testing in the field*. India offers a splendid laboratory for this work. Industry is being developed under all kinds of local conditions. Many experiments in housing have already been undertaken, and more can be stimulated readily. Every type of urban industrial pattern already exists, at least in embryo. The effect of public works programs and credit or tax policies on development patterns can be tested in a hundred or a thousand places. An emer-

---
[25] Chap. xvi.—*Ed.*

gency program such as that now taking shape for Calcutta offers a tremendous opportunity, not only for immediate *ad hoc* improvements but also for the enhancement of basic knowledge for future state-wide planning criteria.

Research-*cum*-experiment, as an integral part of immediate action programs, could have another advantage. By presenting various alternatives for testing in actual use—whether in the form of houses, cities, or opportunities for enterprise and employment—it might stimulate greater public participation in the planning process, and better public as well as expert understanding of the big planning problems. In a way, it means applying upon a far larger scale the basic principle of the Village Development program: learning through doing.

APPENDIX: DATA FROM THE DELHI STUDIES[26]

In preparing a plan for the Delhi area, the staff and consultants of the Town Planning Organization made numerous studies of the physical improvements required to remedy present evils and accommodate future growth. Mr. Echeverria's paper for the Seminar was largely based on the results of this work, and some of the data have been very briefly summarized here. The detailed proposals were published in "Draft Master Plan for Delhi" (Delhi Development Authority, 1960).

THE DEFICIT

The housing situation was analyzed from census material and also from the Socio-Economic Survey conducted by the University of Delhi in 1955. The primary problem is the quantitative shortage. It was estimated that by 1961 there would be 41 per cent more families than available homes of any kind or quality, which means a shortage of around 150,000 dwellings. In addition, about 50,000 homes are so substandard that they should be replaced. Almost 70 per cent of the families live in one-room dwellings, the majority with an area of less than 150 square feet and with no bathroom, water closet, or kitchen.

There is also a water shortage, although this is less serious than in many other Indian cities. The sewerage system is incomplete and provides inadequate treatment. Basic community facilities of all kinds are lacking in many areas.

The present deficit is therefore of emergency proportions, even without allowing for the heavy requirements due to rapid future growth.

---

[26] Condensed from Edward G. Echeverria, "Housing and Urban Services," mimeographed, 1960.—*Ed.*

IMPROVEMENT COSTS

Over-all cost figures for carrying out the Delhi Plan were not yet available. The average unit cost of new development (including housing, utilities, roads, and community facilities) has, however, been estimated from more detailed studies. "If we assume a normal charge for land of 5 rupees per square yard, available in bulk on the edge of most cities, and an acceptable two-room dwelling of low cost, the total per capita is estimated at Rs. 2,000 or about Rs. 9,000 per family as follows":

	Rupees per capita	Percentage of total
1. Cost of land at Rs. 25,000 per acre at density of 60 persons per acre..............................	400	20
2. Cost of site development, assuming Class A level of services......................................	280	14
3. Cost of community facilities (schools, health, etc.)..	138	7
4. Cost of dwelling unit, assuming 450 sq. ft. at Rs. 12, for 4.6 persons average........................	1,180	59
Total per capita cost......................	1,998	100

A program of 25,000 new dwellings per year has been proposed for the Delhi area under the Third Five Year Plan. At Rs. 9,000 per unit, the annual cost would therefore be Rs. 225 million. This does not include transportation, many other non-neighborhood facilities, or central slum clearance and rebuilding on expensive land (where the unit costs would be considerably higher). These estimates of housing construction costs are lower than current price levels, but it is assumed that major economies are possible. In any case, it is evident that a great deal of public initiative and subsidy would be necessary, since the income of most families is less than Rs. 100 per month.

STANDARDS AND COSTS

Prototype housing designs for each income group have been developed, with proposals for new types of cheap housing for low-income families. "The minimum urban dwelling proposed is a stabilized earth one-story structure, with a polyethelene cover over bamboo trusses and sheathing. The estimated cost of the expandable unit is less than Rs. 1,000."

The comparative costs of site development were analyzed, in terms of the differing standards deemed suitable for communities of different size and density. The resulting estimates are summarized as follows:

Site improvement	Rupees per capita, by population size		
	Class A (over 500,000)	Class B (50,000–500,000)	Class C (25,000–50,000)
Water supply..............	47.0	39.0	29.9
Sewerage.................	49.6	41.0	32.8
Surveying, leveling, posts..	30.7	30.7	30.7
Roads and paths..........	70.1	40.3	29.1
Storm water drains.......	29.3	25.3	21.6
Street lighting............	22.6	22.6	21.6
Horticultural work........	12.9	9.6	7.3
Community centers........	6.7	5.0	3.3
Contingencies.............	12.1	9.6	7.8
Total...............	281.0	223.1	184.1

Much simpler and cheaper standards were also worked out for Class D (10,000–25,000) and Class E (under 10,000), but these were asumed to be essentially rural communities and the costs were not included in the paper.

XV

RELATIONS OF TECHNOLOGY
TO THE DESIGN OF
VERY LARGE CITIES

Richard L. Meier

The problems that must be faced in providing for the massive new urbanization of the future are extraordinary in dimension and unusual in type. Simple calculations based upon capital requirements, traffic congestion, or water supply—to name but a few categories in which these problems arise—demonstrate that the experience gained in building the contemporary Western metropolis fails utterly to meet the minimum needs of the urban aggregates in Asia. Much more powerful tools must be employed if urbanization is to contribute to the economic development process. These tools must incorporate technological advances to an important extent, but they require simultaneous innovations in social organization and planning.

If the urbanization experience in the West has not established procedures suited to the scale of urbanization needed in the East, it must be recognized that the Orient, taken as a whole, cannot assemble adequate tools for urbanization, either. If any leverage on these problems exists at all, it is likely to be based upon the relatively unused portions of the stock of technology and seldom-used concepts that has accumulated in the Occident. Since there has been an acceleration in innovation in most fields affecting urban structure and design, with only a small fraction of these innovations achieving widespread use, there is a fair possibility of finding some economic solutions. Also, since a poor society can afford to change only a few factors at a given time, it is evident that we must look for those techniques that combine readily with the old and well-understood building crafts. Our task is one of identifying what fusions of the old with the new may assist in controlling and directing the forces unleashed by the demand for urbanization and its fulfillment.

It is typical of the academic approach that investigators will discuss substance and delineate problems about which something is already known. This tendency is equally true of the analysis of urbanization in India. An *exhaustive* analysis of major problems is not likely to be elicited by such an approach, yet for the planner, the engineer, and the architect the whole development is dependent upon not only identifying, but solving the crucial problems. The process of finding first the crucial limitations and then of suggesting likely solutions has not been formalized. A series of heuristics are involved which change from one set of situations to another. Those that appear to apply to large-scale urbanization will be illustrated by outlining briefly the arguments used in seeking solutions to problems faced in Asia, and more specifically to India, in the course of economic development.

The outcome, a technical solution for very large-scale urbanization at levels of comfort and convenience for the population that are comparable with those enjoyed in populous European metropolitan complexes, has to a large extent already been described.[1] What has been lacking particularly is a discussion of the bases underlying this proposal. If anyone else is to evaluate and add to these investigations, it is desirable that the process of arriving at an urban form for the Indian context of A.D. 1980–2000 and beyond be reviewed in some detail. The procedures that must be used are not at all routine. They depend to a much greater degree upon data and trends to be found in modern science and technology than do most other approaches.

My first study was completed in 1954, although publication was delayed. Its primary intent was to demonstrate that at least one pattern could be found which permitted an adequate scale of living despite the paucity of natural resources. The capital requirements were compatible with reasonable expectations for the pace of economic development. Since that time, some new material has appeared in the technical journals and many of the previous ideas have been more completely tested in experiment stations and in individual practice. Can the first proposal still be defended? More than that, is it possible to go farther and identify even greater potential economies for organizing urban regions? Perhaps a

[1] R. L. Meier, *Science and Economic Development—New Patterns of Living* (Cambridge, Mass., and New York: Technology Press and John Wiley, 1956), pp. 139–222.

whole class of options can be delimited, so that some extra leeway may be provided for cultural and aesthetic choice.

Studies upon urban form spend a great deal of effort on the inductive stage, the elaboration of extensive networks of connected hypotheses, which are extremely difficult to present in a cogent and persuasive fashion. The technique that permits one to work rapidly, and cover a great deal of ground, uses order-of-magnitude calculations in such a manner that the crux of the problem can be pin-pointed. Peripheral issues are set aside at this stage in almost a cavalier fashion. Once the core of the problem has been identified, a concentrated survey of the technical literature is called for. Fortunately, this literature is well organized, as compared to social science documentation, so that comprehensive coverage of the accumulated experience can be achieved in a reasonable amount of time. A quick review of the accomplishments and costs associated with relevant new technology usually suggests new systems, thus opening up new strategies for economizing and leading to a redefinition of the core problem. More order-of-magnitude calculations are then required to elucidate limiting factors. One proceeds in this fashion until the redefined problem can be demonstrated to be insoluble (the most common outcome), whereupon the progression of steps must be retraced to take up the most promising peripheral lead; these leads are followed until a satisfactory technical solution is obtained. When that point has been reached, a series of tests for social, cultural, and political consistency must be applied. If the tests are passed without the appearance of disturbing ambiguities, a candidate solution to the problem has been identified. It stands as the central theme of one of the alternatives for city form.

THE PROBLEM RESTATED

In general terms, the problem is that of finding a structure of society, including its distribution over space, that is most likely to be suited to a long period of economic development. More than ten years ago, after extensive review of the literature, I had come to the conclusion that there was no available means for damming up the flow of population to the cities. The "village industries" program that was much discussed in those days[2] offered no logical

---

[2] A general statement of the thesis is to be found in H. G. Aubrey, "Small Industry in Economic Development," *Social Research*, XVIII (1951), 269. The methods employed in organizing such industries are provided by J. E. Stepanek and C. H. Prien, "The Role of Rural Industries . . . ," *Pacific Affairs*, XXIII (1950), 65. My own critique is found in "Automation and Economic Development," *Bulletin of the Atomic Scientists*, X (1954), 129. A review of the Chinese progress in this direction is to be found in *Small Industry and Handicraft Development in Mainland China, 1952–58* (Misc. Paper No. 2, International Industrial Development Center [Menlo Park, Calif.: Stanford Research Institute, December, 1958]).

next step for improving the productivity of labor. Thus, such a program, despite its intentions, could only be the prelude to the kind of large-scale industrialization that is necessarily associated with cities. The densely populated areas of the world would encounter unprecedented problems of congestion in this industrialization process.

The world's heaviest rural-urban flows of population associated with economic development are expected to appear in China—in the direction of the Shanghai, Peking, and Canton areas—if China finds a way to continue its development. But for China the census is not detailed, and no satisfactory set of detailed maps is available, so that quantitative evaluations are out of the question.

In India the prospective scale of urbanization is almost as great. Excellent topographical maps were available, and the census is reasonably adequate. India offers an appropriate context for analyzing the implications of urban growth.

One could start by making estimates of the labor required for maximum productivity of the land based upon agricultural techniques already employed in Indian agricultural experiment stations or in Japan, where maximum yields were obtained with labor-intensive methods, and then allow the remainder to be urbanized. But what is the total population to be accommodated? *The demographic transition to low birth rate and death rate could (optimistically) be assumed to be completed with only a trebling of population.* The present population of India may be set at 400 million, and that of Pakistan in the neighborhood of 100 million persons. Thus, well over a billion persons would have to make their homes in urban environments in the Indian subcontinent eventually.[3] Most of them would be born in rural areas and be forced to make a personal adjustment to the city. How would these urban residents be distributed?

A map of the urbanizable territory of India based upon three minimal criteria—access to fresh-water supplies, access to raw materials, and the availability of relatively flat land other than flood plain—was prepared. Almost 10 per cent of the area qualified. Putting the ultimate aggregate urban population into that space implied an average population density of 8,000 to 10,000 persons per square mile, which is already an urban density by Western standards. Bengal, Orissa, and the whole Eastern slope seemed to be most favorably situated for urbanization. In this pro-

---

[3] It is assumed that relations between India and Pakistan would become as cordial as those between the United States and Canada. The boundaries would not be defended and a relatively free interchange of population would evolve. Almost any alternative would thwart economic development.

jection Delhi encountered water problems[4] and Bombay's growth was impeded by the hills, although it may decide to fill in much of the bay. Bangalore was found to have serious topographical difficulties, and the territories at the foot of the Himalayas were expected to suffer from restricted access to raw materials.

The Calcutta region seemed to invite the severest agglomeration in these projections. Therefore, using the historic growth rates for metropolitan growth during the exponential phase (6 to 8 per cent per year), and gross population densities of 20,000 to 30,000 per square mile, Calcutta's prospective growth was projected upon the map decade by decade, and at each step the attempt was made to envisage the extra urban services that would need to be installed in order to bring the newly settled territories into the urban economy. We soon encountered insuperable difficulties in estimation. The Hoogli River was a barrier to urban circulation that required expensive bridges, tunnels, and subways, whose construction might not be economically feasible at the time the need first arose. Similarly, the cost of building upon the silt and detritus downstream was likely to be variable. Very possibly, economical solutions existed—London and New York also are based upon estuaries—but we could not judge the physical implications for Calcutta. In New York, however, the existence of the relatively unused Jersey marshes across the river from Manhattan served as a warning. There were too many discontinuities and nonlinearities inherent in Calcutta's location to permit forming a picture of the city at the hundred million mark.

Therefore, other locations where the pressures of urbanization were expected to become extraordinary were investigated. Madras was selected as the focus of an urban region that might attract as many as 60 to 80 million persons—possibly more if other cities encountered difficulties in accepting migrants. The terrain was gently sloping and it was cut by no major rivers. In the case of the geography of Madras it was possible to be far more explicit in our projections.

First, a static solution had to be found—a physical pattern which, on the one hand, permitted the fulfillment of basic human needs (especially the distribution of food, clothing, shelter, and services) and, on the other hand, permitted a level of productivity which was sufficiently greater than these requirements, so that the surplus could be devoted to building and reconstructing the *megapolis* (a name that had already been assigned to such

---

[4] I am told by Britton Harris that solutions to the Delhi regional water problem are available at not too great a cost and will be discussed in the forthcoming Delhi Regional Plan.

large, multinucleated aggregations). A designer calls the relationship between a level of service and physical specifications a *standard,* and it was evident from the start that the standards underlying Western urban settlement were utterly incompatible with the needs of the densely populated regions in the Orient. A unique set of standards for urbanization would have to be invented for such countries as India and China. Therefore, the next task was to place oneself in the shoes of the Indian planners of the future and grope toward a reasonable system of standards that would be relatively impervious to the social changes that were sure to occur.

THE MINIMUM ADEQUATE STANDARD OF LIVING

In the science of man there has been continuing emphasis upon the search for invariant relationships between any individual and his environment. Extreme conditions must be identified which put a stress upon humans and reduce their ability to interact effectively in society and participate in the culture. The findings tend to be species-specific and so must apply equally well to Asiatic and Western peoples, even though the original data have been obtained almost entirely through studies upon the latter. The nutritional needs belong in this category, as well as those associated with thermal comfort.

Superimposed upon such needs are those underlying coöperation with other individuals—nurture of the young, the acquisition of language, security from attack, medicine, and the like. Moreover, the facilities taking the form of dwellings, vehicles, roads, and timesaving equipment must be conveniently assembled so that all of the necessary tasks can be fitted into a twenty-four-hour day.

The standards that were chosen for a *minimum adequate standard of living* were reduced to a basis that was virtually culture-free—so long as the culture retained a commitment to an urban style of life. It was applicable, with indicated adjustment to climate, to any densely settled portion of the world that lived in poverty. It represented a level of living well above subsistence and one which permitted cultural activity as sophisticated as any that has been achieved up to the present day—so long as such cultural activity renounced conspicuous consumption of material goods or energy.

The components of the *minimum standard of living* are reproduced in Table 1. This set of relationships was arrived at in 1949 and has not been noticeably outmoded in any respect by what has been discovered in the interim. The resistance to obsolescence speaks well for the form in which the standards have been framed. The costs have been restated in terms of current Delhi prices, so

TABLE 1

mall caps>Components of a Minimum Adequate Standard of Living</small>
(Based upon population-average physiological requirements for health
and organized production in a tropical urban environment)

Component	Requirement	Unit cost (in rupees)	Yearly cost (in rupees)
Food:[a]			
Rice...................	100 kg/yr	0.75 per kg[b]	75
Wheat flour............	60 kg/yr	0.50 per kg	30
Sugar and syrup	30 kg/yr	0.80 per kg	24
Legumes...............	20 kg/yr	0.75 per kg	15
Vegetables.............	50 kg/yr	0.20 per kg	10
Cooking oil............	20 kg/yr	1.75 per kg	35
Spices, etc.[c].........	......	......	30
Total.............	......	......	219
Shelter:			
Rent and furnishings[d]	6 square meters	20.0 per month	240
Electric (cooking, lighting, communications)..........	12 kw-hr/mo	0.20 per kw-hr	48
Water.................	2–3 tons/yr	......	12
Misc. household expenses.....	......	......	25
Total.............	......	......	325
Personal:			
Clothing...............	20 m/yr	1.25 per meter	25
Shoes.................	3 prs. sandals	7.0	21
Haircuts...............	13	0.30	4
Newspapers............	1/5 of 400 issues	0.12	10
Postage...............	30 messages	0.10 average	3
Telephone.............	50 calls	0.15	8
Local Transport........	200 rides	0.20	40
Total.............	......	......	111
Services:			
Health (enough for life expectancy of 65 years)			
1 professional, 4 technicians/1,000 persons......................			12
Medicines and Supplies..........			30
Equipment (1 bed/200 persons, or Rs. 100 investment).............			20
Education (7 teachers/1,000)........			13
Buildings (Rs. 100 investment)......................			20
Teaching materials and equipment..............			20
Professional training........................			20
Security (police, fire, public health, etc.)............			30
Social insurance (disability, old age)...............			100
Miscellaneous social services...............			50
Cultural activity, recreation, etc..................			50
			c 365
Total for all components[e] (exclusive of national defense items)......			Rs. 1,030

[a] This diet would yield about 2,800–2,900 calories per capita per day and could be easily balanced through minor modifications of the local cuisine. It will be noted that no specific allocation is given to milk, meat, or fish. Actually, a purely vegetarian diet of the kind indicated can be made nutritionally adequate, but may not be culturally satisfying. If such items are added, the quantity of pulses can be reduced, but the over-all cost would be increased.

[b] Prices are based upon quotations in New Delhi, April, 1960. I am indebted to Rodman T. Davis for supplying many of these figures.

[c] Including flavorants, preservatives, condiments, and vitamins.

[d] It was presumed that about a quarter of this would apply to furnishings, some of which may be built into the dwelling, and the remainder for roofed, enclosed space. This suggests that the capital cost of a typical dwelling unit would fall in the range of Rs. 5,000–8,000, including the price of land.

[e] The same standard came to $331 (1950 prices), using world prices and internally consistent values for labor. The present per capita income in Madras State is probably less than Rs. 300.

that comparisons with the present economic status of urban residents can be made with ease. It should be remembered that the costs of unskilled labor and personal services are much cheaper today than in a city where virtually all the population is maintained at the minimum adequate level. At the same time, however, the costs of shelter, communications, and manufactured products are likely to be reduced in price due to economies of scale.

The capital costs for installing a minimum adequate level of living were estimated in 1954 on the basis of equipment and installation prices then being quoted. Each category (food production, apparel, water, shelter, transport, communications, manufacturing, etc.) was taken conservatively, allowing for no more cost-reducing innovations than had already been described. The conservatism was intentional, because it was still impossible to determine whether the postwar flow of cost-saving innovations was going to do more than counterbalance the increasing scarcity of natural resources. Now we can see a resumption of the trend toward a reduction in the capital required to generate a unit of income. Therefore, the total capital calculated then, $1,800 to 3,500, altogether about five to ten times the per capita income required for an adequate level of living, is almost certainly too high. The economies of scale that come into effect, combined with capital-saving innovations that are now more clearly foreseeable, suggest that a factor of three is more appropriate.

The spatial requirements for urbanization can also be deduced to some extent from these standards. For a fully constructed megapolis, where the birth rate in the population must, of necessity, be brought into equilibrium with the death rate, the family units are likely to be small as compared to the present, the most common sizes being three or four persons. Even if the extended family is retained as an urban institution,[5] the size will not actually be very much increased—the most likely membership might run to four or five. Therefore, something in the neighborhood of 20 to 30 square meters of living space would appear to cover most of the needs for apartments and houses. At least an equal amount of built-up, organized space would be required for the social services, transport, and out-of-the-house activities. The great shortage of capital that may be expected to prevail during the construction phase will pre-

---

[5] There is now considerable concrete evidence that even in southern India families send members out to seek employment. If these members, mainly men, remain in the city, they bring in their families. G. M. Woodruff, "Family Migration into Bangalore," *Economic Weekly*, XII (January, 1960), 163–172. S. Epstein has shown that in Mysore the ownership of small amounts of village land stands in the way of rapid urbanization (*ibid.*, XI [July, 1959], 967–972). The evidence suggests that the urban settlements would be made up internally of low-caste families, refugees from disaster, etc.

vent widespread use of multi-story structures and high-rise build-ings. Thus, it was expected that urbanization would be made up predominantly of single-story buildings, with residential densi-ties in the neighborhood of 75 persons per hectare (allowing 10 per cent of the land to be stream, pond, marsh, tank, or otherwise unusable for building) so long as the congestion problems posed by such high densities could be solved. In the city center and sub-centers another ten square meters per employee position would be needed and allocated at the workplace, but office and industrial activities, particularly the ubiquitous lofts needed for low-capitalized light industry, could be conveniently stacked up four stories or more.

The standards helped very little, however, in envisaging the styles of life that might be adopted, or the different ways in which people might choose to spend their nonworking, nonsleeping hours. Nor did they imply very much about the institutions that link to-gether the individuals and households in coöperative large-scale enterprises for the provision of urban services and the organiza-tion of meaningful cultural activities. The scarcity of natural re-sources and the overwhelming magnitude of the flows of persons to the urban areas were expected, however, to impose some unique requirements in the realm of organization.

RULES FOR URBAN ECONOMIZING

The restrictions placed by poverty upon urban design always come as a shock to Western-trained observers. The familiar proportions and relationships that now represent the good and decent life can be made available to, at best, a tiny fraction of the people that must live in cities in India. Commitment of resources according to Western standards would benefit this minority, but would cut off the hopes for improvement on the part of the majority of the population. Such a decision could only lead to political suicide in the long run. Those who were not included in the privileged class could be easily provoked to overrun any pucka apartment blocks and terrace housing that monopolized amenity.

In the early days of these explorations, strenuous attempts were made to discover whether the megapolis in Asia could not take a form similar to that exhibited in the history and the plans of Lon-don and Paris. Each modification that was hypothesized, however, fell far short of requirements. Each demanded many times more capital than was likely to be available if operating costs were to be held at a reasonable level. Tokyo experience offered a precedent for urbanization that was much more helpful, but still far from adequate.

Only one excursion of this sort is worth relating, and this one because it explored the implications of recommendations that are tendered today by some administrators and planners. Such people often suggest that there must be an optimum size for a city so that one objective of large-scale urbanization might well be the allocation of as many people as possible to cities of optimum size. The optimum may be discovered by constructing an index of services and amenities available in cities, as a function of size, or by discovering the per capita overhead costs for providing a standard set of amenities and services. The treatment of such recommendations operationally is rather unclear, but verbal reports of cities in partially developed countries suggested that urban aggregations less than a few hundred thousand population could not support all of the services desired, while cities that had grown beyond a million persons suffered seriously from congestion. Therefore, a half million was taken as a reasonable hypothetical figure for the optimum size.

After that it was a simple exercise to distribute 1,000,000,000 people living at the minimum adequate standard for space utilization over about 120,000 square miles of land otherwise used for intensive agriculture. In order to be economic, these cities would be connected by excellent transport links and the area occupied in such a way that time lost in movement to and from the center of the city would be at a minimum. These assumptions led to 2,000 star-shaped settled areas with the points of the stars coalescing, leaving round blobs of agriculture in a web of urbanism. For 90 per cent of the residents living in urban units of economically ideal size, escape from the urban environment would then be equivalent to that required to get away from a city hundreds of miles in extent and having a population of a billion people. Thus, the aims of the persons recommending cities of reasonable size are defeated by the size of the population expected.

These preliminary unsuccessful explorations did serve to illuminate certain principles underlying urban design that brought about notable reductions in capital requirements and operating costs. A suitable design might be found if it conformed to all of these principles simultaneously. In outline they may be stated as follows:

1. Virtually all the provisions for new migrants, particularly housing and service facilities, must be erected by self-help techniques. The structures and layout must be so simple that untrained labor can put them into place over an extended period of time with a minimum of central control or assistance. Migrants should be settled in satellite communities and tracts at the fringe of the urban area in order to reduce their contribution to congestion.

2. The automobile as a major means of private transport must be

abolished. Automotive vehicles require too much space, too much fuel, and, thus far at least, threaten contamination of the atmosphere. This sacrifice of the private automobile implies that fewer roads are available for trucks, buses, and even bicycles, and that alternative transport services must be supplied. Main routes to communicate on the fringe would be transformed stepwise from roads with buses to transit lines.

3. The morning and evening peak-load phenomenon in the transportation system should be eliminated from the areas of high-density settlement. This can be done by putting all shops, schools, offices, and services on a multiple shift basis. Buildings and equipment are much more efficiently used on two shifts per day, with a third shift reserved for balancing with overtime work, maintenance, and the receiving of supplies. Horticultural labor and construction labor need daylight and therefore constitute an "inter-shift," making altogether six peaks of movement per day. The users of services, especially students, can be manipulated so as to fill in the valleys that remain. Multiple shift operations are known to be difficult to put into practice. The best hope seems to be that of evolving into such a state by means of a carefully planned transition.

4. The inventory of perishable foods that require refrigeration and special warehousing must be kept to a minimum. Two features promise to make great contributions in this respect. Protein production could become largely microbiological, making direct use of photosynthesis and utilizing the swampy margins of the metropolitan region in a mechanical, high-yield endeavor. Vegetables and garden fruits, grown in intensive horticulture, could be produced immediately to the rear of the settlements of new migrants, so that relatively little transport and storage of perishables would be needed prior to consumption.

5. There must be segregation of heavy manufacturing (which is proportionally much less important to a minimum adequate standard of living than it is to patterns of affluence in Western society) into appropriately serviced areas, and distribution of light manufacturing to sites that are within walking distance of the dwellings or the confluences of movement within the city.

6. Devices must be installed for the maintenance of social order and the prevention of the massive riots that disturb the peace and even overthrow governments. The different ethnic communities must be permitted to make their own laws, but not allowed to invade the territory or take away the privileges of others.

7. The principal investment must be in education, as much at the adult level as in the schools. The various electronic media make it

possible for small nuclei of trained teachers to have a much greater effect than formerly. The feedback, especially the questions that arise among the receivers of education, would require the creation of quite a considerable organization. The transition from rural to urban attitudes must be brought about in the shortest possible time. The introduction of family limitation, work habits leading to high productivity, and the organization of community-level welfare services are programs essential to rapid economic development. Each of these requires social contacts that are designed to be educational.

Only with such rules at hand was it possible to propose and evaluate a transportation system and the land-use allocation scheme that is tied to such a system. Simplicity was essential because the engineering and planning capacities of the urban regions would be rudimentary at the time the skeletal network was laid down. The cheapest long-distance movement of passengers was demonstrated by the electric railway (in the neighborhood of 6 cents per mile, including the value of time lost in movement). Short-distance movement away from the termini was most economically handled via bicycle (less than 4 cents per mile, calculated on the same basis). The physical characteristics of a railroad with feeder transportation required high-volume traffic generation from intensely developed centers.

It quickly became apparent that the rate of acceleration and deceleration of rolling equipment on the electric line was a determining factor for the distance from the center or subcenter that could be tolerated in a mass transit system. Surprisingly, the rolling friction of iron upon iron set limits upon the over-all size for the megapolis. The best resolution of these difficulties in the design of appropriate transportation in present and foreseeable technology was offered by some existing additions to the Paris Metro,[6] which employ rubber tires on dry hardwood or concrete. The stops are best put about a mile apart, except in high-density areas, where the distance may be less.

In order to handle the great variety of people and baggage that descends upon a railroad station when no alternative mode of transportation exists, the bicycle must be supplemented by several

[6] Quite a few variations of this approach have been proposed in the last few years. One of the latest to come to my attention ("Pneuways for Rhodesian Transport," in *The New Scientist*, VII [1960], 384) has estimated costs for construction of ways that run less than 10 per cent of monorail, although cruising speed is set at only 40–50 mph. For the scale of urbanism considered here, high rates of acceleration would be advantageous. They would correspond to cruising speeds of 60 mph or more and demand more capital than was indicated for the "pneuway" above. Even more recently, it has been concluded that similar equipment is best suited to conditions in Los Angeles.

other vehicles in its general class—pedicabs and pedicarts primarily, but also some electric warehouse-trucks and gyrobuses for the main stations.

THE URBAN MODULE

The *module,* like the standard, is a simplifying device for the designer. He notes that certain features of an organized structure, such as a city, are unique, complex, indivisible, and subject to rapid and continuous change, while others are iterative and subject to occasional discrete change. The module can be applied to the relatively permanent elements that repeat themselves. It is a form of building block for design—having quite constant dimensions, some assigned structural specifications, and a few fixed functions, yet still permitting differentiation and individuation in many other directions—that can be established as a matter of convenience to designers and builders. For large-scale urbanism, the *communities* of recent migrants from rural areas offer the best opportunity for simplification and rationalization by applying a modular form.[7]

The flood of in-migrants, however, introduces a critical problem. We have already ruled them out of the central areas and adjoining neighborhoods, because of the effects upon circulation. The best-know alternative—that of permitting migrants to settle in camps, *bidonvilles,* and industrial shack-towns on the urban fringe— wastes precious land through disorder and lack of planning, so that no simple route toward economic advance and the accumulation of capital is left open to the settlers. It must also be ruled out, therefore. The chaos in the physical and social environment checks any sustained program for self-improvement. Accordingly, another alternative has been employed: the concept of an *urban village,* a place with fixed boundaries, speaking one mother tongue and holding to the same general set of customs. (A few villages

---

[7] Modules may also be used in the centers and subcenters of new urban regions, but in those instances the dimensions of the appropriate module are smaller in scale and more precise in their other specifications. The basic module for central districts would not contain a community, but might constitute only a block of buildings, or perhaps even a standard plot of land together with the airspace above it. The international styles of elevator buildings may be applied effectively in these central places, and the most educated and urbanized segment of the population may be expected to live in contiguous residential areas. Therefore, modules for high-density central areas can very likely be successfully borrowed from overseas, and do not need to be created *de novo* in the developing country itself. The proper choice of module for central districts cannot be decided upon at the present time. One form may be preferred in Delhi, other forms in Bombay and Madras. It is futile to carry a discussion of general problems of generalized city-center designs any further at this time. Serious economic difficulties cannot be foreseen; therefore, no unusual adaptations of technology need to be brought forward at this stage. The normal working of the real estate market seems likely to generate appropriate land uses when present known methods of regulation are employed.

could be constituted as mixtures of a wide variety of subcultural backgrounds, so that the in-migrant is granted some choice when he arrives.) This is a community that has some bases for coöperation independent of arbitrary authority asserted from the outside.[8] When established, it would be assigned territory along the rail lines that connect with the large employment centers. The land would be surveyed and the water and sewer lines laid down in advance, but the construction would have to be done by the people themselves.

The urban village was proposed primarily as an environment that made possible a rapid adjustment to city life while at the same time it provided a convenient basis for administration. Ambitious young people would have access to technical schools and higher education by taking the train. Many such persons may be expected to move on to better jobs in the factories and offices, and later take up residences elsewhere—primarily adjacent to centers and sub-centers fitted to an international style of life. The construction of the village dwellings and the preparation of the surface for intensive horticulture, followed by extensive work on the maintenance and improvement of such structures, inculcates an acceptance for modes of organizing work that are better adapted to urban institutions. The growing of garden produce on the site provides a chance for the least adaptable members of the new community to become useful. The next generation, one that has spent the whole of its life in this environment, would be much more educated than the in-migrants and hence able to leave the community if it wished and make a decent living in modern industrial and commercial environments.

The *urban village* may be assigned the following specifications when serving as a module:

Area: 200–400 hectares
Population: 15,000–25,000
Transport: one station on transit line, one connecting path for bicycles
Education: several elementary schools, one high school
Health: one clinic, several bath-washhouse combinations
Commerce: one bazaar or market
Gardening: 100–250 hectares

Madras at its limit could maintain perhaps 3,000 to 4,000 of these urban villages, with an extra 10 to 20 million persons living

---

[8] The concept of the *urban village* used here is fully compatible with the detailed descriptions employed by Herbert Gans, of the Institute for Urban Studies, University of Pennsylvania. His studies of the suburbs and immigrant settlements of American cities pay particular attention to the effects of natural, virtually unplanned, ecological forces upon the second generation. ("The Urban Villagers" [1959]; mimeographed, 256 pp.)

in residential areas close to the centers. Many of the communities would have the same languages, dialects, and ethnic origins, and exhibit differences due to timing, location, and choice.

In working out patterns for the organization of urban villages, considerable difficulty was encountered in the course of a search for optimum circulation. An urban village could not be established simply by fiat, so that it immediately yielded the minimum adequate level of living. Instead, it was quite certain to be started at levels very close to subsistence, very likely dependent upon various government authorities to help it through emergencies. The climb up to adequate levels of living for the whole community might be expected to require two or three decades, although many households would reach that stage much earlier. An efficient circulation pattern suited to a community living at subsistence, where almost everyone walks to work or at least to the station, becomes much too congested with light vehicle movement well before the time that minimum adequate levels are reached. Yet, valuable space cannot be wasted by holding it in reserve during this period of development. We did not find a neat solution to the bicycle parking problem. We could provide storage at the station, so that the two hectares (5 acres) of parking space that seemed to be required could be telescoped into a tenth of that area, and the bicycles would be stacked as much as 40 feet high, but only at a price. Investment in bicycle storage at the station was estimated to require at least 30 per cent of the average amortized value of the bicycles themselves. It was assumed that the roads would be metaled in a fashion that is already becoming standard in India. The asphalt and crushed rock necessary for these roads and paths could be financed from a licensing tax on bicycles.

THE GROWTH MODEL

Once the standards and the modules have been chosen, and a view of the long run has been achieved, it is necessary to formulate a program which starts from contemporary conditions and moves step by step toward the desired outcome. At each step the alternative directions for growth can be assessed, the capital and resource requirements be estimated from the standards employed, and the specific difficulties that present themselves be disentangled. Obstacles to growth may require some study. They may be overcome by improved technology, or they may enforce a stunting of the growth that was previously anticipated.

The growth program for the Madras megapolis was set tentatively as follows:

Year	Millions of population	Year	Millions of population
1960	2	2010	48
1970	4	2020	64
1980	8	2030	72
1990	16	2040	80
2000	32	2050	80

Thus, exponential growth was anticipated up to an immigration rate of about 1.3 to 1.4 millions of persons per year, a level that would be maintained for about three decades. If we make a necessary assumption for economic growth, namely, that the practice of family limitation has been spread throughout the rural areas in the 1970–1990 period,[9] this migration rate should have removed the surplus population from the rural areas in the hinterland of Madras by 2020.[10] The remaining growth is attributed primarily to the abnormal age distribution created by migration, and so represents children born to recent arrivals that are in excess of deaths registered locally, even though the nation as a whole must have brought the birth rate into equilibrium by that time.

At the time it was first undertaken, the step-by-step programing encountered difficulties when the population reached 30,000,000 persons. It was found impossible then to obtain additional fresh water. The marginal cost of water was estimated to be already at $100 to $150 per acre foot (0.4–0.6 rupees per metric ton). Water from the Himalayas was likely to have been fully claimed by the nearer urban centers, which would no doubt encounter the same difficulties. We were fortunate to have come across at this time the first reports from the University of California Engineering Experiment Station concerning an adaptation of the Claude process. This process was designed to extract energy from sea water, yielding distilled water as a by-product. The California design emphasized the yield of distilled water, and reduced the production of electric power to a level where turbine design no longer posed any difficulties. This process required a temperature difference in excess of 20° C. between the cold water obtained directly from the ocean depths and the warm surface water in order to obtain the necessary free energy. The crucial factor affecting the cost of water produced

---

[9] A. J. Coale and E. M. Hoover, *Population Growth and Economic Development in Low Income Countries* (Princeton, N.J.: Princeton University Press, 1958), and R. L. Meier, *Modern Science and the Human Fertility Problem* (New York: Wiley, 1959).

[10] It will be noted that these assumptions have attributed greater growth to Madras than is indicated by the rank-size employed by Kingsley Davis. The estimates here reflect specific geographical factors affecting cost of urbanization that were left out of account in the demographic study. (See chap. i.—*Ed.*)

was the length of pipe required for moving cold water from the lower levels of the Indian Ocean to shore installations. The maps showed a rather narrow continental shelf in the vicinity of Madras, so the piping requirement was minimal. The amount of distilled water obtainable seems to be large enough to meet the needs of the megapolis if plants are placed on the beaches about a mile apart. In hot weather, when the need for water would be greatest, they should produce enough by-product power to operate themselves. The shallow slough to the north of Madras could be used as a warming basin for sea water and thereby add significantly to the efficiency. Fortunately, the process is contracyclical, since the yield is reduced in rainy periods and raised markedly when rain does not fall and the weather remains sunny. Other methods for obtaining fresh water from sea water are now being developed in the United States, but none of them promises to be any cheaper for a location like that of Madras.[11]

The transportation system posed another perplexing problem at this time : the traffic flowing in and out of the old central city seemed to require a terminus far more complex than the Grand Central Station—Times Square combination. Was it possible to interchange the population from pedestrian movement and bicycle-class vehicular systems to fast trains, without extravagant terminal costs? It is easy to recommend escalators, moving sidewalks, and automatic shuttles, but these are extravagances in a country with a per capita income still in the neighborhood of 500 rupees per year (projected). The solution appeared to be that of a rental system, very likely with credit cards, which would stock vehicles at convenient points throughout the business and administrative area. The stocks at the central station would be greatest of all, but were still shown to require no more than a fifty-story structure for storage from one working day to the next. Addresses up to three kilometers from the station could be reached within ten minutes after arrival. This simple solution seems most astonishing when it is compared to the present congestion encountered at the major terminals of metropolitan centers much smaller than the megapolis envisaged here. This is one point where multiple benefits derive from the banning of automobiles, the establishment of interlaced multiple daily shifts in offices and services, and the resultant flattening of the peak load.

In these early studies it was already possible to suggest that,

---

[11] Since then much engineering work has been carried out on various other techniques for the desalting of sea water, and standardized cost evaluation has been developed. (Staff report, "Chemists Sum up Water Desalting Progress," *Chemical and Engineering News*, XXXVIII [April 25, 1960], 56–59.)

when the principal purpose is to transmit information, passenger transportation often represents a waste of time and energy; but the manner by which the advancing technology of information transmission could provide substitutes for such movement was less clear. Now we can see, for example, how teaching-machine programs can be sent to students from a central repository, stored temporarily on tape, and erased later to make way for another lesson. Students still need to travel, mainly to acquire laboratory techniques not easily reducible to tape, imbibe enthusiasms and observations from picked teachers, and compare experiences with other students at their own level, but this amount of contact does not require daily commutation. Similarly, the routine aspects of finance and market no longer demand face-to-face interaction. The central city, however, and the specialized subcenters, too, would certainly need trained people on hand for the interpretation and analysis of information, for the negotiation of coöperative arrangements between organizations, and for making decisions in the face of unspecified risks. Altogether, the passenger-carrying capacity in the 21st century may be less than has been anticipated at this time, although it must still remain large. A network of small pipes which conduct high-capacity microwave beams would enable the substitutions to be made. They could carry most of the postal flow, the television content, telephone messages, market data and documentation, cultural materials, etc. The network would naturally parallel the rail lines, but the capacity of channels connecting the centers would be many times greater than those connecting the urban villages. By that time the electromechanical switching-equipment used at present, particularly in telephone exchanges, should be displaced by fully electronic equipment requiring much less space and less maintenance.

After the problems of water shortage and traffic congestion were dealt with, the programing of megapolitan growth encountered no critical problems. One could see from the calculations that the costs for the interchange of persons and goods were mounting with added population, so that a city of 100 million population might easily become as inconvenient as New York is today. At the projected per capita income, a single center with subcenters and special communities reaches its limit at around the 100-million mark. The ability to program growth to 80 million on flat terrain does not mean that critical problems do not exist; it only implies that we lack sufficient information at the present time to discover and describe them. This open-ended future has a considerable advantage, nevertheless, over historic paths of development, all of which seem to be blocked, over the long run, by an insufficiency of resources or by the lack of appropriate technology.

PROSPECTS FOR FOOD, FUEL, AND MATERIALS

How has the passage of time dealt with the assumption underlying the projections and the projections themselves? A nonclassical approach had to be adopted in order to find any kind of future that seemed technically and economically feasible. Novel approaches are risky because they may include hidden flaws which have not been detected. The ideas have not had sufficient exposure to criticism. In this brief review we shall proceed from the major to the minor categories.[12]

FOOD

The principal nutritional shortage in India and other societies living at or close to subsistence is in protein foodstuffs. The predicted revolution in protein synthesis has moved closer to realization in Japan, particularly at the Tokugawa Institute for Biological Research, of the University of Tokyo, where most of the practical studies are being carried out. Organisms that fix their own nitrogen and at the same time manage to grow rapidly in warm water have now been found. Methods of controlling predators have been developed. In both Japan and the United States, methods for removing color and original taste have been found. A fillip from an unexpected quarter—the studies on the survival of man in outer space—has brought about a tenfold increase in research upon the technology associated with photosynthesis in continuous-flow systems. The new emphasis is upon the design of reliable fully automatic production systems.[13] The costs of production may be expected to fall to about the same range as soy bean or ground-nut protein in the 1970's, or sooner; the supply is more dependable than that of those crops and the quality of the protein is considerably better.

The intensive gardening procedures based upon the experience of the South Chinese and the Japanese, and the hydroponics experience in Puerto Rican and Indian experiment stations, are most sensitive to plant virus diseases. Some progress has been made in the control of such diseases through the use of antibiotics. A large number of small advances have been made on many fronts which, taken together, do not increase expectations, but offer greater assurance that, despite local mishaps, some kind of crop can be obtained. Even greater flexibility in food supply should derive from developments in food processing. Synthetic rice, for example,

---

[12] It has been impossible to document the following statements in the standard fashion, due to their brevity. A more detailed evaluation would indicate the technical arguments underlying the conclusions and cite findings to substantiate the conclusions.

[13] R. G. Tischer, "Nutrition in Space Flight," *Advances in Space Science*, I (1959), 341–382.

can be made from whatever bulk starch is in best supply, and has been found to have acceptance in peasant populations.

FUEL

The development of nuclear energy from fission at the technological level has proceeded at a pace very close to the early projections, but costs are high as compared to that of fuel oil on the world market, since extra reserves of petroleum have been found recently. Therefore, most large-scale reactor construction has been postponed for a while.

The fusion process, which aims at obtaining power from the deuterium component in water, is undergoing a thorough researching, but as the details are filled in it appears more and more probable that facilities of economic size would be very large and, therefore, suitable only for the more developed societies where interest rates are comparatively low and the annual increases in demand are large.

The production of liquid hydrocarbon fuels via biological cycles using photosynthesis has now been tested at every step in an engineering experiment station and found to work even more efficiently than had previously been judged. This means that the exhaustion of the reserves of fossil fuels in developing countries need not deal a crippling blow to the development program. The expected cost of using sunlight as an original source of energy sets a ceiling that appears to be equivalent to gasoline at a price no higher than one rupee per liter.

CONSTRUCTION

Building techniques for low-cost, self-help urban housing have not changed very much in the past few years, but the volume of construction undertaken in this category has increased greatly. Perhaps more important than anything else is the evidence, still sketchy and scattered, but nevertheless reassuring, that the organization of self-help construction can be stimulated in such a way that the governmental aid and subsidy is small, compared to the over-all costs. People of rural origin can build houses with their own labor that are really quite decent, and can complete the job within two or three years if they are helped by kinsfolk and friends.

TRANSPORTATION

Although new techniques have appeared in the interim, e.g., hydroplaning, pipelines for solids, "sausage-skin" barges, vertical-take-off aircraft, and guided missiles, there are no striking changes in costs or spatial relationships that must be taken into account.

All of these new developments may easily find a niche in the transportation system that is ultimately built into the economy, but they do not promise to do more than extend the plateau of constant unit costs, pushing back somewhat the points where congestion brings about rapidly increasing marginal costs.

MANUFACTURING

The rapid progress that the Japanese have made in mass-producing light, highly engineered articles—a pattern that is now becoming evident in the industrialization of Hong Kong as well—reinforces the earlier conclusion that Asia can develop most rapidly if it rejects the heavy, bulk-ridden, space-wasting features of European and American consumption and concentrates upon using small amounts of material to best advantage.

The scientific and technological reports coming from India in recent years reflect the need to get the basic metallurgical and chemical industries going. Only scattered suggestions can be found that the experience is being accumulated which will be relevant to the light, consumer-oriented industries of the future. Perhaps the labor shortages in Western countries that result in greater dependence upon imports for labor-intensive products will further stimulate the export firms in Madras, Calcutta, and Bombay, laying the foundation for a linking of the great aptitude for aesthetic synthesis and abstract design that exists in Indian culture with the practicalities of production.

Judgments about what may happen to manufacturing cannot be based upon simple extrapolations drawn from India at present, but primarily from the recent histories of territories, Asian and otherwise, such as Japan, China, Puerto Rico, Israel, Jamaica, Mexico, the Philippines, etc. Each of them in some respect has been ahead of India in organizing its industry and has learned through trial and error what is needed to start and maintain that kind of activity.

ORGANIZING THE URBAN COMMUNITY

How can the rural patterns of living be changed most rapidly into new modes which are consonant with urban life? Very likely, Indian cities will never be in a position to apply all the powers they feel they need. The scarcity of capital and adequately trained professional manpower will contribute to the feeling of impotence on the part of the officials. Is there any relatively simple strategy for administration that seems to be open to the prospective areas of agglomeration?

The principles affecting land use that seem to be an absolute minimum have already been listed. The land and utilities scheme for "planning the slums" so that they could develop over time to a status considerably above that of the typical slum offers a widely used administrative technique. It implies the power to condemn and take over agricultural and other land for residential purposes without paying too much to land speculators. The city would also have to coördinate the railroad lines connecting satellite centers with the public transport that supports the more local circulation. The water and electric utilities, their extension or withholding, offer very simple means for control and guidance of community and neighborhood development. The introduction of the multiple shift system that reduces the peak-load pressures on the transit system and almost doubles the productivity of social overhead capital, will, for example, depend upon the availability of street lighting in the morning and evening hours. Control of the communications systems may rest with the national government, but the local administration of these services should work smoothly enough to enable the police to maintain order and to enable commerce and education to expand rapidly.

Charles Abrams has reviewed the recent experience that is most relevant to the planning of urban metropolitan regions in developing countries.[14] He lists a range of methods that may be drawn upon for the administration of plans, which I shall rearrange and place in order of increasing administrative complexity: (1) compulsion using severe penalties, (2) inducement with subsidies and rewards, (3) education and persuasion, (4) direct operations, (5) joint ventures, (6) planned inevitability. In India, as elsewhere, it seems likely that all of these techniques will need to be employed simultaneously. There is a chance in India, however, that some of the advanced procedures can be used more often than when planning was undertaken before, because it is possible now to transmit information in India at lower relative costs, while the use of the military or the police for enforcement may be expected to become more expensive. The traditions of India foster an open society subject to open criticism and constant revision, so that the political barriers to the flow of information are low. The social and linguistic barriers are diminishing rapidly at the community level, at least, as education increases. (The conflicts between language groups may, however, be exacerbated for a while.)

The communications elements in the undertaking of plans for urban growth have been brought out because they are most subject to revision and improvement over the forthcoming decades. Major advances in communications technology are coming along

---

[14] Charles Abrams, "Regional Planning Legislation in the Underdeveloped Areas," *Land Economics*, XXXV (1959), 85–103.

rapidly and can be quickly adapted to the needs of developing countries.[15] Unit costs for the transmission of messages of various kinds and sizes can be reduced to a striking degree. This means that more complex forms of administration will be possible even at the low income levels anticipated during the early stages of the urbanization process.

Let us explore some of the possibilities for guiding the evolution of the urban village, using its connections with the centers and subcenters as leverage for bringing about change. At this stage of development the welfare needs of the newcomers cannot be met directly by an urban administration. It must encourage the new groups to elect spokesmen, and it must appoint "caretakers" in some crucial categories.[16] Communications are carried on between these middlemen and the people themselves (whose basic reaction upon experiencing a critical need for a social service is to "see someone whom I know who will himself know where to go and what to do") on a verbal level, mostly informal, with many things remaining unspoken, and between the middlemen and the centers with restated requests translated into more formal language. These middlemen require some daily communication with the centers. Previously, such communication has been established through face-to-face contacts (or through another layer of middlemen), but now it can be handled through two-way communications channels and a set of telephone numbers and addresses.

Who are these middlemen? They can be briefly categorized as follows:[17]

The elders, who may serve as a panchayat court and resolve most civil disputes before they become court cases

---

[15] Trade journals such as *Electronics* provide comprehensive news regarding those developments. An excellent nontechnical analysis of recent origin is to be found in *Business Week*, March 26, 1960, pp. 74–121.

[16] I am indebted to Dr. Erich Lindemann of Harvard Medical School for this highly economical conception that interrelates the dependent, not-yet-absorbed population with the formally organized elements in the city. An application of this mode of thinking can be found in the "Tenth Anniversary Report of the Wellesley Human Relations Service, Inc., 1948–1958," by R. L. Bragg, W. C. Klein, and E. B. Lindemann (mimeo, 60 pp.). He has recently completed an extended survey of Indian mental health and community organization and may subsequently publish remarks of his own on the applicability of the "caretaker" concept to the Indian scene.

[17] This list was assembled from experience acquired in the course of observing the urbanization process. It is interesting to compare these roles and functions with those reported for an early nineteenth-century Madras village before British contacts had brought about many changes: headman, accountant, watchman, boundaryman, water superintendent, priest, schoolmaster, astrologer, smith, carpenter, washerman, barber, cowkeeper, doctor, dancing girl, musician, poet. (H. E. Malaviya, *Village Panchayats in India*. [New Delhi; All India Congress Committee, 1956], pp. 88–89, citing Mathai, *Epigraphic India*, IV, 138.)

The salaried administrative group that collects taxes, maintains records, and writes the necessary reports

The police officers, most of whom are, as a matter of policy, drawn from outside the community

The teachers, who will often need to be bilingual

The clinic personnel—nurses, pharmacists, dentists, and doctors

The moneylenders and credit-union secretaries

The water-control technicians, who give advice on the economical use of water in horticulture and elsewhere

The transportation agents, who arrange for trips back to the home village and for the delivery of relatives

The produce marketers, who must assess changes in market prices and advise the horticulturist when to harvest

The retailers, who must buy from catalogues or salesmen

The electrical maintenance men, who must service the power distribution system and perhaps make repairs on communication equipment as well

The building artisans, who must show the settlers first how to construct, then repair and maintain, the houses and service buildings needed by the settlers and their families.

The promoters of sports, exhibitions, festivals, and other cultural activities

The secretaries and local committeemen of the major political parties

An estimated 20 to 100 two-way channels are needed to connect the middlemen directly with their respective organizations. They would operate most efficiently nowadays with small, portable radio sets, similar to those now produced in Japan and the United States, which connect with the telephone exhanges if the latter have antennas within a mile or so. The efficiency of a person so equipped when he moves around the community is much greater than if he sits at a desk with a telephone. Indeed, a portable two-way communications instrument with a distinctive antenna could well become a badge of office in the community. The capital investment required per outlet would be no greater than for a telephone and could perhaps be reduced over the next decade.

This is not the only kind of connection with the truly urban culture that the new community could use to advantage. Perhaps a thousand or more one-way instruments (radio, television, teleprinting, etc.) could be accumulated to serve educational, cultural, and recreational purposes simultaneously. Much of adult education can be channeled through the mass media. The questions that are generated, some of which make up the feedbacks to the broadcasters, can be monitored through the two-way connections. With such capacity for speeding interaction with sources of accumulated, specialized experience, it should be possible to create some highly developed institutions. The markets would have stable prices reflecting visible supply-demand relationships, the police would be able to coördinate their efforts in emergencies, the labor force would become differentiated along non-caste lines, involuntary inventory shortages would almost disappear, and current data would be available for the assembly of detailed plans. The principal difficulty that can be foreseen is one that occurs in every developing society—the persons in responsible positions, from the caretakers on up the hierarchy, and including most business administrators and independent professional men as well, would be overworked. The handling of too many messages can be extremely fatiguing, and can lead to actual breakdowns.

The tape recorder can be introduced at the "hot spots" in a message-relaying network. The persons involved can then queue up the flurries of calls that would otherwise overwhelm them. When a lull occurs, they can then review the backlog and, at the very least, take care of the high-priority items. Techniques such as these increase the peak-load capacity of the communications network by a factor of two or three. Institutions in the most advanced urban centers are only now adjusting to the potentials for organization that are inherent in these instruments, so that we may expect that the crucial operations in the construction of a megapolis can be made to work at least as well as their counterparts in advanced societies, though other aspects are likely to remain rather crude and simple for many decades to come.

Part 4

GOVERNMENT
AND
PLANNING

XVI

PROBLEMS OF INTEGRATING RURAL, INDUSTRIAL, AND URBAN DEVELOPMENT

Tarlok Singh

Large changes are in progress in both the rural and the urban life of India. While studies to assess the impact of rural-urban migration and the employment situation in urban areas have been undertaken, there have been few investigations into the changes which are currently taking place in urban areas. In some ways, more has been done in the evaluation and study of rural change. Work in this field has, however, not extended far enough to permit a comparative analysis of the factors which are bringing about changes in rural and urban life, the pace at which these changes are taking place, and the effects of these changes on different sections of the rural community.

Urbanization is both a consequence and a causal factor in economic development. The rate of urban growth is an important index of progress in the economy. Some allowance should be made for the fact that many of the problems of urbanization are relatively new and that social policies for dealing with the emerging symptoms are being but slowly evolved. Nevertheless, there are some aspects of the present urban situation which point to larger problems. For instance, the recent city surveys almost uniformly report a high degree of unemployment and underemployment. In one city, 40 per cent of all the earners interviewed felt a sense of insecurity in the jobs they held. Planned townships set up for new industries often seem to begin their careers like walled cities of old, isolated from and not too greatly concerned with what develops beyond. The inevitable expansion of these towns and the need to

mark out for future acquisition successive rings of villages intro-
duce in the latter a feeling of decay, to which current policies do not
give enough thought. The tendency to grab land and push up land
prices introduces around every large town undeniable elements of
exploitation and conflict. Farther away from urban areas, there is
discontent on the part of the more conscious opinion in the rural
areas with the growing disparity between urban and rural conditions, opportunities, and levels of income. A more imaginative solution of the problems of urbanization and better urban planning and
administration are essential and will doubtless help, but the issues
go deeper. In what manner are rural and urban development, both
essential parts of the scheme of economic and social development,
to be related to or "integrated" with one another?

"Integration" is never an easy expression to define. In the context of rural and urban development, to "integrate" means to
ensure coördinated development such as will secure even progress
between rural and urban areas, and to minimize social and economic conflict between them and within the urban communities
themselves. In advanced countries, the distinction between urban
and rural life has become less significant. In countries like India, too,
this phenomenon may take place after some forty or fifty years of
growth. The manner in which the distance between rural and urban
life diminishes differs according to such factors as the intensity of
industrialization, density of population, the roles assigned to individual initiative and to coöperative and collective organization,
the system of local administration, and other factors. In the Indian
situation, therefore, there is room for departing in some measure
from the experience, for instance, of the United States or Soviet
Russia and for considering afresh how, over the coming decades,
the rural and urban economies might be developed so that they
would merge into one and become, as it were, parts of a composite
structure. Here it is perhaps pertinent to suggest that at the present
stage of development in India the urban way of life (as contrasted with the rural) cannot yet be said to have been established,
for it is confined to those members of the urban community who
have become wholly identified with industrial and commercial
activity, skilled workers, and others with incomes high enough and
stable enough to sustain the main urban amenities. Large sections
of the population may not be able easily to retreat from the town,
but the situation is sufficiently fluid for them to move from a large
city to a small or middle-sized town. There are also others for
whom the time for a final choice between village and town has not
yet come.

The problem of the integrated development of rural and urban areas is posed in relation to industry because of the leading role of industrialization in changing the pattern of resource allocation within the community and in bringing new productive forces into play. It would be more correct to speak of industry, along with agriculture, as providing the spearhead of the attack upon problems of mass poverty—an attack which can only succeed if, at the same time, a corresponding measure of development is assured in education, the building-up of skills, improvement in the conditions of health and housing, development of power and of transport and, more generally, in scientific and social research and in efforts to raise the productivity of large numbers of persons. If some urban areas generally present greater attraction to new industries than others, perhaps the main explanation is to be sought in the differences in the level of development of economic and social overheads. To a large extent, therefore, the problem of spreading the benefits of industrialization, and of realizing them sooner rather than later, is one of deciding upon the lines along which economic and social overheads should be developed in the future. In this, both long-range and short-range considerations have to be taken into account, the question being one of assessment of economic and social costs in the wider perspective of national development.

In considering the broad approach to this problem, the first observation to be made is that the choices are by no means clear-cut. In any scheme of development, large cities, middle-sized and small towns, and rural areas have to receive, according to the urgent problems to be met, a fair share of the total resources that can be assigned for economic and social overheads. Within these limits, however, there is room for relative emphasis and for a degree of orientation in terms of future development which may exert a significant influence over a period. There is a large measure of agreement that concentration of urbanization in metropolitan cities, unavoidable as it may have seemed, entails high social and economic costs, and that, to the extent possible, other patterns of urbanization should be promoted, with economic and social overheads being used as an important lever of development. For this purpose, four main suggestions have been advanced. The first is that middle-sized towns offer an environment in which, having regard to various economic considerations, industry can find roots strong enough to compare with the attractions of large metropolitan cities. Definitions in terms of the population of towns fulfilling this condition differ, some favoring towns with a population of 250,000 to a million, others 50,000 to 100,000 or even 20,000 to 50,000. The location of industry involves a variety of factors. A rigid view as to size is, therefore, difficult to support and is, indeed, unnecessary. The second broad approach, closely related to the first, is that middle-sized and small towns should be developed as "countermagnets" to the large cities. The third approach which has been put forward is that, in each area, small towns and large villages should be selected for the development of medium-sized and small industries. In the second proposal the emphasis was on finding an efficient alternative to the larger cities. Here the stress is on bringing into the rural areas, in a more direct way than may be otherwise possible, a further dimension in development—namely, the introduction of industry on a sufficient scale to change their occupational structure. Finally, there is an allied proposal, summed up in the expression "village clusters," which involves the development of a local industry and its ancillary facilities in a village selected as being "central" for a small group of adjacent villages.

The important consideration is not so much to choose between these various proposals as if they excluded one another, but to recognize them as gradations in a general scheme of development aiming at a wider dispersal of industry away from the large cities. The different proposals mentioned above are, in reality, parallel patterns of growth, each being adopted in the measure in which it is favored by the prevailing conditions. The problem has to be approached from both ends—outwards from the village, seeking a varied system of work opportunities, and, secondly, away from the large cities, seeking a wider distribution of industrial and economic activity so as to avoid the admittedly undesirable effects of overconcentration. Expressions in common use, such as "decentralization of industry," do not succeed in conveying the more positive idea of balanced development between rural and urban areas, between large, middle-sized, and small towns, between economic and social objectives, appropriately conceived for long-term development. Viewed thus, there is little need to make the point, as some have done, that the individual village is an insufficient basis for rural industrialization. In this form, the proposition has not really been advanced, and those who have appeared to suggest this course have, in fact, done no more than point to one aspect of the balanced development which has to be achieved.

Although urbanization is most frequently associated with industrial development, which will doubtless be the major influence in the future, one could distinguish between the processes associated with the urbanization of at least four different types of towns, namely, (*a*) local trading and marketing centers, (*b*) places of administrative and cultural importance, (*c*) commercial centers, especially those connected with foreign trade, and (*d*) industrial towns. These aspects exist together in most towns, the proportions varying from one to another. This is illustrated, for instance, in the distribution of population on the basis of livelihood in twelve of the cities studied under the auspices of the Research Programmes Committee of the Planning Commission set out in the table below.

PERCENTAGE DISTRIBUTION OF POPULATION
ACCORDING TO MEANS OF LIVELIHOOD

City	Production other than cultivation	Commerce	Transport	Other services and miscellaneous means of livelihood
Allahabad.............	22	20	10	48
Baroda...............	27	22	5	44
Bhopal...............	21	18	7	52
Gorakhpur............	25	19	13	37
Hyderabad............	19	20	8	51
Hubli................	39	22	8	24
Jamshedpur..........	70	11	3	15
Kanpur..............	42	24	4	28
Lucknow.............	24	21	7	45
Madras..............	25	22	9	42
Poona...............	27	18	7	27
Surat...............	44	25	3	27

The existing towns will witness considerable growth in the next fifteen to twenty years. Many new towns will also come into existence. The average rate of growth in urban population is estimated at about 4 per cent per annum although, according to the studies which have been made, in the metropolitan cities it might be even higher. Against this background, the idea of balanced development mentioned above might be interpreted as comprising the following main objectives:

1) As far as possible, new industries should be established away from the large and congested cities. The new centers might be middle-sized towns, small towns, or new locations selected on account of the accessibility of raw materials or other considerations.

2) In the planning of large industries, the concept of region should be adopted. Thus, where a steel plant or a heavy machinery project is established, the area of planning should extend beyond the immediate environs to a larger area for whose development the new industry might serve as a major focal point.

3) Generally, in community development projects or other areas within districts, the rural and the urban components of develop-

ment should be knit into a composite plan. This will involve an attempt to work out carefully the interdependence between each town and the surrounding rural area, emphasizing, for instance, the supplies to be drawn from the villages, the market in the rural area to be served from the town, communications, expansion of power facilities, and the provision of facilities for training and education.

4) Within each area, apart from the medium-sized or other industries located on the basis of economic and other criteria in the selected towns, the effort should be to secure a diversified occupational pattern in place of the present extreme dependence on agriculture. In the main, this will involve the building-up of processing industries, meeting local needs to the extent feasible through local production, and the improvement of tools and equipment in the traditional village industries and their gradual transformation into small-scale industries through the introduction of power.

These objectives are consistent with one another and may be said to be facets of the same basic approach. The next question to be considered concerns the conditions necessary for realizing them. The most important of these is the concept of the pattern of industrialization on which the plans are based. In the Indian situation, it is assumed that, apart from fields in which large capital-intensive industries are unavoidable for technological reasons, the bulk of industry will take the form of medium-sized and small industries making use of the available human resources and, at the same time, applying a forward-looking technology. It is also assumed that as between large or medium-sized and small-scale industries, the object will be to widen the field for small-scale operations by way of the manufacture of parts and components and by arrangements for the production of ancillaries. The general proposition has long been accepted, but its concrete applications have to be worked out systematically, industry by industry, and conditions created in which large numbers of small enterpreneurs and artisans' coöperatives can take up new activities with a measure of assistance in finance, techniques, and designs from the appropriate institutions. Apart, therefore, from big industries, many of which might fall appropriately in India within the sphere of the public sector, these are the essentials of an industrial policy designed to facilitate balanced industrial development and seeking to fulfill the four objectives outlined above. Decisions as to location of industries and the related development of economic and social overheads follow from these broad principles.

In giving effect to these concepts, the next question to examine is whether the machinery of planning below the national and state level is adequate for sustaining development on the lines envisaged. This is a theme by itself, but a few suggestions could, perhaps, be offered.

In the first place, it is clear that the plans for developing economic and social overheads in the larger cities, the new industrial townships, and the more important middle-sized towns, in which industries are located, should become integral parts of the national and state plans, in each case along with the associated regions. Thus, it is no longer adequate to consider the building-up of a township for a steel plant as a scheme by itself without at the same time coördinating the development of a larger area which may be viewed in the future, along with the township, as a planning region.

Secondly, the concept of local administration will need to be strengthened in two ways—in terms of the area within the jurisdiction of a municipal body and in terms of the functions to be undertaken by it. In the past, the municipal limits of towns have been expanded under the pressure of circumstances: because industrial, commercial, and building activities overstepped these limits, because speculation in land disorganized the life of the neighboring villages, or because ribbon development began to disfigure the countryside. It would, therefore, appear desirable from the beginning to provide for larger rather than smaller limits for every growing town. This would bring a city and its hinterland within the same unit of planning and administration, and, extending the idea further, would facilitate the economic and social integration of a large surrounding rural area with the town on rational lines, thus enabling the town and the village to influence each other directly to mutual advantage.

The third aspect which may be considered is the role of the village community and its likely future. It is sometimes thought that the stress on the village community is an attempt to cling to the past, a failure to see the forces of change. This is a misapprehension in relation to the underlying concepts of coöperative development and the community approach in India's plans. It is envisaged that, as technological changes take place in agriculture, and as transport facilities improve, the unit of effective community organization will become larger. Gradually, the operational area of local planning and decision will become a group of villages rather than the individual village. This trend is stimulated both by the growing requirements of the village to be met from without and the institutional arrangements needed for meeting those requirements. The process, however, is seen rather as being one of evolution from below, in response to developing needs, than as an imposition from above justified by convenience of administration alone.

A fourth and more fundamental aspect is the need to assure integrated development of all sections of the village community and through it of rural society as a whole. By their very nature, the composition of urban populations is heterogeneous, and thus the bonds of urban community life are few, the cohesive forces weak. On the other hand, within the rural community there are still vital elements of common obligation and common interest which can be turned to account in the development of a coöperative and diversified rural economy. To the extent that this is achieved, the easier it will be to secure a larger measure of integration between the rural, urban, and industrial economies for the country as a whole.

XVII

NATIONAL IMPLICATIONS OF
URBAN-REGIONAL PLANNING

Albert Mayer

The present paper discusses certain of the national implications of urban-regional planning, basing its arguments upon the Delhi Plan. It deals with major national-policy decisions and actions or requirements which are not controllable by the Delhi Plan alone, but which are necessary for the proper working and the timetable of the plan —or necessary if some of the underlying premises or assumptions of the plan are to prove justified in fact. Also, it notes that the implementation of the Delhi Plan has certain major implications, some of which are national in scope.

Five major items have been selected for analysis.

THE DELHI PLAN AND URBAN-REGIONAL PLANNING GENERALLY —THEIR PLACE AND SCALE IN THE FIVE YEAR PLANS

The Delhi Plan includes a timetable of accomplishment, and it includes very crude cost estimates for achieving, within its twenty-year span, certain goals or stages in housing, slum clearance, development and redevelopment, roads, water supply and distribution, and electric supply. It includes also land acquisition on a very large scale to permit the accomplishment of these results, and to forestall the further speculative rise in land values which would otherwise make over-all costs entirely prohibitive.

The resulting yearly, five-yearly, and total expenditures raise some fundamental issues and dilemmas. For the first time, the economic planners, the Planning Commission, have before them the figures on which to base a policy and course of action. Hitherto,

housing and slum-clearance expenditures have been on a token or
ad hoc basis, under various separate schemes. Most recently (end
of 1959), the Ministry of Works, Housing and Supply has in-
augurated a scheme for central loans to states for advance land
acquisition. "This scheme is intended to help in solving the problem of housing and slum clearance by the provision of loan finance
to State governments for the large-scale acquisition and development of land in selected places" [1]—a larger scale but still frag-
mentary measure. Now, with the Delhi figures at hand, for the
first time the order of magnitude is available by which the scale of
an operation of urban-regional planning can be visualized; and it
is even possible to make highly crude extrapolations for the order
of magnitude of the problem on a nationwide basis. Such questions
as the following can and must now be posed :[2]

Where in the Third Five Year Plan's hierarchy of necessity does
urban development stand, as compared with already fully recognized needs such as more steel production, more hydroelectric development, etc? In short, in the gamut of total needs and individual
categories, where does such an effort and such a timetable as Delhi's
twenty-year program belong? Realistically, must the totality of development and redevelopment called for in the Delhi Plan be
worked out at a much slower rate, with actual work proceeding on
a much more *ad hoc* and selective basis, attending to the urgent and
the critical, pretty much as hitherto, but with the benefit of the plan
skeleton and envelope?

Again, having reached some over-all conclusion and set aside
some total funds for planned urban-regional development and
housing for the Third Five Year Plan, should Delhi, as a pilot
exploration and prototype, receive special attention and expenditure
(predicated on some such timetable and annual capital expenditures
as noted in the Plan) consciously disproportionate to what can be
afforded in other metropolitan situations? Or should such concentrated expenditure, if it is made, be devoted to Calcutta, where
the situation may be more explosive? Such questions as these are
thrown into relief by the Delhi exploration, and demand consideration and decision.

In particular, the question of large-scale land acquisition by pub-

---

[1] Government of India, Ministry of Works, Housing and Supply, *Land Acquisition
and Development Scheme* (October, 1959), p. 1. The "places" are Bombay, Calcutta,
Madras, Kanpur, Admedabad, and Delhi.

[2] Even though the Delhi Plan includes detailed and carefully thought-out recommendations for taxes and revenues to be raised to a great extent locally to meet
capital and recurrent development costs, it must be clear that, in large measure, these
must be considered as part of the totality of funds available to the country for development, and thus to that extent affecting other possible development.

lic authority must be considered and acted on at the earliest moment, as it already has been in Delhi, where over 30,000 acres have been notified. There is an imperative need for public-land acquisition well ahead, as, for example, has for many years been the policy of Stockholm, Rotterdam, and some other European cities. It means an enormous saving in costs because it forestalls speculative increases, already inflated by 200 to 300 per cent in a very short time in many cases. It also gives the public the benefit of legitimate land-value increases created by its own development policies and efforts, which often involves some differential profit and helps to counterbalance the need for subsidies. Fully as important, it permits a much freer hand and a more efficient development operation. Land use and zoning can be optimal, free of the avalanche of private protests which normally accompanies and hamstrings development, since the most effective planning involves necessary differences in uses and densities, sometimes in similarly located land.

Land acquisition poses some difficult problems and suggests possible answers. In a way, this is the most crucial measure to assure the possibility of effective planning over time. Land acquisition differs crucially from actual development and implementation in that it is purely a financial and fiscal transaction which does not involve any physical resources or manpower, and thus does not subtract them from other developments in the Five Year Plans. On the other hand, very large sums, indeed, are involved. Delhi alone, for example, will involve a sum in the neighborhood of 100 crores. Can such sums be managed, no matter how big and crucial the stakes, the ultimate savings, and the advantages? This is the question that needs close discussion and early decision. One possibility might be to consummate the acquisition on somewhat the same basis as the U.P. government met the very large sum involved in liquidating the zamindari (i.e., agricultural land). Most of the payment was in nonnegotiable bonds at very moderate interest rates over a long term, with only a small fraction in cash. If such a method were found to be legal, or could be made legal in the case of urban land, this very big basic problem could be solved. Moreover, a going income might be had from a large portion of the land until it was actually needed for construction, from agricultural and other current use; in this way, the recurring interest cost would be about minimal.

When we consider the urban-regional planned development in the same context as other long-recognized investment categories, another question emerges. How much competition is there, in fact, with other elements in the Five Year Plans? Building construction and road construction, especially under Indian conditions, require a large proportion of labor, which is, of course, in long supply. A large proportion of cost is in terms of such local and noncompetitive products as clay for brick, sand for concrete, and timber—not local, but not in heavy demand—for shuttering and other purposes. Cement is not a scarce product. With the new plants in operation, the relatively small amount of steel needed may now become fairly easily available. The component of long-distance transportation would seem at first glance to be not too serious. These rough-and-ready instances suggest that an investigation should be made to see whether a fairly large and widespread program of urban-regional development could not be undertaken without serious direct competition with other elements of the Five Year Plans. We will see in the next section how very important it is to achieve a widespread synchronized program in urban-regional planning, if we are to avoid excessive imbalances.

Also, within what might be called the urban-regional development sector, certain elements demand even less of competitive products than the sector as a whole—for example, the "urban village" and "center village cum village cluster" projected in the Delhi Plan as well as, to some extent, the development of smaller cities. In these cases, where buildings are predominantly of one or two stories, the proportion of noncompetitive materials is substantially greater.

There is, too, the factor just noted tangentially—the heavy labor component (much of it, under Indian conditions, unskilled). The major consideration here is, however, that employment-intensity on a large scale is just what is so badly needed in the Indian economy.

Further exploration suggests itself; for example, intensified technological investigation into the extended use of noncompetitive or less competitive materials. Examples are: bamboo for reinforcement; jute products for this purpose, for roofing, for forms in shallow arches, etc.

THE DANGER OF EXACERBATING IMBALANCE AND STRESS
BY URBAN-PLANNING DEVELOPMENT

Fundamentally underlying the Delhi Regional Plan are, of course, the population projections, which determine much more than merely the areas and costs required for housing, important as these are. Facilities for commerce, for industry, for services, with the vast requirements of these functions in areas and cost, are all closely dependent on population. We all know from past experience that such population projections may go very much astray. Under

Indian conditions and prospective urban conditions in India, the discrepancy, if any arises, is only too likely to be in an upward direction, the most unfortunate one for the planner. Hence, we must do our level best to make the future population actuals come rather close to our predictions.

In making population projections for the next twenty years for the Delhi region—projections which, if anything, are on the conservative side—assumptions were inherent as to what would happen, or what we could cause to happen, elsewhere, bearing in mind, of course, that the largest component in the Delhi growth, as in that of the other large cities, is the number of in-migrants. In Delhi Territory (Delhi and New Delhi plus a rural area of some 300 villages, now part of Delhi Corporation), the 1961 population is estimated at 2.58 million,[3] and the 1981 figure, taking the average of four projections, will be 5.50 million, the figure that is provided for in the Plan. That this is on the low side is indicated by its assumed growth rate for urban Delhi of less than 4.25 per cent annually and for Delhi Territory of less than 4 per cent, "though," according to the same source, "the normal rate in recent years is estimated as 4.28 per cent. In other words, the assumptions made in our projection for Urban Delhi and Delhi Territory are modest as compared to independently computed figures, based on recent data." But if the not at all unlikely high projection of 4.5 per cent annual increase should prove to be actual, there would be over one million additional people.

But the fact is that even this high projection is by no means the most severe that may well take place. This high may be called the "normal migrational high." But it is a well-known phenomenon everywhere that special improvement in housing and living conditions in one city or area as compared with others attracts an abnormally high immigration, beyond this "normal migrational high." Thus, the execution of a Delhi urban plan itself, without simultaneous or synchronized development beyond, can be a dangerous move.

To follow this thinking and the potential dilemma further, consider the four districts surrounding Delhi, within which is the Metropolitan Region. In this area itself, the average or average-low figure for 1981 is 12.21 million compared to estimates for 1961 of 8.28 million—a growth of 3.93 million. If the normal "high" projection were used, this increase would be greater by 1.48 million, or a total increase of 5.51 million. As a final delicate factor in this dangerous group of mobile equations, the Delhi Plan

---

[3] These and subsequent figures are from "Delhi Regional Master Plan 1960," Part 2, chap. 2, "The Population of Delhi and Its Regions," Table 7. [Mimeographed.]

seeks to divert, by means of centers in this already rapidly growing surrounding metropolitan area, one half-million of the projected population that is otherwise expected to settle in the Delhi Territory itself. The reason for this proposed diversion is that, in examining the physical and geological features and in setting planned limits to the potentially urban central-city area, it is found that beyond a certain point development becomes excessively costly.

Thus, we see that it is anything but a simple matter to make our population projections become reasonably meaningful and a realistic basis for development. Within Delhi City and the territory we may be as much as from over one million to almost two million too low, and chaos could result if any such phenomenon were to happen. The higher estimate could readily befall us unless energetic, comprehensive, and synchronized measures are taken, such as have been taken in Caracas, Venezuela.[4] Similarly, the Metropolitan Region figures, already heavy, may be much exceeded in fact, and the region will be submerged unless there is some concurrent level of action in the area beyond (what in the report on the Plan is called the National Capital Region).

Thus, two major points emerge: (1) that what might be called the natural course of development, i.e., concentration chiefly on the Delhi urban area itself, would certainly accentuate the urbanization crisis rather than improve it, and would exacerbate the growth trend of Delhi itself rather than creatively modify it; and (2) that some form of concurrent development of the Delhi urban area and territory, the metropolitan area, *and* the more remote National Capital Region, must be worked out, so that "normal" imbalances do not get further out of hand and that we do not spend our re-

[4] A vast housing project designed for about 180,000 people was constructed in Caracas, 1954–1958. The resulting social situation was so serious that an international team of specialists, called upon to diagnose and advise, found that "in effect a civil anarchy prevailed." Certain of the findings and recommendations of this team are relevant to Delhi's possibility of being overwhelmed by in-migrants, e.g.:

"In the first place the evaluation project came to the conclusion that the government should suspend all construction of superblocks until there exists a defined housing policy related to the economic and social development of the country and within a process of national planning and coordination. It was found that the massive construction programs in Caracas had served to attract heavy migration to the city from rural areas and, therefore, severely intensified the housing problem in the capital.

"The Banco Obrero and the Venezuelan government are now applying a policy of stimulating rural and regional development and promoting housing construction in the smaller cities and communities of the country, as a basic element in helping to stabilize the population and increase agricultural production. Several new towns with industrial bases are planned for the Caracas region, to aid in diminishing the pressure on the central core." See *Journal of Housing* (Chicago), October, 1959, pp. 311–314. The full report, in Spanish, *Projecto de Evaluacion de los Superbloques del Banco Obrero, Caracas, Venezuela*, is published by Inter-American Housing and Planning Center, Bogota, Colombia.

sources on getting further behind. What this means is that, though results in any one of the outer areas would be less dramatically visible, only by substantial and reasonably early development in the outer areas as well as in the major city would it become possible for the real goals to be ultimately achieved.

This stress on the importance of balance and synchronization naturally applies to other urban-regional areas as well. It can be readily shown to apply, also to the balance between the various regions with respect to each other—though this latter problem may be momentarily less serious. Thus, the analysis called for in the preceding section, to help determine to what resource and money limits we can go in the volume of development of urban-regional planning schemes, is particularly important.

MORE RAPID METHODS OF EXPLORATION AND FORMULATION
TO MEET THE URGENT NEED IN URBAN-REGIONAL PLANNING

It is generally and rightly considered that planning without a reasonably rapid and comprehensive development timetable is not a satisfactory process, since development is obviously the touchstone of realistic planning. Thus, to settle for the one without the other is a dangerous practice and must be avoided in general.

On the other hand, it must be recognized realistically that even if all the measures (and others like them) are undertaken and prove fruitful, as outlined at the end of the first section, physical-regional planning in India cannot leap forward at a tremendous scale of development. And in any case, anywhere, planning is a process which fulfills itself only over a considerable period of years.

Planning, then, has two prongs:

The one is the supplying of a framework and skeleton into which whatever development that may occur (whether public or private) can be organically fitted. This may be thought of as the "defensive" aspect, holding the line as far as possible against further haphazardness and deterioration. This framework should be created and given legal force as soon as possible and over as many critical areas as possible.

The other is the expediting of the more massive and positive development measures required in order that major redirections may take place, which the limited "defensive" scale cannot accomplish. It is obvious that there are distinct limits to the effectiveness of the line-holding operation; wherever major changes in direction and location are required, the single enterprise, or even several enterprises, cannot often afford to change or to establish themselves newly and separately, until whole groups can be changed. Thus, it is quite evident that there are severe limits to what can be accomplished by the first prong, and that the two kinds of purpose in planning cannot be separated. The accomplishment of the first at the very earliest moment is, however, a *must,* so that the line may be held until increased availability of resources permits a more successful effectuation of the second.

Now we come to grips with the real issue of this section: that a very large amount of urban-regional-physical planning must be undertaken and accomplished within the next few years, so that the difficulties shall not pile up excessively before we can make a full-scale attack, causing in the meantime even greater wastes, diseconomies, and extensions of obsolete trends. To make any decisive dent on the situation, rapid preliminary or interim planning will have to be done, setting up broad and unrefined frameworks and directions. In fact, except in certain selected decisive operations— such as the large Rajasthan canal undertaking, the Danda Karanya resettlement, new towns, and any other operations where large, fairly immediate opportunities and needs exist or are being created —it may well be preferable to deploy the very limited trained manpower available into a relatively large number of preliminary or interim urban-regional plans than to do the full, exhaustive job in a relatively few places.

Some techniques for such short cuts are available and have been in some measure tried out in India. The Delhi Interim Plan, done in about six months, is a good example of an urban plan of this character, and future similar ones could be more satisfactory still, because of the work subsequently done in the present Delhi Regional Plan. It was, however, an urban plan only.

Quite a different approach to short-cut but effective regional approximations was developed by A. T. A. Learmonth and Prakasa Rao in Mysore. Very brief examination of their work yielded the distinct impression that here is a creative implement of an unrefined but very sound character, which could and should be carried further than it was there, in an immediate prototype operation. Its unrefined but very sophisticated and confident attack and formulation give great promise, with the precondition that those in over-all charge are, as was the case in the Mysore operation, men of quick grasp, sound training, and conscientious discrimination.

Work on further development, and probably joint development, of the two methods just noted could well produce, in a number of areas, the rapid rate of study, diagnosis, and interim-plan production which the situation would seem to require. Other factors would need to enter in, so that the work should not be superficial or along lines that would later prove not well founded. These factors, however, would justify a paper in themselves, or, indeed, a conference. The purpose here is only to adumbrate the problem and to indicate some ways of handling it.

CREATION OF EFFECTIVE UNDERSTANDING AND OPINION

Originally, when the functions and organizations of the Delhi planning were laid out and presented for consideration, there was provision for a function and staff called "Public Information," whose objective is evident from its title. Though New Delhi is full of sophisticated and cosmopolitan people, and Delhi has its proportion also, it is probably safe to assert that, even of these, only a fraction has a grasp of the terminology of planning or any serious interest in it, and that the number to whom the dynamics of planning are clear is quite negligible. Of that quite negligible number, a good proportion would be opposed.

Another factor in the situation—prevalent even among ministers and other highly placed people favorable to planning—is the obsolete notion that planning is a one-shot effort and that a regional plan is a static event, a single, elaborate blueprint once and for all.

Above all, the meager pro-plan forces and the opposed vested interests are still very unequal. There is no substantial weight of effective opinion behind urban-regional planning as there is behind economic planning. There is as yet no real awareness of the big social and economic stakes involved, or of the urgency of the situation. As for the rate of over-all national population growth, there is a considerable body of opinion that understands its dangerous implications in terms of food output not keeping pace with it or ahead of it, that draws the obvious inference of the need for birth control, and that vigorously pushes its views and conducts systematic propaganda. But the *urban* implications of population growth and migration, and the severity of the problem of urban accommodation for at least a doubling population in twenty years, are not yet adequately vivid; indeed, they are scarcely perceived.

Yet, in the event, it was impossible to prevail on either the sponsoring foundation or the Government of India to authorize a program or even a single staff person for purposes of public education. These same two entities, now initiating a pilot program for increasing food production, announce that "The essential elements in the educational and operational program include:

"An effective approach and explanation to enlist the support of village leaders and institutions, including panchayats.

"Appropriate and thorough explanations to all the cultivators in the village of the nature of the Pilot Program, its potential benefits to them and their families, and the essential action to be taken by them if they wish to participate." [5]

In the urban-regional scene, with its far greater complications and its greater remoteness from people's daily understanding, such efforts are all the more necessary. It is already evident in a number of ways what neglect of opportunity there has already been, what positive harm has been done in the last two years by the rejection of this indispensable function. There is, in the Delhi situation, no feeling or evidence of positive drive, no clear understanding among more than literally a handful of people as to objectives, urgent needs, methods; there is much misinformed comment and a maximum of rumor, including the usual charges of preinformation to a favored few as to proposed land use, etc. What is needed immediately is a dispersal of the negativism and inertia, and a filling of the vacuum in understanding. Equally lacking and needed is the creation of an exciting and expectant atmosphere, so that people at all levels can experience some feeling of participation, some sense of the significance of the city and their place in it.

It may conceivably be possible, under Indian conditions, to effectuate a bare plan with a few important political leaders in favor of it, men who constantly have many other newly arising and compelling assignments, and a few energetic officials pushing it— assuming we have that much—or it may not. But such a setup, which is roughly the present situation, is highly precarious, and whatever development we achieve will be minimal. The fact is: a whole march forward is required, and, in spirit and scope, this should be not less than the equivalent of what has just been described for the Food Production Pilot Program. In fact, we need a great deal more, because in the other case the objectives and urgency are clear and desperately pressing, and continuously *felt to be so* by leaders and by the ranks below, by the country. We do not yet have this condition, even minimally, in urban-regional planning.

To fill the gap, it is necessary to institute and maintain a dynamic communications enterprise that should involve political leaders and officials, local and from the states. These would have to include ministers, members of local Delhi bodies (particularly of the Corporation, the Industrial Advisory Committee, and similar committees), members of the Lok Sabha, and members of the Rajya Sabha. Similarly involved should be local and regional nonofficial groups in the Delhi area; the whole network of public voluntary

---

[5] Quoted from mimeographed document, "Suggestions for 10-Point Pilot Program to Increase Food Production," November 16, 1959 (32 pp.), p. 17. Source not noted thereon, but received from Extension Commissioner, Ministry of Food and Agriculture.

organizations, including trade associations, ought to have an understanding of the total planning operation and of their place in it. Then, too, the press, the All India Radio, and the periodicals have a role to play in the provision of background and interpretive materials on a continuing basis, in place of the occasional press release. Films, lectures, tours, and mobile exhibits are vital, and ought to be kept in circulation, as one way of involving the people. Only in such ways can the people be given a stake in city living.

The efforts involved in such an undertaking should not be sporadic and routine. In one aspect, one thinks of the first-class job achieved by Philadelphia, where an imaginative exhibit has continued for years and has been seen by hundreds of thousands of Philadelphians. Moreover, its renown has attracted many visitors and has sparked conferences that have helped to popularize planning and development throughout the United States. This is exactly the effect that the Delhi Plan deserves and seeks.

NEED FOR A MINISTRY OF HOUSING AND REGIONAL URBAN-PLANNING DEVELOPMENT

One ineluctable implication already visible from the steel towns, and now drastically highlighted by the Delhi experience, is the urgent need for the creation of a Ministry of Housing and Urban-Regional Planning and Development. Only in this way can there be created the strength and determination, the unification of thinking and requirements, necessary to launch the complex efforts and techniques involved in this new and uncharted field, to follow them through with determination, continued and renewed observation and thinking, and, above all, to carry understanding and conviction that this new field is of vital, pervasive importance and urgency to the polity, economy, efficiency, and social effectiveness of India.

This emerging and overdue urban-regional planning and development is invested with an immediacy and a pervasiveness which require it to have the most powerful launching. It cannot continue to be a minuscule effort lodged in odd corners of the Health Ministry, the Home Ministry, the Ministry of Works, Housing and Supply, and the characteristically weak Ministries of Local Self-Government in the states.

And, contrary to the norm, this new ministry ought from the start to be of cabinet rank in the Center and the states, with a strong and influential minister who has personal, vital interest and commitment *to this field*. Its secretariat must be senior in influence and prestige, and yet not so senior as to have lost any of its dynamic urge. Its secretariat and its operational executives must not be just good, interchangeable—and, in practice, frequently interchanged—

civil servants who would just as lief or rather be doing something else, but persons who have shown commitment and understanding, concern and study in this particular field. There are some such— not very many, it is true—and they are to be found both in the Indian Civil Service–Indian Administrative Service and outside it. In this connection, length of experience, or, rather, length of exposure, should not be confused with commitment or real grasp. This point applies to any new type of operation involving new concepts and techniques, but it applies doubly in the case of urban planning. Actually, many or most Indian leaders are indifferent to the city, or even have an antiurban bias. They live in cities, at least during their working lives, but the importance of the city and its social adequacy and excellence for labor productivity, for example, are not yet by any means clear or compelling to them. Their hearts are in the villages, and it is a sort of article of faith that the villages are vastly superior to and ethically more habitable than the city: the city must be tolerated, but there is, generally speaking, no creative concept of it or sense of identification with it. Thus, besides all else, we must accept this strong psychological factor and also a further one: that those in actual charge of the program may have no dynamic interest in it. Indeed, they may actually have something of a set against it. These things can and do occur, and not only in India—one has seen the like in the United States as well—and, of course, they mean death by inanition.

The other requirement, equally significant in the Indian scene, immediately needed and immediately possible, is for certain key men engaged in the technical work of planning and development, and especially in the Delhi situation, to have their cadre made permanent at once. Everywhere, and certainly under Indian conditions, the men engaged in a new governmental effort are at a psychological disadvantage, both vis-à-vis the entrenched services and vis-à-vis their own opinion of themselves. This state of mind is underlined and its harmfulness multiplied by the stigma of temporariness and the absence of tenure and rights. And it is just in pioneer work that all possible buttressing is required. In this category, nothing is more potent or electric than the status and the recognition implied by permanence. Surely there can be no doubt that urban-regional planning and development, particularly in the Delhi area, are here to stay and grow. Let us recognize this fact, let us take all advantage of it, and let us dramatize the advent of this field of enterprise by making this service permanent in whatever ministry it now is or will be.

XVIII

URBANIZATION IN MAHARASHTRA STATE: PROBLEMS AND A PLAN OF ACTION

S. G. Barve

The author of this paper is interested in urban problems in Maharashtra State principally from the viewpoint of prescribing a practicable plan of action for immediate implementation in the field. The subject matter, as in so many other fields of policy, suffers from inadequacy of data. There is a mass of information lying scattered in the books of local authorities and administrative departments of states (to note only two sources) which if compiled and analyzed would furnish extensive documentation relating to conditions in urban centers in India. As it is, the available information is scanty and its coverage patchy. Nevertheless, the lacks and shortcomings of urban social existence in Indian cities are sufficiently known. While socioeconomic surveys and the compilation of scattered data would undoubtedly help, in that they would provide a more comprehensive documentation, both the principal deficiencies and their prescriptions are sufficiently evident to form a basis for action. What follows will highlight the chief features of a suitable plan for the cities of Maharashtra State.

Conditions in Maharashtra State

In common with the rest of the country, in the former State of Bombay—out of which the states of Maharashtra and Gujarat have been formed—there was rapid growth in urban population from 1931 onward, and more especially in cities in the population group of 50,000 and above. In the decade 1941–1951 the percentage increase in population in the urban areas was 62.9 as compared to the figure of only 7.7 in the rural areas.

The urban population of Maharashtra State accounts for 28.8 per cent of the total state population against the all-India average of 17.3 per cent. A significant index of urbanization is the extent of industrial growth. In this regard Maharashtra State accounts for about 20 per cent of the total number of registered factories in the whole country and an equal percentage of the factory labor employed in organized industry in the country. The state's population is, however, only 9.05 per cent of the all-India population. The total number of towns and urban centers of Maharashtra is 382. By size, these towns can be divided as follows:

  1 town with a population of above 1,000,000
  4 towns with a population ranging between 100,000 and 1,000,000
 15 towns with a population ranging between 50,000 and 100,000
125 towns with a population ranging from 10,000 to 50,000
237 towns with a population below 10,000

The occupational pattern in the urban centers of Maharashtra presents two different pictures—one typified by Bombay City and prevalent over half a dozen larger cities, and the other by the rest of the urban centers generally. The outstanding feature of urbanization in the state is the predominant position occupied by the City of Bombay, which is one of the country's two largest complexes of industry and commerce. Persons employed in factory labor constitute about 7.5 per cent of the total urban population in the state; that is to say, assuming an average family size of 4 persons, factory labor would be a source of income for about 30 per cent of the urban population in the state. The figure for Bombay City and one or two larger industrial centers, however, shows a very much higher proportion than this average, so that these proportions are correspondingly lower in the remaining urban centers.

Educational facilities of the whole state for secondary and university education, generally speaking, are concentrated in the urban areas and, even there, among the larger towns. Cinema theaters, which are in present-day Indian conditions a predominant form of entertainment for the urban population, are concentrated in the larger urban centers, the smaller centers being frequently served by peripatetic tent cinemas. So far as electrification is concerned, all the cities with a population of 50,000 and above have electricity facilities, while the proportion of the number of towns served by these facilities decreases steadily with a decrease in the size of the urban unit.

Roughly, about 85 per cent of the total urban population is

covered by municipalities. The annual income of the municipalities per capita of the population, as recorded in a government report of 1954–55, is as high as Rs. 194 in the case of the corporations which account for three of the largest cities—namely, Bombay, Poona, and Nagpur—whereas for the rest of the municipalities the average figure is as low as Rs. 20.

Accurate documentation in respect of certain civic conditions cannot be presented because of the lack of data. Thus, accurate information is not readily available regarding the number of towns in Maharashtra served by (*a*) piped water-supply facilities, (*b*) underground drainage systems, and (*c*) adequate internal transport systems. On the basis of such local information as is available, the position would seem to be:

a) Most of the towns with population below 10,000 and many towns with population ranging between 10,000 and 35,000—that is to say, about one third of the total number—have no piped water supply. In many of the towns where a piped water-supply system exists, extensions and augmentation of supplies are necessary to meet with the increased population. Only half a dozen among the towns with a piped water supply have anything like a satisfactory system of filtration of water.

All towns of population above 50,000 have electric supply, as do all but eleven towns of population between 20,000 and 50,000. Of the towns with a population ranging from 10,000 to 20,000, there are 52 provided with electric supply; the remaining 31 towns have none.

b) Underground drainage facilities exist in about half a dozen towns altogether! In some of these the growth of the population in recent years has outpaced the facilities and they require considerable expansion.

c) Internal transport systems exist only in some half a dozen centers, such as Kolhapur (population 136,835), Sholapur (277,087), Bombay (2,905,456), Nagpur (449,099), and Poona (539,993). In most of the smaller towns the transport system operating in the countryside also serves the needs of the city population, for which a few extra internal schedules are run. Barring the handful of centers mentioned above and the urban schedules of the rural bus services, public conveyance in most of the urban centers is furnished, where it exists at all, by a small number of pony traps locally called "tongas," a few taxis, and cycle-rickshaws—these latter generally power-driven, but in a few centers still propelled by the rickshaw drivers themselves.

In recent years steps have been taken for organizing milk-supply schemes for some of the larger urban centers, notably in the City of Bombay where a government milk-supply scheme accounts for about 40 per cent of the total milk requirements of the metropolis. A number of milk-supply schemes are contemplated to be started in the other urban centers and are at present in varying stages of implementation. (Out of 382 towns in the state, these proposals for the

period of the Third Five Year Plan envisage covering about 22
towns; the magnitude of the task that remains to be done is evident.) In the absence of a regulated milk-supply scheme, it might be
observed that conditions in the milk trade are highly unsatisfactory
from the point of view both of the quantity of supplies and their
quality and standards of hygiene and cleanliness.

Detailed information relating to housing shortage and slums is
not available for most of the towns. While the smaller the size of
the town, the less acute is the housing shortage (the conditions in
Bombay City being most acute), in most of the larger towns a degree of housing shortage has been experienced in postwar years due
to the high cost of building materials, increasing urbanization, and
failure of private housebuilding to keep pace with the additional requirements of residential accommodation. A study group of the
Bombay government reported in 1959 that there was a shortage of
300,000 tenements in the Bombay City area. It recommended as a
very ambitious target an increase in housebuilding activity, including
both private construction and public housing. While most larger
towns have their slums, in the city of Bombay the slum population
is computed to account for 18 per cent of the total population. The
Municipal Corporation has listed 144 slums, and these account for
a population of over 400,000.

A Plan of Action

It is necessary first of all to set out what we are *not* considering in
this paper.

There are certain issues of a general character which do not appropriately fall within the purview of the specific problems of
urbanization. Thus, for instance, it is well known that in the Indian
economy there is a large and unmeasured volume of unemployment
and underemployment. Further, in recent years, with the expansion
of education, the issue has developed a new slant: namely, a significant intensification in the problem of unemployment among the *educated*. Unemployment among the educated has a particular significance for urban communities, wherein the educated, whether employed or unemployed, are principally to be found. Likewise, there
is the overshadowing problem of the growth of population and the
necessity for organizing and propagating family planning measures.
This, again, is not a problem specifically relatable to urbanization,
and it does not call for consideration here. Further, illustratively,
one might mention that there are certain well-known deficiencies in
the Indian system of education: wastage in the early years, lack of
proper screening and selection for admissions to universities and
colleges, an excessive literary bias still inadequately corrected by

emphasis in recent years on technical education, etc. Even though most institutions of higher learning would naturally be—and are—located in urban centers, we cannot treat of these issues in the present context. Also, in the field of public health, it is well known that there is a large incidence of preventable disease in India. Extant measures of public health and medical relief are grossly inadequate to cope with the problem. This, again, is a broad feature of the entire Indian scene and is not particularly relatable to urban centers.

There are one or two broad aspects of policy which have a more direct relevance to the welfare of urban communities and to the problem of urbanization. While we cannot discuss them in detail, we may notice them merely in passing. Each one of these problems is a large and complex issue, important enough to deserve separate consideration. We can here merely note, and that briefly, the bearing that the issues have on the problem of urbanization in India.

The use of electricity in modern industry has opened out great potentialities in the direction of decentralized location. Electric power, compared to other sources of power, can be cheaply and conveniently transported over long distances. Also, its great versatility makes it possible to use the energy not only for industry, but for purposes of traction, lift, and miscellaneous heavy jobs on the farm. If electric power should be made available through transmission grids over the countryside, immense possibilities would open out for the setting-up of factories and agricultural processing establishments away from congested urban centers. The expansion of power generation and its transmission over the countryside has, therefore, a very vital bearing on the extent and character of urbanization itself.

The organization of the dairy industry on a satisfactory footing is another important issue that has a considerable bearing, especially on the rural-urban economic interchange. To state a few bald facts: the average per capita consumption of milk in India is notoriously low; large sections of the Indian population subsist on an entirely or mostly vegetarian diet and need milk and milk products to an even greater extent than meat-eating populations; the milk trade at present is almost entirely disorganized; the supplies of milk are poor in quality, frequently adulterated, and very often deficient in standards of hygiene and sanitation. The milch cattle population suffers from many disabilities—want of selective breeding, proper and adequate feeding, veterinary care, and so forth. Although this is not the place to consider the complex and large issue of organizing the dairy industry in India on a satisfactory basis, it must be mentioned that the improvement of milk supplies and the organization of scientific dairying is capable of making a significant contribution to the improvement of the economic give-and-take between Indian cities and the surrounding countryside. In Indian small-farm economy the keeping of a buffalo on the farm is one of the most welcome, practicable, and ready means for introducing mixed farming in the villages within milk-marketing distance of urban centers. The dairy industry, poultry farming, growing of vegetables, and fruit gardening—all of which can be sustained only by the concentrated demands for these products in urban centers—are important directions in which intensive farming can be readily developed in the areas of influence of all urban centers, to the great advantage of the villages in such areas as well as the urban communities. The deliberate promotion of these subsidiary occupations is, therefore, an important measure of policy.

A MINIMUM PLAN OF ACTION FOR URBAN CENTERS IN MAHARASHTRA STATE

We may now consider a specific plan of action for improvement of living conditions in urban centers in Maharashtra. The plan of action will be limited to the provision of basic amenities which are absent or deficient in so many of the towns. Further improvements in civic amenities would be due to be considered after this program of elementary necessities is completed.

As specific information relating to costs of such amenities in urban centers in Maharashtra is not available, we must base our estimates on the data available in the proposals made in respect of the former Bombay State. Roughly two thirds of these estimates would yield a fair approximation to the likely costs for a similar program in the urban centers of Maharashtra State.

A town-planning study group of the Bombay government framed the following program of action for implementation during the Third Plan period, that is to say, from April, 1961, to March, 1966: the expansion of piped water supply in towns where it exists and the provision of piped water supply in the 55 towns of population of 10,000 to 35,000 where it does not exist, the whole program being estimated to cost, roughly, 25 crores of rupees; also, if towns of the population of 35,000 and above were to be furnished with underground drainage, it was estimated that the further cost would be about 15 crores.

A sum of 40 crores of rupees would, therefore, be needed for carrying out even this modest program in respect of water supply and drainage in the larger urban centers of the former Bombay State. On a rough computation, two thirds of this sum—about 27 crores of rupees—would be adequate for carrying out a similar program in the larger urban centers of Maharashtra.

It may be mentioned that in the period of the Second Five Year Plan the sum of only 7.5 crores had been allotted for these schemes. It is improbable, therefore, that anything more than this size of allocation would be available for these purposes under the Third Five Year Plan. Indeed, owing to the pressure of other priority demands, the allocations may be somewhat or even considerably less.

In this connection it must be pointed out that all such water-supply and drainage schemes are or can be made financially self-sustaining in the long run. In the municipal areas, water rates and drainage taxes can be so fixed as to bring in a sufficient return for servicing the maintenance and running costs as well as the interest and depreciation charges arising from the capital investments involved. The question, therefore, is simply one of finding the necessary capital finance for undertaking the capital outlays involved in the furnishing of towns with these services.

Municipalities are not capable of raising loan funds for such capital outlays. At present, the Maharashtra government gives grants of 50 per cent to district municipalities and 33⅓ per cent to borough municipalities for water-supply and drainage schemes. The remainder of the amount is to be raised by the municipalities themselves. The municipalities being unable to do this, it is imperative that the state government should float government loans for the purpose on the capital market and make grants available to the municipalities. It may be mentioned in this connection that practically the entire outlay for water-supply and drainage schemes would be in local currency with a very small, if any, component of foreign-exchange expenditure. This relatively modest outlay is perfectly feasible of execution and reasonably within the plan allocations that could be expected for this purpose. The author believes that the results of a successful carrying-out of this program would be sensationally dramatic in the field of public health. It is difficult to imagine any other single line of activity which could give such satisfying results with such a modest outlay, and withal meet a clamorous social need of the community.

"DEVELOPMENT PLANS"

Apart from these two basic services, in the present condition of urban centers in the state what is principally wanted is an adequate "development plan" (in terms of the Bombay Town Planning Act, 1954) supported by town-planning measures to provide for zoning, to allocate space for parks, playgrounds, and recreation centers, to regulate the growth of towns, and to reserve spaces for public purposes, such as markets, post offices, police stations, primary and secondary schools, hospitals and dispensaries, industrial estates, theaters, and so forth. The Bombay Town Planning Act, 1954, is a fairly comprehensive and thoroughgoing measure which vests in the development authority large powers for controlling the use of land. The whole scheme of the Act is that the local authority should prepare a "development plan" for the area under its jurisdiction within a few years of the commencement of operation of the Act; "reservations" would be made for various public purposes in this development plan and the local authority would be under obligation to acquire such reserved plots during a period of ten years succeeding the establishing of its development plan. There is provision for the levy of betterment on the incremental value of the sites improved by the development scheme. If the Bombay Town Planning Act is effectively implemented in the urban centers, conditions of living in the towns in the state should significantly improve within a period of a few years.

There are, however, certain prerequisites for an adequate enforcement of the "development plan."

First of all, a large number of the urban centers are not yet "city-surveyed." In Indian land-records terminology, a "city survey" is a mapping-out and demarcation of all plots in the surveyed area, with a record of areas, ownership, tenancies, etc. Without a city survey, a development plan under the Town Planning Act cannot be prepared. The state government must, therefore, forthwith organize the completion of the city survey of all towns not already covered.

For the preparation of the development plans, most of the municipalities have not the necessary technical staff. The work must, therefore, be done by the state agency. The Department of the Consulting Surveyor to Government undertakes the work for preparation of development plans at the request of local authorities. It is essential to extend the Consulting Surveyor's organization sufficiently to enable it to take up the preparation of development plans in as many of the larger urban centers as possible. By March, 1961, it is expected that development plans in respect of some 40 more towns will be completed. It is necessary to step up the rate of completion of development plans. It is estimated that with an expenditure of 25 lacs in the course of the Third Five Year Plan, 125 more towns could be furnished with development plans during the Plan period. Indeed, it would be desirable to step up the preparation of development plans even more, and to aim at completing development plans for all urban centers during the five years of the Third Plan period.

In India today we are on the eve of a rapid spurt in industrial growth. Urbanization has been growing apace and may be expected to intensify still further in the future. The preparation of a development plan furnishes to a growing urban community an "envelope" to control its future growth. The existence of a development plan should save large sums of money by avoiding indiscriminate and disorderly growth and the creation of future slums, deficiencies of playing fields and recreational centers, narrow and crowded streets, and lack of space for public services and amenities. A development plan, so far as it relates to areas not yet urbanized, is only an act of necessary foresight and by itself costs nothing, being principally a measure for regulating the use of land. For all these reasons, one must press for the most rapid possible completion and enforcement of development plans in all the growing urban centers.

The development plan entails acquisition, which could be phased over a ten-year period, of the plots reserved for public purposes. The study group referred to above estimated that the provision of 3.3 crores during the Third Plan period would enable the government to finance an adequate rate of implementation of development plans in the former Bombay State. A similar estimate for Maharashtra State would be of the order of 2.2 crores.

It is not necessary to consider in detail other amenities conducive to civilized urban existence: dispensaries and maternity wards; the dustproofing and maintenance of roads, and their lighting; the provision of primary schools and public libraries, of vegetable and other markets, and slaughterhouses, and of playgrounds, parks, and recreation centers. Most of these involve only a small capital outlay, which it ought to be possible for the local authorities to finance. Moreover, the drawing-up and implementation of a development plan would solve one of the commonest handicaps in the provision of these amenities—namely, a suitable site for their location.

HOUSING

Adequate housing in urban centers implies in Indian conditions concurrent organization of several measures for the promotion of housebuilding activity and slum clearance. Some of the more important may be mentioned here.

Arrangements must be made for long-term finance to be made available against suitable security both to individuals and coöpera-

tive societies of housebuilders. This is an important deficiency today in the setup of credit and financial institutions in India.

In as much as a considerable section of the population in urban
centers cannot have adequate housing without an element of subsidy, one must envisage a large expansion of public housing
schemes under the auspices of state governments and municipalities, for industrial labor, low-income groups, and other such needy
categories.

Most Indian housebuilding is based on materials locally forthcoming. If housebuilding activities are to expand greatly in the
larger urban centers, as they must to cope with the serious shortage of housing, it is essential that measures should be taken for
facilitating the expansion of supplies of building materials. The
reservation of suitable land for brickkilns, the prospecting and
opening of stone quarries, the expansion and cheapening of supplies of other raw materials, such as sand, steel, and cement, all
have a direct bearing on the volume of housing activity. Of these,
cement and steel are factory products (now expected to be in sufficient supply, with the commissioning of a considerably enlarged
capacity of the cement industry and the three large new steel
plants about to be completed), but the rest of the materials are
produced locally everywhere. A good deal can be done by local
administrative authorities to facilitate and cheapen the supply of
such local materials.

Slum clearance is a vast and complex issue. The slum is an extreme illustration of housing shortage. So far as the older slums
are concerned, extensive redevelopment schemes are necessary for
abolishing them. Equally important is the problem of preventing
the emergence of new slums.

I believe that, during the considerable period that will elapse
before housing increases sufficiently to overtake and catch up with
the growth of urban population, it will be necessary to think in
terms of makeshift and cheaper means for preventing slums. The
provision of plinths suitably spaced and laid out on a modest rental,
with water supply and drainage facilities provided, would be a
good interim measure for the prevention of new slums, as well as
for the clearance of existing ones. In Indian conditions, in a large
number of places, the climate admits of persons living satisfactorily
all the year round with quite modestly built shelters. On plinths
so laid out and serviced, the plinth-holder should be permitted to
put up a hutment of whatever material he may be able to afford
for himself. Perhaps some small amount may be loaned by the
authorities for the initial investment and recovered by easy install-
ments. For many years to come, it is very unlikely that the volume

of new public housing for the needy sections of the urban population will be equal to the task of making up the arrears as well as coping with the increasing urban population. Plinth layouts would cost only a fraction of a public housing estate.

ORGANIZATIONAL SETUP

It remains next to consider the organizational setup necessary for carrying out such a plan of action. At present, the nexus between the state administration and the local authorities is defective in certain important respects. The approach of the state administration is often too literal and negative. Proposals made by local authorities are rejected too frequently because of failure to comply with some minor formality or other. In the matter of financial "irregularities" and audit objections, again the approach is often that of finding fault rather than constructively suggesting improvement. Most of the local authorities are not in a position to engage their own qualified technical and administrative staff to formulate technically sound schemes and to execute them competently. Firms of consulting engineers who could do this for them on payment do not exist. It ought to be possible to make available to the local authorities the services of technical agencies, maintained by the state for this purpose. Thus, in the preparation of drainage and water-supply schemes, in the preparation of town-planning schemes, in evolving proposals about building regulations and health codes, in framing bylaws for measures of taxation, etc., the local authorities stand in need of constructive help from the state administration.

In the matter of allocation of tax resources, also, a more generous and understanding approach from the state government is called for. Too often the state government appropriates to itself all the extant tax resources and is jealous of any proposal emanating from local authorities which is likely to benefit local coffers, even if it would cause only the slightest prejudice to the state coffers. The principles of grants-in-aid also need to be liberalized and rationalized.

It must not be supposed, of course, that the municipal administrations are themselves without defects, drawbacks, and deficiencies. There is a chronic reluctance to make an adequate tax effort; there is insufficient rigor in the collection of arrears of taxes; assessments of taxes are too often unduly lenient. There are, also, instances of petty favoritism; of interference with and retardation of administrative measures, particularly those involving coercion or discipline; of nepotism in recruitment and the play of caste and communal prejudices, reflecting the nonhomogeneity of the urban community which the elected members represent.

This is not the place for examining in detail how such a changed and positive outlook with reference to the field of activity of local authorities could be evolved, or into what specific recommendations it could be broken down. The details will readily suggest themselves and could be evolved without difficulty, once steps are taken for the "orientation of outlook." The state administration must look upon the local authorities of the urban centers (as indeed of the countryside as well) as partners in the program of planned development. Municipal authorities of urban centers are responsible for nearly a third of the population of Maharashtra. To equip these agencies with an adequate administrative organization, to furnish them with adequate financial resources, and to maintain a constant liaison and attitude of constructive suggestion and helpfulness toward them ought to be an important component at all times of the policy of planned development in the state.

Various measures of organizational detail have been suggested in this regard from time to time. It has been suggested, for instance, that the heads of the important technical departments under the local authorities, e.g., the chief executive officers, the engineers, the health officers, and the tax assessment officers, should be brought into state-wide cadres to improve the administrative efficiency of the organization and furnish them a measure of security against interference from the locally elected officials. The suggestion has also been made that certain functions, e.g., the assessment of house tax, should be centralized and placed under officers responsible to the state government. Regarding additional resources for municipalities, various suggestions have been made from time to time about the allocation of such tax resources as the entertainment tax, the tax on nonagricultural constructions, the urban immovable-property tax, etc., so that this income might be made over wholly or in part to the local authorities. The state government also owns extensive pieces of land within municipal limits, and it has been suggested that these should be made available free or at modest valuation to municipalities for their requirements of nonprofit-making public use. It is neither necessary nor possible to examine these detailed suggestions in the present context.

Mention may, however, be made of one important recommendation at the level of top organization within the state administration which is capable of comprehending all such detailed possibilities. It has been suggested that a small Local Self-Government Board, with representatives of municipalities, the concerned state departments, and one or two nonofficial members distinguished in the field of local self-government, should be set up at the state level, under the chairmanship of the minister in charge of the local self-government department. It would direct and supervise the entire financial and administrative nexus between the state government and the local authorities. If such an administrative organism is created and properly used, it should be possible to bring about the necessary reorientation of outlook among the state departments on one hand and the municipal administrations on the other. Such a device would also be of great help in nourishing a proper relationship between the elected elements in municipalities and the stipendiary officials under the municipal administration. Successful local self-government can be built up only by a happy fusion of the two important participating elements, namely, local self-rule and enterprise on the one hand, and administrative efficiency of the local agencies on the other.

It must be remembered that the levying of adequate taxes by local representatives, even though for local benefit, calls for a high degree of civic consciousness difficult to find even in countries with centuries of tradition of local self-government, such as the United Kingdom. The background of general poverty, the hiatus between mounting aspirations and paucity of financial resources, the lack of homogeneity in the urban communities—all these make the problem peculiarly difficult in India. A steady and constructive pressure by a friendly and understanding body, on a plane of detachment from local problems that would be attainable at the state level, could do an immense amount of good by the exercise of an unremitting influence toward better local administration.

There is a Local Self-Government Institute in Bombay. The development and strengthening of such an institute could make it into an influential nonofficial forum to promote high professional standards among municipal executives and elected office-bearers; it might be made to work, so to say, as a "spearhead" or "conscience" of a movement toward improvement of municipal administration from within; and it should be a very useful adjunct to the administrative apparatus.

CONCLUSIONS

As in so many other sectors of activity in India, in the field of municipal administration what is necessary and what requires to be done are fairly well known and established. What remains in the main is the actual doing of it.

An important hurdle is the problem of financial resources. In Maharashtra an allocation of the order of about 35 to 40 crores of rupees (which would probably represent about 10 per cent of the total state plan for the period of the Third Five Year Plan) would make a perceptible beginning in organizing the life of the urban communities on a reasonably satisfactory basis.

As important as the problem of "resources" is the problem of "organization." Here, again, the requirements are self-evident. The success of any organizational setup must, however, inevitably depend upon the quality, enterprise, and leadership forthcoming both at the state level and in the local communities, in the political sphere and in the administrative field. If these are available the job can be done.

XIX

THE CHALLENGE OF URBAN GROWTH
TO INDIAN LOCAL GOVERNMENT

P. R. Nayak

Since independence, the mode of life, problems, and aims of the Indian people have been undergoing radical changes. Of these, none probably is more important than the transition from a laissez-faire and largely agricultural economy to planned industrialization and accelerated urban growth. These two are in a sense symbolic of increasing national maturity. But much that is unpleasing is also happening.

At the best of times, our cities were a mixture of magnificence and squalor, of palaces and slums, of great opportunity and deep despondency. Recent urban growth, however, has created problems of an unprecedented character, and their impact has been felt most by the recent migrants, sucked from a poor but undefiled countryside into the crazy pattern of the cities. Housing is deplorably short. Slums spring up all around. Even clean areas become rundown through overcrowding. Water supply and drainage are inadequate. Other vital municipal services, such as education and medical relief, prove unequal to the demand and deteriorate in quality. Milk and vegetables become scarce and costly. Above all, the speed with which the urban areas grow, overflowing their boundaries and forming sprawling agglomerations of buildings and people, makes the tasks of city governments truly formidable.

We shall first examine the structure and resources of the governmental apparatus which has to undertake these tasks, and then move to a discussion of the way in which the challenge is being met.

The Structure and Resources of Local Government

PRESENT FORMS OF LOCAL GOVERNMENT

The main forms of local government in the urban areas are municipal committees and municipal corporations. Municipal committees, which have been established in all towns and in some cities, follow closely the English system of local government. All authority is vested in the elected council and its committees, though perhaps the president of the council has a role superior in character to that of his English counterpart. The permanent officials act as advisers in the making of policy and administrative decisions. They also execute such decisions, subject to the control and supervision of the elected body. All officers are appointed and removable by the council. Latterly, some changes have been taking place. The constitution of state-wide cadres of municipal executive officers has been adopted at some places to give the officials a greater measure of independence in presenting advice, exercising delegated powers, and executing policy decisions.

Municipal corporations have been set up in the larger cities, the earliest of them over seventy years ago. Their functions are generally wider and their powers of taxation larger than those of the municipal committees. They also enjoy a high degree of autonomy. A special feature of their organization is the separation of executive from deliberative or policy-making functions. The former are entrusted to a commissioner or chief executive officer, appointed by the state government for a term of years, and exercising powers or discharging functions prescribed under the municipal statute. The deliberative or policy-making wing of the corporation is the elected council; there are also a number of statutory committees composed of elected members with defined powers. The mayor, who is elected by the council, and the chairmen of committees regulate the conduct of meetings and generally act as the spokesmen of the respective bodies.

This system, it will be noticed, is very different from the English pattern of local government. It owes its origin to the ideas of Sir Pherozshah Mehta, who may be regarded as the father of the city government of Bombay. When a law was under consideration in the late 19th century for the municipal government of Bombay, he said:

The municipal council is not to administer and govern for which it is radically unfit, but has to fulfill its proper function to watch and control the executive Government, to throw the light of publicity on all its acts, to compel a full exposition and justification of all of them; and if the men who compose the executive abuse their trust or fulfill it in a manner which conflicts with the deliberate sense of the people, to expel them from office.[1]

The vesting of executive authority in a municipal council, in his opinion,

would have been to substitute in the place of the responsible executive officer, a heterogeneous body of men equally powerful, men incapable and difficult of being controlled and with their responsibility so attenuated by division and sub-division, as to render them practically and really entirely irresponsible . . . It would be a retrogressive step, plunging the municipality into a gulf of mismanagement, insufficiency and jobbery such as the wildest rumours have not dreamed of . . . The only safe and efficient way of disposing of the executive authority is to vest it in a single responsible officer controlled by a representative assembly. Town councils with executive powers would only prove centres of inefficiency and jobbery." [2]

Despite a great deal of argument over the alleged unsuitability of such a statutory executive for the present democratization of institutions in the country, the system has been gaining increasing adherence; and more and more cities are being patterned at the local government level on the corporation form of administration. With the crystallization of political parties during recent years, the political cleavage that has become common in local governments threatens to make the administration of executive functions by a council degenerate into a "spoils system." A detached executive, capable of executing policies prescribed by the legislature and by the council without fear or favor, is considered to have great merit.

It must not be assumed that the executive can or does function in an irresponsible or unresponsive manner. He must operate within the framework of the policies laid down and the funds sanctioned by the council. Even in spheres which can be considered statutorily within his purview, it is not easy for the executive to ignore the wishes of the council. The council has the right to demand his removal by a majority of five eighths or two thirds of the members, and the appointing government is then bound to withdraw him. In these circumstances, and because of the good sense and restraint that have prevailed on both sides, cases of conflict have been rare.

Recent changes in local government structure—namely, the increasing resort to the corporation form of organization for the bigger cities, and the constitution of state cadres of municipal

---

[1] *The Bombay Municipal Reform Question, 1871.* [Pamphlet.]
[2] *Ibid.*

executive officers—indicate a policy shift of considerable importance. They appear to be dictated partly by the complexity of governing large cities. Urban administration has become today an extremely arduous task; and the part-time duty rendered by elected councilors is perhaps unequal to that task. A recent study by the *Economist,* of London, of the present situation in the U.K. has highlighted the weaknesses that are developing even in that cradle of local government. Government is, after all, a continual experiment in the art of promoting the well-being of the people. Good government, it has been said, is no substitute for self-government. But the latter, too, aims at the general weal, and our administrative forms must, in a changing situation, be adapted so as to promote these aims, rather than merely subserve purely theoretical concepts.

The argument over the right organization of local government in the larger cities is, in a sense, related to the stresses and strains generated by growing city populations. A heterogeneous, impressionable, and, at times, immature electorate has been called upon to exercise its franchise in a new-found atmosphere of considerable political activity, and in the cities the sheet anchor of traditionalism is often missing or weakened. In the result, political rather than civic considerations have dominated the arena of local government. Controversy over the organization of linguistic states and over Chinese aggression against India have, in Bombay and Delhi, created political tensions within the council and affected stability and smooth functioning. Different sections of the population with group or individual problems have appealed to party platforms, rather than to the good sense of the elected council. A tendency, therefore, to do and say things that are politically popular, rather than intrinsically good for the city, has emerged. It may affect slum clearance or the redevelopment of an area, for example, as either is likely to lead to the shifting and loss of valued voting strength. Tension and instability both contribute to create uncertainty of decision and to delay and aggravate problems that demand urgent attention.

Two or three other features which detract from sound local-government organization may be mentioned. Legislation for securing the long-term planning of city growth is halting and inadequate, where it exists. Moreover, the application of such existing laws has, in practice, been of negligible proportions. A paucity of qualified planning personnel has been one factor responsible for this; there have not been enough town planners to study the problems of even the principal cities. A second difficulty has been the financial stringency which renders any plans that may be drawn up extremely difficult of fulfillment. The plans themselves, when drawn up, are not based on properly conceived standards of need, and it is soon found that the gaps that are filled are overtaken by the developing urban situation in a short space of time. The necessity for well-conceived town-planning legislation of a uniform character has only lately been recognized; its enactment is still awaited in many parts of the country. Facilities for the training of town planners are slowly being developed, but until their value is fully understood, and their utilization rendered possible through compulsive legislation, not a great deal will be accomplished.

In both these fields, excellent work has lately been done in Delhi. Comprehensive legislation was enacted over two years ago covering the preparation of a master plan, the establishment of standards of services, and the preservation of the planning process as a continuing one. This has, however, highlighted another age-old problem in the cities, viz., the multiplicity of local government agencies. Improvement trusts operate over a common geographical area with municipal bodies; cantonment boards control small pockets under the occupation of the defense services; service agencies, such as gas or electricity utilities, transport undertakings, water and sewage boards, create a yet further confusing pattern; and the older and newer parts of some cities are governed by different municipalities. With the emergence of planning as a pronounced feature of city governments, a planning agency, working apart from the ordinary government of civic affairs, is a recent addition to the multiplicity of local government bodies. In Delhi, until about two years ago, there were eleven local bodies; three statutory boards controlling electricity, transport, and water supply and sewage disposal; and a Development Authority. After the formation of the Delhi Municipal Corporation, two years ago, there are still three local bodies and a Development Authority. Greater Bombay has now moved to a unified local government, but greater Calcutta still has a multiplicity of municipalities, an Improvement Trust, and separate public utility undertakings. Where the growth of cities makes artificial barriers of administrative control utterly unrealistic, the perpetuation of multiple agencies creates one more problem for the planner, the executor, and the administrator.

THE FINANCES OF LOCAL GOVERNMENT

The remedying of urban problems has been rendered difficult by the pace of urbanization and the paucity of resources. Certain basic problems are common to all city governments today in the matter of their finances, namely (1) population growth, (2) higher price levels and the consequent increase in the recurring cost of rendering municipal services, (3) the need for developmental plans for the augmentation of existing municipal utilities, and (4) a revenue base which does not correspond with factors causing rising expenditure.

The main source of municipal revenue is, of course, the taxes on property, including taxes for services such as water supply, drainage, and fire protection. An octroi or terminal tax on the entry of goods, taxes on vehicles and animals, a tax on professions, trades, and callings, revenues from markets and slaughterhouses, and licensing fees are other conventional sources. Latterly, taxes on theaters and advertisements have also been authorized. In one isolated instance (Delhi) a local government has been given the power to tax sales of immovable property and of electricity, though ordinarily these are sources of revenue exclusively reserved for the benefit of state governments. Table 1 gives an indication of the growth of revenues of certain cities:

TABLE 1

REVENUES OF FIVE LARGE CITIES, 1920–1959
(In millions of rupees)

City	1920–21	1925–26	1940–41	1955–56	1958–59
Greater Calcutta.....	15.56	21.87	25.74	65.98 (1956–57)	...
Greater Bombay.....	20.02	30.66	35.66	58.29	110.67[a]
Delhi..............	2.27	2.16	4.22	28.48	62.10[a]
Madras............	5.24	6.06	8.34	29.38	32.86
Ahmedabad........	1.72	2.93	5.15	...	35.63 (1959–60)

[a] The figures for Bombay and Delhi for 1958–59 relate to greatly enlarged jurisdictions.

The increase has clearly not been commensurate with the growth of population and the increase in the cost of rendering service. Administrative and materials costs have gone up by three to four times between 1940–41 and the present day.

The situation may be looked at from another angle. Below are given figures, in rupees, of the incidence of taxation per head of population in three cities:

	Madras	Bombay	Calcutta
1918–19..............	5.02	15.71	10.15
1940–41..............	7.60	19.84	18.31
1947–48..............	10.94	26.15	11.46
1955–56..............	13.16	35.94	16.53

As new housing has not kept pace with the growth of population, and property values have been kept depressed through rent control and other measures, property taxes, which are the largest single source of revenue, have not yielded a corresponding increase in revenue. In the result, the gap between need and performance in the matter of services has become wider. A study of expenditure on certain items of civic services during a recent period is given in Table 2.

TABLE 2

EXPENDITURE FOR CERTAIN CIVIC SERVICES IN FIVE LARGE CITIES
(In millions of rupees)

Civic service	Madras		Bombay		Delhi		Poona		Bangalore	
	1952–1953	1956–1957	1950–1951	1955–1956	1948–1949	1956–1957	1951–1952	1956–1957	1956–1957	1958–1959
Public instruction..	3.44	4.56	7.80	9.97	1.54	4.60	1.5	2.01	0.19	0.50
Water supply and drainage........	3.44	5.25	...	...	1.65	3.95	0.75	1.10	1.32	3.22
Public works, roads, etc........	4.00	5.14	95.00	76.80	2.04	6.73	0.55	1.78	0.61	1.40
Medical relief and public health....	1.81	2.08	8.92	12.97	4.50	7.63	0.97	1.63	1.64	3.31

While an attempt is being made to increase services, this has been done, in the main, at some sacrifice of quality, as in the case of education or medical relief. The creation of new institutions does not, on the whole, show a corresponding rise. For example, a recent survey by the Reserve Bank of India on investment trends in local governments showed that between 1951–52 and 1956–57, borrowing for capital development in 54 local authorities amounted to only Rs. 380 millions, against their total income in 1956–57 of about Rs. 990 millions.

The necessity for increased financial assistance to local governments for their growing responsibilities has been emphasized by a number of committees and commissions. Little, however, has been done, and local governments are perhaps themselves partly responsible. Examples of underutilized local resources are not uncommon. Politically, a greater exploitation of available sources of income is considered to be a hazardous venture. But the failure to mobilize local resources on the scale needed and practicable itself hinders the accretion of fresh sources of income. Indeed, as has sometimes happened, it may encourage an encroachment on essentially local sources for state or national purposes. The maximum exploitation of available sources of income is, therefore, a pre-requisite for the strengthening of local finances. The problem of mobilization involves a determination of the level of necessary taxation. This is, no doubt, a political decision, but it must pro-ceed on the basis that the services rendered must be paid for, in one form or another. Though varying capacities may be recog-nized, the idea of something for nothing must be discounted. The humblest must make a contribution, however small.

MEETING THE CHALLENGE

It has been said that success in local government depends on an enlightened and alert electorate, a conscientious body of councilors, an efficient municipal civil service, and adequate finance. To these, a fifth may be added: a program of action that is sufficiently far-seeing and dynamic. These requisites can be arranged somewhat differently under the heads of public participation, structure and organization, finances, and the ingredients of the physical pro-gram.

PUBLIC PARTICIPATION

Some of the present weakness or ineffectiveness of local govern-ment results from the apathy of the ordinary citizen. As cities grow, people who by reason of their prominence in business or the professions might be expected to play an important role in civic affairs seem to drop out under the stress of political forces. Local government is then left mainly to political workers whose value and effectiveness in this field may not always be equal to the need. In that situation, the importance of alertness on the part of the common man becomes heightened. In fact, however, his apathy is noticeable at election time, when those who turn up to exercise their franchise rarely exceed 40 or 50 per cent of the electorate; it is evident, also, in the attitude towards Town Hall when things happen that are against good sense or public interest. Small pres-sure groups are able, through an agitational approach, to extort concessions that may actually be harmful to the community. There is a general attitude of helplessness or indifference to the defects and defaults in municipal government, save when they affect an individual personally. The electorate seems to have become a factor of diminishing importance in local government even in some Western countries, where it may be that a generally high level of local services leaves little scope or need for enlightened public par-ticipation or intervention; but where conditions are very different the reasons for apathy must be sought elsewhere. In India the heterogeneous character of the urban community seems partly responsible. Human relations in the cities are largely anonymous, superficial, and transitory. Here is the paradox of close physical contact and distant social relationship. In some measure, the handicapped city dweller has not perhaps himself perceived his disadvantage. His interest in the city has often been ephemeral. City dwelling is a temporary acquisitive phase. He has to concentrate on earning and laying aside as much as possible for the eventual and certain return to his real home. One need not also rule out the effect of the fatalistic outlook our philosophy of life has engendered: social and economic disadvantage is one's destined lot, and calm acquiescence is virtue.

This heterogeneity and this mental attitude have to be overcome if we want to create a keen and alert community that can both participate in local government affairs and apply correctives where necessary. The importance of social organization as a means to the integration of the people into an organized community needs no emphasis. As populations grow arithmetically, the need for a well-coördinated organization that weaves the individual into the group life increases in geometrical progression.

It is in this situation that a program of urban community development has lately been initiated in some Indian cities. The movement does not aim at urban development, which is a task for the local administration, but seeks to create an urban community on the basis of awareness and self-help. The object is not to take social service to the underprivileged, but to evoke in them a desire for and confidence in the success of self-reliance. It is both educational and organizational in character. It is educational in so far as the aim is to promote attitudes and habits that are conducive to social and economic improvement. It is organizational because it seeks to bring people together to pursue common objectives by requiring, where necessary, the reorientation of existing institutions and the creation of new ones to make self-help fully effective. The movement depends for its success on the emergence and training of local leaders, who may help to infuse into city administration a new influence that will be constructive, self-reliant, and attuned to the needs and feelings of the community.

A network of local organizations, neighborhood units, and citizens' forums must be complementary to an extended and improved program of public relations activity. The ordinary man knows too little about the work and the plans of his council. In the midst of a hard and drab existence there is little to arouse his enthusiasm. Public relations work should, therefore, impart information, bring color, present the good points of the city, explain current difficulties, and say what one may look forward to. An exhibition of civic activities that was organized in Bombay four or five years ago was a tremendous success, having been witnessed by over a million people. One felt that the citizen was proud of what his city had done, looked forward to the promised future, and felt that Bombay was indeed *Urbs prima in India.*

The first battle of urbanization must thus be fought on the emotional and intellectual plane. The initial phase of the urban community-development project in Delhi has been encouraging, and there is reason to hope that the physical tasks of city improvement may, as a result, be rendered easier as time passes.

ADEQUACY OF THE LOCAL GOVERNMENT STRUCTURE

The present structure of local government has been discussed in an earlier section. We need a machinery that ensures democratic functioning and, at the same time, delivers the goods speedily and efficiently. The time factor is important. In the midst of much dissatisfaction at prevailing conditions, the time for action is fast running out in our cities. Our policies and administration forms must, therefore, be such as to catch up rapidly with the situation.

Several aspects of the subject of local government organization have been under study in many states since the country gained independence. In the main, however, thinking has been confined to the organization of deliberative and executive functions, and to the finances of local bodies. On the first point, it has been generally agreed that deliberative and executive functions should be separated and that a reasonable degree of independence should be given to the executive in day-to-day working. This view has been increasingly adopted in recent legislation governing the administration of the larger cities. There was, no doubt, a protest by mayors gathered in conference in 1958 against this trend as being undemocratic and bureaucratic-minded, but a meeting of Indian Local Self-Government ministers in October, 1959, reiterated the intrinsic soundness of the policy. Even as regards the smaller towns and cities, the progressive formation of state cadres of municipal executive officers is indicative of the same policy approach. One may, therefore, treat this subject as one of settled policy, at least for the time being, though controversy is unlikely to abate completely.

Our ideas are not as clear, however, on certain other aspects of good organization. There has latterly been a considerable degree of uncertainty and hesitancy over the functions of local government. In the context of national planning, conflicting and alternating trends of centralization or of excessive decentralization have been noticed in spheres such as education, public health, and medical relief. For a while, local responsibility tended to be diluted by compartmentalized agencies or centralized control. The apparent conflict between central and state interests in developmental plans, on the one hand, and the needs of democratic decentralization, on the other, has not so far been rationally resolved. For example, there is considerable discussion today about the provision of public housing. Should this be the responsibility of local governments, or is there need for the creation of separate autonomous agencies, such as housing boards and development authorities? Where funds are provided by an outside agency, it may be natural to think in terms of increasing control over the local authority or the substitution of a separate agency.

A new element in this debate has been the proper organization of city planning. Some cities, Delhi notably, have preferred a separate planning agency, only tenuously connected with the local government authorities. How far an independent planning body can really be an effective instrument for serving the continuously changing needs of a city is arguable. The dynamism of planning and the effects of implementation (by local governments) of the several ingredients of a predetermined plan seem to point to the desirability of integrating the planning process with that of implementation. With the emphasis now being laid on long-term planning, this question is naturally evoking a great deal of discussion. The concept of a separate organization that will control local governments as regards either the desired ingredients of a plan or of its execution does not appear to be sound. Planning should spring from the people themselves. If the responsibility is placed on the local authority, it is probable that the plan that emerges will prove more acceptable and easier of implementation.

In these circumstances, an urgent reëxamination of the functions of local governments is necessary. Should they be comprehensive in character, or should we work more in the direction of independent, specialized agencies that will look after certain sectors of conventionally accepted civic activity? Can some of the advantages claimed for the latter arrangement be secured by making such specialized functions the concern of autonomous committees of the council itself? If local governments are to fulfill their proper role in the estimation of the people and, in turn, enthuse the community, the need today appears to be to amplify and enlarge their functions. Certain directive principles may have to be prescribed for development and service activity in the interests of broad national conformity, but the main task of framing policy and implementation is better left to the local authority itself.

A second, somewhat unexplored aspect of local government organization is the size of the elected body. The tendency in India has been towards large councils. Bombay's corporation has 131 elected members. Delhi has 80 councilors elected by adult franchise and 6 aldermen indirectly elected. The law also provides for an enlargement of the council by 20 more directly elected councilors. These numbers may appear small in comparison with the hundreds that constitute city administrations in some of the Communist countries. But the method of policy formulation and administration there is very different. The council itself meets three or four times in a year and concerns itself with perhaps half a dozen issues of a major character, and day-to-day working is controlled by a small group of twenty or twenty-five elected from the larger council. A more suitable pattern for our way of work would be the one prevailing in the Western democracies. By those standards, our councils tend to be too large, and largeness has imposed certain handicaps in operation. A tendency towards greater fissiparousness, the accentuation of political or group activity, and greater difficulty in agreeing over policy or administration are often noticeable. Many thoughtful individuals have been advocating the constitution of numerically smaller councils. For example, in Bombay, for some time, the idea has been under consideration that the size of the elected council should be reduced to around seventy-five. A compromise between efficient organization, on the one hand, and opportunities on as wide a scale as possible for participation in governmental activity, on the other, has to be struck. Possibly the answer lies in a reasonably small council and a large number of ward or constituency committees that will help to promote and look after local needs better. The creation of such ward committees is envisaged in some recent legislation, for example that relating to the Delhi Municipal Corporation; but there has been a strange reluctance to create these bodies.

In this connection, it has been asked whether the right organization for Indian local government is not one based on the two-tier system that prevails in London. But already some dissatisfaction is being voiced at the disadvantages of that system. On any rational basis, it is difficult to see how development in the spheres of education or water supply or communications can work well if handled on narrow geographical lines. Indeed, some of the current problems in Indian cities have arisen from a multiplicity of local self-government agencies. The urban scene presents such profound disparities that a process of improving and equalizing conditions can be undertaken only by one agency that can redistribute resources according to need. In any case, the paucity of technical, professional, and administrative personnel makes this course inescapable at present.

A third aspect of the question concerns the manner in which municipal functions should be discharged. Should the power of decision remain substantially with the council as a whole, or should the committee system be resorted to in an increasing measure? It is true that certain spheres of civic activity, such as those in the nature of public utilities, are today being entrusted to more or less autonomous committees of the council. There appears, however, to be greater scope for functioning through the committee system. It would ensure quicker decision; the heat and controversy that generally attend public sittings of the council would be avoided; and calm and intelligent discussion would be facilitated. The council could then function as essentially a ratifying body and, besides, help to throw on general civic problems the glare of public debate.

The foregoing issues require careful study, and the same may be said for the performance of local governments in recent times and the fixation of broad priorities and programs for urban areas.

Finally, as regards organization, one may commend the recent example of Bombay in setting up a City Coördination Council. This was one of the recommendations of a Study Group on Greater Bombay, which observed that the lack of coördination among different public authorities concerned with city development was largely responsible for the prevailing unhappy state of affairs. These authorities own land, build houses, regulate trade and industry, and perform several functions that affect the life of the citizen. But because of their position, they are not easily amenable to control of a statutory character. The Coördination Council, which seeks to fill the gap in part, has representatives of the state government, the Bombay Municipal Corporation, the Port Trust, the railways, the Bombay Housing Board, and various control and state government departments. The fact that the council has the Chief Minister of Bombay at its head not only invests it with a special authority, but also holds promise of prompt and decisive action.

THE FINANCIAL PROBLEM

The great impediment to the speedy solution of urban problems has been, and continues to be, the acute financial stringency of local governments. The Taxation Enquiry Commission which made the most recent survey of this situation observed that "the total inadequacy of municipal finance for the work that remains to be undertaken in many cities and towns in respect of important items such as water supply, drainage and slum clearance has been brought pointedly to our notice by many State Governments." [3] The Commission made various recommendations for the allocation of specified tax sources to local governments, for the sharing of certain taxes between local and state governments, and for a rational and definite basis of grants-in-aid. Many of these recommendations have remained on paper, for their implementation would have exposed state and central finances to weaknesses that might have proved detrimental to the Five Year Plans. As the Taxation Enquiry Commission itself said, "any proposal to augment local revenue by merely transferring a share of State taxes only accentuates the problem at the State level." [4]

The crux of the situation is that the financial requirements of local governments have not been taken into account in the formulation of the Five Year Plans to any significant extent. It was only during the Second Five Year Plan that some allocation of funds was made for programs of water supply and slum clearance. A part of the provision for water supply and the whole of that for slum clearance were to be made available to municipal governments. The funds allocated, however, were negligible and were essentially in the nature of token provisions. The financial needs of city governments for education, health and medical relief, communications, and housing were not considered. These needs will never be adequately provided for if local governments are left to make their own arrangements. There seems to be no escape from a total planning that takes the needs of urban areas also into account. It is futile to hope for rapid urban improvement unless resources of a commensurate order are found. Major local governments in the country were able to raise only Rs. 38 crores by way of borrowing in a recent six-year period. A very modest requirement of local governments today is probably Rs. 100 crores per year. A conference of city governments (Bombay, Calcutta, Madras, Bangalore, Ahmedabad, and Poona) held in 1954 estimated that the needs of these six cities only during the period of the Second Five Year Plan would be Rs. 125 crores. The Draft Master Plan for Delhi, over a five-year period, envisages a capital outlay of about Rs. 135 crores. The Master Plan for Bombay that was prepared twelve or thirteen years ago then estimated the developmental expenditure at Rs. 125 crores; at present prices, and in the light of new demands, this may be well over Rs. 200 crores now.

Local governments have not the strength to arrange for funds

---

[3] Ministry of Finance, Department of Economic Affairs, Government of India, *Report of the Taxation Enquiry Commission* (1955), I, 31.
[4] *Ibid.*

of this order on their own. The way out is by the inclusion of the developmental needs of cities within the framework of national five-year plans. It is not enough to cater to these needs in compartments, e.g., for housing or water supply or slum clearance, as has been the practice so far. These services cannot be provided in isolation. They must be integrated with the other essential needs of the community, such as schools, roads, hospitals and dispensaries, markets, and playing fields. Otherwise we shall find, as we do in Delhi, brand-new colonies without many of the essential ancillary services.

This is as far as external assistance goes for developmental purposes. A strengthening of revenue resources must go hand-in-hand with the provisions of larger capital services. The municipalization of public utilities, such as city passenger transport and electricity distribution, is being resorted to as one of the means of strengthening local finances, but the process has not gone far enough. Although administrative difficulties stand in the way in the case of the smaller towns and cities, means can be found whereby some monetary benefit may accrue to local governments from these operations of an essentially local character. Beyond this, however, there is the reluctance over the mobilization of resources that has been referred to earlier. Indeed, one sometimes notices alarming trends toward the sacrifice of current revenue resources. Thus, in Delhi during the last year or two, almost Rs. 10 lacs per annum of revenue has been foregone, though the general financial position is far from satisfactory. It cannot be truly said that the level of local government taxation has today even approached the optimum. Local government leaders frequently proclaim that the satiation point is yet a long way off, but they seem unable to resist pressures for sundry reliefs in existing taxes. It has been said that tax concessions and the reluctance to augment resources through further taxation are probably an outcome of the fact that city councils are still dominated by the middle classes. Their attitude is understandable, as the incidence of taxation falls substantially on that class. At the other end, a political section that professes to speak for the poorer classes strenuously urges their total incapacity to bear any taxation whatsoever. We see then a strange demand for free water supply, exemption from obligatory taxes, subsidized housing, and a variety of other monetary benefits. Amateurishness in local governments often tends to jeopardize their financial strength, as the needs of a developing economy are not adequately appreciated or understood. Here lies real danger. Some safeguards today exist, e.g., the power of state governments to enforce reasonable levels of local taxation; but, if we are likely to move toward a real integration of local government finance with national plan needs, further measures for evoking a matching effort on the part of local governments are clearly necessary. The Taxation Enquiry Commission observed some years ago that a rational and enlarged system of grants-in-aid to local authorities should embody the principle that they exploit their own resources to the extent necessary or indicated from time to time.

THE INGREDIENTS OF THE DEVELOPMENTAL PROGRAM

Many of the present ills of urban areas have resulted from a neglect of the requirements of careful planning. The amelioration of these conditions can, therefore, be achieved only through planned development and redevelopment in a comprehensive manner. The planning process envisages the application of foresight, coördination, and adaptability to public and private improvements and developments. Each new activity is designed to yield its full contribution to the transformation of the community into an increasingly better one. This comprehensive city plan or master plan must be both practical and economically sound; and it must take note of the peculiar and varying conditions, problems, and requirements of each city. A common experience in this matter has, however, been that the process of plan preparation takes too long. Even for cities of modest size a period of two or three years is found necessary; Delhi will have taken five or six years. In cities growing explosively, the plan may, therefore, become outdated or impracticable of fulfillment even before the ink on it is dry. Clearly, the planning process must be quickened, even at some risk of arbitrariness or of a reduction in scope and degree of thoroughness. There have been instances in which town-planning schemes for small sectors of a city have taken more than five or six years to formulate. Much of the present legislation on the subject appears to be based on the needs of a vanished era and an outmoded approach to city growth. A law that obviates inordinate procedural delays is needed.

The most pressing needs to be served by city planning and development are housing and slum clearance. The great paucity of suitable housing in our cities and the rapid growth of slums have been referred to earlier. The slum problem is in reality an integral part of the larger issue of housing. Inadequacy of housing breeds slums, and slums are a blot on a city's housing facilities. The two must not, indeed cannot, be tackled in isolation. For a long time to come, therefore, a sound policy for all public housing should be that it must primarily help to speed the eradication of slums. Different housing authorities today operate without adequate mutual consultation and collaboration, and a good deal of new housing does not subserve the needs of slum rehousing. The needs of new housing development call for the opening-up of large virgin areas. Coördination of public housebuilding activity will make such opening-up easier, as the pooling of sundry requirements will stretch available resources farther. Here, again, the development of areas must be done with an eye to the achievement of quick results and a careful husbanding of resources—for example, by bringing under use, to the maximum possible extent, vacant lands in already serviced areas. Considerations of economy must not lead to the result that the houses built and the development undertaken become the slums of the near future. Certain optimum housing and developmental standards must be set. Recent thinking would stipulate a two-room tenement, comprising two living rooms, a kitchen, and an independent bath and water closet. Notions about adequate housing standards and of environmental facilities change rapidly in a developing social and economic situation. It is better, therefore, to err on the side of some liberality. Paucity of resources no doubt imposes restraints; but these can take other forms than an undue depression of standards. For example, let our new houses be built to last for a modest duration instead of the sixty to eighty years that conventional forms of building predict. Building costs can also be lowered by modifying overrigid building regulations and by the mass production of components. The latter holds great promise, if we are really on the eve of a big housing program in our cities. The Study Group on Bombay estimates the housing needs of the city at 20,000 new units per year and considers that the target is realizable. In Delhi, too, we need a sustained program of constructing about 20,000 new houses every year by private and public agencies, calling for the development of about 1,500 acres of land per year. This development, in the main, can be undertaken only by public authority, preferably the local government which is the servicing agency. The needs of a long-term program of this nature demand a bold measure of large-scale acquisition of urban lands. In Delhi, therefore, proposals have been formulated for the acquisition of over 30,000 acres by government. As the principal landowner, the government will be able, first, to ensure orderly development and, secondly, to control speculative and spiraling land prices, which have become a distressing feature of the urban economy. Where land is plentiful, as in Delhi, new housing will principally come in neighborhood units; but a densification of sparsely populated urban areas will also be necessary, and vertical development will become a more common feature.

While concentrating on new housing activity, we must not overlook the need for preserving and improving the older houses in our cities. A serious attempt to arrest their further decay and disappearance is necessary. This is one aspect of a slum-prevention drive. It requires an urgent survey of all old buildings in our cities. This has lately been undertaken in Bombay. Many such buildings, though structurally sound enough to last for fifteen to twenty years, are deficient in certain important respects, such as size of rooms, light and venilation, sanitary facilities, and water supply. A scheme for securing alterations and improvements in such buildings so as to create desirable living conditions is fully worth while. The preparation of a housing code to regulate these improvements has been undertaken in Bombay. A scheme of subsidizing building-owners as an inducement for the execution of required alterations has also been adopted.

Our slums have to be dealt with through the dual approach of improvement and clearance. The former is, of course, only a short-term measure. It is, nevertheless, valuable, because clearance is a costly and certainly time-consuming process. Slum improvement aims to provide certain basic necessities, such as a piped water supply, adequate sanitary conveniences, conservancy and public health services, and electricity. In tackling the slum problem so far, much more has been done by way of improvement than by clearance. More than 300 slum properties in Delhi have been given basic amenities on these lines. New colonies with basic services laid so as to ensure a decent environment, but providing for the construction of small structures by the people themselves, have been developed. A project for similarly rehousing over 25,000 families in the capital who are now squatting indiscriminately in insanitary clusters of huts is under way.

These are, however, merely steppingstones to a regular program of slum clearance. Resources so far released specifically for clearance are meager, but it is believed that an integrated approach to urban housing will enlarge the success we can achieve in this direction. The prerequisite to any plan for slum clearance is a detailed physical and sociological study of depressed areas. As soon as possible, and even while a survey is in progress, active steps must be taken to educate the people so as to obtain their willing coöperation in any projected clearance scheme. We have not yet acquired sufficient experience of all the personal, social, and economic implications of a large-scale shifting of urban populations. Great care is, therefore, necessary in the preparation and execution of our first schemes, so that the movement as a whole does not get a psychological setback. The preferable course, therefore, is to take up small pilot projects in different types of slum areas. The redevelopment of clearance areas through private owners of land has not proved fruitful, and the responsibility has had to be borne by public authorities.

After houses, our cities need most more drinking water, better drainage and sewerage facilities, and adequate schools, hospitals, dispensaries, and recreational facilities. Of these, the first two are especially urgent, if the needed housing program is to be rendered possible at all. Both involve very large capital outlays, and in some cases new sources of water supply appear problematical. The possibilities of small waterworks based on tube wells are being studied, especially for the townships or neighborhood units that are foreseen. Possibilities of reducing sewage-treatment cost through the use of lagoons are also under study; the Public Health Engineering Institute has been conducting experiments on their adoption for small communities in Indian conditions. In both cases, the objectives are quicker results and a reduction in development costs.

Reasonable standards for the provision of schools, hospitals, and dispensaries have been set under the Five Year Plans for the urban and rural areas. Some of the most striking of our achievements in recent years are to be found in these fields. Still, substantial gaps exist in regard to these and recreational facilities in the older, congested parts of our cities, where naturally the need is greatest. The quick development of new housing facilities alone can bring success nearer in these matters, for the rehousing of populations and the redevelopment of the older areas will release land for parks and open spaces and for schools and dispensaries. From all angles, therefore, a bold program of house construction holds the key to the urban situation.

CONCLUSIONS

The civic problems of our cities are undoubtedly complex and grave, but they are all essentially soluble. A planned approach and an appropriate machinery can resolve them. Even finance is not beyond the range of practical politics. The present time is a very opportune, indeed crucial, moment for crystallizing our attitude toward urban growth and concerting suitable measures for city improvement. With the Third Five Year Plan in the offing, we are on the eve of a large new program of industrialization. The objective of lessening the pressure on already strained urban areas must be promoted through a dispersal of industrial activity and an intensified program of rural civic development. In a sense, the challenge to urban growth must, in part, be met by a retreat from the urbanization process. Natural growth will, of course, always be there, and some accession of population is inevitable—but must we postulate the inexorable march of urbanization in the way we have seen it in

recent years? Must Bombay grow to be a city of 7.5 millions in
ten years? Must Delhi's population rise from the present 2.5
millions to nearly 5.5 millions in two decades? One would like to
answer these questions in the negative; if our policies and actions
are wise and far-seeing, that answer might well turn out to be
right. There are instances in Europe of the stabilization of city
size and population, despite intensive industrialization. In a country
of the size of India, with a tremendous hinterland full of possibilities, scope for the pursuit of a similar aim is truly great.

It is encouraging that good beginnings have been made on the
new tasks of local government in Bombay and Delhi, to give two
examples. The Bombay plan envisages, apart from the conventional programs of a local authority, the shifting of nonconformity
industries, the establishment of numerous industrial estates and
satellite townships, the relocation of government offices away from
centers essentially suited for trade and commerce, the linking of
the island with the mainland at new points through rail-*cum*-road
bridges across creeks, and the reclamation of large areas of marshy
land. The Study Group on Greater Bombay has expressed the
definite view that if the tasks ahead can be tackled with determination, distinct improvements can be achieved within two years and
that, within a further similar period, the problems of the city would
have been set well on the way to a lasting solution. Bombay has
always given a lead to the country in ideas and execution. The
population is more civic-minded and alert; the leadership has been
virile and clear-thinking. It is, therefore, reasonable to hope that
a place endowed with natural beauty, with its hills and creeks and
rivers, with a reasonable developed environment of man's own
making, will be further embellished by a process of orderly redevelopment, by the eradication of slums and congestion, and by a
release from city tensions.

Delhi also is chalking out an imaginative program of activity for
the next two decades. One may not agree with all that Delhi's
Master Plan foresees. There are those who dislike the planned
growth of the city to a population of 5.5 millions by 1981. There
is, however, great intrinsic merit and sociological justification for
the proposed development and redevelopment of Greater Delhi
on the basis of a rationalized distribution of population. There are
large areas of urban Delhi today in which the density of population is as low as 5 to 10 per acre; in others, the figure goes up to
over 1,000. The Draft Master Plan envisages a redistribution of
population densities so as to create more acceptable living conditions all round. For example, the eventual population of the walled
city that Shah Jehan built is to be reduced from nearly 1,000,000 to

380,000. New Delhi will increase from about 250,000 to 750,000. Shahdara, a suburb with a population of about 150,000 today, will be intensively developed into a complete new city of 700,000. The Draft Plan proposes far-reaching changes in the system of communications and sets optimum standards for ancillary civic services such as school buildings, playing fields, community centers, dispensaries, and markets. It has attempted a realistic assessment of developmental cost and of the resources that can and should be mobilized. The Delhi Master Plan is the first really comprehensive attempt to draw up a picture of long-term development. Its implementation is a great challenge both to the Government of India, which must bear the brunt of the financial burden, and to the Delhi Municipal Corporation, which is destined to be the principal agency for the execution of the Plan. The prospect would be exciting at any time, but it is infinitely more so to an infant corporation in whose hands much of the future happiness of the Delhi citizen reposes. Despite inevitable teething troubles, the work done in the last two years in overcoming psychological obstacles and in paving the way for long-term improvements encourages the firm belief that we can and will build a Delhi that is in all respects a worthy capital for a great and prosperous democracy.

THE URBAN CHALLENGE TO LOCAL
AND STATE GOVERNMENT: WEST BENGAL,
WITH SPECIAL ATTENTION TO CALCUTTA

Richard L. Park

Affection for the culture, the people, and the problems of Calcutta
is an acquired taste. At first and second glances, this historic city,
and much of the urban sector of West Bengal that surrounds it,
are among the most unpleasant—even noxious—environments on
the face of the earth. Visitors to the city, foreign and Indian alike,
are apt to be depressed upon first confronting the masses of people,
the jumble of carts and lorries, the professional beggars, the
refuse everywhere; the narrow lanes, the decaying Victorian edifices, the ragged tenements, the smoking and accident-prone factories; the thousands of chaotic sheds, bazaar shops, pye-dogs,
cows, crows, and buzzards. And yet, once having coursed through
the ribbon strips from Dum Dum Airport, or from Howrah or
Sealdah stations, the newcomer, more than likely, finds refuge in
a hotel near the public park—the Maidan—in a government office,
or in the spacious home or flat of a Calcutta friend, hidden and protected by a broken-glass-betopped wall from the apparent madness
beyond. Aside from the curious and continuous tinkling and singing
noises that characterize the tone of the city, the more affluent visitor
then may relax and enjoy the refinement, intelligence, and high
humor that are the Bengali gifts.[1]

---

[1] The finer aspects of life in Bengal, and particularly in Calcutta, often have been
described. Two recent sympathetic but critical statements by Nirmal Kumar Bose are
"Modern Bengal," in *Man in India* (Calcutta), XXXVIII, No. 4 (October–December,
1958), and "Social and Cultural Life of Calcutta," in *Geographical Review of India*,
XX (December, 1958), pp. 1–46. See also the insightful essay by the late Sudhin-

Actually, a closer and more extensive search of the city and its environs would reveal, in physical terms at least, an even more unfavorable set of impressions. In the city proper, over three million people[2] compete for a livelihood, in an area of only 32.32 square miles, and with average densities of about 90,000 persons per square mile.[3] The civic center of Calcutta, abutting the enormous Maidan, is rather regal and genteel, in a Victorian sort of way, as are the wealthy residential areas of Ballygunge, Alipore, and others near by. With fewer multistoried buildings than Bombay, and with much less open space than New Delhi, Calcutta is compact—even dense—in most of its sectors. Extensive ribbon developments have grown along the roadways out of the city center to Dum Dum, to the south, and especially out toward the jute mills.[4] Beyond the government buildings, the business districts, and the upper-middle-class residential areas sprawl the slums and an intermixture of factories, godowns, salt marshes, tenements, schools, temples, mosques, and seemingly endless bazaars.

Calcutta more than doubled in population between 1931 and 1951,[5] including in its expansion since 1947 many hundreds of

---

[dranath] Datta, "The World's Cities: Calcutta," *Encounter*, VIII, No. 6 (June, 1957), pp. 35–45.

The noneconomic base involved in much of Calcutta's early expansion and its later consolidation in the cultural life of the city is explored by Benoy Ghose in "The Colonial Beginnings of Calcutta: Urbanization without Industrialization," *Economic Weekly* (Bombay), XII, No. 33 (August 13, 1960), 1255–1260.

[2] The population of Calcutta was 2,548,677 as of March 1, 1951—an increase from the 1,163,711 of the 1931 census. (*Census of India, 1951*, VI, Part III, "Calcutta City," by A. Mitra [Delhi: Manager of Publications, 1954], vii.) See also International Urban Research, *The World's Metropolitan Areas* (Berkeley and Los Angeles: University of California Press, 1959). On page 48 of the latter publication, note the population of the Calcutta Metropolitan Area: 5,170,830 in 1951, and an estimated 5,700,000 in 1955. Calcutta City proper is estimated (1955) at 2,750,000, and may well be over three million in 1961. The Calcutta Metropolitan Area is defined on pages 82–83. [A subsequent (unpublished) errata sheet corrects the figures for Calcutta published on page 48 of *The World's Metropolitan Areas*. The 1951 population of the Metropolitan Area should read 5,220,739, and the estimated population for the same area in 1955 should read 5,755,000.—*Ed.*]

[3] Figures on the social conditions of life in Calcutta are taken from the *Census of India, 1951*, VI, Part III; from "The City of Calcutta: A Socio-Economic Survey (1954–1958), Summary of Findings," prepared for the Planning Commission, Government of India, by the Department of Economics, Calcutta University (hand-dated December 12, 1959; mimeographed); and from Syamal Chakrabartty, *Housing Conditions in Calcutta* (Calcutta: Bookland Private Limited, 1959), which is based on the work of the socioeconomic survey of Calcutta, previously noted. The completed study is published as S. N. Sen, *The City of Calcutta: A Socio-Economic Survey, 1954–55 to 57–58* (Calcutta: Firma K. L. Mukhopadhyay, 1960).

[4] Personal exploration. I have also drawn from a private paper by Britton Harris, "Impressions of Calcutta," dated March 24, 1958.

[5] See note 2, above, and the article by M. Venkatarangaiya on "Bombay and Calcutta" in William A. Robson (ed.), *Great Cities of the World: Their Government, Politics and Planning* (New York: Macmillan, 1957), p. 140.

thousands of refugees from East Pakistan—probably as many as three million coming to West Bengal, with the vast majority still remaining in the Greater Calcutta region or just beyond.[6] The destructive wear and tear of army operations in and about the city during World War II, the physical and emotional consequences of the Bengal famine of 1942–43, and the communal riots beginning in August of 1946 culminated in the partition of 1947. The partition cut off East Bengal and vastly reduced the territory and revenues of the remaining state, West Bengal, while breaking the back (at least temporarily) of the jute industry that had for so long been the pride of the city.[7] Refugees piled into Calcutta in great numbers just at a time when the state was least well equipped to handle the flow. Calcutta, together with West Bengal generally, has never yet recovered from this series of blows to its well-being. One result has been an increase in the political impact of poor living and working conditions in the city—conditions that were bad enough before the war.

It is estimated that over 300,000 people live on the pavements and sidewalks of the city, with no homes at all.[8] Until very recently, Sealdah Station was crowded with refugees who lived there for months on end, with few if any living facilities. Hawkers' stalls have gone up helter-skelter all over the city. The water supply, for many years inadequate for normal needs, has been strained far beyond capacity,[9] and as a consequence outbreaks of diseases familiar in Calcutta—cholera, smallpox, plague, etc.—have occurred regularly. To make matters worse, the Hooghly River has been silting in recent years more rapidly than it could be dredged, and water for agricultural and other purposes has become increasingly saline.[10] Suburban railway service has deteriorated, and limited funds for maintenance and excessive use have led to a decline in the efficiency of tramways and buses.[11] Taking into account the

---

[6] K. Rangaswami, "Dandakaranya: Slow Progress of a Scheme," *Hindu Weekly Review*, VIII, No. 20 (May 16, 1960), 10.

[7] See S. P. Chatterjee, *The Partition of Bengal: A Geographical Study* (Calcutta Geographical Society, Publication No. 8 [Calcutta, 1947]), and *Calcutta Municipal Gazette,* Thirty-third Anniversary Number, Supplement, LXIX, No. 5 (November 22, 1958), 1–5.

[8] *Calcutta Municipal Gazette*, Thirty-third Anniversary Number, Supplement, p. 1.

[9] *Amrita Bazar Patrika* (Calcutta), November 13, 1959, p. 1, and December 17, 1959, pp. 6–7. On water supply in Calcutta, and on measures to prevent cholera epidemics, see Chakrabartty, *op. cit.,* p. 55.

[10] See D. N. Sengupta, "The Hooghly River," *The Modern Review* (Calcutta), CIV, No. 3 (September, 1958), 201–205, for a review of the silting and salinity of the Hooghly.

[11] *Calcutta Municipal Gazette*, Thirty-third Anniversary Number, Supplement, p. 1. See also "Congestion on Suburban Railways," *The Eastern Economist* (New Delhi), XXVIII, No. 4 (January 25, 1957), 128–129.

humid (or dank) climate of the place from at least March through late October, one must conclude that Calcutta is not the most naturally inviting city in India.

Under what housing conditions do the people of Calcutta live?[12] Only 5 per cent of the city's families live in separate flats, and only 2 per cent in complete houses. Thus only 7 per cent of the families live in exclusive dwellings.[13] Most families live in rented quarters.[14] As for space, 17 per cent of the families have *no* living room at all, and 30 per cent have less than one third of a room for their use. Four per cent possess one half of a room, 33 per cent one room, and only 16 per cent have more than one room.[15] It is estimated that at least 77 per cent of the people of Calcutta live in over-crowded rooms, that is to say with more than two persons per room[16] based on 40 square feet minimum needed for every person.[17]

As for amenities, 30 per cent of Calcutta's families have no water tap of their own. (The custom in these cases is to use the public taps on the street.) Sixty per cent share water taps with others, 9 per cent have one tap for themselves, and only one per cent have more than a single water tap.[18] Ten per cent of the families have one or more latrines for their own use, but 12 per cent have no latrine at all.[19] Forty-nine per cent of multi-member families have no separate bathing facilities, and the Calcutta average for no baths is higher, 61 per cent. (Again, the taps on the streets are used for bathing.)[20] Cooking is done by 36 per cent of Calcutta's multi-member families in the living room, whereas 30 per cent of these have only a "cooking corner"; 34 per cent have separate kitchens. The Calcutta average reveals that 78 per cent of all families have no really usable separate kitchen.[21] Forty-five per cent have no electricity, and 40 per cent have "some" electricity.[22]

---

[12] In the paragraphs that follow on housing conditions, all the statistics are from Chakrabarrty's *Housing Conditions in Calcutta,* which in turn is based on "The City of Calcutta: A Socio-Economic Survey (1954–1958), Summary of Findings." (See note 3 for full citations; hereafter cited as Chakrabarrty and "Socio-Economic Survey.") The survey was based on a sample of 5,204 Calcutta families, of which 57 per cent were single-member, 28 per cent medium-sized (2 to 5 members), and 15 per cent big families (6 members or more).

[13] Chakrabarrty, p. 6.

[14] *Ibid.,* p. 9, Table 2 shows the percentage of families living in different types of houses with different categories of occupancy rights.

[15] *Ibid.,* p. 13.

[16] *Ibid.,* p. 14.

[17] "Socio-Economic Survey," p. 8.

[18] Chakrabarrty, p. 19.

[19] *Ibid.,* p. 21.

[20] *Ibid.,* p. 22.

[21] *Ibid.,* p. 23.

[22] *Ibid.,* p. 20.

To pick out a few of the worst aspects of Calcutta households' living conditions:

30 per cent have no water tap attached to their residences
12 per cent have no latrine
61 per cent have no bathroom
78 per cent have no separate kitchen
45 per cent have no electric connection

It would appear unnecessary to produce additional data to support the view, held by all who have examined Calcutta's housing and living conditions, that this city is in desperate need of emergency measures to improve its deplorable living standards.[23]

When one searches for underlying causes for present circumstances—leaving aside the special problem of refugees—it is noted that "about a quarter of the population of the city live a single life without their families, and they form more than half of the households." [24] Most of these single people are male, married, and migrants. Many of them are illiterate, unskilled workers, with about 87 per cent of them earning less than Rs. 100 per month (an average of Rs. 74 per month).[25] The people of this large group live in about the worst living conditions in the city. For the most part, these men leave their families in their village homes, come to the city to earn cash incomes, spend just as little as possible on themselves while they are in the city, and then leave the job to return to the village as soon as sufficient funds have been saved. Such a group, with no long-range family ties to Calcutta, cannot be expected to coöperate willingly in long-range plans for the city's im-

[23] The unpublished report of the International Bank's mission (1960) to India, headed by Michael Hoffman, makes a strong plea for the rehabilitation of Calcutta and its port at the level of $400 million in emergency allocation. See "Calcutta and the World Bank Mission," *The Economic Weekly* (Bombay), XII, No. 40 (October 1, 1960), 1469–1474.

The literature abounds with evidence of the political consequences of West Bengal's and Calcutta's present physical condition. For example, see K. K. Sinha, "West Bengal: Problems and Prospects," *Freedom First*, No. 80 (January, 1959), pp. 5–6, and another article by the same author, "West Bengal: A Political Report," *Thought*, XI, No. 33 (August 15, 1959), 28. See also Myron Weiner, "Political Leadership in West Bengal: The Implications of Its Changing Patterns for Economic Planning," *The Economic Weekly* (Bombay), XI, No. 46 (November 14, 1959), 925–932. This article makes the case that a rural elite is growing in West Bengal that may be expected to decrease the influence of the more left-wing political influences of Calcutta. A rebuttal of Weiner's thesis by "AM" appeared in the same journal on September 26, 1959; Weiner replied in the same journal on November 14, 1959; and "AM" commented again on November 28, 1959. (It is difficult to get agreement on West Bengal's political circumstances, except that all other than active politicians in the state confess bafflement, to a greater or lesser degree, at the maze of personal influences at work in the politics of the state.)

[24] "Socio-Economic Survey," p. 1.

[25] *Ibid.*

provement. It will also be noted that this large group of migrant men results in a disproportionately small percentage of women in Calcutta. "In 1957–58, the city's population consisted of about 35% women and 65% men . . ." [26] The consequence has been a steady high rate of social crimes and unhealthful patterns of behavior in the slum regions surrounding the factories. On the more favorable side, at least most of the older men have found it possible to get some work. Unemployment among those of working age has been declining steadily, from about 10 per cent in 1954–55 to 7.6 per cent in 1956–57.[27] However, youthful workers (ages 15–24), women, displaced migrants (refugees), and many of the educated have experienced a much more drastic unemployment situation. The higher level of unemployment among these workers, as well as widespread underemployment, has substantially increased the political discontent within the city.[28]

Another problem in the city is that of migration and the migrants. Defining a migrant as anyone who came to Calcutta in 1935 or later, migrants now constitute about 45 per cent of the total population.[29] "Displaced migrants," forming 17 per cent of the total population, are those who have come to the city because of communal disturbances; mostly they are from East Pakistan. These persons constitute a "problem," because a majority come from the middle classes. Among them are many educated persons, and about 50 per cent held trading, ministerial, or technical and professional jobs before migrating to Calcutta.[30] Many of these people came from urban centers; consequently, their demand for more adequate housing and social amenities has been greater in intensity than that of those who came from rural environments.[31]

Before turning to questions of regional, state, and local administration and planning for West Bengal and Calcutta, it may be worth while to assess the costs that would be involved in approaching some decent solution to the Calcutta housing problem, seemingly a key to the rehabilitation of the city.

As has been pointed out earlier, most housing units in Calcutta are rented. The rent schedule worked out in the survey by the Department of Economics, Calcutta University, was as follows:[32]

28 per cent pay rents up to Rs. 5 per month
23 per cent pay rents between Rs. 6 and 10 per month

[26] *Ibid.,* p. 2.
[27] *Ibid.,* p. 6.
[28] Sen, *op. cit.,* pp. 106–121.
[29] "Socio-Economic Survey," p. 8.
[30] *Ibid.,* pp. 8–9.
[31] *Ibid.,* p. 9.
[32] Chakrabarrty, p. 31.

17 per cent pay rents between Rs. 11 and 15 per month
18 per cent pay rents between Rs. 16 and 30 per month
10 per cent pay rents between Rs. 31 and 60 per month
3 per cent pay rents between Rs. 61 and 125 per month
1 per cent pay rents between Rs. 125 and 250 per month

Averages work out at Rs. 10.35 per month for single-member households, and Rs. 27.58 per month for multi-member households.

In Calcutta, probably 70 to 80 per cent of the resident families need to be rehoused, which is to say that new housing would be needed for at least 524,563 families.[33] As a first step toward this goal, the West Bengal Bill of 1957 hopes to provide funds for 30 per cent of the resident families, thus for only 224,812 families. If all those now living in kutcha (country style or makeshift) or semi-kutcha houses were to be rehoused, 382,176 families would be involved. Assuming a Rs. 6,000 minimum investment per new family tenement-unit (one room),[34] the three plans work out as follows:

224,812 family (tenement) units—Rs. 1,348,872,000
382,176 family (tenement) units—Rs. 2,293,056,000
524,563 family (tenement) units—Rs. 3,147,378,000

Where is the money to come from? Certainly not from rentals alone. An assumed investment of about Rs. 6,000 per tenement unit and a 5 per cent per annum return from rentals works out to Rs. 300 rent per annum, or Rs. 25 per month. Yet the average monthly rental in those parts of Calcutta most affected is today somewhat less than Rs. 10![35]

In another assessment of the slum problem in Calcutta and its costs for clearance, S. K. Gupta, I.C.S., the chairman of the Calcutta Improvement Trust, had this to say:[36]

The Government of India's slum clearance scheme says that in multi-storeyed constructions the gross density must not exceed 60 tenements (approximately 250 persons) per acre. This means that for 617,374 people living in *bustees,* we have to find 2,470 acres or 7,310 *bighas,* which is about one and a half times the area now covered by *bustees.*

Mr. Gupta goes on to state that if proper houses were to be built for the bustee dwellers, those from the bustees could not pay the necessary rents. Rental, he estimates, would have to be between

---

[33] *Ibid.,* pp. 50–51.

[34] *Ibid.,* p. 51.

[35] "Socio-Economic Survey," p. 56.

[36] In *Annual Report on the Operations of the Calcutta Improvement Trust, for the Year 1955–1956* (Calcutta: Calcutta Improvement Trust, n.d.), Appendix, "Problem of Slums in Calcutta" (slightly abridged from the *Statesman,* May 19 and 20, 1957), p. 41. The figures in the remainder of the paragraph are from pp. 43–44.

Rs. 60 and Rs. 35 per new tenement per month, and this would be far too dear. He estimates present bustee rentals at between Rs. 4 and Rs. 30 per month. Mr. Gupta concludes that an outright subsidy of at least 50 per cent would be needed from the government for providing housing replacements for the bustees.

The summary of the socioeconomic survey by the Department of Economics, Calcutta University, concludes that at least Rs. 25 crores per year for five years, or Rs. 125 crores, would be needed even to put a dent into the housing needs of Calcutta.[37] In addition to housing construction, there would be need for "increasing capacities in the transport industry, schools, colleges, hospitals, and other social amenities," which would lift the total needed expenditure over a five-year period to between Rs. 350 and Rs. 400 crores, wherefore, "the immensity of the task will be obvious if we remember that this rate of expenditure represents more than 5 per cent of the total investment (public and private) to be incurred during the Second Plan period."[38] Syamal Chakrabartty, in concluding his book on *Housing Conditions in Calcutta*, is more blunt. He asks the question, on housing needs alone, "Can we afford to allocate such huge funds for any immediate programme?" and responds, "The answer is too obvious: We cannot."[39]

II

The preceding brief review of housing and general living conditions in Calcutta gives some sense of the enormity of the problems that face responsible politicians and administrators in the West Bengal government, in the Calcutta Corporation, and in other local governments in the state. It now remains to examine the response of local and state governments to these challenges of urban growth.

Planning in India is a complex and sometimes obscure process, especially as plans focus down to specific localities. West Bengal, like the other states in the Republic of India, is in a position annually to allocate its own revenues, and to participate in sharing national resources through negotiation with the central government. Here the Planning Commission assists in weighing and balancing state-proposed projects, and the cabinet, its committees, and Parliament itself participate in the national allocations. Political pressures, as well as those strictly governmental, come into play in this budgetary dance, and the result is a rough-and-ready plan-

---

[37] "Socio-Economic Survey," p. 13.

[38] *Ibid.*

[39] *Op. cit.,* p. 51. See also the extended comments on Calcutta's housing needs and the cost in Sen, *op. cit.,* pp. 122–163, 264–265, and *Amrita Bazar Patrika* (Calcutta), June 22, 1959, p. 5. On slum clearance see Dipanka, "Calcutta Letter," *The Economic Weekly* (Bombay), X, No. 35 (August 30, 1958), 1128.

ning blueprint that hews as much to the top planners' conceptions of rationality as is politically and administratively feasible. Considering the enormous needs and the consistent pressures from all sides, it is generally agreed that India's national planning, translated into operating programs in the several states, has been a great success over the first two Plan periods. This, then, is the first and highest level of coördination of planning. Unfortunately, a given state's internal plan and operating program may not necessarily live up in practice to the initial high hopes of the central planners.

Largely because of the nature of India's federal system, and based on the fact that certain essential economic and social reform programs overlap state boundaries, an experiment in regional planning was instituted on November 1, 1956.[40] The Zonal Councils scheme and its workings have not been well publicized or critically assessed as yet, though general opinions expressed by highly placed informants to the author in the summers of 1959 and 1960 would lead one to believe that little weight of importance is given to the work of these Councils, except to the extent that they give a psychological sense of regional interdependency among leading politicians. In any event, it should be noted that West Bengal belongs to the Eastern Zone, along with Bihar, Orissa, Assam, Manipur, and Tripura.[41] The Council for this zone first met on April 30, 1957, with Pandit Govind Ballabh Pant, Home Minister of the Central Government, as chairman,[42] and with Dr. B. C. Roy, Chief Minister of West Bengal, as the first vice-chairman; the Chief Minister of Bihar was to follow the next year as vice-chairman, and so on, in rotation. Among the many problems that have come before the Council have been the rehabilitation of refugees,[43] coördination of river problems through the Ganga and Brahmaputra Flood Control Board and the Ganga Water Transport Board, developments

---

[40] See Joan V. Bondurant, *Regionalism versus Provincialism: A Study in Problems of Indian National Unity* (Indian Press Digests, Monograph No. 4 [Berkeley, Calif.: Institute of International Studies, University of California, 1958]), especially pp. 105–150. The Zonal Councils were set up not only to encourage regional coöperation between states, but, as Dr. Bondurant makes clear, also to decrease the possible harmful consequences of the organization of the states along linguistic lines. For a powerful critique of the influence of provincialism in India see Selig S. Harrison, *India: The Most Dangerous Decades* (Princeton, N.J.: Princeton University Press, 1960).

[41] Bondurant, *op. cit.*, p. 107.

[42] Pandit Pant has been chairman of all the Zonal Councils. His views on the Councils are found in the *Hindu Weekly Review*, V, No. 17 (April 29, 1957), 4.

[43] See the article by K. Rangaswami, "Dandakaranya: "Slow Progress of a Scheme," *Hindu Weekly Review*, VIII, No. 20 (May 16, 1960), p. 10, for an example of a program for rehabilitation of refugees that includes the Eastern Zone, but goes beyond it to Madhya Pradesh. For a variety of reasons explained by Rangaswami, provincialisms in West Bengal and in Madhya Pradesh have combined to inhibit a rational development of this project.

of the centrally controlled Damodar Valley Corporation (closely affecting both Bihar and West Bengal), roads, railways, motor vehicles, the iron and steel industry, coals, agricultural productivity, movement of food grains, etc.[44] Especially for the coördination of river-valley schemes, large industrial developments such as the one at Durgapur, and the growing iron and steel industry,[45] to say nothing of the national security and defense issues that affect this region currently, the Zonal Councils could provide India with a regional planning and programing mechanism. It remains to be seen whether state loyalties and regional and national interests can interlock amicably. The Councils appear to be a start toward the goal of regional planning across state boundaries and could be a contributing factor to India's economic development.[46] To date, however, perhaps with the exception of the iron and steel industry, but even here not going much beyond productivity goals, there seems to have been little coördination, especially on housing.[47]

When considering regional planning along Zonal Council lines, it should be recognized that a planning body without a clearly defined jurisdiction, without direct, organic ties to an established bureaucracy, and dependent upon its constituent elements for revenues and sanctions, cannot—in the natural administrative order of things—hope to achieve miracles. Indeed, some critics believe that such a body as the Zonal Council becomes more a nuisance than a constructive force; in the absence of strongly felt mutual interests between states, the Council may become a refuge for debate and cordial political discussion, replacing by convenient default those hard decisions within each state that are unpopular and costly to make. The evidence to date would seem to support the critics.

Within the State of West Bengal, the key agency concerned with urban as well as rural development is the Development Department. Through the Development Commissioner, a great many steps have been taken to improve urban conditions in Calcutta and else-

---

[44] Bondurant, *op. cit.*, pp. 133–135, for the period through about the end of 1957. On the Damodar Valley scheme, see Henry C. Hart, *New India's Rivers* (Bombay: Orient Longmans, 1956).

[45] See Vithal Babu, "Report on a Preliminary Inquiry on the Growth of Steel Towns in India: A Study on the Problems of Urbanization" (Calcutta: UNESCO Research Centre on Social Implications of Industrialization in Southern Asia, 1959). [Mimeographed.]

[46] For a discussion of regional planning and economic policy see Catherine Bauer Wurster, "The Optimum Pattern of Urbanization: Does Asia Need a New Type of Regional Planning?" a paper prepared for the UN Seminar on Regional Planning, Tokyo, July, 1958, especially pp. 15–19. [Mimeographed.]

[47] See Vithal Babu, *op. cit.*

where in the state.[48] For example, the Construction Board of the Development Department has coördinated and supervised a substantial number of building projects in the state, including schools and colleges, medical institutions, refugee townships (such as Habra-Baigachi, thirty miles northeast of Calcutta), industrial housing on 50 per cent subsidy, the development townships of Kalyani and Fulia, a cattle farm at Haringhata, community development townships, and a new secretariat building in Calcutta.[49] The total listing of the Construction Board's completed and planned projects is impressive. Considering the needs, however, the effort must be considered inadequate. In fact, S. Bandopadhyay, the Chief Engineer of the Construction Board, calls their policy "consciously inadequate," because of the lack of resources in materials, personnel, and funds.[50]

It is also important to realize that, although the Development Department has jurisdiction over all West Bengal, there is no formal and considered coöperation and coördination with the Calcutta Corporation, or with other local municipalities. Competition between programs, or else lack of knowledge of competing programs, would seem to be the more accurate description of the current situation.

Furthermore, observers of the housing projects of the Construction Board report a series of major errors in planning that have negated much of the effort expended on them. For example, the Ganguly Began and Poddar Park projects of four-story, single-room tenements, in 1,000 units, built at the expense of Rs. 4 million, are a failure. Having been built far from places of work, with high rentals and few or no community facilities, the projects have remained almost empty for years. The township of Kalyani, some thirty miles north of Calcutta, has no sound economic base, and remains only partially occupied.[51]

As for Calcutta, the two bodies most concerned with urban improvement are the Calcutta Corporation and the Calcutta Improvement Trust.[52] The Corporation, originally created as early as 1863,

---

[48] See S. Bandopadhyay, "West Bengal's Building Program," *Indian Construction News* (Calcutta), December, 1957. For broader considerations of urbanization and its problems in West Bengal, see Sudhansu Bhusan Mukherjee, "Urbanization in Burdwan Division," *Calcutta Statistical Association Bulletin,* VI, No. 21 (March, 1955), 1–16.

[49] See Bandopadhyay, *op. cit.,* pp. 21 ff. On subsidized industrial housing see *Amrita Bazar Patrika* (Calcutta), June 21, 1959, pp. 1–2.

[50] *Op. cit.*

[51] Private memorandum by E. G. Echeverria, April 2, 1958.

[52] There is a considerable literature on the Calcutta Corporation. A short critical survey will be found in M. Venkatarangaiya's essay on "Bombay and Calcutta," in Robson (ed.), *Great Cities of the World.* Much of the historical literature is considered by Ernest Goldsmith in "Municipal Government in Calcutta: The Calcutta Corporation" (Master's thesis, University of California, Berkeley, 1960). As for the Calcutta

has had a checkered career. For many years, particularly under the leadership of Surendranath Banerjea (who helped write the Act of 1923 under whose terms the Corporation operated until 1951), it was a training ground for budding politicians, and much good work along political lines, and in constructive effort as well, was accomplished. The general record of the Corporation in developmental effort, however, has been far from outstanding. In terms of general efficiency and quality of administration, the Calcutta Corporation has been notoriously poor.[53]

In recent years, especially under the pressures of partition, the Corporation became so hopelessly incompetent that the Government of West Bengal superseded it in 1948 and took over its operations until 1951. In the meantime, a Corporation of Calcutta Investigation Commission was appointed to review its functions and organization, and to recommend a new Act to govern the workings of the Corporation.[54]

Unfortunately, the new organization of the Calcutta Corporation (since 1951) does not appear to have increased substantially its efficiency or sense of priority and relevance. One critic, who shall remain anonymous, wrote in 1958 that "the lack of cooperation between different agencies, the multiplicity of jurisdictions, and the lethargy of Corporation officials seem to be worse in the Calcutta area than anywhere else in India." The same critic felt that "drastic steps" were needed to correct the situation, but that such steps seemed improbable of achievement.[55]

The Calcutta Improvement Trust was first established in 1911 by Act V of the Bengal Legislative Council. Attention was to be given, initially, to the improvement of city streets and the providing of open spaces in the city, and likewise in the suburbs if permission were granted by the Bengal government.[56] To give some idea of the substance of the Trust's operations, from 1923 to 1941 it expended some $10 million, mostly on roads, bridges, recreation areas, and sewers. Little was expended on housing.[57] The same

---

Improvement Trust, see the *Annual Reports.* (I have examined those for 1954–55, 1955–56, and 1956–57.) On the workings of the Calcutta Municipal Act, 1951 (Calcutta Corporation), see an article by the head of the Calcutta Improvement Trust, S. K. Gupta, I.C.S., "Second Thoughts on Problems of Municipal Relationships," *Background Papers on Improving City Government* (New Delhi: Indian Institute of Public Administration, n.d.).

[53] See Venkatarangaiya, *op. cit.,* pp. 152 ff.

[54] See the *Report of the Corporation of Calcutta Investigation Commission,* Vols. I and II (Alipore: West Bengal Government Press, 1950).

[55] The general description, alas, might well apply to all too many cities in various parts of the world.

[56] See Goldsmith, *op. cit.,* chap. xi. Note that a city like Howrah, formerly under the Calcutta Improvement Trust—and not "improved" much—now has its own improvement trust.

[57] *Ibid.*

kind of program continues now, though more attention is given to housing. Yet, with a budget in 1954–55, for example, of Rs. 92.48 lakhs,[58] only very modest housing achievements could be attempted.

Organizationally, the Calcutta Corporation and the Improvement Trust are separated, although the Corporation is represented on the Trust by the Commissioner of the Corporation, and by three Corporation representatives.[59] The question often has been raised about the efficiency and suitability of this separation of activities. It is argued, with some force, that the functions performed by the Trust belong as a direct responsibility to the Corporation. Some such reorganization and consolidation of functions might make sense in the abstract, but it did not appeal to the Calcutta Corporation Investigation Commission.[60]

III

West Bengal faces political, economic, and social crises each year, especially in Calcutta. The pressures of urban growth in and around the city have been, and continue to be, among the most critical and disturbing in India. It would appear that little appreciable effort has been made by any of the governmental agencies concerned, aside from some gains in slum clearance and refugee rehabilitation, to alleviate the burdens of incredibly low standards of living experienced by the vast majority of Greater Calcutta residents. Close coördination of the efforts of the iron and steel industry in the region, the Damodar Valley Corporation, new industrial development, the West Bengal Development Department, the Calcutta Corporation, the Calcutta Improvement Trust, and the other municipal governments and trusts in West Bengal remains an urgent necessity. But all too little has been done to date.

Some well-informed students of West Bengal's affairs have little sympathy for what they consider special pleading on behalf of Greater Calcutta, or for the state's cities generally. While recognizing the urban crisis, they believe that the rural sector is entitled to first priority. One such view is given below:[61]

My own view for a long time has been that Calcutta is now paying the price of having prospered in the past by draining the life-blood from the country-

---

[58] *Annual Report on the Operations of the Calcutta Improvement Trust, for the Year 1954–55*, p. 6.

[59] *Ibid.*, p. 4.

[60] See Venkatarangaiya, *op. cit.*, and Prabuddha Nath Chatterjee, "A Plea for Municipal Self-Government in Calcutta," *The Modern Review* (Calcutta), CIV, No. 5 (November, 1958), 396–399.

[61] The excerpts are taken from a letter to the author dated August 5, 1960. The writer of the letter must remain anonymous, but it can be said that he is an experienced hand in both the rural and urban problems of Bengal.

side, both economically as well as in human resources. This prosperity was therefore never securely founded. For a long time action will have to be taken to redress the balance by paying more attention to broad-based economic development, particularly in the countryside. The abysmal hunger in Calcutta for housing, sanitation, water supply, and road reparation will have to wait. At most, on account of the agitational pressure of the metropolitan intelligentsia, we may have to take some kind of "holding action," such as through patchwork repairs of the largest potholes in the roads. We can hardly contemplate more ambitious programmes.

Controlled evacuation of industry and a part of the population will need to be planned. Further, in planning anything at all the obligation must be placed squarely upon the central government rather than the Government of West Bengal, since Calcutta does not serve only this state, and its problems are too vast to be manageable by West Bengal with its very meager resources.

The vast majority of informed observers, however, consider the urban problem in West Bengal, and especially the area of Greater Calcutta, an urgent matter of national—and even international—concern.

Biren Roy, president of the West Bengal Municipal Association, has suggested the need for the framing of a development plan for all of the municipalities of the state, with definite targets for physical improvement, a substantial increase in local revenues, and a direct association with the channels of national planning.[62] No progress on this proposal appears to have been made.

More broadly, the Government of West Bengal, under the Chief Minister, Dr. B. C. Roy, has submitted to the central government an ambitious plan for Calcutta's improvement.[63] This plan would involve the rehabilitation of refugee settlements; vastly improving drainage, sewerage, garbage disposal, and drinking-water supply (along lines suggested by the World Health Organization); the building of a new city south of Calcutta for at least 150,000 people; and many other constructive (and expensive) projects. The "Roy Plan" reflects, in part, the massive program for Calcutta recommended by the International Bank's mission to India of 1960, headed by Mr. Michael Hoffman, whose report is said to include a devastating criticism of present conditions in Calcutta, followed by a plan for its reconstruction.[64] It remains to be seen whether the Government of India will agree to interest itself in the Calcutta problem to the extent of allocating the funds needed to

---

[62] *Amrita Bazar Patrika* (Calcutta), July 11, 1959, p. 5.

[63] *The Economic Weekly* (Bombay), XII, No. 48 (November 26, 1960), 1711.

[64] The so-called "Hoffman Report" (note 23) has not been released for general use at the time of writing. Rather detailed comments on the report will be found in these issues of *The Economic Weekly* (Bombay): XII, No. 40 (October 1, 1960), 1469–1474; XII, No. 47 (November 19, 1960), 1668–1669; XII, No. 48 (November 26, 1960), 1711.

accomplish the minimum of critical goals. The World Bank suggests a $400 million emergency budget item for Greater Calcutta and the Port of Calcutta alone. It does not seem likely that a budget at that level could or would be provided from present available resources, but most observers agree that it would be a major step forward if the central government admitted that cities such as Calcutta are in themselves national resources and, as such, are entitled to a just share of national financial support.

Beyond plans and funds, perhaps the most urgent unfinished business in the Greater Calcutta metropolitan region is the reorganization of administrative structures to consolidate jurisdictions and to give broad powers to one planning and administering body (a development authority) to see the challenging job of rehabilitation through to completion. Such a reorganization is within the competence of the Government of West Bengal to effect. Given a reasonably responsible and competent planning and administrative structure, a major commitment of resources from central revenues, and full coöperation from the Government of West Bengal, multilateral and bilateral international participation in a "Calcutta Plan for Development" would likely follow.

Without drastic action soon, there is every reason to believe that Calcutta will erupt in steadily increasing and organized outbursts of social and economic discontent that arise from the despair within.[65]

---

[65] Since this paper was written, West Bengal has established a Calcutta Metropolitan Planning Organization, reporting to the Chief Minister and the Cabinet of the State Government, to draw up a master plan for the metropolitan region of Calcutta. The Government of India has allocated Rs. 40 crores (approximately $80 million) under the Third Five Year Plan in support of Calcutta's redevelopment, which sum may be matched from the U.S. Wheat Loan Fund. In addition, the Ford Foundation has provided a team of consultants, under Edward G. Echeverria, to assist in the preparation of the master plan. The World Bank and the World Health Organization, among other international bodies, are expected to assist at a later stage. A major assault against the ills of Calcutta outlined in this article now is in progress.

XXI

SOME OPERATIONAL PROBLEMS
IN URBAN AND REGIONAL PLANNING
AND DEVELOPMENT

Albert Mayer

There are certain recognized or classical causes for the failure of plans to develop and produce beneficial or optimum results. One is that they may remain on paper in great measure. This is exactly what happened to so many of the plans made a generation ago in the West, whose creators and whose clients failed to understand the need for close, continuing participation by political leaders and parties (local and above), and by the population for whom the plans were made. Another classical cause of failure has been the inadequacy of the premises: the inability to grasp the underlying conditions and to foresee their changes, or adequately influence them; or the omission of a mechanism to observe and take change into account as time passed.

Failure can—and characteristically does—occur for quite different reasons. Too little recognized is the fact that unless there is sustained emphasis on the quality and thoroughness of execution, physical targets may be met, but the goals of planning missed. By "goals" I mean such objectives as: greater production and productivity; economic utilization of space and the facilities provided; reduction of the friction of space and the improvement of traffic conditions; reduction of social tensions; and the achievement of collateral and over-all effects, of which the particular plan should be only a part or fulcrum. This last objective is particularly critical, for these collateral effects, if achieved, may enhance the value and impact of the plan and widen its radiating effects, with negligible extra cost. Otherwise, the plan may fail to activate them, or unknowingly allow them a negative effect, thus diminishing the effectiveness of the planning. In India the planners, and particularly the executants of plans, tend to be excessively "straight-line" in their thinking and decisions, and, thus, to think and act in terms of a single restricted aim, usually strictly departmental—a characterization which will be illustrated later on.

It is the intention of this paper to highlight the importance of operational considerations in the attainment of planning objectives, to explore these operational requirements, and to see in some detail what is involved. This task will be undertaken chiefly by identifying and describing important types of cases where such considerations are often absent, and by explicating the losses incurred, or the potential advantages missed. Thus, the main purpose of this paper is to pose problems; but at the end it proposes to do some generalizing, which may point toward conclusions or approaches to solutions.

The issue of this paper may become clearer if, at the outset, we focus upon a concrete example of planning which failed largely as the result of an inadequate understanding of operational considerations. The example is taken from Caracas, Venezuela.

In Caracas a vast housing program was undertaken at subsidized rents, with the objectives of clearing slums and of creating good housing for families of low income. The physical program was tackled with energy and determination, and during four years, 1954–1958, housing for about 180,000 people was constructed. Yet, in 1958, conditions were already so deplorable that an international team of specialists was called upon to diagnose the situation and offer advice. There had been tremendous losses accruing from unpaid rents; the lack of social adaptation of the residents had led to maintenance difficulties on a large scale; juvenile delinquency and crime rates had sharply increased. "In effect," as the experts testified, "a civil anarchy prevailed." [1]

Obviously, such a case as this is complicated, and there were a number of contributing factors. From the report on the situation, however, it is evident that there had been, in fact, a serious neglect of operational requirements. The following quotation makes this clear:

The projects cost roughly 200 million dollars for 180,000 persons . . . but the accompanying social, economic and administrative difficulties were found to

[1] The information relating to the Caracas project is taken from a summary of the experts' report in the October, 1959, issue of *The Journal of Housing* (National Association of Housing and Development Officials, 1313 E. 60th St., Chicago), pp. 311–314. Quotations are from this summary, written by Eric Carlson, technical adviser in the Central Coordinating and Planning Office of the Republic of Venezuela.

be so serious that in effect a civil anarchy prevailed . . . [The advisers] recommend long-term steps for the management of the super-blocks and the integration of their inhabitants with the community by means of education and social programs . . . The architectural and technical deficiencies were found to be less important than the administrative and management considerations [since] many of the families . . . have migrated from rural areas and are unequipped culturally, socially and emotionally for the shocks and disciplines imposed by urban standards and living conditions. They will need special guidance and orientation which should be provided initially by a much strengthened and improved social work and community development department.

Thus, the margin between success and failure was not so much in the realm of the physical and quantitative, as in the absence of imaginative and socially sound operation.

ANALYSIS OF TYPICAL CASES IN URBAN-REGIONAL PLANNING

We will now undertake a somewhat close analysis of four major situations which are typically encountered in urban-regional planning, and which embody different aspects of what is here called the operational component; we will relate them to the original act of planning and to planning concepts. These are largely cases that may be expected to arise when urban-regional planning gets fully in motion in India. They are:

1) Provision for a range of industrial employment in an urban-regional master plan, lest planned physical targets may be reached without achievement of major purposes-in-use, due to faulty but common operational practices.
2) Elements in the process of reorganizing the core of a central city—the operational, preparational, and timing factors involved.
3) The need for land reserves, and the operational problem of maintaining their availability until they are needed for development.
4) Gaps in our knowledge and experience—the need and opportunity for alternative solutions in specific areas, accompanied by close observation and evaluation of their operation.

THE CASE OF INDUSTRY

Let us trace the developmental and operational aspects of industrial planning in a metropolitan region. We will first outline the program and intentions of the planners. Then we will discuss what very well may (and frequently does) happen in course of operation, and which, to a substantial degree, negates the intentions and requirements of the plan, though the physical targets are achieved.

We will identify five types of physical and locational provision for industry:

1) "Flatted factories" are multistory concentrated developments intended for locations in the central district—in the case of Delhi, for small firms which need to be grouped centrally—which minimize the rental effect of central land cost by spreading it over a larger area of manufacturing space (i.e., over several stories).

2) Industrial estates, more openly planned, farther from city centers, generally with buildings constructed by the government or other entrepreneur and rented to moderate-sized industries.

3) Industrial areas or districts, consisting of large acreages zoned for industry of an extensive and fairly large character; situated necessarily in outlying areas, close to good transportation, and supplying employment to a substantial local residential area, often not yet in existence.

4) Industrial provision in outlying towns in the metropolitan area. While there will here also be a complement of small industries of the first two categories noted above, it is expected that such provision characteristically will be for extensive industries of the last category noted. These should be most typical because of the lower land and development costs, probable lower labor costs, and because large industries are more independent of the central nexus of services than are smaller ones, or can create what they require.

5) Finally, as worked out for the Delhi Region, development of "Central villages" as centers of village clusters, with a continuing element of agriculture or animal husbandry, but with the particular objective of setting up certain types of small industry which can be successfully competitive with enterprise in urban locations.

The multiple and linked intentions in planning this varied set of provisions for industry are (*a*) to provide for an over-all quantity and for types of employment best suited to the economy of the city and its region, and (*b*) to provide different types of space, intensity of use, and location which will suit the range of industry existing and desirable in a metropolitan area, based on surveys of past and present, and will meet the projections and desiderata for the future, in regard to the growth of population and the labor force, thus providing conditions conducive to growth of the individual industry.

This planning is intended to serve, as well, three other major objectives on behalf of the well-being and efficiency of the region.

The first of these is the amelioration of traffic, which in all cities is increasingly intolerable and dangerous, and particularly in the hearts of Indian cities with their almost inextricably mixed land-uses and their congestion. By means of the flatted factories it is intended to permit small industries which require central location—such as art industries, fashion industries, special metalworking industries, service industries, and repair shops—and to place such small and growing operations in selected central and semi-central locations, taking out the obsolete haphazard industries which make traffic rationalization and reorganization impossible. At the other end of the system are middle- and large-scale industries in the outlying open areas, whose market is largely regional and beyond, and whose generated traffic in materials can largely bypass the central areas. Drawing their working force from the locality largely (and to a very small degree from elsewhere by peripheral roads), local and reasonably self-contained districts are intended, with consequent minimization of traffic and costs of fares to workers.

Second, the extensive industry allocated to surrounding towns is intended to create regional "countermagnets" to divert part of the job-seeking in-migration, which is expected to intensify, and thus make the population projections for the central city reasonably meaningful and not desperately underestimated.

The third of the major collateral purposes of this industrial complex, closely related to the ones just discussed, is to unscramble the intense mixtures of incompatible land uses in the centers by siphoning off a substantial part of one of these uses. This will begin to create some looser conditions, leading into rehabilitation and redevelopment. More will be said of this operation in the next case analysis.

The central village and village-cluster development also bears on these major purposes; namely, to move out of the central city small industries and their workers—workers who need not be in the city, who have never become fully urbanized, and who could live more cheaply and happily in "urban villages." (This applies to art weavers, potters, etc.) Such a move would also help to lessen congestion and ease the process of reorganization. These new entities would likewise play their part in the countermagnet program and would, thus, help to slacken the pressure on the city.

All this *could* happen, *should* happen, and is *planned* to take place. But will it? The outcome depends very heavily on whether the actual operation will or will not follow the interlinked assumptions and requirements of the plan. Consider some specific facets. The plan requires that most of the flatted-factory floor space in the central areas be made available for the rehousing or expansion of existing troublesome small industries, industries in the way of land use rationalization. If, however, those in charge of operations do not carefully observe the purpose, and if most of the desirable space in flatted factories is opportunistically rented out to new firms, then we will not achieve the leverage of vacating a substantial number of existing occupancies, our traffic mix-ups will not have been eased, and our clearance and redevelopment operations will not have been advanced.

Or, again, in this same case let us suppose that the planners' intentions with respect to rental policy for the occupancy of the flatted factories are fairly well adhered to and that, as a result, a substantial amount of the old industrial hovels are vacated. Unless there is very serious determination to keep the vacated premises empty until clearance and development of a sizable area can take place, the vacated areas will be reoccupied by others. The situation then will be worse than before; the original conditions will again exist, and the flatted-factory concentrations will have been superimposed on the traffic and congestion pattern.

Consider next the industrial estate component. The planners would have in mind two types of occupancy. First, the drawing-off from the central areas of small firms which have outgrown the restricted spaces available yet are not big enough to move into the extensive areas where they would need to build for themselves. It is important to set aside a large portion of the available area for this group, so as to continue the process of making the central city viable, an economically and socially effective entity. The second would envisage a proportion of new industry to satisfy part of the need for new jobs for the growing population. These are the intentions and the reasons therefor. Will the operating people effect them?

Very likely not. The tendency will be to rent on a first-come, first-served basis, so as to show the quickest possible results, and in particular to favor new outside concerns which the "booster" psychology thrives on, and which obviously make more interesting news than the orderly moving-in of occupants transferring from the critical areas and congestion of the central city. Thus, here too, the physical targets may all be carried out, but the objectives sought may be seriously undermined or far from fulfilled.

I hope it is clear that such situations are not conjured up to prove a thesis, but are just the kind of thing that happens all the time. It should be equally clear that there should be no intent on the planners' part to specify any exact percentages of desired occupancy, for it obviously is impossible to foresee so closely and certainly is impossible to carry out any such refined operation. On the other hand, there must not be a really serious divergence between the planners' intentions and the execution if there is not to be a fatal breakdown of the plan.

With regard to the provision of large areas for extensive industry on the outskirts of the central city and in the regional cities, two points must be covered, on the tactical side, both involving the question of timing. One of the major purposes of city and regional planning is the creation of more or less self-contained "districts" or subcities, where work and habitation are integrated and are reasonably close to each other. Failure to synchronize the creation of the three major elements—work, residence, and social-commercial facilities—may cause new imbalances as serious as the ones to be cured. The second is this: at what stage do we start locating extensive industries into the regional towns if we are to build these up as countermagnets against excessive pressure impinging on the central city, and how? In their present state of mind, Indian industrialists want overwhelmingly to be attached to the central city or its outskirts, unless there is some special natural resource advantage drawing them elsewhere. In Western countries there is enough disenchantment with the big city and its headaches so that many industrialists readily locate away from the big cities. The Indian industrial climate has not yet reached that point. Also, the industrialists' operating experience or that of their friends or competitors in the smaller city or the specially created township is disappointing. The new towns are never quite finished; a critical road remains unpaved; a promised shopping center is not completed, or a school; the railway station facilities remain Class B, though Class A was promised. All these are operational lapses, and many of them are small, but they are decisive. Thus, there is the problem of how to prepare and get into actual motion the planned intentions of time and place.

Finally, in this industrial-economic regional equation, there is the concept of the central village and cluster in the region. It is an attractive and probably quite feasible idea. It may become one of the serious keys to regional solutions, to controllable urban population dispositions, to the very necessary economy of capital expenditure in an underdeveloped country, because of its considerably cheaper housing and services. It is not, however, the easiest road. It is certainly not a present trend. To realize it, there must be: close coördination of provision of industrial facilities, marketing facilities in the new location, and moving and settlement of workers and their families; acquisition of rural land without arousing local hostility; careful selection, preparation, and training of the new-comers; close working with the existing population to create under-standing and avoid clashes; follow-up after implementation to minimize and help to remedy the major difficulties and inadequacies that inevitably arise.

If new trends are to be set in motion successfully, they must be attacked in terms of full resources and rigorous determination. Otherwise, they should not be attempted, for it too often happens that essentially good ideas, which should and could have succeeded, are discarded in frustration.

OPERATING ON THE CORE OF THE CENTRAL CITY

The reorganization of the city core and its related areas is of course a key objective in any urban-regional plan. The causes of advanced obsolescence are clear: drastic changes in use patterns and a worsening of the traffic problem since the existing physical con-figuration was structured; increases in the quantity and complexity of functions to serve a much larger and more far-flung population and its employments, as well as a changed technological situation; greatly increased congestion; and, in the Indian situation, noxious industries chockablock with living quarters.

One advantage of the situation (or one former advantage that survives, with many countervailing disadvantages) is the close proximity of workplace and residence. To those who are there now, this proximity seems both convenient and economical, which in a sense, indeed, it is: a few minutes to reach work, and no expendi-ture for bus fare; also, one's friends, one's business competitors, one's service arrangements are close at hand. This point of view is that of the "insider," and except for a relatively few, excep-tionally enterprising businessmen who feel the disadvantages and have had the initiative and courage to leave the common competi-tive arena, the people and the business enterprises there see no adequate and compelling reason to be anywhere else. This state of reasonable satisfaction is accentuated by the low living require-ments of the majority of the residential population—who live in slums, are quite used to them, and, in a sense, help make them. This situation, however, is not economic. From the over-all point of view, the ill effects on public health and the traffic congestion and confusion (and consequent time losses) are very costly. The price to the general public of the saving, for example, in bus fares, is the drastically uneconomic occupancy of the most valuable and costly land in the city by the slum dwellers, who can pay only a pittance in rent, and in great measure similarly by slum industry. The same is true of the large residential compounds, uneconomic survivors of a totally different situation. Characteristically, there is the close intermixture of living quarters, wholesale and retail commerce and markets, storage godowns, and hand and machine and noxious industry.

To make available for redevelopment any one area of appreciable size with all these existing uses means synchronized development of seven or eight differentiated new areas where rationalized use can be achieved. This is, of course, a delicate set of operations. It involves a concerted moving of similar and related businesses—and these not by any means all found in the single restricted area to be cleared or rehabilitated—so that the nexus of functions and services, supplies, and marketing operations is not too seriously severed in the new areas; it should, rather, be improved.

The operation involves, further, a great deal of preparatory work over a considerable period among a number of levels of people and enterprises to create an atmosphere favorable to making these moves and adjustments; and it involves finding and buttressing leaders who will help to get them under way and sustain them. It includes identifying and working with private trade associations, producer coöperatives, and private welfare organizations where these can be found. It involves changing the self-held levels of demand into what might be called creative dissatisfaction and intent. In place of definite refusal or sullen acquiescence after endless delays and protests and political obstacles, there must be achieved a general state of mind of understanding and of corporate *élan*. For, to broaden the implications, the plan in the end—or, indeed, any great accomplishment—will not succeed amply on a basis of grudging acceptances, of barely achieved acquiescences.

LAND RESERVES

Another major operating problem concerns land reserves. Land reserves are, of course, of the essence of effective planning. For the planning must cover a long period, not less than twenty to twenty-five years. Unless land is held available in fairly well determined quantities and locations for specific future uses, obviously there is no plan, but merely a continuation of opportunistic development and operation, with government or a development authority paying high prices whenever a specific project is to be undertaken. Indeed, a tremendous problem lies ahead, and is already upon us, with the 4 per cent annual increase in urban population and the already high speculative prices of land.

Reserves are necessary to permit the eradication of the great inefficiencies and congestion of the present, and, especially, to take care of the more than doubling of population and economic activity in large urban areas over the next twenty years—a minimal figure even assuming the persistent development and success of a counter-magnet policy. In addition, there must be reserves for such purposes as green belts and regional recreation, for roads and ample rights of way not needed at this moment, but whose need in the next twenty years can be foreseen and planned.

The question relevant here is actual, continual, physical control over land whose development is not scheduled immediately, but in, say, five years, or eight years, or fifteen years. This physical problem arises from an anarchic attitude to land development which manifests itself in squatting, and in what in India we call "un-authorized constructions," which may be described roughly as a more expensive and elaborate form of squatting. This antiplanning phenomenon takes place on a vast scale around cities all over India, mainly in what might be called logical locations, i.e., locations where proper development would take place a few years later; but it is also quite extensive in illogical locations at considerable distances from transport, or in areas subject to flooding.

In any event, acquisition of needed land is a most serious problem. An extreme and famous case is the successful resistance to displacement, over a period of three years so far, of about 100 families of squatters in the Jamuna Bazaar area of Delhi, which has prevented the completion of a short stretch of the crucially important National By-Pass Road, which is otherwise completed, leaving a gap which has further bedeviled the increasingly troublesome traffic situation.

Complementing the anarchic attitude toward land shown by the city dwellers, there is an official reluctance to take action; and where action is initiated, political backing quails against the immediate and well-organized protests of the persons affected. In any case, the lack of staff makes it extremely difficult even to locate and identify all of the scattered violations—and in Indian cities these are numbered by the thousands. Consequently, a sense of vested interest is built up among those in illegal possession as they are left undisturbed over a length of time. In fact, this spurious vested interest is sometimes transferred to a second "purchaser," who sometimes knows—and often doesn't—that there is no legal title.

These two "natural" phenomena—anarchic attitudes and official failure to take sharp and determined action—are, of course, reinforced by the dire shortage of accommodation of any kind, most dire for housing and industry, and more particularly for the lower levels in those categories. But it is by no means confined to them, especially among the exploiters of the situation. There may be some future amelioration of the supply problem, and to that extent this disease may become less virulent.

The effect of this, however, will not be as conclusive as one might expect, both because the volume of new construction, and of housing in particular, cannot be adequate in an underdeveloped and crowded country for at least a number of years, and because in the lowest levels and lower-middle levels, people's physical-social demands or effectively developed needs are extremely low. Thus, many thousands of families continue to prefer the no-rent or negligible rent of a hovel to the higher rental of even a fairly heavily subsidized minimal-standard dwelling unit. (Incidentally, the modification of this attitude is in itself a problem that must be dealt with creatively by the operating organization.)

The problem is both puzzling and deeply rooted, and the search for a solution would take us more complexly into the Indian situation than would be appropriate for this paper. Nevertheless, if planning intentions are to be transformed into actual development, the exploration must be made and a solution will have to be discovered.

GAPS IN KNOWLEDGE—EXPLORATION BY OBSERVED ALTERNATIVES

In Indian planning today—and, indeed, in planning everywhere, in varying degrees—there are many unknowns in terms of what are optimum units of composition and configuration or texture within the total plan. This is particularly true of social relations. There is simply not enough information, not enough observed past experience, not enough in the way of studies covering many crucial problems. One principal and indispensable way to fill these gaps is now at hand because of the large and diverse numbers of new towns being created, such as the steel towns and towns connected with other new industries, and the large new housing developments in existing cities. There is a double duty incumbent on the operators or executants, not now being fulfilled.

In this vast volume of work there is plenty of opportunity to do some intelligent experimenting; to try out well-considered alternatives, consciously designed as such, that could clearly demonstrate advantages and disadvantages. Moreover, a careful program of observation and comparison is in order, so that lessons might be rapidly learned from which planning would gain in economy and effectiveness.

A few specific but typical examples may be cited to point this up.

In residential areas, democratic planning and outlook call for minimizing economic stratification, for the promotion of some intermingling. But, how do we do it? On how intimate a scale can we intermingle? In the same building unit? In the same street or around the same quadrangle? Or, perhaps, only in the same mohalla? Again, how far up and down can we safely go in the economic scale, in such a healthy attempt at intermingling? What are the other factors that affect such a policy favorably or unfavorably—such as caste, place of origin, type of job? One could readily set up and defend half-a-dozen different intelligent programs. This is just what should be planned, built, and carefully observed.

It would not cost any extra money, because even though we call these alternative programs "experiments" (which, indeed, they are or readily can be), so-many building units are going to be put up anyway. But instead of just building that much shelter, we owe it to ourselves to gain conscious comparative experience—an opportunity we are ignoring, as of now.

We have no real information, moreover, as to optimum sizes of neighborhood and subneighborhood, the desirable degree of homogeneity or heterogeneity, or the economics of placement; nor do we have quantified information on urban shopping. Here, again, if the present unpleasant and uneconomic agglomerations are to be effectively and happily transformed, the quickest way is to create conscious alternatives and observe them.

One additional illustration of this experimental or planned-alternative method is of such particular moment as to deserve fuller exposition.

The desperately questionable element in the urban-regional plan is the possibility of finding resources for carrying it out in any measurable period. This is true of the over-all development costs and of housing costs in particular. There is the capital cost of housing; the cost of subsidy for a large proportion of the people; the cost of community facilities. It seems quite impossible realistically to visualize a full-scale attack in all respects on the totality of the problem, in terms of foreseeable resources. While no one expects everything to happen at once, probably few, if any, have faced up to the scale of what can actually be accomplished, measured against total need.

What commonly happens is that in those projects that are constructed the base housing is first built, in itself much the major part of the cost. Generally, this housing is ready a very long time before community facilities are available; and the all-important skilled community workers and social organization may never get there.

Meantime, there is lack of acceptance by the occupants, and deterioration sets in, to a less or greater degree.

As an experiment, then, one might supply, right at the beginning, a full group or core-heart of simply designed community facilities for the new project, well staffed with competent workers; and various types of less-than-standard housing, or very temporary or embryonic housing, at a total cost much lower than the standard method, to be finished or replaced later on whenever possible by the people themselves. Comparison of the occupants' state of mind and well-being, at various points in time, under each system, would be a vital contribution.

Enough has been noted to demonstrate the importance and significance of such experiment and comparison, provided that it is well observed. Should, however, the enormous advantages of this technique become sufficiently clear, so that it came into operation, the other extreme would loom up as a danger to be avoided: namely, applying everywhere a single solution which experiment and observation had shown to be successful under certain specific (and therefore limited) conditions.

The technique *can* work. It may be noted that in Israel it is used now in considerable measure, so that there the experience is dynamic and is not a mere accumulation or multiplication of projects.

SOME GENERALIZATIONS

Some generalizations emerge from this variety of operational or hypothetical-operational cases, and from the author's actual experience in Indian planning and development. They can legitimately be considered as part of the diagnosis of this paper.

1. The first is that there is nothing like enough interplay, or grasp of the need for it, between the planners and the operating forces. This would account for the hypothetical industrial case, where different types of "wrong" occupants were permitted to occupy the various types of space prepared, to the detriment of the multipurposes of the plan. There are three aspects of this, as follows.

Planners do not sufficiently recognize the exigencies of operations and may set up requirements that are in fact difficult to carry out.

The operating forces may not be sufficiently aware of the planners' intentions. The operating men should be much more heavily and systematically involved in the original planning and its purposes, in the conferences and studies leading to the plan. This is desperately needed and should not be difficult to accomplish, but under Indian conditions it rarely exists, so far.

In the operational or developmental stage, the original planners should remain in the picture as observer-advisers—as the most necessary and least difficult step in the effective transmission of planners' intentions, and as an insurance against operational unawareness or disregard.

2. The second is that vis-à-vis the departments or ministries—central or state, as the case may be—strongly established for years and accustomed to "straight-line" operation on their own, the planning function and planning personnel are considered to be upstarts and, at least, lacking in seniority. Thus, if the operational people are genuinely to perform according to plan, to coördinate with each other and fructify each other's hitherto straight-line efforts, to work out the correct timing of operations, there must be a strong and continued expression of attitude and intention on the part of ministers and political leaders. Only then will they be sending senior men, and regularly, to participate genuinely; only then will the points in the first category have meaning and impact.

3. Of all the negative operational factors which act adversely on the achievement of the purposes, the effectiveness, and the collateral radiating effects of planning, the most pernicious is the failure to employ sufficient operating personnel—in numbers, quality, and varied skills. This is true in a number of ways.

The fact is that, in India, at the skilled or technical level a much higher expenditure on staff is required per unit of physical product or construction than is ever engaged, if maximum efficiency, effectiveness, and economy are to be achieved. Actually, when millions of rupees are being spent on physical development, it is desperately important and highly economical to have enough staff, with the right qualifications, to achieve both lower field costs (for better quality of product) and greater collateral and radiating effects in the result.

While part of the understaffing is due to scarcity of trained personnel, much more is due to failure to recognize the need, and to a curious prejudice against staff as such—possibly stemming from the habitual or traditional excess of clerks on the payrolls of secretariats. It is easier to convince a minister, or the all-powerful Finance Department scrutinizers, to approve a million rupees for physical expenditure, than Rs. 800 a month for a needed staff member—although, where technical and social results are being sought, understaffing is the poorest possible economy.

In so many of our instances in planning and development we are breaking new ground. We are trying to get people to do things that they are not accustomed to doing and are even prejudiced against. We are trying to get them to move into new areas; we are (or should be) trying to convert recent villagers into effective urban citizens. All this involves "atmospheric" change and well-trained preparation, long before actual operations are undertaken. Yet, it is either very difficult or impossible to obtain appreciable preparational staff—indeed, any at all—a year or more ahead of time, which is a minimum requirement. Likewise needed are skilled personnel of varied professional qualifications to prepare the ground and prepare the inhabitants of areas into which we plan to move, to follow through so that the final stages of field work shall be fully implemented, not left with many loose ends; and particularly to help during the critical early period of operations. This work is absolutely essential if we are to give our planning a fair chance and develop anything like a maximum of potential at minimum overall cost. Again, we must observe what we are doing, and evaluate and compare, so as to learn and improve. Thus, the operation must include some staff for field research, which may be an excessively fancy name for a pragmatically necessary operation. This is necessary throughout the system, and in particular, of course, we will not get anything like value out of the very large housing efforts by the Ministry of Works, Housing and Supply, and by the localities, if we cannot consciously set up, and follow through with observation and evaluation, the types of alternatives noted above.

The time is due and overdue for a new attitude toward the whole question of staff. The current habit must be changed, which consists of considering the size of the staff or payroll per se, and operating on the basis that there is some inherent merit in small (and low-paid) staff. The real question is one of relationship: what is the economic or economic-social gain in product-economy, per unit of staff expenditure? This is the critical relationship and the proper criterion. In this light, the smallest staff may, indeed, be the most wasteful. It would be, of course, just as absurd to leave the implication that there is inherent merit in a large staff. Long overdue, however, is the extension and serious application of the input-output concept to the question of staff, a concept which already has proved so fruitful in its other present applications.

There are two other aspects in which a sharply new attitude toward staff is urgently important. It will have been seen that development work is complex, carried forward on a number of planes, with many ramifications. There cannot be just one Deputy Commissioner (Development), with a horde of minor persons under him. Reverting to our examples, the industrial operation requires a highly resourceful, decisive man. So does the central redevelopment and development operation. So does the central-village countermagnet operation. And so on. Not only do the complexity, importance, and scale of these jobs themselves demand it, but in dealing with the entrenched and old-established departments any junior person will get nowhere.

Finally, we have to recognize that the usual peripatetic, shifting civil service concept will not, in this new development arena, "deliver the goods." Specialized knowledge and experience, already present or to be acquired, are the *sine qua non* here. For example, it will take more than the experience of a good district magistrate, with all his rough-and-ready resourcefulness, to cope with development work effectively. The usual concept may afford the best or only way to begin, but let us beware of shifting any competent man after a year or two have begun to yield him the hard-earned experience and skill that are so indispensable.

These, then, are some of the stakes and problems involved in the operation of urban-regional development programs, and some possible illustrative generalizations. We are on the threshold of new concepts and new undertakings which are a good deal more interwoven and involve a good deal more technical, social, and economic complexity than have generally been encountered or, at least, recognized. If planning is to be realized in something approaching its full potential in both development and operations, the two must become much more closely linked. A long, hard look must be taken at the new dimensions required of operation and execution.

XXII

THE FUTURE OF INDIAN CITIES: NATIONAL ISSUES AND GOALS

Asoka Mehta

It is not an easy task to summarize the rich and varied discourses that we had at the Seminar on Urbanization in India.[1] The discussion was always interesting and often exciting and rewarding. Like multicolored printing, every session helped to fill the design further. It is obvious that the participants have emerged from their deliberations with a more profound understanding of the nature of the problems, and with added humility because of the difficulties involved in their solution.

Two tremendous forces have been unleashed in India today: a relatively rapid rate of population growth and an increasingly rapid rate of urbanization. If these forces are allowed to operate unchecked, the results assuredly will be explosive. The population of India can reach by the year 2000 the figure of a billion, with a third of that number crowding into urban areas. A fivefold increase in the urban population in as many decades would pose a challenge unmatched before. These population changes could result in the migration of 85 million people from rural to urban areas. Even allowing for the dislocations caused by the war and the partition of the country, between 1941 and 1951 the rural-to-urban migration involved only some nine million people. Such vast

[1] This chapter is the text of Asoka Mehta's address, delivered at the final session of the Seminar on Urbanization in India at the Claremont Hotel, Berkeley, California, July 1, 1960. Mr. Mehta had been asked to give a personal summing-up of the seminar; his views are his own, and do not necessarily represent those of the Government of India.—*Ed.*

currents of migrants can in time bloat the major cities into metropolises of fantastic size, such as a Calcutta with a population of 66
million. The social implications of such urban agglomerations are
staggering.

On the other hand, the alternative to urbanization, under conditions of rising population, may be even more terrifying. Even
if someone wanted to stop the waves of migrants, he would soon
discover with King Canute that it cannot be done. All that is possible is to devise wise countervailing policies.

Two obvious conclusions need to be accepted immediately: the
economic development in which India is now engaged has to be
accelerated, and, simultaneously, determined support must be given
to family planning. No expenditure on the development of family-
planning science, its techniques, and the diffusion of the knowledge
gained can be deemed excessive. The sooner we slow down the
surge of population growth, the easier will become all other future
tasks of social engineering.

It seems to be a general rule that the more recently in history
the process of industrialization has occurred, the faster is its rate,
including that of urbanization. National policies, however, can
provide, within limits, direction to urbanization and shape the
size and patterns of towns and cities. What happens to the number, location, and condition of the people is not preordained, but
is the result of decisions taken by the people. It is the task of policy
makers to assist the people in making wise decisions.

There is some relationship between urbanization and economic
development, but it is rarely direct and causal. The largest towns
in India have tended to grow fastest and to have more industry,
but the most rapidly growing towns do not necessarily have particularly high proportions of industry. It is significant to note that
at a similar level of urbanization the countries of Europe were
more industrialized than India is now. As India moves forward in
its scale of industrialization, the phenomenon is likely to persist;
economic slack, together with a lack of capital resources needed to
absorb all migrants into meaningful urban occupations, is likely to
result in imperfectly committed urbanites. The cost of providing
urban amenities will be very large and the danger of "a tale of two
cities" will be ever present. In terms of available resources, India
will remain "overurbanized" for a long time. Hence the supreme
need of conscious policy intervention.

Even when we envisage an increase in the urban population by
100 million over the next twenty years, the rural population still
would expand by equal numbers. If urbanization is not to get out
of control, if its flood is not to overwhelm us, determined efforts

will have to be made to improve the texture of life and work both in the urban *and* the rural areas.

Whether in the cities or in the towns, there are today considerable congestion and inadequate social amenities. For a variety of reasons Indian towns have developed highly congested cores, and —whether that density is diluted or not—any increase in the congestion, or its wholesale repetition in the new or growing towns, would be the final condemnation of current trends. To the extent that a higher density is inescapable in the Indian situation, ampler civic amenities must be provided.

It would be wrong to view an urban unit, whether large or small, in isolation. Nor should the problem be posed independently of the rural regions surrounding the urban areas. From the great city to the villages surrounding there is a certain continuum, and a socially worth-while solution will have to plan development for a spectrum of related communities in varying stages of urban life.

If the big cities are not to be flooded, it will not be enough to replan them in order to reopen their "lungs" and to unscramble the intense mixtures and incompatibilities of land uses in their centers. It will be necessary also to siphon off a substantial part of these present land uses to new areas to be opened up, and it will be equally necessary to develop self-sufficient satellite towns to hold the job-seeking migrants from the city. The creation of countermagnet towns around the big cities might raise the status and improve the position of a number of smaller towns on the urban periphery that today are stagnating. Simultaneous attention to outer areas and to the metropolitan area is necessary for effective solutions.

The relationship between towns (or even cities) and the surrounding rural areas still is somewhat obscure. To what extent is the dynamic influence of the city felt, and cultural diffusion achieved, in the rural hinterland? Whatever be its present form, the growth of literacy, the spread of newspapers and other media of communication, the development of transport, and the economic renaissance are likely to make the relationship more intimate and the contacts more stimulating. It will, therefore, be necessary— and perhaps not too difficult—to foster parallel growth of the rural areas; the future development of towns and cities will form an integral part of a well-thought-out regional development. The more that development is tackled regionally, the less will be the surge of city-bound migrants and the fewer the social evils that ultimately would have to be corrected for family survival. A rural-versus-urban conflict would be fatal equally to our democracy and to our economic growth. A regional approach to urban development, with its mixture of occupations, its metropolitan core, satellite towns, and rural communities engaged in a variety of agricultural pursuits and industrial activities sharing many common amenities like transport, electricity, plus educational and health facilities, would bridge the psychological gulf and soften the traditional antagonism of the village to the city, an antagonism that can go as deep as any sense of anticolonialism.

Such parallel or related patterns of development are likely to be more difficult, and face greater problems of administrative coördination, than the simple town-planning known in earlier decades. But such purely localized planning cannot be attempted today; if tried, it would prove self-defeating because of the anticipated unrestricted inrush of migrants. When a river is to be trained, it must be directed both at its source and farther down its flow; similarly, the flood of urbanization must be attended at its source, during its course, and at the metropolitan estuary.

While it will be necessary to give attention to the villages in our development plans, it is obvious that the contrast between them and the cities cannot disappear. But the contrast cannot remain as stark as it is today, nor can the contrast inside the city remain as mocking to our aspirations as it is at present. The accent in the cities will have to be on simplicity and utility. Every effort will have to be made to use locally available resources, to foster self-help among the citizens, and to evoke community solidarity. In that sense, while the villages will have to be stirred with new ambitions and provided with new and varied occupational possibilities, in the towns and cities some of the rustic values will have to be revived. The range of amenities in the two parts will vary, but the difference cannot be very large, nor can the difference inside the city remain as glaring as it is today. This means that regionally articulated towns and cities will afford modernity and beauty mainly in community buildings and recreation areas; other parts will have to move along with simplicity and homespun grace. If the towns and cities are to escape drabness, community life will have to rediscover its inner richness, and centers of community activities—buildings, parks, landscapes—will have to receive fullest aesthetic attention.

Changes in these directions can be made only when economic development is actively pursued. India is now engaged in purposeful development. The perspective opened up proposes a fourfold increase in national income over the next twenty years, and with other new phases of economic transformation brought about by total investments of Rs. 800 billion. These investments would increase the production of key materials like electricity, steel, coal, cement, fertilizers, and machinery, while at the same time increasing the range and output of consumers' goods substantially. Occupational opportunities would be greatly expanded, and over 12 million persons would be engaged in manufacturing and mining. Such development can provide a vital tool for the purposes of region-based urban development through the power held by the government in the locating of industry.

Large factories can be planted deliberately in a small town or a new town, and, as the employment multiplier is high, growing urban communities can crystallize in these locations. Expansion of the facilities of transport, credit, technical aid, etc., can encourage the medium and small industries to move out of the cities. The proliferation of industrial estates holds considerable promise in that direction. Unfortunately, the instruments for aiding small industries have so far not been used, or have not worked, as tools for dispersal, nor have effective district-development campaigns been organized.

Industrial development in established urban surroundings might involve heavy social overheads. Encouragement to industry to set up plants around a town that is provided with good radiating roads and transport and that has an adequate nucleus of banking and other services might help both the industries and the workers. The workers could continue to live in their rural homes, escape the disruption of family life and the inconveniences of city-slum life, and augment their earnings by extra incomes on the farm. The employers would be able to keep wage levels somewhat lower. In the early phase of industrial and economic development, a class that shares the life of the farmer as well as the worker can be of great economic and social importance. It would narrow the distance between agriculture and industry and achieve an intertwining of occupational and social interests.

On the policy level, the Government of India not only accepts the wide distribution of location of industries, but also favors diversion of production to medium and small industries. In practice, the policy has not yielded significant results. Licensing powers have not helped the dispersal of industries much, but often have set hurdles in the way of new entrepreneurs. In practice, the government has not been able to break away from the advantages of industrial constellation or from the assumption that the future lies with big and medium-sized cities. Countervailing forces against the inevitable attraction of these established places remain weak.

Even though the objectives are to spread out industrialization as far as possible and to obtain productive results as quickly as possible, little has been done to reorient technology in the direction of capital-saving or employment-intensive methods of production. Neither in India nor abroad does such research receive adequate sponsorship. The development of agro-industrial activities in rural areas, in spite of some extension of electrification to larger villages, has remained an unrealized objective. Now that in some of the urban development plans there is provision for encouraging clusters of villages with industrial components, perhaps concrete experience will be gained to assist in the making of general policy.

All the ingenuity and creativity of directional development will not arrest the growth of existing cities. To correct inefficiencies, to achieve decongestion, and to provide for inevitable expansion, the greatest attention will have to be given to land reserves. With a 4 per cent annual increase in urban population, a speculative boom in land can heavily load the dice against productive development unless firm measures are taken well in advance. A long-range policy of land reserves can be worked out if the purchase of urban-development land is made on lines somewhat similar to those used in some states in India to extinguish zamindari rights.

While it is better to plan the growth of cities, we cannot overlook the need for a reorganization of existing cities. These cities contain such swamps of urban life that, unless they are partially drained, the life of fresh currents of migrants is bound to get befouled. Both in Bombay and in Calcutta hundreds of thousands of citizens have no homes except the pavements and sidewalks of the city: in the case of Calcutta, four out of ten families sleep on the streets or fend for themselves. Three fourths of the housing shortage is in the four main cities of India. In Bombay, 8 per cent of the family dwellers have no latrines at all; for Calcutta the figure is 12 per cent. Three quarters of the population of Bombay has no bathroom facilities of any kind, and for Calcutta the figure is 61 per cent. Similar details of the congestion and dilapidation of dwellings can be supplied. Such terrifying lags and lacks in the elementary amenities of life cannot be allowed to remain uncorrected, even if such amenities can be provided only as community, as distinct from household, facilities.

While structural reforms are necessary in the big cities—which are apt to become much bigger—equal attention will have to be paid to patchwork improvement. There is no escape from the dual approach of improvement and clearance in the matter of slums. Efforts that can elicit popular participation in civic improvements can play a vital role. Experiments recently carried out suggest that urban people are capable of discovering nuclei of community life in small neighborhood groups. When we realize that the blighted parts of the cities encompass as much as 10 to 60 per cent of the space, the process of rehabilitation achieved through group self-help assumes a key function. While family ties and caste loyalties have proved remarkably resistant to urban influences and have partially compensated against the anonymity and indifference of urban environments, it will be useful to seek leverages of change in the solidarity of small neighborhood groups and groups with linguistic affinities—social cohesions that appear to be significant. While it is difficult to forecast how long and how strongly the recuperative powers of group efforts and self-help can be elicited, it is obvious that in their absence, and in the face of apathy and cynicism, the task of urban reorganization would be well-nigh hopeless for the administration.

It will not be possible to provide even substandard pucka houses for all the people. Temporary dwellings of local and cheap materials will have to be utilized to meet the prevalent difficulties for a considerable time to come. Apart from the urgent need to concentrate research on the use of local and easily obtainable materials, plans must be made to lay out open housing areas with roads, lighting, community sanitation (and the organization of necessary services like post offices, schools, etc.) where the municipal authorities would provide only plinths and the people would put up their own simple dwellings. It perhaps may be useful to divert to general civic amenities in larger proportions than at present the resources that are available for both housing and other improvements. As noted above, we can compensate for substandard housing by more ample civic amenities, including community centers with varied uses and possibilities: for recreation, study, medical attention, etc.

Urban expansion is likely to draw in its vortex 20,000 to 25,000 acres of land annually. The proper development of this land in advance would obviate much later trouble. That means that a very large amount of urban-regional physical planning must be undertaken and accomplished over the next few years.

Substandard housing will be accepted and self-help generated mainly to the extent that ostentatious housing is rigorously curtailed. The places of attraction and adoration will have to be the centers of community life and work, and not the palatial dwellings of the rich. The more adequate the blossoming of such centers, the more rewarding will life appear to the many.

Whether we think of patchwork improvement, of reorganization of the cities that would involve displacement of some people and their moving to other areas, or of planning for future growth, it is patent that without widespread understanding of these objectives and the enlistment of popular interest—and, where possible, active coöperation—the major tasks will remain undone, or will be done badly. The governments and civic authorities have to discover methods of contacting, informing, and interesting citizens in the plans of change and development. A network of local organizations, neighborhood groups, and citizens' forums will have to complement a carefully thought-out program of public relations.

It will be helpful both in city planning and in wider regional development to develop a set of work projects—urban, semiurban, and rural—that can be undertaken to counteract slack in employment or in economic activity, and whose phasing falls into an understandable pattern in the eyes of the people. The key battle of urbanization will have to be fought on the emotional and intellectual rather than the material plane.

The powers, functions, and finances of local administration will have to be considerably revised. Traditional procedural delays will have to yield to practices of dispatch. The boundaries of local bodies, instead of being pushed outwards successively only in the wake of pressures that are allowed to grow, should be extended well in advance of such pressures. Local administration will have to develop flexibility. Just as it has been discovered in rural community development that administrative reorganization involving greater popular participation is a necessary precondition for success, so will it be found that urban community response will demand administrative devolution and decentralization. As we expect from the people group efforts and widening circles of interest and understanding, the administration will have to learn to work not in straight lines, but at many levels and through newly formed habits of consultation and coördination. Not only in local administration, but in the administration as a whole, there will need to be widespread distribution of responsibility and a predilection for the exercise of initiative, if similar responses are to be evoked from the people. The administration will have to realize that both space and time are equally scarce commodities in our cities: one cannot profitably be traded for the other.

As for the finances of local authorities, I believe that the distribution of financial resources should not end with the center and the states, but, rather, should bring within its orbit the needs of local authorities also. To the extent that urban efforts blossom into regional development, when urban and rural problems become enmeshed, it may be easier to siphon greater funds into this work. Regional development will necessitate new forms of administrative coördination. Here, as elsewhere, it would be wise not to impose one set of patterns, but to encourage different regions—at least, regions in different states—to experiment with a variety of methods and procedures. The fact, however, cannot be gainsaid that finance will remain the local authorities' principal bottleneck.

In the West, urbanization had the strength to transform rural areas into its own city image. In the meaningful future in India, such a transformation, whether desirable or not, is not possible. The danger in India is of decaying villages and unlivable cities. The central direction of policy has, therefore, to be to improve the conditions in the villages, in terms of productivity, occupational diversity, and social amenities, as far as possible, and in urban areas to prevent polarization between the submerged many and the cosmopolitan few. The standards of civic amenities in urban areas must be raised, so far as the mass of citizens is concerned, but they cannot be allowed to become wholly unrelated to the rural areas. As in industrialization we conceive of a complex of highly modernized key industries and an expanding spread of employment-intensive medium and small industries, so we will have to think of the solution of urbanization in terms of significantly satisfactory community buildings, parks, etc., and the leveling-off of housing and other facilities, not just for the underprivileged, but as a general norm. If our anchorage in such economic and social policies is abandoned, the nation will face disaster. Our policies have to be sociologically controlled, not ideally envisaged.

Part 5

CONCLUSION

XXIII

A SURVEY OF THE LITERATURE
ON URBANIZATION IN INDIA

Bert F. Hoselitz

During the last few years a flood of publications has appeared on various aspects of urbanization in India. Though it is impossible to give a precise index of the recent and increasing attention paid to this field in India, an indication of the trend is provided by the fact that an annual social science bibliography for India contained one entry on "cities" in its 1953 issue, whereas it contained 23 such entries four years later.[1]

The reason for this increased concern with urbanization seems clear. The census of 1951 revealed an unprecedented growth of towns and cities in India. Urban population, which in 1941 amounted to 13.9 per cent of the total population, made up 17.3 per cent of a larger population in 1951. Whereas the total population of the Indian Union grew by 13.3 per cent in the decade 1941–1951, the urban population grew by 34.8 per cent in the same period. Moreover, there is every indication that the pace of urban growth is continuing, probably at an increasing rate, and that India will boast in 1961 not 77 cities with populations of 100,000 or more (as she had in 1951), but possibly well over 100 cities of that size.

The growth of urban places in and by itself would be of less concern if it did not produce at the same time a number of social

Reprinted, with additions and changes, from *Annals of the Association of American Geographers,* XLIX, No. 2 (June, 1959), 223–231.

[1] UNESCO, Research Centre on the Social Implication of Industrialization in Southern Asia, *Social Science Bibliography, India* (Calcutta, 1953), II, 98, and *Social Science Bibliography, India-Pakistan* (1957), VI, 148.

problems which are new and demand constructive solutions. Unemployment in Indian cities is high, especially among educated persons, and this creates serious social and political problems. The growth of cities is due in large part to immigration, the conditions and causes of which are still little understood. Moreover, housing, water supply, and sanitary services are sorely lacking in Indian cities, and the rapid growth of population creates increasing pressures for supplying even minimum facilities of this kind. This makes necessary some action in the direction of urban planning in order to better balance short-run and long-run needs. Much of the present growth of cities takes place by the building of shantytowns —bustees—which are being established on any piece of land that happens to be available. Indian cities, and especially the smaller towns, suffer from a plethora of slums; and general conditions of overcrowding and absence of facilities in urban places in India are perhaps best characterized if we compare urban densities in India with those in other countries.

In 1951 Greater Bombay had a density of 25,579 persons per square mile; Ahmedabad, 38,834; and Surat, 58,723.[2] Corresponding densities in Chicago (1939) were 21,093 persons per square mile, but one must bear in mind that in India most residential dwellings are only one-story, whereas many residential dwellings in Chicago are several stories. These figures of population density refer to the over-all population and area both of Indian cities and Chicago. More revealing comparisons are possible if we look at densities in specific sections of cities. For example, according to the 1951 census the density in Old Delhi was 136,536 persons per square mile, whereas the corresponding density in New Delhi was 8,419 persons per square mile. In Chicago, in 1939, densities in what were designated as blighted areas were 41,307 persons per square mile; in areas designated as "stable" it was 17,989 persons per square mile. In other words, New Delhi had a lower density than what was considered the urban norm for an American city, but Old Delhi—and this includes areas which would be designated as slums, as well as areas not so considered—had a density almost four times as high as a blighted area in an American city. The vast compression of human beings in small spaces in Indian cities becomes even clearer if we consider that in three of the eighteen wards of Old Delhi densities of over 400,000 persons per square mile were observed, and that another four wards

---

[2] R. K. Patil and K. M. Talati, "Trends in Urbanisation of Surat City: A Case Study," in Indian Economic Association, *Papers Read at the 39th Annual Conference of the I. E. A., 1958* (Bombay, 1958), p. 79.

showed densities of over 275,000 persons per square mile. Only five wards out of the eighteen had densities of less than 100,000 persons per square mile. Similar ranges in density and similar peak densities are reported also from other Indian cities, e.g., Aligarh and Bombay. In the latter city the lowest densities are found in Upper Colaba, with 14,528 persons per square mile in 1951; the highest densities are found in the Bhuleshwar section of C Ward, with 873,984 persons per square mile. Though here multistory buildings are the rule, the terrible overcrowding of the Bombay slums is made vividly clear by these figures. In Aligarh, the differences in density, though substantial, are somewhat less; in 1951 they ranged from 4,928 persons per square mile in the Civil Lines to 136,384 persons per square mile in Kanwariganj Ward.[3]

The immediate impetus for the study of urban conditions in India came from several quarters. In 1952 UNESCO sponsored a comparative study of immigration to cities in several South Asian countries. These studies were published as *The Social Implications of Industrialization and Urbanization;* two of the five studies in the volume relate to Indian cities (Bombay and Delhi).[4] At approximately the same time the Indian Sociological Association, and somewhat later the Indian Economic Association, made the discussion of urbanization processes topics of their annual meetings. Finally, the Research Programmes Committee of the Planning Commission sponsored studies of the socioeconomic conditions prevailing in some twenty major cities of India. Though each research group charged with the analysis of any one city had a fairly high degree of freedom to follow its own method of investigation, many of these studies were patterned after the urban surveys which had

---

[3] The densities for Delhi have been taken from Delhi Development Authority, *Draft Master Plan for Delhi* (Delhi: Delhi Development Authority, 1960), II, 1. The densities for Chicago are taken from W. H. Ludlow, "Urban Densities and Their Costs: An Exploration into the Economics of Population Densities and Urban Patterns," in Coleman Woodbury (ed.), *Urban Redevelopment: Problems and Practices* (Chicago: University of Chicago Press, 1953), p. 213. The data for Bombay and Aligarh wards are taken from C. Rajagopalan, "Bombay: A Study in Urban Demography and Ecology," *Sociological Bulletin,* IX, No. 1 (March, 1960), 37–38, and Howard F. Hirt, "Spatial Aspects of the Housing Problem in Aligarh, U.P., India," *Population Review,* II, No. 1 (January, 1960), 44.

[4] UNESCO, Research Centre on the Social Implications of Industrialization in Southern Asia, *The Social Implications of Industrialization and Urbanization* (Calcutta: Research Centre on the Social Implications of Industrialization in Southern Asia, 1956). See, especially the papers by P. N. Prabhu, "Bombay: A Study of the Social Effects of Urbanization," pp. 49–106, and M. B. Deshmukh, "Delhi: A Study of Floating Migration," pp. 143–226. See also a general study on urbanization in southern Asia: Philip M. Hauser (ed.), *Urbanization in Asia and the Far East* (Calcutta: Research Centre on the Social Implications of Industrialization in Southern Asia, 1957).

been done during the war and the immediate postwar period by
the Gokhale Institute at Poona.[5] The surveys produced under the
auspices of the Research Programmes Committee present, without doubt, the greatest amount of actual data which are becoming
available on socioeconomic conditions in Indian cities.

It is a pity, however, that the researchers who have undertaken
these studies have displayed little imagination and have kept
strictly to preconceived patterns of research. Hence, ecological
problems are left unexplored, little attention is given to the relation between a city and its immediate hinterland, and the spatial
distributions within a city, in general, and within the larger city
region are completely neglected. This is unfortunate, because it
not only robs us of a good deal of geographical knowledge of
Indian cities which might easily have been collected—it also de-
prives these surveys of a good deal of their usefulness for urban
planning, a task which eventually will become indispensable. So
far, several of these surveys have become available in book form,
among which the one on Poona is the largest. The study on Calcutta, though somewhat shorter, shows the greatest degree of original insight, whereas the volumes on Hyderabad-Secunderabad and
Baroda, though containing some interesting data, show no genuine
originality.[6] A brief version of the report on Jamshedpur is also
available, so far only in the form of a journal article, but the full
version in book form will soon become available. The remaining
volumes should appear within the next two or three years. When
the whole series is published, it will constitute the most extensive
collection of data on various social and economic characteristics—
family composition, number and composition of immigrants, earnings, employment and unemployment, housing conditions and associated facilities, and general economic conditions of the urban population—of the city population in any Asian country.

Although the urban studies undertaken under the auspices of the
Research Programmes Committee constitute perhaps the most

---

[5] D. R. Gadgil, *Poona: A Socio-Economic Survey,* Part I (Poona: Gokhale Institute
of Politics and Economics, 1945), and Part II (Poona: Gokhale Institute of Politics and
Economics, 1952); R. G. Kakade, *The Socio-Economic Survey of Weaving Communities in Sholapur* (Poona: Gokhale Institute of Politics and Economics, 1947); N. V.
Sovani, *The Social Survey of Kolhapur City,* Part I (Poona: Gokhale Institute of Politics and Economics, 1948), and Parts II and III (Poona: Gokhale Institute of Politics
and Economics, 1951–52).

[6] N. V. Sovani, D. P. Apte, and R. G. Pendse, *Poona: A Re-Survey* (Poona: Gokhale
Institute of Politics and Economics, 1956); S. N. Sen, *The City of Calcutta: A Socio-
Economic Survey, 1954–55 to 57–58* (Calcutta: Firma K. L. Mukhopadhyay, 1960);
S. Kesave Iyengar, *A Socio-Economic Survey of Hyderabad-Secunderabad City Area*
(Hyderabad: Government Press, 1957); H. C. Malkani, *A Socio-Economic Survey of
Baroda City* (Baroda: Sadhana Press, 1958); B. R. Misra, "Socio-Economic Survey
of Jamshedpur," *Economic Papers* II (November, 1957), 1–26.

massive survey on urban socioeconomic conditions, they do not exhaust the whole body of urban research in India. Basic to all of it are a number of "inventory" studies of recent growth patterns and the spatial distribution of Indian cities, which have been undertaken by different persons at approximately the same time and which have been made as a result of the very extensive details on the demography of Indian cities published in Volume I, Part II-A, of the *Census of India, 1951.*[7] Some of these studies, notably the papers by G. S. Ghurye, V. Nath, S. Guha, C. B. Mamoria, and a number of contributors to the symposium on "Urban Development Trends in India" sponsored by the Indian Economic Association, deal with growth patterns of urban India during the last fifty years.[8] Though these papers present a historical depth, they do not carry the discussion of urbanization trends back of the early censuses, and only one recent article, by R. I. Crane, contains also an analysis of urban patterns in India before the British conquest.[9] The papers by Ghurye, Nath, and some of the contributors to the Indian Economic Association's symposium (notably S. B. Bagal, A. Bose, and N. V. Sovani) contain a number of useful statistical distributions, e.g., by size classes, by differential growth rates according to size classes, and preliminary classifications of cities by function.[10] Sovani also shows that at least since 1921 Indian cities have conformed to the rank-size rule.

The papers by Ghurye, Nath, and Mamoria are based on the census data for all-India and appeared shortly after these data were first published. All these articles contain some gaps and several errors, which are mainly due to the haste with which they were written. They have become superseded by a long and careful doctoral dissertation by Ashish Bose. This dissertation also deals primarily with all-India data, but it does present some distributions for the major Indian states. In this feature Bose's study parallels

---

[7] Registrar General, *Census of India, 1951,* I, Part II-A, "Demographic Tables" (Delhi: Manager of Publications, 1955), 61–97.

[8] G. S. Ghurye, "Cities of India," *Sociological Bulletin,* II, No. 1 (May, 1953), 47–71; V. Nath, "Urbanization in India, with Special Reference to the Growth of Cities," in United Nations, *Proceedings of the World Population Conference, 1954,* II (New York, 1955), 843–854; S. Guha, "Socio-Economic Impact of Urbanization," *All-India Congress Committee Economic Review,* X, No. 3 (June 1, 1958), 16–18; C. B. Mamoria, "Rural and Urban Composition of Indian Population," *Modern Review,* XCIX, Nos. 2 and 3 (February and March, 1956), 118–124 and 195–202; various authors, "Urban Development Trends in India," in Indian Economic Association, *op. cit.,* pp. 3–114.

[9] Robert I. Crane, "Urbanism in India," *American Journal of Sociology,* LX, No. 5 (March, 1955), 107–114.

[10] S. B. Bagal, "Trends of Urbanization and Rural-Urban Migration in India, 1901–51," in Indian Economic Association, *op. cit.,* pp. 15–29; Ashish Bose, "The Pace of Urbanization in India," *ibid.,* pp. 30–42; N. V. Sovani, "Trend of Urbanization in India," *ibid.,* pp. 107–114.

articles by J. M. Datta for Bengal and K. M. Patnaik for Orissa.[11]

In contrast to these papers, a recent essay by Gananathan and a thesis by Amrit Lal emphasize spatial relations, though these works also concentrate on functional distinctions.[12] This is especially true of Lal's work, which, however, uses a rather peculiar statistical measure to arrive at a functional classification of cities. In addition to these works, which deal with the spatial relations of Indian cities on a nationwide basis, several regional studies also are of interest.[13] Outstanding among them are E. Ahmad's study of towns in Uttar Pradesh, and the article by the same author and O. H. K. Spate on cities in the Gangetic plain. Additional regional studies which deserve attention are M. Guha's study of urban centers in West Bengal, D. Mookherjee's study of western India, R. V. Joshi's study of the same region, V. A. Janaki's study of Kerala, B. Sinha's essay on Orissa, and V. V. Ramanandham and Y. Venkatesawarlu's paper on Andhra.

The contrasts and similarities in urban patterns discussed in these papers are of special interest, since they all are written by geographers and deal with regions which topographically, socially, and economically present great differences. Compare, for example, the narrow, densely populated area of Kerala with the vast plain in the Ganges valley, the dry and often inhospitable country of western India, and the relatively sparsely populated and city-poor countryside of Orissa. Contrast all these with the lush tropical region of West Bengal, dominated by the vast urban agglomeration of Calcutta at one end and the growing mass of urban centers of the Damodar Valley–Asansol region at the other. Consider, further, the wide economic differences prevailing in these

---

[11] Ashish Bose, "The Process of Urbanisation in India" (Doctoral dissertation, University of Delhi, 1958). Jatindra Mohan Datta, "Urbanization in Bengal," *Geographical Review of India,* XVIII, No. 4 (December, 1956), 19–23; Khetra Mohan Patnaik, "Urban Development in Orissa," in Indian Economic Association, *op. cit.,* pp. 89–95.

[12] V. S. Gananathan, "Distribution of Urban Settlements in India," in *Proceedings of the 17th International Geographical Congress* (Washington, 1952), pp. 742–745; Amrit Lal, "Some Characteristics of Indian Cities of over 100,000 Inhabitants in 1951 with Special Reference to Their Occupational Structure and Functional Specialization" (Doctoral dissertation, Indiana University, 1958).

[13] E. Ahmad, "Origin and Evolution of the Towns of Uttar Pradesh," *Geographical Outlook,* I (January, 1956), 38–58; O. H. K. Spate and E. Ahmad, "Five Cities of the Gangetic Plain," *Geographical Review,* XL (1950), 260–78; Meera Guha, "Urban Regions of West Bengal," *Geographical Review of India,* XIX, No. 3 (September, 1957), 31–44; D. Mookherjee, "West Bengal: Its Urban Pattern," *ibid.,* No. 4 (December, 1957), 67–72; R. V. Joshi, "Urban Structure in Western India," *ibid.,* XVIII, No. 1 (March, 1956), 7–19; V. A. Janaki, "A Functional Classification of Urban Settlements of Kerala," *Journal of the M. S. University of Baroda,* III (1954), 79–104; V. V. Ramanandham and Y. Venkatesawarlu, "Economic Aspects of Town Formation in Andhra Pradesh," *Indian Geographical Journal,* XXXII, Nos. 3–4 (July–December, 1957), 63–85; B. Sinha, "Urban Geography of Orissa," *ibid.,* pp. 86–94.

various regions: for example, the relatively wealthier, more highly commercialized economy of western India, especially Gujarat, as contrasted with the backward agricultural countryside of Orissa. These differences, in addition to differences in social life, caste structure, and general character of the population, impose conditions which will show up also in the distribution and function of urban places in different parts of India. Just as it is of significance to determine spatial and functional patterns of urban distributions for India as a whole, it is also of importance to make these studies for the various regions into which India is divided, precisely because of the different topographical, social, economic, and climatic conditions prevailing in different regions.

Not only do regional studies of urban distributions not exist as yet for the major regions of India, the situation with regard to descriptive or analytical accounts of individual cities is even less satisfactory. We have already referred to the already published (and the forthcoming) socioeconomic studies of major Indian cities, but these surveys are limited in general scope and leave out of consideration many variables which are of special interest to the geographer. There have appeared, however, in the last few years a few studies, written from the sociological or the geographical viewpoint, which do present what are intended to be rather exhaustive surveys of Indian cities. The three most notable ones, as judged by their size, are the works by Venkatarayappa on Bangalore, by Bopegamage on Delhi, and by Singh on Banaras.[14]

The first two of these books are primarily sociological studies, and the last is a straightforward urban geography. In any overall evaluation of the three books, there is no question but that Singh's work on Banaras is by far the best and most useful. Singh uses a well-established method, his procedures are sure and forceful, the questions he asks and the data he assembles follow an established pattern, and the over-all result is a clear picture of spatial relations—of such significant distributions as population, economic activities, public institutions, neighborhoods, etc., in the city of Banaras and its environs. Since Singh's study is approached from the geographical viewpoint, he pays attention to physical site characteristics. He is concerned not only with the major existing transport arteries, but also with questions concerning drainage, surface configuration, and the impact of different parts of the Umland, or hinterland, upon the present morphology of the city and its potentials for expansion. Hence, when Singh, in the last chap-

---

[14] K. N. Venkatarayappa, *Bangalore: A Socio-Ecological Study* (Bombay: University of Bombay Press, 1957) ; A. Bopegamage, *Delhi: A Study in Urban Sociology* (Bombay: University of Bombay Press, 1957) ; R. L. Singh, *Banaras: A Study in Urban Geography* (Banaras: Nand Kishore & Bros., 1955).

ter of his book, turns to an evaluation of various schemes for the planning and improvement of Banaras, he has laid the groundwork for evaluating the feasibility and appropriateness of such developments in terms not only of the economic and social requirements of Banaras, but also in terms of its physical facilities. As we shall see later, the much less adequate methodology employed by Venkatarayappa and Bopegamage does not lead to results of this kind.

A general survey of the chapters in Singh's work and the other two books reveals a great similarity. After a brief historical introduction, there is in each book a chapter on the physical setting, followed by one on the cultural landscape, population, and economic functions of the city, and some additional chapters on public utilities, housing, traffic, and the prospects of urban planning and developments. Only the study on Banaras has a section relating the city to its hinterland, and only the study on Banaras has a chapter discussing the topographical and morphological features of the city.

In spite of the outward similarities in general structure of the three books, the geographical study is superior to the one labeled "social ecology" and the one labeled "sociology." In part this may be due to the skill of the writer, but in large measure it is due to the uncertainty of method employed by sociologists as contrasted with geographers. The ecological approach, as it is displayed by the books of Venkatarayappa and Bopegamage, consists mainly in a listing of the major functional zones within a city, without explanation of the flow of persons and commodities that takes place between them and without relating them to the topographical or internal morphological features of the city. A city is merely an assemblage of one or more business centers, industrial quarters, residential neighborhoods, etc. Though general account is taken of the historical or locational factors which determine the precise situation of these city regions with respect to one another, this fact is not further explored, and, when it comes to suggestions for planning, proposals are made which in terms of actual feasibility are absolutely fantastic, simply because a number of simple factors pertaining to the physical environment—e.g., drainage characteristics or levels of underground water—are omitted.

The socioecological approach suffers not only from this shortcoming; it suffers also from the absence of a well-rounded set of questions raised at the beginning of the investigation and the lack of tentative hypotheses concerning the functional orientation of a city. What kind of city is Bangalore? How important are its administrative as against its manufacturing and distributive functions? Or, taking the case of Delhi, how important is the function of Greater Delhi as the capital of India, as against its function as the major distributive center in northwest India? Whereas up to 1911 Delhi was a provincial capital of secondary importance, it became a colonial capital in that year. In 1947 it became the capital of a large independent country and, at the same time, with the loss of Lahore to Pakistan, it became the major trading, banking, and transport center in northwest India. It is now the third largest city of India and by far the largest inland city. How have these features—the increasing significance of governmental functions, the increasing importance of transport and communications, the increasing weight as a distributive center, and, last but not least, the growing importance of industry—affected Delhi? What has been the impact of these same factors, in somewhat diminished degree, in Bangalore? What impact have these factors had on the surrounding areas—of special interest in Delhi, since some of the suburbs of Delhi are located in Uttar Pradesh and Punjab—and, most important, what trends have been observable in the spatial distribution of these functions within each city? These are most interesting questions, which are treated only very superficially in the books by Bopegamage and Venkatarayappa and which would have deserved extensive and careful research.

The comparison of these three books, all three of which emanated from doctoral dissertations, seems to point out that, in India at least, standard geographical methods of research are superior to socioecological ones, and that the points investigated and the answers obtained are more satisfactorily handled if a research pursues "urban geography" rather than "social ecology." Yet there are some highly perceptive studies, notably of smaller cities, written from the sociological viewpoint. An interesting example of such a study is a paper by Mrs. H. Acharya on the town of Nasik in the State of Maharashtra.[15] But such studies are, as yet, rare, and only a few of them have been written by Indians.

Further shortcomings of the books on Bangalore and Delhi also should be mentioned. There happen to exist a number of subsidiary studies on both cities which could have been used with advantage. This is especially true of Delhi. Above all, there had been published, in 1956, an Interim Plan for Greater Delhi, which contains a large amount of extremely useful material. Similarly, on Bangalore there had appeared two suggestive papers by N. P. Gist, which treat of social ecology in that city in a rather ingenious

---

[15] Hemalata Acharya, "Urbanizing Role of a One-Lakh City," *Sociological Bulletin*, V, No. 2 (September, 1956), 89–101.

fashion.[16] These, and a number of other government reports, have been left unexploited by the authors of the two socioecological city studies. In a way, the publication of the book on Delhi was a bit premature, since in the past year (1959), as a consequence of the work on the Greater Delhi Development Plan by the Town Planning Organization of the Ministry of Health, a number of additional useful studies have appeared. This is especially true of a pamphlet issued under the auspices of the National Council of Applied Economic Research on commodity flows in Delhi.[17] This pamphlet breaks some new ground as concerns the locational study of Indian cities. It poses the questions: what major commodities come into Delhi, how are they distributed within Delhi, what institutions and what spatial patterns are employed in getting them distributed, and how is trade in such major commodities as fuels, foods, and textiles carried out in its social and spatial aspects in an Indian city? The report by the National Council exhibits data on these points, supported by graphs in which the major flows and the intensity of flows are mapped and in which the main distributional points are indicated.

It might be mentioned that the National Council pamphlet, as well as the books by Bopegamage and Venkatarayappa, contain quite a few maps, some of which are designed to provide new information. Yet, the sheer technique of map making could have been vastly improved. The lettering is poor, and in cases in which maps are colored, the colors are not well chosen. More important, the maps are drawn with little imagination, major points are often omitted, and the maps sometimes contain too much and sometimes too little information. There is no question but that Indian researchers in fields related to geography could profit greatly from some technical aid in the design and execution of maps.

The works which have been discussed so far almost all deal with a set of urban centers or a single city and are concerned with a multitude of social, economic, or demographic problems in the city or cities analyzed. A large part of the literature relating to urbanism in India, however, is directed toward certain single special aspects, and we shall now turn briefly to an evaluation of these other writings. The most widely discussed problems are those of labor conditions in Indian cities and of unemployment, especially

[16] Ministry of Health, *Interim General Plan for Greater Delhi* (Delhi: Manager of Publications, 1956); Noel P. Gist, "Ecology of Bangalore, India: An East-West Comparison," *Modern Review*, CI, No. 5 (May, 1957), 357–364, and "The Ecological Structure of an Asian City: An East-West Comparison," *Population Review*, II, No. 1 (January, 1958), 17–25.

[17] National Council of Applied Economic Research, *Commodity Disposition Survey in Delhi* (Bombay: Asia Publishing House, 1959), vii +48 pp., maps, tables. [Rs. 7.25.]

in urban areas. On this second topic an extensive series of articles was published in the *Indian Journal of Commerce,* in its December, 1954, and March, 1955, issues. These articles suffered from a lack of adequate data; they were speculative rather than factual, and even in analysis they became superseded soon by a concise and well-designed essay on this topic by W. Malenbaum.[18] In the meantime, the National Sample Survey has collected a considerable amount of data on unemployment in urban areas all over India and has published them in several statistically extensive publications.[19] Also, other government offices have collected information on this problem, which is taking on increasing importance in the minds of Indian planners. The latest and most up-to-date study is a recent pamphlet produced by the National Employment Service of the Ministry of Labour.[20] This last study presents a summary view of the problem, but for details one must turn to the various publications of the National Sample Survey, as well as some other surveys which have been made at the local level—for example, in Lucknow, Baroda, and Nagpur.[21] Among all these reports, the National Sample Survey's report on employment and unemployment in Calcutta[22] is a model—in its coverage, in the occupational classification of the labor force, and in the over-all presentation of data. It is to be hoped that this publication (which is as yet available only in mimeographed form) will become a standard according to which other surveys of urban employment and unemployment may be patterned.

Next to the question of employment, that of urban labor conditions is the most burning. The problem of wages and general labor conditions was of such concern to the Indian government that it undertook as one of its earliest postwar survey tasks a far-flung

---

[18] See the symposium on "Urban Unemployment in India," in which participated A. C. Shukla, K. P. Sundharam, K. B. Dangayach, P. K. Chosh, B. N. Misra, P. Brahmanand, and M. L. Mishra, *Indian Journal of Commerce,* VII, No. 28 (December, 1954), 1–62, and VIII, No. 29 (March, 1955), 1–10; also Wilfred Malenbaum, "Urban Unemployment in India," *Pacific Affairs,* XXX, No. 2 (June, 1957), 138–150.

[19] National Sample Survey, *Special Report on the Survey of Persons on the Live Register of the Delhi Employment Exchange* (New Delhi: Manager of Publications, 1954), and *Report on Preliminary Survey of Urban Unemployment in September 1953* (New Delhi: Manager of Publications, 1956).

[20] National Employment Service, *Unemployment in Urban Areas* (New Delhi: Manager of Publications, 1959).

[21] B. Singh, *A Report on Unemployment in the City of Lucknow* (Lucknow: Lucknow University Press, 1955); Y. V. Kolhatkar and C. T. Shah, "A Survey of Unemployment and Underemployment in the City of Baroda," *Journal of the M. S. University of Baroda,* V, No. 1 (March, 1956), 75–121; Madhya Pradesh, Directorate of Economics and Statistics, *Survey of Educated Unemployed in Nagpur City* (Nagpur, 1956).

[22] National Sample Survey, *Report on Sample Survey of Employment in Calcutta: 1953* (Calcutta: Indian Statistical Institute, 1956), 74 pp. + 38 unpaginated tables. [Mimeographed; n.p.]

investigation of the family budgets of urban working-class families. These studies were published, one small pamphlet for each major city, and though they are not of outstanding interest from a methodological viewpoint, they do contain many data on differences in consumption patterns among the lower classes in many urban centers of India (and Pakistan). It should be noted that coverage of North Indian cities is much more complete than for those of South India.[23]

Of greater interest than these studies of family budgets are analytical studies of labor conditions and the labor supply in Indian cities. Apart from the study by Prabu on Bombay (cited in note 4, above), there are two valuable studies on the urban cotton-mill workers in western India, one with a historical slant by M. D. Morris and another comparing features of the factory and nonfactory populations by R. D. Lambert.[24] These two studies by Americans may be supplemented by (1) a study on the Bombay textile-mill labor force written from the social service standpoint and (2) a book on the Bombay cotton-mill workers which attempts to provide a comprehensive and well-rounded picture of all aspects of the life and work cycle of the Bombay mill workers.[25] But in analytical power these remain far behind the essays by Morris and Lambert. It may be worth reporting also that attention has been given not only to the working class in Bombay, but also to the socioeconomic conditions of the middle and upper classes.[26] These studies, together with the surveys of the workers, provide a fairly well-rounded survey of social and economic conditions among all social classes in Bombay, especially those associated with the textile industry.

None of the other industrial cities has been surveyed as exten-

[23] Ministry of Labour, *Report on an Enquiry into the Family Budgets of Workers in Delhi* (Delhi: Manager of Publications, 1954), is one of the studies. Others cover the following major cities: Ajmer, Ahmedabad, Bombay, Dehra Dun, Gauhati, Howrah, Jamshedpur, Jharia, Jubbulpore, Kanpur, Kharagpur, Ludhiana, Sholapur; in addition some reports on cost of living in minor cities have been published. All are located in North India and a few (Lahore, Karachi, Sialkot) in Pakistan.

[24] M. D. Morris, "The Supply of Labour to the Bombay Cotton Textile Industry, 1854–1951," *Indian Economic Journal,* I, No. 2 (October, 1953), 138–152; Richard D. Lambert, "Factory Workers and the Non-Factory Population in Poona," *Journal of Asian Studies,* XVIII, No. 1 (November, 1958), 21–42.

[25] A. N. Biraj, "Textile Labour in Bombay City," *Indian Journal of Social Work,* XIV, No. 2 (September, 1953), 168–177; A. G. Gokhale, *The Bombay Cotton Mill Worker* (Bombay: Millowners' Association, 1957), 126 pp.

[26] S. K. Kadri, "An Inquiry into the Socio-Economic Position of Employers in the City of Bombay," *Journal of the University of Bombay; History, Economics, and Sociology Series,* XXI, No. 4 (January, 1953), 91–93; C. S. Patil, "A Socio-Economic Survey of the Middle Class in Bombay," *ibid.,* XXV, No. 49 (July, 1956), 20–24.

In addition to the materials on the Bombay middle class, we also possess a parallel study on Ahmedabad in the pamphlet by L. V. Dani, *Middle Class Social Survey of Ahmedabad City* (Ahmedabad: Gujerat Vepari Mahamandal, 1955).

sively as Bombay during the last few years, and the Bombay data will have to be compared with those produced for other cities by the urban surveys in process under the auspices of the Research Programmes Committee (see note 6). A general socioeconomic survey of Bombay is also in progress, but so far only portions of the survey have appeared in print. Moreover, these portions deal mostly with the structure of industry and other services in the Greater Bombay region—e.g., with engineering plants and commercial establishments. A general summary of the demographic and ecological features of Bombay has recently been published in an essay by C. Rajagopalan.[27]

Calcutta, which up to World War II was probably the most widely studied city, but where relatively little research was done in the first ten years after independence, has again been subjected to extensive study. The determining factors were the large influx of refugees from East Pakistan, the establishment of the UNESCO Research Centre in Calcutta, which showed great interest in urban studies, and the impetus exerted by the socioeconomic survey for the Research Programmes Committee of the Planning Commission. The most important fruit of these efforts is the book by S. N. Sen, but it is supplemented by two important articles by N. K. Bose and A. B. Chatterjee on social, cultural, and demographic aspects of the city, and an extensive survey of labor conditions in the Calcutta textile industry undertaken by the UNESCO Research Centre.[28]

Compared to Bombay and Calcutta, the social and labor conditions of other Indian cities have been studied only superficially. However, Mr. V. Agnihotri, an employee of the Uttar Pradesh Labour Department, has published several articles on the conditions of the working class in Kanpur which constitute a fairly comprehensive survey of living and working conditions of the laboring classes in this city.[29]

---

[27] D. T. Lakdawala and B. V. Mehta, "Small and Medium Scale Engineering Factories in Bombay City," *Journal of the University of Bombay; History, Economics, and Sociology Series,* XXVI, No. 4 (January, 1958), 50–103; D. T. Lakdawala and J. C. Sandesara, "Shops and Establishments in Greater Bombay," *ibid.,* XXV, No. 4 (January, 1957), pp. 56–103; C. Rajagopalan, *op. cit.,* pp. 16–38.

[28] S. N. Sen, *op. cit.;* Nirmal Kumar Bose, "Social and Cultural Life of Calcutta," *Geographical Review of India,* XX (December, 1958), 1–46; A. B. Chatterjee, "Demographic Features of Howrah City," *ibid.,* pp. 150–169; UNESCO Research Centre on Social Implications of Industrialization in Southern Asia, *Report on Social and Cultural Factors Affecting Productivity of Industrial Labour* (3 vols.; Calcutta, 1958).

[29] Among the more interesting papers by V. Agnihotri are the following: "Poverty among Factory Workers in Kanpur," *Labour Bulletin, Uttar Pradesh,* XIV, No. 10 (October, 1954), 13–19; "Employment and Education among the Blind in Kanpur," *ibid.,* XV, No. 1 (January, 1955), 16–19; and *Housing Conditions of Factory Workers in Kanpur* (Lucknow: Fine Press, 1954), 63 pp.

In part, labor conditions in Indian cities are dependent upon migratory patterns. It has been estimated that 40 per cent of the urban labor force consists of migrants, and, although there are no precise data on this point, the proportion of migrants increases as the skill of the laborer decreases. This means that the most poorly paid jobs in most Indian cities are filled by migrants, or, in other words, that immigrants normally attach themselves to the lower fringe of the urban social structure. Unfortunately, there is as yet little known about migratory patterns in Indian cities. Some interesting facts, especially on the lowest earners in an Indian city, have been brought to light in a recent socioeconomic survey of the slums of Delhi, which follows in its methodology the traditional pattern set by the Gokhale Institute and the studies sponsored by the Research Programmes Committee of the Planning Commission (see notes 5 and 6).[30] In addition, the studies done under the auspices of the Research Programmes Committee stress the analysis of migration and the conditions of recent migratory workers. In Delhi, the number of recent immigrants is rather larger than in most other Indian cities, chiefly because almost 500,000 refugees settled there after partition. The refugees constitute a special case, however, and few urban centers face the refugee problem as a more or less permanent one. Calcutta is a major exception, because of its proximity to East Pakistan.

More important in the long run than the immigration of refugees is the migration of nonrefugees to Indian cities. The patterns of this migration are, as yet, little understood. A few pilot surveys have been done, among them the study by Deshmukh, referred to earlier (note 4). Deshmukh traced the migratory pattern of workers from Central India to Delhi. Only a few similar studies exist, among them one on North India by E. Eames, two studies by N. P. Gist on migratory patterns in South India, and one general and rather superficial survey on over-all migratory pattern by P. K. Rao.[31] Although these articles present some interesting facts on a rather limited scale, the methodology for the study of the social and economic impact of cityward migration has been exhibited best in a study dealing with the migration of displaced

---

[30] Bharat Sevak Samaj, Delhi Pradesh, *Slums of Old Delhi* (Delhi: Atma Ram & Sons, 1958).

[31] E. Eames, "Some Aspects of Urban Migration from a Village in North Central India," *Eastern Anthropologist*, VIII, No. 1 (September–November, 1954), 13–26; Noel P. Gist, "Selective Migration in Urban South India," in United Nations, *Proceedings of the World Population Conference, 1954* (New York, 1955), II, 811–822, and "Selective Migration in South India," *Sociological Bulletin*, IV, No. 2 (September, 1955), 147–160; P. K. Rao, "Urban Pull in India," in International Institute of Differing Civilizations, *Record of the 27th Meeting Held in Florence* (Brussels, 1952), pp. 217–225.

persons in the urban areas of Bombay State, done by the National Sample Survey.[32] The prestige of the National Sample Survey is so great that we may expect several other parallel studies in the near future using the techniques proposed there; it is to be hoped that these techniques will also be applied to the study of non-refugee migrants.

As is well known, rural-urban migration is responsible also for the demographic peculiarities of urban areas in India. The high sex ratios in Indian cities have often been observed, especially in the northern cities. Another general observation is the youthfulness of the urban population. These characteristics, though well known, have as yet been little related to migratory patterns and ecological distributions in urban areas, but two interesting essays exhibiting somewhat novel approaches have recently appeared. One is a study of migration to the three major cities (Calcutta, Bombay, and Madras), and the age and sex composition of this migration, by S. N. Agarwala; the other is a study of differential age and sex compositions in various subdivisions of Delhi by A. Bopegamage.[33]

The study of migrants evokes two further aspects of urbanism which we must discuss before concluding this survey of research on Indian cities. The first is the relation between cities and the rural areas, especially the hinterland, or Umland of a city. The second is the problem of town planning as a measure which will preserve cities from developing the characteristic urban sprawl which has proven too costly to remove and so uneconomical in Western countries.

As has already been pointed out, the study of urban-rural relations is as yet little explored. The various socioecological studies, and the socioeconomic surveys, pay scarcely any attention to areas outside the city limits. The only study reviewed in this essay which pays explicit attention to the relationships between a city and its Umland is Singh's book on Banaras. However, some attention to the problem is given in a few transportation studies, notably one by the National Council of Applied Economic Research on goods transport by road in the Delhi region, and an essay by M. Guha on transport in the Calcutta region.[34] Some attention to this prob-

---

[32] National Sample Survey, *Report on the Sample Survey of Displaced Persons in the Urban Areas of the Bombay State* (Delhi: Manager of Publications, 1957).

[33] S. N. Agarwala, "A Method for Estimating Decade Internal Migration in Cities from Indian Census Data," *Indian Economic Review*, IV, No. 1 (February, 1958), 59–76; A. Bopegamage, "A Demographic Approach to the Study of Urban Ecology," *Sociological Bulletin*, IX, No. 1 (March, 1960), 82–93.

[34] National Council of Applied Economic Research, *Some Aspects of Goods Transport by Road in the Delhi Region* (Bombay: Asia Publishing House, 1959); Meera Guha, "Transport in and around Calcutta," *Geographical Review of India*, VII (1955), 4–8.

lem is also given in an essay by A. Vasanta. Although he is concerned primarily with describing methods of delimiting the area of urban concentration, in the course of this task he wrestles with the problem of urban boundaries and the relations between the nucleus within and the region outside the boundary. Finally, there exist several studies of towns of secondary importance which are within the wider reaches of a larger city, which exhibit a dependency relationship to the larger city, and which dominate the countryside immediately surrounding them. Among the abler studies of this kind should be mentioned an essay by R. L. Singh on Mirzapur, a town within the wider Umland of Banaras; a study by D. Mookherjee on Siliguri, a small town in northern West Bengal; a careful paper by A. R. Tiwari on Agra; a dissertation and an article by H. F. Hirt on Aligarh, which lies within the region of Delhi; and the study by Singh on Gorakhpur, which tends to hold a position marginal to the Banaras Umland and yet constitutes an urban center showing little difference in life patterns from those of a large village.[35] Gorakhpur is a railway center and a market town, but it has few of the characteristics of a genuine city; in spite of its size of around 150,000 inhabitants, it clearly exhibits many transitional features from rural to urban conditions.

There appear to exist some genuine differences in the social life of the larger cities, especially the four giant metropolitan centers, and the smaller towns with populations between 50,000 and 300,000 inhabitants. The small-town peculiarities, though not absent even in the capital of India, are especially pronounced in one-industry towns—such as railway centers or steel towns—which have a core of highly modern industry surrounded by settlements of village-like and quasi village-like character. This is exhibited also, to a fair extent, in a study by the UNESCO Research Centre on the various steel towns, which is available in a preliminary form, but due to appear shortly in a more definitive version.[36]

These studies present analyses of the morphological and socio-

[35] A. Vasanta, "A Method to Delimit Areas of Urban Concentration," *Indian Geographical Journal,* XXXII, Nos. 3–4 (July–December, 1957), 95–100; R. L. Singh, "Mirzapur, A Study in Urban Geography," *Geographical Outlook,* I, No. 1 (January, 1956), 16–27, and "Gorakhpur, A Study in Urban Morphology," *National Geographical Journal of India,* I (September, 1953), 1–10; D. Mookherjee, "The Urban Pattern of Siliguri," *Geographical Review of India,* XIX, No. 3 (September, 1957), 15–20; A. R. Tiwari, "Urban Regions of Agra," *Agra University Journal of Research,* VI, No. 1 (January, 1958), 101–114; H. F. Hirt, "Aligarh, Uttar Pradesh, A Geography of Urban Growth" (Doctoral dissertation, Syracuse University, 1955), and *op. cit.,* pp. 37–45.

[36] UNESCO Research Centre on Social Implications of Industrialization in Southern Asia, *Report on a Preliminary Inquiry on the Growth of Steel Towns in India: A Study on Problems of Urbanization* (Calcutta, 1959).

economic aspects of the transition from rural to urban distributions. They are supplemented by an essay by Srinivas, which deals with the cultural dimension and contrast in value structure accompanying this transition from rural to urban settlement patterns. The persistence of rural settlement types in what are essentially urban environments has, of course, been observed often. A. Bopegamage has devoted an article to describing a village within the metropolitan area of Delhi, and B. F. Hoselitz has stressed the village-like character of many neighborhoods of Indian cities.[37]

The heterogeneity in Indian cities is one of the chief factors demanding the early application of rehabilitation and development plans. Urban planning involves a multiplicity of problems, many of which are as yet little explored and understood in India. There is still confusion and doubt on urban land policy, zoning, and local tax and improvement legislation; above all, there is lack of understanding in many places of the basic requirements and conditions of urban planning. Whatever progress has been made in the last few years is described briefly and superficially in an essay by J. Wood in *Land Economics,* and, with special reference to the administrative problems, by N. K. Gandhi in a paper on the construction of new towns.[38] The delicate problem of urban land policies in India has been described in a recent paper of C. C. Desai, and O. H. Koenigsberger has presented a magnificent essay on plans for new towns in India.[39] This essay also contains good maps which clearly show the problems faced by urban planners in India.

As for the plans themselves, little has been published as yet, except from the purely architectural viewpoint. The famous new capital of Chandigarh has not been described in detail, nor has the less famous, but perhaps better planned, new capital of Orissa, Bhubaneshwar.[40]

---

[37] M. N. Srinivas, "The Industrialization and Urbanization of Rural Areas," *Sociological Bulletin,* V, No. 2 (September, 1956), 79–88; A. Bopegamage, "A Village within a Metropolitan Area," *ibid.,* pp. 102–110; Bert F. Hoselitz, "Urbanization and Town Planning in India," *Confluence,* VII, No. 2 (Summer, 1958), 115–127. See also the recent essay on a slum village in the New Delhi area: "Kotla-Mubarakhpur, an Urban Village," *Urban and Rural Planning Thought,* I, No. 1 (January, 1958), 41–54.

[38] J. Wood, "Development of Urban and Regional Planning in India," *Land Economics,* XXXIV, No. 4 (November, 1958), 310–315; N. K. Gandhi, "New Towns Construction in India," *Quarterly Journal of the Local Self-Government Institute,* XVIII (October, 1957), 435–445.

[39] C. C. Desai, "Urban Land Policies in India," in United Nations, *Urban Land Problems and Policies* (New York, 1953), pp. 76–82; O. H. Koenigsberger, "New Towns in India," *Town Planning Review,* XXIII, No. 2 (July, 1952), 94–132.

[40] A rather superficial account of Chandigarh is contained in M. Fry and J. B. Drew, "Chandigarh and Development in India," *Asian Review,* XLI (1955), 110–125.

There exist apparently only two published proposals of development plans for large Indian cities: an early and rather sketchy plan for Bombay, which was proposed in 1948, and the very detailed and highly elaborate plan for Greater Delhi.[41] But there are clear signs that the need for urban planning is more and more widely recognized. In many of its aspects the Delhi Master Plan should be regarded as a model for analogous urban plans elsewhere in India, and, indeed, in Asia as a whole; moreover, the urban socio-economic surveys sponsored by the Planning Commission have been responsible for pointing up the crying need for city planning. Finally, we witness a growth of the number of urban planners in India, a greater degree of professionalization of their trade, and in 1958 even the founding of a special journal entirely devoted to problems of urban and rural planning.[42] This developing need has led to the publication of a number of stimulating essays on urban planning in India, its present state and its future, which may form the basis upon which further studies in this field can be built. The most noteworthy essays along these lines are two articles by Britton Harris, a paper by Jack Wood, an essay by Edward Echeverria, and a paper by J. A. Stein. It is perhaps also noteworthy that Indian scholars not only have begun to survey more intensively the urban situation and problems in their own country, but have become interested in comparative studies of urbanization, as is evidenced, for example, by a recent paper of A. G. Khan on United States metropolitan areas.[43]

Thus it is becoming more generally recognized that in spite of the scarcity of resources, present trends of urban growth in India make town and city planning imperative at this time, if serious future costs are to be minimized. Increased emphasis on the study of urban centers, not merely in their socioeconomic, but also in their topographical and morphological aspects, is a precondition

---

[41] M. V. Modak and A. Mayer, *Outlines of a Master Plan for Greater Bombay* (Bombay, 1948); and Delhi Development Authority, *op. cit.*, 2 vols., 184 and 165 pp.

[42] This journal is *Urban and Rural Planning Thought,* edited by T. J. Manickam, director of the School of Town and Country Planning at New Delhi. It appears four times a year, and began publication in January, 1958.

[43] Britton Harris, "Urbanization Policy in India," in Gerald A. P. Carrothers, (ed.), *Papers and Proceedings of the Regional Science Association,* V (1959), 181–203, and "Urban Problems in the Third Plan: Some of Their Implications," *Economic Weekly,* XII, Nos. 23–25 (June, 1960), 875–878; Jack Wood, "Town Planning in India: Status and Education," *Urban and Rural Planning Thought,* I, No. 4 (October, 1958), 223–243; Edward Echeverria, "How Much Land Do Indian Cities Need," *ibid.,* pp. 253–263; J. A. Stein, "Neighborhood Planning for Modern Industrial Towns," *ibid.,* I, No. 1 (January, 1958), 29–40; A. G. Khan, "The Metropolitan Areas of the United States: A Brief Survey of Research in Urban Economics," *Economic Weekly,* XII, No. 26 (June 25, 1960), 1043–1046.

of adequate town planning. Although this survey of the literature suggests that more is now known than ever before concerning Indian urbanization, India is still far from possessing adequate inventories of its urban centers, their functions, their populations, and their problems.

EDITOR'S POSTSCRIPT

Despite the fact that India has engaged in farsighted economic planning since independence, and despite the considerable success of the Five Year Plans, remarkably little constructive attention has been paid to the spatial aspects of social and economic change. For this reason, solid information relating to questions of population movement and industrial distribution is sadly lacking, and it seems likely that the lack will remain unless some thoroughgoing and sophisticated thinking goes into the conceptualization of the problem. The purpose of the Berkeley seminar, therefore, was not to provide blueprints for development, but rather to move toward some consensus regarding the nature of the processes at work and the probable outcome of present trends.

There is no difficulty in securing agreement that the social and physical conditions of Indian cities today are bad, from almost any standpoint, and that they are deteriorating. Many Indian urban dwellers are without employment, many more are literally homeless—and yet, year by year, each of the major cities becomes measurably larger. Natural increase (the excess of births over deaths) does not alone account for this situation; by far the greatest proportion of the growth of city populations comes from the migration of villagers.[1] Edward Echeverria, consultant to the team of experts working on the Delhi Regional Plan, indicated that the housing deficit, far from being reduced in the decade 1951–1961, has probably increased by at least three million.[2] Marshall B. Clinard and B. Chatterjee, consultant and director, respectively, of the Delhi Urban Community Development Program, described the dirt, dilapidation, and lack of social cohesion that characterize the poorer residential quarters of the typical Indian city.[3] P. R. Nayak, formerly Commissioner for Delhi, agreed that Indian

---

This Postscript is based in part on two earlier articles, appearing in *The Economic Weekly* and *Asian Survey*, with the permission of the editors of those journals.

[1] See especially Bogue and Zachariah, chap. ii of this volume.

[2] Unpublished seminar paper, "Housing and Urban Services: Status, Standards, Costs."

[3] Chap. iv.

municipalities today confront appalling physical and social conditions, and spoke of the inadequacy of the resources of local governments to meet the challenge.[4]

The migrant stream gives promise of a continued flow. Kingsley Davis, using a variety of means for estimating the number of migrants moving into cities of 100,000 population or more, suggested, for example, that the lowest probable figure for the quarter century beginning in 1975 would be a little more than 37 millions, and that the highest estimate involved the movement of some 200 million Indians into cities of this size, from places outside.[5] Whether they are "pushed" by the meager material and psychological satisfactions to be obtained at home, or are "pulled" by the promise of employment (and greater social freedom) in the metropolis, the villagers are on the move. So little reluctance to go to the city did Donald J. Bogue and K. C. Zachariah find, on the part of the Indian villager, that they concluded that, despite urban unemployment, "with villagers becoming progressively more oriented toward the new urbanized economy, and with migration channels firmly established, the nation seems to be all set to enter a phase of unprecedented urbanization, assisted by the prevailing family system and culture rather than hindered by it." [6]

The in-migrants, then, seek—but do not always find—nonagricultural employment, and they constitute a potential industrial labor force. This last fact is extremely important, since it leads to the heart of a crucial ambivalence. I shall take a few pages to examine this ambivalence, in the belief that it helps to set the scene for the papers that precede.

In a general way, India's present situation resembles a stage that the more highly industrialized countries have already passed through. The historical experience has been that urbanization, slow to commence, increases rapidly during the early phases of industrialization and falls off only when it can virtually go no further, since it has by then involved the vast majority of the population. Such a model is no sure guide to the future, admittedly, but, in Bert F. Hoselitz's words, an examination of "India's progress of effective urbanization shows approximately the same characteristics as the corresponding trend in the various European countries." [7] That India will complete the pattern is highly probable, and there is no substantial evidence to the contrary.

The four objectives of the Second Five Year Plan, according to

---

[4] Chap. xix.
[5] Chap. i.
[6] Chap. ii, p. 65.
[7] Chap. viii, p. 162.

a report published by the Planning Commission, were: a sizable increase in national income; rapid industrialization; a large expansion in employment opportunities; and a reduction in inequalities in income and wealth.[8] Clearly, the rapid expansion of industrial production has a special status among these goals, since it must be the chief instrument by which the others are achieved.[9] Rough logic would suggest that, if India conforms to the regularity observed between the progress of industrialization and that of urbanization elsewhere, an increase in urbanization in India would be associated with an increase in the national income, an expansion of job opportunities, and, possibly, a decrease in the inequalities of income and wealth.[10] Viewed in this light, India's present situation might be viewed as the painful transition from a predominantly rural and agricultural society to a predominantly urban and industrial society.

We should then expect to see government policies aimed at easing the transition and attempting to maximize the achievement of national economic goals through judicious influences upon the urbanization process. This suggests utilizing the potentiality of the urban labor force, promoting the expansion of successful industries, and encouraging new enterprises. Various incentives can be imagined, and one set might have to do with the furnishing of the social overheads of metropolitan efficiency. Housing, medical and educational facilities, coherent community development, transportation—the industrial workers would require all of these, and their provision would, directly or indirectly, increase the productivity of labor.[11]

But here we encounter a paradox. In fact, not only is there scarcely any support, in India, for the assignment of resource priorities to the cities, but exactly the opposite is found to be true. "The abysmal hunger in Calcutta for housing, sanitation, water supply, and road reparation will have to wait," wrote a Bengali correspondent to Richard L. Park.[12] "My own view," continues the same correspondent, "[is] that Calcutta is now paying the

---

[8] *The New India: Progress Through Democracy* (New York: Planning Commission, Government of India, 1958), p. 43.

[9] This is not strictly true of the goal to reduce inequalities, but no doubt the real intention is to give more nearly equal shares of a larger pie; the general experience has been that industrialization does lead to lessened inequality.

[10] Unless, that is, India is "overurbanized," i.e., more urbanized than European countries at a comparable stage of industrialization, and continuing in this direction. Professor Sovani discussed this concept, in seminar and in an unpublished seminar paper.

[11] The context requires gross simplification. A concern for metropolitan efficiency might well dictate timing and locational strategies intended to slow down or redirect the migrant stream. This introduces distinctions between short- and long-term plans.

[12] See chap. xx, pp. 394–395.

price of having prospered in the past by draining the lifeblood from the countryside, both economically as well as in human resources. . . . For a long time action will have to be taken to redress the balance . . ." These are strong words, and probably few of the Indians attending the seminar would express themselves with such bitterness. And yet, as Sachin Chaudhuri points out,[13] despite an ancient tradition of urbanism in India, there has been in recent centuries a powerful anti-city sentiment. In part this stems from the fact that the major cities in India today—Calcutta, Bombay, Madras, New Delhi, for example—had their origins as centers of colonial economic exploitation, and that they turned their faces away from their hinterlands and toward London. Gandhi was clearly troubled by this association, which no doubt explained his belief that industrial centralization "cannot be sustained and defended without adequate force."[14]

Surprising reinforcement of these views turns up in the Planning Commission itself. Thus we find the Commission quoting, with approval, Gandhi's "prophetic" statement of 1916 to the effect that "India's salvation lies in the villages, with the Indian farmer."[15] Moreover, the Commission tells us, underlying those objectives of the Second Five Year Plan which we have already discussed are certain fundamental decisions, of which one is that India would first develop its agriculture and its rural people, and another is that the villagers would be "awakened," so that their energies might serve as a principal instrument of the devolpment effort (but not that they might depart, awake, to the cities).[16] It appears, then, that the bias against big cities and a concentration of industry is built into the goal structure which the Plans are meant to subserve. On the one hand, as the draft outline of the Third Plan reiterates, "there is an over-riding need to lay the foundations for rapid industrialization over the next 15 years, if long-term objectives in regard to national income and employment are to be achieved;"[17] on the other hand, "India is now, and in the foreseeable future will remain, a predominantly agricultural nation [and] for many decades, even generations, rural people and rural society will characterize Indian culture and economy."[18]

Official India, it seems, aims to break the traditional link be-

---

[13] Chap. xi.

[14] Krishnalal Shridharani, *The Mahatma and the World* (New York, 1946), p. 229.

[15] *The New India*, p. 43. This report has as its frontispiece, incidentally, a portrait of Gandhi.

[16] *Ibid.*, p. 60.

[17] *The Third Five Year Plan: A Draft Outline*, Planning Commission, Government of India (June, 1960), p. 204.

[18] *The New India*, p. 42.

tween large cities and the growth of modern industrial production methods; and it intends to secure rapid industrialization while maintaining a predominantly rural society, chiefly by manipulating the location of industry. Both the goal of a rural-industrial society and the policy of industrial decentralization repeatedly came to the fore during the course of the seminar, for of all the issues under discussion these seemed best to activate the conflicts latent in the situation.

Many of the conferees went on record as opposing any policy that would assist rapid urbanization to take place, though there was no consensus as to whether the government should throw up a stone wall against the movement to the cities or should rather play the role of midwife to an emerging urban India. Thus Ashok Mitra, an economist from the International Bank for Reconstruction and Development, held that an increase in population of the order predicted by Kingsley Davis would absorb, in the form of urban overheads, resources desperately needed elsewhere in the economy, and spoke confidently of "not permitting" the anticipated trek of migrants. Pitambar Pant, on the other hand, though deeming it desirable to ensure a better balance between the urban and rural sectors—meaning that the life of the villages must be made more attractive—conceded that there would, in fact, be urbanization on a "problematic" scale, and that future Indian economic planning would have to make provision for urban adaption. Indeed, Mr. Pant has gone so far as to quantify the solution and to indicate its place in the national plans.[19]

The question remains, however, that, supposing the policy makers place a negative value upon large-scale metropolitan growth, what degrees of freedom are open to them? Will the migrants steadily pour into the major cities, seemingly irrationally, regardless of the national decisions on rural community development, industrial location, and housing? Or, by a suitable control of such factors, can the holding power of the Indian villages be increased?[20]

Industry enjoys a reputation as the magnet exerting an attractive pull on population (much as it was once said that trade followed the flag). In India, certainly, a great deal of hope is invested in the

---

[19] See chap. ix.

[20] It should by no means be assumed that the effects of rural community development are all in the direction of increasing the holding power of the villages. It has been estimated that the program has given more than half of India's villages "a glimpse of a new future," and it is at least arguable that the city appears to be the locus of a full view of what has merely been glimpsed in the village. See Selig S. Harrison, *India: The Most Dangerous Decades* (Princeton, N. J., 1960), *passim* and especially p. 5.

promise of industrial decentralization. A significant amount of large industry is found in the public sector, and there it is reasonably easy for the government to make and carry out locational decisions. In its dealings with private industry the government must restrict itself to relatively mild positive and negative incentives, dedicated as it is to democratic methods and the promulgation of the maximum amount of freedom. Moreover, the government must always be aware of the risk of penalizing the most successful industries and of inhibiting (rather than redirecting) investment if it pursues a stern and inflexible policy on location. In practice, too, it is severely hampered by the lack of agreement as to what constitutes the *proper* manipulation of industrial location.

Centralization and concentration are fairly easily understood, and it is generally recognized that, if there is no interference, the projected migrations will in all probability take place and Calcutta and Bombay will strengthen their existing industrial supremacy.[21] A recent study of New York, in discussing the tendency for large central offices to be congregated there, noted that:

The needs of the elite group in the central office of a large company are as variable and unpredictable as those of any "producer." From week to week, their interests vary from some esoteric provision of the Internal Revenue Code to the political situation in Cuba; from the effectiveness of spot television commercials to the efficacy of operations research; from the best place to build a factory to the best time to issue stock. Once again, it is uneconomical for such offices to staff themselves internally to deal with every such problem; the only feasible pattern is to draw upon specialists as the need arises. And the most efficient locational arrangement is one which permits the specialists and those they serve to be congregated at a common point.[22]

Assuredly, as India modernizes her productive system and begins to acquire more of the associated paraphernalia so familiar in the West, similar situations will arise in Calcutta, Bombay, and Delhi.

What is concretely implied by "decentralization," the vaunted alternative to the otherwise inevitable "centralization," is far from agreed upon. Obvious questions arise. Does decentralization signify a movement out of the large cities on the part of population and industry already there? Or does it mean that future

---

[21] William Bredo and Richard Ellefsen have attempted to measure this ascendancy. Their figures show that the combined metropolitan areas of Bombay and Calcutta have 40 per cent of the total number of all industrial plants in India. See Appendix to chap. xii. Hoselitz indicated, in seminar, that in his opinion the next ten years' development in India will undoubtedly take place in already developed areas, and suggested that this had the positive value of ensuring the maximum use of resources. (In no country, as Hoselitz further pointed out, is there an even spread of industry over the landscape; most nations have their Ruhr or their Midlands.)

[22] Raymond Vernon, *Metropolis: 1985* (Cambridge, Mass., 1960), p. 81.

urban and industrial growth will be redirected to more suitable locations? And what, precisely, *are* more suitable locations? Are they to be chosen because of the social structure they promote? Or are they to be chosen strictly on a basis of alternative costs?

A number of answers have been given to these questions, indicating a variety of viewpoints. Thus, Shanti Tangri, who believes that the swollen populations of the great Indian cities spell political unrest and social instability and at the same time constitute a waste of resources, advocates *reversing* the flow of "human and material capital" which now streams from the rural to the urban sector: "Communist China is doing it by coercive measures. India has to do it by economic inducement and persuasion." [23] Tarlok Singh, Joint Secretary of the Planning Commission, speaks of the necessity for a balanced development of town and countryside. "Large sections of the population may not be able easily to retreat from the town," he argues, "but the situation is sufficiently fluid for them to move from a large city to a small or middle-sized town." [24] William Bredo and Britton Harris, pursuing somewhat similar lines of inquiry,[25] proceed more cautiously. Each seems to believe that there is a tendency in India to underrate the value of metropolitan areas as nurseries of economic growth. Harris, for example, while agreeing that the metropolises place a heavy burden upon the total national resources available for development, argues that "the high proportion of jobs in government, railways, and organized commerce and industry is not, and probably never can be, duplicated in the rural areas. . . . *To a very considerable extent, the price which must be paid for urban development is a price paid for conducting these activities at all in the Indian economy.*" [26] (Emphasis supplied.)

Both Bredo and Harris proceed on the assumption that if decentralization is to proceed—in the sense that industry is to be promoted outside the metropolitan areas—great care ought to be exercised in selecting nuclei that can be shown to possess a social and economic climate making for industrial viability. Bredo, therefore, warns against pushing industry too far into the rural areas, where the proportion of failures could be dangerously high, and urges research into the factors making for entrepreneurial success. Harris is of the opinion that cities of less than 200,000 population tend to be without many of the environmental factors which stimulate manufacturing growth, and suggests that carefully chosen cities

---

[23] Chap. x, p. 211.
[24] Chap. xvi, p. 328.
[25] Chaps. xii and xiii.
[26] Chap. xiii, p. 266.

of between 250,000 and one million persons might provide the best sites alternative to the cities now possessing a virtual industrial monopoly.[27]

Harris's suggestions are intended to ensure a successful and rapid industrialization, and it is significant that they hardly provide for ruralizing industry; rather, they outline an alternative pattern of continued urban growth, one which would ultimately lead to a larger number of cities above the million mark. Richard L. Meier argues that a future consequence of policies diverting industry and population to medium-sized towns would be the spread of massive agglomerations of contiguous urbanization. His alternative[28] is to accept the inevitability of Indian cities of a size not previously seen in world history—e.g., some 80 million inhabitants for Madras by the year 2050. In this context, the problems of the immediate future would cluster around finding an efficient metropolitan design, one that would solve the social and physical problems of cities of this order. Planned megapolises, Meier argues, would be far preferable to the haphazard growth of conurbations. Meier's own solution to the design problem is the cellular megapolis, each cell taking the form of an "urban village."

Clearly, the whole problem of finding feasible means of decentralization is in need of clarification. It rarely occurs that a nation can decide its goals with a great deal of specificity without reference to the possibilities (and impossibilities) inherent in its *status quo,* and it seems at least possible that India will find some of its cherished goals to be mutually exclusive. Given the initial situation, it may be that a predominantly rural way of life on the one hand and a steadily rising national income on the other are not fully compatible. Perhaps a form of decentralization can be devised which will help to mediate the desired balance of goals; almost certainly, any attempt to establish a wasteful industrial-location pattern, with its accompanying aggravation of present population-distribution problems, would jeopardize the whole planning endeavor.[29]

---

[27] It seems likely that, if only because of lower land costs, the provision of urban overheads would be considerably cheaper in such medium-sized towns than in the largest cities. Moreover, the medium cities may be expected to have the rudiments of the required facilities, unlike the smallest towns. See chap. xiv, where Catherine Bauer Wurster explores the whole question of comparative costs.

[28] See chap. xv.

[29] I wish to make it quite clear that I am *not* suggesting that the rural population— the majority of Indians, after all!—should not have its plight ameliorated, or that as many as possible should crowd into congested cities. My discussion is concerned primarily with the ideological and philosophical aspects of rural-urban conflicts. Officials and politicians, sensitive to the needs and wishes of the electorate, obviously do not make decisions solely on ideological grounds. My suggestion amounts to no

My discussion would tend to suggest that the content of the seminar papers and discussions is food for pessimists. There was no evidence that any measures under consideration would significantly dry up the stream of urbanward migration, and to many must have come the thought that things must get worse before they get better. Lower standards emerged as an unfortunate but likely necessity, particularly in the way of housing and urban facilities. (The reality of this situation is less harsh than its formulation would suggest, for the standards may have been inflated to begin with—particularly where they derived from the West—and to the Indian who sleeps on the pavements the simplest shelter distinctly represents a rise in level of living.) Again, conflicts were exposed —between economic and social goals, for instance, and between long-range and short-run goals.

And yet, somehow, the seminar itself, taken as a datum, re-established a measure of optimism. Despite all the warnings against monolithic policies and inflexible procedures, there was nothing either monolithic or inflexible about the give-and-take of discussion—all the more significant, given the mixture of Indians and Americans, scholars and officials. There was no one academic or official point of view, and no unified American or Indian approach. Behind the arguments for particular forms of decentralization lay a realization that in fact no effective mechanism for the enforcement of uniformity exists; calls for extensive slum-clearance existed side-by-side with proposals to build low-standard "disposable" houses; along with rural community development there now emerges urban community development. K. N. Misra, Town and Village Planner to the government of Uttar Pradesh, pointed to the experience of his state that adding new neighborhoods to existing cities proved to be a better way of handling migrants than establishing more costly new towns. The presence of ambivalence does, after all, imply the existence of "sociological" as well as "ideological" attitudes; the hope must be that the former will be reinforced through learning.[30]

What the seminar suggested, then, was that despite admitted

---

more than this: that industrialization will be more rapid if decisions are based on sound judgments concerning relative costs and probable outcomes, unencumbered by notions of the moral superiority of rural life. India will probably remain predominantly rural for many years, it is true. Agriculture is not improved, however, by extolling the ethics of the village.

I am not assuming, either, that Western experience in handling urban problems has much to offer India. The anti-city bias of many city planners is too well known to need comment, and the nations of the West have not urbanized gracefully or without strain. India's chance is not to emulate, therefore, but to do better.

[30] I am indebted to Asoka Mehta both for the terms, in this context, and for the thought.

rigidities and inflexibilities in the prevailing situation many Indians, in and out of government, are keenly critical of unrealistic policies relating to urbanization and are attempting to find creative solutions to the problems they are facing. The character of the seminar may be taken as evidence of the desire, the energy, and the ability, on the part of those responsible, to tackle heroically the challenges offered by a coming urban population growth of unprecedented scale.[31]

Roy Turner
International Population and Urban
Research
University of California, Berkeley

[31] Catherine Bauer Wurster and Richard Park, in personal communications, suggest that I have imputed a conflict to the seminar that was not apparent. Mrs. Wurster writes that "there was no emotional split between 'centrists' and 'decentrists.' Among both the Indian and the American participants there were differing viewpoints as to the desirable or feasible urban pattern, but these differences are beginning to be resolved in rational terms."

INDEX

INDEX

Abrams, Charles, 320
Acharya, Mrs. Hemalata, 128–129, 131, 433
Adorno, T. W., 204n
Africa, 30, 132, 177
Agarwala, S. N., 169n, 439
Agnihotri, V., 437
Agra, 69–70, 214, 440
Agriculture: within cities, 68–69, 118; intensification, 69; in city hinterland, 96, 106; share of labor force, 164–169 passim; rationalization of, 169–170, 186; role in economic development, 183–184, 195–198; projections of expansion, 185–188; underemployment and productivity, 226–227; industrialization and, 248–249; research in protein production, 317; dairy industry reorganization, 351–352
Ahatas, 72
Ahmad, E., 430
Ahmedabad: population projection, 25 (table); morphology of, 63; community development project, 92n; tax revenues, 366; population density, 426
Ajmer, 40, 204
Aligarh: population density, 64, 427; morphology of, 65–66; Muslim fanaticism, 202; political extremism, 204; socioeconomic study of, 440
Allahabad, 69, 118
Alliganj, 122
All-India Village Industries Association, 216
Ambar Charka, 241
Amritsar, 41

Anand, 97
Anandavali, 128
Andhra, 430
Andhra Pradesh, 142–143, 241, 242
Apte, D. P., 428n
Architecture: urban, 58–60 passim, 104; village houses, 124; urban density, costs, and, 284–285; technology and, 299–323 passim; of Calcutta, 383
Arya Samaj, 120
Asansol industrial complex, 119
Assam, 30, 39–40, 41, 390
Aubrey, H. G., 301n
Australia, 159
Austria, 162, 163

Bihar, 132
Babu, Vithal, 119n, 139–140, 391n
Bagal, S. B., 429
Bailey, F. G., 124–125
Balogh, Thomas, 231
Banaras: population density, 64, 65; hinterland relationships, 95, 130–131, 439; origins of, 159, 214; reactionary leadership, 202; political trends, 204; geographical study of, 431–432
Bandopadhyay, S., 392
Banerjea, Surendranath, 393
Bangalore: population increase, 9–10, 25 (table); residential segregation, 60; decentralization, 67; slum social structure, 119; Pariah romanticization of, 132; migrant transitional area, 135, 136; industrialization, 268; physical growth pattern, 292; limits to growth, 303; expenditures for utilities and welfare,

367; socioeconomic study of, 431, 432–433

Baroda: city-hinterland relationships, 94–116 *passim;* kinship pattern, 134; industrialization, 293; socioeconomic survey of, 428

Bauer, Peter T., 193n, 194n

Bazaars, 59–60, 72–76, 86–88

Beggars, 72–73

Belgium, 162, 163

Bengal: success of Communists, 200; famine of 1942, 211, 384; colonial social and political life, 215–216; urbanization prospects, 302; communal riots, 384; demographic study of, 430. *See also* West Bengal

Bengal Nagpur railway, 62

Bhadkad, 123–124

Bhadrad-Nadiad railway, 124

Bhilai, 139–140

Bhilaspur, 40

Bhopal, 40

Bhubaneshwar, 441

Bhuleshwar, 427

Bihar: migration, 40; pattern of villages, 142; village industrialization, 241; planning, 294, 390

Bikaner, 41

Biraj, A. N., 436n

Birth control, 414

Birth rate, 6, 27, 314

Bogue, Donald J., 23n, 30n, 97, 444n

Bombay: population growth, 9–10, 25 (table); migration to, 31–40, 42, 43, 132, 133, 427, 439; characteristics of migrants, 40; population loss, 41; morphology of, 58; population density, 64, 65, 426, 427; commerce, 66, 128; automobile commuting, 69; railway service and suburban growth, 70; beggars, 72–73; magnitude of problems of, 75; food supply, 97; city-hinterland relationships, 94–116 *passim,* 128; local government, 131, 362–363, 365, 372; rural and urban culture in, 142, 171–172; political trends, 204, 207, 364; social anomie, 206; colonial period, 215; industrialization, 250, 258–259, 282, 293; housing costs, 284; housing and transportation needs, 291, 350, 377, 418; limits to growth, 303; division of state of, 347; occupational pattern, 348; internal transport system, 349; municipal income, 349, 366; program under Third Plan, 352–360; Local Self-Government Institute, 359; municipal expenditures for utilities and welfare, 367; community development public relations, 370; coordination of local agencies, 373; community development financing, 374; slum prevention, 378; architecture in, 383; UNESCO study of migration to, 427; labor conditions, 436; socioeconomic survey of, 437; city plan for, 442

Bombay Town Planning Act, 1954, 353–360 *passim*

Bondurant, Joan V., 204n, 390n, 391n

Bopegamage, A., 119n, 131, 176n, 431, 439, 441

Bose, Ashish, 6n, 158n, 160n, 166n, 429, 430n

Bose, Nirmal Kumar, 382n, 437

Bose, Subhash, 202

Bragg, R. L., 321n

Brahmanand, P., 435n

Brahmans, 79, 125

Brazil, 159, 178

Bredo, William, 243n, 256n, 282, 449n

Bridenbaugh, Carl, 192n

Brinton, Crane, 201, 204n

Burma, 30, 43

Bustees, 71–72, 77–78

Calcutta: population growth, 9–10, 25, 278, 383–384; birth and death rates, 28; migration, 42–43, 439; characteristics of migrants, 48–54 *passim;* morphology of, 58; population density, 64, 65; commerce, 66, 175, 217; automobile commuting, 69; railway service and suburban development, 70, 133; slums, 71; magnitude of problems of, 75; urban culture, 171–172; political problems, 201, 202, 204; famine of 1942, 211; colonial period, 215–216; industrialization, 250, 258–259, 282; cholera, 280–281; housing costs, 284, 287–289; housing and transportation needs, 291, 384, 385–388, 418, 439; urbanization prospects, 303, 382–396, 414; exports, 319; development planning, 336; local government, 365, 392–393; tax revenues, 366; morphology of, 382–383; effects of partition, 384; social unrest, 396; socioeconomic studies of, 428, 437, 439; unemployment survey, 435; displaced persons, 438

Calcutta Improvement Trust, 392–394

Candada, 159

Canton, 302

Caracas, 340, 398

Carlson, Eric, 398n

Carrothers, Gerald A. P., 442n

Casis, Ana, 177n, 178n

Caste: residential segregation, 60, 61, 65; and urban living conditions, 73–74;

breakdown of, 74, 128, 173–174; and power and property, 125; and migration propensity, 134; and village relationships, 144–146, 147–148. *See also* Kinship; Social structure and relationships

Central Uttar Pradesh. *See* Uttar Pradesh

Ceylon, 30, 132

Chakrabartty, Syamal, 383*n*, 384*n*, 385*n*, 387*n*, 389

Chandigarh, 58, 68, 291, 441

Charity, 73

Chatterjee, A. B., 437

Chatterjee, Prabuddha Nath, 394*n*

Chatterjee, S. P., 384*n*

Chauk, 59

Chawls, 71

Cheris, 72

Chicago, 426

Chile, 177

China: urbanization, 159, 181; asset creation, 195; mobilization of labor resources, 211; intensive gardening, 317; industrialization, 319; aggression, 364

Chitpur, 217

Chosh, P. K., 435*n*

Chowk, 59

Citizens' development councils. *See* Vikas Mandals

City-hinterland relationships, 94–116. *See also* specific cities

City planning: British colonial influence, 58, 60–64; Delhi, 95, 296–298, 365 (*see also* Delhi Plan); medieval European cities, 174–175; Jaipur, Lucknow, New Delhi, 175; villages, 222–223; resources and, 223–226; location of industry and population, 261–276 *passim;* model communities, 291; shortcomings of, 294–295; Bombay Third Plan program, 352–360; role of Department of the Consulting Surveyor, 354; organization for action, 357–359, 371; local government inadequacy, 364–365; comprehensiveness vs. compartmentalization, 376, 395–396; Calcutta program, 395–396; operational problems, 397–412; studies of, 441–442. *See also* Community development; Regional planning

Claude water conversion process, 314–315

Coale, Ansley, 11*n*, 21, 184*n*, 314*n*

Cohn, Bernard, 121, 122–123

Coimbatore, 290

Collver, O. Andrew, 3*n*

Colonial period. *See* England

Commerce: location of, 57–70 *passim;* bazaar characteristics and functions, 59–60, 72–76, 86–88; urbanization and, 99, 108–109, 110–116 *passim,* 175, 215;

rural-urban contacts, 121–122, 126, 128–129; service-center villages, 151–154; employment in, 166; exports, 183, 250, 319; and industrialization, 244; study of commodity flow in Delhi, 434

Communism: urbanization and, 200; leadership, 202; resources of, 203

Community development: goals, 67–93 *passim;* resources for, 223–226; local government role, 361–381; public participation, 368–370; centralization vs. decentralization, 370–371; Calcutta, 392–396; city center rehabilitation, 404–405; land reserves for, 405–407; understaffing, 410–412. *See also* City planning; Economic development; Five Year Plans; Housing; Local government; Regional planning; Self-help

Community Development Program: problems of, 140, 397–412; premises of, 141; aims of, 146, 154; caste and, 147–148; concentration on service facilities, 152, 153; and village industrialization, 241–242; successes and failures, 248

Community organizers, 79–93 *passim*

Company towns, 62

Consumption: capital accretion vs., 207–208, 262; size of city and, 283; variations in, 435. *See also* Income

Cooperatives, 149

Cooum, River, 66

Crane, R. I., 429

Culture: and geographic mobility, 29–30; Indo-British urbanism, 58–59, 60–64; level of and population concentration, 66; diffusion of urban standards, 129–131, 214; village traditionalism, 144–149; rural-urban transition, 158–160, 441; foreign influences, 171–172; materialism vs. spiritualism, 200; substitutes for political involvement, 200–201; rural-urban gap, 215–218. *See also* Ideology; Social structure and relationships

Custodian of Evacuee Property, 78

Dacca, 202, 214

Dalmia industries, 64

Damle, Y. B., 129, 130

Damodar Valley Corporation, 391, 394

Damodar Valley scheme, 294, 295

Danda Karanya resettlement, 342

Dandekar, Mrs. Kumudini, 134

Dandekar, V. M., 228*n*

Dangayach, K. B., 435*n*

Dani, L. V., 436*n*

Datta, J. M., 430

Datta, Sudhin, 216, 382*n*

Davis, Kingsley, 6*tn,* 18*n,* 29*n,* 158*n,* 177*n,* 178*n,* 278, 314*n*

Davis, Rodman T., 305*tn*

Deccan, 133

Decentralization. *See* Community development; Economic development; Industrialization

Dehri-Dalmianagar, 63–64

Delhi: population growth, 9–10, 25, 150, 272–273; migration, 39, 43; characteristics of migrants, 40, 438; displaced persons, 66; beggars, 73; city-hinterland relationships, 94–116 *passim,* 131; food supply, 97 hinterland utilities, 97–98; local government, 131, 132; origins of, 159, 214; reactionary leadership, 202; political trends, 204, 364; community development, 218 (*see also* Delhi Plan); transportation needs, 286; research for planning, 296–298; legislation for planning, 365; tax revenues, 366, 375; expenditures for utilities and welfare, 367; community development financing, 374; housing needs, 377; slums, 378; citizen participation, 380–381; hinterland industrialization, 400; resistance to planning, 406; UNESCO study of migration, 427; socioeconomic study of, 431, 432–433; demographic study of, 439; study of goods transport, 439. *See also* New Delhi; Old Delhi

Delhi City Planning Team, 223

Delhi Employment Exchange, 199

Delhi Pilot Project, 71–93

Delhi Plan, 95, 294, 335–346, 376, 380–381, 442

Delhi Seminar on Rural Industrialization, 241–242

Democracy: decentralization of municipal services and, 76; hierarchical vs. egalitarian values, 148–149; problems of development of, 199–205; and economic development pattern, 232, 262–263; and local government, 362–365 *passim,* 364, 370–373

Demographic Training and Research Centre (Bombay), 28

Demography, 3–26; urban-rural differences, 95–98, 99, 117–118, 130–131; family size, 127; characteristics of migrants, 132–134; and delimitation of villages, 141–142; African and Latin American cities, 177–180; Calcutta household composition, 386–387; urban surveys, 427–430. *See also* Density of population; Population

Density of population: urban, 4–7, 64–66,

426–427; and city-hinterland delimitation, 99; suburban wards, 100; of city hinterlands, 103–105, 109–116 *passim;* rural "push" to migration, 169–170; and political extremism, 199–201; in villages, 225; and housing costs, 284–285; and sanitation, 285–286; and transportation, 286–287; projections of, 302–303

Desai, C. C., 441

Desai, I. P., 127

Deshmukh, M. B., 427*n,* 438

Deshpande, C. D., 57–58

Deva, 124

Dharwar, 58, 68

Disease. *See* Health, sanitation and disease; Mortality

Displaced persons: housing congestion, 66; in Delhi Pilot Project, 78, 79; industrialization and, 139; receptiveness to political extremism, 206; new towns for, 291; in Calcutta, 384, 387, 438; in Delhi, 438

Drew, J. B., 441*n*

Dumont, René, 197

Durgapur, 139, 391

East Punjab. *See* Punjab

Eames, Edwin, 134, 438

East India Company, 62, 215

Echeverria, Edward G., 189*n,* 284, 296, 392*n,* 396*n,* 442

Economic development: urbanization and, 3, 7–8, 157–181, 263–268; migration and, 20; in villages, 29, 123–126 *passim,* 128–129; goals of, 74, 92, 261–263; city-hinterland relationships and, 94–116; cash economy and, 125–126, 128–129; jajmani system and, 144–146; service-center villages, 151–154; capitalization needs, problems, and potentials, 167–168, 182–183, 185–186, 193–195, 196–197, 219, 262 (*see also* Financing); role of agriculture, 169–170, 185–188; and urbanization, 178–179, 219; long-range strategy, 182–191; political stability and, 192–212; Russian model, 195; ideological problems, 195–198; unemployment and, 198–200; mobilization of human resources, 211–212 (*see also* Self-help); centralization-decentralization problems, 213–239, 248–250, 266–269; efficiency vs. employment, 235–236; regional disparities, 246–247; role of industry, 248–249 (*see also* Industrialization); international trade and, 250; and location of industry, 250–260; phased programs, 255–256; consumption and, 262; rationalization and redistribution of employment, 267; urban pattern and, 288; integration of, 327–334; need for acceleration, 414; research and, 425–443 *passim. See also* Agriculture; Community development; Five Year Plans; Planning; Self-help

Education: and migration, 51–54, 135–136; of community organizers, 79; role in self-help projects, 84, 86; European influence, 172; and unemployment, 198–199, 350–351; and political extremism, 199–205 *passim;* investment needs for, 309–310; transportation and, 316; public opinion and planning, 343–344; concentration in cities, 348. *See also* Literacy

Ellefsen, Richard, 256*n,* 449*n*

England: urbanization, 4–10 *passim,* 162; colonial influence of, 58, 60–64, 215; size of farms, 169; autonomy of cities, 174; social costs of industrialization, 197; suburban development, 278; local government model for India, 362; local government weakness, 364

Epstein, S., 306*n*

Etawah Pilot Project, 290

Europe: social structure and urbanization, 159–160; rate of urbanization and industrialization, 160–181 *passim;* capitalization and industrialization, 167–168; rationalization of agriculture, 169–170; housing discrimination, 173; autonomy of cities, 174

Exports, 183, 250, 319

Faridabad, 31, 291

Federal Reserve Bank (India), 281

Ferozepur, 41

Feuer, Lewis, 199

Financing: of Delhi Pilot Project, 75; local resources, 75, 364–365; self-help educational subsidies, 86; Ahmedabad community development project, 92*n;* capitalization needs, problems, and potentials, 167–168, 182–183, 185–186, 193–195, 196–197, 219, 262; interest rates, 196–197; housing, 223–224, 281–282, 306–307, 388–389; industrialization, 227–228, 243–244; investment policy and urban growth, 265–266; timing of investments, 287–288, 290; new towns, 290–291; land acquisition, 336–337; land speculation control, 337; local development, 353, 373–376; tax problems and, 357–358; local government resources, 365–368; Calcutta rehabilitation, 395–396. *See also* Self-help

First Plan: industry, trade, and agriculture, 227; small-scale industry, 236–237; housing, 281–282

Fisher, Margaret, 204*n*

Five Year Plans: effects on urbanization, 9; village ignorance of, 130; urban-regional planning under, 335–338. *See also* First Plan; Third Plan; Fourth Plan; Planning; Second Plan

Food Production Pilot Program, 344

Ford Foundation, 75, 92*n,* 396*n*

Fourth Plan, 264

France: rate or urbanization, 162; labor force distribution, 164; size of farms, 169; autonomy of cities, 174

Fry, M., 441*n*

Fulia, 392

Gadgil, R., 428*n*

Galenson, Walter, 196*n*

Galbraith, J. K., 204*n*

Gamble, Richard B., 3*n,* 18*n*

Gananathan, V. S., 430

Gandhi, M. K.: attitudes toward, 202; distrust of urban life, 216; emphasis on village development, 236

Gandhi, N. K., 289*n,* 441

Ganga and Brahmaputra Flood Control and Water Transport boards, 390

Gangapur, 128

Ganges, 122. *See also* Hooghly River.

Ganguli, B. N., 228*n*

Gans, Herbert, 312*n*

Geographic mobility. *See* Migration

George Town, 66

Germany: rate of urbanization, 162, 163; employment distribution, 166; size of farms, 169; autonomy of cities, 174; role of sports in politics, 201

Ghat, 134

Ghose, Benoy, 383*n*

Ghurye, G. S., 429

Gibbs, Jack P., 7*n*

Gist, Noel P., 58*n,* 60, 67, 433, 438

Goalpara, 41

Gokhale, A. G., 436*n*

Gokhale Institute, 428, 438

Golden, Hilda Hertz, 8*n*

Goldsmith, Ernest, 392*n,* 393*n*

Gorakhpur, 440

Gough, Kathleen, 125

Government; financial limitations in slum projects, 75; influence on village economy and social structure, 125; land acquisition and resettlement of villagers, 138–140; centralization in cities, 160; and urbanization, 175; African independence and urbanization, 177; and centralization vs. decentralization, 213–

239; and origin of cities, 214–215; promotion of rural industry, 240–260 *passim;* licensing of industry, 256–260, 282; as entrepreneur, 262; restriction of migration by, 264–265; defense manufacturing, 268; development policy, 271; industrial location and housing policy, 275; institutionalization of planning, 279; role in urban organization problems, 319–323 *passim;* organization of planning, 333, 389–390; sponsorship of milk-supply schemes, 349–350; role of states in urbanization, 382–396; regulation of tenement density, 388; housing subsidies, 389; Development Department (West Bengal), 391–392; policy on industry size and location, 417; research and reports on urban problems, 425–443 *passim;* concern for wages and labor conditions, 435. *See also* Community Development Program; Local government; Planning Commission

Granguly Began, 392

Granshof, F. L., 175*n*

Greater Bombay. *See* Bombay (and similarly for respective cities)

Guha, Meera, 70*n*, 430, 439

Guha, S., 429

Guindy industrial estate, 70, 292

Gujerat: literacy, 108; village life in, 124, 127; formation of, 347; commerce, 431

Gupta, S. K., 388, 393*n*

Habra-Baigachi, 392

Haikerwal, B. S., 206*n*

Hamlets, 142, 143

Harijan Basti, 142

Harijans, 79

Haringhata, 392

Harris, Britton, 292, 303*n*, 383*n*, 442

Harris, Dorothy L., 23*n*

Harrison, Selig S., 390*n*, 448*n*

Hart, Henry C., 391*n*

Haufe, Helmut, 161*tn*

Hauser, Philip M., 427*n*

Health, sanitation, and disease: in slums, 72; self-help improvements, 83; in city hinterlands, 97–98; migration and insanity, 134; cholera in Calcutta, 280–281; city size and, 280–281, 285–286; minimum adequate standard of living components, 304–307; water resources, 314–315; food supplies for megapolis development, 317; milk-supply schemes, 349–350, 351–352; Bombay Third Plan program for, 352–360 *passim;* local

government expenditures, 367; local facilities needs, 379; conditions in Calcutta, 384

Health Ministry, 345

Health and welfare councils, 76

Higgins, Benjamin H., 195*n*, 200*n*

Himachal Pradesh, 40, 143

Himalayas as water source, 314

Hindus, 43

Hindu Code Bill, 140

Hinterland-city relationships, 94–116

Hinterlands, 117–140 *passim*

Hirt, Howard F., 58*n*, 66*n*, 427*n*, 440

Hoffer, Eric, 204, 212

Hoffman, Michael, 386*n*, 395

Holland, 162, 295

Home Ministry, 345

Hong Kong, 319

Hooghly River: industrialization, 63, 66, 70, 217; transportation problems, 303; water supply, 384

Hooghlyside conurbation, 70

Hoover, Edgar M., 11*tn*, 21, 184*n*, 314*n*

Hoselitz, Bert F., 170*n*, 199, 205, 207*n*, 293, 441, 449*n*

Housing: urban congestion, 66; segregation breakdown, 73–74; rent, 90; segregation, 173–174; urbanization and, 189–190; self-help rehabilitation, 194; costs in cities, 223–224, 265–266, 284–285, 293; decentralization, 273; conditions by size of city, 280, 350, 418–419; public expenditures, 281–282; location problems, 286–287; needs, 291, 306–307, 376–377; Delhi studies of, 296–298; construction technology, 318, 355–357; planning and land acquisition, 335–338 *passim;* need for Ministry of, 345; financing, 355–357; conditions in Calcutta, 384–388 *passim;* cost of solution in Calcutta, 387–389; planning errors, 392; Calcutta Improvement Trust efforts, 393–394. *See also* Slums

Howrah, 70, 132

Hungary, 164

Hussain, A. F. A., 137, 138, 207

Hyderabad: population growth, 10*t*, 25*t*; city-hinterland relationships, 94–116 *passim;* socioeconomic survey, 428

Ideology: urbanization and, 129–131, 200–201; of migrants, 136; problem in panchayats, 147; hierarchical vs. egalitarian, 148–149; urban elite vs. masses, 171–172; persistance of rural values, 178–179; theory and dogma in economic development, 195–198; welfare values and costs of urbanization, 197; extremism, 199–205; intergroup contact and, 208–209; bias for village development, 222, 236–237; traditionalism, 263; urban vs. rural development priority, 394–395; national goals and urban development, 413–421. *See also* Democracy

Illiteracy. *See* Education; Literacy

Income: rural-urban differences, 266; city size and, 282–283; projection of, 416; studies of, 435–438. *See also* Consumption

Indraprastha, 159

Industrialization: urbanization and, 3, 7–8, 12, 263–267, 301–302; company towns, 62; and segregation breakdown, 73–74; caste-occupation patterns, 74; in villages, 117–119 *passim*, 216–217, 227–239 *passim*, 290; and social change, 137–140 *passim*; and European urbanization, 162; and labor force distribution, 164–169; capitalization and size of unit, 167–168; capitalization problems, 178, 179–180; and Latin American urbanization, 179–180; resource allocation problems, 195–198; role in economic development, 195–198; and pattern of urban growth, 220–221; decentralization of, 232–239 *passim*, 240–260, 266–269, 401–403; industrial estates, 242–244, 254; electrification and, 243–244, 251; and curbing migration, 246–247; location considerations, 250–260, 309, 329–332; market and resource requirements, 252–253; licensing, 256–260; working conditions, 267–268, 435–438; lag behind migration, 273–274; city size and, 282–283; of moderate-size cities, 292–293; technology and, 319; role in development, 327–334; in Maharashtra, 348; urban-regional planning and, 399–404; government policy on location and size, 417. *See also* Economic development

International Bank Calcutta report, 395

Ireland, 163–164

Israel, 295, 319

Italy, 174

Iyengar, S. Kesave, 428*n*

Jaipur, 175

Jajmani system, 144–146

Jalda colony, 139

Jamaica, 319

Jamshedpur: morphology of, 58, 63, 68; kinship and migration, 135; industrialization, 268; socioeconomic survey of, 428

Janaki, V. A., 430

Jana Sangha, 204

Japan: urbanization, 4–10 *passim*, 181; economic development, 221; sanitation, 286; decentralization of industry, 234; agricultural productivity, 302, 317; industrialization, 319

Jaunpur, 70

Jhirpani colony, 139

Joshi, C. B., 69*n*

Joshi, R. V., 58*n*, 67, 69, 430

Kadri, S. K., 436*n*

Kahl, Joseph A., 179

Kaira, 123–124

Kakade, R. G., 428*n*

Kakinada, 241

Kalyam, 127

Kalyani, 291, 392

Kanpur: population, 25*t;* morphology of, 63; slum compound, 72; migration, 122; socioeconomic study of, 437

Kanwariganj ward (Aligarh), 427

Kapadia, K. M., 74*n*, 119*n*, 126–127

Karachi, 202

Karan, Pradyumna Prasad, 58*n*, 63, 68*n*

Karim, A. K. Nazmul, 73*n*

Karve Committee report, 240–241

Karve, Iravati, 173

Kashmir, 97

Katras, 71

Kelley, Burnham, 198*n*, 208*n*

Kerala: literacy, 108; village pattern, 143; development workers in, 144; success of Communists, 200; village industry, 241; study of, 430

Khan, A. G., 442

Kharagpur, 62, 63

Khatiks, 79

Kinship: joint family unit, 118; and village social structure, 120–122 *passim*, 144–146; breakdown of joint family system, 125, 126–127; impact of migration on, 134–135; impact of industrialization on, 138–140; and political patterns, 201–202; urban family size, 306

Kish, L., 97

Klein, W. C., 321*n*

Knolb, William L., 192*n*

Knowles, William H., 205

Koenigsberger, O. H., 441

Kolaba, 133

Kolar Gold Field City, 41

Kolhapur, 349

Kolhatkar, Y. V., 435*n*

Konkan, 133

Kumbapettai, 125

Kutch, 40

Kutcha construction, 59
Kuznets, Simon, 8*n*, 165*tn*

Labor force. *See* Occupation
Lahore, 202, 433
Lakadawala, D. T., 437*n*
Lal, Amrit, 430
Lambert, Richard D., 137*n,* 436
Lampard, Eric, 159, 193*n*
Latin America, 177–180, 201
Leadership: citizens' development councils, 76, 77–93 *passim;* community organizers, 79–93 *passim;* self-help training program for, 87–88; urbanism, education, and extremism, 201–203; communications middlemen in village development, 321–322; role in planning, 344–345
Learmonth, A. T. A., 230, 295, 342
Lewis, Oscar, 145*n*, 178
Lewis, W. Arthur, 207*n,* 209
Liebenstein, Harvey, 196*n*
Lindemann, Erich, 321*n*
Literacy; in slums, 72, 78; urbanization and, 99; in city hinterlands, 107–108, 109–116 *passim;* and resistance to change, 130
Local government: antagonism and apathy toward, 72, 73, 81, 89–90; Delhi city welfare council proposal, 88–89; expenditures of, 281; reorganization of, 333, 370–373; town planning authority of, 354, 357–359; Local Self-Government Institute (Bombay), 359; urbanization and, 361–381, 382–396; forms of, 362–365; political expedience of, 364; financing problems of, 364–365, 373–376; financing resources of, 365–368; Calcutta Corporation, 392–393; control of land-use, 406; reform of, 420. *See also* Community development
Lok Sabha, 344
London, 307, 372
Lucknow, 121, 122, 175, 435
Ludlow, W. H., 427*n*

McCully, Bruce T., 201*n*
Madhya Bharat, 40
Madhya Pradesh, 40, 142, 259
Madras: population growth, 25 (table), 313–314; migration, 31, 42, 43; population loss, 41; morphology, 58; population density, 64; commercial concentration, 66; automobile commuting, 69; railway service and suburban development, 70; slums, 72; magnitude of problems of, 75; city-hinterland relationships, 94–116 *passim;* food supply for

Delhi, 97; primary industries in, 118; village pattern, 142–143; urban culture, 171–172; political trends, 204; colonial period, 215; location of industry, 259; transportation, 292; community development, 303; urban villages, 312–313; water supply, 314–315; export prospects, 319; tax revenues, 366; expenditures for utilities and welfare, 367; study of migration to, 439
Madura, 215
Magadha empire, 159
Mahabharata, 159
Mahalanobis, Prof., 227
Maharashtra, 126, 132, 134, 347–360
Majumdar, D. N., 120, 121–122, 130, 198, 199, 210
Malabar, 125
Malaviya, H. E., 321*n*
Malaya, 30, 43, 132
Malenbaum, Wilfred, 193*n,* 195*n,* 198, 205*n,* 283*n,* 435
Malhotra, Dr., 243
Malkani, H. C., 428*n*
Mamoria, C. B., 429
Mandis, 244
Mandi towns, 153
Manhalli, 129
Manickam, T. J., 442*n*
Manipur, 390
Marathas, 78
Marriage. *See* Kinship
Marriott, McKim, 119*n,* 121, 122–123, 146*n,* 195*n,* 225*n*
Martindale, Don, 174*n,* 192*n*
Marwari moneylenders, 126
Maslow, A. H., 204*n*
Mayer, Albert, 195*n,* 292, 442*n*
Mehta, Asoka, 413*n,* 452*n*
Mehta, B. V., 437*n*
Mehta, J. J., 291*n*
Mehta, Sir Pherozshah, 362
Meier, Richard, 285, 292, 300*n,* 314*n*
Methodology, 95–98
Meuriot, P., 169*n*
Mexico, 177, 178–179, 319
Migrants: occupations of, 45, 46–51; attitudes and values, 136, 178–179; employment problem, 167–169; maintenance of ties to village, 172; self-help housing, 308; "urban village" settlements, 311–312; in Calcutta, 386–387. *See also* Displaced persons
Migration to cities, 5–7, 27–54; potential increase, 9–10, 12–22, 264–265; proportion of urbanization, 23; rural immobility, 29–30; 1941–1951, 31–44; sex distribution, 40; to metropolises, 41–44;

age distribution, 43, 44; partition and, 43, 45; unemployment "push," 45; education and, 51–54; and segregation breakdown, 73–74; "resting stage" enclaves, 119; and village stability, 131–133; "rotation," 132; poverty "push," 133–134; kinship structure and, 134–135; "feedback," 135–136; population "push," 169–170; agricultural productivity and, 187–188; and anomie, 205–206; and rural-urban "balance," 222–223; and rural-urban differences, 218–239, 246–247; rural-urban wage differentials and, 226–227, 283; decentralization of industry as brake on, 233–234, 401; lag of industrialization, 273–274; China, 302; Madras, 314; rate, 413; UNESCO study of, 427; and labor conditions, 438; studies of, 438–439

Millikan, M. F., 203n
Ministry of Community Development, 241
Ministry of Works, Housing and Supply, 336, 345
Mirzapur, 440
Mishmi Hills, 40, 41
Mishra, M. L., 435n
Misra, B. N., 435n
Misra, B. R., 119n, 135, 428n
Mithbaon, 134
Mitra, A., 383n
Modak, M. V., 442n
Modi family mills, 68
Modinagar, 68, 69
Mohalla, 60
Mohalla committees, 67–68, 76
Mohana, 120, 121
Mohone, 291
Mookherjee, D., 430, 440
Moorthy, M. V., 73n
Moradabad, 118
Morphology of cities, 57–70 *passim;* and urban conditions, 73–74; and city-hinterland delimitation, 94–116 *passim;* of villages, 141–144, 150–154; city planning, 175; and transportation, 286–287; technology and, 299–323; module design, 311–313; reports on various cities, 425–443 *passim*
Morris, Morris David, 133, 207n, 436
Morrison, William A., 127, 130
Mortality, 6, 27, 280; in slums, 72; sanitation and, 197
Motivation: apathy and antagonism to development, 72, 73, 81, 89–90, 343–344, 368–369; women's interest in self-help programs, 91; urban growth, social change, and, 163–164; political activity, 199–205 *passim*

Mukherjee, Mrs. B., 58n
Mukherjee, Sudhansu Bhusan, 392n
Mukherji, A. B., 68, 69n, 204
Mulug, 242
Muslims: migration to Pakistan, 43; influence on city morphology, 59; residential segregation, 60; redevelopment of property of, 78
Mysore: migration, 39, 40; urban population loss, 41; village change, 129; village pattern, 142; village social system, 147; industrialization, 259, 268; regional planning, 342
Mysore Survey, 295

Nagpur: population growth, 25 (table); reactionary leadership, 202; internal transport, 349; municipal income, 349; unemployment survey, 435
Nargong, 40
Nasik, 128, 131, 433
Nath, V., 294, 429
National Buildings Organizations, 281–282, 285
National income, 183, 185–188
National Planning Commission. *See* Planning Commission
National Rayon Corporation, 291
National Seminar on Urban Community Development, 75n, 92, 93
Natural increase of urban population, 12–21 *passim,* 27–28
Navsari, 127
Nehru, Jawaharlal, 130, 196, 202, 217–218
Netherlands, 162, 295
Neuwirth, Gertrude, 174n, 192n
New Delhi: population density, 65, 426; decentralization, 67; automobile commuting, 69; city planning, 175; morphology, 383. *See also* Delhi
Newman, K. S., 204n
Newspapers, 130–131
New York, 25, 303, 316
Neyyattinkara, 241
Nimroff, M. F., 127
Nurkse, Ragnar, 195, 249n

Occupation: and migration, 45, 46–51; and residential segregation, 60–63 *passim;* urbanization and, 99, 108–109, 110–116 *passim;* city hinterlands, 105–107, 109–116 *passim;* classification of, 118; caste and, 134, 144, 146; distribution relative to urbanization, 164–169; city size and, 282–283, 330–331; pattern in Maharashtra, 348; of displaced persons, 387
Oka, Takashi, 196n

Old Delhi: population density, 64, 426–427; morphology of, 66; decentralization, 67; housing and transportation needs, 291. *See also* Delhi

Opler, Morris, 120–121, 131

Orissa: migration, 40; self-help financing, 89*n;* village social and economic change, 124–125; displaced persons resettlement, 139; village pattern, 142; urbanization, 302; regional planning, 390; study of, 430; agriculture, 431; new capital for, 441

Overstreet, Gene D., 202*n*

Pakistan: Muslim migration to, 43; impact of technological change, 137; social disorganization, 207; population, 302; refugees from, 384 (*see also* Displaced persons)

Panchayats, 147–149, 232

Panama, 177

Panjabi, R. M., 68*n*

Pant, Pandit Govind Ballabh, 390

Pant, Pitambar, 198*n,* 277, 285, 294

Pareto's Law of Income Distribution, 251

Pariahs, 119, 132, 135

Paris, 307, 310

Park, Richard L., 195*n*

Partition. *See* Displaced persons; Pakistan

Pataliputra, 159

Patil, R. K., 426*n,* 436*n*

Patnaik, K. M., 430

Peking, 302

Penang, 132

Pendse, R. G., 428*n*

People's development councils. *See* Vikas Mandals

Pepsu, 40

Peshawar, 202

Philadelphia, 345

Philippines, 319

Pickard, Jerome P., 24*n*

Planning: village characteristics and, 143–144; population growth and, 150; centralization vs. decentralization, 213–239; goals of, 261–263; urbanization and development alternatives, 278–279; need for comprehensiveness, 294–295; research and, 277–294 *passim,* 295–296, 425–443 *passim;* megapolis design, 299–323; organization of, 319–323 *passim;* public opinion and, 343–344; political and administrative considerations, 389–390; errors in, 392; departmentalization of, 398. *See also* City planning; Community development; Delhi Plan; Eco-nomic development; Planning Commission; Regional planning

Planning Commission: mandate of, 236; Karve Committee report, 240–241; small-industry program, 243–244; estimates of costs, 286; area-development survey, 295; research in occupation distribution, 331. *See also* Planning

Poddar Park, 392

Polai, S. L., 204*n*

Poland, 196*n*

Political life: village power structure, 125; autonomy of cities, 174–175; as frustration outlet, 199–201; sources and patterns of extremism, 201–205; control of unions, 206–207; and centralization vs. decentralization, 213–239 *passim;* population growth and, 364; instability in West Bengal, 394, 396. *See also* Social structure and relationships

Poona: population growth, 25 (table); population density, 64; decentralization, 67; suburb development, 69; health and welfare council 76*n;* commerce, 129; diffusion of urban values, 130; reactionary leadership, 202; internal transport, 349; municipal income, 349; expenditures for utilities and welfare, 367; socioeconomic survey, 428

Population: growth and projected growth, 11–13, 22–26, 30–43, 184–188, 223, 264–265, 302, 339–340, 347–348, 383–384, 413–414; proportion in slums, 71; of villages, 143, 150–151; of service-center villages, 152–153; growth rates, 157–158, 160–164; Latin American cities, 177–178; optimum distribution of, 251; city size and industrial growth, 256–260; city size and living conditions, 279–283; optimum city size, 292–293, 329; and local tax base lag, 366–367; stabilization of city size, 380; redistribution in Delhi, 380–381. *See also* Demography; Density; Migration

Port cities, 58

Portugal, 164

Poverty: and urban congestion, 66, 69, 272–273; and self-help prospects, 90; and migration, 133. *See also* Income; Slums

Prabhu, P. N., 74*n,* 133, 427*n,* 436

Prabhu, V. R., 58*n,* 68

Pradesh, 241

Pradesh, Madhya, 435*n*

Praja Socialist party, 203

Prien, C. H., 301*n*

Prussia, 163

Public Health Engineering Institute, 379

Public utilities. *See* Health, sanitation, and disease
Pucka construction, 59, 61
Puerto Rico, 177, 317, 319
Punjab: migration, 39–41 *passim;* displaced persons, 43, 66; population stability, 132; villages, 142; development planning, 143; development workers in, 144; location of industries in, 259; industrialization, 293; Delhi suburbs in, 433

Railways. *See* Transportation
Rajagopalan, C., 427*n*, 437
Rajasthan, 40, 142
Rajasthan canal, 342
Raj, K. N., 198*n*
Rajkot, 293
Rajya Sabha, 344
Ramanandham, V. V., 430
Rampur, 118
Rangaswami, K., 384*n*, 390*n*
Rao, M. S. A., 125, 127
Rao, Prakasa, 295, 342, 438
Rashtriya Swayam-Sewak Sangh, 200
Ratnagiri, 132, 133, 134
Rawalpindi, 202
Redfield, Robert, 119
Refugees. *See* Displaced persons
Regional planning, 335–346; Delhi, 95 (*see also* Delhi Plan); centralization vs. decentralization, 230–231; Tennessee Valley development, 294; population growth and, 339–340; interim plans, 341–342; Zonal Councils scheme, 390–392; urban vs. rural priority, 394–395; operational problems, 397–412; need for, 415–416; regional differences, 430–431. *See also* Planning
Revenue Survey, 142–143
Roads. *See* Transportation
Robson, William A., 383*n*, 392*n*
Rosenstein-Rodan, P. N., 193*n*, 195, 198
Rostow, W. W., 197*n*, 203*n*
Rotterdam, 337
Rourkela, 139
Roy, B. C., 390, 395
Rural Arts and Crafts Training Centre (Mulug), 242
Russia: rate of urbanization, 162; capital investment vs. consumption, 196*n;* role of sports in politics, 201; diversion of resources to war production, 221; rural-urban economic integration, 328

St. Thomas Mount, 70
Salsette Island, 70, 108
Samuelson, Paul A., 208

Sandesara, J. C., 437*n*
Sanitation. *See* Health, sanitation, and disease
Sansis, 78
Santiniketan, 217
Satara, 133
Saurashtra, 40, 293
Savarkar, 202
Scandinavia, 162–163
Sealday, 70
Second Plan: emphasis on village development, 227–228; emphasis on basic industries, 230; socialist aims, 237; electrification, 243; successes and failures, 248; costs estimates, 265–266; public housing, 281–282; utilities development, 353; allocation of funds to local authorities, 374
Segregation: residential, 60–63 *passim;* breakdown of, 73–74, 90–91
Self-help: in urban community development, 74–93 *passim,* 418–419; in Delhi Pilot Project, 81–93 *passim;* and rural asset creation, 194; Gandhi's village industries emphasis, 216–217; housing construction, 265, 308, 318; displaced-persons settlements, 291
Seminar on Rural Industrialization and Economic Development (New Delhi), 244
Senapur, 121
Sen, S. N., 383*n*, 387*n*, 389*n*, 428*n*, 437
Sengupta, D. N., 384*n*
Sewage. *See* Health, sanitation, and disease
Shah, C. T., 435*n*
Shah Jahan, 66
Shahjahanpur, 41
Shanghai, 302
Sholapur, 63, 349
Sharif, 241
Shridharani, Krishnalal, 447*n*
Shri, R. A., 170*n*
Shukla, A. C., 435*n*
Siberia, 159
Siliguri, 440
Silone, Ignazio, 204*n*
Singer, Milton, 202
Singh, Hari Har, 70
Singh, K. N., 58*n*, 63–64
Singh, Lal, 70*n*
Singh, Rudra Dutt, 119*n*
Singh, R. L., 58*n*, 95, 119*n*, 130–131, 431–432, 435*n*, 439, 440
Singh, Tarlok, 295
Singh, Ujagir, 69*n*
Sinha, B., 430
Sinha, K. K., 386*n*

Slums: population in, 71; Delhi Pilot Project, 71–93; conditions in, 72–74; community development approach, 75–83; self-help in, 90; village social structure in, 119; and costs of urbanization, 197–198; and social stability, 205; Bombay, 350; prevention of, 356, 377–378; Calcutta clearance costs, 388. *See also* Housing

Slum Clearance Program, 284

Small Industries Service Institutes and Extension Centres, 243

Small Scale Industries Organization, 242

Social structure and relationships: urban morphology and, 73–74; community development approach and, 74–93 *passim;* Brahman influence, 79, 125; "community feeling" and self-help, 82–83; religious barrier breakdown, 90–91; urban impact on village life, 116–140; cash economy and, 128–130 *passim;* industrialization and, 138–140; villages, 141–154; traditionalism, 144–149; caste as basic unit, 146, 147–148 (*see also* Caste); and urban growth, 158–160; and urban-rural values, 171–172; special interest groups, 173–174; and Latin American economic development, 178; and political patterns, 201–203; anomie, 205–206; intergroup contact, 208–209; colonial Calcutta, 215–216; urbanization and, 270; large cities, 299–323 *passim;* urban village homogeneity, 311–313; urban organization problems, 319–323; and public participation in local development, 368–369; of Calcutta migrants, 386–387; studies of, 435–438, 440–441; migrant's position in, 438. *See also* Caste; Kinship

Sovani, N. V., 428*n,* 429

Soviet Union. *See* Russia

Spate, O. H. K., 430

Srikakulam, 41

Sriniketan, 217

Srinivas, M. N., 129*n,* 133, 146*n,* 147, 441

Stamp, Dudley, 130

State-of-birth statistics, 30

Stein, J. A., 442

Stepanek, J. E., 301*n*

Stockholm, 337

Strong, Josiah, 197

Subrahamanyam, N., 70*n*

Sundharam, K. P., 435*n*

Surat, 426

Swadeshi movement, 216

Sweden, 164

Switzerland, 162, 164

Tagore, Rabindranath, 217

Talati, K. M., 426*n*

Tanjore, 125, 215

Tata Iron and Steel Company, 63

Taxation Enquiry Commission, 283, 373–374, 376

Technology: lag behind ideology, 196–198; and decentralization of industry, 233; and agricultural productivity, 248–249; and design of large cities, 299–323; and food, fuel, and materials supplies for megapolises, 317–319; and housing construction, 377

Tennessee Valley development, 294

Third Plan: investment rate, 183, 185–186; village industries, 217; urban development, 223–224, 336; formulation of, 256; acceleration of industrialization, 264, 379; milk-supply schemes, 349–350; Bombay program, 352–360

Thorner, Daniel, 8*n,* 9

Tillman, Durdin, 195*n*

Tischer, R. G., 317

Tiwari, A. R., 440

Tokugawa Institute for Biological Research, 317

Tokyo, 307

Town Planning Organization, 95, 296

Trade unions, 206–208

Transportation: and location of residence, 69, 70, 292; and urbanization, 99; and city morphology, 99–103 *passim,* 292; and rural-urban contacts, 128, 144–146; urban systems, 132–133, 349; employment in, 166; and industrialization, 244, 247; and urban congestion, 272–273; city size and, 286–287; metropolitan needs, 291, 310–311; restriction of automobile use, 308–309; and storage of food, 309; and Madras growth potential, 315; technology and, 318–319; and location of industry, 401–402; studies of, 439–440

Travancore-Cochin, 40

Trent, Mrs. T. S., 129

Tripura, 39, 40, 41, 390

Ulhasnagar, 31

Underdeveloped countries, 177–180

Unemployment: and migration, 45; and economic development, 198–200; in major cities, 283; of educated persons, 350–351; in Calcutta, 387; research and reports on, 434–435

UNESCO Centre (Calcutta), 132

Unions, 206–208

United Nations, 11, 24*n*

United States: urbanization, 3–12 *passim*, 221; population distribution, 158–163 *passim;* capitalization of foreign industry, 180; sanitation and mortality, 197; decentralization of industry, 234; suburban development, 278; land prices, 287; research in protein production, 317; rural-urban economic integration, 328; popularization of regional planning, 345

Untouchables, 79

Upper Colaba (Bombay), 427

Urban community development, 71–93. *See also* City planning; Community development; Urbanization

Urbanization, 3–26; and industrialization, 7–8, 12, 250–251, 327–334; prospects of, 11–26, 187–188, 413–414; reclassification of rural places, 13–14, 28; and population density, 26, 103–105, 109–116 *passim* (*see also* Density); by states, 31–40; by districts, 32–39, 40–41; size of major town and, 45; company towns, 62; centralization vs. decentralization, 67–70, 213–239, 261–276, 277–298, 401–403; city-hinterland relationships, 94–116; and literacy, 107–108, 109–116 *passim;* sex ratio, 108, 109–116 *passim;* impact on village life, 117–140; primary industries in urban areas, 118; and ideology, 129–131; commuting, 132–133; social structure and, 158–160, 173–174 (*see also* Social structure and relationships); and labor force distribution, 164–169; and economic development, 157–181, 182–191, 219–220, 263–255; foreign influence, 171–172, 215–216; political autonomy and, 174–175; in Africa and Latin America, 177–180; barriers to, 178–179; and housing problem, 189–190 (*see also* Housing); political stability, economic growth, and, 192–212; and unemployment, 198–200; and political extremism, 199–200; and productivity, 206–208 *passim,* 288–289; trade union role in, 206–208; and consumption patterns, 207–208, 209; and intergroup contact, 208–209; and education, 214; stages and rates, 218–219, 264–266, 425–426; and service facilities needs, 265; "parasitism" arguments against, 266–267; policy for, 271–276; and living conditions and costs, 277–298; new towns, 290–291; metropolitan, 291–292; optimal city size, 292–293, 308; technology and design of large cities, 299–323; available land, 302–303;

standards for, 304–323 *passim;* module design, 311–313; food, fuel, and materials problem, 317–319; organization problems, 319–323; in Maharashtra, 347–360; and lag in tax base, 366–367; role of local and state governments, 361–381, 382–396; national goals and, 413–421; research and reports on, 425–443. *See also* City planning; Community development; Migration; Population

Uttar Pradesh: migration, 40, 134; primary industries in urban areas, 118; village patterns, 142, 430; village social system, 147; suburb development, 443

Values. *See* Ideology

Vasanta, A., 440

Venkatarangaiya, M., 383*n*, 392*n*, 393*n*, 394*n*

Venkatarayappa, K. N., 431

Venkatesawarlu, Y., 430

Venezuela, 177

Vernon, Raymond, 449*n*

Vikas Mandals, 76, 77–93 *passim*

Villages: urbanization, 94–116 *passim,* 117–140; physical amenities in, 97–98; population density, 104–105, 109–116 *passim;* commerce, 108–109, 110–116 *passim;* dormitory populations, 132–133; selective migration from, 133–134; apathy and antagonism to change, 137–140; as community development unit, 141–154; isolation of, 144–146; hierarchical vs. egalitarian values, 148–149; physical change trends, 150–154; development of service centers, 151–154; industrialization, 216–217, 227–239 *passim,* 240–260 *passim;* future development, 222–223. *See also* Community development

Vindhya Pradesh, 40

Wales, 169

Walker, Gordon, 211*n*

Warangal, 242

Washington, D. C., 23*n*

Water supply. *See* Health, sanitation, and disease

Wealth, 124

Weber, Adna F., 160*n*, 161*tn*

Weber, Max, 166*n*, 174, 192*n*

Weiner, Myron, 201, 386*n*

West Bengal: migration, 39–40; occupational distribution, 48–51; educational level of workers, 52; State Statistical Bureau, 71; village pattern, 142; location of industries, 259; cholera, 280–281; industrialization, 282; local and state government role in urbanization, 382–396; shortcomings of planning, 294; role of Development Department, 391–392; study of cities, 430. *See also* Bengal

Windmiller, Marshall, 202*n*, 207
Wood, J., 441, 442
Woodbury, Coleman, 427*n*

Woodruff, Gertrude, 119, 132, 135, 136, 306*n*
World Bank, 396
Wurster, Catherine Bauer, 225*n*, 391*n*, 451*n*

Yamey, Basil S., 193*n*, 194*n*

Zachariah, K. C., 28*n*, 30*n*, 39*tn*, 444*n*
Zinkin, Taya, 203*n*